THE CLASSIC 1000
INDIAN RECIPES

Everyday Eating made more exciting

Foulsham books are available from all good bookshops; or you can telephone Macmillan Direct on 01256 329242 or order on our website www.foulsham.com

THE CLASSIC 1000 INDIAN RECIPES

EDITED BY WENDY HOBSON

foulsham

LONDON • NEW YORK • TORONTO • SYDNEY

foulsham

The Publishing House, Bennetts Close,
Cippenham, Berkshire, SL1 5AP England

ISBN 978-0-572-02807-7

Cover photographs: Top left, bottom left and bottom right
© The Anthony Blake Photo Library

Photographs by Carol and Terry Pastor

With thanks to the following companies for providing items for the photographs:
Oriental rugs, textiles, furniture and decorative objects from Country and Eastern Ltd,
The Old Skating Rink, 34–36 Bethel Street, Norwich, Norfolk, NR2 1NR.
Tel: 01603 663890. Web site: www.countryandeastern.co.uk.
Spices from Rafi's Spice Box, 15 Goal Street, Sudbury, Suffolk, CO10 1JL.
Tel: 01787 881992. Web site: www.spicebox.co.uk.
Pottery plate opposite page 160 by Dorothy Gorst from the Kersey Pottery,
Kersey, Suffolk, IP7 6DY. Tel: 01473 822092. Also available from Posting House
Pottery, Hall Street, Long Melford, Suffolk, CO10 9JA. Tel: 01787 311165.
Web site: www.longmelford.co.uk/pottery.
Tiles from Fired Earth Ltd, 7 St Giles Street, Norwich, Norfolk, NR2 1JL.
Tel: 01603 618461. Web site: www.firedearth.com.

Printed in Great Britain by St Edmundsbury Press Ltd, Bury St Edmunds, Suffolk.

Contents

Introduction

Indian cookery comprises a wealth of variety and excitement. From such a vast sub-continent come different styles of cooking, different flavours, textures and ingredients. In this collection of recipes, you will find classic recipes from all over India, including both many of the favourites which have become popular in the West, and also many others which are less well known – but no less delicious.

As with any unfamiliar style of cooking, it takes time to absorb the techniques and find out about the ingredients used. So it is a good idea to start cooking some of the dishes which are at least slightly familiar to you. That way, you have more idea of the results to expect. It will also help you to learn about the cooking techniques so that you can then transfer that knowledge to the new recipes you try out.

Combining dishes together also takes some experience. Start simply by combining one or two curry dishes with a dal, raita and breads, then begin to branch out as you learn more about the delights and delicacies of Indian cookery.

Glossary

To make the recipes accessible and easy to follow, we have used the English terms for ingredients. Some Indian terms have become anglicised, however, by common use, and you will already be familiar with many of those that do appear. Also, if you are shopping for ingredients in Indian food stores, you may find this checklist of Indian names useful. You will find different spellings of translated Indian names on many products.

Grains and Lentils

Barley jo
Blackyeye beans lobhiya
Chick peas kabuli channa
Corn maki
Cornflour maki ka atta
Red kidney beans rajma dal
Flour maida
Flour, gram basin
Flour, millet bajre ka atta
Lentil, red dal
Lentil, whole black mah ki dal
Lentil, whole green sabat moong ki hari dal
Mung beans moong dal
Peas, pink split masoor dal
Peas, yellow split arhar dal
Semolina sooji
Vermicelli seviya

Fruit

Apple seb
Apricot khubani
Banana kela
Fig anjeer
Grapes angoor
Guava amrud
Mango aam
Orange santra

Papaya papita
Peaches aaru
Pears nashpati
Pineapple ananas
Pomegranate annar

Milk Products

Paneer Indian cheese
Khoyal solidified milk

Nuts

Almond badam
Cashew nuts kaju
Coconut nariel
Groundnut (peanut) moong-phali
Pistachio pista

Spicing and Flavouring Ingredients

Aniseed saunf
Asafoetida hing
Bay leaf tej patta
Cardamom, black bari elaichi
Cardamom, green choti elaichi
Chilli mirch
Chilli, green hari mairch
Chilli, red lal mirch
Cinnamon dal chini

Clove laung
Coriander (cilantro) dhaniya
Coriander (cilantro) leaves hara dhaniya
Cumin jeera
Curry leaves meedi neem ki patti
Fenugreek methi
Fenugreek leaves methi ka patta
Garlic lahsun
Ginger adrak
Ginger, dry sondh
Jaggery (treacle) gur
Mace javitri
Mango powder amchoor
Mint hara pudeena
Nutmeg jaiphal
Onion seeds pyaj ke beej
Oregano seeds ajwain
Parsley ajmood ka patta
Pomegranate seeds anardana
Poppy seeds khus-khus
Raisin/sultana kismish
Rose water gulab water
Saffron kesar
Sesame seeds til
Tamarind imli
Turmeric haldi or haldar
Tymol seeds ajwain
Vinegar sirka

Vegetables

Aubergine (eggplant) bengun or baingan
Beans sem
Beans, French fansi
Beetroot (red beet) chuquander
Bitter gourd karela
Cabbage bandh gobhi
Carrot gazar

Cauliflower gobhi
Celery leaves ajwain ka patta
Colocasia arbi
Courgette taroi
Cucumber khira
Gourd, bitter karela
Gourd, ridge taroi
Gourd, snack chichinda
Mushroom kukar moote or khumb
Onion pyaz
Okra bhindi
Peas matar
Pepper (bell), green pahari mirch or bari mirch

Potato aloo
Pumpkin kaddu
Radish mooli
Spinach palak
Turnip shalgam
Tomato tamatar
Yam suran

Notes on the Recipes

1. Do not mix metric, Imperial or American measurements. Follow one set only.

2. Spoon measurements are level.

3. Eggs are size 3. If you use a different size, adjust the amount of liquid added to obtain the right consistency.

4. Always wash fresh foods before preparing them.

5. Peel or scrub ingredients as appropriate to the recipe. For example, onions are always peeled, so it is not listed in the recipe. Carrots can be washed, scrubbed or peeled, depending on whether they are young or old.

6. Seasoning and the use of strongly flavoured ingredients, such as onions, garlic and hot spices, are very much a matter of personal taste. Taste the food as you cook and adjust seasoning to suit your own taste.

7. Use freshly ground black pepper, where appropriate.

8. Try to obtain a selection of spice ingredients from supermarkets or Indian stores. Most herbs are used fresh, and can be obtained from supermarkets. Always use fresh herbs for garnishing or sprinkling on cooked dishes. Otherwise, if you do use dried herbs, use half the amount specified for fresh.

9. Use your own discretion in substituting ingredients and personalising the recipes. Make notes of particular successes as you go along.

10. Wash and strain lentils, beans and seeds such as oregano or poppy seeds before use, and remove any dirt.

Seasoning Mixtures and Basic Recipes

A curry is basically a casserole of meat, poultry or vegetables cooked in a masala – a combination of spices in a paste. *Garam masala* literally means 'hot spice', and it is made by roasting and grinding a variety of dried spices to achieve different flavours. The basic art of Indian cooking lies in the careful blending of different spices to yield subtle variations in the flavour of foods. The kitchen shelves of any south Indian home will always have at least two or three instant powders called *podis*. Made from a variety of dals and seasonings, they make a quick instant meal mixed with rice and ghee.

Chillies – both fresh and dried – are an important spice in Indian cooking. The seeds are the hottest part, so remove the seeds if you prefer a milder flavour. Always wash your hands after preparing chillies as the oil from the chilli will sting if you touch your mouth, lips or eyes.

This section also includes the preparation of other basic ingredients, such as tamarind, for use in the recipes.

Yoghurt is used extensively in Indian cuisine, so it is worth making your own. The milk must first be sterilized, so it is easier to use long-life milk, which is already sterile. Fresh milk should be brought to the boil then allowed to cool. Once you have made the first batch, save a tablespoonful to start the second one.

Paneer is Indian cheese, made by curdling milk and leaving it in a muslin cloth (cheesecloth) to strain off the whey.

Curry Powder
Makes 50 g/2 oz/½ cup

30 ml/2 tbsp coriander (cilantro) seeds ● 10 ml/2 tsp cumin seeds

10 ml/2 tsp ground turmeric ● 5 ml/1 tsp ground red chilli

Roast the spices in a small, heavy-based pan over a medium heat for 4-5 minutes, stirring constantly until they become a shade darker than their original colour. The spices will also give out a distinct aroma and the pan will emit light fumes of smoke. Remove the spices from the pan and grind them to a fine powder in a spice or coffee grinder. Store in an airtight jar for up to 6 months.

Mild Curry Powder
Makes 225 g/8 oz

50 g/2 oz/½ cup coriander (cilantro) seeds ● 25 g/1 oz/¼ cup cumin seeds

25 g/1 oz/¼ cup fenugreek seeds ● 25 g/1 oz/¼ cup gram flour

25 g/1 oz/¼ cup garlic powder ● 30 ml/2 tbsp paprika

30 ml/2 tbsp ground turmeric ● 30 ml/2 tbsp garam masala

5 ml/1 tsp ground ginger ● 5 ml/1 chilli powder

5 ml/1 tsp mustard powder ● 5 ml/1 tsp ground black pepper

5 ml/1 tsp ground dried curry leaves ● 5 ml/1 tsp asafoetida

Dry roast the coriander, cumin and fenugreek seeds in a pan until lightly coloured. Grind them to a paste and mix with the remaining ingredients. Store in an airtight container.

Savoury Curry Powder
Makes 50 g/2 oz/½ cup

30 ml/2 tbsp coriander (cilantro) seeds ● 10 ml/2 tsp cumin seeds

15 ml/1 tbsp ground turmeric ● 5 ml/1 tsp ground ginger

3 dried red chillies

Roast the spices in a small, heavy-based pan over a medium heat for 4-5 minutes, stirring constantly until they become a shade darker than their original colour. The spices will also give out a distinct aroma and the pan will emit light fumes of smoke. Remove the spices from the pan and grind them to a fine powder in a spice or coffee grinder. Store in an airtight jar for up to 6 months.

Spicy Hyderabad-style Curry Powder   Makes 100 g/4 oz/1 cup

20 green cardamom pods ● 2 cinnamon sticks, broken into pieces

5 bay leaves ● 2.5 ml/½ tsp cloves ● 1.5 tsp/¼ tsp grated nutmeg

30 ml/2 tbsp aniseeds ● 5 ml/1 tsp black peppercorns

5 dried red chillies ● 10 dried curry leaves

90 ml/6 tbsp coriander (cilantro) seeds ● 45 ml/3 tbsp cumin seeds

45 ml/3 tbsp ground turmeric ● 15 ml/1 tbsp fenugreek seeds

30 ml/2 tbsp black mustard seeds

Roast the spices in a small, heavy-based pan over a medium heat for 4-5 minutes, stirring constantly until they become a shade darker than their original colour. The spices will also give out a distinct aroma and the pan will emit light fumes of smoke. Remove the spices from the pan and grind them to a fine powder in a spice or coffee grinder. Store in an airtight jar for up to 6 months.

Garam Masala 1   Makes 100 g/4 oz/1 cup

25 g/1 oz/¼ cup black cardamom seeds ● 25 g/1 oz/¼ cup cloves

25 g/1 oz cinnamon stick ● 25 g/1 oz/¼ cup black peppercorns

Grind the ingredients together in a coffee grinder to a fine powder.

Garam Masala 2   Makes 100 g/4 oz/1 cup

25 g/1 oz/¼ cup black cardamom pods ● 5 cinnamon sticks, broken into pieces

30 ml/2 tbsp cloves ● ¼ whole nutmeg, grated

25 g/1 oz/¼ cup black peppercorns ● 25 g/1 oz/¼ cup caraway or cumin seeds

Roast the spices in a small, heavy-based pan over a medium heat for 4-5 minutes, stirring constantly until they become a shade darker than their original colour. The spices will also give out a distinct aroma and the pan will emit light fumes of smoke. Remove the spices from the pan and grind them to a fine powder in a spice or coffee grinder. Store in an airtight jar for up to 6 months.

South Indian Garam Masala

Makes 150 g/6 oz/1½ cups

3 cinnamon sticks, broken into pieces

50 g/2 oz/½ cup green cardamom pods, husked

30 ml/2 tbsp black cardamom pods, husked ● 25 g/1 oz/¼ cup cloves

25 g/1 oz/¼ cup black peppercorns ● 3 dried red chillies

¼ whole nutmeg, grated ● 25 g/1 oz/¼ cup cumin seeds

50 g/2 oz/½ cup coriander (cilantro) seeds

Roast the spices in a small, heavy-based pan over a medium heat for 4-5 minutes, stirring constantly until they become a shade darker than their original colour. The spices will also give out a distinct aroma and the pan will emit light fumes of smoke. Remove the spices from the pan and grind them to a fine powder in a spice or coffee grinder. Store in an airtight jar for up to 6 months.

Mughal-style Garam Masala

Makes 100 g/4 oz/1 cup

100 g/4 oz/1 cup green cardamom pods, husked

2 cinnamon sticks, broken into pieces ● 25 g/1 oz/¼ cup cloves

25 g/1 oz/¼ cup black peppercorns

15 ml/1 tbsp grated nutmeg

Roast the spices in a small, heavy-based pan over a medium heat for 4-5 minutes, stirring constantly until they become a shade darker than their original colour. The spices will also give out a distinct aroma and the pan will emit light fumes of smoke. Remove the spices from the pan and grind them to a fine powder in a spice or coffee grinder. Store in an airtight jar for up to 6 months.

Kashmir-style Garam Masala

Makes 100 g/4 oz/1 cup

100 g/4 oz/1 cup green cardamom pods, husked

5 cinnamon sticks, broken into pieces

50 g/2 oz/½ cup black cumin seeds ● 25 g/1 oz/¼ cup black peppercorns

50 g/1 oz/¼ cup cloves ● ½ whole nutmeg, grated

50 g/2 oz/½ cup aniseeds or fennel seeds

Roast the spices in a small, heavy-based pan over a medium heat for 4-5 minutes, stirring constantly until they become a shade darker than their original colour. The spices will also give out a distinct aroma and the pan will emit light fumes of smoke. Remove the spices from the pan and grind them to a fine powder in a spice or coffee grinder. Store in an airtight jar for up to 6 months.

Mysore Rasam Powder
Makes 225 g/8 oz/2 cups

100 g/4 oz coriander (cilantro) seeds ● 25 g/1 oz/¼ cup black peppercorns

25 g/1 oz/¼ cup cumin seeds ● 20 ml/4 tsp fenugreek seeds

1 bunch fresh curry leaves ● 15 ml/1 tbsp oil

3 dried red chillies ● 10 ml/2 tsp ground turmeric

Dry roast the coriander seeds, peppercorns, cumin, fenugreek and curry leaves until lightly browned, then set aside. Heat the oil and fry the chillies. Grind all the ingredients together until fine. Store in an airtight container.

Dosai Chilli Powder
Makes 100 g/4 oz/1 cup

10 ml/2 tsp oil ● 50 g/2 oz/1 cup dried red chillies

75 g/3 oz/½ cup split black beans ● 75 g/3 oz/½ cup yellow split peas

25 g/1 oz/¼ cup sesame seeds ● 5 ml/1 tsp asafoetida

30 ml/2 tbsp ground jaggery ● 2.5 cm/1 in piece of tamarind

salt

Heat the oil and fry the chillies until lightly browned. Dry roast the split beans, split peas, sesame seeds and asafoetida until lightly coloured. Grind all the ingredients to a fine powder, adding salt to taste.

Green Curry Paste
Makes about 175 g/6 oz/1½ cups

5 ml/1 tsp fenugreek seeds, soaked overnight ● 5 cloves garlic, chopped

30 ml/2 tbsp chopped ginger root ● 45 ml/3 tbsp chopped fresh mint

45 ml/3 tbsp chopped fresh coriander (cilantro)

120 ml/4 fl oz/½ cup wine vinegar ● 15 ml/1 tbsp salt

15 ml/1 tbsp ground turmeric

10 ml/2 tsp chilli powder ● 2.5 ml/½ tsp ground cloves

5 ml/1 tsp ground cardamom ● 120 ml/4 fl oz/½ cup oil

45 ml/3 tbsp sesame oil

Drain and rinse the fenugreek seeds then purée with all the remaining ingredients except the oils. Heat the oils and fry the paste for about 5 minutes until thick and the oil appears on the surface. Spoon into jars. Heat a little more oil to cover the paste then seal and store to use as required.

Madras-style Curry Paste
Makes 225 g/8 oz/2 cups

100 g/4 oz/1 cup ground coriander (cilantro) ● 50 g/2 oz/½ cup ground cumin

5 ml/1 tsp ground black pepper ● 30 ml/2 tbsp ground turmeric

15 ml/1 tbsp ground black mustard seeds ● 5 ml/1 tsp ground red chilli

12 cloves garlic ● 5 cm/2 in ginger root, chopped

45 ml/3 tbsp wine vinegar ● 150 ml/¼ pt/⅔ cup oil

Purée all the ingredients except the oil in a blender or food processor. Heat the oil in a small, heavy-based pan over a medium heat. Add the purée and fry for 5-6 minutes, stirring constantly, until the oil separates from the spices. Discard the oil and let the paste cool. Store in an airtight jar for up to 1 month.

Fresh Green Curry Paste
Makes 50 g/2 oz/½ cup

6 cloves garlic ● 2.5 cm/1 in ginger root, chopped

25 g/1 oz/1 cup fresh mint leaves ● 25 g/1 oz/1 cup fresh coriander (cilantro)

10 ml/2 tsp ground turmeric ● 2.5 ml/½ tsp cloves

seeds from 10 cardamom pods ● 100 ml/4 fl oz/½ cup wine vinegar

5 ml/1 tsp fenugreek seeds ● 100 ml/4 fl oz/½ cup oil

Purée all the ingredients except the oil in a blender or food processor. Heat the oil in a small, heavy-based pan over a medium heat. Add the purée and fry for 5-6 minutes, stirring constantly, until the oil appears on the surface. Discard the oil and let the paste cool. Store in an airtight jar for up to 1 month.

Sambar Powder
Makes 200 g/7 oz/2 cups

15 ml/1 tbsp oil ● 100 g/4 oz/2 cups dried red chillies

200 g/7 oz/1 cup coriander (cilantro) seeds ● 25 g/1 oz/¼ cup cumin seeds

30 ml/2 tbsp fenugreek seeds ● 30 ml/2 tbsp black peppercorns

30 ml/2 tbsp mustard seeds ● 10 ml/2 tsp yellow split peas

10 ml/2 tsp red lentils ● 10 ml/2 tsp poppy seeds

2 large cinnamon sticks, broken into pieces ● 2-3 curry leaves

10 ml/2 tsp ground turmeric

Heat the oil and fry the chillies until darkened. Dry roast the other ingredients except the turmeric until lightly coloured. Grind all the ingredients to a fine powder. Store in an airtight container.

Sambar Powder 2   Makes 350 g/12 oz/3 cups

225 g/8 oz/2 cups coriander (cilantro) seeds

100 g/4 oz/2 cups dried red chillies ● 25 g/1 oz/¼ cup black peppercorns

25 g/1 oz/¼ cup cumin seeds ● 10 ml/2 tsp fenugreek seeds

10 ml/2 tsp mustard seeds ● 75 g/3 oz/½ cup yellow split peas

10 ml/2 tsp poppy seeds ● 1 coconut

1 large cinnamon stick, broken into pieces ● 1 large bunch fresh curry leaves

10 ml/2 tsp ground turmeric

Dry roast all the ingredients except the turmeric in a heavy-based pan until lightly coloured. Grind everything to a fine powder. Store in an airtight container.

Rasam Powder   Makes 450 g/1 lb/4 cups

275 g/10 oz/2½ cups coriander (cilantro) seeds ● 50 g/2 oz/1 cup dried red chillies

50 g/2 oz/½ cup black peppercorns ● 100 g/4 oz/⅔ cup red lentils

50 g/2 oz/⅓ cup yellow split peas ● 7.5 ml/1½ tsp cumin seeds

1 small bunch fresh curry leaves ● 5 ml/1 tsp ground turmeric

Dry roast all the ingredients except the turmeric in a heavy-based pan until lightly coloured. Grind everything to a fine powder. Store in an airtight container.

Chutney Powder   Makes 200 g/7 oz/2 cups

75 g/3 oz/½ cup yellow split peas ● 75 g/3 oz/½ cup split black beans

50 g/2 oz/½ cup grated (shredded) copra ● 10 dried red chillies

2.5 ml/½ tsp asafoetida ● 10 ml/2 tsp oil

15 ml/1 tbsp jaggery or sugar ● 15 ml/1 tbsp tamarind pulp

2-3 curry leaves ● salt

Dry roast the split peas, split beans and copra for 2 minutes. Fry the chillies and asafoetida in the oil until lightly browned. Grind all the ingre-dients to a fine powder, adding salt to taste. Store in an airtight container and serve with hot rice and ghee.

Dal Powder
Makes 175 g/6 oz/1½ cups

100 g/4 oz/ cup red lentils ● 15 ml/1 tbsp yellow split peas

15 ml/1 tbsp split black beans ● 15 ml/1 tbsp ghee

5 ml/1 tsp black peppercorns ● 5 ml/1 tsp cumin seeds

5 dried red chillies ● 2.5 ml/½ tsp asafoetida

salt

Dry roast the lentils, split peas and split beans in a pan for 4-5 minutes over a low heat. Heat the ghee and fry the peppercorns, cumin seeds, chillies and asafoetida powder for a few minutes until lightly browned. Grind everything to a powder, adding salt as required. Store in an airtight container and serve with hot rice and ghee.

Coconut Powder
Makes 175 g/6 oz/1½ cups

½ coconut, grated (shredded) ● 30 ml/2 tbsp red lentils

30 ml/2 tbsp yellow split peas ● 2.5 ml/½ tsp asafoetida

8 dried red chillies ● 5 ml/1 tsp oil ● salt

Dry roast the grated coconut until golden. Dry roast the lentils and split peas for a few minutes. Fry the asafoetida and chillies in the oil until lightly browned. Grind all the ingredients to a coarse powder, adding salt to taste. Store in an airtight container for 3-4 days and serve with hot rice and ghee.

Curry Leaves Powder
Makes 200 g/4 oz/1 cup

1 large bunch fresh curry leaves ● 10 ml/2 tsp coriander (cilantro) seeds

15 ml/1 tbsp black peppercorns ● 15 ml/1 tbsp cumin seeds

10 ml/2 tsp fenugreek seeds ● 10 ml/2 tsp mustard seeds

15 ml/1 tbsp split black beans ● 15 ml/1 tbsp yellow split peas

5 ml/1 tsp asafoetida ● 30 ml/2 tbsp jaggery or sugar

30 ml/2 tbsp tamarind pulp ● salt

Dry roast the curry leaves for 2 minutes then set aside. Roast the coriander seeds, peppercorns, cumin, fenugreek and mustard seeds, split beans, split peas and asafoetida until golden. Grind everything to a fine powder, adding the jaggery or sugar, tamarind and salt to taste. Store in an airtight container and serve with hot rice and ghee.

Peanut Powder

Makes 225 g/8 oz/2 cups

50 g/2 oz/½ cup sesame seeds ● 15 dried red chillies

5 ml/1 tsp asafoetida ● 10 ml/2 tsp oil

salt ● 225 g/8 oz/2 cups roasted peanuts

Dry roast the sesame seeds until lightly browned. Fry the chillies and asafoetida in the oil for a few minutes. Grind the chillies and asafoetida to a fine powder. Add the sesame seeds and grind again. Add the peanuts and grind again, seasoning to taste with salt. Store in an airtight container and serve with hot rice and ghee.

Sesame Seed Powder

Makes 175 g/6 oz/1½ cups

100 g/4 oz sesame seeds ● 50 g/2 oz/½ cup grated (shredded) copra

10 dried red chillies ● 5 ml/1 tsp asafoetida

20 ml/4 tsp oil ● salt

Fry the sesame seeds, copra, chillies and asafoetida in the oil for a few minutes until lightly browned. Grind to a coarse powder, adding salt to taste. Store in an airtight container and serve with plain hot rice and ghee.

Garlic Purée

Makes 100 g/4 oz

30-35 large cloves garlic

Peel the garlic cloves and blend them to a paste in a blender or food processor, adding just a small amount of water if necessary. Store in an airtight container or freeze in ice cube trays. Add to dishes as required.

Ginger Purée

Makes 450 g/1 lb

450 g/1 lb ginger root, chopped

Purée the ginger in a blender or food processor then freeze in ice cube trays. Add to dishes as required.

Onion Purée

Makes 450 g/1 lb

450 g/1 lb onions, chopped

Bring a pan of water to the boil, add the onions then boil for 3 minutes. Drain well. Purée in a blender or food processor then freeze in ice cube trays or small containers. Add to dishes as required.

Tamarind Pulp
Makes 600 ml/1 pt/2½ cups

300 g/11 oz dried tamarind ● 600 ml/1 pt/2½ cups hot water

Soak the dried tamarind overnight in the hot water or boil it for 15 minutes over a medium heat.

Rub the tamarind through your fingers to reduce it to a pulp then rub through a sieve and collect the pulp. Discard the husks, which should not exceed 15 ml/1 tbsp. Excess pulp can be frozen.

Tamarind Juice
Makes 250 ml/8 fl oz/1 cup

1 lemon-sized tamarind ● 250 ml/8 fl oz/1 cup warm water

Soak the tamarind in warm water for about 10 minutes. Squeeze and extract as much juice as possible from the pulp, adding a little extra warm water, if necessary.

Ghee
Makes 450 g/1 lb/2 cups

450 g/1 lb/2 cups unsalted butter

Heat the butter in a pan, stirring until the butter has melted. When the solids (whey) appear at the bottom and the clear part (ghee) is at the top, reduce the heat to low. Continue to stir over a low heat until light brown. Turn off the heat and keep stirring so that it does not boil over. Allow to cool slightly.

Put a muslin (cheesecloth) cloth over a container or jar and pour the butter through the cloth so that the ghee strains through into the container. Squeeze the remaining ghee from the cloth and discard the residue. Leave to cool then put the lid on the container and keep until required.

Khoya
Makes about 75 g/3 oz

1.2 1/2 pts/5 cups gold top milk

Place the milk in a heavy-based pan and bring to the boil. Simmer gently and stir over a low heat for about 2 hours until it solidifies.

Quick Khoya
Makes about 75 g/3 oz

50 g/2 oz/½ cup full cream milk powder ● 10 ml/2 tsp ghee, melted

30 ml/2 tbsp lukewarm milk

Combine all the ingredients in a bowl until a soft dough forms.

Fresh Coconut Milk

Makes 250 ml/8 fl oz/1 cup

1 coconut ● 250 ml/8 fl oz/1 cup hot water

Remove the white flesh from the coconut and grate it. Place it in a muslin (cheesecloth) bag and squeeze as much milk as possible. Soak the coconut in the bag in the water for about 30 minutes. Squeeze out the milk into a bowl until all the milk has been extracted.

Quick Coconut Milk

Makes 250 ml/8 fl oz/1 cup

100 g/4 oz/1 cup desiccated (shredded) coconut

300 ml/½ pt/10 cups lukewarm water

Blend the coconut and 250 ml/8 fl oz/1 cup of water to a smooth paste in a blender or food processor. Put the paste in a muslin bag and squeeze out as much coconut milk as possible. Place the remaining water in a bowl and knead the coconut bag in the water to squeeze out any remaining milk.

Yoghurt

Makes 600 ml/1 pt/2½ cups

15 ml/1 tbsp live natural (plain) yoghurt

15-30 ml/1-2 tbsp skimmed milk powder

600 ml/1 pt/2½ cups long-life milk

Mix together the yoghurt and skimmed milk powder to a smooth paste. Heat the milk to lukewarm then stir it into the yoghurt paste. Pour it into a clean vacuum flask and leave for about 6 hours until the yoghurt has set. Empty the yoghurt into a clean container and store in the refrigerator for up to 5 days.

Paneer

Makes 150 g/5 oz

1.2 1/2 pts/5 cups gold top milk ● 30 ml/2 tbsp lemon juice

Bring the milk to the boil. Add the lemon juice so that the milk separates into curds and whey. Add a little more if necessary to achieve this. Leave to set for 5 minutes.

Line a strainer with a muslin (cheesecloth) cloth and strain the milk. Reserve the whey to use in curries instead of water to add extra flavour and minerals. Squeeze the excess whey out of the curd and fold the cloth around the paneer to form a square about 10 cm/4 in. Place the paneer on an upturned plate and place a heavy weight on top to squeeze out excess whey. Leave for about 4 hours to set.

Sambars

Thick and fiery sambars are the first course in any south Indian meal. They are served steaming hot with plain cooked rice and a vegetable accompaniment. Almost any vegetable can be used in a sambar. The tart tamarind juice, besides having a cooling effect, has the unique property of preserving the vitamins of the vegetables cooked in it. Sambar powder can be bought ready-made in an Indian food store, or you can make your own from the recipes on pages 14 and 15.

Basic Sambar
Serves 4

75 g/3 oz/½ cup red lentils ● 15 ml/1 tbsp oil
5 ml/1 tsp mustard seeds ● 2.5 ml/½ tsp asafoetida
2.5 ml/½ tsp fenugreek seeds ● 2.5 ml/½ tsp cumin seeds
1 dried red chilli, halved ● 2-3 curry leaves ● 2 green chillies, halved
225 g/8 oz mixed vegetables, cubed (radish, onion, potato, aubergine (eggplant), courgette (zucchini), green (bell) pepper etc.)
30 ml/2 tbsp tamarind juice ● 250 ml/8 fl oz/1 cup water
15 ml/1 tbsp Sambar Powder 2 (page 15)
2.5 ml/½ tsp ground turmeric ● salt ● 15 ml/1 tbsp rice flour (optional)
30 ml/2 tbsp water (optional) ● 15 ml/1 tbsp chopped fresh coriander (cilantro)

Cook the lentils in boiling water for about 1 hour until tender then drain and set aside. Heat the oil and fry the mustard seeds, asafoetida, fenugreek and cumin seeds, red chilli and curry leaves until the mustard seeds start crackling. Add the green chillies and vegetables and fry for 2 minutes. Add the tamarind juice, water, sambar powder, turmeric and salt, cover and simmer over a low heat until the vegetables are tender. Stir in the cooked lentils and simmer for 5 minutes. If the sambar needs to be thickened, blend the rice flour with the water, stir it into the pan and simmer for a further few minutes. Garnish with coriander and serve hot with rice.

Sambar Masala
Serves 4-6

15 ml/1 tbsp oil ● 50 g/2 oz/½ cup desiccated (shredded) coconut

15 ml/1 tbsp coriander (cilantro) seeds ● 10 ml/2 tsp split black beans

10 ml/2 tsp yellow split peas ● 5 ml/1 tsp fenugreek seeds ● 4 dried red chillies

Sambar: 250 g/9 oz/1½ cups yellow split peas ● 1.2 1/2 pts/5 cups water

5 ml/1 tsp ground turmeric ● salt to taste

250 g/9 oz aubergine (eggplant) or okra, cut into 5 mm/¼ in thick pieces

15 ml/1 tbsp tamarind pulp (page 19)

Tarka: 90 ml/6 tbsp oil ● large pinch of asafoetida

5 ml/1 tsp mustard seeds ● 3 curry leaves or bay leaves

3 small onions, thinly sliced ● 5 ml/1 tsp garam masala

400 g/14 oz canned tomatoes ● 90 ml/6 tbsp chopped fresh coriander (cilantro)

Heat the oil in a frying pan (skillet) on a medium-low heat and roast the coconut, coriander seeds, split beans, split peas, fenugreek seeds and chillies for about 5 minutes until light brown. Leave to cool then grind to a fine paste.

Place the split peas, water, turmeric and salt in a large pan, bring to the boil and skim off any scum. Reduce the heat, cover and simmer for 30 minutes until the split peas are tender. Meanwhile, cook the aubergine in the tamarind pulp for 5 minutes. Bring to the boil then add the spice paste.

Cook on a medium-low heat for 10 minutes or until the aubergine is tender. Mix in the cooked peas.

Meanwhile, heat the oil and fry the asafoetida and mustard seeds until they start crackling. Add the curry or bay leaves and onion and fry until golden brown. Stir in the garam masala and tomatoes and cook until all the liquid has been absorbed and the oil appears on the surface. Add the coriander and mix in the cooked dal. Bring to the boil, reduce the heat then simmer for 5 minutes. Serve hot with rice, raita and cauliflower or potato.

Cauliflower Sambar
Serves 4

76 g/3 oz/½ cup red lentils ● 5 ml/1 tsp oil

5 ml/1 tsp coriander (cilantro) seeds ● 2.5 ml/½ tsp black peppercorns

5 ml/1 tsp split black beans ● 2.5 ml/½ tsp asafoetida

30 ml/2 tbsp desiccated (shredded) coconut

1 medium cauliflower, cut into florets ● 2 tomatoes, quartered

15 ml/1 tbsp Sambar Powder 2 (page 15) ● 2.5 ml/½ tsp ground turmeric

salt ● 10 ml/2 tsp rice flour ● 120 ml/4 fl oz/½ cup water

120 ml/4 fl oz/½ cup coconut milk

Seasoning: 10 ml/2 tsp ghee ● 5 ml/1 tsp mustard seeds

5 ml/1 tsp split black beans ● 1 dried red chilli, halved ● 2 curry leaves

Cook the lentils in boiling water for about 1 hour until tender then drain and set aside. Heat the oil and fry the coriander seeds, peppercorns, split beans and asafoetida for 2 minutes. Add the desiccated coconut and grind to a paste with a little water. Cook the cauliflower in boiling water with the tomatoes, sambar powder, turmeric and salt until the cauliflower is tender.

Dissolve the rice flour in the water then stir it into the cauliflower with the ground paste and cooked lentils. Simmer for 10 minutes until the ingredients are well blended.

Heat the ghee and fry the seasoning ingredients until the mustard seeds start crackling. Add to the sambar with the coconut milk and simmer for 3 minutes. Serve hot with rice.

Curry Leaves Sambar

Serves 4

6 dried red chillies ● 5 ml/1 tsp black peppercorns

5 ml/1 tsp asafoetida ● 10 ml/2 tsp split black beans

5 ml/1 tsp long-grain rice ● 1 lemon-sized tamarind

20 curry leaves ● 450 ml/¾ pt/2 cups water ● salt

30 ml/2 tbsp oil ● 5 ml/1 tsp mustard seeds

1.5 ml/¼ tsp fenugreek seeds

Dry roast 5 of the red chillies, the peppercorns, asafoetida, split beans and rice until lightly coloured. Add the tamarind and curry leaves and grind to a fine paste with a little of the water. Add the remaining water and the salt and set aside. Heat the oil and fry the mustard and fenugreek seeds and the remaining halved chilli until the mustard seeds start crackling. Stir in the paste and simmer until the sambar thickens. Serve hot with rice and papadums.

Dumpling Sambar

Serves 4

1 lemon-sized tamarind ● 450 ml/¾ pt/2 cups water

4 dried red chillies ● 175 g/6 oz/1 cup red lentils

2.5 ml/½ tsp asafoetida ● salt ● 15 ml/1 tbsp oil

2 curry leaves

Seasoning: 30 ml/2 tbsp gingelly oil ● 5 ml/1 tsp mustard seeds

2.5 ml/½ tsp fenugreek seeds ● 2 dried red chillies, halved

2-3 curry leaves ● 2.5 ml/½ tsp asafoetida

5 ml/1 tsp split black beans ● 5 ml/1 tsp yellow split peas

5 ml/1 tsp red lentils ● 15 ml/1 tbsp Sambar Powder 1 (page 14)

30 ml/2 tbsp ground jaggery

Soak the tamarind in the water, extract the juice and set aside.

To make the dumplings, soak the lentils and chillis in water for 2 hours then grind to a thick paste with the asafoetida and a pinch of salt. Heat the oil and fry the paste and curry leaves for a few minutes then remove from the heat and shape into small balls. Steam on a rack in a pan of boiling water for 10-20 minutes until cooked through. Leave to cool.

Meanwhile heat the seasoning oil and fry the mustard and fenugreek seeds, chillies, curry leaves and asafoetida until the mustard seeds start crackling. Add the split beans, split peas and lentils and fry until golden. Add the sambar powder and fry for 1 minute. Add the tamarind juice, jaggery and a pinch of salt, cover and simmer for 10 minutes. Add the dumplings and simmer for a further 10 minutes. Serve hot with rice.

Lentil Sambar
Serves 4

75 g/3 oz/½ cup red lentils • 15 ml/1 tbsp oil • 5 ml/1 tsp mustard seeds

2.5 ml/½ tsp fenugreek seeds • 2.5 ml/½ tsp cumin seeds

2.5 ml/½ tsp asafoetida • 1 dried red chilli, halved

2-3 curry leaves • 2 green chillies, halved

225 g/8 oz mixed vegetables, diced (radish, onion, potato, aubergine (eggplant), courgette (zucchini), green (bell) pepper etc.)

15 ml/1 tbsp tamarind pulp (page 19)

250 ml/8 fl oz/1 cup water • 15 ml/1 tbsp Sambar Powder 2 (page 15)

2.5 ml/½ tsp ground turmeric • salt

15 ml/1 tbsp chopped fresh coriander (cilantro)

Cook the lentils in boiling water for about 1 hour until tender then drain. Heat the oil and fry the mustard, fenugreek and cumin seeds, asafoetida, red chilli and curry leaves until the mustard seeds start crackling. Add the green chillies and vegetables and fry for 2 minutes. Add the tamarind pulp, water, sambar powder, turmeric and salt. Cover and simmer for 2 minutes. Stir in the lentils, cover and simmer for 10 minutes. Sprinkle with coriander and serve hot with rice.

Mysore Sambar
Serves 4

100 g/4 oz/⅔ cup red lentils • 15 ml/1 tbsp coriander (cilantro) seeds

100 g/4 oz/1 cup grated (shredded) coconut • 5 ml/1 tsp mustard seeds

15 ml/1 tbsp long-grain rice • 4 dried red chillies

2.5 ml/½ tsp asafoetida • 225 g/8 oz green beans, coarsely chopped

30 ml/2 tbsp peas • 1 potato, chopped

2.5 ml/½ tsp ground turmeric • salt

Seasoning: 10 ml/2 tsp oil ● 5 ml/1 tsp mustard seeds
5 ml/1 tsp cumin seeds ● 1 dried red chilli, halved
2-3 curry leaves

Cook the lentils in boiling water for about 1 hour until tender then drain and set aside. Grind the coriander seeds, coconut, mustard seeds, rice, chillies and asafoetida to a paste with a little water then set aside. Place the beans, peas and potato in a pan and just cover with water. Bring to the boil and simmer until tender. Add the lentils, turmeric, salt and ground paste and simmer over a low heat until the ingredients are well blended. Heat the seasoning oil and fry the seasoning ingredients until the mustard seeds start crackling. Add to the sambar and simmer for a few minutes. Serve hot with rice.

Onion Sambar   Serves 4

75 g/3 oz/½ cup red lentils ● 45 ml/3 tbsp oil

2.5 ml/½ tsp asafoetida ● 5 ml/1 tsp cumin seeds

10 ml/2 tsp poppy seeds ● 45 ml/3 tbsp coriander (cilantro) seeds

6 dried red chillies ● 25 g/1 oz/3 tbsp yellow split peas

45 ml/3 tbsp grated (shredded) coconut

225 g/8 oz spring onions (scallions), chopped

300 ml/½ pt/1¼ cups water ● 30 ml/2 tbsp tamarind juice

2.5 ml/½ tsp ground turmeric ● salt ● chopped fresh coriander (cilantro)

Seasoning: 5 ml/1 tsp mustard seeds ● 5 ml/1 tsp cumin seeds

1.5 ml/¼ tsp fenugreek seeds ● 1 dried red chilli, halved

2-3 curry leaves

Cook the lentils in boiling water for about 1 hour until tender then drain and set aside. Heat half the oil and fry the asafoetida, cumin, poppy and coriander seeds, chillies and split peas for a few minutes. Add the coconut, a few of the onions and a little water. Grind the mixture to a fine paste then set aside. Heat the remaining oil and fry the seasoning ingredients until the mustard seeds start crackling. Add the remaining onions and fry over a low heat for 5 minutes. Add the tamarind juice, turmeric and salt to taste, cover and simmer for 5-7 minutes. Add the cooked lentils and ground paste and cook for another 5 minutes until everything is well blended. Garnish with chopped coriander and serve hot with rice.

Pepper Sambar
Serves 4

1 lemon-sized tamarind ● 450 ml/¾ pt/2 cups water

15 ml/1 tbsp black peppercorns ● 15 ml/1 tbsp yellow split peas

5 ml/1 tsp coriander (cilantro) seeds ● 2 dried red chillies

2.5 ml/½ tsp asafoetida ● 30 ml/2 tbsp oil

5 ml/1 tsp mustard seeds ● salt ● 15 ml/1 tbsp chopped fresh curry leaves

Soak the tamarind in the water and extract the juice then set aside. Dry roast the peppercorns, split peas, coriander seeds, chillies and asafoetida until lightly coloured then grind to a fine powder. Add a little water to make a paste then set aside. Heat half the oil and fry the mustard seeds until they start crackling. Add the tamarind juice and salt to taste, cover and simmer over a low heat for 2 minutes. Add the paste and bring to the boil. Stir in the remaining oil and curry leaves and simmer for 10 minutes until the ingredients are well combined. Serve hot with rice.

Spicy Tamarind Sambar
Serves 4

1 lemon-sized tamarind ● 450 g/¾ pt/2 cups water

45 ml/3 tbsp oil ● 2 dried red chillies, halved

5 ml/1 tsp mustard seeds ● 2.5 ml/½ tsp fenugreek seeds

2.5 ml/½ tsp asafoetida ● 5 ml/1 tsp red lentils

5 ml/1 tsp yellow split peas ● 5 ml/1 tsp split black beans

2-3 curry leaves ● 150 g/5 oz pickling onions

15 ml/1 tbsp Sambar Powder 1 (page 14) ● 30 ml/2 tbsp ground jaggery

30 ml/2 tbsp salt ● 30 ml/2 tbsp gram flour

120 ml/4 fl oz/½ cup water

Soak the tamarind in the water, extract the juice and set aside. Heat the oil and fry the chillies, mustard and fenugreek seeds and asafoetida until the mustard seeds start crackling. Add the lentils, split peas, split beans and curry leaves and fry until the lentils are golden. Add the onions and fry for 2 minutes. Add the sambar powder and fry for 1 minute. Add the tamarind juice, jaggery and salt, cover and simmer over a low heat for about 10 minutes. Meanwhile, blend the flour and water to a batter then stir it into the sambar and simmer for 2 minutes. Serve hot with rice.

Vegetable Coconut Sambar

Serves 4

75 g/3 oz/½ cup red lentils ● 45 ml/3 tbsp oil ● 2.5 ml/½ tsp fenugreek seeds

2.5 ml/½ tsp asafoetida ● 45 ml/3 tbsp coriander (cilantro) seeds

25 g/1 oz/3 tbsp yellow split peas ● 5 ml/1 tsp cumin seeds

45 ml/3 tbsp grated (shredded) coconut ● 300 ml/½ pt/1¼ cups water

6 spring onions (scallions), chopped ● 1 small aubergine (eggplant), cubed

1 celery stick, chopped ● 1 small potato, quartered

1 green (bell) pepper, chopped ● 6 dried red chillies, halved

30 ml/2 tbsp tamarind juice ● 2.5 ml/½ tsp ground turmeric

salt ● 15 ml/1 tbsp chopped fresh coriander (cilantro)

Seasoning: 5 ml/1 tsp mustard seeds ● 5 ml/1 tsp cumin seeds

1.5 ml/¼ tsp fenugreek seeds ● 1 dried red chilli, halved

2-3 curry leaves

Cook the lentils in boiling water for about 1 hour until tender then drain and set aside. Heat half the oil and fry the fenugreek seeds, asafoetida, coriander seeds, split peas and cumin seeds for a few minutes. Add the coconut and a little water and grind to a fine paste. Heat the remaining oil and fry the seasoning ingredients until the mustard seeds start crackling. Add the onions and fry for 2 minutes. Add the vegetables, chillies, tamarind juice, turmeric and salt to taste. Cover and simmer for 10 minutes until the vegetables are tender. Add the cooked lentils and ground paste and simmer for a further 5 minutes until all the ingredients are well blended. Garnish with coriander and serve hot with rice.

Rasams

The second course of any south Indian meal is the thin, watery rasam, which is served as a digestive in small cups - or sometimes used to wet rice. Rasam is quick and easy to prepare. Tamarind, tomatoes and lime give it a piquant, tangy taste. Health-conscious south Indians often make a light meal of an easily digestible rasam, rice and chutney. Rasam powder can be bought ready-made in an Indian food store, or you can make your own (page 14).

Rasam   Serves 4

45 ml/3 tbsp red lentils ● 2 tomatoes, cubed

15 ml/1 tbsp tamarind pulp (page 19) ● 2.5 ml/½ tsp asafoetida

10 ml/2 tsp rasam powder (page 14) ● salt

600 ml/1 pt/2½ cups water ● 10 ml/2 tsp ghee

5 ml/1 tsp mustard seeds ● 2.5 ml/½ tsp cumin seeds

1 dried red chilli, halved ● 2-3 curry leaves

15 ml/1 tbsp chopped fresh coriander (cilantro)

Cook the lentils in water for about 1 hour until tender. Drain and set aside. Put the tomatoes, tamarind pulp, asafoetida, rasam powder and salt into a pan. Add 250 ml/8 fl oz/1 cup of water and bring to the boil, crushing everything together. Simmer for 15 minutes. Add the cooked lentils and remaining water and bring to the boil. Heat the ghee and add the remaining ingredients except the coriander. Fry until the mustard seeds start crackling then stir into the rasam. Serve hot garnished with coriander.

Tomato Rasam   Serves 4

45 ml/3 tbsp red lentils ● 10 ml/2 tsp ghee ● 5 ml/1 tsp mustard seeds

5 ml/1 tsp cumin seeds ● 1 dried red chilli, halved

5 ml/1 tsp ground black pepper ● 2.5 ml/½ tsp asafoetida

2-3 curry leaves ● 4 large tomatoes, finely chopped

3 green chillies, split lengthways ● 2.5 cm/1 in ginger root, finely chopped

600 ml/1 pt/2½ cups water ● 2.5 ml/½ tsp ground turmeric

salt ● 15 ml/1 tbsp chopped fresh coriander (cilantro)

Cook the lentils in water for about 1 hour until tender then drain and set aside. Heat the ghee and fry the mustard and cumin seeds, chilli, pepper, asafoetida and curry leaves until the mustard seeds start crackling. Add the tomatoes, chillies and ginger. Add 250 ml/8 fl oz/1 cup of water, the turmeric and salt, bring to the boil and simmer for 5 minutes. Add the lentils and the remaining water, return to the boil and stir together well for a few minutes until hot. Serve hot, garnished with the coriander.

Lemon Rasam
Serves 4

30 g/1½ oz/¼ cup red lentils ● 4 green chillies

2.5 cm/1 in ginger root, finely chopped ● 2 tomatoes, quartered

2.5 ml/½ tsp ground turmeric ● 300 ml/½ pt/1¼ cups water

salt ● 10 ml/2 tsp ghee ● 5 ml/1 tsp mustard seeds

2.5 ml/½ tsp asafoetida ● 1 dried red chilli, halved

2-3 curry leaves ● 5 ml/1 tsp ground black pepper

2.5 ml/½ tsp ground cumin ● juice of 1 lemon

1 small bunch fresh coriander (cilantro), chopped

Cook the lentils in water for about 1 hour until tender. Drain. Grind together the chillies and ginger and stir them into the lentils with the tomatoes, turmeric, water and salt and bring to the boil over a low heat.

In a separate pan, heat the ghee and fry the mustard seeds, asafoetida, chilli and curry leaves for 1 minute. Add the pepper and cumin and fry until the mustard seeds start crackling. Add to the rasam and remove from the heat. Stir in the lemon juice, garnish with the coriander and serve hot with rice.

Ginger Rasam
Serves 4

45 ml/3 tbsp red lentils ● 600 ml/1 pt/2½ cups water

15 ml/1 tbsp cumin seeds ● 5 ml/1 tsp black peppercorns

3 green chillies ● 5 cm/2 in ginger root, chopped

15 ml/1 tbsp desiccated (shredded) coconut ● 15 ml/1 tbsp ground jaggery

salt ● 10 ml/2 tsp ghee ● 5 ml/1 tsp mustard seeds

5 ml/1 tsp cumin seeds ● 2.5 ml/½ tsp asafoetida

1 dried red chilli, halved ● 2-3 curry leaves

15 ml/1 tbsp chopped fresh coriander (cilantro)

Soak the lentils in half the water for 30 minutes. Grind the cumin, peppercorns, chillies, ginger, coconut, jaggery and salt to a fine paste then stir it into the lentils. Add the remaining water, bring to the boil and simmer until the lentils are tender. Add some more water if the rasam becomes too thick during cooking.

Heat the ghee and fry the mustard and cumin seeds, asafoetida, chilli and curry leaves until the seeds start crackling. Stir into the rasam and serve hot, garnished with coriander.

Cumin and Pepper Rasam
Serves 4

15 ml/1 tbsp ghee ● 5 ml/1 tsp red lentils ● 7.5 ml/1½ tsp black peppercorns

5 ml/1 tsp cumin seeds ● 2 dried red chillies, halved

2.5 ml/½ tsp asafoetida ● 5 ml/1 tsp mustard seeds ● 2.5 ml/½ tsp cumin seeds

2-3 curry leaves ● 15 ml/1 tbsp tamarind pulp (page 19) ● salt

Heat 5 ml/1 tsp of ghee and fry the lentils, peppercorns, cumin, 1 chilli and the asafoetida until lightly coloured. Grind to a fine powder. Heat the remaining ghee and fry the mustard and cumin seeds, the remaining chilli and the curry leaves until the mustard seeds start crackling. Add the tamarind pulp and simmer for a few minutes until the raw smell of the tamarind disappears. Add the ground spices and simmer for a few minutes. Serve hot with rice.

Garlic Rasam
Serves 4

20 ml/4 tsp oil ● 6 dried red chillies, halved

5 ml/1 tsp black peppercorns ● 10 ml/2 tsp coriander (cilantro) seeds

5 ml/1 tsp yellow split peas ● 5 ml/1 tsp cumin seeds

30 ml/2 tbsp tamarind pulp (page 00) ● salt ● 2-3 curry leaves

20-25 cloves garlic ● 5 ml/1 tsp mustard seeds

Heat half the oil and fry 4 chillies, the peppercorns, coriander seeds and split peas until lightly coloured. Grind to a fine paste with the cumin seeds. Heat the tamarind pulp with the salt and curry leaves and simmer until the raw smell of the tamarind disappears. Meanwhile, fry the garlic in the remaining oil then stir in the ground paste. Stir into the tamarind mixture and simmer until all the ingredients are well blended, adding a little more water if the rasam becomes too thick. Heat the remaining oil and fry the mustard seeds and remaining chillis until the seeds start crackling. Stir into the rasam and serve hot.

Spicy Lentil Rasam
Serves 4

75 g/3 oz/½ cup red lentils ● 30 g/1½ oz/¼ cup green lentils

10 ml/2 tsp oil ● 15 ml/1 tbsp coriander (cilantro) seeds

5 ml/1 tsp cumin seeds ● 5 ml/1 tsp black peppercorns

2 dried red chillies, halved ● 10 ml/2 tsp split black beans

2.5 ml/½ tsp asafoetida ● 45 ml/3 tbsp desiccated (shredded) coconut

4-5 curry leaves ● 10 ml/2 tsp ghee ● 5 ml/1 tsp mustard seeds

5 ml/1 tsp cumin seeds ● 1 tomato, chopped ● pinch of ground turmeric

450 ml/¾ pt/2 cups water ● salt ● juice of 1 lemon

1 bunch fresh coriander (cilantro), finely chopped

Cook the lentils in boiling water for about 1 hour until tender then drain and set aside.

Heat the oil and fry the coriander and cumin seeds, peppercorns, 1 red chilli, the split beans and asafoetida until lightly coloured. Add the coconut and 2-3 curry leaves and grind to a fine paste using a very little water.

Heat the ghee and fry the mustard and cumin seeds, the remaining chilli and curry leaves until the mustard seeds start crackling. Add the cooked lentils, tomato, turmeric, water and salt and simmer for a few minutes. Add the ground paste and simmer for 5 minutes until well blended. Add the lemon juice, garnish with the coriander and serve hot with rice.

Mysore Rasam
Serves 4

75 g/3 oz/½ cup red lentils ● 15 ml/1 tbsp ghee

5 ml/1 tsp mustard seeds ● 5 ml/1 tsp cumin seeds ● 1 dried red chilli, halved

2.5 ml/½ tsp asafoetida ● 2-3 curry leaves ● 3-4 small tomatoes, chopped

30 ml/2 tbsp tamarind pulp (page 19) ● 150 ml/¼ pt/⅔ cup water

15 ml/1 tbsp Mysore Rasam Powder (page 14) ● 30 ml/2 tbsp ground jaggery

1.5 ml/¼ tsp ground turmeric ● salt ● 90 ml/6 tbsp coconut milk

1 small bunch fresh coriander (cilantro), chopped

Cook the lentils in boiling water for about 1 hour until tender. Heat the ghee and fry the mustard and cumin seeds, chilli, asafoetida and curry leaves until the mustard seeds start crackling. Add the tomatoes, tamarind pulp, water, rasam powder, jaggery, turmeric and salt. Simmer over a low heat for 15-20 minutes until the raw smell of the tamarind disappears. Add the cooked lentils and simmer for 5 minutes to blend the flavours. Just before serving, stir in the coconut milk and coriander and serve hot with rice and papadums.

Soups

India does not have a particularly strong tradition of soup-making. Perhaps the best known Indian soup is mulligatawny, which is in fact an Anglo-Indian invention! There are countless recipes for this popular, spicy soup and you can use any meat – beef, chicken or lamb – to ring the changes.

Mulligatawny Soup
Serves 4

75 g/3 oz/½ cup yellow split peas, soaked in water for 20 minutes

450 g/1 lb lean stewing beef, cubed ● 450 g/1 lb beef bones

salt ● 2.25 l/4 pts/10 cups water ● 4 cloves garlic

15 ml/1 tbsp coriander (cilantro) seeds ● 15 ml/1 tbsp black mustard seeds

12 black peppercorns ● 10 ml/2 tsp cumin seeds

1.5 ml/¼ tsp fenugreek seeds ● 5 curry leaves

Put the split peas, beef, bones, salt and water into a large saucepan. In a small frying pan (skillet), roast all the remaining ingredients except the curry leaves until lightly coloured. Add to the pan, bring to the boil and simmer for 30-45 minutes until tender. Stir in the curry leaves and cook for a further 5 minutes. Remove the bones and strain the stock to remove the whole spices and seeds. Return the meat to the soup. Serve hot.

Mulligatawny Soup with Lentils
Serves 4-6

100 g/4 oz/1 cup split moong beans, soaked for 20 minutes

900 g/2 lb lean stewing beef, cubed ● salt

2.5 ml/½ tsp ground turmeric ● 2.5 ml/½ tsp ground red chilli

2.5 ml/½ tsp black peppercorns ● 2 cinnamon sticks

3 bay leaves ● 2.25 l/4 pts/10 cups water ● 1 large onion, chopped

5 cloves garlic, chopped ● 2.5 cm/1 in ginger root, finely chopped

10 ml/2 tsp ground cumin ● 15 ml/1 tbsp ground coriander (cilantro)

15 ml/1 tbsp Basic Curry Powder (page 11) ● 45 ml/3 tbsp oil

15 ml/1 tbsp black mustard seeds ● 1.5 ml/¼ tsp fenugreek seeds

1 potato, cubed ● 3 carrots, cubed ● 2 tomatoes, skinned and chopped

Place the first nine ingredients in a pan, bring to the boil and simmer for 15-20 minutes until tender. Blend the next six ingredients to a paste. Heat the oil and fry the mustard and fenugreek seeds until the seeds start crackling. Stir in the paste and fry for 5-6 minutes until the oil appears on the surface. Add to the meat, cover and cook for 20 minutes, stirring occasionally. Add the vegetables and cook for 8-10 minutes, stirring occasionally, until tender. Discard the bay leaves and cinnamon before serving hot with rice.

Cabbage Soup
Serves 6

50 g/2 oz/¼ cup ghee ● 1 onion, chopped

900 g/2 lb cabbage, chopped ● 1 large potato, quartered

2 tomatoes, halved ● 600 ml/1 pt/2½ cups water

300 ml/½ pt/1¼ cups vegetable stock ● 5 ml/1 tsp cornflour (cornstarch)

salt and pepper

Heat the ghee in a pan and fry the onion until soft. Add the cabbage and stir until wilted and coated with ghee. Add the potato, tomatoes and water, bring to the boil, cover and cook over a medium heat for about 10 minutes. Add the stock, return to the boil and cook for 5 minutes. Remove from the heat and mash or purée the soup. Blend the cornflour with a little of the soup then stir it into the pan and bring to the boil, stirring, until slightly thickened. Season to taste with salt and pepper and serve hot.

Carrot Soup
Serves 6

25 g/1 oz/2 tbsp unsalted butter ● 450 g/1 lb carrots, diced

1 onion, chopped ● 5 ml/1 tsp coriander (cilantro) seeds, roasted and crushed

5 ml/1 tsp sugar ● 900 ml/1½ pts/3 cups stock

salt and pepper ● 15 ml/1 tbsp cream (optional)

Melt the butter in a large pan and fry the carrots and onion until soft but not browned. Add the coriander, sugar, stock, salt and pepper. Bring to the boil, cover and simmer gently for 15 minutes until the carrots are tender. Purée the soup, diluting with a little more water if it is too thick. Reheat before serving topped with cream, if liked.

Cauliflower Soup
Serves 6

1 cauliflower, cut into florets ● 1 bay leaf ● 2.5 ml/½ tsp salt

25 g/1 oz/2 tbsp butter or margarine ● 1 onion, finely chopped

1 potato, sliced ● 25 g/1 oz/¼ cup plain (all-purpose) flour

900 ml/1½ pts/3 cups milk ● salt and pepper

Put the cauliflower, bay leaf and salt into a pan and add just enough water to cover. Bring to the boil, cover and cook for 7 minutes. Drain, reserving the liquid.

Meanwhile, melt the butter or margarine and fry the onion and potato for 5 minutes until soft but not browned. Blend in the flour and cook, stirring continuously for 2 minutes. Blend in the milk and bring to the boil, stirring. Add the cauliflower, reduce the heat and simmer gently until tender. Purée in a blender or food processor then return to the pan and stir in enough of the reserved liquid to obtain the consistency you prefer. Check and adjust the seasoning to taste and reheat before serving.

Chick Pea Soup
Serves 4

100 g/4 oz/⅔ cup chick peas (garbanzos), soaked overnight

750 ml/1½ pts/3¾ cups water ● 5 ml/1 tsp cumin seeds

10 ml/2 tsp coriander (cilantro) seeds ● 5 ml/1 tsp fenugreek seeds

3 dried red chillies ● 15 ml/1 tbsp grated (shredded) coconut ● 30 ml/2 tbsp ghee

225 g/8 oz tomatoes, skinned and chopped ● 5 ml/1 tsp ground turmeric

5 ml/1 tsp sugar ● 5 ml/1 tsp salt

Bring the chick peas and 600 ml/1 pt/ 2½ cups of water to the boil, cover and simmer for 1 hour until tender. Grind the cumin, coriander and fenugreek seeds, chillies and coconut. Heat the ghee and fry the spices for 1 minute. **Purée the chick peas then stir in the fried spices, tomatoes, turmeric, sugar and salt and the remaining water. Bring to the boil, cover and simmer gently for 20 minutes.**

Corn Soup
Serves 4-6

25 g/1 oz/2 tbsp butter or margarine ● 1 small onion, chopped

1 clove garlic, crushed ● 1 green chilli, chopped

10 ml/2 tsp chopped fresh coriander (cilantro)

2 tomatoes, skinned and chopped

450 g/1 lb sweetcorn kernels ● 900 ml/1½ pts/3¾ cups stock

salt and pepper ● 45 ml/3 tbsp cream or milk

Melt the butter or margarine in a large pan and fry the onion, garlic and chilli until soft but not browned. Add the coriander and tomatoes and fry until the tomatoes are soft and the fat separates. Add half the corn and fry for a few minutes. Add half the stock **and purée until smooth in a blender or food processor. Add the remaining stock and corn, season with salt and pepper, bring to the boil and simmer for 20 minutes. Stir in the cream or milk and heat through gently before serving.**

Lentil Soup
Serves 4

15 ml/1 tbsp ghee ● 100 g/4 oz/⅔ cup red lentils, soaked for 3 hours

2 onions, chopped ● ½ carrot, chopped ● 1 potato, chopped

½ turnip, chopped ● 600 ml/1 pt/2½ cups vegetable stock

salt and pepper ● 150 ml/¼ pt/⅔ cup milk

15 ml/1 tbsp plain (all-purpose) flour ● fried bread croûtons

Heat the ghee in a large pan and fry the lentils and vegetables until the vegetables are soft but not browned. Add the water, salt and pepper, bring to the boil and simmer gently for 30-40 minutes until the lentils and vegetables are tender. Purée the soup in a blender or food processor then return to the pan and simmer for 3 minutes. Blend together the milk and flour, stir into the soup and simmer, stirring occasionally, for 5 minutes. Serve hot with crispy fried bread croûtons.

Mushroom Soup
Serves 4

25 g/1 oz/2 tbsp butter or margarine ● 3 spring onions (scallions), chopped

100 g/4 oz mushrooms, chopped ● 25 g/1 oz/¼ cup plain (all-purpose) flour

450 ml/¾ pt/2 cups stock ● 120 ml/4 fl oz/½ cup milk ● salt and pepper

Melt the butter in a large pan and fry the spring onions until soft but not browned. Add the mushrooms and fry for 5 minutes. Stir in the flour and cook for 2 minutes. Gradually add the stock, stirring until the soup thickens. Cover and simmer gently for 10 minutes. Add the milk and season with salt and pepper. Heat through gently before serving.

Pea Soup
Serves 4-6

450 g/1 lb peas ● 900 ml/1½ pts/3¾ cups chicken or vegetable stock

5 ml/1 tsp chopped fresh mint ● 2.5 ml/½ tsp sugar

25 g/1 oz/2 tbsp unsalted butter ● 25 g/1 oz/¼ cup plain (all-purpose) flour

300 ml/½ pt/1¼ cups milk ● salt and pepper

Put the peas, stock, mint and sugar into a large pan, bring to the boil, cover and simmer gently for 25-30 minutes.

Meanwhile, melt the butter, stir in the flour and cook for 2 minutes. Gradually blend in the milk, bring to the boil then reduce the heat, season with salt and pepper and simmer gently for 5 minutes. Purée the pea mixture in a blender or food processor then stir it into the milk. Check and adjust the seasoning to taste before serving.

Pea Pod Soup

Serves 4-6

pods from 450 g/1 lb peas ● 1 onion, finely chopped

900 ml/1½ pts/3¾ cups vegetable stock

15 ml/1 tbsp chopped fresh coriander (cilantro) ● 5 ml/1 tsp chopped fresh mint

25 g/1 oz/2 tbsp butter or margarine ● 25 g/1 oz/¼ cup plain (all-purpose) flour

5 ml/1 tsp sugar ● salt and pepper

Put the pods, onion, stock, coriander and mint into a pan, bring to the boil, cover and simmer gently for about 25 minutes until the pods are tender. Drain, reserving the liquid, then purée the pods in a blender or food processor.

Mix the purée into the reserved liquid. Meanwhile, melt the butter or margarine, stir in the flour and cook for 2 minutes. Blend in the puréed mixture and bring to the boil. Season to taste with sugar, salt and pepper.

Potato Soup

Serves 4

15 ml/1 tbsp ghee ● 2.5 ml/½ tsp cumin seeds

pinch of asafoetida ● 4 potatoes, diced

1 tomato, quartered ● salt and pepper

600 ml/1 pt/2½ cups water ● 300 ml/½ pt/1¼ cups milk

Heat the ghee and fry the cumin seeds and asafoetida until the seeds start crackling. Add the potatoes and tomato, season with salt and pepper and cook for 2-3 minutes. Add the water, bring to the boil and simmer over a medium

heat for about 20 minutes. Purée the soup in a blender or food processor or rub through a sieve. Stir in the milk, return to the boil and simmer for 2 minutes before serving.

Prawn and Celery Soup

Serves 4

15 ml/1 tbsp oil ● 15 ml/1 tbsp ghee ● 1 onion, sliced

5 cm/2 in ginger root, sliced ● 1 green chilli, sliced

2.25 l/4 pts/10 cups water from cooked rice ● 4 sticks celery, cut into chunks

225 g/8 oz cooked, peeled prawns (shrimp) ● 5 ml/1 tsp sugar

2.5 ml/½ tsp ground turmeric ● salt ● 1 lemon, sliced

Heat the oil and ghee in a large pan and fry the onion, ginger and chilli until soft but not browned. Add the rice water and simmer for 10-15 minutes until the celery is tender. Add

the prawns and simmer until they are just heated through. Season with turmeric, sugar and salt and serve with rice and slices of lemon.

Pumpkin Soup
Serves 4

45 ml/3 tbsp oil ● 2 onions, chopped ● 2 bay leaves

1 cm/½ in ginger root ● 2 cloves garlic ● 1 green chilli

450 g/1 lb pumpkin, diced ● 1 tomato, skinned and chopped

15 ml/1 tbsp chopped fresh coriander (cilantro) ● 750 ml/1¼ pts/3 cups stock

45 ml/3 tbsp single (light) cream ● 5 ml/1 tsp lemon juice ● salt

Heat the oil and fry the onions and bay leaves until soft. Purée the ginger, garlic and chilli then add it to the pan and fry for 1 minute. Add the pumpkin and fry for 2-3 minutes. Add the tomato, coriander and stock, bring to the boil then simmer for 30 minutes. Purée in a blender and thin with a little more stock, if necessary. Reheat gently, stir in the cream, lemon juice and salt to taste and serve.

Rice Water Soup
Serves 6

225 g/8 oz/1 cup long-grain rice ● 900 ml/1½ pts/3¾ cups water

1 onion, chopped ● salt and white pepper

2.5 ml/½ tsp chilli powder ● 5 ml/1 tsp chopped fresh coriander (cilantro)

5 ml/1 tsp lemon juice

Put the rice and water in a pan, bring to the boil and simmer for 15 minutes. Drain the water into a separate pan and reserve the rice for another dish. Add the onion, salt, pepper and chilli powder to the rice water. Return to the boil and simmer gently for 10 minutes. Stir in the coriander and lemon juice to taste.

Spinach Soup
Serves 6

225 g/8 oz/½ lb fresh spinach, chopped ● 900 ml/1½ pts/3 cups water

salt ● 30 ml/2 tbsp ghee ● 1 onion, chopped

pepper ● 30 ml/2 tbsp cream

Place the spinach, water and salt in a large pan, bring to the boil and simmer until the spinach is soft. Purée until smooth in a blender or food processor or rub through a sieve. In a separate pan, heat the ghee and fry the onion until golden. Gradually blend in the spinach purée and simmer for 5 minutes, stirring occasionally. Season with pepper and serve hot, topped with cream.

Tomato Soup
Serves 4

500 g/18 oz ripe tomatoes, cut into large chunks ● 1 medium potato, chopped

1 small onion, coarsely chopped ● 900 ml/1½ pts/3¾ cups water

oil for deep-frying ● 2 brown bread slices, cut into 1 cm/½ in squares

salt and pepper

Place the tomatoes, potato, onion and water in a large pan over a medium heat and bring to the boil. Reduce the heat to medium-low, cover and cook for about 20 minutes until the potato and tomato pieces are tender and mushy. Remove the tomato skin. Purée the soup in a blender or food processor. Return to the pan to reheat, then boil until the soup is the consistency you prefer.

Meanwhile, heat the oil in a deep frying pan (skillet) over a medium heat. Fry the bread squares until golden brown. Serve the soup in bowls, sprinkled with the crispy croûtons and salt and pepper to taste.

Tomato and Coconut Soup
Serves 4

30 ml/2 tbsp oil ● 1 onion, chopped ● 2 bay leaves

30 ml/2 tbsp plain (all-purpose) flour ● 450 g/1 lb tomatoes, chopped

100 g/4 oz desiccated (shredded) coconut ● 2 green chillies

2.5 cm/1 in ginger root ● 500 ml/17 fl oz/2¼ cups water ● salt

45 ml/3 tbsp coconut milk ● 15 ml/1 tbsp chopped fresh coriander (cilantro)

Heat the oil and fry the onion and bay leaves until soft. Add the flour and fry for 2 minutes, stirring. Add the tomatoes and coconut and fry for 3 minutes. Purée the chillies and ginger then add to the pan with the water and salt. Bring to the boil then simmer for about 12 minutes. Purée or rub through a sieve then add the coconut milk and boil for a few minutes until the soup is the consistency you prefer. Garnish with the coriander before serving.

Mixed Vegetable Soup
Serves 4

450 g/1 lb mixed vegetables (of your choice), cut into chunks

900 ml/1½ pts/3⅔ cups water ● few drops of almond essence (extract)   ·

salt and pepper ● oil for frying ● 2 slices of brown bread, diced

Place the vegetables and water in a heavy-based pan and bring to the boil. Cover and simmer gently until the vegetables are tender and mushy. Purée the soup in a blender or food processor then return to the pan, add the almond essence and season to taste with salt and pepper. Simmer until the soup is the consistency you prefer. Just before serving, heat the oil in a separate pan and fry the bread until crispy. Sprinkle over the soup and serve hot.

Walnut Soup
Serves 6

50 g/2 oz/½ cup walnuts ● 300 ml/½ pt/10 cups milk

25 g/1 oz/2 tbsp butter or margarine ● 1 small onion, finely chopped

25 g/1 oz/¼ cup plain (all-purpose) flour ● 900 ml/1½ pts/3¾ cups chicken stock

salt and pepper ● 1 egg yolk ● 60 ml/4 tbsp cream

Grind the walnuts to a smooth paste, adding a little water. Heat the milk to almost boiling and pour over the paste. Leave to stand for 30 minutes.

Melt the butter or margarine in a heavy-based pan and fry the onion gently until soft. Stir in the flour and cook for 2 minutes. Stir in the stock and walnut milk and season with salt and pepper. Bring almost to boiling point. Blend together the egg yolk and cream. Pour a little hot soup on to the mixture then stir it back into the pan and stir over a medium heat until the soup thickens. Serve immediately or leave to cool, chill then serve cold.

Yoghurt Soup
Serves 4

2 green chillies ● 1 onion, chopped ● 1 cm/½ in ginger root

4 cloves garlic ● 30 ml/2 tbsp ghee ● 5 ml/1 tsp cumin seeds

5 ml/1 tsp mustard seeds ● 2-3 curry leaves ● 2.5 ml/½ tsp ground turmeric

300 ml/½ pt/1¼ cups natural (plain) yoghurt

300 ml/½ pt/1¼ cups single (light) cream ● 10 ml/2 tsp sugar

salt ● 15 ml/1 tbsp chopped fresh coriander (cilantro)

Purée the chillies, onion, ginger and garlic. Heat the ghee and fry the cumin and mustard seeds and curry leaves until the seeds start crackling. Add the turmeric and purée and fry until browned. Add the yoghurt and cream and season to taste with sugar and salt. Whisk over a gentle heat until the soup comes to the boil. Serve garnished with fresh coriander.

Creamy Lettuce Soup
Serves 6

25 g/1 oz/2 tbsp unsalted butter ● 2 small lettuces, torn into bite-sized pieces

1 small onion, finely chopped ● 25 g/1 oz/¼ cup plain (all-purpose) flour

900 ml/1½ pts/3¾ cups milk ● salt and pepper ● 1 egg yolk

60 ml/4 tbsp cream ● 30 ml/2 tbsp grated cheese

Melt the butter in a large pan, add the lettuce and onion and fry gently for 8-9 minutes. Stir in the flour and cook for 2 minutes, stirring. Gradually whisk in the milk until well blended. Bring to the boil, cover and simmer gently for 15-20 minutes. Remove from the heat and leave to cool. Purée the soup and season to taste with salt and pepper. Gradually reheat the soup but do not let it boil. Blend together the egg yolk, cream and cheese. Stir a little of the hot soup into the mixture, then stir it back into the pan and blend together over a low heat. Cook until slightly thickened. Leave to cool then chill before serving.

Cucumber Cooler

Serves 4

1 large cucumber ● 450 ml/¾ pt/2 cups natural (plain) yoghurt

15 ml/1 tbsp chopped fresh coriander (cilantro) ● salt and pepper

5 ml/1 tsp sugar ● 2-3 mint leaves, finely chopped

Peel and seed the cucumber. Blend all the ingredients except the mint until smooth in a blender or food processor. Check and adjust the seasoning to taste then chill. Serve garnished with mint.

Tangy Tomato Soup

Serves 4

450 g/1 lb tomatoes, skinned and quartered ● 1 small onion, sliced

1 small green (bell) pepper, quartered

5 ml/1 tsp chopped fresh dill (dill weed)

juice of ½ lime ● 450 ml/¾ pt/2 cups chicken or vegetable stock

salt and pepper

Purée all the ingredients until smooth in a blender or food processor. Check and adjust the seasoning to taste. Chill well then serve sprinkled with black pepper.

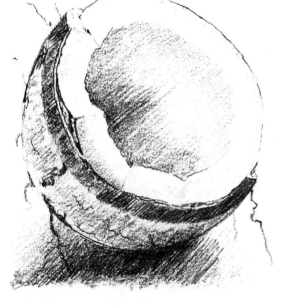

Seafood

Not surprisingly, fish dishes are more popular on the coasts of India where seafood is readily available. The fish purchased in India are very different from those available elsewhere, so these recipes have been adapted to suit Western species. Bengali fish dishes are often cooked in mustard oil. Fish are often cooked with skin, bones and head intact, as this retains the maximum nutritional value and flavour.

Fish Curry   Serves 4-6

4 large garlic cloves ● 2 onions, cut into chunks

2.5 cm/1 in ginger root, chopped ● 50 ml/2 fl oz/3½ fl oz wine vinegar

500 g/18 oz cod or haddock fillets, cut into 5 cm/2 in pieces ● 90 ml/6 tbsp oil

Sauce: 60 ml/4 tbsp oil ● 5 ml/1 tsp mustard seeds

1 onion, finely chopped ● 4 cloves ● 4 peppercorns

2 bay leaves ● 1 black cardamom pod ● 1.5 cm/½ in cinnamon stick

5 ml/1 tsp ground roasted cumin ● 5 ml/1 tsp ground turmeric

2.5 ml/½ tsp ground red chilli ● salt ● 225 g/8 oz canned tomatoes

150 ml/¼ pt/⅔ cup natural (plain) yoghurt ● 15 ml/1 tbsp sugar

200 ml/7 fl oz/scant 1 cup water

Garnish: 2.5 ml/½ tsp garam masala

15 ml/1 tbsp chopped fresh coriander (cilantro) ● 1 small green chilli, chopped

Purée the garlic, onions, ginger and wine vinegar to a smooth paste in a blender or food processor. Marinate the fish in half the paste for 30 minutes. Reserve the other half for the sauce.

Make the sauce while the fish is marinating. Heat the oil in a heavy-based pan and fry the mustard seeds until they start crackling. Add the onion and whole spices and fry until golden brown. Mix in the reserved paste and fry for a few minutes until golden brown. Stir in the ground spices and salt then the tomatoes and cook until all the liquid has been absorbed. Add the yoghurt and sugar and cook again until all the liquid has been absorbed and the oil appears on the surface. Add the water, bring to the boil then simmer over a low heat for 5 minutes.

Meanwhile, heat the oil and fry the fish over a medium heat for 15 minutes until light brown, turning once or twice. Remove from the pan and place on a serving dish. Pour the sauce over the fish, sprinkle with the garnish ingredients and serve hot with chapatis, rice, dal, raita and a bean and potato dish.

Fish Cutlets
Makes 12

500 g/18 oz cod or haddock fillets, skinned

45 ml/3 tbsp desiccated (shredded) coconut

45 ml/3 tbsp chopped fresh coriander (cilantro) • 5 ml/1 tsp garam masala

5 ml/1 tsp dried pomegranate seeds • 2.5 ml/½ tsp ground red chilli

salt • 2 slices bread, soaked in warm water and squeezed

1 onion, finely chopped • 1 small green chilli, finely chopped • 1 egg, beaten

75 ml/5 tbsp breadcrumbs • oil for frying

Bake the fish in a preheated oven at 240°C/475°F/gas mark 9 for 20 minutes. Mix the fish with the remaining ingredients except the egg and breadcrumbs and divide into 12 equal portions. With oiled hands, roll the portions of fish mixture and flatten to about 5 mm/¼ in thick. Heat a frying pan (skillet) and smear with a little oil. Dip the cutlets into egg then breadcrumbs and fry until golden brown underneath. Pour some more oil around, turn the cutlets over and fry until golden brown. Serve hot with chutney.

Fish in Coconut Cream
Serves 6

1 coconut, grated (shredded) • 1.5 l/2½ pts/6 cups hot water

4 onions, chopped • 10 cloves garlic, chopped • 2.5 cm/1 in ginger root

60 ml/4 tbsp ghee • 2 curry leaves

900 g/2 lb cod fillets, cut into chunks • 3 green chillies

salt • 15 ml/1 tbsp chopped fresh coriander (cilantro)

Soak the coconut in 300 ml/½ pt/1¼ cups of hot water then strain to remove the milk. Pour over the remaining hot water to extract more milk. Purée or grind the onions, garlic and ginger to a fine paste. Warm the ghee in a frying pan (skillet) and fry the curry leaves until browned. Add the ground spices and fry, stirring occasionally. Add the fish and cook for 1 minute, stirring carefully to coat the fish in the spices. Stir in the coconut milk so that the fish is completely covered. Add the chillies, cover and simmer for 5 minutes. Season to taste with salt and turn the fish over. Simmer, uncovered, for a further 10 minutes until the fish is tender and the sauce has thickened. Garnish with coriander and serve hot with plain rice.

Fish in Tomato Sauce
Serves 4-6

30 ml/2 tbsp plain (all-purpose) flour • 5 ml/1 tsp garam masala

2.5 ml/½ tsp ground red chilli • 2.5 ml/½ tsp ajwain

50 ml/2 fl oz/3½ tbsp water • 500 g/18 oz cod fillets, skinned and cubed

30 ml/2 tbsp oil

Sauce: 3 large cloves garlic • 2.5 cm/1 in ginger root, coarsely chopped

1 onion, coarsely chopped • 75 ml/3 tbsp oil

2.5 ml/½ tsp mustard seeds • 5 ml/1 tsp garam masala

5 ml/1 tsp ground coriander (cilantro) • 5 ml/1 tsp ground roasted cumin

2.5 ml/½ tsp ground red chilli • 2.5 ml/½ tsp ground turmeric

salt • 400 g/14 oz canned tomatoes • 15 ml/1 tbsp sugar

375 ml/13 fl oz/1½ cups water

Garnish: 15 ml/1 tbsp chopped fresh coriander (cilantro)

1 green chilli, chopped

Mix the flour, garam masala, chilli, ajwain and water to a smooth batter and dip the fish in the batter. Heat the oil and fry the fish until golden brown on all sides.

To make the sauce, purée the garlic, ginger and onion to a smooth paste in a blender or food processor. Heat the oil and fry the mustard seeds until they start crackling. Stir in the blended paste and fry until golden brown. Stir in the ground spices and salt then the tomatoes and sugar and cook until all the liquid has been absorbed and the oil appears on the surface. Add 45 ml/3 tbsp of water and cook until the water has been absorbed. Add the remaining water, bring to the boil then simmer over a low heat for 5 minutes. Pour the hot sauce over the fried fish and sprinkle with the garnish ingredients. Serve hot with plain rice, puris, a potato dish and raita.

Bengali-style Fish in Yoghurt
Serves 4-6

30 ml/2 tbsp plain (all-purpose) flour • 5 ml/1 tsp garam masala

2.5 ml/½ tsp ground red chilli • 2.5 ml/½ tsp ajwain • 50 ml/2 fl oz/3½ tbsp water

500 g/18 oz cod fillet, cut into 4 cm/1½ in pieces • 30 ml/2 tbsp oil

Sauce: 300 ml/½ pt/1¼ cups natural (plain) yoghurt

60 ml/1 tbsp chopped fresh coriander (cilantro) • 1 green chilli

75 ml/5 tbsp oil • 5 ml/1 tsp mustard seeds • 4 cloves

4 black peppercorns • 4 bay leaves • 2.5 cm/1 in cinnamon stick

1 black cardamom pod • 5 ml/1 tsp garam masala

5 ml/1 tsp ground roasted cumin • 5 ml/1 tsp sugar

5 ml/1 tsp ground turmeric • 2.5 ml/½ tsp ground ginger

2.5 ml/½ tsp ground red chilli • 100 ml/3½ fl oz/6½ tbsp water

Garnish: 1.5 ml/¼ tsp garam masala

Mix together the flour, garam masala, chilli, ajwain and water and rub the mixture into the fish pieces. Heat the oil and fry the fish gently for 15 minutes until golden brown on all sides. Place in a serving dish.

Make the sauce while the fish is cooking. Purée the yoghurt, coriander and chilli to a smooth paste in a blender or food processor. Heat the oil in a heavy-based pan and fry the mustard seeds until they start crackling. Add the whole and ground spices. Add the paste and water and bring to the boil, stirring continuously, then simmer over a low heat for 5 minutes. Pour the sauce over the fish and sprinkle with garam masala. Serve hot with plain rice, chapatis and stuffed aubergine or okra.

Malabari Fish
Serves 6

1 coconut, grated (shredded) • 1.5 l/2½ pts/6 cups hot water

45 ml/3 tbsp oil • 3 onions, thinly sliced • 10 cloves garlic, chopped

5 cm/2 in ginger root, chopped • 6 green chillies, slit

100 g/4 oz/1 cup plain (all-purpose) flour • 5 ml/1 tsp ground turmeric

2 tomatoes, chopped • 900 g/2 lb cod or white fish, thickly sliced

45 ml/3 tbsp white wine vinegar • salt

Add 300 ml/½ pt/⅔ cup hot water to the grated coconut and extract a thick milk. Add the remaining hot water to the coconut and strain to extract the second milk.

Heat the oil and fry the onions, garlic and ginger for 2 minutes. Add the chillies, flour and turmeric, stirring well to avoid lumps. Add the tomatoes and thin coconut milk, bring to the boil then simmer for 10 minutes. Add the fish and white wine vinegar and simmer for 15 minutes. Add the thick coconut milk and salt and simmer for 5 minutes. Serve hot with plain rice or idlis.

Fish Shaslik
Serves 4

4 dried red chillies ● 2.5 cm/1 in ginger root ● 4 cloves garlic, crushed

450 g/1 lb cod or white fish fillets, cubed ● 6 cloves

6 black peppercorns ● 1 black cardamom pod ● ½ cinnamon stick

150 ml/¼ pt/⅔ cup natural (plain) yoghurt ● salt

100 g/4 oz onions, cubed ● 45 ml/3 tbsp ghee ● 5 ml/1 tsp garam masala

Grind the chillies and ginger together. Add the garlic to a pan of water and wash the fish in the water to get rid of any fishy smell then drain. Grind together the cloves, peppercorns, cardamom and cinnamon then mix with the fish. Mix in the yoghurt and salt to taste.

Fix alternate cubes of fish and onion on skewers and grill (broil) under a moderate grill (broiler) until cooked through and browned, brushing occasionally with a little melted ghee. When cooked through, remove from the skewers, sprinkle with garam masala and serve hot.

Fish Kofta Curry
Serves 4

450 g/1 lb cod fillets ● 3 onions, sliced ● 8 green chillies, sliced

15 ml/1 tbsp chopped fresh coriander (cilantro) ● 4 cloves

5 ml/1 tsp black peppercorns ● 6 cardamom pods ● 4 cinnamon sticks

5 ml/1 tsp cumin seeds ● 90 ml/6 tbsp ghee ● 2 tomatoes, skinned and chopped

1.2 l/2 pts/5 cups water ● 10 ml/2 tsp ground coriander (cilantro)

2.5 cm/1 in ginger root, chopped ● salt

Poach the fish in a little water for about 15 minutes until tender. Flake the flesh. Add 1 of the onions and 4 green chillies to the fish with the coriander. Grind together the cloves, peppercorns, 3 cardamom pods and the cinnamon and cumin seeds and add to the fish. Mix well and mash to a paste, then shape into round balls. Heat half the ghee and fry the fish balls until browned.

Heat the remaining ghee and fry the remaining onions and chillies until browned. Add the tomatoes and half the water and simmer gently until the liquid has evaporated. Add the remaining cardamom, the coriander and ginger and season to taste with salt. Add the remaining water, bring to the boil and simmer for 5 minutes. Add the fish and simmer for a further 15 minutes. Serve hot with plain rice.

Fish with Okra
Serves 4

30 ml/2 tbsp ghee ● 30 ml/2 tbsp mustard oil ● 4 cardamom pods

5 ml/1 tsp sugar ● 225 g/8 oz onions, sliced

150 ml/¼ pt/⅔ cup natural (plain) yoghurt ● 450 g/1 lb cod fillets, cut into chunks

225 g/8 oz okra, chopped ● 4 dried red chillies, seeded and ground

2.5 cm/1 in ginger root, chopped ● salt

Heat the ghee and oil and fry the cardamom pods for 1 minute. Add the sugar and stir until it turns brown. Add the onions and fry until browned. Beat the yoghurt to a smooth paste and add to the pan with the fish, okra, chillies, ginger and salt. Cover and simmer for 10 minutes until the fish is tender. Serve hot or cold with rice.

Steamed Bengali-style Fish
Serves 6

900 g/2 lb white fish fillets, cut into chunks ● salt

10 ml/2 tsp ground turmeric ● 3 dried red chillies ● 10 ml/2 tsp mustard seeds

15 ml/1 tbsp water ● 5 green chillies, slit ● 30 ml/2 tbsp mustard oil

Season the fish with salt and set aside. Grind the turmeric, chillies, mustard seeds and water to a smooth paste. Mix together the fish, ground paste, chillies and oil, place in a steamer and steam for 10 minutes or until tender. Serve hot with plain rice.

Fish Vindaloo
Serves 4-6

675 g/1½ lb white fish fillets, cut into chunks ● salt

6 dried red chillies ● 10 cloves garlic ● 5 cm/2 in ginger root

10 ml/2 tsp cumin seeds ● 675 g/1½ lb onions, chopped

300 ml/½ pt/1¼ cups wine vinegar ● 45 ml/3 tbsp ghee

½ cinnamon stick ● salt ● 25 g/1 oz/2 tbsp sugar

5 ml/1 tsp garam masala ● 6 green chillies

Sprinkle the fish with salt and leave to stand for 10 minutes. Rinse then pat dry. Grind the red chillies, garlic, ginger, cumin seeds and onions to a fine paste with a little of the wine vinegar. Heat the ghee and fry the ground spices for a few minutes. Add the cinnamon and fish, sprinkle with salt, and fry over a high heat for 5 minutes. Lower the heat and simmer until the fish is tender. Add the wine vinegar, sugar, garam masala and chillies and simmer until the sauce thickens.

Fish Shifta

Serves 4

450 g/1 lb white fish, minced ● 4 large onions, minced

1 sprig fresh coriander (cilantro), chopped ● 1 sprig fresh mint, chopped

3 cloves garlic, chopped ● 2.5 cm/1 in ginger root, chopped

10 ml/2 tsp ground turmeric ● 30 ml/2 tbsp oil

salt and pepper ● oil for frying

Mix together all the ingredients except the frying oil and shape into fat sausage shapes. Heat the oil and shallow-fry for about 10 minutes until cooked through and browned. Serve hot with chutney and tomato sauce.

Spicy Fish with Tomatoes

Serves 4

60 ml/4 tbsp ghee ● 700 g/1½ lb cod fillets, cubed

5 ml/1 tsp coriander (cilantro) seeds ● 5 ml/1 tsp black peppercorns

1 clove garlic, crushed ● 5 ml/1 tsp ground turmeric

1.5 ml/¼ tsp chilli powder ● 5 ml/1 tsp salt ● 4 tomatoes, skinned and chopped

300 ml/½ pt/1¼ cups water ● 2.5 ml/½ tsp garam masala

15 ml/1 tbsp chopped fresh coriander (cilantro)

Heat the ghee and fry the fish for 2-3 minutes then remove from the pan. Grind the coriander seeds, peppercorns and garlic to a paste. Add the paste to the pan with the turmeric, chilli powder and salt and fry gently for 2 minutes. Stir in the tomatoes and water, bring to the boil then simmer gently for 5 minutes. Return the fish to the pan and simmer gently for 10 minutes, shaking the pan occasionally but not stirring. Add the garam masala, cover and leave to stand for 2 minutes. Serve garnished with coriander.

Eastern Fried Fish

Serves 4-6

5 large cloves garlic ● 2 onions, coarsely chopped ● 2.5 cm/1 in ginger root

1 small green chilli ● 100 ml/3½ fl oz/6½ tbsp wine vinegar

5 ml/1 tsp dried pomegranate seeds ● 5 ml/1 tsp garam masala

5 ml/1 tsp ground cumin ● 5 ml/1 tsp ground coriander

2.5 ml/½ tsp ground red chilli ● salt

500 g/18 oz cod fillets, skinned and cut into 5 cm/2 in pieces ● 60 ml/4 tbsp oil

Blend the garlic, onions, ginger, chilli, wine vinegar and pomegranate seeds to a smooth paste in a blender or food processor. Mix in the ground spices and salt and rub into the fish pieces. Cover and marinate for 2 hours.

Remove the fish from the marinade and set aside. Place the marinade in a pan and dry off all the liquid over a medium heat for about 30 minutes. Return the fish to the marinade and coat the pieces evenly. Heat the oil and fry the fish until golden brown on all sides. Serve hot with pulao rice, dal and a potato and bean dish.

Bengali Fish Koftas

Serves 4-6

500 g/18 oz cod, haddock or mackerel fillets, skinned

30 ml/2 tbsp chopped fresh coriander (cilantro)

10 ml/2 tsp poppy seeds, ground ● 1 small onion, finely chopped

2 large cloves garlic, crushed ● 1.5 cm/½ in ginger root, finely chopped

1 egg, beaten ● 2.5 ml/½ tsp garam masala ● 1.5 ml/¼ tsp ground red chilli

salt ● oil for deep-frying

Sauce: 3 large cloves garlic, chopped ● 2.5 cm/1 in ginger root, chopped

1 onion, chopped ● 75 ml/5 tbsp oil ● large pinch of asafoetida

5 ml/1 tsp mustard seeds ● 2 bay leaves ● 1 small onion, finely chopped

5 ml/1 tsp ground coriander (cilantro) ● 5 ml/1 tsp ground roasted cumin

2.5 ml/½ tsp garam masala ● 2.5 ml/½ tsp ground red chilli

2.5 ml/½ tsp ground turmeric ● salt ● 225 g/8 oz canned tomatoes

150 ml/¼ pt/⅔ cup natural (plain) yoghurt ● 250 ml/8 fl oz/1 cup water

Garnish: 15 ml/1 tbsp chopped fresh coriander (cilantro)

1 small green chilli, chopped

Bake the fish in a preheated oven at 240°C/475°F/gas mark 9 for 20 minutes. Mix together the coriander, poppy seeds, onion, garlic, ginger, egg, garam masala, chilli and salt and add to the baked fish. Divide the mixture into 18 equal portions and roll them into rounds. Heat the oil and fry the koftas until golden brown.

Make the sauce while the fish is cooking. Blend the garlic, ginger and onion to a smooth paste in a blender or food processor. Heat the oil and fry the asafoetida and mustard seeds until the seeds start crackling. Add the bay leaves and small onion and fry until golden brown. Add the blended paste and fry until golden brown. Stir in the ground spices, salt and tomatoes and cook until all the liquid has been absorbed and the oil appears on the surface. Stir in the yoghurt and cook until all the liquid has evaporated. Pour in the water, bring to the boil then simmer for 5 minutes. Pour the hot sauce over the koftas, sprinkle with the garnish ingredients and serve hot with rice, chapatis, raita and a potato dish.

Fish Korma
Serves 4-6

30 ml/2 tbsp lemon juice • 5 ml/1 tsp garam masala

2.5 ml/½ tsp ground red chilli • 2 large cloves garlic • 1.5 cm/½ in ginger root

1 onion, coarsely chopped • salt

500 g/18 oz cod or haddock fillets, skinned and cut into 5 cm/2 in pieces

1 egg, beaten • 25 g/1 oz/¼ cup breadcrumbs • 60 ml/4 tbsp oil

Sauce: 2 large cloves garlic • 1.5 cm/½ in ginger root, coarsely chopped

1 onion, coarsely chopped • 60 ml/4 tbsp oil • 5 ml/1 tsp mustard seeds

1 small onion, finely chopped • 4 cloves • 4 black peppercorns

2 bay leaves • 1.5 cm/½ in cinnamon stick • 1 black cardamom pod

15 ml/1 tbsp poppy seeds, ground

90 ml/6 tbsp desiccated (shredded) coconut, ground

5 ml/1 tsp ground coriander (cilantro) • 5 ml/1 tsp ground roasted cumin

2.5 ml/½ tsp ground red chilli • 2.5 ml/½ tsp ground turmeric

salt • 225 g/8 oz canned tomatoes • 300 ml/½ pt/1¼ cups water

Garnish: 2.5 ml/½ tsp garam masala

15 ml/1 tbsp chopped fresh coriander (cilantro) • 1 small green chilli, chopped

Blend the lemon juice, garam masala, chilli, garlic, ginger, onion and salt to a smooth paste in a blender or food processor. Rub the mixture over the fish and leave to marinate for 1 hour.

Dip the marinated fish in the egg then roll in breadcrumbs. Heat half the oil and fry the fish pieces until golden brown on the underside. Add the remaining oil, turn the fish over and fry for 7 minutes until golden brown. Place on a serving dish.

Make the sauce while the fish is cooking. Blend the garlic, ginger and onion to a smooth paste in a blender or food processor. Heat the oil in a heavy-based pan and fry the mustard seeds until they start crackling. Add the onion and whole spices and fry until golden brown. Add the blended paste and fry for 2 minutes. Add the poppy seeds and fry for 2 minutes. Add the coconut and fry until golden brown. Stir in the ground spices and salt then the tomatoes and cook until all the liquid has been absorbed and the oil appears on the surface. Add one-third of the water and cook until all the water has been absorbed. Add the remaining water, bring to the boil then simmer over a low heat for 3 minutes. Pour the hot sauce over the fish, sprinkle with the garnish ingredients and serve hot with plain rice, chapatis, raita and okra.

Haddock Parcel
Serves 4

450 g/1 lb fresh coriander (cilantro) leaves ● 10 green chillies

600 ml/1 pt/2½ cups natural (plain) yoghurt ● salt

450 g/1 lb haddock fillets ● 1 lemon, sliced

Grind the coriander (cilantro) and chillies to a paste. Blend in the yoghurt and season with salt. Cut the fish into 4 and rub with the paste. Wrap the pieces individually in kitchen foil and place in a steamer over boiling water. Steam for about 20 minutes until the fish is tender. Garnish with lemon slices and serve hot with chapatis and rice.

Masala-stuffed Fish
Serves 6-8

1 large haddock or salmon ● juice of 3 lemons ● salt and pepper

45 ml/3 tbsp ghee ● 25 g/1 oz/¼ cup blanched almonds

25 g/1 oz/3 tbsp raisins ● 6 spring onions (scallions), sliced

100 g/4 oz peas ● 100 g/4 oz mashed potatoes

5 ml/1 tsp ground turmeric ● 5 ml/1 tsp garam masala

15 ml/1 tbsp chopped ginger root ● 5 green chillies, thinly sliced

45 ml/3 tbsp chopped fresh mint

45 ml/3 tbsp chopped fresh coriander (cilantro)

1 egg, beaten ● 45 ml/3 tbsp mustard oil

Clean the fish, rub inside and out with the juice of a lemon and sprinkle with salt and pepper. Leave to stand for 1 hour.

Heat the ghee and fry the almonds and raisins for 2 minutes then remove from the pan. Add the onions and fry until soft. Stir in the peas, potatoes, turmeric, garam masala and ginger then remove from the heat and leave to cool. Stir in the lemon juice, almonds, raisins, green chillies, mint and coriander. Bind the mixture with the egg and stuff into the fish. Tie up to hold the fish together. Heat the mustard oil and fry the fish for about 30 minutes until cooked through. Serve hot with fried tomatoes and potatoes.

Fish Korma
Serves 4

450 g/1 lb haddock fillets ● 100 g/4 oz onions

5 cm/2 in ginger root ● 1 bulb garlic ● 2 dried red chillies

15 ml/1 tbsp lime juice ● salt ● 1 egg, beaten

100 g/4 oz/1 cup breadcrumbs ● 120 ml/4 fl oz/½ cup ghee

2 cinnamon sticks ● 2 cardamom pods

2.5 ml/½ tsp ground turmeric ● 600 ml/1 pt/2½ cups hot coconut milk

2 green chillies

Cut the fish into chunks. Purée the onions, ginger, garlic and red chillies to a smooth paste in a blender or food processor. Rub half of the paste over the fish pieces, sprinkle with lime juice and season with salt.

Dip the fish pieces in egg then roll in breadcrumbs. Heat 90 ml/6 tbsp of ghee and fry the fish until golden.

Heat the remaining ghee and fry the cinnamon, cardamom and reserved paste for 2 minutes. Add the turmeric and half the coconut milk and simmer for 15 minutes. Add the remaining coconut milk and bring to the boil. Add the fish and chillies and cook for a further 10 minutes. Serve hot with rice.

Ten-minute Mustard Fish   Serves 4

30 ml/2 tbsp mustard powder ● 450 ml/¾ pt/2 cups water

2.5 ml/½ tsp ground turmeric ● salt ● 75 ml/5 tbsp mustard oil

5 ml/1 tsp onion seeds ● 3 onions, finely chopped

450 g/1 lb herring ● 3 green chillies, chopped

Dissolve the mustard powder in the water then stir in the turmeric and salt. Leave to stand for at least 30 minutes.

Heat 60 ml/4 tbsp of oil almost to smoking point and fry the onion seeds for 30 seconds. Add the onions and fry until golden. Pour in the mustard water and bring to the boil. Add the fish, cover and simmer for 6-7 minutes. Add the chillies, cover and simmer for 2 minutes. Stir in the remaining mustard oil and serve hot with plain rice.

Kerala-style Fish   Serves 6

1.5 kg/3 lb herring fillets ● 30 ml/2 tbsp coriander (cilantro) seeds

2 dried red chillies, split ● 5 ml/1 tsp ground turmeric

5 ml/1 tsp black peppercorns ● 375 ml/13 fl oz/1½ cups coconut milk

30 ml/2 tbsp cider vinegar ● 45 ml/3 tbsp oil ● 15 ml/1 tbsp black mustard seeds

1 red onion, chopped ● 8 cloves garlic ● 2.5 cm/1 in ginger root, crushed

2 sprigs fresh curry leaves ● 2 dried red chillies

10 ml/2 tsp tamarind concentrate ● salt

Cut the fish into 5 cm/2 in pieces. Dry roast the coriander seeds, chillies, turmeric and peppercorns in a small pan. Purée or grind to a paste with 45 ml/3 tbsp of the coconut milk and the cider vinegar.

Heat the oil and fry the mustard seeds over a medium heat until they start crackling. Add the onion, garlic, ginger, curry leaves and chillies and fry until the onion is browned. Add the ground spices and fry for 3 minutes. Add a further 45 ml/3 tbsp of the coconut milk and stir over a medium heat until the liquid has evaporated. Add the tamarind, fish and salt and simmer for 5 minutes. Add the remaining coconut milk, stir thoroughly and simmer for 5-10 minutes until thick, stirring occasionally. Serve hot with plain rice and a vegetable dish.

Spiced Grilled Mackerel
Serves 4

4 mackerel, filleted ● juice of 1 lemon

60 ml/4 tbsp chopped fresh coriander (cilantro) ● 10 ml/2 tsp garam masala

5 ml/1 tsp ground cumin ● 5 ml/1 tsp chilli powder ● salt and pepper

45 ml/3 tbsp ghee ● 1 lemon, cut into wedges

Score the skin of the fish in several places with a sharp knife. Mix the lemon juice, half the coriander, the garam masala, cumin, chilli powder and salt and pepper. Pour over the mackerel and leave to marinate for 2 hours, turning once and brushing with the marinade.

Brush half the ghee over the skin and grill (broil) for 5 minutes. Turn over, brush with the remaining ghee and grill for a further 5 minutes. Serve garnished with the remaining coriander and lemon wedges.

Mughal-style Fish Curry in Almond Sauce
Serves 6

2 large plaice ● 2.5 cm/1 in ginger root, chopped ● 6 cloves garlic

salt ● 15 ml/1 tbsp black mustard seeds ● juice of 1 lemon

45 ml/3 tbsp oil ● 1 large onion, chopped

45 ml/3 tbsp hot water ● 25 g/1 oz/¼ cup blanched almonds

30 ml/2 tbsp coriander (cilantro) seeds ● 10 ml/2 tsp cumin seeds

2 dried red chillies ● 5 ml/1 tsp ground turmeric

2.5 ml/½ tsp saffron threads ● 45 ml/3 tbsp hot milk ● 6 cardamom pods

1 cinnamon stick ● 2.5 ml/½ tsp black peppercorns ● 2 bay leaves

1.5 ml/¼ tsp cloves ● 45 ml/3 tbsp natural (plain) yoghurt

Make incisions 2.5 cm/1 in apart on both sides of the fish from head to tail. Blend the ginger, garlic, salt, mustard seeds and lemon juice in a blender or food processor. Spread the purée over and into the fish. Leave to marinate in the fridge for 3 hours.

Heat the oil and fry the onion until soft. Purée the water, almonds, coriander and cumin seeds, chillies and turmeric in a blender or pestle and mortar. Dissolve the saffron in the hot milk and leave to soak for 15 minutes. Stir the cardamom, cinnamon, peppercorns, bay leaves and cloves into the onions and cook for 2 minutes. Add the puréed spices and cook for 6-8 minutes until the oil appears on the surface, stirring constantly. Lightly whisk the saffron milk and yoghurt with a fork then stir it into the pan and simmer for 2 minutes.

Put the fish in a casserole dish and pour over the sauce. Bake in a preheated oven at 180°C/350°F/gas mark 4 for 15 minutes until the fish is cooked and the sauce starts bubbling. Serve hot with rice, chapatis, vegetables and dal.

Monkfish with Mustard Seeds
Serves 4-6

45 ml/3 tbsp mustard seeds ● 60 ml/4 tbsp water

900 g/2 lb monkfish fillet, cubed ● 30 ml/2 tbsp plain (all-purpose) flour

60 ml/4 tbsp oil ● 1 onion, sliced

300 ml/½ pt/1¼ cups natural (plain) yoghurt ● 2 cloves garlic, crushed

15 ml/1 tbsp lemon juice ● salt and pepper

15 ml/1 tbsp chopped fresh coriander (cilantro)

Soak half the mustard seeds in the water for 3 hours. Grind the remainder and toss the fish in the seeds. Heat the oil and fry the onion until golden. Drain the seeds and add to the pan with the fish. Fry for 3 minutes. Stir in the yoghurt, garlic, lemon juice, salt and pepper, bring to the boil then simmer for 15 minutes until tender. Serve garnished with coriander.

Hot Goan-style Fish Curry
Serves 6

2 large plaice ● 150 ml/¼ pt/⅔ cup coconut milk

5 ml/1 tsp ground turmeric ● 4 dried red chillies

75 g/3 oz/¾ cup desiccated (shredded) coconut ● 5 ml/1 tsp cumin seeds

15 ml/1 tbsp coriander (cilantro) seeds ● 45 ml/3 tbsp oil

1 large onion, finely chopped ● 1 sprig fresh curry leaves

2 large tomatoes, skinned and quartered ● 5 ml/1 tsp tamarind concentrate ● salt

Cut the fish into 10 cm/4 in pieces. Purée the coconut milk, turmeric, chillies, coconut, cumin and coriander seeds. Heat the oil and fry the onion until browned. Stir in the coconut purée, curry leaves, tomatoes and tamarind and cook for 5 minutes, stirring constantly. Add the fish and season to taste with salt. Simmer for 10-15 minutes until the fish is cooked, stirring occasionally. Serve hot with rice, papadums and vegetables.

Stuffed Plaice
Serves 6

2 large plaice ● 10 ml/2 tsp ghee ● 1 large onion, chopped

24 cooked, peeled prawns (shrimp) ● 10 ml/2 tsp tomato purée (paste)

3 green chillies, chopped ● 2 hard-boiled (hard-cooked) eggs, chopped

1 clove garlic, chopped ● 120 ml/4 fl oz/½ cup water ● 1 egg ● salt and pepper

Cut slits in the sides of the fish and remove the centre bone if possible. Heat the ghee and fry the onion until browned. Stir in the prawns, tomato purée, chillies, hard-boiled eggs, garlic and water and simmer gently until thick. Leave to cool. Mix in the egg, divide the mixture in half and use to stuff the fish. Season the fish with salt and pepper and wrap in oiled kitchen foil. Bake in a preheated oven at 200°C/400°F/gas mark 6 for 45 minutes until the fish is tender. Serve with fried potatoes.

Parsi Fish

Serves 6

2 large plaice ● 4 cloves garlic ● 4 green chillies

2.5 ml/½ tsp cumin seeds ● 30 ml/2 tbsp ghee ● 2 onions, sliced

450 ml/¾ pt/2 cups water ● 15 ml/1 tbsp plain (all-purpose) flour

15 ml/1 tbsp sugar ● 45 ml/3 tbsp wine vinegar ● 2 eggs

salt ● 15 ml/1 tbsp chopped fresh coriander (cilantro)

Slice the fish into 6 pieces. Purée the garlic, chillies and cumin seeds to a smooth paste in a blender or food processor. Heat the ghee and fry the onions until golden. Add the ground spices and fry for 2 minutes. Add the water, bring to the boil and simmer for 10 minutes. Blend the flour to a smooth paste with a little water then stir it into the pan and cook until the sauce thickens, stirring continuously. Add the fish and simmer for 15 minutes until tender. Blend together the sugar, wine vinegar and eggs. Remove the sauce from the heat and stir in the mixture. Season with salt and stir in the coriander. Serve with yellow rice.

Plaice Parcels

Serves 6

½ coconut, grated (shredded) ● 1 bunch fresh mint leaves

1 bunch fresh coriander (cilantro) ● 10 green chillies

10 cloves garlic ● 5 ml/1 tsp sugar ● 1 large onion

30 ml/2 tbsp cumin seeds ● salt ● 675 g/1½ lb plaice fillets

juice of 2 lemons ● 30 ml/2 tbsp ghee

Purée the coconut, mint, coriander, chillies, garlic, sugar, onion, cumin seeds and salt to a fine paste in a blender or food processor. Cut the fish into about 6 pieces and lay each piece on a piece of kitchen foil. Rub the fish with the ground paste, sprinkle with lemon juice and dot with ghee. Wrap the foil around the fish, arrange in a baking tin and bake in a preheated oven at 200°C/400°F/gas mark 6 for about 15 minutes until cooked. Serve with rice and dal.

Mustard Curry

Serves 6

30 ml/2 tbsp mustard seeds ● 5 ml/1 tsp ground turmeric

2.5 cm/1 in ginger root ● 6 cloves garlic ● 45 ml/3 tbsp oil

6 green chillies, slit ● 2 onions, thinly sliced ● 150 ml/¼ pt/⅔ cup coconut milk

salt ● 675 g/1½ lb plaice fillets

15 ml/1 tbsp chopped fresh coriander (cilantro)

Grind the mustard seeds, turmeric, ginger and garlic to a paste. Heat the oil and fry the ground mixture for 2 minutes. Add the chillies and fry until browned. Add the onions and fry until soft, adding a little water occasionally. Stir in the coconut milk and salt and simmer for 3 minutes. Add the fish and simmer for about 15 minutes until the fish is tender, stirring occasionally and adding a little more water if necessary. Garnish with the coriander and serve with rice and dal.

Plaice with Fenugreek   Serves 4

45 ml/3 tbsp oil ● 450 g/1 lb plaice fillets, cut into pieces

5 ml/1 tsp cumin seeds ● 2 onions, finely chopped

60 ml/4 tbsp chopped fresh or 20 ml/4 tsp dried fenugreek leaves

1-2 green chillies ● 1 small bunch fresh coriander (cilantro)

4 cloves garlic ● 2.5 cm/1 in ginger root

1.5 ml/¼ tsp ground turmeric ● 5 ml/1 tsp ground coriander (cilantro)

5 ml/1 tsp sugar ● 2 tomatoes, skinned and chopped ● salt

Heat the oil and fry the fish lightly. Remove from the pan and set aside. Add the cumin seeds to the pan and fry for 30 seconds. Add the onions and fry until golden brown. Grind together the fenugreek, chillies, coriander, garlic and ginger then stir the paste into the pan with the remaining ingredients. Simmer for 5 minutes. Add the fish, stir well, cover and cook for 15 minutes until the fish is tender, adding a little water if necessary. Serve hot with rice and okra.

Spiced Fried Plaice   Serves 4

Marinade: juice of 1½ limes ● grated rind of 1 lime

pinch of ground turmeric ● 45 ml/3 tbsp chopped fresh coriander (cilantro)

15 ml/1 tbsp chopped fresh mint ● 4 cloves garlic, chopped

2.5 ml/½ tsp salt ● 2.5 ml/½ tsp black pepper

2 green chillies, seeded and chopped

450 g/1 lb plaice fillets ● 1 egg, beaten

30 ml/2 tbsp water ● 100 g/4 oz/1 cup breadcrumbs

oil for deep-frying

Mix together the marinade ingredients. Make cuts on each side of the fish and rub in the marinade. Leave to marinate for at least 30 minutes.

Beat together the egg and water. Dip the fish in the egg then in the breadcrumbs. Heat the oil and fry the fish until golden brown. Drain on kitchen paper and serve immediately.

Sweet and Sour Plaice
Serves 4-6

675 g/1½ lb plaice fillets ● 45 ml/3 tbsp oil

25 g/1 oz/¼ cup plain (all-purpose) flour ● 2 egg whites, lightly beaten

salt and pepper

Marinade: juice of ½ lime ● 15 ml/1 tbsp oil ● 2.5 cm/1 in ginger root, ground

4 cloves garlic, crushed ● 2.5 ml/½ tsp salt ● 2.5 ml/½ tsp black pepper

1.5 ml/¼ tsp chilli powder

Sauce: 30 ml/2 tbsp oil ● 1 dried red chilli

10 ml/2 tsp cornflour (cornstarch) ● 120 ml/4 fl oz/½ cup water

30 ml/2 tbsp white wine vinegar ● 5 ml/1 tsp soy sauce

30 ml/2 tbsp tomato purée (paste) ● 30 ml/2 tbsp clear honey

Cut the fish into large pieces and make incisions in each with a sharp knife. Mix together all the marinade ingredients and rub well into the fish. Marinate for at least 30 minutes.

Heat the oil. Make a paste of the flour, egg whites, salt and pepper. Coat the fish in the batter and fry until golden brown. Drain on kitchen paper.

To make the sauce, heat the oil and fry the chilli until it darkens then remove it from the pan and discard it. Blend the cornflour with a little of the water then mix with the remaining sauce ingredients. Stir into the hot oil and bring to the boil, stirring. Add the fish to the sauce, cover and simmer for 10 minutes.

Tomato Fish
Serves 4

60 ml/4 tbsp oil ● 3 onions, finely chopped

450 g/1 lb plaice fillets ● 5 ml/1 tsp salt ● 2 green chillies, thinly sliced

5 cm/2 in ginger root, thinly sliced ● 2 green (bell) peppers, sliced

8 mint leaves, finely chopped

Sauce: 450 g/1 lb tomatoes, chopped ● 1 onion, finely chopped

4 cloves garlic, crushed ● 5 ml/1 tsp salt ● 5 ml/1 tsp chilli powder

15 ml/1 tbsp arrowroot ● 120 ml/4 fl oz/½ cup water

30 ml/2 tbsp oil ● 10 ml/2 tsp white wine vinegar ● 15 ml/1 tbsp sugar

To make the sauce, simmer the tomatoes, onion, garlic, salt and chilli powder together for 20 minutes. Sieve the sauce and discard the tomato skins, then return the sauce to a clean pan. Mix the arrowroot and water to a smooth paste. Heat the oil then add it to the tomato sauce with the arrowroot paste, wine vinegar and sugar, stirring until the sauce thickens.

Heat the oil and fry the onions until soft. Remove from the oil and set aside. Add the fish and salt to the oil and fry for 5 minutes. Return the onions to the pan with the chillies, ginger and peppers. Stir in the tomato sauce. Cover and cook for about 10 minutes until the fish is cooked and the sauce has thickened. Garnish with mint and serve with rice and vegetables.

Baked Plaice
Serves 4

1 large plaice • salt

Stuffing: 15 ml/1 tbsp ghee • 2 onions, finely chopped

2 green chilli, finely chopped • 45 ml/3 tbsp chopped fresh coriander (cilantro)

1 large tomato, finely chopped • pinch of ground turmeric

5 ml/1 tsp ground jaggery • 300 ml/½ pt/1¼ cups water

5 ml/1 tsp lemon juice

Make a slit in one side of the fish then rub it all over with salt. Heat the ghee and fry the onions, chilli and coriander until golden. Add the remaining ingredients and season to taste with salt. Fry until the mixture thickens and all the liquid has been absorbed.

Remove from the heat. Pack the stuffing into the fish and place in a greased roasting tin. Bake in a preheated oven at 180°C/350°F/gas mark 4 for about 15 minutes until cooked through. Serve with rice.

Salmon Curry
Serves 6

900 g/2 lb salmon steaks • juice of 1 lemon • 5 ml/1 tsp ground turmeric

salt • 45 ml/3 tbsp oil • 1 large onion, finely chopped

6 cloves garlic, crushed • 2.5 cm/1 in ginger root, finely chopped

5 ml/1 tsp poppy seeds • 1.5 ml/¼ tsp crushed black peppercorns

15 ml/1 tbsp ground coriander (cilantro) • 10 ml/2 tsp ground cumin

2.5 ml/½ tsp chilli powder • 1 large tomato, skinned and chopped

30 ml/2 tbsp chopped fresh coriander (cilantro)

Put the salmon on a plate and sprinkle with the lemon juice, turmeric and salt. Leave to marinate for 30 minutes.

Heat the oil and fry the onion, garlic and ginger until lightly browned. Add the poppy seeds and peppercorns and fry for 1 minute. Add the coriander, cumin and chilli powder and cook for 5 minutes, stirring. Add the tomato and stir together well. Add the salmon and gently stir the fish into the paste. Cover and simmer for 10-15 minutes until the fish is cooked. Garnish with coriander and serve hot with plain rice.

Salmon with Yoghurt Sauce
Serves 6

6 salmon steaks ● 30 ml/2 tbsp lemon juice ● salt and pepper

pinch of cayenne ● 5 ml/1 tsp ground cumin ● 30 ml/2 tbsp ghee, melted

Sauce: 45 ml/3 tbsp olive oil ● 10 ml/2 tsp mustard seeds

450 g/1 lb tomatoes, skinned and quartered

1 spring onion (scallion), cut into rings ● 1 green chilli, chopped

1.5 ml/¼ tsp dried thyme ● 60 ml/4 tbsp chopped fresh mint

900 ml/1½ pts/3¾ cups natural (plain) yoghurt, lightly beaten

Sprinkle the steaks with the lemon juice then season with salt, pepper, cayenne and cumin. Brush with melted ghee and leave to stand while you make the sauce.

Heat the oil and fry the mustard seeds until they start crackling. Add the tomatoes, spring onion, chilli and thyme and cook for 2 minutes until the tomatoes have softened. Add the mint, season with salt and pepper and keep warm.

Grill (broil) the salmon steaks for about 8 minutes until cooked through and golden brown. Meanwhile, heat the yoghurt very gently until warm then stir into the sauce. Serve the steaks with a spoonful of the sauce on top and the rest passed separately.

Himalayan Fish Curry
Serves 6

900 g/2 lb trout ● 90 ml/6 tbsp mustard oil

2 white radishes, sliced ● 4 tomatoes, skinned and chopped

2.5 ml/½ tsp ground turmeric ● 2.5 ml/½ tsp chilli powder

pinch of asafoetida ● 2.5 ml/½ tsp ground ginger

4 cloves ● 2 cinnamon sticks ● 2 cardamom pods ● salt

Cut the fish into 5 cm/2 in cubes and wash in salted water. Pat dry. Heat 60 ml/4 tbsp of oil and fry the fish and radishes until golden brown. Set aside. Heat the remaining oil and add the tomatoes, turmeric, chilli powder, asafoetida, ginger and remaining spices and simmer gently for 10 minutes, adding a little water if the sauce becomes too thick. Add the fish, season with salt and simmer until the fish is tender. Leave to stand for 2 hours. Serve reheated or cold with plain rice.

Tandoori Fish
Serves 4-6

900 g/2 lb whole trout or cod ● salt ● 60 ml/4 tbsp lemon juice

60 ml/4 tbsp wine vinegar ● 6 large cloves garlic

2.5 cm/1 in ginger root, coarsely chopped ● 1 onion, coarsely chopped

10 ml/2 tsp garam masala ● 5 ml/1 tsp ground cumin

5 ml/1 tsp ground turmeric ● 2.5 ml/½ tsp ground mace

2.5 ml/½ tsp grated nutmeg ● 2.5 ml/½ tsp ground red chilli

30 ml/2 tbsp oil ● 60 ml/4 tbsp ghee, melted

Garnish: 250 g/9 oz small boiled potatoes, deep-fried

2.5 ml/½ tsp garam masala ● 1 onion, thinly sliced

30 ml/2 tbsp chopped fresh coriander (cilantro) ● 1 small green chilli, chopped

Clean the fish but do not remove the bones. Remove the eyes, scrape the skin with a sharp knife to remove the scales and make 4-5 gashes on each side. Rub inside and out with salt, wash and pat dry.

Blend the lemon juice, wine vinegar, garlic, ginger and onion to a smooth paste in a blender or food processor. Add the ground spices and a pinch of salt then rub the paste into the fish inside and out. Cover and leave to marinate for 2 hours, turning occasionally.

Heat the oil in a non-metallic pan. Lift the fish from the marinade and fry lightly on both sides for 5 minutes.

Remove the skin and place the fish in a large, non-metallic ovenproof dish. Pour the marinade into the pan and cook until all the liquid has been absorbed and it is light brown. Rub it over the fish then pour over half the ghee. Bake the fish in a preheated oven at 200°C/400°F/gas mark 6 for 10 minutes. Carefully turn over the fish, baste with the marinade and bake for a further 15 minutes. Transfer the fish to a serving dish, surround with the potatoes, sprinkle with the garnish ingredients and serve hot with puris, plain rice, dal and a mixed vegetable dish.

Tandoori Fish
Serves 6

1 × 900 g/2 lb whole trout ● 45 ml/3 tbsp oil ● 15 ml/1 tbsp garam masala

1 lemon, cut into wedges

Seasoning: 2.5 cm/1 in ginger root ● 8 cloves garlic

5 cm/2 in cube green papaya ● 5 ml/1 tsp ground turmeric

1.5 ml/¼ tsp chilli powder ● juice of 2 lemons ● salt

Cut and scale the fish and wash well and make 4 incisions on either side of the fish. Grind all the seasoning ingredients together to a smooth paste then rub all over the fish, inside and out. Leave to stand for 1 hour.

Cook under a hot grill, turning

frequently and brushing with the oil, for about 10 minutes until the fish is almost cooked. Sprinkle with garam masala and grill (broil) until a dark golden brown. Garnish with lemon wedges and serve hot with rice.

Grilled Stuffed Trout

Serves 4-6

2 large trout ● 45 ml/3 tbsp wine vinegar ● 6 large cloves garlic

2.5 cm/1 in ginger root ● 1 onion, coarsely chopped ● 5 ml/1 tsp garam masala

1.5 ml/½ tsp ground turmeric ● salt ● 45 ml/3 tbsp butter or ghee

Filling: 60 ml/4 tbsp ghee ● 1 onion, finely chopped ● 5 black peppercorns

4 cloves ● 2 bay leaves ● 2.5 cm/1 in cinnamon stick

1 black cardamom pod ● 100 g/4 oz/½ cup basmati or patna rice

5 ml/1 tsp garam masala ● 5 ml/1 tsp ground cumin

1.5 ml/¼ tsp ground mace ● 1.5 ml/¼ tsp grated nutmeg

150 g/5 oz mixed vegetables, cubed ● 100 g/4 oz/⅔ cup raisins

50 g/2 oz/½ cup blanched almonds, halved

25 g/1 oz/¼ cup cashew nuts, halved

300 ml/½ pt/10 cups water

Garnish: 2.5 ml/½ tsp garam masala

15 ml/1 tbsp chopped fresh coriander (cilantro)

1 small green chilli, chopped

Clean the trout and remove the eyes but do not remove the bones. Scrape the skin with a sharp knife to remove the scales and make 4-6 gashes on each side. Rub inside and out with salt then wash thoroughly.

Blend the wine vinegar, garlic, ginger, onion, garam masala, turmeric and salt to a smooth paste in a blender or food processor. Rub the paste all over inside and outside the fish, cover and leave to marinate for 4 hours.

To make the filling, heat the ghee in a heavy-based pan and fry the onion and whole spices over a medium heat until golden. Add the rice and fry for 2 minutes. Stir in the ground spices then the mixed vegetables, raisins, nuts and water. Bring to the boil, cover and simmer over a low heat for 15 minutes until the rice is tender. Stir carefully.

While the rice is cooking, remove the fish from the marinade and fry it lightly on both sides for 5 minutes. Gently remove the skin and place the fish on a grill. Pour the marinade into the pan and fry until golden brown. Rub it over the fish. Grill (broil) the fish under a low heat, basting as it cooks with the butter or ghee. Arrange the fish on a serving dish and place the filling between and around them. Pour over the sauce, sprinkle with the garnish ingredients and serve hot with nan, raita and dal.

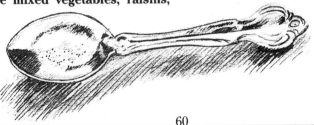

Stuffed Fish

Serves 4-6

2 large trout • salt • 45 ml/3 tbsp wine vinegar • 6 large cloves garlic

2.5 cm/1 in ginger root • 1 onion, coarsely chopped • 5 ml/1 tsp garam masala

1.5 ml/½ tsp ground turmeric • 30 ml/2 tbsp oil

Filling: 60 ml/4 tbsp ghee • 1 onion, finely chopped

5 black peppercorns • 4 cloves • 2 bay leaves

2.5 cm/1 in cinnamon stick • 1 black cardamom pod

100 g/4 oz/½ cup basmati or patna rice • 5 ml/1 tsp garam masala

5 ml/1 tsp ground roasted cumin • 1.5 ml/¼ tsp ground mace

1.5 ml/¼ tsp grated nutmeg • 150 g/5 oz mixed vegetables, cubed

100 g/4 oz/ cup raisins • 50 g/2 oz/½ cup blanched almonds, halved

25 g/1 oz/¼ cup cashew nuts, halved • 300 ml/½ pt/1¼ cups water

Sauce: 4 large cloves garlic • 2.5 cm/1 in ginger root

1 onion, coarsely chopped • 90 ml/6 tbsp oil • 5 ml/1 tsp mustard seeds

1 small onion, finely chopped • 30 ml/2 tbsp ground almonds

15 ml/1 tbsp ground coriander • 2.5 ml/½ tsp ground red chilli

2.5 ml/½ tsp ground turmeric • 2.5 ml/½ tsp garam masala • salt

400 g/14 oz canned tomatoes • 150 ml/¼ pt/⅔ cup natural (plain) yoghurt

45 ml/3 tbsp lemon juice • 15 ml/1 tbsp sugar • 150 ml/¼ pt/⅔ cup water

Garnish: 2.5 ml/½ tsp garam masala

15 ml/1 tbsp chopped fresh coriander (cilantro) • 1 small green chilli, chopped

Clean the trout and remove the eyes but do not remove the bones. Scrape the skin with a sharp knife to remove the scale and make 4-6 gashes on each side. Rub inside and out with salt then wash thoroughly.

Blend the wine vinegar, garlic, ginger, onion, garam masala, turmeric and salt to a smooth paste in a blender or food processor. Rub the paste all over inside and outside the fish, cover and leave to marinate for 4 hours.

To make the filling, heat the ghee in a heavy-based pan and fry the onion and whole spices over a medium heat until golden. Add the rice and fry for 2 minutes. Stir in the ground spices then the mixed vegetables, raisins, nuts and water. Bring to the boil, cover and simmer over a low heat for 15 minutes until the rice is tender. Stir carefully.

While the rice is cooking, heat the oil, lift the fish from the marinade and fry it lightly on both sides for 5 minutes. Gently remove the skin and place the fish on a baking dish. Pour the marinade into the pan and fry until golden brown. Rub it over the fish. Bake the fish in a preheated oven at 200°C/400°F/gas mark 6 for 20 minutes.

The sauce can be made in advance. Blend the garlic, ginger and onion to a smooth paste in a blender or food processor. Heat the oil in a heavy-based pan and fry the mustard seeds until they start crackling. Add the onion and fry until lightly browned. Add the blended paste and fry until golden. Stir in the ground spices and salt and cook for 1 minute then stir in the tomatoes and cook until all the water has been absorbed and the oil appears on the surface. Stir in the yoghurt, cover as the mixture tends to spit, and cook until all the liquid has been absorbed. Add the lemon juice, sugar and water, bring to the boil then simmer over a low heat for 2 minutes.

Arrange the fish on a serving dish and place the filling between and around them. Pour over the sauce, sprinkle with the garnish ingredients and serve hot with nan, raita and dal.

South Indian-style Fish Curry

Serves 6

1.5 kg/3 lb trout or other fish fillets ● 45 ml/3 tbsp oil

5 ml/1 tsp black mustard seeds ● 2.5 ml/½ tsp fenugreek seeds

2 dried red chillies, crushed ● 2.5 ml/½ tsp black peppercorns

1 large onion, chopped ● 6 cloves garlic, chopped

2.5 cm/1 in ginger root, chopped ● 5 ml/1 tsp ground turmeric ● salt

250 ml/8 fl oz/1 cup coconut milk ● 10 ml/2 tsp tamarind concentrate

30 ml/2 tbsp chopped fresh coriander (cilantro)

Cut the fish into 5 cm/2 in pieces. Heat the oil and fry the mustard and fenugreek seeds, chillies and peppercorns until the mustard seeds start crackling. Add the onion, garlic and ginger and cook until soft. Add the turmeric and salt and stir together for 1 minute. Add the fish, coconut milk and tamarind and simmer for 10-15 minutes until the fish is cooked, stirring occasionally. Garnish with coriander and serve hot with plain rice.

Trout in Yoghurt

Serves 4

2.5 ml/½ tsp ground turmeric ● 2.5 ml/½ tsp salt

450 g/1 lb trout, cut into pieces ● 120 ml/4 fl oz/½ cup mustard oil

2 bay leaves ● 2 green chillies, sliced ● 2 onions, finely chopped

2.5 cm/½ in ginger root, finely chopped

120 ml/4 fl oz/½ cup natural (plain) yoghurt ● 5 ml/1 tsp sugar

120 ml/4 fl oz/½ cup water ● 5 ml/1 tsp ghee ● 2.5 ml/½ tsp garam masala

Mix together the turmeric and salt and rub over the fish. Leave to marinate for at least 30 minutes.

Heat the mustard oil and fry the fish until golden brown. Remove from the pan and set aside. Remove all but 30 ml/2 tbsp of oil from the pan then fry the bay leaves and chillies for 1 minute. Add the onions and fry until golden. Add the ginger and fry for 2 minutes. Stir in the yoghurt and sugar. Add the fish pieces and stir to coat them in the sauce. Add a little salt, if necessary, stir in the water, cover and simmer for about 15 minutes until the fish is cooked. Stir in the ghee, sprinkle with the garam masala and serve hot with rice, okra and chapatis.

Grilled Spiced Trout
Serves 4

4 fresh trout • 5 ml/1 tsp ground turmeric • 5 ml/1 tsp ground cumin

5 ml/1 tsp black pepper • 60 ml/4 tbsp chopped fresh coriander (cilantro)

45 ml/3 tbsp mustard oil • 5 ml/1 tsp salt

Clean the trout and pat dry. Mix together the remaining ingredients, coat the trout and leave to marinate for 1 hour. Grill (broil) the fish for about 10 minutes until tender then serve at once with plain rice.

South Indian Hot Fried Prawns
Serves 4-6

15 ml/1 tbsp coriander (cilantro) seeds • 5 ml/1 tsp cumin seeds

5 ml/1 tsp fenugreek seeds • 5 ml/1 tsp mustard seeds

90 ml/4 tbsp oil • 4 large cloves garlic, crushed

2.5 cm/1 in ginger root, finely chopped • 2 bay leaves

2 onions, finely chopped • 50 g/2 oz/½ cup desiccated (shredded) coconut

5 ml/1 tsp garam masala • 2.5 ml/½ tsp ground red chilli

2.5 ml/½ tsp ground turmeric • salt • 500 g/18 oz peeled prawns (shrimp)

400 g/14 oz canned tomatoes • 50 g/2 oz tamarind pulp • 15 ml/1 tbsp sugar

Garnish: 1.5 ml/¼ tsp garam masala

15 ml/1 tbsp chopped fresh coriander (cilantro) • 1 small green chilli, chopped

Dry roast the coriander, cumin, fenugreek and mustard seeds over a medium heat until lightly browned. Cool and grind to a fine powder. Heat the oil in a heavy-based pan and fry the garlic, ginger, bay leaves and onions until golden brown. Add the coconut and fry until lightly browned. Stir in the ground spices, salt and prawns then the tomatoes and fry until the liquid has been absorbed and the oil appears on the surface. Stir in the tamarind pulp and sugar and cook over a medium-low heat for a few minutes until the prawns are tender. Sprinkle with the garnish ingredients and serve hot with rice, dal, raita and a potato and bean dish.

Prawn Curry with Yoghurt
Serves 4

450 g/1 lb cooked, peeled prawns (shrimp) ● juice of 1 lemon

30 ml/2 tbsp oil ● 5 ml/1 tsp black mustard seeds

1.5 ml/¼ tsp fenugreek seeds ● 1 onion, chopped

6 cloves garlic, chopped ● 2.5 ml/½ tsp ground turmeric

1.5 ml/¼ tsp chilli powder ● 50 g/2 oz desiccated (shredded) coconut

30 ml/2 tbsp natural (plain) yoghurt ● salt

Place the prawns in a bowl and squeeze over the lemon juice. Heat the oil and fry the mustard and fenugreek seeds until they start crackling. Add the onion and fry until golden. Add the garlic, turmeric, chilli powder, coconut, yoghurt and salt and stir over a low heat for 2 minutes. Add the prawns and salt and simmer for 10 minutes, stirring occasionally. Serve hot with rice, sambar and papadums.

South Indian Prawns in Coconut
Serves 6

900 g/2 lb cooked, peeled prawns (shrimp) ● 5 ml/1 tsp ground turmeric

salt ● 75 ml/5 tbsp coconut milk ● 100 g/4 oz/1 cup grated (shredded) coconut

30 ml/2 tbsp coriander (cilantro) seeds ● 15 ml/1 tbsp cumin seeds

2 dried red chillies ● 1.5 ml/¼ tsp black peppercorns

15 ml/1 tbsp black mustard seeds ● 10 ml/2 tsp tamarind concentrate

1 red onion, chopped ● 5 cloves garlic, chopped

2.5 cm/1 in ginger root, chopped ● 45 ml/3 tbsp water

45 ml/3 tbsp oil ● 2 sprigs fresh curry leaves

30 ml/2 tbsp chopped fresh coriander (cilantro)

Mix together the prawns, turmeric and salt and set aside for 10 minutes. Purée the coconut milk, coconut, coriander and cumin seeds, chillies, peppercorns, mustard seeds, tamarind, onion, garlic and ginger to a paste, adding the water if necessary. Heat the oil and fry the purée for 10 minutes, stirring continuously. Stir in the prawns and curry leaves and simmer for 10 minutes. Garnish with the coriander and serve hot with rice, chutney and vegetables.

Red Prawns
Serves 4

1 red (bell) pepper ● 1 onion, chopped ● 10 cashew nuts

60 ml/4 tbsp oil ● 5 ml/1 tsp mustard seeds

2 cloves garlic, chopped ● 450 g/1 lb prawns (shrimp), peeled

5 ml/1 tsp salt ● 2.5 ml/½ tsp cayenne ● 5 ml/1 tsp paprika ● 60 ml/4 tbsp water

Purée the pepper, onion and nuts to a paste. Heat 45 ml/3 tbsp of oil and fry the mustard seeds until they start crackling. Add the garlic and prawns and a little salt and fry for 2-3 minutes. Remove the prawns with a slotted spoon. Add the remaining oil to the pan and fry the pepper paste for 4-5 minutes until dry. Add the remaining salt, the cayenne and paprika and stir well. Return the prawns to the pan with the water and simmer gently for 1 minute until the sauce is very thick. Serve hot with rice and vegetables.

Prawns in Pink Sauce
Serves 4-6

60 ml/4 tbsp tomato purée (paste) ● 175 ml/6 fl oz/¾ cup water

250 ml/8 fl oz/1 cup single (light) cream ● 5 ml/1 tsp grated ginger root

2.5 ml/½ tsp cayenne ● 20 ml/4 tsp lemon juice ● 5 ml/1 tsp ground cumin

salt and pepper ● 2.5 ml/½ tsp sugar ● 45 ml/3 tbsp oil

15 ml/1 tbsp mustard seeds ● 3 cloves garlic, chopped

900 g/2 lb peeled prawns (shrimp)

Mix together the tomato purée, water, cream, ginger, cayenne, lemon juice, cumin, salt, pepper and sugar. Heat the oil and fry the mustard seeds until they start crackling. Add the garlic then the prawns and stir-fry for 2 minutes. Pour in the sauce mixture and stir over a low heat until the sauce starts bubbling. Serve at once with rice and vegetables.

Prawns in Coconut Milk
Serves 6

45 ml/3 tbsp oil ● 5 ml/1 tsp black mustard seeds

1.5 ml/¼ tsp asafoetida ● 1 onion, chopped

5 cloves garlic, crushed ● 2.5 cm/1 in ginger root

5 ml/1 tsp ground turmeric ● 2 green chillies, cut into strips

12 curry leaves ● 450 ml/¾ pt/2 cups coconut milk

salt ● 900 g/2 lb peeled prawns (shrimp)

Heat the oil and fry the mustard seeds until they start crackling. Add the asafoetida and cook for 30 seconds then add the onion, garlic and ginger and cook until the onion is browned. Add the turmeric, chillies and curry leaves and fry for 2 minutes. Add the coconut milk and salt and bring to a simmer. Add the prawns and simmer for about 15 minutes. Serve hot with plain rice, vegetable sambar and papadums.

Malabar-style Prawn Curry
Serves 6

900 g/2 lb peeled prawns (shrimp) ● 5 ml/1 tsp tamarind concentrate

30 ml/2 tbsp cider vinegar ● salt ● 5 ml/1 tsp ground turmeric

150 ml/¼ pt/⅔ cup coconut milk ● 30 ml/2 tbsp coriander (cilantro) seeds

10 ml/2 tsp cumin seeds ● 3 dried red chillies ● 1 onion, chopped

5 cloves garlic ● 2.5 cm/1 in ginger root, chopped

1.5 ml/¼ tsp black peppercorns ● 45 ml/3 tbsp oil

5 ml/1 tsp black mustard seeds ● 50 g/2 oz/½ cup grated (shredded) coconut

250 ml/8 fl oz/1 cup water ● 30 ml/2 tbsp chopped fresh coriander (cilantro)

Mix together the prawns, tamarind, cider vinegar, salt and turmeric and leave to marinate for 30 minutes.

Purée the coconut milk, coriander and cumin seeds, chillies, onion, garlic, ginger and peppercorns to a paste in a blender or food processor. Heat the oil and fry the mustard seeds until they start crackling. Add the paste and fry for 2 minutes. Add the coconut and fry for 2 minutes. Add the prawn mixture and water and simmer for 20 minutes, stirring occasionally. Garnish with the coriander and serve hot with plain rice, papadums, chutney and vegetables.

Butterfly Prawns
Serves 4

900 g/2 lb raw prawns (shrimp), peeled ● 50 g/2 oz/¼ cup butter

6 cloves garlic, crushed ● juice of 2 lemons

2.5 cm/1 in ginger root, chopped ● 15 ml/1 tbsp ground coriander (cilantro)

30 ml/2 tbsp ground cumin ● 2.5 ml/½ tsp ground cardamom

15 ml/1 tbsp ground turmeric ● 15 ml/1 tbsp paprika ● 5 ml/1 tsp salt

Split the prawns along the inner curve and spread flat. Melt the butter and mix in the garlic, lemon juice, ginger, spices and salt. Add the prawns and marinate for 3-4 hours.

Grill (broil) the prawns for about 2 minutes until cooked then serve immediately with the juice served separately.

Prawns in Black Pepper and Mustard Seeds
Serves 6

900 g/2 lb peeled prawns (shrimp) ● 5 ml/1 tsp ground turmeric

salt ● juice of 1 lemon ● 45 ml/3 tbsp oil

15 ml/1 tbsp black mustard seeds ● 1 onion, finely chopped

5 cloves garlic, crushed ● 2.5 ml/1 in ginger root, finely chopped

2 green chillies, chopped ● 2.5 ml/½ tsp black peppercorns, crushed

1.5 ml/¼ tsp chilli powder ● 1 tomato, skinned and chopped

30 ml/2 tbsp chopped fresh coriander (cilantro)

Mix the prawns with the turmeric, salt and lemon juice and leave to marinate for 15 minutes.

Heat the oil and fry the mustard seeds until they start crackling. Add the onion, garlic, ginger and chillies and cook for 5 minutes. Stir in the peppercorns and chilli powder and cook for 2 minutes. Add the tomato and prawn mixture, cover and simmer for 10-15 minutes, stirring occasionally. Garnish with the coriander and serve hot with plain rice, chapatis, chutney and vegetables.

Sweet and Sour Prawns   Serves 4-6

Batter: 100 g/4 oz/1 cup gram flour ● 15 ml/1 tbsp oil

15 ml/1 tbsp chopped fresh coriander (cilantro) ● 5 ml/1 tsp ajwain

2.5 ml/½ tsp garam masala ● 2.5 ml/½ tsp ground red chilli

salt ● 150 ml/¼ pt/⅔ cup water

oil for deep-frying ● 450 g/1 lb peeled prawns (shrimp)

225 g/8 oz vegetables (cauliflower, carrots, (bell) pepper, aubergine (eggplant) etc.), cut into 3 cm/1½ in pieces

Sauce: 75 ml/5 tbsp oil or ghee ● 2 onions, finely chopped

4 large cloves garlic, ● 2.5 cm/1 in ginger root, coarsely chopped

10 ml/2 tsp ground coriander (cilantro) ● 5 ml/1 tsp garam masala

5 ml/1 tsp ground roasted cumin ● 2.5 ml/½ tsp ground red chilli

2.5 ml/½ tsp ground turmeric ● 1.5 ml/¼ tsp ground mace

1.5 ml/¼ tsp grated nutmeg ● salt ● 225 g/8 oz canned tomatoes, chopped

60 ml/4 tbsp wine vinegar ● 15 ml/1 tbsp honey

200 ml/7 fl oz/scant 1 cup water

Garnish: 2.5 ml/½ tsp garam masala

15 ml/1 tbsp chopped fresh coriander (cilantro) ● 1 small green chilli, chopped

Place the flour in a bowl, mix in the oil then add the ground spices, salt and water and mix to a smooth batter. Heat the oil. Dip the prawns in the batter then place gently in the oil and fry until golden brown. Remove with a slotted spoon. Dip the vegetable pieces in the batter and fry until golden brown. Place with the prawns.

To make the sauce, heat the oil or ghee in a heavy-based pan and fry 1 onion until golden brown. Blend the remaining onion, the garlic and ginger to a smooth paste then stir it into the pan and fry for 2 minutes. Add the ground spices, salt and tomatoes and cook until all the liquid has been absorbed and the oil appears on the surface. Add the wine vinegar and cook until all the liquid has been absorbed. Add the honey and cook for 2 minutes. Add the water, bring to the boil then reduce the heat and simmer for 2 minutes. Pour the hot sauce over the chicken and vegetables, sprinkle with the garnish ingredients and serve hot with rice, puris, raita and chutney.

Hot Malayalee Prawns
Serves 6

5 ml/1 tsp black peppercorns ● 5 ml/1 tsp mustard seeds

5 ml/1 tsp fenugreek ● 15 ml/1 tbsp ground coriander (cilantro)

5 ml/1 tsp ground turmeric ● 20 dried red chillies

45 ml/3 tbsp oil ● 1 sprig fresh curry leaves

10 ml/2 tsp tamarind concentrate ● 450 g/1 lb onions, finely chopped

10 cloves garlic, crushed ● 2.5 cm/1 in ginger root, chopped

10 green chillies, chopped ● 450 g/1 lb peeled prawns (shrimp) ● salt

Dry roast the peppercorns, mustard seeds, fenugreek, coriander and turmeric for 1 minute then grind together. Grind the red chillies to a paste. Heat the oil and fry the curry leaves and tamarind for 1 minute. Add the onions, garlic, ginger, red chilli paste and green chillies and fry for 2 minutes. Add the prawns, ground spices and salt. Cover with water and simmer until the water has been absorbed. Serve hot with rice.

Prawn Curry
Serves 4

45 ml/3 tbsp ghee ● 1 onion, chopped

2.5 cm/1 in ginger root, chopped ● 3 cloves garlic, crushed

10 ml/2 tsp ground coriander (cilantro) ● 10 ml/2 tsp ground cumin

5 ml/1 tsp ground turmeric ● 5 ml/1 tsp chilli powder

450 g/1 lb peeled prawns (shrimp) ● 3 tomatoes, skinned and chopped

30 ml/2 tsp wine vinegar ● 10 ml/2 tsp tomato purée (paste)

Heat the ghee and fry the onion, ginger and garlic until soft and lightly browned. Add the spices and fry for 2 minutes, stirring. Add the prawns and fry for 5 minutes, stirring.' Add the tomatoes, wine vinegar and tomato purée and fry until the liquid has evaporated and serve hot with rice.

Shell Prawn Curry
Serves 6

450 g/1 lb raw prawns (shrimp) ● 10 dried red chillies ● 2 onions, chopped

600 ml/1 pt/2½ cups water ● salt ● 10 ml/2 tsp ground turmeric

45 ml/3 tbsp coconut oil ● 2-3 coriander (cilantro) leaves

Remove the heads and tails from the prawns but not the shells. Grind the chillies to a powder then mix with the onions and grind to a paste. Place the prawns in a pan with the water, a pinch of salt and the turmeric. Bring to the boil and simmer for 30 minutes until the curry is almost dry.

In another pan, heat the oil and fry the onion paste for 5 minutes. Add the prawn mixture and simmer over a low heat until it forms a thick gravy. Garnish with the coriander leaves and serve hot with rice and vegetables.

Prawn and Pumpkin Curry
Serves 6

½ coconut, grated (shredded) ● 5 dried red chillies, crushed

15 ml/1 tbsp coriander (cilantro) seeds ● 5 ml/1 tsp ground turmeric

1 onion, chopped ● 4 cloves garlic, crushed ● 5 ml/1 tsp tamarind concentrate

450 g/1 lb pumpkin, cubed ● 450 g/1 lb peeled prawns (shrimp) ● salt

Fry the coconut, chillies, coriander, turmeric, onion, garlic and tamarind for 2 minutes then grind to a smooth paste. Place the pumpkin in a pan with water to cover and simmer for 4 minutes. Add the prawns and simmer for 5 minutes. Add the spices and salt, bring to the boil and simmer for 4 minutes until the ingredients are cooked and the sauce is thick.

Prawn Kofta
Serves 4-6

450 g/1 lb peeled prawns (shrimp), minced ● salt ● 2 onions, finely chopped

2 green chillies, finely chopped ● 1 egg, beaten

50 g/2 oz/½ cup breadcrumbs ● 30 ml/2 tbsp mustard oil

30 ml/2 tbsp ghee ● 2 bay leaves ● 1 large onion, chopped

10 ml/2 tsp garam masala ● 10 ml/2 tsp ground turmeric

2.5 cm/1 in fresh ginger, chopped ● 300 ml/½ pt/1¼ cups coconut milk

15 ml/1 tbsp chopped fresh coriander (cilantro)

Season the prawns with salt then mix with the onions and chillies. Shape into 12 balls or koftas, dip in egg then roll in breadcrumbs. Heat the mustard oil and fry until browned.

Heat the ghee and fry the bay leaves, onion, garam masala, turmeric and ginger for 5 minutes, stirring continuously and adding a little water as necessary. Stir in the coconut milk and salt and bring to the boil. Add the koftas and simmer for 10 minutes until the sauce is thick. Garnish with coriander and serve hot with rice.

Prawn Cutlets
Serves 4-6

450 g/1 lb peeled prawns (shrimp), minced

50 g/2 oz/¼ cup desiccated (shredded) coconut

4 green chillies, chopped ● 1 bunch fresh coriander (cilantro), chopped

2 cloves garlic, crushed ● 5 ml/1 tsp cumin seeds

2.5 ml/½ tsp ground turmeric ● 1 egg, beaten

50 g/2 oz/½ cup breadcrumbs ● 45 ml/3 tbsp ghee

Mix together all the ingredients except the egg, breadcrumbs and ghee and shape into flat cutlets. Dip in beaten egg then in breadcrumbs. Heat the ghee and fry the cutlets for about 10 minutes each side until cooked through and nicely browned. Serve hot with rice and vegetables.

Prawn Sambol
Serves 4

450 g/1 lb peeled prawns (shrimp), chopped ● 3 green chillies, chopped

4 cloves garlic, chopped ● 5 ml/1 tsp cumin seeds

5 ml/1 tsp ground turmeric ● salt ● 30 ml/2 tbsp ghee

2 onions, sliced ● 225 g/8 oz spinach, chopped ● 300 ml/½ pt/1¼ cups water

Mix the prawns, chillies, garlic, cumin seeds, turmeric and salt. Heat the ghee and fry the onions until soft. Add the spinach and prawn mixture and fry for 5 minutes. Add the water, bring to the boil and simmer for about 5 minutes until the sauce is thick and the ingredients are well combined. Serve hot with plain rice.

Prawn Mustard Curry
Serves 6

6 dried red chillies ● 5 ml/1 tsp ground turmeric

15 ml/1 tbsp cumin seeds ● 6 cloves garlic ● 10 ml/2 tsp mustard seeds

6 onions, chopped ● 450 g/1 lb peeled prawns (shrimp)

45 ml/3 tbsp ghee ● 900 ml/1½ pts/3¾ cups water

1 sprig fresh curry leaves ● salt ● 15 ml/1 tbsp lemon juice

Grind the chillies, turmeric, cumin seeds, garlic, mustard seeds and onions to a paste then mix in the prawns. Heat the ghee and fry the prawn mixture for 2 minutes. Add the water, curry leaves and salt and bring to the boil. Simmer for about 10 minutes until the gravy is thick. Stir in the lemon juice and serve hot with rice or chapatis.

Prawns in Spinach
Serves 4-6

450 g/1 lb peeled prawns (shrimp) ● salt

60 ml/4 tbsp chopped fresh coriander (cilantro) ● 5 ml/1 tsp cumin seeds

5 cloves garlic ● 4 green chillies, seeded ● 2 dried red chillies, seeded

75 ml/5 tbsp oil ● 45 ml/3 tbsp ghee ● 5 onions, sliced

450 g/1 lb spinach, chopped ● 5 ml/1 tsp ground turmeric

600 ml/1 pt/2½ cups water

Sprinkle the prawns with salt and set aside. Grind the coriander, cumin seeds, garlic and chillies to a paste and mix the paste with the prawns. Heat half the oil and ghee and fry the onions until browned. Add the prawn mixture, spinach, turmeric and salt and simmer, stirring, until the mixture is well browned. Add the water, bring to the boil then simmer until the ingredients are cooked and the ghee appears on the surface. Serve hot with rice and vegetables.

Prawns with Tomato and Spinach   Serves 4

30 ml/2 tbsp ghee ● 4 tomatoes, skinned and chopped

4 cloves garlic, chopped ● 3 onions, chopped ● 2.5 ml/½ tsp chilli powder

1 green chilli, slit ● 2.5 ml/½ tsp garam masala ● salt

225 g/8 oz spinach, chopped ● 450 g/1 lb peeled prawns (shrimp)

Heat the ghee and fry the tomatoes, garlic and onions until browned. Add the chilli powder, chilli, garam masala and salt and fry for 2 minutes. Stir in the spinach and cook over a low heat for about 15 minutes. Stir in the prawns and cook for 3 minutes until heated through. Serve hot with rice and vegetables.

Prawn and Bitter Gourd   Serves 6

450 g/1 lb bitter gourd or cucumber ● 6 dried red chillies

2.5 ml/½ tsp cumin seeds ● 5 ml/1 tsp ground turmeric

5 ml/1 tsp tamarind concentrate ● 15 ml/1 tbsp ghee

30 ml/2 tbsp coconut oil ● 2 green chillies, chopped

2.5 cm/1 in ginger root, chopped ● 3 cloves garlic, chopped

30 ml/2 tbsp white wine vinegar ● salt ● 450 g/1 lb peeled prawns (shrimp)

100 g/4 oz ground jaggery

Cut the gourd or cucumber into thick slices and remove the seeds and pith. Grind the chillies, cumin seeds, turmeric and tamarind to a paste. Heat the ghee and oil and fry the green chillies, ginger and garlic for 2 minutes. Add the ground spices and wine vinegar and season to taste with salt. Bring to the boil. Add the bitter gourd and simmer gently for 5 minutes. Add the prawns and simmer for 5 minutes. Stir in the jaggery and serve hot with rice and a vegetable dish.

Prawn and Mango Curry   Serves 4

2 large green mangoes ● 1 coconut, grated (shredded) ● 6 green chillies

4 cloves garlic ● 4 onions, chopped ● 450 g/1 lb peeled prawns (shrimp)

1 sprig fresh curry leaves ● 15 ml/1 tbsp oil ● salt

300 ml/½ pt/1¼ cups water

Peel the mangoes, chop into small pieces then leave in a bowl of water to avoid discolouration. Grind the coconut, chillies, garlic and onions to a paste then place in a pan with the drained mangoes, prawns, curry leaves and oil. Simmer gently until hot then add the water and season to taste with salt. Bring to the boil and simmer gently until the ghee appears on the surface. Serve hot with plain rice.

Fried Prawns
Serves 4

450 g/1 lb peeled prawns (shrimp)

100 g/4 oz/1 cup grated (shredded) coconut

5 ml/1 tsp chilli powder ● 5 ml/1 tsp ground turmeric

2-3 curry leaves ● 30 ml/2 tbsp ghee ● 1 onion, sliced

Place the prawns, coconut, chilli powder, turmeric and curry leaves in a pan and just cover with water. Bring to the boil then simmer gently until the sauce is thick. Meanwhile, heat the ghee and fry the onion until golden brown. Stir into the prawn mixture and serve hot with rice and vegetables.

Prawn Vindaloo
Serves 4

30 ml/2 tbsp ghee or oil ● 3 onions, sliced

8 dried red chillies, seeded ● 5 cloves garlic, chopped

1.5 ml/¼ tsp cumin seeds ● 15 ml/1 tbsp ground turmeric

2.5 cm/1 in ginger root ● 5 ml/1 tsp tamarind concentrate

2.5 ml/½ tsp mustard seeds ● 15 ml/1 tbsp chopped fresh coriander (cilantro)

60 ml/4 tbsp white wine vinegar ● 450 g/1 lb peeled prawns (shrimp)

Heat the ghee or oil and fry the onions until lightly browned. Grind the chillies, garlic, cumin seeds, turmeric, ginger, tamarind, mustard seeds and coriander to a paste with a little of the wine vinegar. Add to the pan with the remaining wine vinegar and fry for 5 minutes, stirring. Add the prawns and salt and mix well. Simmer for about 15 minutes, adding a little water if necessary. Serve hot or cold with rice, raita and chapatis.

Mustard Prawns
Serves 4

½ coconut, grated (shredded) ● 15 ml/1 tbsp mustard seeds

2 green chillies ● 450 g/1 lb peeled prawns (shrimp)

10 ml/2 tsp ground turmeric ● 5 ml/1 tsp chilli powder ● salt

1 bunch fresh coriander (cilantro), chopped ● 60 ml/4 tbsp oil or ghee

Grind the coconut, mustard seeds and chillies to a paste then mix with the prawns, turmeric, chilli powder, salt and coriander. Heat the oil or ghee and fry the prawn mixture gently, stirring, for about 15 minutes. Serve hot with plain rice and dal.

Tandoori Prawns
Serves 6-8

900 g/2 lb prawns (shrimp), peeled ● juice of 1 lemon ● salt

2 cloves garlic, grated ● 2.5 cm/1 in ginger root, grated

pinch of pepper ● 5 ml/1 tsp paprika ● 5 ml/1 tsp garam masala

5 ml/2 tsp ground roasted cumin ● 5 ml/1 tsp ground coriander (cilantro)

5 ml/1 tsp ground turmeric ● 45 ml/3 tbsp natural (plain) yoghurt

75 ml/5 tbsp oil

Sprinkle the prawns with the lemon juice and salt. Purée all the remaining ingredients except 60 ml/4 tbsp of the oil. Mix with the prawns, cover and refrigerate for 1 hour.

Heat the remaining oil and fry the prawns and marinade for about 5 minutes until the oil appears on the surface and the sauce is thick. Serve hot with mint chutney.

Prawn Patia
Serves 6

150 ml/¼ pt/⅔ cup oil ● 3 onions, sliced ● 8 green chillies

6 dried red chillies ● 2 cloves garlic

30 ml/2 tbsp chopped fresh coriander (cilantro) ● salt

2.5 ml/½ tsp ground coriander (cilantro) ● 2.5 ml/½ tsp cumin seeds

10 ml/2 tsp ground turmeric ● 150 ml/¼ pt/⅔ cup water

1 small mango, sliced ● juice of 1 lemon ● 450 g/1 lb peeled prawns (shrimp)

Heat the oil and fry the onions until browned. Grind together the chillis, garlic, coriander and salt and stir into the pan with the remaining spices and cook for 2 minutes. Add the water, mango, lemon juice and prawns and bring to the boil. Simmer gently, stirring occasionally, until the mixture is quite dry. Serve hot with chapatis and vegetables.

Bitter Gourd Stuffed with Prawns
Serves 6

12 bitter gourds ● 75 ml/5 tbsp ghee ● 225 g/8 oz peeled prawns (shrimp)

1 tomato, skinned and chopped ● juice of 1 lemon ● salt

Masala: 1 onion ● 3 dried red chillies ● 2.5 ml/½ tsp ground turmeric

2.5 ml/½ tsp coriander (cilantro) seeds ● 4 cloves garlic

Lightly scrape the gourd skins, make a split lengthways and remove the seeds. Soak in salted water for 30 minutes. Drain and pat dry. Grind all the masala ingredients to a smooth paste, adding a little water if necessary. Heat half the ghee and fry the paste for 2 minutes. Add the prawns and tomato and cook for 5 minutes. Add the lemon juice and leave to cool. Stuff the gourds with the mixture and tie with string. Heat the remaining ghee until almost smoking and fry the gourds until the skins turn brown and crisp. Serve hot with chapatis.

Spinach Chorchori with Prawns   Serves 4

45 ml/3 tbsp mustard oil ● 450 g/1 lb peeled prawns (shrimp)

450 g/1 lb spinach, chopped ● 30 ml/2 tbsp mustard seeds

5 dried red chillies ● 30 ml/2 tbsp oil

5 ml/1 tsp ground turmeric ● salt

Heat the mustard oil and fry the prawns quickly until browned. Remove from the pan. Reheat the oil and fry the spinach for 2 minutes. Remove from the pan and discard the oil. Grind the mustard seeds and chillies to a paste. Heat the oil until smoking then fry the spinach for 1 minute. Add the ground paste and turmeric and fry for 2 minutes. Add the prawns and salt and cook for 5 minutes. Serve hot with rice and chapatis.

Cabbage Dalna with Prawns   Serves 4

5 ml/1 tsp coriander (cilantro) seeds ● 5 ml/1 tsp cumin seeds

4 cloves garlic ● 5 dried red chillies ● 2.5 cm/1 in ginger root

45 ml/3 tbsp oil ● 2 onions, sliced ● 2 cardamom pods ● 2 cloves

2.5 cm/1 in cinnamon stick ● 5 ml/2 tsp ground turmeric

5 ml/1 tsp sugar ● 1 medium cabbage, shredded

300 ml/½ pt/1¼ cups natural (plain) yoghurt, beaten

450 g/1 lb peeled prawns (shrimp) ● salt

Grind the coriander and cumin seeds, garlic, chillis and ginger to a paste. Heat the oil and fry the onions until browned. Add the ground paste and remaining spices and fry until browned. Add the cabbage and fry for 5 minutes, stirring continuously. Add the yoghurt, cover and simmer until the liquid has been absorbed. Add the prawns and salt and simmer until the sauce is thick. Serve hot with chapatis, rice and vegetables.

Madras Prawn Curry   Serves 6

900 g/2 lb peeled prawns (shrimp) ● 5 ml/1 tsp ground turmeric

salt ● 45 ml/3 tbsp coconut cream ● 30 ml/2 tbsp coriander (cilantro) seeds

10 ml/2 tsp cumin seeds ● 2 dried red chillies

1.5 ml/¼ tsp fenugreek seeds ● 10 ml/2 tsp tamarind concentrate

75 ml/5 tbsp coconut milk ● 45 ml/3 tbsp oil

5 ml/1 tsp black mustard seeds ● 2.5 ml/½ tsp asafoetida

1 large onion, thinly sliced ● 6 cloves garlic, crushed

2.5 cm/1 in ginger root, finely chopped ● 1 green chilli, finely chopped

45 ml/3 tbsp natural (plain) yoghurt

30 ml/2 tbsp chopped fresh coriander (cilantro)

Mix the prawns with the turmeric and salt and leave to stand for 10 minutes. Grind the coconut cream, coriander, cumin seeds, chillies, fenugreek seeds, tamarind and coconut milk to a paste. Heat the oil in a large pan and fry the mustard seeds until they start crackling. Stir in the asafoetida then add the onion, garlic, ginger and chilli and cook until the onion is browned. Add the paste and yoghurt and cook for 5 minutes until the mixture bubbles. Stir in the prawns and simmer for 15 minutes. Garnish with coriander and serve hot with plain rice, papadums, vegetable sambar and chutney.

Prawns with Herbs   Serves 4

2 onions, chopped • 30 ml/2 tbsp chopped fresh coriander (cilantro)

15 ml/1 tbsp green masala paste • 15 ml/1 tbsp chopped fresh mint

3 green chillies, chopped • 1 green (bell) pepper, chopped

30 ml/2 tbsp grated (shredded) coconut • 45 ml/3 tbsp ghee

900 g/2 lb prawns (shrimp), peeled • salt and pepper

Purée the onions, coriander, masala paste, mint, chillies, pepper and coconut to a paste in a blender or food processor. Heat the ghee and fry the paste for about 5 minutes. Add the prawns and fry for a further 5 minutes, stirring well. Season with salt and pepper. Serve hot with rice.

Coromandel-style Crab Curry   Serves 6

1 coconut, grated (shredded) • 30 ml/2 tbsp coriander (cilantro) seeds

75 ml/5 tbsp coconut milk • 150 ml/¼ pt/⅔ cup water • 45 ml/3 tbsp oil

15 ml/1 tbsp black mustard seeds • 2 dried red chillies

2.5 ml/½ tsp black peppercorns • 5 cloves garlic, crushed

2.5 cm/1 in ginger root, finely chopped • 1 onion, finely chopped

5 ml/1 tsp ground coriander (cilantro) • 5 ml/1 tsp ground cumin

salt • 5 ml/1 tsp ground turmeric • 15 ml/1 tbsp chilli powder

30 ml/2 tbsp chopped fresh coriander (cilantro) • 1.5 kg/3 lb crab meat

Purée the coconut, coriander seeds, coconut milk and water to a paste in a blender or food processor, adding a little more water if necessary. Strain through muslin (cheesecloth); there should be about 300 ml/½ pt/1¼ cups of milk. Blend the purée again with a further 100 ml/4 fl oz/½ cup of water and strain again to give 600 ml/1 pt/2½ cups in total.

Heat the oil and fry the mustard seeds and chillies until the seeds start crackling. Add the peppercorns, garlic and ginger and fry for 1 minute. Add the onion and fry until browned. Add the coriander, cumin, salt, turmeric and chilli powder and cook for 3 minutes. Add the coconut milk and bring to the boil. Mix in half the coriander and the crab meat. Simmer for 5 minutes until the crab meat is cooked. Garnish with the remaining coriander and serve hot with plain rice, vegetables and papadums.

Crab Jhal
Serves 8

45 ml/3 tbsp mustard oil ● 900 g/2 lb crab meat

4 onions, sliced ● 5 green chillies, seeded and sliced

1 clove garlic, crushed ● 4 large tomatoes, skinned and quartered

salt ● 5 ml/1 tsp sugar ● 2 potatoes, boiled and cubed

5 ml/1 tsp ground turmeric

Heat the oil and fry the crab meat quickly until browned. Remove and set aside. Reheat the oil and fry the onions until lightly browned. Add the chillies, garlic and crab meat, cover and simmer for 4 minutes. Add the tomatoes, potatoes, sugar and salt and simmer for about 10 minutes until tender. Serve hot with chapatis, plain rice and a vegetable dish.

Lobster Curry
Serves 6-8

15 ml/1 tbsp ghee ● 5 cloves garlic, crushed ● 900 g/2 lb lobster meat

juice of 1 lemon ● 5 ml/1 tsp chilli powder ● 5 ml/1 tsp ground turmeric

5 ml/1 tsp sugar ● salt ● 15 ml/1 tbsp chopped fresh coriander (cilantro)

Heat the ghee and fry the garlic until lightly browned. Add the lobster and fry for 5 minutes. Add the lemon juice, chilli powder, turmeric, sugar and salt, cover and simmer gently until tender, adding a little water if necessary and stirring occasionally. Garnish with the coriander and serve hot with rice and vegetables.

Lamb

In India, lamb is the most commonly used meat. Indians cook the meat with the bones to add extra flavour and also because people usually eat with their hands. All the recipes here are suitable for British-style meat; anyone using the recipes in India must add more water and allow longer cooking times, as Indian meat is a little tougher. This has the advantage that the spices mature very well with longer cooking. For people using British, European or New Zealand meat, it is best to cook the dish a few hours before serving to help mature the spices, then reheat before serving. This does not apply to rice dishes.

Potato, Lamb and Cauliflower   Serves 4-6

250 g/9 oz cauliflower, cut into 2.5 cm/1 in pieces

150 g/5 oz potatoes, cut into 2.5 cm/1 in pieces ● oil for deep-frying

75 ml/5 tbsp oil or ghee ● 5 ml/1 tsp mustard seeds

5 ml/1 tsp cumin seeds ● 5 large garlic cloves, crushed

4 cm/1½ in ginger root, finely chopped ● 1 onion, finely chopped

6 black peppercorns ● 4 cloves ● 2.5 cm/1 in cinnamon stick

2 bay leaves ● 1 black cardamom pod

450 g/1 lb boned lamb shoulder, cubed ● 10 ml/2 tsp ground coriander (cilantro)

2.5 ml/½ tsp ground turmeric ● 2.5 ml/½ tsp ground red chilli

salt ● 400 g/14 oz canned tomatoes ● 150 ml/¼ pt/⅔ cup water

Garnish: 2.5 ml/½ tsp garam masala

15 ml/1 tbsp chopped fresh coriander (cilantro) ● 1 small green chilli, chopped

Fry the cauliflower and potatoes in hot oil until golden brown. Drain and set aside. Heat the oil or ghee and fry the mustard seeds until they start crackling. Add the cumin seeds and fry until browned. Add the garlic, ginger, onion and whole spices and fry gently until golden brown. Add the lamb and fry for 5 minutes. Stir in the ground spices, salt and tomatoes and cook until all the water has been absorbed. Add one-third of the water and cook until all the water has been absorbed. Add the remaining water, cover and simmer gently for about 30 minutes until the meat is tender. Stir in the fried vegetables and cook over a low heat for a further 5 minutes. Sprinkle over the garnish ingredients and serve hot with chapatis, rice, raita and dal.

Moughal-style Lamb
Serves 4-6

90 ml/6 tbsp ghee or oil ● 5 ml/1 tsp cumin seeds

3 onions, finely chopped ● 4 large cloves garlic, crushed

2.5 cm/1 in ginger root, finely chopped ● 2.5 cm/1 in cinnamon stick

4 cloves ● 4 black peppercorns ● 2 bay leaves

1 black cardamom pod ● 500 g/18 oz boned lamb, cubed

50 g/2 oz/½ cup desiccated (shredded) coconut

15 ml/1 tbsp ground coriander (cilantro) ● 5 ml/1 tsp ground turmeric

5 ml/1 tsp ground roasted cumin ● 2.5 ml/½ tsp ground red chilli

1.5 ml/¼ tsp ground mace ● 1.5 ml/¼ tsp grated nutmeg ● salt

225 g/8 oz canned tomatoes ● 150 ml/¼ pt/⅔ cup natural (plain) yoghurt

100 g/4 oz/⅔ cup raisins ● 50 g/2 oz/½ cup blanched almonds, halved

50 g/2 oz/½ cup cashew nuts, halved ● 50 g/2 oz/½ cup walnuts, quartered

25 g/1 oz/¼ cup pistachios, halved ● 150 ml/0 pt/ cup water

Garnish: 2.5 ml/½ tsp garam masala

15 ml/1 tbsp chopped fresh coriander (cilantro) ● 1 small green chilli, chopped

Heat the ghee or oil in a heavy-based pan and fry the cumin seeds over a medium heat until lightly browned. Add the onions, garlic, ginger and whole spices and fry until golden brown. Stir in the meat and coconut and fry for 5 minutes. Stir in the ground spices, salt and tomatoes and cook until the liquid has been absorbed and the ghee appears on the surface. Add the yoghurt and cook until all the liquid has evaporated. Add the raisins, nuts and water, bring to the boil, cover and simmer over a low heat for about 20 minutes until the meat is tender. If you are serving the dish with rice, you can add an extra 150 ml/¼ pt/⅔ cup of water. Sprinkle over the garnish ingredients and serve hot with nan, raita and a vegetable dish.

Lamb with Beetroot
Serves 6

675 g/1½ lb lamb, cubed ● 450 g/1 lb beetroot (red beets)

90 ml/6 tbsp oil ● 3 onions, sliced ● 2.5 cm/1 in ginger root, chopped

3 cloves garlic, crushed ● 15 ml/1 tbsp ground coriander (cilantro)

5 ml/1 tsp ground cumin ● 5 ml/1 tsp ground turmeric

750 ml/1¼ pts/3 cups water ● 2.5 ml/½ tsp chilli powder

5 ml/1 tsp garam masala

Trim the meat and trim and dice the beetroot. Heat 75 ml/5 tbsp of oil and fry the onions until golden. Add the ginger and garlic and fry until lightly browned. Stir in the coriander, cumin and turmeric and fry for 3-4 minutes, stirring. Add the meat and fry for about 15 minutes until lightly browned. Remove the meat from the pan. Stir in the beetroot and fry for 2 minutes, stirring, adding a little more oil if necessary. Add the water and bring to the boil then simmer for 20-25 minutes. Return the meat to the pan with the chilli powder, cover and simmer for about 1 hour until the meat is tender, adding a little more water if necessary. Stir in the garam masala and simmer for about 10-15 minutes until the liquid has evaporated.

Dry Meat Masala
Serves 4-6

500 g/18 oz boned lamb shoulder, cubed ● 400 ml/14 fl oz/1¾ cups water

75 ml/5 tbsp ghee or oil ● 5 ml/1 tsp onion seeds

5 ml/1 tsp sesame seeds ● 4 bay leaves ● 3 large cloves garlic, chopped

2.5 cm/1 in ginger root, chopped ● 1 onion, finely chopped

15 ml/1 tbsp ground almonds ● 15 ml/1 tbsp ground coriander (cilantro)

5 ml/1 tsp ground roasted cumin ● 5 ml/1 tsp garam masala

2.5 ml/½ tsp ground red chilli ● 2.5 ml/½ tsp ground turmeric

1.5 ml/¼ tsp ground mace ● 1.5 ml/¼ tsp grated nutmeg ● salt

200 ml/7 fl oz/scant 1 cup water

Garnish: 2.5 ml/½ tsp garam masala

15 ml/1 tbsp chopped fresh coriander (cilantro) ● 1 small green chilli, chopped

Place the lamb and water in a pan and bring the boil. Reduce the heat, cover and cook for 30 minutes. Remove the lid and increase the heat to dry off any remaining water.

Heat the ghee or oil and fry the onion seeds for a few seconds until browned. Add the sesame seeds then the bay leaves, garlic, ginger and onion and fry until golden brown. Stir in the ground spices, salt and cooked meat and fry until all the liquid has been absorbed. Add 50 ml/2 fl oz/3½ tbsp of water and fry until all the water has been absorbed and the ghee appears on the surface. Repeat this until all the water has been absorbed and the meat is tender. Sprinkle over the garnish ingredients and serve hot with dal, raita and a kofta dish.

Tikka Kebabs
Serves 6

900 g/2 lb boneless lamb, cubed • juice of ½ lemon • salt

45 ml/3 tbsp oil • 450 ml/¾ pt/2 cups natural (plain) yoghurt

1 onion, chopped • 10 ml/2 tsp garam masala • 2 cloves garlic, chopped

1 cm/½ in ginger root, chopped • 5 ml/1 tsp paprika

1.5 ml/¼ tsp ground red chilli • pinch of pepper

Mix the meat with the lemon juice, salt and oil. Purée the yoghurt, onion, garam masala, garlic, ginger, paprika, chilli and pepper in a blender or food processor. Mix into the meat, cover and refrigerate overnight.

Thread the meat on to metal skewers and cook in a preheated oven at 180°C/350°F/gas mark 4 for about 20 minutes, turning and basting occasionally. Serve hot with coriander chutney.

Lamb with Spinach
Serves 4-6

450 g/1 lb spinach, coarsely chopped • 300 ml/½ pt/1¼ cups water

90 ml/6 tbsp ghee or oil • 6 large cloves garlic, crushed

4 bay leaves • 4 cm/1½ in ginger root, finely chopped

1 onion, finely chopped • 450 g/1 lb boned lamb shoulder, cubed

10 ml/2 tsp ground coriander (cilantro) • 5 ml/1 tsp ground roasted cumin

5 ml/1 tsp garam masala • 2.5 ml/½ tsp ground red chilli

2.5 ml/½ tsp ground turmeric • salt • 400 g/14 oz canned tomatoes

250 ml/8 fl oz/1 cup water

Garnish: 2.5 ml/½ tsp garam masala • 1 green chilli, chopped

Place the spinach and water in a pan and bring to the boil. Cover and simmer over a medium-low heat for about 20 minutes until the spinach is tender and the water has been absorbed. Leave to cool then blend to a smooth paste.

Heat the ghee or oil in a heavy-based pan and fry the garlic, bay leaves, ginger and onion over a medium heat until golden brown. Add the meat and fry for 5 minutes until lightly browned. Stir in the ground spices, salt and tomatoes and cook until all the liquid has been absorbed and the ghee appears on the surface. Add the water and cooked spinach, bring to the boil, cover and simmer over a medium-low heat for 20 minutes until the meat is tender, stirring occasionally. Sprinkle over the garnish ingredients and serve hot with chapatis, rice, dal and raita.

Lamb with Yoghurt and Tomato
Serves 4-6

60 ml/4 tbsp oil or ghee ● 5 large cloves garlic, crushed

4 cm/1½ in ginger root, finely chopped ● 2 onions, finely chopped

4 cloves ● 4 black peppercorns ● 2 bay leaves

2.5 cm/1 in cinnamon stick ● 1 black cardamom pod

500 g/18 oz boned lamb, cubed ● 10 ml/2 tsp ground coriander (cilantro)

2.5 ml/½ tsp ground red chilli ● 2.5 ml/½ tsp ground turmeric

400 g/14 oz canned tomatoes ● salt 150 ml/¼ pt/⅔ cup natural (plain) yoghurt

30 ml/2 tbsp chopped fresh fenugreek ● 100 ml/3½ fl oz/6½ tbsp water

Garnish: 2.5 ml/½ tsp garam masala

15 ml/1 tbsp chopped fresh coriander (cilantro) ● 1 small green chilli, chopped

Heat the oil or ghee and fry the garlic, ginger, onions and whole spices until golden. Add the meat and fry for 10 minutes until golden. Stir in the ground spices, tomatoes and salt and cook for 10 minutes until the liquid has been absorbed and the oil appears on the surface. Add the yoghurt and fenugreek and cook for 10 minutes until the liquid has been absorbed. Add the water and cook over a low heat for 5 minutes until the meat is tender. Sprinkle over the garnish ingredients and serve hot with chapatis, dal, fried bitter gourd or cauliflower, raita and plain rice.

Lamb Curry
Serves 4

75 ml/5 tbsp ghee or oil ● 2.5 ml/½ tsp fenugreek seeds

2.5 ml/½ tsp cumin seeds ● 3 large cloves garlic, crushed

2 onions, finely chopped ● 2.5 cm/1 in ginger root, chopped

4 cloves ● 4 black peppercorns ● 2 bay leaves

2.5 cm/1 in cinnamon stick ● 500 g/18 oz boned lamb, cubed

5 ml/1 tsp ground coriander (cilantro) ● 2.5 ml/½ tsp ground roasted cumin

2.5 ml/½ tsp ground red chilli ● 2.5 ml/½ tsp ground turmeric

salt ● 300 ml/½ tsp/1¼ cups water

Garnish: 2.5 ml/½ tsp garam masala

15 ml/1 tbsp chopped fresh coriander (cilantro) ● 1 small green chilli, chopped

Heat the ghee or oil in a heavy-based pan and fry the fenugreek and cumin seeds until browned. Add the garlic, onions, ginger and whole spices until golden. Add the meat and fry for 5 minutes. Stir in the ground spices, salt and 45 ml/3 tbsp of water and fry until the water has been absorbed and the ghee appears on the surface. Add the remaining water, bring to the boil then cook over a medium-low heat for 20 minutes until the meat is tender, stirring occasionally. Sprinkle with the garnish ingredients and serve hot with chapatis, cauliflower, rice and raita.

Lamb with Yoghurt, Mint and Coriander

Serves 4-6

150 ml/¼ pt/⅔ cup natural (plain) yoghurt

45 ml/3 tbsp chopped fresh coriander (cilantro) ● 30 ml/2 tbsp chopped fresh mint

5 ml/1 tsp garam masala ● 5 ml/1 tsp ground roasted cumin

2.5 ml/½ tsp ground mace ● 2.5 ml/½ tsp grated nutmeg

2.5 ml/½ tsp ground red chilli ● 2.5 ml/½ tsp ground turmeric

500 g/18 oz boned lamb, cubed ● 75 ml/5 tbsp oil or ghee

large pinch of asafoetida ● 5 ml/1 tsp mustard seeds

5 ml/1 tsp ground anise ● 1 onion, finely chopped

4 large cloves garlic, crushed ● 2.5 cm/1 in ginger root, finely chopped

225 g/8 oz canned tomatoes ● 100 ml/3½ fl oz/6½ tbsp wine vinegar

100 ml/3½ fl oz/6½ tbsp water

Garnish: 1.5 ml/¼ tsp garam masala

15 ml/1 tbsp chopped fresh coriander (cilantro) ● 1 green chilli, chopped

Blend the yoghurt, coriander and mint to a smooth paste in a blender or food processor then stir in the ground spices. Stir into the meat and leave to marinate for 2 hours.

Heat the oil or ghee in a heavy-based pan and fry the asafoetida and mustard seeds until they start crackling. Add the anise and fry until browned. Add the onion, garlic and ginger and fry gently until golden brown. Lift the lamb from the marinade, add to the pan and fry until lightly browned on all sides. Stir in the remaining marinade and cook until all the liquid has been absorbed. Add the tomatoes and cook until all the liquid has been absorbed. Stir in the wine vinegar and cook until the liquid has been absorbed and the oil appears on the surface. Stir in the water, bring to the boil and simmer for 2 minutes until the meat is tender. Sprinkle over the garnish ingredients and serve hot with nan or puris, rice, dal, raita and a vegetable dish.

North Indian Lamb and Okra Curry

Serves 4-6

105 ml/7 tbsp ghee or oil ● 5 ml/1 tsp cumin seeds

4 large cloves garlic, crushed

2.5 cm/1 in ginger root, finely chopped ● 2 onions, finely chopped

10 ml/2 tsp ground coriander (cilantro) ● 5 ml/1 tsp garam masala

5 ml/1 tsp ground roasted cumin ● 2.5 ml/½ tsp ground red chilli

2.5 ml/½ tsp ground turmeric ● salt ● 500 g/18 oz boned lamb, cubed

400 g/14 oz canned tomatoes ● 200 ml/7 fl oz/scant 1 cup water

250 g/9 oz okra, cut into 1.5 cm/½ in pieces

Garnish: 1.5 ml/¼ tsp garam masala

15 ml/1 tbsp chopped fresh coriander (cilantro) ● 1 green chilli, chopped

Heat the ghee or oil in a heavy-based pan and fry the cumin seeds over a medium heat until browned. Add the garlic, ginger and onions and fry until golden brown. Stir in the ground spices and salt then the meat and tomatoes, cover and cook until all the liquid has been absorbed and the ghee appears on the surface, stirring occasionally. Add the water, bring to the boil, cover and cook over a medium-low heat for 20 minutes until the meat is tender, stirring occasionally. Add the okra and cook for a further 10 minutes. Sprinkle over the garnish ingredients and serve hot with onion paratha, raita and dal.

Lamb Vindaloo
Serves 4-6

15 ml/1 tbsp coriander (cilantro) seeds ● 10 ml/2 tsp cumin seeds

10 ml/2 tsp mustard seeds ● 5 black peppercorns

5 cloves ● 5 dried red chillies ● 2.5 cm/1 in cinnamon stick

2.5 ml/½ tsp cardamom seeds ● 2.5 ml/½ tsp ground turmeric

salt ● 5 large cloves garlic, chopped ● 4 cm/1½ in ginger root, chopped

200 ml/7 fl oz/scant 1 cup wine vinegar ● 500 g/18 oz boned lamb, cubed

75 ml/5 tbsp oil ● 2 onions, finely chopped

400 g/14 oz canned tomatoes ● 250 ml/8 fl oz/1 cup water

Garnish: 2.5 ml/½ tsp garam masala

15 ml/1 tbsp chopped fresh coriander (cilantro) ● 1 green chilli, chopped

Heat a frying pan (skillet) over a medium heat and fry the whole spices until browned. Grind them to a fine powder. Stir in the turmeric and salt to taste. Blend the powder with the garlic, ginger and 60 ml/4 tbsp of wine vinegar to a smooth paste in a blender or food processor. Rub the paste into the meat and leave to marinate overnight.

Heat the oil in a heavy-based pan and fry the onions over a medium heat until golden brown. Add the lamb and fry for 15 minutes until golden. Stir in the tomatoes and fry until all the liquid has been absorbed and the oil appears on the surface. Add the remaining wine vinegar and water, bring to the boil, cover and cook over a medium-low heat for 40 minutes until the meat is tender. Sprinkle with the garnish ingredients and serve hot with rice, chapatis, raita and a bean and potato or okra dish.

Rogan Josh
Serves 6

120 ml/4 fl oz/½ cup ghee or oil ● pinch of asafoetida

900 g/2 lb lamb, cubed ● 150 ml/¼ pt/⅔ cup natural (plain) yoghurt

600 ml/1 pt/2½ cups boiling water ● 5 ml/1 tsp aniseeds

2.5 ml/½ tsp ground ginger ● 5 ml/1 tsp caraway sees

10 ml/2 tsp chilli powder ● 6 cloves ● 10 cm/3 in cinnamon stick

6 large cardamom pods ● 1 sprig fresh curry leaves

5 ml/1 tsp ground saffron ● salt

Heat the ghee or oil and fry the asafoetida and meat until the meat is well coated in the oil. Continue to cook, stirring, until the meat browns and separates from the bone. Add the yoghurt and cook until the yoghurt has been absorbed. Add the boiling water and spices. Simmer for 2 hours over a low heat until the water has evaporated and the ghee appears on the surface. Serve hot with rice and vegetables.

Kashmiri Rogan Josh
Serves 4-6

15 ml/1 tbsp coriander (cilantro) seeds ● 5 ml/1 tsp cumin seeds

5 ml/1 tsp poppy seeds ● 4 cloves ● 4 black peppercorns

2.5 cm/1 in cinnamon stick ● 5 ml/1 tsp black cardamom seeds

15 ml/1 tbsp desiccated (shredded) coconut ● 15 ml/1 tbsp ground almonds

1.5 ml/½ tsp ground mace ● 1.5 ml/½ tsp grated nutmeg

75 ml/5 tbsp ghee or oil ● 5 ml/1 tsp onion seeds ● 1 onion, finely chopped

4 cloves garlic, crushed ● 2.5 cm/1 in ginger root, finely chopped ● 3 bay leaves

500 g/18 oz boned lamb, cubed ● 2.5 ml/½ tsp ground red chilli

2.5 ml/½ tsp ground turmeric ● salt ● 225 g/8 oz canned tomatoes

150 ml/¼ pt/⅔ cup natural (plain) yoghurt ● 200 ml/7 fl oz/scant 1 cup water

Garnish: 2.5 ml/½ tsp garam masala

15 ml/1 tbsp chopped fresh coriander (cilantro) ● 1 small green chilli, chopped

Heat a frying pan (skillet) and fry the coriander, cumin and poppy seeds, the cloves, peppercorns, cinnamon and cardamom until golden. Cool then grind to a powder. Heat a pan and fry the coconut, almonds, mace and nutmeg until lightly browned.

Heat the ghee or oil in a heavy-based pan and fry the onion seeds for 30 seconds. Add the onion, garlic, ginger and bay leaves and fry until golden brown. Stir in the lamb and fry for 5 minutes. Stir in the roasted spices, the chilli, turmeric and salt then add the tomatoes and cook until all the liquid has been absorbed and the ghee appears on the surface. Add the yoghurt and cook until all the liquid has been absorbed. Add the water, bring to the boil, cover and cook over a low heat for 10 minutes until the meat is tender. Sprinkle over the garnish ingredients and serve hot with chapatis, raita, dal and rice.

Lamb Dansak
Serves 6-8

675 g/1½ lb boned lamb, cubed ● 45 ml/3 tbsp red lentils

45 ml/3 tbsp yellow split peas ● 45 ml/3 tbsp whole green lentils

1 small aubergine (eggplant), chopped ● handful of fenugreek, chopped

200 g/7 oz pumpkin, chopped ● 2 potatoes, peeled and chopped

2 onions, chopped ● 1.5 ml/¼ tsp ground turmeric ● salt

45 ml/3 tbsp oil ● 3 spring onions (scallions), sliced

2.5 ml/½ tsp fenugreek seeds ● 5 ml/1 tsp cumin seeds

10 ml/2 tsp ground coriander (cilantro) ● 2.5 cm/1 in ginger root, ground

5 cloves garlic, crushed ● 15 ml/1 tbsp garam masala

lime-sized ball of tamarind, soaked in 300 ml/½ pt/1¼ cups water

10 ml/2 tsp ground jaggery, soaked with the tamarind

Put the meat, pulses, vegetables, turmeric and salt into a heavy-based pan and add just enough water to cover. Bring to the boil then simmer gently for about 50 minutes until the meat is tender. Remove the meat then purée the pulse and vegetable mixture and return all the ingredients to the pan.

Heat the oil and fry the onions until golden brown. Reserve half of them for garnish and add the rest to the meat. Fry the fenugreek and cumin seeds, coriander, ginger and garlic until well browned then add to the meat with the garam masala. Extract the pulp from the tamarind, discard the seeds and add the pulp to the meat. Simmer for 10 minutes then garnish with the reserved onions and serve hot with rice and vegetables.

Baruchi Braised Lamb
Serves 4

45 ml/2 tbsp oil ● 150 g/5 oz onions, sliced ● 1 cm/½ in ginger root

1 bulb garlic ● salt ● 675 g/1½ lb boned lamb, cubed

450 g/1 lb potatoes ● 120 ml/4 fl oz/½ cup ghee

2.5 ml/½ tsp cardamom seeds, ground ● 2.5 cm/1 in cinnamon stick, ground

2 dried red chillies ● 2.5 ml/½ tsp ground saffron

150 ml/¼ pt/⅔ cup coconut milk ● 300 ml/½ pt/1¼ cups milk ● juice of ½ lemon

Heat 30 ml/2 tbsp of oil and fry the onions until browned and crisp. Grind to a powder then mix to a paste with the ginger, garlic and salt. Rub the paste over the meat and leave to marinate for 1 hour.

Boil the potatoes, peel and halve then fry in a little oil until crisp. Heat the ghee and fry the meat until browned. Add the cardamom, cinnamon and chillies and simmer until the meat is tender. Add the saffron, potatoes, coconut milk, milk and lemon juice and simmer for 10 minutes. Serve hot with rice, chapatis and vegetables.

Kuchha Korma
Serves 6

900 g/2 lb boned lamb, cut into chunks ● 100 ml/3½ fl oz/6½ tbsp ghee

225 g/8 oz onions, sliced ● 600 ml/1 pt/2½ cups natural (plain) yoghurt

2 curry leaves ● 1 cinnamon stick ● 6 cardamom pods

8 cloves ● 10 peppercorns ● 10 ml/2 tsp ground coriander (cilantro)

6 dried red chillies

Place all the ingredients in a heavy-based pan and add just enough water to cover. Bring to the boil and simmer over a low heat for about 1 hour until the meat is tender, stirring occasionally and adding a little more water if necessary. When the onions have dissolved and the ghee appears on the surface, the curry is ready. Serve hot with chapatis.

Lamb Chilli Fry
Serves 4-6

90 ml/6 tbsp ghee ● 20 dried red chillies

45 ml/3 tbsp coriander (cilantro) seeds ● 10 cloves garlic, sliced

10 cm/4 in ginger root, sliced ● 4 onions, sliced ● 6 cloves

6 cardamom pods ● 1 cinnamon stick ● 675 g/1½ lb boned lamb, cubed

5 ml/1 tsp ground turmeric ● salt

300 ml/½ pt/1¼ cups natural (plain) yoghurt ● juice of 1 lemon

15 ml/1 tbsp chopped fresh coriander (cilantro)

Heat 15 ml/1 tbsp of ghee and fry the chillies until dark then remove from the pan. Using a little more ghee each time, fry the coriander seeds, garlic and ginger separately and set aside. Heat the remaining ghee in a large pan and fry the onions until golden brown. Drain and set aside. Add the cloves, cardamom pods and cinnamon to the ghee and fry for 1 minute. Add the lamb, turmeric and salt, cover and simmer for about 20 minutes, stirring occasionally, until the meat is half-cooked. Add the yoghurt, lemon juice and fried spices and simmer for a further 20 minutes until the meat is tender, stirring occasionally and adding a little water if necessary. Stir in the onion slices and simmer for 2 minutes then garnish with the coriander and serve hot with rice, chapatis and vegetables.

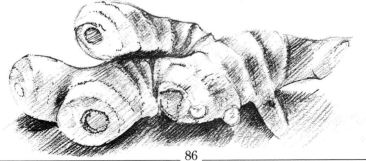

Lamb in Yoghurt
Serves 4

450 g/1 lb boned lamb, cubed ● 600 ml/1 pt/2½ cups natural (plain) yoghurt

salt ● 30 ml/2 tbsp ghee ● juice of 1 lemon

Masala: 8 green chillies ● 1 onion

15 ml/1 tbsp poppy seeds ● 5 ml/1 tsp chopped fresh coriander (cilantro)

2.5 cm/1 in ginger root ● 6 cloves garlic

15 ml/1 tbsp desiccated (shredded) coconut ● 15 ml/1 tbsp yellow split peas

4 cloves ● 1 cinnamon stick

Place the lamb, yoghurt and salt in a heavy-based pan and simmer over a low heat for about 40 minutes until the meat is tender and almost dry. Grind together all the masala ingre- dients and add them to the pan. Sim- mer for 10 minutes. Add the ghee and fry until the meat turns a reddish brown. Add the lemon juice and serve hot with papadums and vegetables.

Lamb Gosht
Serves 4-6

15 ml/1 tbsp poppy seeds ● 15 ml/1 tbsp melon seeds

15 ml/1 tbsp blanched almonds ● 5 ml/1 tsp chopped ginger root

5 ml/1 tsp chopped garlic ● 5 ml/1 tsp ground cardamom

5 ml/1 tsp peppercorns, cracked ● 5 cm/2 in piece papaya

15 ml/1 tbsp chopped fresh coriander (cilantro) ● 1 cinnamon stick

5 ml/1 tsp cumin seeds ● 900 g/2 lb boned lamb, cut into chunks

100 g/4 oz/½ cup ghee ● 5 ml/1 tsp ground turmeric

Roast the poppy and melon seeds with the almonds in a dry pan until lightly browned then grind to a paste. Grind together the ginger, garlic, car- damom, peppercorns, papaya and coriander. Crumble in the cinnamon and mix in the whole cumin seeds. Rub both the spice mixtures over the meat and leave to marinate for 1 hour.

Heat the ghee in a large ovenproof pan and fry the meat for 5 minutes, stirring continuously. Reduce the heat and simmer gently for 15 minutes. Transfer to a preheated oven and cook at 180°C/350°F/gas mark 4 for 1 hour until the meat is tender. Sprinkle with turmeric and serve hot with rice and vegetables.

Curried Lamb with Saffron
Serves 6

900 g/2 lb lean lamb, cubed ● 3 cloves garlic, chopped

1 cm/½ in ginger root, chopped ● 2.5 ml/½ tsp ground cumin

1.5 ml/¼ tsp chilli powder ● 1.5 ml/¼ tsp black pepper

pinch of ground cinnamon ● 90 ml/6 tbsp oil ● pinch of saffron

250 ml/8 fl oz/1 cup warm water ● 4 onions, sliced

5 ml/1 tsp ground coriander (cilantro)

15 ml/1 tbsp chopped fresh coriander (cilantro) ● 45 ml/3 tbsp lemon juice

Place the meat in a bowl and rub in the garlic, ginger, cumin, chilli powder and pepper. Stir the cinnamon into the oil, pour over the meat, add the saffron and marinate for 3 hours.

Transfer the meat to a heavy-based pan and add the water. Bring to the boil, cover and simmer for about 30 minutes until the meat is tender.

Remove the meat from the pan. Add the onions and ground coriander and simmer until the onions are soft and the sauce slightly thickened. Return the meat to the pan, sprinkle with coriander and return to the boil. Cover and simmer gently for 15 minutes. Stir in the lemon juice and simmer for 1 minute before serving.

Coconut Lamb with Nuts
Serves 6

10 ml/2 tsp ground coriander (cilantro) ● 30 ml/2 tbsp chopped almonds

30 ml/2 tbsp chopped peanuts ● 10 ml/2 tsp cumin seeds

5 ml/1 tsp poppy seeds ● 3 cardamom pods ● 8 cloves ● 10 black peppercorns

pinch of ground mace ● pinch of grated nutmeg

30 ml/2 tbsp desiccated (shredded) coconut ● 5 cm/1 in ginger root, chopped

12 cloves garlic, chopped ● 5 dried red chillies, soaked in hot water

60 ml/4 tbsp ghee ● 2 onions, finely chopped

1.5 ml/¼ tsp ground turmeric ● 300 ml/½ pt/1¼ cups natural (plain) yoghurt

3 tomatoes, skinned and chopped ● 900 g/2 lb lean lamb, cubed

600 ml/1 pt/2½ cups boiling water ● 5 ml/1 tsp garam masala

45 ml/3 tbsp chopped fresh coriander (cilantro)

Dry roast the coriander for 30 seconds then remove from the pan. Stir in the almonds, peanuts, cumin and poppy seeds, cardamom, cloves, peppercorns, mace, nutmeg and coconut and fry for 1½ minutes. Purée the mixture with the coriander, ginger, garlic, chillies and soaking water. Heat the ghee and fry the onions until golden. Add the purée and turmeric and fry for 4-5 minutes. Stir in the yoghurt and cook, stirring, until the yoghurt dries up. Add the tomatoes and simmer for 4-5 minutes. Add the meat and fry until browned. Stir in the water, cover and simmer gently for about 1½ hours until the meat is tender, adding water if necessary. Sprinkle with garam masala and coriander and cook for a further 1 minute before serving.

Light Lamb and Potato Curry   Serves 6

75 ml/5 tbsp oil ● 4 onions, sliced ● 3 cloves garlic, chopped

2.5 cm/1 in ginger root, chopped ● 15 ml/1 tbsp ground coriander

5 ml/1 tsp ground cumin ● 2.5 ml/½ tsp ground turmeric

4 tomatoes, skinned and chopped ● 675 g/1½ lb lamb, cubed

5 curry leaves ● 750 ml/1¼ pts/3 cups water ● 450 g/1 lb potatoes, cubed

30 ml/2 tbsp chopped fresh coriander (cilantro)

Heat the oil and fry the onions until golden, stirring occasionally. Add the garlic and ginger and fry until lightly browned. Stir in the coriander, cumin and turmeric and fry for 1 minute, stirring. Add the tomatoes and fry until the mixture resembles a thick, lumpy purée and oil appears around the sides of the pan. Add the meat and curry leaves and fry until browned, stirring occasionally. Add the water and bring to the boil, cover and simmer for 20 minutes. Reduce the heat to low and cook for a further 20 minutes. Add the potatoes and stir thoroughly. Cover and simmer for about 40-45 minutes until the meat and potatoes are tender. Sprinkle with coriander and simmer for 1 minute before serving hot with rice.

South Indian Fried Lamb   Serves 4

45 ml/3 tbsp ghee ● 3 onions, sliced ● 1 sprig fresh curry leaves

2 sprigs fresh coriander (cilantro), chopped ● 4 cloves garlic, chopped

2.5 cm/1 in ginger root, chopped ● 450 g/1 lb lamb, cubed

Spices: 10 ml/2 tsp cumin seeds ● 5 dried red chillies ● 6 cloves

1 cinnamon stick ● 5 ml/1 tsp aniseeds

5 ml/1 tsp ground turmeric ● pinch of mustard seeds

Heat the ghee and fry the onions and curry leaves until golden. Add the coriander, garlic and ginger and fry until browned. Grind all the spices together then add them to the pan, adding a little water if necessary so that they do not brown. Add the lamb and fry for several minutes. Add just enough water to cover the meat, bring to the boil then cover and simmer for about 45 minutes until the meat is tender. Remove the lid and continue to simmer until almost all the water has evaporated and the sauce is thick.

Lamb Sindhi
Serves 4

450 g/1 lb lamb, cubed ● 2 onions, sliced ● 2 tomatoes, skinned and sliced

6 cloves garlic, chopped ● 300 ml/½ pt/1¼ cups natural (plain) yoghurt

3 cardamom pods ● 6 cloves ● 2.5 ml/½ tsp garam masala

2.5 ml/½ tsp ground turmeric ● salt ● 30 ml/2 tbsp ghee

Place the lamb, onions, tomatoes and garlic in a heavy-based pan then stir in the yoghurt. Add all the spices, mix well and leave to stand for 30 minutes. Stir the ghee into the pan, cover and seal tightly so that the steam cannot escape. Place on a medium heat and cook for 2 hours until the meat is very tender.

Lamb and Cabbage Curry
Serves 4

450 g/1 lb boneless lamb, cubed ● 675 ml/10 pts/3 cups coconut milk

1 small cabbage, chopped ● salt ● 5 ml/1 tsp cumin seeds

5 ml/1 tsp ground coriander (cilantro) ● 5 ml/1 tsp ground turmeric

5 ml/1 tsp black pepper ● 2.5 ml/½ tsp mustard seeds

3 cloves garlic, crushed ● 2 onions, chopped

25 g/1 oz/¼ cup grated (shredded) coconut ● 30 ml/2 tbsp ghee

30 ml/2 tbsp wine vinegar ● 300 ml/½ pt/1¼ cups coconut cream

Place the lamb and coconut milk in a pan and simmer gently for about 20 minutes until the lamb is almost tender. Add the cabbage and salt and simmer while you roast the spices. Roast the spices in a dry pan then grind them to a paste with the garlic, 1 onion and the grated coconut. Add to the pan with the remaining onion, ghee, wine vinegar and coconut cream and simmer for 15 minutes until the lamb is tender and all the ingredients are thoroughly blended. Serve hot with rice and vegetables.

Lamb with Aubergine and Dal
Serves 4

60 ml/4 tbsp ghee ● 900 g/2 lb lamb, cubed

3 cloves garlic, crushed ● 2.5 cm/1 in ginger root, chopped

75 g/3 oz/½ cup yellow split peas ● 75 g/3 oz/½ cup chick peas (garbanzos)

75 g/3 oz/½ cup green lentils ● 1 small aubergine (eggplant), diced

4 tomatoes, skinned and chopped ● 1 green chilli, halved and seeded

5 ml/1 tsp ground turmeric ● 10 ml/2 tsp salt ● 30 ml/2 tbsp chopped fresh mint

2.5 cm/1 in cinnamon stick, crushed ● 4 cardamom pods

10 ml/2 tsp coriander (cilantro) seeds ● 10 ml/2 tsp cumin seeds

5 black peppercorns ● 2 dried red chillies ● 45 ml/3 tbsp water

30 ml/2 tbsp chopped fresh coriander (cilantro)

Heat the ghee and fry the meat until well browned on all sides. Remove from the pan. Add the garlic and ginger and fry for 1 minute until golden. Add the meat, split peas, lentils, aubergine and tomatoes and stir well. Add the chilli, turmeric, salt and mint. Pour in enough water just to cover the vegetables, bring to the boil, cover and simmer for 1 hour, stirring occasionally and adding a little more water if necessary. Stir well to break up the pulses and thicken the sauce. Grind the coriander and cumin seeds, peppercorns, chillies and water to a paste then stir into the pan, cover and simmer until the meat is tender. Serve garnished with coriander.

Kerala Lamb in Coconut Milk   Serves 6

1 coconut, grated (shredded) ● 1.5 l/2½ pts/6 cups hot water ● 4 onions

15 ml/1 tbsp ghee ● 5 cloves ● 5 cardamom pods ● 1 cinnamon stick

675 g/1½ lb lamb, cubed ● salt ● 10 green chillies, split

5 cm/1 in ginger root, grated ● 225 g/8 oz small potatoes, boiled and peeled

15 ml/1 tbsp plain (all-purpose) flour ● 15 ml/1 tbsp butter

juice of 1 lemon ● 15 ml/1 tbsp chopped fresh curry leaves

Pour 300 ml/½ pt/1¼ cups of boiling water over the coconut then squeeze out the coconut milk. Add the remaining hot water to the coconut and leave to cool. When cool, strain and squeeze out the liquid. Slice 1 onion and quarter the remainder.

Heat the ghee and fry the sliced onion, cloves, cardamom and cinnamon until browned. Add the thin coconut milk and bring to the boil. Add the meat and salt, cover and simmer over a low heat for about 30 minutes until the meat is almost tender. Add the remaining onions, the chillies and ginger and simmer until tender. Add the potatoes. Mix the flour with the thick coconut milk and add this to the curry. Simmer over a low heat until the sauce thickens. Add the butter, lemon juice and curry leaves and mix together well. Serve hot with idlis.

Lamb Madras   Serves 4

10 ml/2 tsp chilli powder ● 10 ml/2 tsp ground coriander (cilantro)

10 ml/2 tsp ground turmeric ● 1.5 ml/¼ tsp ground ginger

salt and pepper ● 300 ml/½ pt/1¼ cups coconut milk

60 ml/4 tbsp ghee ● 1 onion, chopped ● 3 cloves garlic, crushed

900 g/2 lb lamb, cubed ● 300 ml/½ pt/1¼ cups beef stock

5 ml/1 tsp tamarind concentrate

Mix the spices, salt and pepper to a paste with a little of the coconut milk. Heat the ghee and fry the onion and garlic until golden. Add the paste and fry for 3 minutes, stirring. Add the meat and stock, bring to the boil, cover and simmer gently for 1½ hours until tender. Stir in the remaining coconut milk and the tamarind and simmer for 10 minutes until thick.

Mughal-style Saffron Rice with Spicy Lamb   Serves 4-6

1.1 kg/2½ lb boneless lamb, cubed ● 5 ml/1 tsp ground turmeric
30 ml/2 tbsp oil ● 2 onions, sliced ● 5 cloves garlic, chopped
2.5 cm/1 in ginger root, chopped ● 15 ml/1 tbsp curry powder
2.5 ml/½ tsp ground red chilli ● 15 ml/1 tbsp lemon juice ● salt
10 ml/1 tsp Mughal-style Garam Masala (page 13)
2.5 ml/½ tsp ground cardamom ● 2 green chillies
30 ml/2 tbsp chopped fresh mint ● 3 tomatoes, skinned and chopped
15 ml/1 tbsp chopped fresh coriander (cilantro)
Pulau: 30 ml/1 tbsp oil ● 1 onion, sliced ● 2.5 cm/1 in cinnamon stick
5 cardamom pods ● 5 cloves ● 4 bay leaves ● 5 ml/1 tsp cumin seeds
600 ml/1 pt/2½ cups water ● 225 g/8 oz/1 cup long-grain rice, soaked for 2 hours
pinch of grated nutmeg ● pinch of ground saffron
30 ml/2 tbsp blanched almonds

Coat the meat with the turmeric and leave to stand for 15 minutes. Heat the oil and fry the onions, garlic and ginger over a medium heat until soft and golden brown. Add the curry powder and chillies and fry for 1 minute. Stir in the lemon juice and salt. Add the meat, stirring until it is coated with the spices. Add the garam masala, cardamom, chillies, mint and tomatoes, cover and simmer over a low heat for 1 hour, stirring occasionally, until the lamb is tender. Remove from the heat, garnish with coriander and leave to stand while you prepare the rice.

Heat the oil and fry the onions, cinnamon, cardamom, cloves and bay leaves over a medium heat until golden brown. Add the cumin seeds and continue to fry until the onions are dark brown. Add the water and bring to the boil. Add the rice, nutmeg and saffron, cover and simmer over a medium heat for about 15 minutes until the liquid has been absorbed and the rice is cooked. Put half the rice into a deep casserole dish. Place the lamb on top and cover with the remaining rice. Cover with foil, put on the lid and bake in a preheated oven at 120°C/250°F/gas mark ½ for 10 minutes until hot. Garnish with almonds and serve hot.

Boti Kebabs
Serves 6

120 ml/4 fl oz/½ cup natural (plain) yoghurt • 1 onion, chopped

2.5 cm/1 in ginger root, chopped • 3 cloves garlic, chopped

5 ml/1 tsp poppy seeds • 15 ml/1 tbsp chopped fresh coriander (cilantro)

2.5 ml/½ tsp pepper • 5 ml/1 tsp cumin seeds • 2.5 ml/½ tsp ground turmeric

1.5 ml/¼ tsp ground red chilli • salt • 900 g/2 lb boneless lamb, cubed

30 ml/2 tbsp oil

Purée all the ingredients except the meat and oil to a paste. Pour over the meat and leave to marinate for 1 hour. Thread the meat on to metal skewers **and grill (broil) for about 15 minutes, turning and basting with oil occasionally, until the meat is cooked to your taste. Serve hot with mint chutney.**

Meat Rolls with Nut Stuffing
Serves 6

900 g/2 lb lamb, cut into 5 cm/2 in cubes • 2.5 cm/1 in ginger root, chopped

4 cloves garlic, crushed • 2.5 ml/½ tsp black pepper

90 ml/6 tbsp oil • 3 onions, chopped • 25 g/1 oz/½ cup cashew nuts

30 ml/2 tbsp pistachios • 5 ml/1 tsp ground cumin

15 ml/1 tbsp desiccated (shredded) coconut • 15 ml/1 tbsp lemon juice

3 onions, sliced • 150 ml/¼ pt/⅔ cup natural (plain) yoghurt

5 ml/1 tsp garam masala • 30 ml/2 tbsp chopped fresh coriander (cilantro)

2 green chillies, chopped

Mix the meat with the ginger, garlic and pepper and leave to stand for at least 1 hour, preferably overnight.

Flatten the meat slightly until the pieces are as thin as possible without tearing. They should be about 5 × 9 cm/2 × 3½ in. Heat 30 ml/1 tbsp of oil and fry the chopped onions until browned. Crush the nuts and add them to the pan with the cumin and coconut and fry for 1 minute, stirring. Remove from the heat and stir in the lemon juice. Allow to cool slightly.

Spoon about 5 ml/1 tsp of the mixture on to the strips, roll them tightly and tie with string if you wish. Heat 60 ml/4 tbsp of oil and fry the meat rolls for about 10 minutes until browned, turning carefully. Meanwhile, heat the remaining oil and fry the sliced onions until browned. Stir in the yoghurt, garam masala, coriander and chillies and simmer for 4-5 minutes. Pour over the browned meat, cover and simmer for about 8-10 minutes before serving.

Mughal-style Kheema Masala

Serves 6

45 ml/3 tbsp oil • 1 onion, finely chopped

6 cloves garlic, finely chopped • 2.5 cm/1 in ginger root, finely chopped

2 green chillies, finely chopped • 8 cloves • 8 cardamom pods

4 bay leaves • 2 cinnamon sticks • 5 ml/1 tsp poppy seeds

2.5 ml/½ tsp black peppercorns • 10 ml/2 tsp Mughal-style Garam Masala (page 13)

10 ml/2 tsp ground cumin • 20 ml/4 tsp ground coriander (cilantro)

5 ml/1 tsp ground turmeric • 5 ml/1 tsp paprika

25 g/1 oz/¼ cup ground almonds • 1 tomato, skinned and chopped

1.5 kg/3 lb minced (ground) lamb • 250 ml/8 fl oz/1 cup natural (plain) yoghurt

salt • 30 ml/2 tbsp chopped fresh mint

Heat the oil and fry the onion, garlic, ginger and chillies over a medium heat until browned. Add the cloves, cardamom, bay leaves, cinnamon, poppy seeds and peppercorns and cook for about 2 minutes, stirring, until the spices darken. Add the garam masala, cumin, coriander, turmeric and paprika and cook for 2 minutes. Add the almonds and tomato and mix well. Stir in the meat, yoghurt and salt, cover and simmer for 20 minutes, stirring occasionally, until the meat is tender. Garnish with mint and serve hot with rice, nan and vegetables.

Hyderabad-style Biryani Gosht

Serves 6

6 cloves garlic • 2.5 cm/1 in ginger root, chopped • 2 green chillies

30 ml/2 tbsp chopped fresh coriander (cilantro)

30 ml/2 tbsp chopped fresh mint • 10 cloves • 1 cinnamon stick

5 ml/1 tsp cumin seeds • 2.5 ml/½ tsp grated nutmeg

seeds from 8 cardamom pods • 5 ml/1 tsp saffron strands • 45 ml/3 tbsp hot milk

120 ml/4 fl oz/½ cup oil • 3 onions, sliced • 2.5 ml/½ tsp ground red chilli

900 g/2 lb/4 cups basmati rice, soaked for 20 minutes

900 g/2 lb boneless lamb, cubed • juice of 1 lemon

450 ml/¾ pt/2 cups natural (plain) yoghurt • salt • 2 1/3½ pts/8½ cups water

Purée the garlic, ginger, chillies, coriander and mint to a paste in a blender or food processor. Grind half the cloves with the cinnamon, cumin seeds, nutmeg and half the cardamom seeds. Soak the saffron in the hot milk for 15 minutes. Heat the oil and fry the onions until golden brown. Add the chillies, ground and puréed spices and cook for 5 minutes, stirring. Add the drained rice and fry until coated in the spices. Add the meat, lemon juice, yoghurt, salt and water, bring to the boil, cover and simmer gently for 30 minutes until the water has been absorbed and the meat is tender. Serve hot with rice, nan, puris and vegetables.

Hyderabad-style Korma
Serves 6

1 onion, chopped ● 2.5 cm/1 in ginger root ● 5 cloves garlic

2 green chillies ● 10 ml/2 tsp ground coriander (cilantro)

10 ml/2 tsp ground cumin ● 1.5 ml/¼ tsp ground cinnamon

1.5 ml/¼ tsp ground cloves ● 1.5 ml/¼ tsp ground cardamom

2.5 ml/½ tsp saffron strands ● 45 ml/3 tbsp hot milk ● 45 ml/3 tbsp oil

1.5 kg/3 lb boneless lamb, cubed ● salt

150 ml/¼ pt/⅔ cup natural (plain) yoghurt ● 25 g/1 oz/¼ cup cashew nuts

25 g/1 oz/¼ cup blanched almonds ● 120 ml/4 fl oz/½ cup water

30 ml/2 tbsp chopped fresh coriander (cilantro)

Purée half the onion, the ginger, garlic and chillies to a fine paste in a blender or food processor. Add the ground spices and blend together. Soak the saffron in the hot milk for 15 minutes. Heat the oil and fry the remaining onion over a medium heat until browned, stirring frequently. Add the spice mixture and fry until the oil appears on the surface. Stir in the meat, season with salt and fry until browned on all sides. Mix together the saffron milk and yoghurt and stir into the pan with the nuts and water. Reduce the heat and simmer for 1 hour until the meat is tender, stirring occasionally. Garnish with coriander and serve hot with pulao rice, nan, puris and vegetables.

Shahi Padshah Korma
Serves 6

1.5 kg/3 lb boneless lamb, cubed ● 900 ml/1½ pts/3¾ cups water

2.5 cm/1 in cinnamon stick ● 3 bay leaves ● 5 ml/1 tsp black peppercorns

salt ● 30 ml/2 tbsp lemon juice ● 6 cloves garlic

5 cm/2 in ginger root, chopped ● 5 ml/1 tsp cardamom seeds ● 8 cloves

15 ml/1 tbsp coriander (cilantro) seeds ● 45 ml/3 tbsp oil

1 onion, thinly sliced ● 250 ml/8 fl oz/1 cup natural (plain) yoghurt

45 ml/3 tbsp soured (dairy sour) cream ● 2.5 ml/½ tsp saffron strands

25 g/1 oz/¼ cup blanched almonds ● 25 g/1 oz/3 tbsp raisins

Place the lamb, 750 ml/1¼ pts/3¾ cups of water, the cinnamon, bay leaves, peppercorns, salt and lemon juice in a pan, bring to the boil and simmer for 20 minutes. Reserve the lamb and stock separately. Purée the garlic, ginger, cardamom seeds, cloves, coriander seeds and remaining water. Heat the oil and fry the onion over a medium heat until soft. Add the spices and cook for 5 minutes, stirring. Add the lamb and cook for 5 minutes, stirring. Add the stock, yoghurt and soured cream, cover and simmer for 30 minutes. Remove the lid and stir in the saffron, almonds and raisins and continue to cook for a further 10 minutes until the lamb is tender. Serve hot with rice, nan, parathas and vegetables.

Shafi's Shali Lamb
Serves 6

15 ml/1 tbsp coriander (cilantro) seeds • 5 ml/1 tsp cumin seeds

5 ml/1 tsp poppy seeds • 25 g/1 oz/¼ cup blanched almonds

1.5 ml/¼ tsp black peppercorns • seeds from 4 black cardamom pods

4 cloves • pinch of ground mace

25 g/1 oz/¼ cup desiccated (shredded) coconut

2 dried red chillies, soaked for 15 minutes

2.5 cm/1 in ginger root, chopped • 6 cloves garlic • 450 ml/¾ pt/2 cups water

45 ml/3 tbsp oil • 3 bay leaves • 1 cinnamon stick

5 ml/1 tsp cardamom seeds • 1 onion, grated

5 ml/1 tsp ground turmeric • 150 ml/¼ pt/ cup natural (plain) yoghurt

1.5 kg/3 lb boneless lamb, cubed • 2 tomatoes, skinned and chopped

Roast the coriander, cumin and poppy seeds, the almonds, peppercorns, cardamom seeds, cloves, mace and coconut in a pan over a medium heat until slightly darkened. Purée in a blender with the chillies and their soaking water, the ginger, garlic and 45 ml/3 tbsp of the water. Heat the oil and fry the bay leaves, cinnamon and cardamom seeds over a medium heat for 1 minute. Add the onion and fry until browned. Stir in the purée and turmeric and cook for 5 minutes. Add the yoghurt and cook for 5 minutes, stirring. Add the meat and tomatoes and the remaining water. Cover and simmer gently for about 40 minutes until the meat is tender. Serve hot with rice, nan, vegetables and raita.

Lamb with Spinach in Yoghurt Sauce
Serves 6

45 ml/3 tbsp oil • 15 ml/1 tbsp black mustard seeds

15 ml/1 tbsp cardamom seeds • 15 ml/1 tbsp ground coriander (cilantro)

2.5 ml/½ tsp crushed black peppercorns • 2 green chillies, chopped

4 cloves garlic, crushed • 2.5 cm/1 in ginger root, chopped

1.5 kg/3 lb boneless lamb, cubed • 1 onion, chopped • 5 ml/1 tsp ground turmeric

1.5 kg/3 lb spinach, chopped • salt • 45 ml/3 tbsp natural (plain) yoghurt

Heat the oil and fry the mustard seeds until they start crackling. Add the spices and fry for 1 minute. Stir in the meat and fry for 10 minutes until browned. Add the onion and fry until browned. Add the turmeric, spinach and salt and cook for 5 minutes. Transfer to a casserole dish, cover and cook in a preheated oven at 180°C/350°F/gas mark 4 for 30 minutes until the lamb is tender. Serve hot with rice, chapatis and pulses.

Photograph opposite: *Cauliflower Sambar (page 22)*

Lamb Sundia
Serves 4-6

900 g/2 lb lamb, chopped ● 5 ml/1 tsp ground turmeric

15 ml/1 tbsp ground coriander (cilantro) ● 10 ml/2 tsp chilli powder

30 ml/2 tbsp oil or ghee ● 10 ml/2 tsp poppy seeds

100 g/4 oz/⅔ cup red lentils ● 2 cardamom pods ● 6 onions, chopped

2.5 cm/1 in ginger root, chopped ● 2 bulbs garlic, chopped

1 coconut, grated (shredded) ● juice of 3 lemons ● salt

oil for deep-frying

Place the lamb in a pan with the turmeric, coriander and chilli powder and pour in just enough water to cover. Bring to the boil and simmer gently for about 45 minutes until the meat is tender. Remove the meat and shred it. Heat a little oil or ghee and fry the poppy seeds, lentils and cardamom separately until lightly browned. Add these to the meat with the remaining ingredients and season to taste with salt. Mix together well and shape into balls. Deep-fry in hot oil over a low heat until nicely browned. Serve hot with papadums, rice and a curry sauce.

Fried Chops
Serves 4

500 g/18 oz lamb chops ● 4 large cloves garlic, crushed

2.5 cm/1 in ginger root, finely chopped ● 1 onion, finely chopped

1 small green chilli, finely chopped

30 ml/2 tbsp chopped fresh coriander (cilantro)

15 ml/1 tbsp ground coriander (cilantro) ● 5 ml/1 tsp garam masala

5 ml/1 tsp ground roasted cumin ● 1.5 ml/¼ tsp ground red chilli

salt ● 200 ml/7 fl oz/scant 1 cup water ● 30 ml/2 tbsp oil

1 egg, beaten

Place all the ingredients except the oil and egg in a heavy-based pan and bring to the boil. Cover and simmer over a medium-low heat for 20 minutes. Remove the lid and increase the heat to dry off any remaining water. Push the meat and spices up the bones to leave about 2.5 cm/1 in of clean bone so that the chops are easier to eat with your fingers. Heat the oil in a frying pan (skillet). Dip the chops in beaten egg and fry until golden brown on both sides. Serve hot at tea with chutney or at a meal with pulao, chapatis, dal and a potato-bean dish.

Photograph opposite: *Prawn and Celery Soup (page 36)*

Potato Fried Chops
Serves 4

500 g/18 oz lamb chops ● 4 large cloves garlic, crushed

2.5 cm/1 in ginger root, finely chopped ● 1 onion, finely chopped

1 small green chilli, finely chopped

30 ml/2 tbsp chopped fresh coriander (cilantro)

15 ml/1 tbsp ground coriander (cilantro) ● 5 ml/1 tsp garam masala

5 ml/1 tsp ground roasted cumin ● 1.5 ml/¼ tsp ground red chilli

200 ml/7 fl oz/scant 1 cup water ● salt

Coating: 225 g/8 oz mashed potatoes

15 ml/1 tbsp chopped fresh coriander (cilantro)

2.5 ml/½ tsp garam masala ● 1.5 ml/¼ tsp ground red chilli

30 ml/2 tbsp oil ● 1 egg, beaten

Place the chops, garlic, ginger, onion, chilli, coriander, ground spices, salt and water in a heavy-based pan and bring to the boil. Cover and simmer over a medium-low heat for 20 minutes. Remove the lid and increase the heat to dry off any remaining water. Push the meat and spices up the bones to leave about 2.5 cm/1 in of clean bone.

Mix together the coating ingredients and press around the chops, leaving the top of the bone clear. Heat the oil in a frying pan (skillet). Dip the chops in beaten egg and fry until golden brown on both sides. Serve hot at tea with chutney or at a meal with pulao, chapatis, dal and a potato-bean dish.

Chops with Spices and Vinegar
Serves 4

225 g/8 oz canned tomatoes ● 75 ml/5 tbsp wine vinegar

4 large cloves garlic ● 2.5 cm/1 in ginger root, coarsely chopped

1 large onion, coarsely chopped ● 10 ml/2 tsp ground coriander (cilantro)

5 ml/1 tsp garam masala ● 2.5 ml/½ tsp ground red chilli

salt ● 500 g/18 oz lamb chops ● 60 ml/4 tbsp oil

Garnish: 1.5 ml/¼ tsp garam masala

15 ml/1 tbsp chopped fresh coriander (cilantro) ● 1 small green chilli, chopped

Blend the tomatoes, wine vinegar, garlic, ginger and onion to a smooth paste. Mix in the ground spices and salt then rub the mixture over the chops and leave to marinate for 3-4 hours.

Place the chops and marinade in a heavy-based pan and cook over a medium heat for 20 minutes. Remove the chops from the pan and set aside.

Continue to cook the marinade until all the liquid has been absorbed. Remove from the heat and rub the cooked marinade over the chops.

Heat the oil and fry the chops over a medium heat until cooked through and golden brown. Sprinkle over the garnish and serve hot with vegetable pulao, dal and raita.

Lamb Chops Moghlai   Serves 4

2.5 cm/1 in ginger root ● 3 dried red chillies ● 2.5 ml/½ tsp ground turmeric

4 cloves garlic ● 4 lamb chops ● 100 g/4 oz/½ cup ghee

1 potato, parboiled and sliced ● 1 onion, thinly sliced

Grind the ginger, chillies, turmeric and garlic to a smooth paste. Rub over the chops and marinate for 2 hours.

Heat the ghee and fry the chops until thoroughly browned. Drain and set aside. Fry the potatoes until golden. Return the chops to the pan and continue to fry for a few minutes. Transfer to a warm oven. Fry the onion until crisp and sprinkle over the chops.

Marinated Lamb Chops   Serves 4

150 ml/¼ pt/⅔ cup natural (plain) yoghurt ● 5 cm/2 in ginger root, ground

5 cloves garlic, crushed ● 2.5 ml/½ tsp ground cumin

5 ml/1 tsp chilli powder ● salt ● 4 large lamb chops

30 ml/2 tbsp oil ● 15 ml/1 tbsp Worcestershire sauce

7.5 ml/1½ tsp white wine vinegar ● 20 ml/4 tsp sugar

45 ml/3 tbsp double (heavy) cream ● 45 ml/3 tbsp natural (plain) yoghurt

Mix the yoghurt with the ginger, garlic, cumin, chilli powder and salt. Rub well into the chops and leave to marinate overnight.

Heat the oil and fry the Worcestershire sauce, wine vinegar and sugar for a few seconds. Add the chops and marinade, stir well, cover and simmer gently for about 20 minutes. Arrange the chops in an ovenproof dish. Mix together the cream and yoghurt and spread over the chops. Cover the dish with foil and bake in a preheated oven at 180°C/350°F/gas mark 4 for about 45 minutes until the chops are tender and moist.

Lamb Chops Dopiaza   Serves 4

45 ml/3 tbsp oil ● 2.5 ml/½ tsp ground cumin

1-2 green chillies, seeded and chopped ● 5 ml/1 tsp sugar

5 onions, sliced ● 5 cm/2 in ginger root, ground

6 cloves garlic, crushed ● 4 large lamb chops ● salt and pepper

30 ml/2 tbsp white wine vinegar ● 250 ml/8 fl oz/1 cup water

Heat the oil in a heavy-based pan and fry the cumin and chillies for a few seconds. Add the sugar and fry for a few seconds. Add 3 onions and fry until golden. Stir in the ginger and garlic and fry until browned. Add the chops and fry until browned on both sides. Add the salt, pepper, wine vinegar and water, stir well and bring to the boil. Cover and simmer for about 40 minutes until the chops are tender. Add the remaining onions, cover and simmer for a further 20 minutes. Serve immediately with rice and aubergines.

Tamarind Chops
Serves 4

1 small ball of tamarind ● 450 g/1 lb lamb chops

15 ml/1 tbsp ghee ● 8 onions, halved

1 large potato, halved ● 6 green chillies, slit

2.5 ml/½ tsp mustard ● salt

Soak the tamarind in a little water for 5 minutes then extract the juice. Place all the remaining ingredients in a heavy-based pan and add just enough water to cover. Bring to the boil then simmer gently over a medium heat for about 1 hour until the meat is tender. Add the tamarind juice and simmer for a further 5 minutes. Serve with nan bread.

Moghlai Lamb Malai
Serves 6-8

1.2 1/2 pts/5 cups milk ● 25 g/1 oz/¼ cup ground almonds

900 g/2 lb boned leg of lamb ● 10 ml/2 tsp chilli powder

5 ml/1 tsp black pepper ● 2.5 ml/½ tsp ground ginger

6 cloves ● 6 cardamom pods ● 10 cm/4 in ginger root, grated

5 ml/1 tsp aniseeds ● pinch of asafoetida

150 ml/¼ pt/⅔ cup sherry ● salt ● 50 g/2 oz/ raisins

25 g/1 oz/½ pistachios ● 1.5 ml/¼ tsp ground saffron

450 g/1 lb/2 cups ghee

Mix together the milk and ground almonds in a shallow pan and simmer over a low heat until a thick layer of cream forms. Make a slit in the side of the cream and gently drain out the milk. Pour the milk back on top of the cream and replace over a very low heat. Repeat this until no milk is left. Turn the cream out on to a plate and leave to cool.

Pound the meat to flatten it to about 5 mm/¼ in thick. While pounding, sprinkle with spices, sherry and salt.

Cut the cream into strips and lay on the meat, leaving a 1 cm/½ in border all round. Sprinkle with raisins, pistachios and saffron. Roll up the meat and fasten with cocktail sticks (toothpicks) or string. Leave to stand for 30 minutes.

Heat the ghee and fry the meat gently for about 1 hour until cooked through and tender. Remove the cocktail sticks (toothpicks) or string before serving.

Curried Leg of Lamb
Serves 8-10

15 ml/1 tbsp coriander (cilantro) seeds ● 30 dried red chillies

pinch of saffron ● 1 sprig fresh curry leaves ● 15 ml/1 tbsp garam masala

50 g/2 oz/¼ cup desiccated (shredded) coconut

50 g/2 oz/½ cup blanched almonds ● 50 g/2 oz/ cup raisins

5 cm/2 in ginger root ● 6 cloves garlic ● 5 cm/2 in green papaya

150 ml/¼ pt/⅔ cup natural (plain) yoghurt ● salt juice of 1 lemon

1 leg of lamb ● 100 g/4 oz/½ cup ghee

Grind together the coriander seeds, chillies, saffron, curry leaves and garam masala. Grind together the coconut, almonds and raisins. Grind together the ginger, garlic and papaya and mix with the yoghurt, salt and lemon juice. Cut gashes all over the surface of the lamb. Spread the yoghurt mixture over the lamb and leave to marinate for 10 minutes. Spread the coriander mixture over the lamb then spread over the almond mixture. Heat the ghee in an ovenproof pan and fry the lamb until lightly browned on all sides. Cover the pan and cook in a pre-heated oven at 200°C/400°F/gas mark 6 for about 45 minutes until the meat is reddish-brown and tender. Serve with roast potatoes and rotis.

Roast Leg of Lamb
Serves 4-6

6 large cloves garlic ● 2.5 cm/1 in ginger root ● 4 dried red chillies

150 ml/¼ pt/ cup natural (plain) yoghurt ● 30 ml/2 tbsp wine vinegar

30 ml/2 tbsp chopped fresh coriander (cilantro) ● 5 ml/1 tsp garam masala

2.5 ml/½ tsp ground turmeric ● salt ● 675 g/1½ lb leg of lamb

90 ml/6 tbsp ghee or oil ● 2 onions, chopped ● 4 cloves

4 black peppercorns ● 3 bay leaves ● 2.5 cm/1 in cinnamon stick

1 black cardamom pod ● 15 ml/1 tbsp ground coriander (cilantro)

5 ml/1 tsp ground roasted cumin ● 2.5 ml/½ tsp ground turmeric

1.5 ml/¼ tsp ground mace ● 1.5 ml/¼ tsp grated nutmeg

400 g/14 oz canned tomatoes ● 500 ml/17 fl oz/20 cups water

Garnish: 250 g/9 oz small potatoes ● oil for deep-frying

2.5 ml/½ tsp garam masala ● 15 ml/1 tbsp chopped fresh coriander (cilantro)

1 small green chilli

Blend the garlic, ginger, chillies, yoghurt, wine vinegar, coriander, garam masala, turmeric and salt to a smooth paste in a blender or food processor. Rub over the lamb, cover and leave to marinate for 4 hours.

Heat the ghee or oil in a heavy-based pan and fry the onions and whole spices over a medium heat until golden brown. Add the lamb and fry until it is light golden brown on all sides. Pour in the rest of the marinade and cook until all the liquid has evaporated. Stir in the ground spices then the tomatoes and cook until all the liquid has been absorbed and the ghee appears on the surface. Gradually add the water and cook until the meat is tender and the water has all been absorbed.

Meanwhile, boil the potatoes in their skins then peel them and deep-fry until golden brown. Sprinkle the garnish ingredients over the lamb and serve hot with nan or chapatis, dal, vegetable pulao and raita.

Seekh Kebab   Makes 20

250 g/9 oz minced (ground) lamb ● 3 large cloves garlic

2.5 cm/1 in ginger root ● 1 egg ● 1 small green chilli

2 slices bread, soaked in water for 1 minute then squeezed

30 ml/2 tbsp chopped fresh coriander (cilantro)

5 ml/1 tsp garam masala ● 5 ml/1 tsp ground roasted cumin

2.5 ml/½ tsp ground mace ● 2.5 ml/½ tsp grated nutmeg

2.5 ml/½ tsp ground red chilli ● oil for basting

Blend the lamb, garlic, ginger, egg and chilli to a smooth paste in a blender or food processor. Mix in the bread and ground spices. Divide the mixture into 20 equal portions and shape into sausages. Push an oiled skewer through each one and shape the meat to a thin, round strip about 7.5 cm/3 in long. Rest the skewers on a tray about 18 cm/7 in below a pre-heated grill and grill (broil) until golden brown on all sides, turning occasionally. Serve hot with a meal or at tea.

Husseini Seekh Kebabs   Serves 4-6

5 cm/2 in ginger root ● 8 cloves garlic

5 ml/1 tsp cumin seeds, roasted ● 6 dried red chillies

few fresh coriander (cilantro) leaves ● salt

900 g/2 lb leg of lamb, cubed ● 450 g/1 lb small onions

30-45 ml/2-3 tbsp ghee ● 600 ml/1 pt/2½ cups milk

600 ml/1 pt/2½ cups single (light) cream

25 g/1 oz/¼ cup blanched almonds, finely grated (shredded)

25 g/1 oz/¼ cups pistachios ● 5 ml/1 tsp ground cardamom

Grind the ginger, garlic, cumin seeds, chillies and coriander to a fine paste, adding salt to taste. Rub this mixture over the lamb and leave to marinate for 2½ hours.

Fix the meat on to skewers, placing an onion between each cube of meat.

Grill (broil) on a low heat until tender and browned.

Meanwhile, heat the ghee, milk, cream, almonds and pistachios. Mix well and simmer until slightly thickened. Garnish with the cardamom and serve with the kebabs.

Moghlai Shami Kebabs
Serves 4

45 ml/3 tbsp ghee ● 10 ml/2 tsp garam masala

2.5 ml/½ tsp ground turmeric ● 4 green chillies, chopped

2.5 ml/½ tsp chopped ginger root ● 5 cloves garlic, chopped

2 onions, chopped ● 450 g/1 lb minced (ground) lamb

15 ml/1 tbsp gram flour ● 15 ml/1 tbsp lemon juice

salt ● 3 hard-boiled (hard-cooked) eggs, chopped

1 onion, cut into rings ● 1 lemon, sliced

Heat 15 ml/1 tbsp of the ghee and fry the spices and 1 onion for 3 minutes. Add the meat and fry for 10 minutes. Stir in the flour, lemon juice and salt. Turn the mixture out to cool then grind it to a fine paste. Mix together the remaining onions with the eggs. Shape the meat mixture into cutlets with a spoonful of onion and egg mixture in the centre. Heat the remaining ghee and fry the cutlets until golden brown on both sides. Serve hot with onion rings and lemon slices.

Keema Kebabs
Makes 16

75 g/3 oz/½ cup split yellow peas, soaked overnight in 500 ml/17 fl oz/2 cups water

250 g/9 oz minced (ground) lamb ● 1 onion, coarsely chopped

1 large clove garlic, chopped ● 2.5 cm/1 in ginger root, coarsely chopped

10 ml/2 tsp garam masala ● 2.5 ml/½ tsp ground red chilli

salt ● 300 ml/½ pt/1¼ cups water

Filling: 1 onion, coarsely chopped ● 1 small green chilli, finely chopped

45 ml/3 tbsp chopped fresh coriander (cilantro) ● oil for frying

Place the split peas, lamb, onion, garlic, ginger, garam masala, chilli, salt and water in a pan and bring to the boil. Cook over a medium-low heat for 30 minutes until the split peas and meat are tender, adding a little extra boiling water during cooking, if necessary. Dry off any remaining liquid over a high heat. Leave to cool. Blend to a smooth paste, in batches if necessary, then divide into 16 portions. Mix the filling ingredients and divide into 16 portions.

Flatten a portion of meat in oiled hands, place a portion of filling in the centre and shape the meat into a ball covering the filling. Flatten to about 5 mm/¼ in thick. Make the remaining kebabs in the same way. Heat a flat frying pan (skillet) over a medium heat and smear it with 15 ml/1 tbsp of oil. Fry a few kebabs at a time over a medium-low heat for 2 minutes. Add another 15 ml/1 tbsp of oil, turn the kebabs and fry until golden brown. Serve hot with a meal or at tea with chutney.

Nargisi Kebabs
Serves 4-6

500 g/18 oz minced (ground) lamb ● 30 ml/2 tbsp ground poppy seeds

15 ml/1 tbsp chopped fresh coriander (cilantro)

15 ml/1 tbsp natural (plain) yoghurt ● 5 ml/1 tsp garam masala

3 large cloves garlic, crushed ● 1.5 cm/½ in ginger root, coarsely chopped

1 onion, coarsely chopped ● 1 egg, beaten ● salt

10 hard-boiled (hard-cooked) eggs ● oil for deepy-rying

Garnish: 2.5 ml/½ tsp garam masala

15 ml/1 tbsp chopped fresh coriander (cilantro) ● 1 small green chilli, chopped

Blend all the ingredients except the hard-boiled eggs and oil to a smooth paste. Divide into 10 equal portions. Using oiled hands, shape the meat around the hard-boiled eggs.

Heat the oil and fry the koftas until golden brown on all sides. Remove with a slotted spoon. Sprinkle with the garnish and serve hot with chutney and vegetable pulao.

Kaccha Kebabs
Serves 4

5 ml/1 tsp ground coriander (cilantro) ● 5 ml/1 tsp aniseeds

1.5 ml/¼ tsp cumin seeds ● 6 cloves ● 10 peppercorns

1 cinnamon stick ● 5 ml/1 tsp garam masala ● 6 cardamom pods

450 g/1 lb minced (ground) lamb ● ½ slice green papaya

onion skins ● 15 ml/1 tbsp ghee

15 ml/1 tbsp red lentils, coarsely ground salt ● ghee for frying

Dry roast the coriander and aniseeds for a few seconds then grind all the spices together. Mix the meat with the papaya then grind to a paste. Place the mixture in a pan and make a hole in the centre. Place a live piece of charcoal in the space then cover it with onion skins. Add the ghee to the coal

then close the pan tightly so that the smoke cannot escape. When the smoking stops, discard the onion skins and charcoal. Add the lentils and salt to the meat and mix well. Shape into kebabs and fry on both sides in very hot ghee until cooked through and well browned.

Lucknow-style Shami Kebabs
Serves 4-6

900 g/2 lb minced (ground) lamb ● 2 onions, chopped

100 g/4 oz/ cup yellow split peas ● 10 black peppercorns

2.5 cm/1 in cinnamon stick ● 6 black cardamom pods ● 8 cloves

4 bay leaves ● 2.5 cm/1 in ginger root, chopped

10 cloves garlic, chopped ● 3 dried red chillies ● 675 ml/1¼ pts/3 cups water

5 ml/1 tsp garam masala ● salt ● oil for frying

Mix all the ingredients except the oil and simmer for about 25 minutes until the meat is tender, stirring occasionally. Drain and discard the liquid and leave to cool. Remove and discard the cardamom skins. Blend the mixture then shape into flat patties. Fry in a lightly greased pan for about 15 minutes on each side until browned.

Shahi Kofta
Serves 4

450 g/1 lb minced (ground) lamb ● 1 egg ● 120 ml/4 fl oz/½ cup ghee

1 large onion, sliced ● 1 onion, chopped

2.5 cm/1 in ginger root, chopped ● 6 peppercorns

1 cm/½ in cinnamon stick ● 1 bunch fresh coriander (cilantro)

4 green chillies ● salt ● 15 ml/1 tbsp coriander (cilantro) seeds

5 ml/1 tsp ground turmeric ● 15 ml/1 tbsp cumin seeds

2.5 ml/½ tsp chilli powder ● 1 blade mace

5 ml/1 tsp cardamom seeds ● salt ● 120 ml/4 fl oz/½ cup water

Mix the lamb with the egg and shape into 2.5 cm/1 in balls. Heat the ghee and fry until golden brown. Remove from the pan. Fry the onion until golden brown. Grind all the spices to a paste, add to the pan fry for 7 minutes. Add the meatballs and water and simmer over a medium heat until the sauce is thick. Serve hot with rice and vegetables.

Nargisi Kofta
Serves 4-6

500 g/18 oz minced (ground) lamb ● 30 ml/2 tbsp ground poppy seeds

15 ml/1 tbsp chopped fresh coriander (cilantro)

15 ml/1 tbsp natural (plain) yoghurt ● 5 ml/1 tsp garam masala

3 large cloves garlic, crushed ● 1.5 cm/½ in ginger root, coarsely chopped

1 onion, coarsely chopped ● 1 egg, beaten ● salt

10 hard-boiled (hard-cooked) eggs ● oil for deep-frying

Sauce: 75 ml/5 tbsp ghee or oil ● 4 cloves

4 black peppercorns ● 2 bay leaves ● 2.5 cm/1 in cinnamon stick

1 black cardamom pod ● 2 onions, finely chopped

3 large cloves garlic ● 2.5 cm/1 in ginger root, coarsely chopped

45 ml/3 tbsp water ● 10 ml/2 tsp ground coriander (cilantro)

5 ml/1 tsp ground roasted cumin ● 2.5 ml/½ tsp ground red chilli

2.5 ml/½ tsp ground turmeric ● salt ● 400 g/14 oz canned tomatoes, chopped

150 ml/¼ pt/⅔ cup natural (plain) yoghurt ● 500 ml/17 fl oz/2¼ cups water

Garnish: 2.5 ml/½ tsp garam masala

15 ml/1 tbsp chopped fresh coriander (cilantro) ● 1 small green chilli, chopped

Blend all the main ingredients except the hard-boiled eggs and oil to a smooth paste in a blender or food processor. Divide into 10 equal portions. Using oiled hands, shape the meat around the hard-boiled eggs. Heat the oil and fry the koftas, in batches if necessary, until golden brown on all sides. Remove with a slotted spoon.

To make the sauce, heat the ghee or oil in a heavy-based pan and fry the whole spices and 1 onion until golden brown. Blend the remaining onion, the garlic, ginger and water to a smooth paste in a blender or food processor then stir it into the pan and cook until golden brown. Stir in the ground spices, salt and tomatoes and cook until all the liquid has been absorbed and the ghee appears on the surface. Stir in the yoghurt and cook until all the liquid has been absorbed. Add the water and bring to the boil. Add the fried kofta to the sauce and simmer for 10 minutes, uncovered. Sprinkle with the garnish ingredients and serve hot with vegetable pulao, nan or chapatis, raita and a bean and potato dish.

Oudh-style Kofta   Serves 6

8 cloves garlic ● 2.5 cm/1 in ginger root, chopped
2 green chillies ● 15 ml/1 tbsp poppy seeds
10 ml/2 tsp garam masala ● 1.5 ml/¼ tsp ground black pepper
salt ● 5 ml/1 tsp paprika ● 120 ml/4 fl oz/½ cup water
1.5 kg/3 lb minced (ground) lamb ● 2 eggs, lightly beaten
25 g/1 oz/¼ cup gram flour ● 45 ml/3 tbsp oil
1 onion, chopped ● 5 ml/1 tsp ground turmeric
1.5 ml/¼ tsp ground red chilli ● 5 ml/1 tsp ground cumin
10 ml/2 tsp ground coriander (cilantro) ● 2 tomatoes, skinned and chopped
120 ml/4 fl oz/½ cup natural (plain) yoghurt
30 ml/2 tbsp chopped fresh coriander (cilantro)

Purée the garlic, ginger, chillies, poppy seeds, pepper, salt, paprika and water to a paste. Stir into the meat with the eggs and flour and shape into 20 meatballs. Heat the oil and fry the onion over a medium heat until browned. Stir in the turmeric, chillies, cumin and coriander. Add the tomatoes and cook until soft. Add the meatballs and bring to the boil. Stir in the yoghurt and simmer gently for 20 minutes. Turn the meatballs over and cook for a further 20 minutes. Garnish with coriander and serve hot with rice, nan, puris and vegetables.

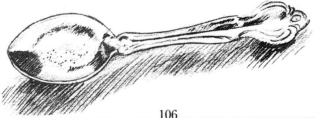

Meatballs in Yoghurt
Serves 4

120 ml/4 fl oz/½ cup natural (plain) yoghurt • 1 onion, chopped

2 cloves garlic, chopped • 1 cm/½ in ginger root, chopped

1 green chilli, chopped • 5 ml/1 tsp ground coriander (cilantro)

5 ml/1 tsp ground cumin • 30 ml/2 tbsp chopped fresh mint

450 g/1 lb minced (ground) lamb • 45 ml/3 tbsp oil

Purée the yoghurt, onion, garlic, ginger, chilli, coriander, cumin and mint then mix with the meat and divide into 20 meatballs. Heat the oil and fry the meatballs for about 20 minutes until golden brown and crisp on all sides. Remove the lid and stir until all the liquid has evaporated. Serve hot with chutney.

Peppers Stuffed with Meat and Mint
Serves 4

4 large green (bell) peppers • 900 g/2 lb minced (ground) lamb

1 onion, chopped • 5 cloves garlic, crushed

5 mm/¼ in ginger root, chopped • 15 ml/1 tbsp ground almonds

1 green chilli, finely chopped • salt • 30 ml/2 tbsp chopped fresh mint

45 ml/3 tbsp oil • 5 ml/1 tsp cardamom seeds • 1 cinnamon stick

5 cloves • 1.5 ml/¼ tsp black peppercorns

2 bay leaves • 5 ml/1 tsp ground coriander (cilantro)

5 ml/1 tsp cumin seeds • 2.5 ml/½ tsp ground turmeric

5 ml/1 tsp garam masala

Slice the top off the peppers and scoop out the seeds. Mix the meat, half the onion, garlic and ginger, the almonds, chilli, salt and mint. Heat the oil and fry the cardamom seeds, cinnamon, cloves, peppercorns and bay leaves over a medium heat until the spices darken slightly. Add the remaining onion, garlic and ginger and fry for 2 minutes, stirring. Stir in the coriander, cumin seeds, turmeric and garam masala and fry for 1 minute. Add the meat, cover and sim-mer for 10 minutes, stirring occasionally. Leave to cool slightly. Preheat the oven to 200°C/400°F/gas mark 6. Remove and discard the bay leaves, cinnamon, cardamom pods, pepper-corns and cloves. Stuff the peppers with the meat mixture and stand in a lightly greased casserole dish. Reduce the oven temperature to 150°C/300°F/gas mark 2 and cook the peppers for 10 minutes. Serve hot with rice, dal and chutney.

Keema Matar
Serves 4-6

75 ml/5 tbsp ghee or oil • 2 onions, thinly sliced

3 large cloves garlic, crushed • 2.5 cm/1 in ginger root, finely chopped

4 cloves • 4 black peppercorns • 2 bay leaves

1.5 cm/½ in cinnamon stick • 1 black cardamom pod

5 ml/1 tsp ground coriander (cilantro) • 5 ml/1 tsp ground roasted cumin

2.5 ml/½ tsp garam masala • 2.5 ml/½ tsp chilli powder

2.5 ml/½ tsp ground turmeric • salt • 500 g/18 oz minced (ground) lamb

225 g/8 oz canned tomatoes • 100 ml/3½ fl oz/6½ tbsp water

250 g/9 oz peas

Garnish: 1.5 ml/½ tsp garam masala

15 ml/1 tbsp chopped fresh coriander (cilantro)

Heat the ghee or oil in a heavy-based pan and fry the onions, garlic, ginger and whole spices over a medium heat until golden brown. Stir in the ground spices, salt and lamb and fry for 2 minutes. Add the tomatoes and water, bring to the boil, then cover and cook over a low heat for 20 minutes until the meat is tender, stirring occasionally. Remove the lid and increase the heat to dry off any remaining water. Stir in the peas and cook for a further 5 minutes. Sprinkle over the garnish ingredients and serve hot with chapatis or puris, dal, raita and a vegetable pulao.

Cocktail Kofta
Serves 6

900 g/2 lb minced (ground) lamb • 5 ml/1 tsp ground coriander (cilantro)

5 ml/1 tsp ground cumin • 2.5 ml/½ tsp chilli powder

45 ml/3 tbsp natural (plain) yoghurt • 1 egg, beaten

30 ml/2 tbsp chopped fresh coriander (cilantro) • salt

Sauce: 450 ml/¾ pt/2 cups water • 6 cloves garlic

2.5 cm/1 in ginger root, chopped • 5 ml/1 tsp ground cumin

5 ml/1 tsp ground coriander (cilantro) • 2.5 ml/½ tsp chilli powder

5 ml/1 tsp paprika • salt • 45 ml/3 tbsp oil

1 cinnamon stick • 5 cardamom pods • 5 cloves

1 onion, chopped • 2.5 ml/½ tsp ground turmeric

45 ml/3 tbsp natural (plain) yoghurt

Mix all the meatball ingredients together and shape into 20 balls.

Purée 60 ml/4 tbsp of the water with the garlic, ginger, cumin, coriander, chilli powder, paprika and salt. Heat the oil and fry the cinnamon, cardamom and cloves until slightly darkened. Add the onion and fry until soft and browned. Add the garlic paste, turmeric and yoghurt and fry for 1 minute. Add the meatballs and remaining water to the pan, stirring thoroughly. Cover and simmer gently for 20 minutes, stirring occasionally. Remove the lid and increase the heat. Boil until the liquid has evaporated. Transfer the meatballs to a serving dish. Remove and discard the whole spices and pour the sauce over the meatballs. Serve with mint chutney.

Potato Kheema Matar   Serves 4

30 ml/2 tbsp oil ● 1 onion, finely chopped ● 4 cloves garlic, finely chopped

1 cm/½ in ginger root, finely chopped ● 1 green chilli, finely chopped

2.5 ml/½ tsp ground turmeric ● 5 ml/1 tsp ground coriander (cilantro)

5 ml/1 tsp ground cumin ● 5 ml/1 tsp garam masala

900 g/2 lb minced (ground) lamb ● 3 potatoes, peeled and quartered

salt ● 1 tomato, skinned and chopped ● 225 g/8 oz peas

30 ml/2 tbsp chopped fresh coriander (cilantro)

Heat the oil and fry the onion, garlic, ginger and chilli over a medium heat until browned. Stir in the turmeric, coriander, cumin and garam masala and fry for 1 minute. Add the meat, potatoes, salt and tomato and stir thoroughly. Cover and simmer for 20 minutes, stirring occasionally. Stir in the peas and coriander, cover and simmer for about 5 minutes until the meat is cooked and the peas are tender. Serve hot with chapatis, dal and chutney.

Spicy Kebabs   Serves 6

900 g/2 lb minced (ground) lamb ● 1 onion, grated

4 cloves garlic, grated ● 1 cm/½ in ginger root, grated

1 green chilli, grated ● 2.5 ml/½ tsp garam masala

1 egg, beaten ● 1.5 ml/¼ tsp black pepper ● 2.5 ml/½ tsp paprika

25 g/1 oz/¼ cup gram flour ● 5 ml/1 tsp chopped fresh mint

30 ml/2 tbsp natural (plain) yoghurt ● salt ● 60 ml/4 tbsp oil

Mix all the ingredients except 45 ml/3 tbsp of the oil and shape into 20 meatballs. Flatten to about 2.5 cm/1 in thick. Heat the remaining oil and fry the meatballs for about 20 minutes until browned on all sides. Serve hot with mint chutney.

Ginger, Cardamom and Mint Kebabs

Serves 6

900 g/2 lb minced (ground) lamb • 2 onions, chopped

175 g/6 oz/1 cup yellow split peas • 10 black peppercorns

2.5 cm/1 in cinnamon stick • 5 cardamom pods • 8 cloves

3 bay leaves • 2.5 cm/1 in ginger root, chopped

2 dried red chillies • 675 ml/1¼ pt/3 cups water

30 ml/2 tbsp chopped fresh mint • salt • 1 egg, beaten

45 ml/3 tbsp oil • 25 g/1 oz/¼ cup plain (all-purpose) flour

Place all the ingredients except the egg, oil and flour in a large pan, bring to the boil then simmer until the water has evaporated and the meat is tender, stirring occasionally. Drain and discard any excess liquid and let the mixture cool.

Purée the mixture to a smooth paste then mix in the egg and divide into 12 balls, flattening each to about 5 cm/ 2 in thick. Heat the oil. Dust the meatballs with flour and fry for about 10 minutes until browned on all sides. Serve hot with mint chutney.

Lamb-stuffed Marrow

Serves 4-6

1 large marrow (squash) • 1 cinnamon stick

30 ml/2 tbsp ghee • 1 onion, chopped • 1 clove garlic, chopped

2.5 cm/1 in ginger root, chopped • 1 green chilli, chopped

225 g/8 oz minced (ground) lamb • 2 tomatoes, skinned and chopped

2.5 ml/½ tsp ground turmeric • 2.5 ml/½ tsp garam masala

salt • 10 ml/2 tsp chopped fresh coriander (cilantro)

Cut the marrow in half lengthways and scoop out the seeds. Cook in boiling water with the cinnamon for about 10 minutes then drain. Heat 30 ml/ 2 tbsp of ghee and fry the onion, garlic, ginger and chilli for 1 minute. Add the lamb and fry for 5 minutes. Add the tomatoes and turmeric and simmer over a very low heat until the meat is tender, adding a little water if necessary. Sprinkle with garam masala and salt. Fill the marrow with the meat mixture then tie the halves together with string. Coat lightly with butter then bake in a preheated oven at 180°C/350°F/gas mark 4 for 20-30 minutes until crisp and brown. Garnish with coriander and serve hot with fried onions.

Mughal-style Lamb in Almond Sauce   Serves 6

45 ml/3 tbsp oil • 1 onion, finely chopped

6 cloves garlic, finely chopped • 2.5 cm/1 in ginger root, finely chopped

2 green chillies, finely chopped • 8 cloves • 10 cardamom pods

4 bay leaves • 2 cinnamon stick • 5 ml/1 tsp poppy seeds

2.5 ml/½ tsp pepper • 10 ml/2 tsp Mughal-style Garam Masala (page 13)

10 ml/2 tsp ground cumin • 20 ml/4 tsp ground turmeric

5 ml/1 tsp paprika • 25 g/1 oz/¼ cup ground almonds

1 tomato, skinned and chopped • 1.5 kg/3 lb minced (ground) lamb

250 ml/8 fl oz/1 cup natural (plain) yoghurt • salt

30 ml/2 tbsp finely chopped fresh mint

Heat the oil and fry the onion, garlic, ginger and chillies over a medium heat until browned. Add the cloves, cardamom, bay leaves, cinnamon, poppy seeds and pepper and cook for 2 minutes, stirring, until the spices darken. Add the garam masala, cumin, turmeric and paprika and stir for 2 minutes. Stir in the ground almonds and tomato. Stir in the meat, yoghurt and salt, cover and cook for 20 minutes, stirring occasionally. Garnish with mint and serve hot with rice or nan and vegetables.

Southern-style Lambs' Liver Curry   Serves 4-6

75 ml/5 tbsp ghee or oil • large pinch of asafoetida

4 large cloves garlic, crushed • 2.5 cm/1 in ginger root, finely chopped

2 onions, thinly sliced • 75 ml/5 tbsp desiccated (shredded) coconut

500 g/18 oz lambs' liver, cubed • 5 ml/1 tbsp garam masala

5 ml/1 tsp ground roasted cumin • 2.5 ml/½ tsp ground red chilli

2.5 ml/½ tsp ground turmeric • salt • 225 g/8 oz canned tomatoes

150 ml/¼ pt/⅔ cup natural (plain) yoghurt • 45 ml/3 tbsp wine vinegar

150 ml/¼ pt/⅔ cup water

Garnish: 1.5 ml/¼ tsp garam masala

15 ml/1 tbsp chopped fresh coriander (cilantro) • 1 small green chilli, chopped

Heat the ghee or oil in a heavy-based pan and fry the asafoetida over a medium heat until it starts sizzling. Add the garlic, ginger and onions and fry until golden brown. Add the coconut and fry for 2 minutes. Add the liver and fry for 5 minutes. Add the ground spices, salt and tomatoes and cook until all the liquid has been absorbed and the ghee appears on the surface. Add the yoghurt and cook until all the liquid has been absorbed. Add the wine vinegar and water, bring to the boil, cover and simmer over a medium-low heat for 5 minutes until the liver is tender. Sprinkle over the garnish ingredients and serve hot with rice, chapatis, raita, cauliflower and peas.

Quick Fried Liver
Serves 4

30 ml/2 tbsp oil ● 3 onions, sliced

3 green chillies, seeded and chopped ● 2 tomatoes, skinned and chopped

30 ml/2 tbsp tomato sauce ● 5 ml/1 tsp Worcestershire sauce

15 ml/1 tbsp chopped fresh coriander (cilantro) ● 450 g/1 lb lambs' liver, cubed

5 ml/1 tsp garam masala ● 5 ml/1 tsp sugar

Heat the oil and fry the onions until soft. Add the chillies, tomatoes and sauces and cook until the oil appears on the surface. Add the coriander and liver and fry for about 10 minutes until the liver is tender and the liquid has evaporated. Add the garam masala and sugar and cook for 5 minutes. Serve with rice.

Spiced Liver
Serves 6

1.5 kg/3 lb lambs' liver, cut into strips ● 15 ml/1 tbsp plain (all-purpose) flour

juice of 1 lemon ● 2.5 ml/½ tsp crushed black peppercorns

45 ml/3 tbsp oil ● 2 onions, grated ● 6 cloves garlic, grated

2.5 cm/1 in ginger root, grated ● 5 ml/1 tsp ground turmeric

30 ml/2 tbsp cider vinegar ● 2.5 ml/½ tsp ground red chilli ● salt

Sprinkle the liver with the flour, squeeze over the lemon juice and sprinkle on the crushed peppercorns. Heat the oil and fry the onions, garlic and ginger over a medium heat until lightly browned. Stir in the turmeric, cider vinegar and chilli. Stir in the liver and salt, reduce the heat, cover and simmer gently over a low heat for 20 minutes until the liver is tender. Serve hot with rice, vegetables and dal.

Moghlai Korma
Serves 4

2.5 cm/1 in ginger root, chopped ● 6 cloves garlic, chopped

30 ml/2 tbsp chopped fresh coriander (cilantro) ● 6 green chillies, seeded

900 g/2 lb/4 cups ghee ● 6 onions, thinly sliced

450 g/1 lb lambs' liver, diced ● 4 lambs' kidneys, quartered

15 ml/1 tbsp salt ● 1.75 l/3 pts/7½ cups water

225 g/8 oz potatoes, peeled and diced ● 225 g/8 oz yam, peeled and diced

100 g/4 oz pumpkin, peeled and diced ● 2 cooking bananas, diced

225 g/8 oz peas ● 60 ml/4 tbsp water ● 10 ml/2 tsp ground turmeric

2.5 ml/½ tsp garam masala ● 5 ml/1 tsp black pepper

2-3 saffron strands ● 45 ml/3 tbsp wine vinegar

15 ml/1 tbsp Worcestershire sauce ● 5 ml/1 tsp sugar

Grind the ginger, garlic, coriander and chillies to a paste. Heat 45 ml/3 tbsp of ghee and fry the onions until browned. Add the ground spices and fry until browned. Add the liver and kidneys and half the salt and fry until browned. Add the water and simmer for 20 minutes. Fry the potatoes, yam, pumpkin and bananas separately in the remaining ghee then place in a bowl. Cook the peas for 5 minutes in boiling water then drain. Mix the remaining salt with the water and sprinkle over the vegetables. Melt the remaining ghee and fry the turmeric, garam masala and pepper for a few minutes. Add the saffron and crush into the spices. Add the peas and fried vegetables and stir well. Add the fried mixture to the meat with the wine vinegar, Worcestershire sauce and sugar, bring to the boil and simmer until the lamb is tender and all the ingredients well blended. Serve hot with chapatis and rice.

Liver Dopiaza
Serves 6

45 ml/3 tbsp ghee ● 450 g/1 lb onions, sliced
450 g/1 lb tomatoes, skinned and chopped ● 10 ml/2 tsp ground turmeric
2.5 cm/1 in ginger root, chopped ● 6 cloves garlic, crushed
4 green chillies, seeded and chopped ● 450 g/1 lb lambs' liver, diced
150 ml/¼ pt/⅔ cup natural (plain) yoghurt ● 5 ml/1 tsp chilli powder
10 ml/2 tsp garam masala ● salt
30 ml/2 tbsp chopped fresh coriander (cilantro)

Melt the ghee and fry the onions, tomatoes and turmeric until soft and reddish-brown. Add the ginger, garlic and chillies and fry for 2 minutes. Add the liver and fry until browned. Add the yoghurt and remaining spices and season with salt. Cook over a low heat until the liver is tender and the ghee appears on the surface, sprinkling with a little water if necessary. Garnish with coriander and serve hot with a tandoori dish.

Beef

Since many Indians are vegetarian, cows are not farmed for beef in India. They also have a religious significance, so beef is not as popular as other meats in Indian cuisine. It is used by the Muslim community. The cow is considered by Hindus as a 'mother' because when a mother cannot feed a baby for any reason, then cow's milk is used. However, there are some interesting beef recipes, and you can also adapt some traditional lamb recipes, if you choose.

Marinated Beef   Serves 4

300 ml/½ pt/1¼ cups natural (plain) yoghurt ● 2.5 cm/1 in ginger root, minced

4 cloves garlic, crushed ● 5 ml/1 tsp ground cumin

5 ml/1 tsp ground cardamom ● 5 ml/1 tsp ground cloves

30 ml/2 tbsp chopped fresh coriander (cilantro) ● salt

450 g/1 lb beef, cubed ● 45 ml/3 tbsp oil ● 2 cloves

2 onions, sliced ● 2 green chillies, chopped

pinch of ground cinnamon ● 5 ml/1 tsp dried fenugreek leaves

250 ml/8 fl oz/1 cup water

Mix the yoghurt with the ginger, garlic, cumin, cardamom, cloves, coriander and salt, spread over the meat and leave to marinate overnight.

Heat the oil and fry the cloves until they darken. Add the onions and fry until golden. Add the chillies, cinnamon and fenugreek and fry for a few seconds. Add the meat, marinade and water, cover and simmer for about 1½ hours until the meat is tender.

Aniseed Beef   Serves 4

300 ml/½ pt/1¼ cups natural (plain) yoghurt ● 2.5 cm/1 in ginger root, ground

5 cloves garlic, crushed ● 5 ml/1 tsp ground cardamom

5 ml/1 tsp ground cinnamon ● 2 cloves, ground

450 g/1 lb beef, cubed ● 45 ml/3 tbsp oil ● 3 large onions, sliced

5 ml/1 tsp ground coriander (cilantro) ● 5 ml/1 tsp ground anise

2.5 ml/¼ tsp ground turmeric ● salt and pepper

15 ml/1 tbsp chopped fresh coriander (cilantro)

Mix 15 ml/1 tbsp of the yoghurt with the ginger, garlic, cardamom, cinnamon and cloves, rub into the meat and leave to marinate for 2 hours.

Heat the oil and fry the onions until golden. Remove from the pan and set aside. Add the meat and fry until lightly browned on all sides. Mix all the remaining ingredients except the fresh coriander into the remaining yoghurt and add to the meat. Cover and simmer gently for about 1 hour until the meat is tender. Garnish with coriander and serve hot with rice and a vegetable dish.

Boti Kebabs
Serves 6

120 ml/4 fl oz/½ cup natural (plain) yoghurt ● 1 onion, chopped

2.5 cm/1 in ginger root, chopped ● 3 cloves garlic, chopped

5 ml/1 tsp poppy seeds ● 15 ml/1 tbsp chopped fresh coriander (cilantro)

2.5 ml/½ tsp black pepper ● 5 ml/1 tsp cumin seeds

2.5 ml/½ tsp ground turmeric ● 1.5 ml/¼ tsp ground red chilli ● salt

900 g/2 lb boneless beef, cubed ● 30 ml/2 tbsp oil

Purée all the ingredients except the meat and oil to a paste. Pour over the meat and leave to marinate for 1 hour.
Thread the meat on to metal skewers and grill (broil) for about 15 minutes, turning and basting with oil occasionally, until the meat is cooked to your taste. Serve hot with mint chutney.

Beef Rolls with Nut Stuffing
Serves 6

900 g/2 lb beef, cut into 5 cm/2 in cubes ● 2.5 cm/1 in ginger root, grated

4 cloves garlic, crushed ● 2.5 ml/½ tsp black pepper

90 ml/6 tbsp oil ● 3 onions, chopped ● 25 g/1 oz/½ cup pistachios

30 ml/2 tbsp cashew nuts ● 5 ml/1 tsp ground cumin

15 ml/1 tbsp desiccated (shredded) coconut ● 15 ml/1 tbsp lemon juice

3 onions, sliced ● 150 ml/¼ pt/⅔ cup natural (plain) yoghurt

5 ml/1 tsp garam masala ● 30 ml/2 tbsp chopped fresh coriander (cilantro)

2 green chillies, chopped

Mix the meat with the ginger, garlic and pepper and leave to stand for at least 30 minutes, preferably overnight.
Flatten the meat slightly until the pieces are as thin as possible without tearing. They should be about 5 × 9 cm/2 × 3½ in. Heat 30 ml/1 tbsp of oil and fry the chopped onions until browned. Crush the nuts and add them to the pan with the cumin and coconut and fry for 1 minute, stirring. Remove from the heat and stir in the lemon juice. Allow to cool slightly.
Spoon about 5 ml/1 tsp of the mixture on to the strips, roll them tightly and tie with string if you wish. Heat 60 ml/ 4 tbsp of oil and fry the meat rolls for about 10 minutes until browned, turning carefully. Meanwhile, heat the remaining oil and fry the sliced onions until browned. Stir in the yoghurt, garam masala, coriander and chillies and simmer for 4-5 minutes. Pour over the browned meat, cover and simmer for about 8-10 minutes before serving.

Tikka Kebabs
Serves 6

900 g/2 lb boneless beef, cubed ● juice of ½ lemon ● salt

45 ml/3 tbsp oil ● 450 ml/ pt/2 cups natural (plain) yoghurt

1 onion, chopped ● 10 ml/2 tsp garam masala

2 cloves garlic, chopped ● 1 cm/½ in ginger root, chopped

5 ml/1 tsp paprika ● 1.5 ml/¼ tsp ground red chilli

pinch of pepper

Mix the meat with the lemon juice, salt and oil. Purée the yoghurt, onion, garam masala, garlic, ginger, paprika, chilli and pepper. Mix into the meat, cover and refrigerate overnight. Thread the meat on to metal skewers and cook in a preheated oven at 180°C/350°F/gas mark 4 for about 20 minutes, turning and basting occasionally. Serve hot with coriander chutney.

Beef with Beetroot
Serves 6

675 g/1½ lb beef, cubed ● 450 g/1 lb beetroot (red beets)

90 ml/6 tbsp oil ● 3 onions, sliced ● 2.5 cm/1 in ginger root, minced

3 cloves garlic, crushed ● 15 ml/1 tbsp ground coriander (cilantro)

5 ml/1 tsp ground cumin ● 5 ml/1 tsp ground turmeric

750 ml/1¼ pts/3 cups water ● 2.5 ml/½ tsp chilli powder

5 ml/1 tsp garam masala

Trim the meat and trim and dice the beetroot. Heat 75 ml/5 tbsp of oil and fry the onions until golden. Add the ginger and garlic and fry until lightly browned. Stir in the coriander, cumin and turmeric and fry for 3-4 minutes, stirring. Add the meat and fry for about 15 minutes until lightly browned. Remove the meat from the pan. Stir in the beetroot and fry for 2 minutes, stirring, adding a little more oil if necessary. Add the water and bring to the boil then simmer for 20-25 minutes. Return the meat to the pan with the chilli powder, cover and simmer for about 1 hour until the meat is tender, adding a little more water if necessary. Stir in the garam masala and simmer for about 10-15 minutes until the liquid has evaporated.

Beef Madras
Serves 4

10 ml/2 tsp chilli powder ● 10 ml/2 tsp ground coriander (cilantro)

10 ml/2 tsp ground turmeric ● 1.5 ml/¼ tsp ground ginger

salt and pepper ● 300 ml/½ pt/1¼ cups coconut milk ● 60 ml/4 tbsp ghee

1 onion, chopped ● 3 cloves garlic, crushed ● 900 g/2 lb beef, cubed

300 ml/½ pt/1¼ cups beef stock ● 5 ml/1 tsp lemon juice

Mix the spices, salt and pepper to a paste with a little of the coconut milk. Heat the ghee and fry the onion and garlic until golden. Add the paste and fry for 3 minutes, stirring. Add the meat and stock, bring to the boil, cover and simmer gently for 1½ hours until tender. Stir in the remaining coconut milk and the lemon juice and simmer for about 10 minutes until thickened.

Dry Beef Curry
Serves 6

900 g/2 lb lean stewing beef, cubed ● 2.5 ml/½ tsp ground turmeric

15 ml/1 tbsp cider vinegar ● 30 ml/2 tbsp oil

6 cloves garlic, finely chopped ● 1 large onion, finely chopped

1 green chilli, finely chopped ● 5 mm/¼ in fresh root ginger, finely chopped

15 ml/1 tbsp Basic Curry Powder (page 11)

15 ml/1 tbsp desiccated (shredded) coconut ● salt

1 large tomato, chopped

Mix the meat, turmeric and cider vinegar and leave to stand for 10 minutes.

Heat the oil and fry the garlic, onion, chilli and ginger over a medium heat until lightly browned. Add the curry powder and coconut and fry for 3-4 minutes, stirring occasionally, until the oil rises to the surface. Stir in the meat mixture, salt and tomato and fry over a high heat for 3-4 minutes.

Transfer to a casserole dish, cover with foil and the lid and bake in a pre-heated oven at 200°C/400°F/gas mark 6 for 30 minutes. Reduce the heat to 150°C/300°F/gas mark 2 and bake for a further 15 minutes until the meat is tender. Serve hot with rice or chapatis, a vegetable dish and salad.

Beef with Almonds
Serves 6

900 g/2 lb beef, cubed ● 300 ml/½ pt/1¼ cups natural (plain) yoghurt

5 ml/1 tsp ground turmeric ● 14 dried red chillies

salt ● 90 ml/6 tbsp ghee ● 6 cloves ● 4 cinnamon sticks

4 cardamom pods ● 2.5 ml/½ tsp caraway seeds ● 225 g/8 oz onions, sliced

2.5 cm/1 in ginger root, finely chopped ● 6 cloves garlic, finely chopped

300 ml/½ pt/1¼ cups coconut milk ● 100 g/4 oz/1 cup ground almonds

Place the meat in a bowl, stir in the yoghurt and turmeric and leave to marinate for 1 hour. Grind the chillies to a fine paste with a little salt.

Heat the ghee and fry the cloves, cinnamon, cardamom, caraway and onions until lightly browned. Stir in the ginger and garlic then the ground chillies and fry until well browned.

Add the beef mixture, cover and cook for about 30 minutes, stirring occasionally, until the meat is half-cooked. Stir in the coconut milk, cover and cook until the meat is tender. Stir in the ground almonds and simmer over a very low heat until the ghee appears on the surface. Serve hot with parathas.

Light Beef and Potato Curry
Serves 6

75 ml/5 tbsp oil ● 4 onions, sliced ● 3 cloves garlic, chopped

2.5 cm/1 in ginger root, chopped ● 15 ml/1 tbsp ground coriander (cilantro)

5 ml/1 tsp ground cumin ● 2.5 ml/½ tsp ground turmeric

4 tomatoes, skinned and chopped ● 675 g/1½ lb beef, cubed

5 curry leaves ● 750 ml/1¼ pts/3 cups water ● 450 g/1 lb potatoes, cubed

30 ml/2 tbsp chopped fresh coriander (cilantro)

Heat the oil and fry the onions until golden, stirring occasionally. Add the garlic and ginger and fry until lightly browned. Stir in the coriander, cumin and turmeric and fry for 1 minute, stirring. Add the tomatoes and fry until the mixture resembles a thick purée and oil appears around the sides of the pan. Add the meat and curry leaves and fry until browned, stirring occasionally. Add the water and bring to the boil, cover and simmer for 20 minutes. Reduce the heat to low and cook for a further 20 minutes. Add the potatoes and stir thoroughly. Cover and simmer for about 40-45 minutes until the meat and potatoes are tender. Sprinkle with coriander and simmer for 1 minute before serving.

Beef with Yoghurt
Serves 4

45 ml/3 tbsp ghee ● 900 g/2 lb beef, cubed

2 green chillies, seeded and chopped ● 2 onions, chopped

225 g/8 oz tomatoes, skinned and chopped ● 10 ml/2 tsp garam masala

5 ml/1 tsp ground ginger ● 2.5 ml/½ tsp cayenne ● salt and pepper

300 ml/½ pt/1¼ cups natural (plain) yoghurt

Heat the ghee in an ovenproof pan and fry the beef until browned on all sides. Remove from the pan. Add the chillies and onions and fry for about 10 minutes until soft. Add the tomatoes and fry for about 5 minutes, stirring. Add the spices, salt and pepper. Stir the beef back into the pan. Gradually add the yoghurt, a spoonful at a time, stirring constantly. Cover tightly and bake in a preheated oven at 170°C/325°F/gas mark 3 for 1½ hours until tender.

Beef and Spinach in Yoghurt Sauce
Serves 6

45 ml/3 tbsp oil ● 5 ml/1 tsp black mustard seeds ● 15 ml/1 tbsp cardamom seeds

15 ml/1 tbsp ground coriander (cilantro) ● 2.5 ml/½ tsp crushed black peppercorns

2 green chillies, chopped ● 6 cloves garlic, crushed

2.5 cm/1 in ginger root, chopped ● 1.5 kg/3 lb stewing steak, cubed

1 onion, chopped ● 5 ml/1 tsp ground turmeric ● 1.5 kg/3 lb spinach, chopped

salt ● 45 ml/3 tbsp natural (plain) yoghurt

Heat the oil and fry the mustard seeds over medium heat until they start crackling. Add the cardamom, coriander, peppercorns, chillies, garlic and ginger and fry for 1 minute. Stir in the meat and fry for 10 minutes until browned on all sides. Add the onion and fry until browned. Stir in the turmeric, spinach and salt and cook for 5 minutes. Stir in the yoghurt. Transfer to a casserole, cover and cook in a preheated oven at 180°C/350°F/gas mark 4 for about 30 minutes until beef is tender. Serve hot with rice, nan and papadums.

Palak Beef   Serves 4

225 g/8 oz spinach, chopped • 4 green chillies • 45 ml/3 tbsp ghee

5 ml/1 tsp sugar • 450 g/1 lb beef, cubed • 150 ml/¼ pt/⅔ cup milk

5 ml/1 tsp chilli powder • salt • 10 ml/2 tsp ground coriander (cilantro)

5 ml/1 tsp ground turmeric • 250 ml/8 fl oz/1 cup water

10 ml/2 tsp garam masala

Boil the spinach and chillies for a few minutes in a little water until tender. Drain and leave to cool then grind to a fine paste.

Heat the ghee and fry the sugar for 1 minute. Stir in the beef and fry for 2 minutes. Add the milk and fry for 3 minutes. Stir in the chilli powder, salt and coriander and fry until the meat is well browned. Add the spinach paste and turmeric and fry for 5 minutes. Add the water and simmer until the meat is cooked and the water has evaporated. Stir in the garam masala, cover and simmer very gently until the meat is very tender and the spices have permeated thoroughly. Serve hot with chapatis.

Hyderabad Spiced Beef   Serves 4

60 ml/4 tbsp ghee • 450 g/1 lb beef, cubed

1 large onion, sliced • 2.5 cm/1 in ginger root, chopped

10 cloves garlic, chopped • 3 dried red chillies, coarsely chopped

5 ml/1 tsp ground turmeric • 300 m/1½ pt/1¼ cups natural (plain) yoghurt

6 black peppercorns • 3 cinnamon sticks • 2 cardamom pods

4 cloves

Heat half the ghee to smoking point then add the meat and stir well. Stir in all the remaining ingredients, cover and simmer over a very low heat for 45 minutes. Add the remaining ghee and simmer, uncovered, until the meat is reddish-brown. Serve hot with rice and salad.

Beef and Cauliflower Ghosht
Serves 6

8 cloves garlic ● 2.5 cm/1 in ginger root ● 900 g/2 lb beef, cubed

30 ml/2 tbsp ghee ● 2 onions, finely chopped ● 6 dried red chillies

6 black peppercorns ● 30 ml/2 tbsp ground coriander (cilantro)

2.5 cm/1 in cinnamon stick ● 4 cloves

15 ml/1 tbsp desiccated (shredded) coconut

1 small cauliflower, cut into florets ● 1 tomato, chopped

2.5 ml/½ tsp ground turmeric ● salt

15 ml/1 tbsp chopped fresh coriander (cilantro)

Grind the garlic and ginger to a fine paste. Rub the paste on to the meat and leave to stand.

Heat the ghee and fry the onions until lightly browned. Grind the chillies, peppercorns, coriander, cinnamon, cloves and coconut to a fine paste then stir them into the pan and fry for 2 minutes. Add the beef, cauliflower and tomato and fry for 1 minute. Stir in the turmeric and add just enough water to cover the meat. Cover and simmer for about 1 hour until the meat is tender, stirring occasionally. Sprinkle with salt to taste and cook for a further 10 minutes. Garnish with coriander and serve hot with chapatis.

Bhindi Beef Curry
Serves 4

60 ml/4 tbsp ghee ● 2 large onions, chopped

4 cloves garlic, crushed ● 2.5 cm/1 in ginger root, crushed

450 g/1 lb beef, cubed ● 2.5 ml/½ tsp ground turmeric

4 dried red chillies ● 2.5 ml/½ tsp ground coriander (cilantro)

2.5 ml/½ tsp cumin seeds ● 2.5 ml/½ tsp ground black pepper

5 ml/1 tsp salt ● 225 g/8 oz okra ● 225 g/8 oz tomatoes, skinned and mashed

5 ml/1 tsp garam masala ● 15 ml/1 tbsp chopped fresh coriander (cilantro)

Heat 45 ml/3 tbsp of ghee and fry the onions until browned. Add the garlic and ginger and fry for 1 minute. Add the beef, turmeric, chillies, coriander, cumin seeds, pepper and salt and simmer gently, adding a little water if necessary, until the meat is browned.

Meanwhile heat the remaining ghee and lightly fry the okra. When the meat is brown, add the okra and tomatoes and simmer until the meat is tender and reddish-brown, adding a little water if necessary. Garnish with garam masala and coriander and serve hot with chapatis.

Beef and Mushrooms   Serves 4

45 ml/3 tbsp ghee ● 1 onion, chopped ● 2 cloves garlic, crushed

15 ml/1 tbsp ground coriander (cilantro) ● 10 ml/2 tsp garam masala

2.5 ml/½ tsp chilli powder ● 30 ml/2 tbsp natural (plain) yoghurt

900 g/2 lb stewing beef, cubed ● 30 ml/2 tbsp plain (all-purpose) flour

450 ml/¾ pt/2 cups water ● salt ● 225 g/8 oz mushrooms, sliced

30 ml/2 tbsp chopped fresh coriander (cilantro)

Heat the ghee and fry the onion and garlic until golden. Mix the spices to a paste with the yoghurt. Add the beef to the pan and fry until browned on all sides. Add the spice paste and flour and fry for 5 minutes, stirring to coat the meat. Add the water and salt, bring to the boil then cover and simmer gently for 1½-2 hours until the beef is almost tender, stirring occasionally. Add the mushrooms and cook for a further 30 minutes until the beef is tender. Serve sprinkled with coriander.

Beef and Tomatoes   Serves 4

45 ml/3 tbsp oil ● 2 bay leaves ● 2 dried red chillies

2.5 ml/1 in cinnamon stick ● 2 onions, finely chopped

2.5 cm/1 in ginger root, minced ● 5 cloves garlic, crushed

1 green chilli, chopped ● 5 ml/1 tsp ground coriander (cilantro)

5 ml/1 tsp ground cumin ● 5 tomatoes, skinned and chopped

2.5 ml/½ tsp sugar ● salt ● 450 g/1 lb beef, cubed

120 ml/4 fl oz/½ cup water

Heat the oil and fry the bay leaves and chillies until they darken then remove and discard them. Add the cinnamon and onions and fry until golden. Add the ginger and garlic then the green chilli and spices and fry for a few seconds. Add the tomatoes, sugar and salt and fry until the fat appears on the surface. Add the meat and fry until browned. Add the water, bring to the boil, cover and simmer for about 1 hour until the meat is tender. Serve hot with rice and a vegetable dish.

Beef with Cashews
Serves 4

250 ml/8 fl oz/1 cup natural (plain) yoghurt

5 ml/1 tsp ground coriander (cilantro) ● salt

450 g/1 lb beef, cubed ● 45 ml/3 tbsp oil

5 ml/1 tsp ground cardamom ● 5 ml/1 tsp cumin seeds

3 onions, sliced ● 5 cm/2 in ginger root, grated

2 green chillies, chopped ● 250 ml/8 fl oz/1 cup water

25 g/1 oz/½ cup cashew nuts, ground ● 45 ml/3 tbsp cream ● juice of ½ lime

Mix the yoghurt, coriander and a little salt. Rub into the meat and leave to marinate for 1 hour.

Heat the oil and fry the cardamom and cumin for a few seconds. Add the onions and fry until golden. Add the ginger and chillies then the meat, marinade and water. Bring to the boil, cover and simmer for about 1 hour until the meat is tender. Stir in the cashews and cream, cover and simmer for 15 minutes. Stir in the lime juice and serve hot with rice and vegetables.

Kebab Curry
Serves 4

450 g/1 lb beef, cubed ● 5 cm/2 in ginger root, sliced

225 g/8 oz pearl onions ● 6 green chillies, cut into chunks

1 head garlic, separated ● 30 ml/2 tbsp ghee ● 1 large onion, sliced

2 tomatoes, chopped

Masala: 3 dried red chillies ● 6 cloves garlic

2.5 cm/1 in ginger root ● 5 ml/1 tsp ground coriander (cilantro)

1.5 ml/¼ tsp cumin seeds ● 30 ml/2 tbsp poppy seeds

1 cinnamon stick ● 3 cloves ● 2 cardamom pods

5 ml/1 tsp ground turmeric

salt ● 2 potatoes, quartered ● 15 ml/1 tbsp tamarind juice

2 hard-boiled (hard-cooked) eggs, quartered

15 ml/1 tbsp chopped fresh coriander (cilantro)

Thread the beef, ginger, pearl onions, chillies and garlic on to kebab skewers.

Heat the ghee and fry the sliced onion until lightly browned. Add the tomatoes and cook until soft. Grind the masala ingredients to a fine paste, add to the pan and cook until the ghee appears on the surface. Add the kebabs and stir gently until they are well coated with the sauce. Add salt to taste and enough water to cook the meat. Simmer until the meat is almost tender. Add the potatoes and simmer until tender. Stir in the tamarind juice, boil for 2 minutes then remove from the heat. Garnish with the coriander and eggs and serve hot with rice and salad.

Nargisi Kebabs
Serves 6

675 g/1½ lb minced (ground) beef ● 1 onion, chopped

7.5 ml/1½ tsp ground turmeric ● 2.5 cm/1 in ginger root

5 ml/1 tsp cumin seeds ● 3 green chillies ● 5 ml/1 tsp garam masala

salt ● 3 eggs ● 12 hard-boiled (hard-cooked) eggs

60 ml/4 tbsp ghee ● 1 lime, sliced

Place the beef, onion and 2.5 ml/½ tsp of turmeric in a pan with a little water and boil until the meat is cooked and the water has evaporated. Grind the ginger, cumin seeds, chillies, garam masala and salt to a paste then add the cooked meat and grind again until soft. Mix in the raw eggs and season to taste with salt. Shape the mixture round the hard-boiled eggs. Heat the ghee and fry the coated eggs until well browned on all sides. Garnish with lime slices and serve hot on its own or with a tomato sauce.

Shami Kebabs
Serves 6

675 g/1½ lb minced (ground) beef ● 100 g/4 oz/⅔ cup yellow split peas

2.5 cm/1 in ginger root ● 3 cloves garlic

5 ml/1 tsp ground coriander (cilantro) ● 5 ml/1 tsp garam masala

1 dried red chilli ● 1 egg ● 1 hard-boiled (hard-cooked) egg

1 onion ● 2 green chillies ● 25 g/1 oz/¼ cup blanched almonds

5 ml/1 tsp chopped fresh coriander (cilantro) ● 45 ml/3 tbsp ghee

Place the beef and split peas in a pan, cover with water, bring to the boil, cover and simmer for about 1 hour until tender and dry. Grind the ginger, garlic, coriander, garam masala and chilli to a paste and mix into the meat with the raw egg. Shape into balls or flat patties. Coarsely chop the remaining ingredients and mix together. Put a little of the chopped mixture in the centre of each kebab. Heat the ghee and fry the kebabs until richly browned. Serve with onion rings and slices of lime.

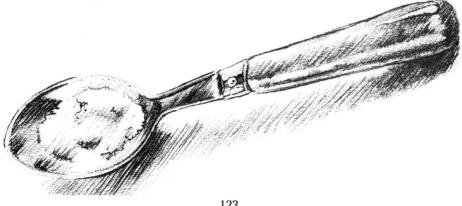

Shikampooree Kebabs
Serves 4

45 ml/3 tbsp ghee • 1 onion, minced • 2 cloves garlic, crushed

1 cm/½ in ginger root, minced • 4 dried red chillies

5 ml/1 tsp ground coriander (cilantro) • 5 ml/1 tsp ground turmeric

2.5 ml/½ tsp ground cumin • 2.5 ml/½ tsp garam masala

pinch of ground cinnamon • pinch of ground cardamom

pinch of ground cloves • 2.5 ml/½ tsp ground almonds

15 ml/1 tbsp gram flour • 450 g/1 lb minced (ground) beef • salt

15 ml/1 tbsp coconut cream • 150 ml/¼ pt/⅔ cup natural (plain) yoghurt

5 ml/1 tsp chopped fresh mint

Heat half the ghee and fry the onion, garlic, ginger and chillies for 3-4 minutes. Stir in the spices and almonds and cook over a low heat for 5 minutes. Stir in the flour, beef, salt and coconut cream and cook for 10 minutes. Remove from the pan and grind the mixture to a fine paste.

Blend the yoghurt, mint and salt to taste. Shape spoonfuls of the meat mixture into balls and place 2.5 cm/½ tsp of yoghurt in the centre. Shape the meat around the yoghurt to form flat, round cutlets. Heat the remaining ghee and fry the cutlets until golden brown. Serve hot with onion rings and salad.

Baked Kebabs
Serves 4

5 cm/2 in ginger root • 1 unripe fig • 15 ml/1 tbsp salt

450 g/1 lb steak, cubed • 2 onions, chopped

45 ml/3 tbsp ghee • 2 potatoes, cubed • 1 large tomato, chopped

1 sprig fresh coriander (cilantro), chopped

1 sprig fresh mint, chopped • 10 ml/2 tsp chilli powder

3 eggs, beaten

Grind the ginger, fig and salt to a smooth paste, mix it well into the meat and leave to marinate for 2 hours.

Heat 15 ml/1 tbsp ghee and fry the onions until crisp and golden then grind them to a paste. Add a further 15 ml/1 tbsp of ghee and fry the potatoes until golden. Mix the onions, potatoes, remaining ghee, tomato, coriander, mint and chilli powder into the meat and spread in an ovenproof dish. Pour the eggs on top of the meat, cover tightly and bake in a preheated oven at 200°C/400°F/gas mark 6 for 30 minutes until the meat is cooked and the eggs set.

Meatballs in Yoghurt
Serves 4

120 ml/4 fl oz/½ cup natural (plain) yoghurt • 1 onion, chopped

2 cloves garlic, chopped • 1 cm/½ in ginger root, chopped

1 green chilli, chopped • 5 ml/1 tsp ground coriander (cilantro)

5 ml/1 tsp ground cumin • 30 ml/2 tbsp chopped fresh mint

450 g/1 lb minced (ground) beef • 45 ml/3 tbsp oil

Purée the yoghurt, onion, garlic, ginger, chilli, coriander, cumin and mint in a blender or food processor then mix with the meat and divide into 20 meatballs. Heat the oil and fry the meatballs for about 20 minutes until golden brown and crisp on all sides. Remove the lid and stir until all the liquid has evaporated. Serve hot with chutney.

Spicy Kebabs
Serves 6

900 g/2 lb minced (ground) beef • 1 onion, grated

4 cloves garlic, grated • 1 cm/½ in ginger root, grated

1 green chilli, grated • 2.5 ml/½ tsp garam masala

1 egg, beaten • 1.5 ml/¼ tsp black pepper • 2.5 ml/½ tsp paprika

25 g/1 oz/¼ cup gram flour • 5 ml/1 tsp chopped fresh mint

30 ml/2 tbsp natural (plain) yoghurt • 60 ml/4 tbsp oil • salt

Mix all the ingredients except 45 ml/ 3 tbsp of the oil and shape into 20 meatballs 2.5 cm/1 in thick. Heat the remaining oil and fry the meatballs for 20 minutes until browned. Serve hot with mint chutney.

Ginger, Cardamom and Mint Kebabs
Serves 6

900 g/2 lb minced (ground) beef • 2 onions, chopped

175 g/6 oz/1 cup yellow split peas • 10 black peppercorns

2.5 cm/1 in cinnamon stick • 5 cardamom pods • 8 cloves

3 bay leaves • 2.5 cm/1 in ginger root, chopped

2 dried red chillies • 675 ml/1¼ pt/3 cups water

30 ml/2 tbsp chopped fresh mint • salt • 1 egg, beaten

45 ml/3 tbsp oil • 25 g/1 oz/¼ cup plain (all-purpose) flour

Place all the ingredients except the egg, oil and flour in a large pan, bring to the boil then simmer until the water has evaporated and the meat is tender, stirring occasionally. Drain and discard any excess liquid and let the mixture cool.

Purée the mixture to a smooth paste then mix in the egg and divide into 12 balls, flattening each to about 5 cm/2 in thick. Heat the oil. Dust the meatballs with flour and fry for about 10 minutes until browned on all sides. Serve hot with mint chutney.

Pasand Kebabs
Serves 6

60 ml/2 tbsp ghee or butter • 2 onions, sliced

900 g/2 lb minced (ground) beef • 5 cm/2 in ginger root, minced

8 green chillies, finely chopped

1 bunch fresh coriander (cilantro), finely chopped

600 ml/1 pt/2½ cups natural (plain) yoghurt • 10 ml/2 tsp ground black pepper

10 ml/2 tsp ground cloves • 5 ml/1 tsp ground turmeric

salt • 1 onion, cut into rings • 1 lemon, slices

Heat half the ghee or butter and fry the onions until golden brown. Mix them with the remaining ingredients and season to taste with salt. Cover and leave to marinate for 2½ hours.

Shape the mixture into small balls and thread on to kebab skewers. Melt the remaining ghee or butter, brush over the kebabs and grill (broil) for about 20 minutes until golden brown on all sides. Serve hot with onion rings and lemon slices.

Cocktail Kofta
Serves 6

900 g/2 lb minced (ground) beef • 5 ml/1 tsp ground coriander (cilantro)

5 ml/1 tsp ground cumin • 2.5 ml/½ tsp chilli powder

45 ml/3 tbsp natural (plain) yoghurt • 1 egg, beaten

30 ml/2 tbsp chopped fresh coriander (cilantro) • salt

Sauce: 450 ml/¾ pt/2 cups water • 6 cloves garlic

2.5 cm/1 in ginger root, chopped • 5 ml/1 tsp ground cumin

5 ml/1 tsp ground coriander (cilantro) • 2.5 ml/½ tsp chilli powder

5 ml/1 tsp paprika • salt • 45 ml/3 tbsp oil

1 cinnamon stick • 5 cardamom pods • 5 cloves

1 onion, chopped • 2.5 ml/½ tsp ground turmeric

45 ml/3 tbsp natural (plain) yoghurt

Mix all the meatball ingredients together and shape into 20 balls.

To make the sauce, purée 60 ml/4 tbsp of the water with the garlic, ginger, cumin, coriander, chilli powder, paprika and salt. Heat the oil and fry the cinnamon, cardamom and cloves until slightly darkened. Add the onion and fry until soft and browned. Add the garlic paste and fry for 1 minute. Add the meatballs and remaining water to the pan, stirring thoroughly. Cover and simmer gently for 20 minutes, stirring occasionally. Remove the lid and increase the heat. Boil until the liquid has evaporated. Transfer the meatballs to a serving dish. Remove and discard the whole spices, stir in the yoghurt and pour the sauce over the meatballs. Serve with mint chutney.

Kofta Curry
Serves 4

4 green chillies ● 2.5 cm/1 in ginger root

3 onions, thinly sliced ● 8 peppercorns

15 ml/1 tbsp chopped fresh coriander (cilantro)

675 g/1½ lb minced (ground) beef ● 1 egg ● salt

oil or ghee for deep-frying ● 15 ml/1 tbsp ghee

10 ml/1 tsp ground coriander (cilantro) ● 5 ml/1 tsp ground turmeric

5 ml/1 tsp ground cumin ● 5 ml/1 tsp chilli powder

1 cinnamon stick ● 2 black cardamom pods ● 3 cloves

3 cloves garlic, thinly sliced ● 1 sprig fresh curry leaves

1 sprig fresh coriander (cilantro) leaves ● 1 tomato, chopped

600 ml/1 pt/2½ cups water

Purée the chillies, ginger, 1 onion, the peppercorns and coriander to a paste in a blender or food processor. Mix with the beef, egg and salt and shape into egg-sized balls. Heat the oil or ghee and deep-fry the koftas until browned. Drain and set aside.

Heat the ghee and fry the remaining onions and spices for 5 minutes, adding salt to taste. Add the tomato and cook until the ghee appears on the surface, adding a little water if necessary. Add the koftas and water and simmer until the gravy thickens. Serve hot with rice and a vegetable dish.

Muslim-style Spicy Meatballs
Serves 6

900 g/2 lb minced (ground) beef ● 5 cloves garlic, crushed

salt ● 5 ml/1 tsp paprika ● 45 ml/3 tbsp oil

5 cloves ● 5 cardamom pods ● 6 black peppercorns

1 cinnamon stick ● 3 bay leaves ● 1.5 ml/¼ tsp grated nutmeg

10 ml/2 tsp garam masala ● 1 onion, finely chopped

3 tomatoes, skinned and quartered ● 2.5 ml/½ tsp chilli powder

45 ml/3 tbsp natural (plain) yoghurt ● 450 ml/¾ pt/2 cups water

30 ml/2 tbsp chopped fresh coriander (cilantro)

Mix together the meat, garlic, salt and paprika and shape the mixture into 24 balls. Heat the oil and fry the cloves, cardamom, peppercorns, cinnamon, bay leaves, nutmeg and garam masala over a medium heat for 3 minutes. Add the onion and fry until golden brown. Add the tomatoes and chilli powder and fry for 2 minutes. Mix in the yoghurt and water and bring to the boil. Add the meatballs and spoon the sauce over them. Cover and simmer gently for 20 minutes. Remove the lid and cook for a further 5 minutes. Garnish with coriander and serve hot with rice and a vegetable dish.

Keema Tikka
Serves 6

900 g/2 lb minced (ground) beef ● 1 egg

30 ml/2 tbsp breadcrumbs ● 1 onion, finely chopped

3 cloves garlic, finely chopped ● 1 cm/½ in ginger root, finely chopped

1.5 ml/¼ tsp ground black pepper ● 1.5 ml/¼ tsp ground black mustard seeds

30 ml/2 tbsp chopped fresh mint or coriander (cilantro) ● salt ● 30 ml/2 tbsp oil

Mix together all the ingredients except the oil and divide the mixture into 6 equal patties. Heat the oil and fry the patties over a medium heat until golden brown on both sides. Serve hot with chapatis and chutney.

Sweet and Sour Beef
Serves 4

30 ml/2 tbsp oil ● 2 onions, chopped ● 2 green chillies, seeded and chopped

4 curry leaves, torn ● 2.5 cm/1 in ginger root, minced ● 4 cloves garlic, crushed

5 ml/1 tsp ground roasted cumin ● 1.5 ml/¼ tsp ground turmeric

2.5 ml/½ tsp ground black pepper ● 450 g/1 lb minced (ground) beef

2 tomatoes, skinned and chopped ● 5 ml/1 tsp wine vinegar

120 ml/4 fl oz/½ cup water ● 10 ml/2 tsp sugar ● 15 ml/1 tbsp cream

15 ml/1 tbsp chopped fresh coriander (cilantro)

Heat the oil and fry 1 onion until golden. Add the other onion, the chillies, curry leaves, ginger and garlic and fry for 5 minutes. Add the spices and fry for a few seconds. Add the beef and fry until lightly browned and the moisture has evaporated. Add the tomatoes, wine vinegar and water, bring to the boil, cover and simmer for 15 minutes. Stir in the sugar and cream, season to taste with salt, cover and simmer for a further 10 minutes. Garnish with coriander and serve hot with rice and aubergine.

Potato and Mince
Serves 4

45 ml/3 tbsp oil ● 2 onions, finely chopped

2 cloves garlic, finely chopped ● 450 g/1 lb minced (ground) beef

4 tomatoes, skinned and chopped ● 15 ml/1 tbsp tomato purée (paste)

2.5 ml/½ tsp dried oregano ● 5 ml/1 tsp dried basil

2 green chillies, seeded and chopped ● 50 ml/2 fl oz/3½ tbsp water

salt and pepper ● 6 potatoes ● 30 ml/2 tbsp butter

30 ml/2 tbsp milk ● 25 g/1 oz/¼ cup grated cheese

Photograph opposite: *South Indian Hot Fried Prawns (page 63)*

Heat the oil and fry the onions until soft. Add the garlic and fry for 1 minute. Add the mince and fry until browned. Add the tomatoes, tomato purée, oregano, basil, chillies and water and season with salt and pepper. Cover and simmer for about 20 minutes until the meat is cooked.

Meanwhile, boil the potatoes until tender then drain, peel and mash them with the butter, milk and half the cheese. Season with salt and pepper. Spoon the mince into an ovenproof dish, spread the potatoes on top and sprinkle with the remaining cheese. Bake in a preheated oven at 200°C/400°F/gas mark 6 for about 15 minutes until the top is golden brown.

Beef with Peas
Serves 4

30 ml/2 tbsp oil ● 1.5 ml/¼ tsp crushed black peppercorns

1 small onion, finely chopped ● 3 cloves garlic, finely chopped

15 ml/1 tbsp Basic Curry Powder (page 11) ● 3 tomatoes, skinned and chopped

450 g/1 lb minced (ground) beef ● 30 ml/2 tbsp chopped fresh mint

15 ml/1 tbsp natural (plain) yoghurt ● salt ● 275 g/10 oz peas

Heat the oil and fry the peppercorns for 30 seconds. Add the onion and garlic and fry over a medium heat until lightly browned. Stir in the curry powder and fry for 1 minute. Stir in the tomatoes and fry for 2-3 minutes until soft. Stir in the beef, mint, yoghurt and salt, cover and simmer for 10 minutes. Stir in the peas, cover and cook for a further 5 minutes. Serve hot with rice, mango chutney, salad and papadums.

Curried Beef with Aubergine
Serves 4

45 ml/3 tbsp oil ● 1 cinnamon stick ● 6 cardamom pods

2 bay leaves ● 2.5 ml/½ tsp black peppercorns ● 1.5 ml/¼ tsp cloves

1 onion, grated ● 4 cloves garlic, crushed

1 cm/½ in ginger root, grated ● 1 green chilli, grated

15 ml/1 tbsp Basic Curry Powder (page 11) ● 1 large tomato, skinned and chopped

900 g/2 lb minced (ground) beef ● salt

1 medium aubergine (eggplant), cut into strips

Heat the oil and fry the spices over a medium heat until slightly darkened. Add the onion, garlic, ginger and chilli and fry until golden. Add the curry powder and fry for 1 minute. Add the tomato and fry for 1 minute. Stir in the meat and salt, cover and simmer for 10 minutes, stirring occasionally, Stir in the aubergine, cover and cook for 7-10 minutes, stirring occasionally. Serve hot with rice or chapatis, dal and chutney.

Photograph opposite: *Curried Leg of Lamb (page 101)*

Pork

There are few Indian dishes that use pork as it is not eaten by Muslims. However, there are a few pork recipes, such as Goan Portuguese-style Spicy Pork, which was introduced by Portuguese settlers in India.

Coorgi Pork   Serves 8

1.5 kg/3 lb pork ● 30 dried red chillies, ground

12 onions ● 250 ml/8 fl oz/1 cup water

15 ml/1 tbsp cumin seeds ● 5 ml/1 tsp ground turmeric

15 ml/1 tbsp coriander (cilantro) seeds ● 10 ml/2 tsp peppercorns

30 ml/2 tbsp white wine vinegar ● 4 boiled potatoes, quartered

salt

Cut the pork into small pieces and mix with the ground chillies. Leave to stand for 15 minutes then place in a pan. Slice 10 of the onions and add to the pork with the water. Bring to the boil, cover and simmer for 1 hour until the meat is cooked.

Grind the remaining onions with the cumin seeds, turmeric, coriander seeds, peppercorns and wine vinegar and stir into the pan. Simmer for a further 15 minutes. Add the potatoes and season to taste with salt. Simmer until heated through. Serve hot with vegetables, papadums and rice.

Sundia   Serves 4-6

900 g/2 lb pork, chopped ● 5 ml/1 tsp ground turmeric

15 ml/1 tbsp ground coriander (cilantro) ● 10 ml/2 tsp chilli powder

30 ml/2 tbsp oil or ghee ● 10 ml/2 tsp poppy seeds

100 g/4 oz/⅔ cup red lentils ● 2 cardamom pods

6 onions, chopped ● 2.5 cm/1 in ginger root, chopped

2 bulbs garlic, chopped ● 1 coconut, grated (shredded)

juice of 3 lemons ● salt ● oil for deep-frying

Place the pork in a pan with the turmeric, coriander and chilli powder and pour in just enough water to cover. Bring to the boil and simmer gently for about 45 minutes until the meat is tender. Remove the meat and shred it. Heat a little oil or ghee and fry the poppy seeds, lentils and car-

damom separately until lightly browned. Add these to the meat with the remaining ingredients and season to taste with salt. Mix together well and shape into balls. Deep-fry in hot oil over a low heat until nicely browned. Serve hot with papadums, rice and a curry sauce.

Pork Vindaloo

Serves 4-6

15 ml/1 tbsp coriander (cilantro) seeds ● 10 ml/2 tsp cumin seeds

10 ml/2 tsp mustard seeds ● 5 black peppercorns

5 cloves ● 5 dried red chillies ● 2.5 cm/1 in cinnamon stick

2.5 ml/½ tsp cardamom seeds ● 2.5 ml/½ tsp ground turmeric

salt ● 5 large cloves garlic, chopped

4 cm/1½ in ginger root, chopped ● 60 ml/4 tbsp wine vinegar

500 g/18 oz boned pork, cubed ● 75 ml/5 tbsp oil

2 onions, finely chopped ● 400 g/14 oz canned tomatoes, chopped

150 ml/¼ pt/⅔ cup wine vinegar ● 250 ml/8 fl oz/1 cup water

Garnish: 2.5 ml/½ tsp garam masala

15 ml/1 tbsp chopped fresh coriander (cilantro)

1 green chilli, chopped

Heat a frying pan (skillet) over a medium heat and fry the whole spices until browned. Grind them to a fine powder. Stir in the turmeric and salt to taste. Blend the powder with the garlic, ginger and wine vinegar to a smooth paste in a blender or food processor. Rub the paste into the meat and leave to marinate overnight.

Heat the oil in a heavy-based pan and fry the onions over a medium heat until golden brown. Add the pork and fry for 15 minutes until golden. Stir in the tomatoes and fry until all the liquid has been absorbed and the oil appears on the surface. Add the wine vinegar and water, bring to the boil, cover and cook over a medium-low heat for 40 minutes until the meat is tender. Sprinkle with the garnish ingredients and serve hot with rice, chapatis, raita and a bean and potato or okra dish.

Pork Korma

Serves 4

60 ml/4 tbsp ghee ● 3 onions, thinly sliced

4 cloves garlic, chopped ● 1.5 ml/¼ tsp ground cumin

1 cinnamon stick ● 3 bay leaves ● 10 cloves

6 cardamom pods ● 450 g/1 lb pork, cubed

300 ml/½ pt/1¼ cups natural (plain) yoghurt

4 large tomatoes, skinned and chopped

2.5 ml/½ tsp black pepper ● salt

Heat the ghee and fry the onions and garlic until soft. Add the spices and fry until browned. Add the meat and fry until browned. Stir in the yoghurt, tomatoes, pepper and salt and simmer for about 20 minutes until the meat is tender and the sauce is thick. Serve hot with pilau rice and dal.

Pork Sorpotel
Serves 6-8

900 g/2 lb fatty pork • 225 g/8 oz pigs' liver

900 ml/1½ pts/3¾ cups water • 10 dried red chillies

10 ml/2 tsp ground turmeric • 10 ml/2 tsp cumin seeds

16 black peppercorns • 5 cm/2 in cinnamon stick

14 cloves • 18 cloves garlic, crushed

2.5 cm/1 in ginger root, chopped • 3 onions, chopped

5 ml/1 tsp tamarind concentrate • 5 ml/1 tsp white wine vinegar

5 ml/1 tsp salt • 5 ml/1 tsp sugar

Cook the pork and liver in the water for about 1 hour until tender. Drain and leave to cool then cut into small cubes. Grind the spices to a smooth paste and mix with the pork and liver. Cook over a gentle heat for about 10 minutes. Add the onions, tamarind, wine vinegar, salt and sugar and simmer until the gravy is thick. Serve hot with rice, vegetables and dal.

Goan Portuguese-style Spicy Pork
Serves 8

15 ml/1 tbsp cumin seeds • 10 ml/2 tsp black mustard seeds

5 ml/1 tsp ground turmeric • 2.5 ml/½ tsp black peppercorns

5 ml/1 tsp ground cinnamon • 5 ml/1 tsp cardamom pods

2.5 ml/½ tsp cloves • 2.5 ml/½ tsp grated nutmeg

1 onion, chopped • 8 cloves garlic, chopped

2.5 cm/1 in ginger root, chopped • 5 ml/1 tsp paprika

6 dried red chillies, soaked in 30 ml/1 tbsp cider vinegar

45 ml/3 tbsp mustard oil • 250 ml/8 fl oz/1 cup cider vinegar

15 ml/1 tbsp brown sugar • salt • 1.5 kg/3 lb lean pork, cubed

Dry roast the spices in a pan until lightly coloured then grind them together with the onion, garlic and ginger, paprika, chillies and soaking vinegar. Blend in 30 ml/2 tbsp of the oil, the cider vinegar, sugar. Add the pork, stir well then cover and marinate overnight in the refrigerator.

Heat the remaining oil and fry the meat over medium heat until browned. Pour in the marinade and stir for 5 minutes until the oil appears on the surface. Reduce the heat, cover and simmer gently for 1 hour until the meat is tender. Serve hot with plain rice, vegetables and papadums.

Pork Dopiaza
Serves 4

900 g/2 lb onions 120 ml/4 fl oz/½ cup ghee

30 ml/2 tbsp lemon juice ● 750 g/1½ lb boneless pork, cubed

10 ml/2 tsp ground coriander (cilantro) ● 10 ml/2 tsp ground turmeric

5 ml/1 tsp fenugreek seeds ● 5 ml/1 tsp salt

5 ml/1 tsp chilli powder

Thinly slice half the onions and chop the remainder. Heat the ghee and fry the chopped onions with the lemon juice for about 20 minutes until golden and dry, stirring frequently. Remove from the pan. Fry the pork in the same pan until browned on all sides then remove from the pan. Add the sliced onions, coriander, turmeric, fenugreek, salt and chilli powder to the pan and fry for about 10 minutes until the onions are soft. Return the pork to the pan with a little water, cover and simmer gently for 1 hour until tender. Stir in the fried onions and simmer for 15 minutes until the sauce is thick, stirring continuously.

Mild Pork Curry
Serves 4

60 ml/4 tbsp ghee ● 1 onion, chopped ● 4 cloves garlic, crushed

seeds from 4 cardamom pods ● ½ cinnamon stick ● 4 cloves

5 ml/1 tsp ground ginger ● 2 green chillies, chopped

900 g/2 lb boneless pork, cubed ● juice of 1 lemon

5 ml/1 tsp grated lemon rind ● 5 ml/1 tsp grated orange rind

5 ml/1 tsp salt ● 300 ml/½ pt/1¼ cups water

30 ml/2 tbsp chopped fresh coriander (cilantro)

Heat the ghee and fry the onion and garlic until golden. Grind the cardamom seeds, cinnamon and cloves then add to the pan with the ginger and chillies and fry for 2 minutes, stirring. Add the pork and fry until well browned on all sides. Add the lemon juice, lemon and orange rinds, salt and water, bring to the boil then simmer gently for 1½ hours until the pork is tender. Serve garnished with the coriander.

Pork Chops with Almond Sauce
Serves 4

4 cloves ● 4 cardamom pods ● 5 ml/1 tsp black peppercorns

½ cinnamon stick ● 75 ml/5 tbsp ghee ● 2 onions, sliced

2.5 cm/1 in ginger root, chopped ● 4 pork chops, trimmed

600 ml/1 pt/2½ cups milk ● 5 ml/1 tsp ground turmeric

salt ● 50 g/2 oz/½ cup ground almonds

150 ml/¼ pt/⅔ cup double (heavy) cream

Dry roast the cloves, cardamom, peppercorns and cinnamon until lightly coloured then grind. Heat 60 ml/ 4 tbsp of ghee and fry the onions, ginger and spices for 10 minutes until soft then remove from the pan. Heat the remaining ghee and fry the chops until browned on both sides. Stir the milk, turmeric and salt into the onion mixture, pour over the chops, bring to the boil, cover and simmer for about 45 minutes until the chops are tender and the sauce is thick, basting the chops occasionally during cooking. Mix together the almonds and cream and leave to stand for 30 minutes. Remove the chops from the pan and boil the sauce until reduced to a thick consistency. Stir in the almond cream, return the chops to the pan and simmer for 10 minutes, making sure the chops are covered in the sauce.

Pork Chops with Plums
Serves 4

120 ml/4 fl. oz/½ cup lemon juice ● 3 cloves garlic, crushed

10 ml/2 tsp ground ginger ● 5 ml/1 tsp paprika

5 ml/1 tsp chilli powder ● 4 pork chops, trimmed

450 g/1 lb plums in syrup ● salt

Mix half the lemon juice with the garlic, ginger, paprika and chilli powder. Place the chops in a dish and pour over the marinade. Cover and leave to marinate overnight.

Rub the plums through a sieve and place the purée in a heavy-based pan with the remaining lemon juice and salt. Bring to the boil and simmer until thick. Brush over the chops and grill (broil) for about 20 minutes until cooked through and glazed on both sides, basting with the marinade when you turn the chops.

Poultry

In Indian cookery, chicken is considered more of a delicacy than in the West. It is usually skinned and marinated before cooking. This helps to mature the spices thoroughly. Chicken dishes are a treat because in India they are expensive.

Anniversary Chicken
Serves 6-8

Marinade: 150 ml/¼ pt/⅔ cup natural (plain) yoghurt

45 ml/3 tbsp wine vinegar ● 4 cloves garlic

2.5 cm/1 in ginger root, coarsely chopped ● 1 onion, coarsely chopped

1 small green chilli (optional) ● 5 ml/1 tsp garam masala

5 ml/1 tsp ground roasted cumin ● 5 ml/1 tsp ground turmeric

2.5 ml/½ tsp ground red chilli ● salt

1 medium chicken, skinned and pricked with a fork

30 ml/2 tbsp ghee, melted

Filling: 30 ml/2 tbsp ghee ● 90 ml/6 tbsp desiccated (shredded) coconut

150 g/5 oz Khoya (page 19) ● 150 g/5 oz/1 cup raisins

50 g/2 oz/½ cup blanched almonds, halved ● 50 g/2 oz/½ cup cashew nuts, halved

50 g/2 oz/½ cup walnuts, chopped ● 30 ml/2 tbsp sugar

2.5 ml/½ tsp ground cardamom

2.5 ml/½ tsp saffron soaked in 15 ml/1 tbsp warm milk

1.5 ml/¼ tsp ground cinnamon ● 1.5 ml/¼ tsp ground mace

1.5 ml/¼ tsp ground mixed spice ● 1.5 ml/¼ tsp grated nutmeg

Sauce: 2 cloves garlic, crushed ● 1.5 cm/½ in ginger root, coarsely chopped

1 large onion, chopped ● 45 ml/3 tbsp water ● 60 ml/4 tbsp oil

15 ml/1 tbsp ground coriander (cilantro) ● 5 ml/1 tsp garam masala

2.5 ml/½ tsp ground red chilli ● 2.5 ml/½ tsp ground turmeric

salt ● 15 ml/1 tbsp lemon juice

200 ml/7 fl oz/scant 1 cup water

Blend the marinade ingredients to a smooth paste in a blender or food processor. Rub the marinade over the chicken inside and out and leave to marinate for 2 hours.

Push 2 skewers into the chicken and place it on a baking dish so that the skewers rest on the dish and the chicken is lifted up. Place any remaining marinade in a pan and fry off the liquid over a high heat. Pour it over the chicken and pour over the melted ghee. Roast in a preheated oven at 200°C/400°F/gas mark 6 for about 1 hour, turning and basting regularly.

To make the filling, heat the ghee and fry the coconut until lightly browned. Add the remaining ingredients and cook for 3 minutes. Set aside.

To make the sauce, blend the garlic, ginger, onion and water to a smooth paste in a blender or food processor. Place in a pan and dry off the liquid over a medium heat. Pour in the oil and fry until golden brown. Stir in the ground spices, salt, lemon juice and one-quarter of the water and cook until all the water has been absorbed and the oil appears on the surface. Add the remaining water and bring to the boil. Set aside.

Stuff the roasted chicken with the filling, pour over the sauce and place the chicken back in the oven for a further 10 minutes until tender, basting occasionally. Serve hot with nan.

Barbecued Chicken   Serves 6

5 cm/1 in ginger root, chopped • 10 cloves garlic, crushed

1 onion, chopped • 300 ml/½ pt/1¼ cups natural (plain) yoghurt

1 chicken, skinned and cut into portions • 10 ml/2 tsp chilli powder

5 ml/1 tsp cumin seeds • salt • 150 ml/¼ pt/⅔ cup lemon juice

45 ml/3 tbsp butter, melted • 5 ml/1 tsp garam masala

1 lemon, sliced • 1 onion, sliced into rings

Seasoning: 1 cinnamon stick • 1 bay leaf • 8 cloves

7 black peppercorns • 3 cardamom pods

Grind together the ginger, garlic and onion and blend to a paste with the yoghurt. Rub over the chicken and leave to marinate for 5 hours.

Grind together all the seasoning ingredients then mix with the chilli powder, cumin seeds, salt and lemon juice. Make a few slashes on each chicken piece and smear with the mixture. Leave to stand for 1 hour.

Brush the chicken with melted butter and barbecue or grill (broil) for about 30 minutes until cooked through and browned, turning frequently. Sprinkle with garam masala and serve garnished with lemon slices and onion rings.

Barley-fried Chicken   Serves 6

900 g/2 lb boned chicken, chopped • 100 g/4 oz/1 cup oats, ground

50 g/2 oz/½ cup barley, ground • 3 onions, minced

5 ml/1 tsp grated ginger root • 1 clove garlic, minced

5 ml/1 tsp garam masala • 5 ml/1 tsp chopped green chillies

1 egg • 1 egg yolk • 15 ml/1 tbsp lemon juice

30 ml/2 tbsp chopped fresh mint • 15 ml/1 tbsp sesame seeds

oil for deep-frying

Mix together all the ingredients except the oil and knead to a pliable mixture. Divide into 16 and shape into flat patties about 2.5 cm/1 in thick. Heat the oil to almost smoking point then lower the heat for 1 minute. Fry a few patties at a time for about 6 minutes then turn them over and fry for a further 5-6 minutes until browned. Drain on kitchen paper and serve at once.

Chicken Baffatte
Serves 4

7 dried red chillies ● 2.5 cm/1 in ginger root ● 5 cloves garlic

5 ml/1 tsp ground coriander (cilantro) ● 5 ml/1 tsp cumin seeds

15 ml/1 tbsp wine vinegar ● 45 ml/3 tbsp ghee

450 g/1 lb onions, sliced ● 1 chicken, skinned and cut into portions

300 ml/½ pt/1¼ cups water ● 450 g/1 lb potatoes, quartered

450 g/1 lb small onions ● 15 ml/1 tbsp tamarind concentrate

salt ● 300 ml/½ pt/1¼ cups thick coconut milk

Blend the chillis, ginger, garlic, coriander and cumin seeds to a paste with the wine vinegar in a blender or food processor. Heat the ghee and fry the onions until browned. Add the ground spices and fry for 4 minutes. Add the chicken and fry until lightly browned. Add the water, using enough almost to cover the chicken. Bring to the boil and simmer for 30 minutes. Add the potatoes and cook for 15 minutes. Add the small onions and cook for 15 minutes. Add the tamarind and salt and cook for 10 minutes. Add the coconut milk and continue to cook until the chicken is tender and the sauce has thickened.

Chicken Bhoona
Serves 4

4 boneless chicken breasts, skinned and cut into strips

90 ml/6 tbsp natural (plain) yoghurt ● juice of 1 lemon

3 cloves garlic, crushed ● 5 ml/1 tsp ground turmeric

15 ml/1 tbsp paprika ● seeds from 3 cardamom pods

salt ● 60 ml/4 tbsp ghee ● 2.5 ml/½ tsp garam masala

30 ml/2 tbsp chopped fresh coriander (cilantro)

Place the chicken strips in a bowl and mix in the yoghurt, lemon juice, garlic, turmeric, paprika, cardamom seeds and salt. Melt half the ghee and stir into the marinade. Cover and refrigerate for 2 hours.

Heat the remaining ghee and fry the chicken and marinade for 10 minutes, stirring. Add the garam masala and coriander and fry for a further 10 minutes until the chicken is tender.

Coriander Chicken
Serves 4

5 cloves garlic, chopped ● 2.5 cm/1 in ginger root, chopped

1 chicken, skinned and cut into 8 ● 60 ml/4 tbsp ghee

50 g/2 oz/½ cup flaked almonds ● 50 g/2 oz/½ cup raisins

225 g/8 oz Khoya (page 19) ● 600 ml/1 pt/2½ cups natural (plain) yoghurt

5 ml/1 tsp ground turmeric ● salt ● 10 green chillies, slit

45 ml/3 tbsp chopped fresh coriander (cilantro)

600 ml/1 pt/2½ cups coconut milk

Grind the garlic and ginger to a paste then rub it into the chicken pieces. Heat the ghee and fry the chicken until browned then remove from the pan. Add the almonds and raisins to the pan and fry for 1 minute. Blend the khoya, yoghurt, turmeric and salt and add it to the pan with the chicken. Simmer until only a little liquid is left. Add the chillies and simmer until dry. Add the coriander and coconut milk and simmer gently until the chicken is tender and the ghee appears on the surface.

Chicken Chilli Fry
Serves 4

1 chicken, skinned and cut into 4 ● 2.5 cm/1 in ginger root

5 cloves garlic ● 5 green chillies ● ½ lemon

salt and pepper ● 4 eggs, beaten

100 g/4 oz/1 cup breadcrumbs ● ghee or oil for deep-frying

Place the chicken in a heavy-based pan, just cover with water, bring to the boil, cover and simmer gently for about 45 minutes until tender. Drain.

Grind together the ginger, garlic and chillies. Rub the chicken with the lemon then coat with the ground paste and season with salt and pepper. Dip in egg then breadcrumbs, then egg and breadcrumbs again. Fry in hot ghee or oil until crisp and browned. Serve at once.

Chicken Cutlets
Serves 4-6

225 g/8 oz canned tomatoes ● 75 ml/5 tbsp lemon juice

45 ml/3 tbsp wine vinegar ● 45 ml/3 tbsp chopped fresh coriander (cilantro)

6 cloves garlic, chopped ● 5 cm/2 in ginger root, chopped

1 onion, chopped ● 1 small green chilli, chopped

10 ml/2 tsp garam masala ● 5 ml/1 tsp ajwain

5 ml/1 tsp ground roasted cumin ● 5 ml/1 tsp ground turmeric

2.5 ml/½ tsp ground red chilli ● salt

1.25 kg/3 lb chicken pieces, skinned and pricked with a fork

2 eggs, beaten ● 60 ml/4 tbsp oil

Blend the tomatoes, lemon juice, wine vinegar, coriander, garlic, ginger, onion and chilli to a smooth paste in a blender or food processor. Add the ground spices and salt and mix thoroughly. Rub the marinade over the chicken pieces and leave to marinate overnight.

Place the chicken pieces and marinade in a heavy-based pan and cook over a medium heat for 25 minutes until tender. Increase the heat to dry off all the liquid.

Heat the oil in a frying pan (skillet). Dip the cooked chicken pieces into the eggs then fry over a medium heat until golden brown, adding a little more oil if necessary. Serve hot with chutney at tea or as a meal with vegetable pulao and dal.

Chicken Curry
Serves 4-6

75 ml/5 tbsp oil or ghee • 2 onions, thinly sliced

5 cloves garlic, chopped • 2.5 cm/1 in ginger root, chopped

1.5 cm/½ in cinnamon stick • 4 cloves • 4 black peppercorns

2 bay leaves • 1 black cardamom pod

12 chicken pieces, skinned • 15 ml/1 tbsp ground aniseeds

15 ml/1 tbsp ground almond • 15 ml/1 tbsp ground coriander (cilantro)

5 ml/1 tsp ground roasted cumin • 2.5 ml/½ tsp ground red chilli

2.5 ml/½ tsp ground turmeric • 400 g/14 oz canned tomatoes, chopped

salt • 150 ml/¼ pt/⅔ cup natural (plain) yoghurt

175 ml/6 fl oz/¾ cup water

Garnish: 2.5 ml/½ tsp garam masala

15 ml/1 tbsp chopped fresh coriander (cilantro)

1 small green chilli, chopped

Heat the oil and fry the onions, garlic, ginger and whole spices over a medium heat until golden brown. Add the chicken and fry until golden brown on all sides. Stir in the ground spices, tomatoes and salt and cook until all the liquid has been absorbed and the oil appears on the surface. Add the yoghurt and cook until all the liquid has been absorbed. Add two-thirds of the water, cover and simmer over a low heat for 20 minutes until the chicken is tender, stirring occasionally. Add the remaining water, increase the heat to medium and cook for a further 2 minutes until the sauce is the consistency you prefer. Sprinkle over the garnish ingredients and serve hot with rice or chapatis, cauliflower, a potato dish and chutney.

Chicken Dhansak
Serves 4

225 g/8 oz/1⅓ cups yellow split peas, soaked

225 g/8 oz/1⅓ cups mixed lentils, soaked

1 chicken, skinned and cut into portions ● 1 potato, diced

1 aubergine (eggplant), diced ● 2 onions, sliced

45 ml/3 tbsp ghee ● 1 bunch fresh fenugreek, finely chopped

1 slice pumpkin, diced ● 3 tomatoes, skinned and diced ● salt

Seasoning: 2.5 ml/½ tsp cumin seeds ● 2.5 ml/½ tsp ground turmeric

2.5 ml/½ tsp fenugreek seeds ● 2.5 ml/½ tsp mustard seeds

2.5 ml/½ tsp black pepper ● 5 ml/1 tsp chilli powder

10 ml/2 tsp ground coriander (cilantro) ● 2-3 mint leaves

2.5 cm/1 in ginger root ● 6 cloves garlic ● 2.5 cm/1 in ginger root

5 green chillies ● 2-3 coriander (cilantro) leaves

15 ml/1 tbsp tamarind concentrate

Drain the split peas and lentils then place in a pan with the chicken, potato, aubergine and 1 onion. Bring to the boil and simmer for about 40 minutes until cooked.

Meanwhile, grind all the seasoning ingredients to a paste. Heat the ghee and fry the remaining onion then add the ground spices, fenugreek, pumpkin, tomatoes and salt. Remove the meat from the first pan then grind the lentil mixture to a paste. Add to the onion mixture with the meat with a little salt and a little more water if necessary. Simmer for 10 minutes then serve hot with rice and shami kebabs.

Chicken Dopiaza
Serves 6

5 onions, sliced ● 5 cloves garlic, sliced

2.5 cm/1 in ginger root, sliced ● 3 green chillies

120 ml/4 fl oz/½ cup oil ● 12 chicken pieces, skinned

15 ml/1 tbsp ground cumin ● 5 ml/1 tsp ground turmeric

1.5 ml/½ tsp ground red chilli ● 2.5 ml/½ tsp black pepper

salt ● 5 ml/1 tsp aniseeds ● 750 ml/1¼ pts/3 cups chicken stock

2.5 ml/½ tsp saffron strands ● 120 ml/4 fl oz/½ cup hot milk

250 ml/8 fl oz/1 cup natural (plain) yoghurt

45 ml/3 tbsp soured (dairy sour) cream

Blend half the onions with the garlic, ginger and chillies to a smooth paste in a blender or food processor. Heat the oil and fry the chicken pieces until browned on all sides then remove from the pan. Add the remaining onions and fry until soft. Add the cumin, turmeric, chilli, pepper, salt and aniseeds and fry for 3 minutes, stirring. Add the puréed mixture and cook for 5 minutes, stirring. Add the chicken and stock, bring to the boil and simmer for 15 minutes. Meanwhile, soak the saffron in the milk for 15 minutes. Blend together the yoghurt and cream then stir in the saffron milk and stir into the pan, cover and simmer for a further 15 minutes until the chicken is tender and the sauce has thickened.

Dry Chicken Curry   Serves 6

90 ml/6 tbsp oil ● 4 onions, chopped

2.5 cm/1 in ginger root, minced ● 4 cloves garlic, chopped

1.5 ml/¼ tsp ground turmeric ● 2.5 ml/½ tsp black pepper

10 ml/2 tsp ground cumin ● 4 tomatoes, skinned and chopped

250 ml/8 fl oz/1 cup natural (plain) yoghurt ● 5 curry leaves

900 g/2 lb chicken pieces, skinned ● 2.5 ml/½ tsp garam masala

10 ml/2 tsp chilli powder

Heat half the oil and fry the onions until golden. Add the ginger and garlic and fry until lightly browned. Add the turmeric, pepper and cumin and fry for 4 minutes, stirring. Add the tomatoes, yoghurt and curry leaves and stir for 1 minute then reduce the heat and simmer gently for 20 minutes, stirring occasionally. Heat the remaining oil and fry the chicken pieces until golden brown on all sides. Pour the onion mixture over the chicken, stir well then cover and simmer for 20-25 minutes until the chicken is cooked through, stirring occasionally. Stir in the garam masala and chilli powder and simmer for a few minutes, uncovered, until the sauce is thick.

Spicy Baked Chicken   Serves 6

6 chicken portions, skinned ● 2.5 cm/1 in ginger root, grated

3 cloves garlic, crushed ● 45 ml/3 tbsp ground coriander (cilantro)

15 ml/1 tbsp cumin seeds, ground

250 ml/8 fl oz/1 cup natural (plain) yoghurt

2.5 ml/½ tsp garam masala ● 2.5 ml/½ tsp chilli powder

2.5 ml/½ tsp mango powder ● 45 ml/3 tbsp oil

Place the chicken in a bowl then rub with the ginger and garlic. Leave to stand for 1 hour.

Dry roast the coriander and cumin seeds for a few seconds then stir into the yoghurt with the garam masala, chilli and mango powders. Stir into the chicken, cover and refrigerate for 24 hours.

Arrange the chicken pieces in a baking dish and pour over any remaining marinade. Brush with a little oil and roast in a preheated oven at 180°C/350°F/gas mark 4 for about 1 hour until the chicken is tender. Pour off the liquid then spoon 60 ml/4 tbsp of stock over the chicken. Transfer to a hot grill and grill (broil) until browned.

Mughlai Chicken
Serves 6

45 ml/3 tbsp oil ● 3 onions, sliced

2.5 cm/1 in ginger root, grated ● 3 cloves garlic, chopped

900 g/2 lb chicken pieces, skinned ● 5 ml/1 tsp ground turmeric

5 dried red chillies ● 5 ml/1 tsp ground cardamom

5 cm/2 in cinnamon stick ● 4 bay leaves

250 ml/8 fl oz/1 cup natural (plain) yoghurt

30 ml/2 tbsp cashew nuts, halved ● 2.5 ml/½ tsp garam masala

15 ml/1 tbsp lemon juice ● 45 ml/3 tbsp chopped fresh coriander (cilantro)

Heat the oil and fry the onions until golden. Stir in the ginger and garlic and fry for 3 minutes. Add the chicken, turmeric, chillies, cardamom, cinnamon and bay leaves and fry until the chicken is lightly browned. Stir in half the yoghurt, cover and simmer for about 30 minutes until the chicken is cooked through. Meanwhile, dry roast the nuts until lightly browned and grind and stir into the remaining yoghurt. Stir into the pan with the garam masala and lemon juice and simmer, uncovered, for 5 minutes until the sauce is thick. Serve garnished with coriander.

Hot Chicken Curry
Serves 4

45 ml/3 tbsp oil ● 5 cardamom pods ● 2 bay leaves

1 cinnamon stick ● 4 cloves ● 2.5 ml/½ tsp black peppercorns

2 onions, sliced ● 4 cloves garlic, chopped

1 cm/½ in ginger root, chopped ● 1 green chilli, chopped

15 ml/1 tbsp ground coriander (cilantro) ● 5 ml/1 tsp ground turmeric

5 ml/1 tsp ground cumin ● pinch of chilli powder

1 medium chicken, skinned and cut into 8 ● salt

450 ml/¾ pt/2 cups water

Heat the oil and fry the cardamom, bay leaves, cinnamon, cloves and peppercorns over a medium heat until slightly darkened. Add the onions, garlic, ginger and chilli and fry until golden brown, stirring occasionally. Stir in the coriander, turmeric, cumin and chilli powder and cook for 2 minutes. Stir in the chicken pieces and salt and make sure they are coated in oil and spices. Add the water, bring to the boil, cover and simmer for 20-30 minutes until the chicken is tender, stirring occasionally. Serve hot with rice, vegetables and coriander relish.

Chicken in Coriander, Mint and Yoghurt
Serves 4-6

4 large cloves garlic, chopped ● 2.5 cm/1 in ginger root, chopped

1 onion, chopped ● 1 kg/2 lb chicken pieces, skinned

120 ml/4 fl oz/½ cup oil ● 5 ml/1 tsp mustard seeds

5 ml/1 tsp cumin seeds ● 5 ml/1 tsp garam masala

5 ml/1 tsp ground coriander (cilantro) ● 2.5 ml/½ tsp ground red chilli

2.5 ml/½ tsp ground roasted cumin ● 2.5 ml/½ tsp ground turmeric

salt ● 450 ml/¾ pt/2 cups natural (plain) yoghurt

100 g/4 oz fresh coriander (cilantro) leaves ● 25 g/1 oz fresh mint leaves

1 small green chilli, chopped ● 45 ml/3 tbsp lemon juice

Blend the garlic, ginger and onion to a smooth paste in a blender or food processor. Rub over the chicken and leave to marinate for 1 hour.

Heat half the oil and fry the marinated chicken pieces over a medium heat for about 30 minutes until light brown. Heat the remaining oil in a separate pan and fry the mustard seeds until they start crackling. Add the cumin seeds and fry until browned. Stir in the ground spices and salt. Blend the yoghurt, coriander, mint and chilli to a paste then stir it into the pan and bring to the boil. Add the fried chicken pieces and cook for 20 minutes until the sauce is the consistency you prefer. Add the lemon juice. Serve hot with rice, dal and a cauliflower-potato dish.

Chicken in Cashew Sauce
Serves 6

1 chicken, skinned ● 45 ml/3 tbsp oil ● 2 onions, chopped

5 cloves garlic, chopped ● 2.5 cm/1 in ginger root, chopped

2 green chillies, chopped ● 45 ml/3 tbsp curry powder

10 ml/2 tsp garam masala ● salt ● 5 ml/1 tsp ground turmeric

5 ml/1 tsp paprika ● 25 g/1 oz/¼ cup cashews, ground

450 ml/¾ pt/2 cups chicken stock ● 45 ml/3 tbsp natural (plain) yoghurt

4 tomatoes, skinned and chopped ● 30 ml/2 tbsp chopped fresh coriander (cilantro)

Cut the chicken into about 12 pieces. Heat the oil and fry the onions, garlic, ginger and chillies over a medium heat until browned. Add the curry powder, garam masala, salt, turmeric, paprika and cashews and cook for 5 minutes, stirring, until the oil appears on the surface. Stir in the stock and simmer for 3 minutes. Stir in the yoghurt, tomatoes and chicken, cover and simmer for 40 minutes until the chicken is tender, stirring occasionally. Garnish with coriander and serve hot with rice, chapatis and vegetables.

Chicken with Cashews and Yoghurt   Serves 4

50 g/2 oz/½ cup cashew nuts • 3 cloves garlic, chopped

2.5 cm/1 in ginger root, chopped • 150 ml/¼ pt/⅔ cup water

5 cm/2 in cinnamon stick, crushed • 2 cloves

seeds from 4 cardamom pods • 50 g/2 oz poppy seeds

10 ml/2 tsp coriander (cilantro) seeds • 5 ml/1 tsp cumin seeds

5 ml/1 tsp salt • 5 ml/1 tsp chilli powder

5 ml/1 tsp saffron strands • 300 ml/½ pt/1¼ cups boiling water

45 ml/3 tbsp ghee • 2 onions, chopped

150 l/¼ pt/⅔ cup natural (plain) yoghurt • 4 chicken breasts, skinned

30 ml/2 tbsp chopped fresh coriander (cilantro)

30 ml/2 tbsp chopped fresh mint • 45 ml/3 tbsp lemon juice

Blend the nuts, garlic, ginger and water to a smooth paste in a blender or food processor. Grind the cinnamon, cloves, cardamom, poppy, coriander and cumin seeds to a powder. Mix the paste and powder with the salt and chilli powder. Soak the saffron in the boiling water for 15 minutes. Heat the ghee and fry the onions until golden. Add the spice mixture and yoghurt and fry until the ghee appears on the surface. Add the saffron water and stir well. Add the chicken, bring to the boil, then lower the heat, cover and simmer gently for 45 minutes, stirring occasionally. Add the coriander and mint and sprinkle with the lemon juice. Cover and simmer for a further 15 minutes until the chicken is tender and the sauce has thickened.

Chicken in Coconut Milk   Serves 4

60 ml/4 tbsp oil • 8 chicken pieces, skinned

2 onions, chopped • 5 cloves garlic, chopped

5 cm/2 in ginger root, chopped • 4 dried red chillies

4 cloves • 2.5 cm/1 in cinnamon stick • 5 ml/1 tsp fenugreek seeds

10 ml/2 tsp coriander (cilantro) seeds • 10 ml/2 tsp cumin seeds

75 ml/5 tbsp lemon juice • 600 ml/1 pt/2½ cups coconut milk

salt • 2-3 curry leaves • 15 ml/1 tsp sesame seeds, toasted

Heat the ghee and fry the chicken until golden brown then remove from the pan. Blend the onions, garlic, ginger, chillies, cloves, cinnamon, fenugreek, coriander, cumin seeds and lemon juice to a smooth paste in a blender or food processor, adding a little water if necessary. Add this mixture to the pan and fry gently for 5 minutes until lightly coloured, stirring continuously. Add the coconut milk and salt and return the chicken to the pan. Bring to the boil, cover and simmer gently until the chicken is tender and the sauce is thick. Serve garnished with curry leaves and sesame seeds.

Creamed Chicken
Serves 6

75 ml/5 tbsp oil or ghee ● 3 onions, chopped

4 large cloves garlic, crushed ● 4 cm/1½ in ginger root, chopped

4 cloves ● 4 black peppercorns ● 2 bay leaves

2.5 cm/1 in cinnamon stick ● 1 black cardamom pod

1.25 kg/3 lb chicken, skinned and cut into 16

5 ml/1 tsp ground roasted cumin ● 2.5 ml/½ tsp ground red chilli

2.5 ml/½ tsp ground turmeric ● 1.5 ml/¼ tsp grated nutmeg

1.5 ml/¼ tsp ground mace ● salt ● 300 ml/½ pt/1¼ cups milk

150 g/5 oz/1 cup raisins ● 75 g/3 oz/¾ cup blanched almonds, halved

75 g/3 oz/¾ cup cashew nuts, halved ● 25 g/1 oz/¼ cup pistachios, halved

1.5 ml/¼ tsp ground cardamom ● 300 ml/½ pt/1¼ cups single (light) cream

Garnish: 2.5 ml/½ tsp garam masala

15 ml/1 tbsp chopped fresh coriander (cilantro)

1 small green chilli, chopped

Heat the oil or ghee in a heavy-based pan and fry the onions, garlic, ginger and whole spices over a medium heat until light brown. Add the chicken and fry for 10 minutes until golden brown on all sides. Stir in the ground spices, salt and milk, bring to the boil, cover and simmer gently for 15 minutes, stirring occasionally. Remove the lid and add the nuts, raisins and cardamom. Cook over a medium heat until the chicken is tender, all the liquid has been absorbed and the ghee appears on the surface. Reduce the heat to low, stir in the cream and simmer gently for 2 minutes. Sprinkle over the garnish ingredients and serve hot with rice and aubergine.

Dill Chicken
Serves 4

30 ml/2 tbsp oil ● 4 cardamom pods ● 1 cinnamon stick

2 onions, chopped ● 5 cloves garlic, crushed

2.5 cm/1 in ginger root, chopped ● 2 tomatoes, skinned and chopped

45 ml/3 tbsp chopped fresh dill (dill weed) ● pinch of ground turmeric

5 ml/1 tsp ground roasted cumin ● 5 ml/1 tsp chilli powder

salt and pepper ● pinch of garam masala

1 chicken, cut into portions ● 450 ml/¾ pt/2 cups water

Heat the oil and fry the cardamom and cinnamon for 1 minute. Add the onions and fry until lightly browned. Add the garlic and ginger and fry for 2 minutes. Add the tomatoes and dill and fry until the oil appears on the surface. Add the spices, salt and pepper and fry for a few seconds. Add the chicken and fry until the moisture from the chicken evaporates. Add the water, bring to the boil, cover and simmer gently for about 40 minutes until the chicken is tender and the sauce has thickened.

Chicken Dhansak
Serves 4-6

800 g/1 lb boned chicken, skinned and cut into 5 cm/2 in pieces

200 g/7 oz mixed dals ● 2.5 ml/½ tsp ground turmeric ● salt

200 g/7 oz mixed vegetables (choose 4 types from pumpkin, aubergine (eggplant), potato, marrow (squash)), cut into chunks

45 ml/3 tbsp chopped fresh fenugreek leaves ● 45 ml/3 tbsp chopped fresh mint

45 ml/3 tbsp chopped fresh coriander (cilantro)

30 ml/2 tbsp desiccated (shredded) coconut ● 5 large cloves garlic, crushed

2.5 cm/1 in ginger root ● 2 onions, chopped

1.2 1/2 pts/5 cups water ● 90 ml/6 tbsp ghee or oil

5 ml/1 tsp mustard seeds ● 5 ml/1 tsp cumin seeds ● 5 ml/1 tsp garam masala

5 ml/1 tsp ground coriander (cilantro) ● 5 ml/1 tsp ground roasted cumin

5 ml/1 tsp ground red chilli ● 5 ml/1 tsp Sambar Powder (page 15)

2.5 ml/½ tsp ground turmeric ● 60 ml/4 tbsp lemon juice

150 ml/¼ pt/⅔ cup water

Garnish: 2.5 ml/½ tsp garam masala ● 1 small green chilli, chopped

Place the chicken, dal, turmeric, vegetables, fenugreek, mint, coriander, coconut, garlic, ginger, 1 onion and the water in a pan over a medium heat. Bring to the boil, skim off any scum, reduce the heat, cover and simmer for 40 minutes until the chicken is tender. Remove the chicken and cook the lentil mixture for a further 20 minutes until tender. Leave to cool then blend to a smooth paste.

Meanwhile, heat the ghee or oil and fry the mustard seeds until they start crackling. Add the cumin seeds and fry until browned. Add the remaining onion and fry until golden brown. Add the cooked chicken pieces and fry for 5 minutes until light brown. Stir in the ground spices and cook for 2 minutes. Stir in the lentil paste, lemon juice and water, bring to the boil then simmer gently for 10 minutes. Sprinkle over the garnish ingredients and serve hot with rice, puris and raita.

Fried Spiced Chicken
Serves 4

225 g/8 oz chopped fresh coriander (cilantro) ● 1 onion, chopped

5 dried red chillies ● 1 tomato, skinned ● 5 ml/1 tsp peppercorns

5 ml/1 tsp cumin seeds ● 2.5 ml/½ tsp ground turmeric

1 chicken, skinned and cut into 4 ● 45 ml/3 tbsp ghee

Grind all the seasoning ingredients to a paste. Make several slashes on either side of the chicken and rub in the paste. Marinate for 3 hours.

Heat the ghee and fry the chicken over a medium heat for about 1 hour until tender and browned.

Cocktail Chicken Drumsticks
Serves 6-8

1.5 kg/3 lb chicken drumsticks, skinned ● juice of 1 lemon

4 cloves garlic, chopped ● 1 cm/½ in ginger root, chopped

pinch of pepper ● 2.5 ml/½ tsp garam masala

1.5 ml/¼ tsp ground red chilli ● 2.5 ml/½ tsp paprika

2.5 ml/½ tsp ground coriander (cilantro) ● 2.5 ml/½ tsp ground cumin

30 ml/2 tbsp natural (plain) yoghurt ● 15 ml/1 tbsp oil

Squeeze the lemon juice over the drumsticks and set aside. Purée the remaining ingredients to a fine paste, stir into the chicken, cover and refrigerate for 4 hours. Place the drumsticks on a flat baking tray and brush with the marinade. Bake in a preheated oven at 180°C/250°F/gas mark 4 for about 25 minutes until cooked through and browned. Serve hot with chutney.

Spiced Grill Chicken
Serves 4-6

225 g/8 oz canned tomatoes ● 45 ml/3 tbsp wine vinegar

5 large cloves garlic ● 2 dried figs

2.5 cm/1 in ginger root, coarsely chopped ● 1 small green chilli

10 ml/2 tsp garam masala ● 5 ml/1 tsp ground coriander (cilantro)

5 ml/1 tsp ground roasted cumin ● 2.5 ml/½ tsp black pepper

2.5 ml/½ tsp ground red chilli ● 2.5 ml/½ tsp ground turmeric

salt ● 6 chicken pieces, skinned and pricked with a fork

30 ml/2 tsp ghee, melted

Garnish: 225 g/8 oz small potatoes ● oil for deep-frying

2.5 ml/½ tsp garam masala ● 2.5 ml/½ tsp ground roasted cumin

Blend the tomatoes, wine vinegar, garlic, figs, ginger, chilli, ground spices and salt to a smooth paste in a blender or food processor. Rub the paste into the chicken pieces and leave to marinate for 2 hours.

Lift the chicken from the marinade, brush with ghee and place in a flameproof dish. Grill (broil) under a hot grill for 10 minutes. Place the remaining marinade in a pan and reduce over a medium heat. Turn over the chicken pieces, baste evenly with half the marinade, brush with ghee and return to the grill for a further 10 minutes. Turn them over again, baste with the remaining marinade and grill (broil) under a medium-low grill and cook until golden brown and tender, turning and basting as they cook.

Meanwhile, boil the potatoes in their jackets then peel and deep-fry them in hot oil until golden brown.

Sprinkle the garnish ingredients over the chicken and serve hot with the sautéed potatoes, a vegetable pulao, nan or chapatis, raita and chick peas in sauce.

Herbed Chicken
Serves 4

45 ml/3 tbsp oil ● 5 curry leaves ● 1 green chilli

2.5 cm /1 in ginger root, chopped ● 5 cloves garlic, crushed

3 onions, chopped ● 2 tomatoes, skinned and chopped

45 ml/3 tbsp chopped fresh coriander (cilantro)

30 ml/2 tbsp tomato purée (paste) ● 5 ml/1 tsp chopped fresh basil

5 ml/1 tsp oregano ● salt and pepper

1 chicken, skinned and cut into portions ● 2 potatoes, sliced

100 g/4 oz peas

Heat the oil and fry the curry and chilli for 1 minute. Add the ginger and garlic and cook for 2 minutes, stirring. Add the onions and fry until golden. Add the tomatoes, coriander, tomato purée, basil, oregano, salt and pepper and fry until the oil appears on the surface. Add the chicken, potatoes and peas and enough water almost to cover the chicken. Cover and simmer gently for about 40 minutes until the chicken is tender and the sauce has thickened.

Hyderabad-style Chicken
Serves 6

1 onion, chopped ● 5 cloves garlic, chopped

25 g/1 oz/¼ cup blanched almonds ● 2.5 cm/1 in ginger root, chopped

2 dried red chillies, soaked ● 45 ml/2 tbsp water

250 ml/8 fl oz/1 cup natural (plain) yoghurt

45 ml/3 tbsp soured (dairy sour) cream ● 45 ml/3 tbsp oil

1 cinnamon stick ● 8 cardamom pods ● 2.5 ml/½ tsp black peppercorns

10 cloves ● 5 bay leaves ● 5 ml/1 tsp paprika

5 ml/1 tsp ground turmeric ● salt ● 1 chicken, skinned

Blend the onion, garlic, almonds, ginger, chillies and water to a smooth paste in a blender or food processor. Mix together the yoghurt and soured cream. Heat the oil in a flameproof, ovenproof pan and fry the spices over a medium heat for about 5 minutes until they darken slightly. Add the chicken and fry until browned on all sides. Stir in the yoghurt mixture, cover tightly and cook in a preheated oven at 180°C/350°F/gas mark 4 for 30 minutes. Turn the chicken over and cook for a further 30 minutes. Remove the lid and cook for 5-10 minutes until cooked through and browned. Serve the chicken with the sauce.

Koh-i-noor Chicken
Serves 6

1.5 kg/3 lb chicken portions, skinned ● 3 green chillies

8 cloves garlic ● 2.5 cm/1 in ginger root, chopped

5 ml/1 tsp ground turmeric ● 5 ml/1 tsp garam masala ● salt

1.5 ml/¼ tsp cayenne pepper ● 250 ml/8 fl oz/1 cup natural (plain) yoghurt

12 cloves ● 10 black peppercorns ● 1 cinnamon stick

seeds from 8 cardamom pods ● 5 ml/1 tsp cumin seeds

10 ml/2 tsp coriander (cilantro) seeds ● 25 g/1 oz/¼ cup blanched almonds

120 ml/4 fl oz/½ cup oil ● 3 onions, sliced ● 250 ml/8 fl oz/1 cup water

3 tomatoes, skinned and chopped ● 30 ml/2 tbsp chopped fresh coriander (cilantro)

**Prick the chicken pieces with a fork.
Blend the chillies, garlic and half the
ginger to a paste then rub over the
chicken with turmeric, garam masala,
salt and cayenne. Coat the chicken
with yoghurt and marinate for 2 hours.
Dry roast the whole spices and
almonds. Heat the oil and fry the
onions until golden then remove from**
the pan and grind with the roasted
spices and half the water. Reheat the
oil and fry the chicken pieces until
browned. Add the onion paste,
tomatoes and remaining water, bring
to the boil, cover and simmer gently
for about 30 minutes until the chicken
is tender and the gravy has thickened.
Serve garnished with coriander.

Chicken Korma
Serves 6

1 large chicken ● 5 ml/1 tsp ground turmeric ● salt

45 ml/3 tbsp natural (plain) yoghurt ● 250 ml/8 fl oz/1 cup water

2 onions, chopped ● 8 cloves garlic, chopped

2.5 cm/1 in ginger root, chopped ● 2 dried red chillies

20 ml/4 tsp coriander (cilantro) seeds ● 10 ml/2 tsp cumin seeds

50 g/2 oz grated (shredded) coconut ● 5 cloves

2.5 ml/½ tsp black peppercorns ● seeds from 4 cardamom pods

1 cinnamon stick, broken ● 1.5 ml/¼ tsp grated nutmeg

2.5 ml/½ tsp mustard seeds ● 2.5 ml/½ tsp fenugreek seeds ● 2 bay leaves

45 ml/3 tbsp oil ● 30 ml/2 tbsp chopped fresh coriander (cilantro)

**Remove the skin and fat from the chic-
ken and cut into about 12 pieces. Rub
in the turmeric, salt and yoghurt and
leave to marinate for 1 hour.
Purée the water with all the remaining ingredients except the oil and
fresh coriander. Heat the oil and fry
the purée over a medium heat for 10**
minutes until the oil appears on the
surface. Stir in the chicken with its
marinade and bring to the boil. Reduce
the heat, cover and simmer for 45
minutes until the chicken is tender.
Garnish with coriander and serve hot
with rice.

Spicy Kerala Chicken
Serves 6

1 chicken, cut into 12 ● 10 ml/2 tsp ground turmeric

salt ● 150 ml/¼ pt/⅔ cup natural (plain) yoghurt

225 g/8 oz/2 cups grated (shredded) coconut ● 250 ml/8 fl oz/1 cup coconut milk

45 ml/3 tbsp oil ● 10 cloves garlic, crushed

2.5 cm/1 in ginger root, chopped ● 2.5 ml/½ tsp black peppercorns

5 ml/1 tsp aniseeds ● 1 cinnamon stick ● 10 cloves

5 ml/1 tsp coriander (cilantro) seeds ● 10 ml/2 tsp cumin seeds

1 onion, chopped ● 5 dried red chillies, soaked in hot water

2 tomatoes, skinned and chopped ● 750 ml/1¼ pts/3 cups water

Place the chicken in a bowl and rub in the turmeric, salt and yoghurt. Leave to marinate. Soak the coconut in the coconut milk. Heat 15 ml/1 tbsp of oil and fry the garlic, ginger, peppercorns, aniseeds, cinnamon, cloves, coriander and cumin for 1 minute. Grind with 45 ml/3 tbsp of the coconut mixture.

Heat the remaining oil and fry the onion until lightly browned. Add the puréed mixture, chillies and tomatoes and fry for 5 minutes, stirring. Add the remaining coconut mixture, cover and bring to the boil. Gradually stir in the water, cover and simmer for 30 minutes until the chicken is tender.

Chicken Kadukus
Serves 4-6

1 small chicken, skinned ● 900 ml/1½ pts/3¾ cups water

90 ml/6 tbsp oil or ghee ● 10 ml/2 tsp ground anise

5 ml/1 tsp cumin seeds ● 4 cloves garlic, crushed

2.5 cm/1 in ginger root, finely chopped ● 2 onions, finely chopped

5 ml/1 tsp garam masala ● 5 ml/1 tsp ground coriander (cilantro)

5 ml/1 tsp ground roasted cumin ● 2.5 ml/½ tsp ground turmeric

salt ● 400 g/14 oz canned tomatoes, chopped

45 ml/3 tbsp wine vinegar ● 100 ml/3½ fl oz/6½ tbsp coconut milk

Garnish: 2.5 ml/½ tsp garam masala

15 ml/1 tbsp chopped fresh coriander (cilantro)

1 small green chilli, chopped

Place the chicken and water in a large pan and bring to the boil. Cover, reduce the heat to medium-low and cook for 30-40 minutes until tender. Remove the chicken from the stock, take the meat off the bones and shred the meat.

Meanwhile, heat the oil in a heavy-based pan and fry the anise and cumin seeds until browned. Add the garlic, ginger and onion and fry until golden brown. Stir in the shredded chicken and fry for 5 minutes until lightly browned. Stir in the ground spices, salt and tomatoes and cook until all the liquid has been absorbed and the oil appears on the surface. Pour in the coconut milk and cook until all the liquid has been absorbed. Pour in the stock, bring to the boil, reduce the heat to medium-low and cook for a further 5 minutes. Sprinkle with the garnish ingredients and serve hot with puris or paratha, raita, dal, rice and a cauliflower dish.

Chicken Khobani
Serves 4

30 ml/2 tbsp ghee ● 2 onions, sliced

3 cloves garlic, chopped ● 2.5 cm/1 in ginger root, chopped

4 green chillies, slit ● 1 chicken, skinned and cut into portions

2 tomatoes, skinned and chopped ● 1 cinnamon stick

4 cardamom pods ● salt ● 250 ml/8 fl oz/1 cup hot water

100 g/4 oz dried apricot halves ● 2.5 ml/½ tsp saffron strands

45 ml/3 tbsp hot milk

Heat the ghee and fry the onions, garlic, ginger and chillies until lightly browned. Add the chicken and fry until browned. Add the tomatoes, cinnamon, cardamom and salt and fry over a gentle heat for about 30 minutes until the chicken is almost cooked. Add the apricots. Crush the saffron in the milk and add to the pan. Continue cook for about 5 minutes until the chicken is tender and the apricots are just soft.

Chicken Kebabs
Serves 6

4 chicken breasts ● juice of 1 lemon ● salt

250 ml/8 fl oz/1 cup natural (plain) yoghurt ● 45 ml/3 tbsp oil

4 cloves garlic, crushed ● 2.5 cm/1 in ginger root, grated

5 ml/1 tsp ground cumin ● 1.5 ml/¼ tsp chilli powder

2.5 ml/½ tsp garam masala ● 5 ml/1 tsp paprika

Remove and discard the fat, skin and bones from the chicken and cut into 2.5 cm/1 in cubes. Sprinkle with the lemon juice and salt and leave to marinate for 30 minutes.

Mix the yoghurt with half the oil. Blend in the garlic, ginger, cumin, chilli powder, garam masala and paprika. Pour over the chicken and marinate in the refrigerator overnight.

Thread the chicken pieces on to metal skewers and bake in a pre-heated oven at 240°C/475°F/gas mark 9 for 15 minutes. Baste with the marinade and remaining oil, turn over and bake for a further 15 minutes.

Chicken in Lemon and Yoghurt
Serves 6

1 chicken, skinned ● salt ● 10 ml/2 tsp paprika

juice of 3 lemons ● 5 ml/1 tsp saffron strands ● 30 ml/2 tbsp hot water

20 ml/4 tsp coriander (cilantro) seeds ● 10 ml/2 tsp cumin seeds

5 ml/1 tsp ground turmeric ● 1.5 ml/¼ tsp chilli powder

30 ml/2 tbsp garam masala ● 450 ml/¾ pt/2 cups natural (plain) yoghurt

30 ml/2 tbsp oil ● 5 cloves garlic

2.5 cm/1 in ginger root, chopped ● 1 green chilli, chopped

Cut slits all over the chicken. Rub with salt and paprika and squeeze over the lemon juice. Leave to marinate for 30 minutes. Soak the saffron strands in hot water for 15 minutes.

Dry roast the coriander and cumin seeds, turmeric, chilli powder and garam masala for 1 minute. Purée the yoghurt, oil, garlic, ginger, chilli and saffron water. Spread this paste over the chicken, cover with foil and leave to marinate in the fridge overnight.

Place the chicken in a greased baking tray and pour over the marinade. Roast in a preheated oven at 200°C/400°F/gas mark 6 for 15 minutes. Reduce the heat to 180°C/350°F/gas mark 4 and cook for a further 30 minutes until the chicken is dark red and cooked through.

Moghulai Chicken
Serves 6

1 chicken, skinned and cut into portions ● 5 cm/2 in ginger root, chopped

10 cloves garlic, chopped ● 2.5 ml/½ tsp saffron strands

30 ml/2 tbsp hot milk ● 15 ml/1 tbsp cream

600 ml/1 pt/2½ cups natural (plain) yoghurt

8 dried red chillies ● 15 ml/1 tbsp water

100 g/4 oz/1 cup blanched almonds ● 100 g/4 oz/½ cup ghee

2 onions, sliced ● 2 cardamom pods ● 600 ml/1 pt/2½ cups water

Prick the chicken flesh with a fork. Grind together the ginger and garlic then rub over the chicken. Grind the saffron, milk and cream then mix with the yoghurt, add the chicken and leave to marinate for 1 hour.

Grind the chillies and water to a paste. Grind the almonds to a paste. Heat the ghee and fry the onions until soft but not browned. Add the chicken and fry until lightly browned. Add the yoghurt, chillies, cardamom, water, nuts and salt and simmer for about 1 hour until the chicken is tender and the ghee appears on the surface, stirring occasionally. Serve hot with rice and okra.

Maimoos
Serves 6

6 cloves garlic ● 2.5 cm/1 in ginger root ● 4 green chillies

1 chicken, skinned and cut into 8 ● 45 ml/3 tbsp ghee

3 onions, sliced ● 8 cardamom pods ● 8 cloves

4 cinnamon sticks ● 45 ml/3 tbsp chilli powder

30 ml/2 tbsp poppy seeds ● 25 g/1 oz/¼ cup blanched almonds

25 g/1 oz/¼ cup pistachios ● 900 g/2 lb tomatoes, skinned and chopped

225 g/8 oz Khoya (page 19), cubed ● 150 ml/¼ pt/⅔ cup milk

1.5 ml/¼ tsp saffron strands ● 30 ml/2 tbsp chopped fresh mint

30 ml/2 tbsp chopped fresh coriander (cilantro)

Grind the garlic, ginger and 2 chillies to a paste then rub it over the chicken. Heat half the ghee and fry the onions until browned and crisp. Remove and crush. Heat the remaining ghee and fry 4 cardamom pods, 4 cloves and 2 cinnamon sticks until lightly coloured. Add the chicken and fry for 2 minutes. Add the chilli powder. Grind the poppy seeds, almonds and pistachios to a paste, add to the pan and fry until browned. Add the chicken and fry for 5 minutes. Add the tomatoes and simmer for 15 minutes. Blend the khoya with the milk and saffron. Grind the remaining cardamom pods, cloves and cinnamon and add to the milk with the mint and coriander and remaining chillies. Add to the pan, cover tightly and simmer gently for about 25 minutes until the chicken is tender and the sauce has thickened.

Mushroom Chicken
Serves 4

1 chicken, skinned and cut into portions

50 g/2 oz/½ cup plain (all-purpose) flour

45 ml/3 tbsp butter ● 4 onions, sliced

3 cloves garlic, crushed ● 2 green (bell) peppers, chopped

4 tomatoes, skinned and chopped ● 30 ml/2 tbsp tomato purée (paste)

5 ml/1 tsp chopped fresh oregano ● 225 g/8 oz mushrooms, halved

Dust the chicken with the flour. Heat the butter and fry the chicken until lightly browned then remove from the pan. Add the onions and garlic and fry until the onions are soft. Add the remaining ingredients except the chicken and mushrooms. Cook for 7-8 minutes, stirring occasionally. Add the chicken, cover and simmer gently for about 30 minutes until the chicken is tender. Add the mushrooms, cover and simmer for 10 minutes until the chicken is cooked through and very tender.

Chicken Masala
Serves 6

1 chicken, skinned • pinch of saffron strands

15 ml/1 tbsp hot milk • 15 ml/1 tbsp ground coriander (cilantro)

5 ml/1 tsp aniseeds • 5 ml/1 tsp cumin seeds

4 dried red chillies • 4 cardamom pods • 4 cloves

2.5 ml/½ tsp black peppercorns • 100 g/4 oz/⅔ cup yellow split peas

90 ml/4 tbsp ghee • 45 ml/3 tbsp desiccated (shredded) coconut

1 onion, thinly sliced • 300 ml/½ pt/1¼ cups natural (plain) yoghurt

1.2 1/2 pts/5 cups water • salt

25 g/1 oz/¼ cup blanched almonds, chopped

Joint the chicken. Soak the saffron in the hot milk. Dry roast all the spices and split peas until lightly coloured then grind them together. Heat half the ghee and brown the chicken on all sides then remove from the pan. Heat the remaining ghee and fry the onion until browned. Add the coconut and ground spices and fry for 5 minutes. Return the chicken to the pan. Blend together the yoghurt and water, pour over the chicken and season with salt. Cover tightly and cook until the chicken is tender and the liquid has dried up. Pour in the saffron milk and stir well. Garnish with the almonds and serve hot with rice and papadums.

Gajjar Chicken Masala
Serves 4

60 ml/4 tbsp ghee • 1 chicken, quartered • 2 onions, sliced

2.5 cm/1 in ginger root • 5 cloves garlic

15 ml/1 tbsp ground coriander (cilantro) • 10 ml/2 tsp ground turmeric

10 ml/2 tsp chilli powder • 10 ml/2 tsp garam masala

150 ml/¼ pt/⅔ cup wine vinegar • 2 cardamom pods

1 cinnamon stick • 1 bay leaf • 450 g/1 lb carrots, grated

salt • 300 ml/½ pt/1¼ cups water

4 hard-boiled (hard-cooked) eggs, halved

15 ml/1 tbsp chopped fresh coriander (cilantro)

Heat half the ghee and fry the chicken until well browned then remove from the pan. Add the onions to the pan and fry until soft. Grind the ginger, garlic, coriander, turmeric, chilli powder, garam masala and wine vinegar together then add to the pan and fry for 5 minutes. Add the cardamom, cinnamon, bay leaf and carrots and simmer for 5 minutes. Add the chicken, salt and water and simmer for about 30 minutes until the chicken is tender. Meanwhile, heat the remaining ghee and fry the hard-boiled egg halves until nicely browned. Garnish with the eggs and coriander and serve hot with rice and raita.

Chicken Masala
Serves 6

1 chicken, skinned ● salt ● 5 ml/1 tsp paprika

120 ml/4 fl oz/½ cup water ● 1 onion, chopped

6 cloves garlic, chopped ● 2.5 cm/1 in ginger root, chopped

5 ml/1 tsp ground turmeric ● 30 ml/2 tbsp garam masala

15 ml/1 tbsp ground coriander (cilantro) ● 10 ml/2 tsp ground cumin

2.5 ml/½ tsp chilli powder ● 45 ml/3 tbsp oil

450 ml/ pt/2 cups chicken stock ● 45 ml/3 tbsp soured (dairy sour) cream

120 ml/4 fl oz/½ cup natural (plain) yoghurt

Rub salt and paprika all over the chicken. Blend the water, onion, garlic, ginger, turmeric, garam masala, coriander, cumin and chilli powder to a smooth paste in a blender or food processor. Heat the oil and fry the paste for 10 minutes, stirring. Add the stock and cook for 5 minutes. Mix the soured cream and yoghurt then stir it into the pan, bring to the boil then remove from the heat. Rub the mixture all over the chicken, inside and out. Cover with foil and bake in a preheated oven at 200°C/400°F/gas mark 6 for 20 minutes. Reduce the oven temperature to 180°C/350°F/gas mark 4, baste the chicken with the juices and bake for a further 15 minutes. Remove the foil and bake for a further 10 minutes until the chicken is cooked through and browned.

Stuffed Chicken Masala
Serves 6-8

8 large cloves garlic ● 4 cm/1½ in ginger root ● 2 dried figs

1 small green chilli (optional) ● 5 ml/1 tsp garam masala

2.5 ml/½ tsp ground red chilli ● 2.5 ml/½ tsp ground turmeric

1.5 ml/¼ tsp black pepper ● salt ● 150 ml/¼ pt/⅔ cup natural (plain) yoghurt

1 large chicken, skinned and pricked with a fork

Filling: 60 ml/4 tbsp ghee ● 1 onion, thinly sliced

200 g/7 oz minced (ground) lamb ● 150 g/5 oz/⅔ cup basmati or patna rice

200 g/7 oz peas ● 100 g/4 oz/⅔ cup raisins

75 g/3 oz/¾ cup blanched almonds, halved ● 75 g/3 oz/¾ cup cashew nuts, halved

25 g/1 oz/¼ cup pistachios ● 15 ml/1 tbsp chopped fresh dill (dill weed)

2.5 ml/½ tsp saffron ● 10 ml/2 tsp ground coriander

5 ml/1 tsp garam masala ● 5 ml/1 tsp ground anise

2.5 ml/½ tsp ground red chilli ● 2.5 ml/½ tsp ground turmeric ● salt

300 ml/½ pt/1¼ cups water

Sauce: 150 ml/¼ pt/⅔ cup oil ● 5 ml/1 tsp cumin seeds

1 onion, finely chopped ● 6 cloves ● 6 black peppercorns

2 bay leaves ● 2 cardamom pods ● 2.5 cm/1 in cinnamon stick

5 large cloves garlic ● 3 onions, coarsely chopped

2.5 cm/1 in ginger root ● 5 ml/3 tbsp water ● 15 ml/1 tbsp ground almonds

15 ml/1 tbsp ground coriander (cilantro) ● 10 ml/2 tsp ground roasted cumin

2.5 ml/½ tsp ground red chilli ● 400 g/14 oz canned tomatoes, chopped

salt ● 30 ml/2 tbsp lemon juice

200 ml/7 fl oz/scant 1 cup water

Garnish: 6 hard-boiled (hard-cooked) eggs, halved

5 ml/1 tsp garam masala ● 30 ml/2 tbsp chopped fresh coriander (cilantro)

1 small green chilli, chopped

Blend the garlic, ginger, figs, chilli, ground spices, salt and yoghurt to a smooth paste in a blender or food processor. Rub the paste over the chicken and leave to marinate for 2-3 hours.

Cook the marinated chicken in a preheated oven at 200°C/400°F/gas mark 6 for 45 minutes, turning and basting with the marinade.

Meanwhile, prepare the filling. Heat the ghee in a heavy-based pan and fry the onion over a medium heat until golden brown. Add the lamb and fry for 3 minutes. Add the rice and fry for 2 minutes. Stir in the remaining filling ingredients and bring to the boil then reduce the heat to low, cover and cook for 10 minutes until the meat and rice are tender and all the water has been absorbed. Stuff the chicken tightly with the filling mixture.

Prepare the sauce while the filling is cooking. Heat the oil in a heavy-based pan and fry the cumin seeds until lightly browned. Add the onion and whole spices and fry until golden brown. Blend the garlic, onions, ginger and water to a smooth paste, add to the pan and cook until golden brown. Stir in the almonds, ground spices, tomatoes and salt and cook until all the liquid has been absorbed. Stir in the lemon juice and cook until all the liquid has evaporated and the oil appears on the surface. Pour in the water and bring to the boil. Place the stuffed chicken in the sauce and baste the chicken with the sauce for a further 10 minutes over a medium-low heat until all the water has been absorbed, turning the chicken 2 or 3 times during cooking. Arrange on a serving dish with the eggs, sprinkle with the garnish ingredients and serve hot with nan, raita and cauliflower and peas.

Chicken Palak
Serves 4

30 ml/2 tbsp ghee • 2 onions, sliced • 5 cloves garlic, crushed

2 cloves • 5 ml/1 tsp ground coriander (cilantro)

2 tomatoes, skinned and chopped • 450 g/1 lb spinach, chopped

salt and pepper • 1 chicken, skinned and cut into portions

Heat the ghee and fry the onions and garlic until soft. Add the cloves, coriander, tomatoes and spinach and cook for 5 minutes until the spinach is softened and wilted. Season with salt and pepper and add the chicken. Cover and simmer gently for about 45 minutes until the chicken is tender.

Parsi Creamed Chicken
Serves 6

6 green chillies • 6 cloves garlic • 2.5 cm/1 in ginger root

450 g/1 lb ghee • 5 onions, sliced

1 chicken, skinned and cut into portions • salt

1.5 l/2½ pts/5½ cups water • 225 g/8 oz/2 cups flaked almonds

225 g/8 oz/1⅓ cup raisins • 1.2 l/2 pts/5 cups milk

1.2 l/2 pts/5 cups single (light) cream • 4 eggs

Blend the chillis, garlic and ginger to a paste in a blender or food processor. Heat a little ghee and fry 1 onion until golden. Add the chicken pieces and paste, more ghee and salt and fry until the chicken is lightly browned. Add the water, bring to the boil then simmer for about 40 minutes until the chicken is tender and a little gravy remains. Fry the remaining onions in a little ghee with the almonds and raisins. Remove the chicken from the pan, take the meat off the bones and shred it. Cook the shredded chicken in the milk over a medium heat until the milk is reduced by half. Pour the chicken gravy into a greased baking dish and top with the milk-cooked chicken. Add a layer of fried onions then a layer of cream. Repeat these layers and finally break the eggs on top of the last layer, taking care that the yolks remain whole. Bake the dish in a preheated oven at 190°C/375°F/gas mark 5 for about 15 minutes until the eggs are well set.

Party Chicken
Serves 4

45 ml/3 tbsp oil • 4 onions, sliced

1 chicken, skinned and cut into portions

150 ml/¼ pt/⅔ cup natural (plain) yoghurt

60 ml/4 tbsp single (light) cream • 5 ml/1 tsp ground cardamom

8 cloves garlic, chopped • 25 g/1 oz/¼ cup cashew nuts, ground

1 green chilli, seeded and chopped • 1-2 drops of kewra or rose water

juice of 1 lime • 15 ml/1 tbsp chopped fresh coriander (cilantro)

Heat the oil and fry the onions until golden brown. Add the chicken and fry until golden. Add all the remaining ingredients except the lime juice and coriander, bring to the boil then cover and simmer for about 40 minutes until the chicken is tender and the sauce has thickened. Stir in the lime juice and serve garnished with coriander.

Papatu with Chicken Curry   Serves 6

45 ml/3 tbsp oil ● 2 onions, sliced ● 2 green chillies

100 g/4 oz grated (shredded) coconut ● 2.5 cm/1 in ginger root, chopped

5 ml/1 tsp poppy seeds ● 4 cloves garlic, chopped

5 ml/1 tsp cumin seeds ● 8 dried red chillies

5 ml/1 tsp coriander (cilantro) seeds ● 5 ml/1 tsp lemon juice

1 chicken, skinned and cut into portions ● salt

600 ml/1 pt/2½ cups water

Papatu: 450 g/1 lb semolina ● 450 ml/¾ pt/2 cups milk

300 ml/½ pt/1¼ cups water ● 50 g/2 oz grated (shredded) coconut

pinch of ground cardamom

Heat the oil and fry 1 onion and the chillies until lightly browned. Blend the remaining ingredients except the chicken, salt and water to a smooth paste in a blender or food processor. Add the chicken to the pan and fry until browned on all sides. Add the ground spices, salt and water, bring to the boil, cover and simmer for about 1 hour until the chicken is tender and the sauce has thickened.

Meanwhile, mix together all the papatu ingredients to a dough. Divide into 6 flat circles, arrange in the top of a double boiler and steam for about 45 minutes. Serve with the chicken.

Pahari Chicken   Serves 4

30 ml/2 tbsp ghee ● 4 green chillies, slit

3 cardamom pods ● 2.5 cm/1 in ginger root, chopped

5 cloves garlic, chopped ● 1 chicken, skinned and cut into portions

1.2 1/2 pts/5 cups natural (plain) yoghurt ● salt

30 ml/2 tbsp chopped fresh coriander (cilantro)

Heat the ghee and fry 2 of the chillies with the cardamom, ginger and garlic for 2 minutes. Add the chicken and fry until browned on all sides. Add the yoghurt and salt, cover and simmer gently for about 45 minutes until the chicken is tender and the gravy thick and creamy. Chop the remaining chillies and use to garnish the dish with the coriander. Serve hot with rice, dal and okra.

Chicken with Rice Dumplings

5 ml/1 tsp black peppercorns • 4 dried red chillies • 1 cinnamon stick

5 cloves • 30 ml/2 tbsp coriander (cilantro) seeds

2 onions, sliced • 45 ml/3 tbsp ghee

1 chicken, skinned and cut into portions

600 ml/1 pt/2½ cups coconut milk • 5 ml/1 tsp ground turmeric

salt • 225 g/8 oz long-grain rice, soaked

150 ml/¼ pt/⅔ cup coconut cream • 25 g/1 oz grated (shredded) coconut

5 ml/1 tsp mustard seeds

Grind the peppercorns, chillies, cinnamon, cloves, coriander seeds and 1 onion to a paste. Heat half the ghee and fry the remaining onion until browned. Add the paste and fry for 5 minutes. Add the chicken and fry until browned. Add the coconut milk, turmeric and salt and simmer gently for at least 1 hour until the chicken is tender.

Meanwhile, drain the rice and grind it to a thick paste with just enough of the coconut cream. Stir in a pinch of salt and shape into balls about the size of an egg. Add to the chicken and simmer for 30 minutes until the rice balls are cooked. Heat the remaining ghee and fry the grated coconut and mustard seeds for 1 minute then mix them into the chicken with any remaining coconut cream and simmer for 5-10 minutes before serving.

Stuffed Roast Chicken

1 chicken, skinned • juice of ½ lemon • salt

60 ml/4 tbsp ghee • 2 onions, sliced • 300 ml/½ pt/1¼ cups water

Stuffing: ½ coconut, grated (shredded) • 100 g/4 oz Khoya (page 19)

2.5 ml/½ tsp salt • 15 ml/1 tbsp raisins

25 g/1 oz/¼ cup blanched almonds, chopped • 2.5 ml/½ tsp ground saffron

Gravy: 1 onion • 3 cloves garlic

2.5 cm/1 in ginger root • 5 ml/1 tsp chilli powder

5 ml/1 tsp ground turmeric • 5 ml/1 tsp ground coriander (cilantro)

2 cloves • 1 cinnamon stick • 5 ml/1 tsp wine vinegar

Rub the chicken with lemon juice and salt. Mix together the stuffing ingredients and stuff the chicken then sew it up securely. Heat the ghee and fry the onions until golden. Add the chicken and fry until browned. Cover the pan and simmer gently for about 1 hour, basting occasionally, until cooked through and tender.

Blend together all the gravy ingredients in a blender or food processor. Remove the chicken from the pan and fry the gravy until the ghee appears on the surface. Return the chicken to the pan with the water and simmer for a further 10 minutes.

Chicken with Sweetcorn
Serves 4

60 ml/4 tbsp ghee ● 3 onions, sliced ● 5 ml/1 tsp black peppercorns

4 dried red chillies ● 15 ml/1 tbsp ground coriander (cilantro)

5 ml/1 tsp ground turmeric ● 50 g/2 oz grated (shredded) coconut

600 ml/1 pt/1½ cups coconut milk ● 450 g/1 lb chicken meat, cubed

2-3 curry leaves ● 5 ml/1 tsp mustard seeds ● 225 g/8 oz sweetcorn

Heat half the ghee and fry 1 onion and the spices until lightly browned. Grind the mixture and mix with the turmeric, coconut and coconut milk. Add the chicken and curry leaves, bring to the boil, cover and simmer for about 25 minutes until tender.

Meanwhile, heat the remaining ghee and fry the mustard seeds until they start crackling. Add the remaining onions and fry until lightly browned. Add to the curry with the sweetcorn and heat through gently. Serve hot with rice and vegetables.

Steamed Coriander Chicken
Serves 4

225 g/8 oz chopped fresh coriander (cilantro) ● 1 onion, chopped

5 dried red chillies ● 1 tomato, skinned ● 5 ml/1 tsp peppercorns

5 ml/1 tsp cumin seeds ● 2.5 ml/½ tsp ground turmeric ● 1 chicken, skinned

Blend the seasoning ingredients to a paste. Make several slashes on either side of the chicken and rub in the paste. Marinate for 3 hours. Wrap the chicken in foil and steam for 1-1½ hours until tender.

Saffron Chicken
Serves 4

2.5 ml/½ tsp saffron strands ● 45 ml/3 tbsp hot milk

1 onion, chopped ● 4 cloves garlic, chopped

2.5 cm/1 in ginger root, chopped ● 1 green chilli, chopped

45 ml/3 tbsp water ● 45 ml/3 tbsp oil ● salt

10 ml/2 tsp Mughal-style garam masala (page 13) ● 5 ml/1 tsp ground cardamom

45 ml/3 tbsp natural (plain) yoghurt ● 1 chicken, skinned

Soak the saffron in the hot milk for 15 minutes. Blend the onion, garlic, ginger, chillies and water to a smooth paste. Heat the oil and fry the paste and salt over medium heat until the oil appears on the surface. Add the garam masala and cardamom and cook for 1 minute, stirring. Whisk the saffron milk into the yoghurt then stir it into the pan and cook for 2 minutes. Remove from the heat and rub the mixture all over the chicken, inside and out. Place in a baking tin, seal tightly with foil and bake in a preheated oven at 180°C/350°F/gas mark 4 for 45 minutes. Remove the foil and cook for 15 minutes. Serve hot with rice and vegetables.

Photograph opposite: *Beef with Almonds (page 117)*

Spice-stuffed Chicken   Serves 4

225 g/8 oz papaya ● 1 chicken, skinned ● 3 onions, chopped

2.5 cm/1 in ginger root, chopped ● 3 cloves garlic, chopped

2 green chillies, chopped ● 4 hard-boiled (hard-cooked) eggs, chopped

50 g/2 oz/½ cup blanched almonds ● 50 g/2 oz/½ cup pistachios

50 g/2 oz poppy seeds ● 10 ml/2 tsp garam masala

100 g/4 oz/½ cup ghee ● 2 tomatoes, skinned and chopped

300 ml/½ pt/1¼ cups natural (plain) yoghurt ● salt

Grind the papaya and smear it over the chicken inside and out. Mix together 2 onions with the ginger, garlic, chillies and eggs and use the mixture to stuff the chicken. Grind together the almonds, pistachios, poppy seeds and garam masala and smear the chicken with the paste. Heat the ghee and fry the remaining onion until browned. Add the chicken to the pan with the tomatoes, yoghurt and salt, cover tightly and simmer over a medium heat for 45-60 minutes until the chicken is tender.

Saucy Chicken   Serves 4

120 ml/4 fl oz/½ cup tomato purée (paste) ● 5 ml/1 tsp soy sauce

few drops of chilli sauce ● 8 cloves garlic, chopped

2.5 cm/1 in ginger root, chopped ● 15 ml/1 tbsp chopped fresh coriander (cilantro)

15 ml/1 tbsp honey ● 1 green chilli, chopped

salt and pepper ● 1 chicken, skinned and cut into portions

30 ml/2 tbsp oil

Mix together all the ingredients except the oil and chicken. Prick the chicken all over with a fork and rub in the marinade. Leave to marinate overnight.   Heat the oil and fry the chicken and marinade for about 40 minutes until the chicken is tender.

Photograph opposite:
Chicken Korma (page 149)

Sirdari Chicken
Serves 4

15 ml/1 tbsp ghee ● 225 g/ 8 oz onions, sliced

4 cloves garlic, sliced ● 2.5 cm/1 in ginger root, chopped

150 ml/¼ pt/⅔ cup natural (plain) yoghurt

350 g/12 oz tomatoes, skinned and chopped

75 g/3 oz/¾ cup aniseeds ● 15 ml/1 tbsp blanched almonds

6 black peppercorns ● 1 cinnamon stick ● 3 cardamom pods

2.5 ml/½ tsp chilli powder ● 2.5 ml/½ tsp cumin seeds

2.5 ml/½ tsp ground turmeric ● 1 chicken, skinned and cut into portions

600 ml/1 pt/2½ cups water ● salt

Heat the ghee and fry the onions until golden. Grind together the garlic and ginger then add it to the pan and fry for 1 minute. Add the yoghurt and simmer for 5 minutes. Add the tomatoes, aniseeds, almonds and spices and simmer for 10 minutes, stirring. Add the chicken and fry for a few minutes until well coated in the sauce. Add the water and salt, cover and simmer over a medium heat for about 40 minutes until the chicken is tender and the gravy reduced to about half.

Shredded Chicken
Serves 4

1 chicken, skinned ● 1.2 l/2 pts/5 cups water

2.5 ml/½ tsp cumin seeds ● 2.5 ml/½ tsp ground coriander (cilantro)

2.5 cm/1 in cinnamon stick ● 4 cloves ● salt

60 ml/4 tbsp ghee ● 4 onions, sliced ● 4 green chillies, sliced

15 ml/1 tbsp tomato purée (paste) ● 5 ml/1 tsp wine vinegar

Seasoning: 1 onion ● 2.5 ml/½ tsp aniseeds

1.5 ml/¼ tsp cumin seeds ● 5 cm/2 in ginger root ● 2 cloves garlic

Place the chicken in a pan with the water, cumin seeds, coriander, cinnamon, cloves and salt, bring to the boil then simmer for about 1 hour until tender. Drain the chicken then remove the meat from the bones and shred it. Heat the ghee and fry the onions and chillies until well brow- ned then remove from the pan. Add the chicken and fry until lightly brown- ed. Grind together all the seasoning ingredients and add them to the pan with the onions and chillies. Stir in the tomato purée and wine vinegar and simmer until the sauce is dry.

Sweet and Sour Chicken
Serves 4-6

6 chicken pieces, skinned ● 259 ml/8 fl oz/1 cup water

225 g/8 oz vegetables (cauliflower, carrots, (bell) pepper, aubergine (eggplant) etc.), cut into 3 cm/1½ in pieces ● oil for deep-frying

Batter: 100 g/4 oz/1 cup gram flour ● 15 ml/1 tbsp oil

15 ml/1 tbsp chopped fresh coriander (cilantro) ● 5 ml/1 tsp ajwain

2.5 ml/½ tsp garam masala ● 2.5 ml/½ tsp ground red chilli

salt ● 150 ml/¼ pt/⅔ cup water

Sauce: 75 ml/5 tbsp oil or ghee ● 2 onions, finely chopped

4 large cloves garlic, ● 2.5 cm/1 in ginger root, coarsely chopped

10 ml/2 tsp ground coriander (cilantro) ● 5 ml/1 tsp garam masala

5 ml/1 tsp ground roasted cumin ● 2.5 ml/½ tsp ground red chilli

2.5 ml/½ tsp ground turmeric ● 1.5 ml/¼ tsp ground mace

1.5 ml/¼ tsp grated nutmeg ● salt ● 225 g/8 oz canned tomatoes, chopped

60 ml/4 tbsp wine vinegar ● 15 ml/1 tbsp honey

200 ml/7 fl oz/scant 1 cup water

Garnish: 2.5 ml/½ tsp garam masala

15 ml/1 tbsp chopped fresh coriander (cilantro)

1 small green chilli, chopped

Place the chicken and water in a heavy-based pan, bring to the boil, cover and simmer over a medium-low heat for 20 minutes. Remove the lid, increase the heat and dry off any remaining water.

To make the batter, place the flour in a bowl, mix in the oil then add the ground spices, salt and water and mix to a smooth batter. Heat the frying oil. Dip the cooked chicken pieces in the batter then place gently in the oil and fry until golden brown. Remove with a slotted spoon. Dip the vegetable pieces in the batter and fry until golden brown. Place with the chicken.

To make the sauce, heat the oil or ghee in a heavy-based pan and fry 1 onion until golden brown. Blend the remaining onion, the garlic and ginger to a smooth paste then stir it into the pan and fry for 2 minutes. Add the ground spices, salt and tomatoes and cook until all the liquid has been absorbed and the oil appears on the surface. Add the wine vinegar and cook until all the liquid has been absorbed. Add the honey and cook for 2 minutes. Add the water, bring to the boil then reduce the heat and simmer for 2 minutes. Pour the hot sauce over the chicken and vegetables, sprinkle with the garnish ingredients and serve hot with rice, puris, raita and chutney.

Tandoori Chicken
Serves 4-6

60 ml/4 tbsp lemon juice ● 6 large cloves garlic

5 cm/2 in ginger root ● 1 onion, coarsely chopped

1 small green chilli ● 150 ml/¼ pt/⅔ cup natural (plain) yoghurt, whisked

15 ml/1 tbsp ground coriander (cilantro) ● 30 ml/2 tbsp garam masala

5 ml/1 tsp ground roasted cumin ● 5 ml/1 tsp ground turmeric

2.5 ml/½ tsp ground red chilli ● 1.5 ml/¼ tsp ground mace

1.5 ml/¼ tsp grated nutmeg ● salt

1 medium chicken, skinned and pricked with a fork

75 ml/5 tbsp ghee or butter

Garnish: 5 ml/1 tsp garam masala ● 1 onion, cut into rings

1 lemon, sliced ● 30 ml/2 tbsp chopped fresh coriander (cilantro)

1 small green chilli, chopped

Blend the lemon juice, garlic, ginger, onion and chilli to a smooth paste in a blender or food processor. Place the yoghurt, ground spices and salt in a bowl and stir in the paste. Put the chicken into the marinade and rub it all over the inside and outside of the chicken. Cover and leave to marinate for 8-10 hours, turning the chicken 2 or 3 times.

Place 2 skewers in the marinated chicken and put the chicken in a deep ovenproof dish, resting the skewers on the top of the dish so that the chicken is not touching the bottom of the dish. Roast in a preheated oven at 180°C/350°F/gas mark 4 for about 2 hours until the chicken is tender, turning and basting with the marinade and the ghee as it cooks. Transfer the chicken to a serving dish, sprinkle over the garnish ingredients and serve hot with nan, pulao, matar paneer or a vegetable kofta dish.

Tandoori Chicken Kebabs
Serves 4

4 chicken breasts, skinned and cut into chunks

150 ml/¼ pt/⅔ cup natural (plain) yoghurt ● 2.5 cm/1 in ginger root, crushed

4 cloves garlic, crushed ● 1 onion, grated

15 ml/1 tbsp wine vinegar ● 5 ml/1 tsp chilli powder

2.5 ml/½ tsp red food colour ● 5 ml/1 tsp salt ● 45 ml/3 tbsp ghee

1 lemon, cut into wedges

Place the chicken in a bowl. Mix together all the ingredients except the ghee and lemon, pour over the chicken and stir well. Cover and leave to marinate overnight.

Thread the chicken on to skewers, arrange on a grill (broiler) or barbecue and brush with marinade and ghee. Barbecue or grill the chicken for about 15 minutes until cooked through, turning and brushing with the marinade and ghee as you cook.

Chicken with Tamarind
Serves 4

45 ml/3 tbsp tamarind pulp • 90 ml/6 tbsp hot water

30 ml/2 tbsp jaggery • 2.5 ml/½ tsp chilli powder

15 ml/1 tbsp grated ginger root • 1.5 ml/¼ tsp ground ginger

2.5 ml/½ tsp garam masala • 900 g/2 lb chicken pieces, skinned

15 ml/1 tbsp oil • 15 ml/1 tbsp soy sauce • 3 spring onions (scallions), chopped

Soak the tamarind in the hot water for 10 minutes. Add the jaggery to the water and soak for a further 10 minutes. Squeeze the pulp thoroughly and strain. Discard the pulp. Mix the tamarind juice with the chilli powder, ginger and garam masala then rub into the chicken, cover and leave to marinate for 4 hours.

Rub the oil and soy sauce into the chicken then bake in a preheated oven at 180°C/350°F/gas mark 4 for 30 minutes. Turn the chicken over and baste thoroughly then bake for a further 30 minutes until cooked through. Serve garnished with spring onions.

Chicken with Vegetables and Paneer
Serves 4-6

75 ml/5 tbsp oil or ghee • 200 g/7 oz cauliflower, cut into small florets

100 g/4 oz Paneer (page 20), cubed • 2 onions, finely chopped

4 cloves garlic, crushed • 2.5 cm/1 in ginger root, finely chopped

4 cloves • 4 black peppercorns • 2 bay leaves

1.5 cm/½ in cinnamon stick • 1 black cardamom pod

500 g/18 oz boned chicken, skinned and cut into 4 cm/1½ in pieces

10 ml/2 tsp ground coriander (cilantro) • 5 ml/1 tsp ground roasted cumin

2.5 ml/½ tsp ground red chilli • 2.5 ml/½ tsp ground turmeric

salt • 400 g/14 oz canned tomatoes, chopped

300 ml/½ pt/1¼ pts water • 250 g/9 oz mixed vegetables, cubed

Garnish: 2.5 ml/½ tsp garam masala

15 ml/1 tbsp chopped fresh coriander (cilantro) • 1 small green chilli, chopped

Heat a little oil or ghee and fry the cauliflower and paneer until golden brown. Remove from the pan and set aside. Heat the remaining oil or ghee in a heavy-based pan and fry the onion, garlic, ginger and whole spices until golden brown. Add the chicken and fry for 5 minutes until light brown. Stir in the ground spices and salt then mix in the tomatoes and cook until all the liquid has been absorbed

and oil appears on the surface. Pour in two-thirds of the water and simmer gently until the chicken is tender and all the water has been absorbed. Add the frozen and fried vegetables, the paneer and the remaining water and simmer for 2 minutes. Sprinkle with the garnish ingredients and serve hot with puris or chapatis, raita, dal and okra.

Chicken in Vinegar

Serves 4

1 chicken, skinned and cut into portions ● 1.2 1/2 pts/5 cups wine vinegar

30 dried red chillies ● 10 cloves garlic ● 100 g/4 oz cumin seeds

900 ml/1½ pts/3 cups gingelly oil ● 100 g/4 oz jaggery

Boil the chicken in half the wine vinegar for about 30 minutes until tender. Grind the chillies, garlic and cumin seeds to a paste with a little of the wine vinegar. Heat the oil and fry the ground paste over a low heat for a few minutes. Add the chicken, remaining wine vinegar and jaggery and simmer until the sauce has thickened.

Chicken Vindaloo

Serves 6

900 g/2 lb chicken pieces, skinned ● 3 cloves garlic

2.5 cm/1 in ginger root, chopped ● 45 ml/3 tbsp white wine vinegar

15 ml/1 tbsp treacle ● 5 ml/1 tsp ground turmeric

2 green chillies, chopped ● 1.5 ml/¼ tsp fenugreek seeds

5 ml/1 tsp mustard seeds ● 15 ml/1 tbsp coriander (cilantro) seeds

5 ml/1 tsp cumin seeds ● pinch of asafoetida

2.5 ml/½ tsp chilli powder ● 450 g/1 lb small potatoes

90 ml/6 tbsp mustard oil ● 3 onions, minced

2 tomatoes, skinned and chopped

30 ml/2 tbsp chopped fresh coriander (cilantro)

Wash the chicken and leave to drain. Blend the garlic, ginger, wine vinegar, treacle, turmeric and chillies to a paste in a blender or food processor. Grind together the fenugreek, mustard, coriander and cumin seeds. Rub the blended and ground spices, asafoetida and chilli powder into the chicken, cover and leave to stand for 3 hours.

Boil the potatoes until tender then peel and cut in halves. Heat the oil and fry the onions until golden. Add the tomatoes and fry, stirring, until the oil appears on the surface. Add the chicken and marinade and cook for 10 minutes, stirring occasionally, then cover and simmer for a further 10 minutes. Add the potatoes, cover and simmer gently until the chicken is tender. Serve garnished with coriander.

Chicken with Vegetables and Mushrooms   Serves 4

45 ml/3 tbsp ghee • 3 onions, sliced

1 chicken, skinned and cut into portions • 1 cm/½ in ginger root, sliced

3 green chillies, sliced • salt and pepper

250 ml/8 fl oz/1 cup boiling water • 225 g/8 oz cauliflower florets

50 g/2 oz peas • 5 ml/1 tsp cumin seeds • 3 dried red chillies

2 tomatoes, skinned and halved • 100 g/4 oz button mushrooms

100 g/4 oz Paneer (page 20), diced • 30 ml/2 tbsp chopped fresh coriander (cilantro)

Heat the ghee and fry the onions until golden then remove from the pan. Add the chicken and fry for 15 minutes until half-cooked. Add the ginger, chillies, salt and pepper and fry for 5 minutes. Add the water and simmer gently until the chicken is tender, stirring occasionally. Remove the chicken from the sauce and keep it warm.

Add the cauliflower, peas, cumin seeds and chillies to the chicken sauce and simmer for 10 minutes, stirring. Add the tomatoes, mushrooms and paneer and cook for 5 minutes, stirring. Arrange the chicken on a serving plate with the vegetables around the edge and pour over the sauce. Garnish with coriander.

Chicken in Yoghurt   Serves 4

1 chicken, skinned and cut into portions

250 ml/8 fl oz/1 cup natural (plain) yoghurt

2 onions, chopped • 10 garlic cloves, crushed

2.5 cm/1 in ginger root, chopped • 10 ml/2 tsp ground coriander (cilantro)

5 ml/1 tsp chilli powder • 2 onions, sliced • 45 ml/2 tbsp wine vinegar

2.5 ml/½ tsp sugar • 2.5 ml/½ tsp salt • 250 ml/8 fl oz/1 cup oil

juice of 1½ limes • 15 ml/1 tbsp chopped fresh coriander (cilantro)

Prick the chicken all over with a fork. Mix together the yoghurt, onions, garlic, ginger, coriander and chilli powder and rub into the chicken. Leave to marinate overnight.

Soak the sliced onions in the wine vinegar for 1 hour. Stir in the sugar and salt and leave to stand until they turn pink. Put the chicken and marinade into a pan, cover and simmer for about 45 minutes until the chicken is tender and the juices have dried up. Heat the oil and fry the chicken pieces until lightly browned. Arrange the chicken on a serving dish and squeeze over the lime juice. Serve garnished with coriander. Serve the onions separately.

Chicken in Yoghurt Mint Sauce
Serves 6

1 large chicken, skinned ● 5 ml/1 tsp ground turmeric ● salt

120 ml/4 fl oz/½ cup natural (plain) yoghurt ● 45 ml/3 tbsp oil

1 onion, grated ● 5 cloves garlic, grated ● 2.5 cm/1 in ginger root, grated

5 cardamom pods ● 8 cloves ● 4 bay leaves

2 cinnamon sticks ● 2.5 ml/½ tsp black peppercorns

15 ml/1 tbsp garam masala ● 5 ml/1 tsp paprika

1.5 ml/¼ tsp grated nutmeg ● 450 ml/¾ pt/2 cups chicken stock

30 ml/2 tbsp chopped fresh mint

Cut the chicken into about 12 pieces, place in a bowl and rub in the turmeric, salt and yoghurt. Leave to marinate for 1 hour.

Heat the oil and fry the onion, garlic and ginger over a medium heat until browned. Add the whole spices and fry for 2 minutes, stirring. Add the ground spices and fry for 3 minutes, stirring. Add the chicken and marinade and the stock, bring to the boil, cover and simmer for 45 minutes until the chicken is tender. Add the mint, cover and simmer for a further 5 minutes. Serve hot with rice, nan and a vegetable dish.

Creamy Stuffed Chicken
Serves 6

2.5 cm/1 in ginger root ● 2 dried figs ● 1 chicken, skinned

225 g/1 lb onions ● 450 g/1 lb/2 cups ghee ● 5 ml/1 tsp aniseeds

15 ml/1 tbsp ground coriander (cilantro) ● 5 ml/1 tsp cumin seeds

5 ml/1 tsp black peppercorns ● 5 ml/1 tsp chilli powder

6 cloves ● 2 cardamom pods ● 1 cinnamon stick

225 g/8 oz minced (ground) lamb ● pinch of saffron ● salt

175 g/6 oz/¾ cup long-grain rice, soaked ● 100 g/4 oz/⅔ cup raisins

12 pistachios ● 15 ml/1 tbsp natural (plain) yoghurt

150 ml/¼ pt/⅔ cup single (light) cream ● 15 ml/1 tbsp chopped fresh dill (dill weed)

300 ml/½ pt/1¼ cups milk ● 5 ml/1 tsp sugar

Grind together the ginger and figs then rub the mixture all over the chicken. Leave to marinate for 3 hours.

Chop 2 onions and slice the remainder into rings. Heat 30 ml/2 tbsp of ghee and fry the chopped onion until tender. Add all the spices and fry for a few minutes. Add the lamb, saffron and salt and simmer until tender. Drain the rice and add it to the pan with enough water to cook the rice.

Add the raisins and pistachios and simmer for about 10 minutes until the rice is just cooked. Leave to cool. Stir in the yoghurt, cream and dill. Stuff the chicken and sew it up.

Heat the remaining ghee and fry the chicken until lightly browned on all sides. Add the milk and sugar and simmer gently for about 1 hour until tender. Gently fry the onion rings and use to garnish the chicken.

Curried Chicken Livers
Serves 4

450 g/1 lb chicken livers ● 150 ml/¼ pt/⅔ cup natural (plain) yoghurt

2 onions, sliced ● 6 cloves garlic ● 2.5 cm/1 in ginger root

2 sticks celery, chopped ● 30 ml/2 tbsp ghee ● 6 cloves

2 cinnamon sticks ● 2 cardamom pods ● 5 ml/1 tsp ground turmeric

2 green chillies, chopped ● salt

Chop the liver into 2.5 cm/1 in pieces and arrange them on skewers. Leave to marinate in the yoghurt. Blend 1 onion, the garlic, ginger and celery to a paste. Heat the ghee and fry the cloves, cinnamon and cardamom for 2 minutes, Add the ground spices, turmeric and chillies and fry for 15 minutes until browned. Add the liver kebabs and remaining onion and simmer over a low heat for about 10 minutes until the liver is cooked and the sauce has thickened.

Duck with Pistachios
Serves 6

1 duck ● juice of 1 lemon ● 45 ml/3 tbsp soured (dairy sour) cream

8 cloves garlic, crushed ● 5 ml/1 tsp ground turmeric ● 5 ml/1 tsp paprika

salt ● 2.5 ml/½ tsp chilli powder ● 2.5 ml/½ tsp saffron strands

45 ml/3 tbsp hot milk ● 2 potatoes, boiled and mashed ● 45 ml/3 tbsp oil

2 onions, finely chopped ● 2.5 cm/1 in ginger root, chopped

2 green chillies, chopped ● 25 g/1 oz/¼ cup pistachios, chopped

30 ml/2 tbsp chopped fresh mint ● 15 ml/1 tbsp ground coriander (cilantro)

10 ml/2 tsp ground cumin ● 15 ml/1 tbsp garam masala

2.5 ml/½ tsp grated nutmeg ● 5 ml/1 tsp mustard seeds, ground ● pepper

Cut off the duck wings. Cut the giblets into small pieces and boil the neck, wings and giblets in a small pan of water until the meat is tender and separates from the bones. Remove the meat and set the meat and stock aside.

Mix the lemon juice, soured cream, garlic, turmeric, paprika, salt and chilli powder and rub this mixture over the duck. Leave to marinate for 2 hours. Soak the saffron in the milk for 15 minutes. Strain the stock and mix it with the potatoes. Heat the oil and fry the onions, ginger, chillies, pistachios and mint until the onions are browned. Stir in the coriander, cumin, garam masala, nutmeg, mustard seeds and pepper and fry for 5 minutes, stirring. Add the cooked giblets and mashed potatoes and stir for 5 minutes.

Place the duck in a roasting pan and stuff the cavity with the potato mixture. Pour over the saffron milk, cover with foil and cook in a preheated oven at 200°C/400°F/gas mark 6 for 30 minutes. Reduce the oven temperature to 150°C/300°F/gas mark 2 and bake for a further 30 minutes. Remove the lid and foil, baste well then cover again and bake for a further 1 hour until the duck is tender. Remove the foil and cook for a further 30 minutes until browned, turning the duck over after 15 minutes.

Kerala Fried Duck
Serves 4

1 duck, skinned and cut into portions ● 15 ml/1 tbsp chilli powder

5 ml/1 tbsp black pepper ● 5 ml/1 tsp ground coriander (cilantro)

2.5 ml/½ tsp ground turmeric ● 1.5 ml/½ tsp ground cloves

1.5 ml/¼ tsp ground cinnamon ● 1 l/1¾ pts/4¼ cups water

1 egg, beaten ● 100 g/4 oz/1 cup breadcrumbs ● 60 ml/4 tbsp ghee

30 ml/2 tbsp grated (shredded) coconut ● 1 lemon, sliced

Place the duck in a pan with the spices and water. Bring to the boil then simmer for about 40 minutes until the water has evaporated and the duck is tender. Dip each piece of duck in egg then in breadcrumbs. Heat the ghee and fry the duck until golden brown on all sides. Serve garnished with grated coconut and lemon slices.

Duck Vindaloo
Serves 4

1 duck, jointed ● 2 cinnamon sticks ● 2 cardamom pods

5 cloves ● salt ● 5 dried red chillies

5 green chillies ● 3 onions ● 15 ml/1 tbsp cumin seeds

10 cloves garlic ● 2.5 cm/1 in ginger root

5 ml/1 tsp ground turmeric ● 45 ml/3 tbsp wine vinegar

15 ml/1 tbsp sugar ● 2.5 ml/½ tsp poppy seeds

225 g/8 oz potatoes, quartered ● 45 ml/3 tbsp ghee

Place the duck in a pan and just cover with water. Add the cinnamon, cardamom, cloves and salt, bring to the boil and simmer for 1 hour until the duck is tender. Grind all the remaining ingredients except the potatoes and ghee to a paste. Heat the ghee and fry the duck until browned on all sides then remove from the pan. Add the paste and fry until dry. Add 300 ml/½ pt/1¼ cups of water and simmer until the liquid has disappeared. Add the duck and potatoes and simmer gently until the potatoes are tender and the sauce is very thick.

Duck with Nut Stuffing
Serves 4

1 duck, boned ● 45 ml/3 tbsp ghee ● 1 onion, chopped
2 cloves garlic, chopped ● 10 ml/2 tsp ground cumin
5 ml/1 tsp ground cardamom ● 10 ml/2 tsp ground cumin
2.5 ml/½ tsp ground turmeric ● 100 g/4 oz/1 cup breadcrumbs
75 g/3 oz/¾ cup cashew nuts ● 50 g/2 oz/⅓ cup raisins
30 ml/2 tbsp chopped fresh coriander (cilantro) ● salt and pepper
1 egg, beaten

Wash the duck and pat dry on kitchen paper. Heat the ghee and fry the onion and garlic until soft and golden. Add the spices and fry for 2 minutes. Stir in the breadcrumbs, nuts, raisins, coriander, salt and pepper then bind with the egg. Stuff the duck with the stuffing and sew closed. Weigh the stuffed duck then place it on a rack in a roasting tin and prick the skin with a fork. Cook in a preheated oven at 180°C/350°F/gas mark 4 for 35 minutes per 450 g/1 lb. Slice thickly to serve.

Pigeon Vindaloo
Serves 4

12 dried red chillies ● 5 ml/1 tsp cumin seeds ● 2.5 ml/½ tsp mustard seeds
2.5 cm/½ in ginger root, chopped ● 5 ml/1 tsp ground turmeric
5 cloves garlic ● 15 ml/1 tbsp wine vinegar ● 45 ml/3 tbsp oil
2 onions, sliced ● 4 pigeons, quartered ● salt

Blend the chillies, cumin and mustard seeds, ginger, turmeric, garlic and wine vinegar to a paste in a blender or food processor. Heat the oil and fry the onions until lightly browned. Add the spice paste and fry for 5 minutes, stirring. Add the pigeons and fry until lightly browned. Add enough water just to cover the pigeons, season with salt and simmer gently for about 30 minutes until tender.

Eggs and Cheese

Eggs are not much used in Indian cooking. However, an egg curry is quick and easy to make and can taste just as good as meat or poultry. You will also find some interesting dishes using eggs in other sections of the book, such as Egg Roti on page 306.

Indian cheese, known as paneer, is often used. You will find the basic recipe on page 20.

Parsi Egg with Lentils   Serves 6

225 g/8 oz/1 cups red lentils ● 10 ml/2 tsp salt ● 5 ml/1 tsp ground turmeric

1 large bunch fresh coriander (cilantro) ● 10 green chillies

12 large onions ● 20 button onions ● 4 cloves garlic

2.5 cm/1 in ginger root ● 2.5 ml/½ tsp cumin seeds

900 g/2 lb/4 cups ghee ● 12 eggs, beaten

100 ml/4 fl oz/½ cup tamarind juice

Place the lentils in a pan and cover with water. Add the salt and turmeric, bring to the boil and simmer until all the water has been absorbed. Blend half the coriander, chillies, onions, garlic and ginger with all the cumin seeds. Finely chop the remainder. Heat the ghee and fry the chopped onions until soft. Add all the ground and chopped ingredients and fry until soft and well combined. Add the cooked lentils and stir together well. Stir in the eggs and cook over a low heat until the eggs are well combined. Stir in the tamarind juice and simmer until the ghee appears on the surface.

Duck's Egg Balchow   Serves 6-8

18 duck's eggs ● 30 ml/2 tbsp ghee ● 675 g/1½ lb onions, minced

5 ml/1 tsp cumin seeds ● 10 ml/2 tsp black peppercorns

10 dried red chillies ● 7.5 cm/3 in piece turmeric root

6 green chillies, thinly sliced ● 1 clove garlic, thinly sliced

2.5 cm/1 in fresh root ginger, thinly sliced ● 4 curry leaves

2-3 coriander (cilantro) leaves ● salt

Scramble the eggs then set aside. Heat the ghee and fry the onions until lightly browned. Grind the cumin seeds, peppercorns, red chillies and turmeric to a powder and add to the onions. Stir in the scrambled egg and fry over a low heat until lightly browned. Add the remaining spices and simmer until the ghee appears on the surface.

Egg Malai Masala
Serves 4

6 eggs ● 2 onions ● 2.5 cm/1 in ginger root

4 green chillies ● 30 ml/2 tbsp ghee

300 ml/½ pt/1¼ cups milk ● salt

15 ml/1 tbsp chopped fresh coriander (cilantro)

2.5 ml/½ tsp garam masala

Hard-boil the eggs then shell and halve them. Blend the onions, ginger and chillies to a paste in a blender or food processor. Heat the ghee and fry the paste for 1 minute. Add the eggs and fry until the onion turns pale golden. Add the milk, season with salt and bring to the boil. Add the coriander and simmer, stirring very gently, until the sauce thickens. Sprinkle with garam masala and serve with parathas or roti.

Egg Patties
Serves 4

3-4 potatoes ● ghee ● 1 onion, finely chopped

1 tomato, chopped ● 1 small bunch fresh coriander (cilantro), chopped

salt ● 6 eggs, lightly beaten

100 g/4 oz/1 cup breadcrumbs (optional)

Boil the potatoes then peel and mash them thoroughly. Heat a little ghee and fry the onion until soft but not browned. Stir in the tomato and cook for 2 minutes. Add the coriander and salt and stir in 5 of the eggs, mixing well until the mixture thickens and sets. Remove from the heat and leave to cool. Beat the remaining egg well. Knead the potato and shape into thick, flat patties. Place a spoonful of the egg mixture in the centre and fold the sides over the top to enclose the stuffing. Press into a flat cake shape. Heat a little more ghee in a frying pan (skillet). Dip each patty in the beaten egg then in breadcrumbs, if using, and fry until golden brown on both sides. Serve hot with tomato sauce or chutney.

Egg Cutlets
Serves 4-6

15 ml/1 tbsp ghee ● 45 ml/3 tbsp gram or plain (all-purpose) flour

250 ml/8 fl oz/1 cup milk ● 3 slices bread ● warm water

6 hard-boiled (hard-cooked) eggs, coarsely chopped

50 g/2 oz/½ cup cooked long-grain rice ● 1 small green chilli, finely chopped

1 small onion, finely chopped ● 5 ml/3 tbsp chopped fresh coriander (cilantro)

15 ml/1 tbsp lemon juice ● 5 ml/1 tsp garam masala

5 ml/1 tsp ground roasted cumin ● 5 ml/1 tsp dried pomegranate seeds

2.5 ml/½ tsp ground red chilli ● salt ● 90 ml/6 tbsp oil

Heat the ghee in a saucepan and fry the flour until lightly browned. Pour in the milk and stir until thick. Remove from the heat. Soak the bread in warm water for a few minutes then squeeze out all the water. Stir into the pan with all the remaining ingredients except the oil. Divide the mixture into 12 and shape into 5 mm/¼ in thick ovals. Heat half the oil and fry half the cutlets until golden brown on both sides. Heat the remaining oil and fry the remaining cutlets. Serve hot with samosas and chutney.

Egg Halwa
Serves 4

60 ml/4 tbsp ghee ● 4 eggs, beaten ● 30 ml/2 tbsp sugar

25 g/1 oz/3 tbsp sultanas ● 30 ml/2 tbsp blanched almonds, finely chopped

30 ml/2 tbsp pistachios, finely chopped ● 2.5 ml/½ tsp ground cardamom

Heat the ghee over a medium heat and add the eggs and sugar, stirring occasionally. When the egg mixture forms a few small lumps and stops sticking to the pan, mix in the sultanas, nuts and spice and stir for a further 1 minute. Serve hot at breakfast or after a meal.

Egg Curry
Serves 4-6

150 ml/¼ pt/⅔ cup oil or ghee ● 5 ml/1 tsp cumin seeds

1 medium onion, finely chopped ● 4 cloves ● 4 peppercorns

2.5 cm/1 in cinnamon stick ● 1 black cardamom pod

5 cloves garlic, coarsely chopped ● 3 onions, coarsely chopped

2.5 cm/1 in ginger root, coarsely chopped ● 30 ml/2 tbsp water

25 g/1 oz poppy seeds, ground

75 g/3 oz/¾ cup desiccated (shredded) coconut, finely ground

10 ml/2 tsp ground coriander (cilantro) ● 5 ml/1 tsp ground turmeric

2.5 ml/½ tsp ground red chilli ● 2.5 ml/½ tsp garam masala ● salt

400 g/14 oz canned tomatoes, chopped ● 400 ml/14 fl oz/1¾ cups water

15 ml/1 tbsp lemon juice ● 6 hard-boiled (hard-cooked) eggs, halved

Garnish: 2.5 ml/½ tsp garam masala ● 1 small green chilli, chopped

Heat the oil and fry the cumin seeds until brown. Add the onion and whole spices and fry until golden brown. Blend the garlic, onion, ginger and 30 ml/2 tbsp of water in a blender or food processor to a smooth paste, then add it to the pan and fry for 5 minutes. Add the poppy seeds and fry for 2 minutes. Add the coconut and fry for 2 minutes until golden brown. Stir in the ground spices and tomatoes and fry until all the liquid has been absorbed and the oil appears on the surface. Pour in 45 ml/3 tbsp of water and fry until the water is absorbed. Repeat twice so that the spices can mature in the sauce. Finally add the remaining water and lemon juice, bring to the boil then cover and simmer gently for 3 minutes. Pour the sauce into a serving dish, arrange the eggs on top and sprinkle with the garnish ingredients. Serve hot with rice, puris and a potato or bean dish.

Egg Kofta
Serves 4

4 eggs ● 1-2 slices bread, crumbled ● 10 ml/2 tsp ghee, melted

1 green chilli, finely chopped ● 5 ml/1 tsp minced onion ● salt

For the sauce: 15 ml/1 tbsp butter or ghee ● 1 small onion, chopped

450 g/1 lb ripe tomatoes, skinned

10 ml/2 tsp chopped fresh coriander (cilantro)

2.5 ml/½ tsp garam masala ● 5 ml/1 tsp chilli powder

Hard-boil the eggs, shell and set aside. Soak the bread in cold water until soft then drain and squeeze out any liquid. Slice the eggs lengthways and remove the yolks. Mash the egg yolks into the bread and ghee. Stir in the chilli, onion and salt. Heap the mixture into the halved egg whites and place in a flat flameproof dish.

To make the sauce, melt the butter or ghee and fry the onion until soft but not browned. Stir in the remaining ingredients and simmer for 10 minutes until tender. Pour the sauce over the eggs, cover and cook in a preheated oven at 180°C/350°F/gas mark 4 for about 20 minutes until the sauce is hot. Serve with hot chapatis.

Egg Korma
Serves 6

6 eggs, separated ● 150 ml/¼ pt/⅔ cup milk ● salt

45 ml/3 tbsp ghee ● 30 ml/2 tbsp cashew nuts, chopped

6 onions, coarsely chopped ● 8 green chillies

15 ml/1 tbsp desiccated (shredded) coconut

45 ml/3 tbsp ground coriander (cilantro) ● 6 cloves

1 cinnamon stick ● 2 cardamom pods ● 2.5 cm/1 in ginger root

2.5 ml/½ tsp ground turmeric ● 300 ml/½ pt/1¼ cups warm water

Whisk the egg whites until stiff. Fold in the yolks, milk and salt to taste and beat for 10 minutes. Pour into a shallow dish and place the dish into a large pan filled with water to come half way up the sides of the dish. Bring to the boil, cover and steam for about 10 minutes until set. Turn out the egg and cut into cubes.

Heat the ghee in a heavy-based pan and fry the cashew nuts until golden brown. Add the onions. Blend the remaining ingredients to a paste in a blender or food processor then stir into the pan. Cook over a low heat, stirring occasionally, until the mixture is well cooked and the ghee appears on the surface. Add the water and bring to the boil. Add the egg cubes and simmer gently until the korma thickens. Serve with rice or parathas.

Egg and Bean Curry
Serves 6

6 eggs ● 30 ml/2 tbsp ghee or oil ● 450 g/1 lb French beans

salt ● 1 onion, chopped ● 2.5 cm/1 in ginger root

6 cloves garlic ● 15 ml/1 tbsp chilli powder

10 ml/2 tsp coriander (cilantro) seeds ● 10 ml/2 tsp cumin seeds

5 ml/1 tsp ground turmeric ● 300 ml/½ pt/2½ cups water

Hard-boil the eggs then shell them. Heat the ghee or oil and fry the eggs until golden brown. Cut them in half and set aside, reserving the ghee or oil. String the beans and cut into 2.5 cm/1 in pieces. Boil in salted water for 10 minutes, drain and set aside. Reheat the ghee or oil and fry the onion until soft. Blend the ginger and garlic to a paste in a blender or food processor then add to the pan with the spices. Stir over a medium heat until the ghee appears on the surface. Add the water and simmer gently to form a thickish gravy, adding extra water if preferred. Add the halved eggs and beans and simmer for a further 15 minutes.

Parsi Akoori
Serves 6

12 eggs ● 30 ml/2 tbsp ghee or oil ● 3 onions, finely chopped

2 tomatoes, skinned and chopped ● 2.5 ml/½ tsp ground turmeric

2.5 ml/½ tsp garam masala ● 3 green chillies, sliced

15 ml/1 tbsp chopped fresh coriander (cilantro) ● salt ● 4 bananas

Boil 10 eggs, shell them and chop them coarsely. Heat the ghee or oil and fry the onions until soft. Add the tomatoes, turmeric and garam masala and fry until the tomatoes are tender. Add the cooked eggs, the chillies, coriander and salt to taste. Lightly beat the remaining eggs and stir them into the pan. Cook over a low heat, stirring constantly, until the mixture thickens but does not dry up. Meanwhile, lightly grill (broil) the bananas then peel them and halve them lengthways. Pile the egg mixture in the centre of a serving dish and arrange the bananas around the edge.

Spiced Eggs on Toast
Serves 4

15 ml/1 tbsp ghee or butter ● 2 onions, chopped ● 1 tomato

15 ml/1 tbsp chopped fresh coriander (cilantro)

2.5 ml/½ tsp garam masala ● 3 green chillies, chopped

5 ml/1 tsp chopped green mango ● 1.5 ml/¼ tsp ground turmeric

salt and pepper ● 6 eggs ● 4 slices toast

Heat the ghee or butter and fry the onions until golden brown. Add all the remaining ingredients except the eggs and toast and fry for a few minutes. Remove from the heat, break in the eggs, stir well then return to the heat. Cook over a low heat for a few minutes then serve on hot toast.

Eggs and Kheema

Serves 4

30 ml/2 tbsp ghee • 2 onions, chopped

2.5 cm/1 in ginger root, chopped • 3 cloves garlic, chopped

450 g/1 lb minced (ground) beef • 5 ml/1 tsp chilli powder

5 ml/1 tsp ground coriander (cilantro) • 5 ml/1 tsp ground turmeric

5 ml/1 tsp garam masala • salt

1 tomato, skinned and chopped • 6-8 eggs

Heat the ghee and fry the onions, ginger and garlic until golden brown. Add the beef, chilli powder, coriander, turmeric, garam masala and salt to taste and cook until the liquid dries up. Add the tomato and cook until the meat is tender, adding a little warm water if necessary. Spoon the meat into an ovenproof dish and break the eggs on top, side by side. Place in a preheated oven at 200°C/400°F/gas mark 6 and bake for 20 minutes until the eggs are cooked. Serve immediately with nan.

Egg Cutlets

Serves 4

15 ml/1 tbsp butter • 25 g/1 oz/¼ cup plain (all-purpose) flour

300 ml/½ pt/1¼ cups milk • 50 g/2 oz/2 tbsp cooked long-grain rice

4 hard-boiled (hard-cooked) eggs, chopped • 2 green chillies, chopped

pinch of grated nutmeg • 1.5 ml/¼ tsp chopped fresh coriander (cilantro)

salt and pepper • 100 g/4 oz/1 cup white breadcrumbs

1 egg, lightly beaten • oil for deep-frying

Melt the butter, stir in the flour and cook for a few seconds. Stir in the milk, bring to the boil and simmer, stirring for 5 minutes. Stir in the rice, eggs, chillies, nutmeg and coriander. Season with salt and pepper and stir in enough breadcrumbs to make a thick mixture. Spread the mixture on a floured surface and leave to cool.

Divide the mixture into equal portions and shape into cutlets. Coat in egg and the remaining breadcrumbs and deep-fry in hot fat. Drain on kitchen paper and serve with tomato purée or chutney.

Egg Vindaloo

Serves 4

4 dried red chillies • 5 cloves garlic • 2.5 cm/1 in ginger root

2.5 ml/½ tsp cumin seeds • 450 ml/¾ pt/2 cups wine vinegar

salt • 30 ml/2 tbsp ghee • 225 g/8 oz/½ lb onions, chopped

½ cinnamon stick • 5 ml/1 tsp garam masala • 15 ml/1 tbsp sugar

4 hard-boiled (hard-cooked) eggs, halved

Blend the chillies, garlic, ginger and cumin seeds with a little wine vinegar and salt to a smooth paste in a blender or food processor. Heat the ghee and fry the onions until soft. Add the cinnamon and ground paste and cook over a low heat for 5 minutes. Add the remaining wine vinegar, garam masala and sugar. Add the eggs and cook until the gravy thickens. Serve with rice or rotis.

Spiced Onion Omelette   Serves 1

15 ml/1 tbsp chopped fresh coriander (cilantro)

2.5 ml/½ tsp garam masala ● 1.5 ml/¼ tsp ground turmeric

1 small onion, finely chopped ● salt ● 2 eggs, beaten

30 ml/2 tbsp oil

Whisk the spices, onion and salt into the eggs. Heat half the oil in a frying pan (skillet) and pour in the egg mixture. Fry without stirring until golden brown on the bottom. Turn it over carefully and pour the remaining oil around the edge. Cook until golden brown. Fold in half and serve hot at breakfast with chutney.

Scrambled Egg   Serves 4-6

45 ml/3 tbsp oil ● 5 ml/1 tsp cumin seeds

2 medium onions, finely chopped ● 5 ml/1 tsp garam masala

5 ml/1 tsp ground coriander (cilantro) ● 2.5 ml/½ tsp ground red chilli

2.5 ml/½ tsp ground turmeric ● salt ● 6 eggs, beaten

15 ml/1 tbsp chopped fresh coriander (cilantro)

1 green chilli, chopped

Heat the oil in a frying pan (skillet) and brown the cumin seeds over a medium heat. Add the onions and fry until golden. Stir in the ground spices and salt and cook for 30 seconds. Pour in the eggs and stir for 3-4 minutes until firm then mix in the coriander and chilli. Serve hot with onion paratha at breakfast or as a side dish at a meal.

Shai Paneer   Serves 4

30 ml/2 tbsp oil ● 2 onions, chopped

1 cm/½ in ginger root, grated ● 2 green chillies, chopped

pinch of ground turmeric ● 30 ml/2 tbsp chopped fresh coriander (cilantro)

2 tomatoes, skinned and chopped ● 15 ml/1 tbsp tomato purée (paste)

2.5 ml/½ tsp black pepper ● 2.5 ml/½ tsp garam masala ● salt

350 g/12 oz Paneer (page 20), cubed

250 ml/8 fl oz/1 cup soured (dairy sour) cream

Heat the oil and fry the onions until lightly browned. Add the ginger, chillies and turmeric and fry for 1 minute. Add the coriander and tomatoes and fry until the oil appears on the surface. Add the tomato purée, pepper garam masala and salt and cook for a few seconds. Add the paneer and cream and heat through gently before serving.

Paneer Kofta
Serves 4-6

300 g/11 oz Paneer (page 20) ● oil for frying ● 120 ml/4 fl oz/½ ghee or oil

1 small onion, finely chopped ● 4 cloves ● 4 black peppercorns

2 bay leaves ● 1 cm/½ in cinnamon stick ● 1 black cardamom pod

3 large cloves garlic ● 2.5 cm/1 in ginger root, coarsely chopped

1 large onion, coarsely chopped ● 45 ml/3 tbsp water

15 ml/1 tbsp white poppy seeds, ground

60 ml/4 tbsp desiccated (shredded) coconut, ground

5 ml/1 tsp ground coriander (cilantro) ● 5 ml/1 tsp ground roasted cumin

2.5 ml/½ tsp garam masala ● 2.5 ml/½ tsp ground red chilli

2.5 ml/½ tsp ground turmeric ● salt

400 g/14 oz canned tomatoes, chopped

350 ml/12 fl oz/1½ cups whey water (from paneer)

Garnish: 1.5 ml/¼ tsp garam masala

15 ml/1 tbsp chopped fresh coriander (cilantro) ● 1 small green chilli, chopped

Divide the paneer into 16 equal portions and shape into balls. Heat the oil and fry until light golden brown. Remove and drain. Heat the ghee in a heavy-based pan and fry the onion and whole spices until golden brown. Blend the garlic, ginger, onion and water to a smooth paste in a blender or food processor, add to the pan and fry until golden brown. Add the poppy seeds and fry for 2 minutes. Add the coconut and fry for a few minutes until golden brown. Stir in the spices and tomatoes and cook until the liquid has been absorbed and the ghee appears on the surface. Pour in 45 ml/3 tbsp of the whey water and cook again until the liquid has evaporated. Repeat twice so that the spices can be matured. Finally add the remaining whey water and paneer kofta. Bring to the boil, reduce the heat to low then simmer for 5 minutes. Sprinkle with the garnish ingredients and serve hot with vegetable pulao, raita and puris.

Paneer Keema
Serves 4-6

100 ml/3½ fl oz/6½ tbsp ghee or oil ● 3 large garlic cloves, crushed

2.5 cm/1 in ginger root, finely chopped ● 2 onions, finely chopped

300 g/11 oz Paneer (page 20), crumbled ● 2 bay leaves

5 ml/1 tsp garam masala ● 5 ml/1 tsp ground coriander (cilantro)

5 ml/1 tsp ground roasted cumin ● 2.5 ml/½ tsp ground red chilli

2.5 ml/½ tsp ground turmeric ● salt

25 g/8 oz canned tomatoes, chopped ● 150 ml/¼ pt/⅔ cup natural (plain) yoghurt

450 g/1 lb peas ● 150 ml/¼ pt/⅔ cup whey water (from paneer)

100 g/4 oz/⅔ cup raisins ● 50 g/2 oz/½ cup blanched almonds, halved

50 g/2 oz/½ cup cashew nuts, halved

Garnish: 2.5 ml/½ tsp garam masala

15 ml/1 tbsp chopped fresh coriander (cilantro)

1 small green chilli, chopped (optional)

Heat the ghee or oil in a heavy-based pan and fry the garlic, ginger and onions until lightly browned. Add the paneer and fry until golden brown. Stir in the bay leaves and ground spices and then the tomatoes and cook until all the liquid has been absorbed and the ghee appears on the surface. Add the yoghurt and cook until all the liquid has evaporated. Stir in the peas, whey water, raisins and nuts and bring to the boil. Reduce the heat to low and simmer for 5 minutes until the peas are tender. Sprinkle with the garnish ingredients and serve hot with puris, vegetable pulao and a meat curry.

Spiced Paneer
Serves 4

30 ml/2 tbsp ghee ● 100 g/4 oz Paneer (page 20), cubed

15 ml/1 tbsp chopped onion ● 2 bay leaves ● pinch of ground turmeric

350 g/12 oz peas ● 2.5 ml/½ tsp grated ginger root

1 green chilli, chopped ● 300 ml/½ pt/1¼ cups stock

salt ● 5 ml/1 tsp garam masala

15 ml/1 tbsp chopped fresh coriander (cilantro)

Heat the ghee and fry the paneer until deep golden then drain and remove from the pan. Fry the onion, bay leaves and turmeric until the ghee appears on the surface. Add the peas, ginger and chilli. Add the stock, bring to the boil and simmer over a medium heat for about 15 minutes until the peas are almost cooked. Add the paneer and season to taste with salt, cover and simmer for 5 minutes. Add the garam masala and serve hot, sprinkled with coriander.

Matar Paneer
Serves 4-6

300 g/11 oz Paneer (page 20) ● oil for deep-frying

60 ml/4 tbsp ghee or oil ● 5 ml/1 tsp cumin seeds

1 small onion, finely chopped ● 4 cloves ● 4 peppercorns

2 bay leaves ● 1 black cardamom pod ● 3 large garlic cloves

2.5 cm/1 in ginger root ● 1 onion, cut into chunks

45 ml/3 tbsp water ● 7.5 ml/1½ tsp ground coriander (cilantro)

2.5 ml/½ tsp ground red chilli ● 2.5 ml/½ tsp ground turmeric

225 g/8 oz canned tomatoes, chopped ● salt

600 ml/1 pt/2½ cups whey water (from paneer) ● 500 g/18 oz peas

Garnish: 2.5 ml/½ tsp garam masala

15 ml/1 tbsp chopped fresh coriander (cilantro)

2 small green chillies, chopped

Chop the paneer into 1 cm/½ in cubes and fry in the oil until lightly browned. Remove with a slotted spoon and set aside.

Heat the ghee or oil in a heavy-based pan and fry the cumin seeds until lightly browned. Add the onion, cloves, peppercorns, bay leaves and cardamom and fry until golden brown. Blend the garlic, ginger, onion and water to a smooth paste in a blender or food processor. Stir into the pan and fry for a few minutes until golden brown. Add the coriander, chilli, turmeric, tomatoes and salt and cook over a medium heat until all the liquid has been absorbed. Add 60 ml/4 tbsp of whey water to the pan and fry until all the water has been absorbed and the ghee appears on the surface. Add the remaining whey water and the fried paneer and simmer for 10 minutes. Add the peas and simmer for a further 5 minutes until the peas are cooked and the paneer is soft and spongy. Sprinkle over the garnish ingredients and serve hot with puris, pulao, cauliflower and a chicken dish.

Palk Paneer   Serves 4

500 g/18 oz spinach leaves ● 300 ml/½ pt/1¼ cups water

150 g/5 oz Paneer (page 20), cut into 1 cm/½ in squares

oil for deep-frying ● 60 ml/4 tbsp ghee or oil ● 1 onion, finely chopped

2 large garlic cloves, crushed ● 2.5 cm/1 in ginger root, finely chopped

5 ml/1 tsp ground coriander (cilantro) ● 5 ml/1 tsp ground roasted cumin

2.5 ml/½ tsp ground red chilli ● 2.5 ml/½ tsp garam masala

1.5 ml/¼ tsp ground turmeric ● salt ● 225 g/8 oz canned tomatoes

Garnish: 2.5 ml/½ tsp garam masala ● 1 small green chilli, chopped

Boil the spinach and water together for a few minutes until the spinach is tender. Cool, then blend to a smooth paste in a blender or food processor. Fry the paneer in a deep frying pan (skillet) until golden brown. Drain.

Heat the ghee or oil in a heavy-based pan and fry the onion, garlic and ginger until golden brown. Stir in the ground spices, salt and tomatoes and cook until the ghee appears on the surface. Add the spinach and paneer, cover and simmer for about 10 minutes until the paneer is soft and spongy, adding a little more water during cooking if necessary. Sprinkle with the garnish ingredients and serve hot with nan or maize chapatis, dal, raita and tandoori chicken.

Paneer with Green Pepper   Serves 4

30 ml/2 tbsp oil ● 5 ml/1 tsp cumin seeds ● 4 onions, sliced

salt and pepper ● 225 g/8 oz Paneer (page 20), cubed

4 green (bell) peppers, cut into rings

Heat the oil and fry for cumin seeds for 1 minute. Add the onions and fry until softened but not browned. Add salt and pepper and paneer, cover and simmer until the oil appears on the surface and the liquid has evaporated. Add the peppers and simmer for 5 minutes. Cover and leave to stand for 2 minutes before serving.

Vegetables and Vegetarian Dishes

In India, a large number of people are vegetarian, and Indian soil produces lovely different varieties of vegetables. Also, everyone likes to eat a lot of vegetables as it is often too hot to eat meat and meat can be very expensive to buy. There is therefore a vast range of vegetable and vegetarian cooking throughout all the regions, giving ample scope for vegetarian cooking, or using vegetable dishes with meat courses. Many of the dishes in the Dals chapter are also vegetarian.

Apple Curry   Serves 4-6

6 small cooking (tart) apples ● oil for deep-frying

150 ml/¼ pt/⅔ cup oil or ghee ● 5 ml/1 tsp cumin seeds

2 medium onions, chopped ● 4 cloves ● 4 peppercorns

2.5 cm/1 in cinnamon stick ● 1 black cardamom pod

4 large garlic cloves, chopped ● 2.5 cm/1 in ginger root, coarsely chopped

450 ml/¾ pt/2 cups water ● 25 g/1 oz/¼ cup poppy seeds, finely ground

75 g/3 oz/¾ cup desiccated (shredded) coconut, ground

10 ml/2 tsp ground coriander (cilantro) ● 5 ml/1 tsp ground turmeric

2.5 ml/½ tsp ground red chilli ● 2.5 ml/½ tsp garam masala

salt ● 400 g/14 oz canned tomatoes, chopped ● 15 ml/1 tbsp lemon juice

Garnish: 2.5 ml/½ tsp garam masala

15 ml/1 tbsp chopped fresh coriander (cilantro) ● 1 small green chilli, chopped

Peel the apples and remove the pips and core with a sharp knife. Prick the apples all over with a fork then deep-fry in hot oil until golden brown. Drain and reserve.

Heat the oil or ghee in a large heavy-based pan and fry the cumin seeds until lightly browned. Add 1 chopped onion and the cloves, peppercorns, cinnamon and cardamon and fry gently over a medium heat until golden brown. Blend the remaining onion, the garlic, ginger and 30 ml/2 tbsp of water to a smooth paste in a blender or food processor. Stir into the pan and fry for 5 minutes. Add the poppy seeds and fry for 2 minutes.

Add the coconut and fry for a further few minutes until golden brown. Stir in the coriander, turmeric, chilli, garam masala, salt and tomatoes and fry until all the liquid has been absorbed and the oil appears on the surface of the mixture. Add 45 ml/3 tbsp of water and fry until it is absorbed. Repeat this twice, then add the remaining water and the lemon juice. Bring to the boil, cover and simmer gently for 3 minutes. Pour the sauce into a serving dish and top with the fried apples. Sprinkle over the garnish ingredients and serve hot with rice and a potato or bean dish.

Cooking Apple Bhaji
Serves 4

45 ml/3 tbsp oil ● 5 ml/1 tsp mustard seeds

5 ml/1 tsp ground roasted cumin ● 2.5 ml/½ tsp garam masala

2.5 ml/½ tsp ground turmeric ● 1.5 ml/¼ tsp ground red chilli

1.5 ml/¼ tsp ground mace ● 1.5 ml/¼ tsp grated nutmeg

salt ● 450 g/1 lb cooking (tart) apples, peeled, cored and cut into 1 cm/½ in pieces

225 g/8 oz canned tomatoes ● 45 ml/3 tbsp sugar

100 g/4 oz/⅔ cup raisins

Garnish: 1.5 ml/¼ tsp garam masala

15 ml/1 tbsp chopped fresh coriander (cilantro) ● 1 small green chilli, chopped

Heat the oil in a heavy-based pan and fry the mustard seeds over a medium heat until they start crackling. Add the cumin, garam masala, turmeric, chilli, mace, nutmeg, salt. Add the apples and tomatoes and fry over a low heat for about 10 minutes until the apples are tender. Stir in the sugar and raisins, increase the heat and cook until any remaining liquid has evaporated. Sprinkle over the garnish ingredients and serve hot with puris or paratha, raita, dal and a kofta dish.

Curried Asparagus
Serves 4

450 g/1 lb asparagus ● 60 ml/4 tbsp oil

1.5 ml/¼ tsp fenugreek seeds ● 1.5 ml/¼ tsp cumin seeds

1.5 ml/¼ tsp fennel seeds ● 1.5 ml/¼ tsp mustard seeds

1.5 ml/¼ tsp onion seeds ● pinch of chilli powder

30 ml/2 tbsp lemon juice ● 2.5 ml/½ tsp paprika

Tie the asparagus into bundles and steam for 5 minutes. Drain well then cut into 2.5 cm/1 in pieces. Heat the oil and fry the seeds and chilli powder for 30 seconds. Add the asparagus and stir-fry for 1 minute. Stir in the lemon juice and paprika and serve at once.

Sweet and Sour Aubergine
Serves 4

450 g/1 lb aubergines (eggplants), thickly sliced ● salt

120 ml/4 fl oz/½ cup oil ● 2.5 cm/1 in cinnamon stick

4 onions, thinly sliced ● 2 green chillies, thinly sliced

10 ml/2 tsp chopped fresh coriander (cilantro) ● 5 ml/1 tsp ground cumin

2.5 ml/½ tsp garam masala ● pepper

60 ml/4 tbsp tamarind concentrate ● 15 ml/1 tbsp jagggery

Sprinkle the aubergine with salt and leave to drain for 30 minutes. Heat the oil and fry the aubergine until golden then remove from the pan. Add the cinnamon and fry until it darkens slightly. Add the onions and fry until lightly browned. Add the chillies, coriander, cumin, garam masala, salt and pepper and fry for a few seconds, stirring. Add the tamarind extract and jaggery and simmer for 3 minutes. Add the aubergines and heat through before serving.

Spicy Aubergine
Serves 6

6 small aubergines (eggplants) ● 30 ml/2 tbsp gingelly oil

45 ml/3 tbsp coriander (cilantro) seeds ● 8 dried red chillies

2 onions, chopped ● 2.5 ml/½ tsp ground turmeric

¼ coconut, grated (shredded) ● 2 cloves garlic

30 ml/2 tbsp gingelly seeds ● 1 lemon-sized tamarind pulp

1.2 1/2 pts/5 cups water ● 15 ml/1 tbsp jaggery ● 30 ml/2 tbsp ghee

30 ml/2 tbsp mustard seeds ● 2 green chillies, chopped

1 sprig fresh curry leaves

Cut the aubergines in half lengthways and fry in half the oil until the skins turn light brown then remove from the pan. Add the remaining oil and fry the coriander, chillies, onions and turmeric until soft. Grind them with the coconut and garlic. Dry roast the gingelly seeds then grind them. Soak the tamarind in the water then strain out the pulp then boil the water with the ground spices for 5 minutes. Add the aubergines and gingelly seeds, cover and cook until the sauce thickens. Add the jaggery. Heat the ghee and fry the mustard seeds, chillies and curry leaves until the seeds start crackling then add to the curry and stir well before serving.

Gujrati-style Aubergine and Potato
Serves 4

75 ml/5 tbsp oil ● large pinch of asafoetida ● 2.5 ml/½ tsp fenugreek seeds

2.5 ml/½ tsp mustard seeds ● 2 large garlic cloves, crushed

1 cm/½ in ginger root, chopped ● 1 small onion, finely chopped

225 g/8 oz potato, cut into 2.5 cm/1 in pieces

15 ml/1 tbsp desiccated (shredded) coconut

225 g/8 oz aubergine (eggplant), cut into 2.5 cm/1 in pieces

5 ml/1 tsp ground coriander (cilantro) ● 5 ml/1 tsp ground roasted cumin

2.5 ml/½ tsp garam masala ● 2.5 ml/½ tsp ground red chilli

2.5 ml/½ tsp ground turmeric ● salt ● 225 g/8 oz canned tomatoes, chopped

15 ml/1 tbsp sugar ● 15 ml/1 tbsp lemon juice

Garnish: pinch of garam masala

15 ml/1 tbsp chopped fresh coriander (cilantro) ● 1 small green chilli, chopped

Heat the oil in a heavy-based pan and fry the asafoetida, fenugreek and mustard seeds over a medium heat until the mustard seeds start crackling. Add the garlic, ginger and onion and fry until lightly browned. Add the potato and fry until golden brown. Add the coconut and aubergine and fry for 1 minute. Stir in the coriander, cumin, garam masala, chilli, turmeric and salt. Stir in the tomatoes. Reduce the heat to low, cover and simmer for 20 minutes until the vegetables are tender, stirring occasionally. Add a little water if the mixture becomes too thick. Add the sugar and lemon juice, increase the heat and fry until any remaining liquid has evaporated. Sprinkle with the garnish ingredients and serve hot with dal, rice, raita, chapatis or paratha and a chicken dish.

Stuffed Aubergine Poriyal   Serves 4

5 ml/1 tsp oil ● 15 ml/1 tbsp coriander (cilantro) seeds

15 ml/1 tbsp split black beans ● 15 ml/1 tbsp yellow split peas

5 ml/1 tsp cumin seeds ● pinch of asafoetida ● 5 dried red chillies

salt ● 100 g/4 oz grated (shredded) coconut, toasted

15 ml/1 tbsp tamarind concentrate ● 450 g/1 lb aubergines (eggplants), quartered

45 ml/3 tbsp ghee ● 5 ml/1 tsp mustard seeds

5 ml/1 tsp cumin seeds ● 5 ml/1 tsp split black beans

5 ml/1 tsp yellow split peas ● 1 dried red chilli, halved ● 2-3 curry leaves

Heat the oil and fry the coriander seeds, split beans, split peas, cumin seeds, asafoetida, chillies and salt for 2 minutes. Add the coconut and tamarind and grind to a paste with a little water, if necessary. Fill the aubergines with the stuffing. Heat the ghee and fry the remaining ingredients until the mustard seeds start crackling. Add the stuffed aubergines, salt and a little water, cover and simmer over a low heat until the aubergines are tender. Remove the lid and fry for a few more minutes before serving.

North Indian-style Mashed Aubergine   Serves 4-6

500 g/18 oz aubergines (eggplants) ● 60 ml/4 tbsp oil

2.5 ml/½ tsp mustard seeds ● 2.5 ml/½ tsp cumin seeds

3 large garlic cloves, crushed ● 2 onions, finely chopped

2.5 cm/1 in ginger root, finely chopped ● 30 ml/2 tbsp ground coriander (cilantro)

2.5 ml/½ tsp ground red chilli ● 2.5 ml/½ tsp ground turmeric

2.5 ml/½ tsp garam masala ● 400 g/14 oz canned tomatoes, chopped

salt ● 250 g/9 oz peas

Garnish: 2.5 ml/½ tsp garam masala

15 ml/1 tbsp chopped fresh coriander (cilantro) ● 1 small green chilli, chopped

Bake the aubergine in a preheated oven at 200°C/400°F/gas mark 6 for about 45 minutes until tender. Peel off the skin and mash or purée the flesh.

Heat the oil in a heavy-based pan and fry the mustard seeds over a medium heat until they start crackling. Add the cumin seeds, garlic, onion and ginger and fry over a medium heat until golden brown. Stir in the mashed aubergine and fry for a further 2 minutes. Add the coriander, chilli, turmeric, garam masala and tomatoes and simmer until all the water has been absorbed and the oil appears on the surface. Stir in the peas and simmer for 3 minutes. Sprinkle with the garnish ingredients and serve hot with puris or chapatis, rice, dal and a chicken dish.

Coconut-stuffed Aubergine   Serves 4

450 g/1 lb small aubergines (eggplants) • 30 ml/2 tbsp ghee

4 curry leaves • 8 dried red chillies

15 ml/1 tbsp coriander (cilantro) seeds • 2.5 ml/½ tsp cumin seeds

5 ml/1 tsp ground fenugreek • 5 ml/1 tsp ground turmeric

5 ml/1 tsp salt • 5 ml/1 tsp tamarind concentrate

½ coconut, grated (shredded) • 2.5 ml/½ tsp mustard seeds

2 onions, chopped

Slit the aubergines into fours, keeping the stem intact, and leave to soak in water. Heat half the ghee and fry the curry leaves, chillies, coriander, cumin seeds, fenugreek and turmeric until lightly coloured. Grind with the salt, tamarind and coconut, adding a little water. Stuff the aubergines with three-quarters of this mixture.

Heat the remaining ghee and fry the mustard seeds until they start crackling. Add the onions and fry until golden brown. Arrange the aubergines carefully in the same pan and add the reserved stuffing and a little more water. Cover and simmer over a low heat for about 20 minutes until the aubergines are tender and the gravy has thickened.

Aubergine Bhurta   Serves 4

50 g/2 oz/¼ cup ghee • pinch of cumin seeds • 1 onion, chopped

2 cloves garlic, chopped • 1 cm/½ in ginger root, grated

2 tomatoes, skinned and quartered

450 g/1 lb aubergines (eggplants), cubed and boiled • salt

2 green chillies, chopped • 2.5 ml/½ tsp garam masala

15 ml/1 tbsp chopped fresh coriander (cilantro)

Heat the ghee and fry the cumin seeds, onion, garlic and ginger for 2 minutes. Add the tomatoes, aubergine, salt and chillies and cook for 10 minutes, stirring. Sprinkle with the garam masala and coriander before serving.

Aubergine Rasavangy
Serves 4

50 g/2 oz yellow lentils ● 5 ml/1 tsp oil

30 ml/2 tbsp coriander (cilantro) seeds ● 2 dried red chillies

2.5 ml/½ tsp asafoetida ● 60 ml/4 tbsp grated (shredded) coconut

10 ml/2 tsp ghee ● 5 ml/1 tsp mustard seeds ● 2 green chillies, slit

150 g/5 oz aubergines (eggplants), quartered

1 tomato, skinned and chopped ● 2.5 ml/½ tsp Sambar Powder (page 15)

30 ml/1 tbsp jaggery ● 5 ml/1 tsp tamarind concentrate ● salt

2-3 curry leaves ● 15 ml/1 tbsp chopped fresh coriander (cilantro)

Cook the lentils in boiling water for about 20 minutes until tender then drain. Heat the oil and fry the coriander, chillies and asafoetida until slightly darkened. Grind to a paste with the coconut and a very little water, if necessary. Heat the ghee and fry the mustard seeds until they start crackling. Add all the remaining ingredients except the lentils and coriander and cook until the vegetables are tender. Stir in the lentils and paste and simmer for 10 minutes, stirring. Garnish with coriander and serve hot with rice.

Stuffed Aubergine
Serves 4-6

90 ml/6 tbsp oil ● 2.5 ml/½ tsp mustard seeds

1 small onion, finely chopped ● 1 large onion ● 4 garlic cloves

2.5 cm/1 in ginger root ● 45 ml/3 tbsp water

15 ml/1 tbsp ground coriander (cilantro) ● 15 ml/1 tbsp sugar

5 ml/1 tsp ground roasted cumin ● 2.5 ml/½ tsp ground red chilli

2.5 ml/½ tsp ground turmeric ● 2.5 ml/½ tsp garam masala

1.5 ml/¼ tsp grated nutmeg ● 1.5 ml/¼ tsp ground mace ● salt

400 g/14 oz canned tomatoes, chopped

30 ml/2 tbsp tamarind pulp (page 19) or lemon juice

500 g/18 oz small aubergines (eggplants)

Garnish: 2.5 ml/½ tsp garam masala

15 ml/1 tbsp chopped fresh coriander (cilantro) ● 1 small green chilli, chopped

Heat half the oil in a heavy-based pan and fry the mustard seeds over a medium heat until they start crackling. Add the chopped onion and fry gently until golden brown. Blend the large onion, garlic, ginger and water to a fine paste in a blender or food processor. Stir it into the pan and fry for a few minutes until golden brown. Add the coriander, sugar, cumin, chilli, turmeric, garam masala, nutmeg, salt and tomatoes and cook until all the water has been absorbed and the oil appears on surface. Stir in the tamarind or lemon juice and cook for a few minutes until the liquid has been absorbed. Leave to cool slightly.

Slit the aubergines lengthways without cutting right through. Push the stuffing into the centre of the aubergines; there may be a little left over. Heat the remaining oil in a heavy-based pan on a low heat and add the stuffed aubergine. Cover and cook for 25 minutes, stirring occasionally, until tender and browned on all sides. Arrange the aubergines in a serving dish with the remaining stuffing and sprinkle over the garnish ingredients. Serve hot with onion paratha, rice, a lentil dish, a meat dish and raita.

Aubergines with Mustard Seeds   Serves 6

3 medium aubergines (eggplants) • 60 ml/4 tbsp ghee

30 ml/2 tbsp mustard seeds, ground • 2.5 ml/½ tsp chilli powder

60 ml/4 tbsp chopped fresh coriander (cilantro) • 5 ml/1 tsp salt

300 ml/½ pt/1¼ cups natural (plain) yoghurt

Grill (broil) the aubergines for about 15 minutes until the skins are charred and the flesh is soft. When cool enough to handle, peel off the skins and roughly chop the flesh. Heat the ghee and fry the mustard seeds, aubergine and chilli powder for 5 minutes, stirring. Add the coriander. Beat the salt into the yoghurt then stir into the pan until well blended. Serve at once.

Curried Bananas   Serves 6

6 green bananas • 2 onions, chopped • 6 cloves garlic

5 ml/1 tsp salt • 4 dried red chillies • 10 ml/2 tsp coriander (cilantro) seeds

5 ml/1 tsp garam masala • 5 ml/1 tsp mango powder • 45 ml/3 tbsp ghee

45 ml/3 tbsp natural (plain) yoghurt • 15 ml/1 tbsp chopped fresh coriander (cilantro)

Peel the bananas and slit them lengthways. Blend the onions, garlic, salt, chillies and spices to a paste. Stuff the bananas with the paste and secure with string. Heat the ghee and fry the bananas until browned. Add the yoghurt and cook until soft and tender, adding a little water if necessary. Serve garnished with coriander.

Banana Foogath   Serves 4

30 ml/2 tbsp ghee • 4 bananas, chopped • juice of 1 lemon

½ green (bell) pepper, sliced • 2 tomatoes, skinned and chopped

5 ml/1 tsp chilli powder • salt

Heat the ghee then add all the ingredients and stir gently over a medium heat until sizzling. Serve at once.

Olan
Serves 6

1 green banana ● 100 g/4 oz green beans ● 100 g/4 oz carrots

100 g/4 oz potatoes ● 100 g/4 oz peas ● 50 g/2 oz pumpkin

½ cucumber ● 8 green chillies ● pinch of salt

450 ml/¾ pt/2 cups coconut milk ● 1 sprig fresh curry leaves

Slice the vegetables and cook with the chillies in boiling salted water until tender and the water has evaporated. Add the coconut milk and curry leaves, bring to the boil then serve at once.

Green Banana Curry
Serves 4-6

Kofta: 500 g/18 oz green bananas ● 1 l/1¼ pts/4¼ cups water

30 ml/2 tbsp gram flour ● 15 ml/1 tbsp oil ● 5 ml/1 tsp garam masala

1 large cloves garlic, crushed ● 1 cm/½ in ginger root, finely chopped

1 small onion, finely chopped ● 45 ml/3 tbsp chopped fresh coriander (cilantro)

salt ● oil for frying

Sauce: 75 ml/5 tbsp ghee or oil ● 4 cloves ● 4 black peppercorns

2.5 cm/½ in cinnamon stick ● 2 bay leaves ● 1 black cardamom pod

3 cloves garlic ● 1 cm/½ in ginger root, chopped

1 onion, coarsely chopped ● 45 ml/3 tbsp water

5 ml/1 tsp ground coriander (cilantro) ● 5 ml/1 tsp ground roasted cumin

2.5 ml/½ tsp ground red chilli ● 2.5 ml/½ tsp ground turmeric

2.5 ml/¼ tsp ground mace ● 1.5 ml/¼ tsp grated nutmeg ● salt

225 g/8 oz canned tomatoes ● 45 ml/3 tbsp tamarind chutney

350 ml/12 fl oz/1⅔ cups water

Garnish: 2.5 ml/½ tsp garam masala

15 ml/1 tbsp chopped fresh coriander (cilantro) ● 1 small green chilli, chopped

Place the bananas and water in a large pan and simmer for 30 minutes until tender. Remove the skins and mash the bananas. Sift the gram flour into a pan and roast until golden. Remove from the heat and mix into the banana with the garam masala, garlic, ginger, onion, coriander and salt. Divide the mixture into 14 sausage shapes. Heat the oil and fry the koftas until crispy golden brown. Remove and cool.

To make the sauce, heat the ghee or oil and fry the whole spices until golden brown. Blend the garlic, ginger, onion and water to a paste, then stir it into the pan and fry until golden brown. Stir in the ground spices and tomatoes and fry until all the liquid has been absorbed. Stir in the chutney and 45 ml/3 tbsp of water and cook until all the liquid has evaporated. Add the remaining water, bring to the boil and simmer for 5 minutes. Pour the hot sauce over the koftas and sprinkle with the garnish ingredients. Serve hot with pulao, raita and okra.

North Indian-style Beans and Potato
Serves 4

75 ml/5 tbsp oil or ghee ● 2.5 ml/½ tsp mustard seeds

2.5 ml/½ tsp cumin seeds ● 2 large garlic cloves, crushed

2.5 cm/1 in ginger root, finely chopped ● 1 medium onion, finely chopped

250 g/9 oz potatoes, cut into 1 cm/½ in pieces

250 g/9 oz beans, cut into 1 cm/½ in pieces

5 ml/1 tsp garam masala ● 5 ml/1 tsp ground coriander (cilantro)

5 ml/1 tsp ground roasted cumin ● 2.5 ml/½ tsp ground red chilli

2.5 ml/½ tsp ground turmeric ● salt

250 g/9 oz canned tomatoes, chopped ● 50 ml/2 fl oz/3½ tbsp water

15 ml/1 tbsp lemon juice

Garnish: pinch of garam masala ● 1 small green chilli, chopped

Heat the oil or ghee in a large heavy-based pan and fry the mustard seeds over a medium heat until they start crackling. Add the cumin seeds and fry until browned. Add the garlic, ginger and onion and fry until lightly browned. Add the potatoes and fry for 5 minutes. Add the beans and fry for 2 minutes. Stir in the garam masala, coriander, cumin, chilli, turmeric, salt, tomatoes and water. Bring to the boil, reduce the heat to low, cover and simmer for 15 minutes until tender, stirring occasionally. Increase the heat and simmer until the remaining liquid has evaporated. Sprinkle over the garnish ingredients and serve hot with onion paratha, puris, dal, rice and a chicken or meat dish.

Green Beans
Serves 4

100 g/4 oz green beans ● 600 ml/1 pt/2½ cups water ● salt

2.5 ml/½ tsp ground turmeric ● 2.5 ml/½ tsp grated ginger root

4 cloves garlic ● 225 g/8 oz tomatoes, sliced

2.5 ml/½ tsp garam masala ● 50 g/2 oz/¼ cup ghee

1 onion, chopped ● 2.5 ml/½ tsp cumin seeds ● 1 green chilli, chopped

Boil the beans in the water with the salt, turmeric, ginger and garlic for 20 minutes. Add the tomatoes and garam masala and cook for a further 10 minutes. Heat the ghee and fry the onion and cumin seeds until lightly browned. Stir in the chilli. Pour the onion mixture over the beans and serve hot.

Fried Green Beans
Serves 4

450 g/1 lb green beans, soaked overnight ● oil for deep-frying

salt ● large pinch of chilli powder ● pinch of mango powder

Drain the beans and leave to dry completely. Heat the oil to smoking point then fry the beans for about 1 minute. Remove, drain on kitchen paper and leave to cool. Place in an airtight container and mix in the salt, chilli and mango powders. Shake well and serve hot or cold.

Beans Poriyal
Serves 4

10 ml/2 tsp oil ● 5 ml/1 tsp mustard seeds ● 5 ml/1 tsp cumin seeds

5 ml/1 tsp split black beans ● 5 ml/1 tsp yellow split peas

1 dried red chilli, halved ● 2.5 ml/½ tsp asafoetida ● 2-3 curry leaves

450 g/1 lb green beans, chopped ● salt ● 30 ml/2 tbsp water

30 ml/2 tbsp grated (shredded) coconut

Heat the oil and fry the spices until the seeds start crackling. Add the beans, salt and water, cover and simmer until the beans are tender. Stir in the coconut and heat through before serving.

Bean Foogath
Serves 4

30 ml/2 tbsp ghee ● 225 g/8 oz green beans, cut into chunks

juice of 1 lemon ● ½ green (bell) pepper, sliced

2 tomatoes, skinned and chopped ● 5 ml/1 tsp chilli powder ● salt

Heat the ghee then add all the ingredients and stir gently over a medium heat until sizzling. Serve at once.

Beans and Lentil Poriyal
Serves 6

100 g/4 oz/⅔ cup red lentils ● 5 dried red chillies

pinch of asafoetida ● salt ● 450 g/1 lb green beans

30 ml/2 tbsp oil ● 5 ml/1 tsp mustard seeds ● 5 ml/1 tsp yellow split peas

5 ml/1 tsp split black beans ● 2.5 ml/½ tsp cumin seeds ● 2-3 curry leaves

Soak the lentils and 4 chillies in water for 1 hour then grind to a smooth paste with the asafoetida and salt. Cook the green beans in a heavy-based pan with very little water until tender. Heat the oil and fry the remaining ingredients until the seeds start crackling. Add the lentil paste and fry over a low heat, stirring occasionally, until the mixture is well cooked and looks like crisp breadcrumbs. Add the beans and fry for a few minutes, stirring. Serve at once.

Photograph opposite: *Tandoori Chicken Kebabs (page 164)*

Masala Beans Poriyal
Serves 4

10 ml/2 tsp oil • 45 ml/3 tbsp yellow split peas

15 ml/1 tbsp split black beans • 30 ml/2 tbsp coriander (cilantro) seeds

4 dried red chillies • 2.5 ml/½ tsp asafoetida

60 ml/4 tbsp grated (shredded) coconut • 5 ml/1 tsp tamarind concentrate

salt • 450 g/1 lb green beans, chopped • 30 ml/2 tbsp ghee

Seasoning: 5 ml/1 tsp mustard seeds • 5 ml/1 tsp yellow split peas

5 ml/1 tsp split black beans • 1 dried red chilli

2.5 ml/½ tsp asafoetida • 5 ml/1 tsp cumin seeds • 2-3 curry leaves

Heat the oil and fry the split peas, split beans, coriander seeds, chillies and asafoetida for 1 minute. Add the coconut and tamarind and grind to a paste with a very little water. Season with salt. Cook the green beans in a heavy-based pan with a little salt and water until tender. Heat the ghee and fry the seasoning ingredients until the mustard seeds start crackling. Stir in the masala paste and cook over a low heat for 5-7 minutes until the mixture is dry. Add the beans and cook for 2-3 minutes until well blended.

Green Beans with Coconut
Serves 6

45 ml/3 tbsp oil • 15 ml/1 tbsp mustard seeds • 4 dried red chillies

pinch of asafoetida • 2 onions, chopped • 1 cm/½ in ginger root, chopped

4 cloves garlic, crushed • 1.5 kg/3 lb green beans, cut into 2.5 cm/1 in pieces

50 g/2 oz grated (shredded) coconut • salt

Heat the oil and fry the mustard seeds until they start crackling. Add the chillies and asafoetida and fry for 30 seconds. Add the onions, ginger and garlic and cook until browned. Add the beans, coconut and salt, cover and simmer gently for 8-10 minutes until cooked. Remove the lid and cook for 5 minutes until the water has evaporated. Serve hot with rice and curry.

Stuffed Bitter Gourd
Serves 4-6

250 g/9 oz bitter gourd • salt • 2 onions, coarsely chopped

4 large cloves garlic • 2.5 cm/1 in ginger root

1 small green chilli (optional) • 105 ml/7 tbsp oil

10 ml/2 tsp ground coriander (cilantro) • 5 ml/1 tsp ground roasted cumin

5 ml/1 tsp garam masala • 2.5 ml/½ tsp ground turmeric

2.5 ml/½ tsp ground red chilli • salt • 25 g/1 oz tamarind pulp (page 19)

Photograph opposite: *Green Beans*
(page 191)

Scrape the bitter gourd, cut into 5 mm/¼ in rounds and scoop out and discard the seeds. Bring a pan of salted water to the boil, add the bitter gourd and boil for 1 minute. Drain and repeat 3 times then leave to cool and squeeze out any excess water.

Blend the onions, garlic, ginger and chilli, if using, in a blender or food processor to a smooth paste. Place the paste in a pan and cook over a medium heat until all the water has been absorbed. Add 75 ml/5 tbsp of oil and fry until golden brown. Stir in the ground spices and salt to taste

then mix in the tamarind pulp and cook until all the liquid has been absorbed. Add 45 ml/3 tbsp of water and cook until the water is absorbed. Repeat twice so that the spices have time to mature. Remove from the heat.

Meanwhile, fry the bitter gourd in the remaining oil over a medium-low heat for about 15 minutes until crispy and golden brown. Make a slit in the bitter gourd rounds and spoon in the filling. Serve hot or cold with puris, rice, dal and a meat or chicken dish.

Bitter Gourd with Onion   Serves 4

250 g/9 oz bitter gourd ● 500 ml/17 fl oz/2¼ cups water

5 ml/1 tsp salt ● 75 ml/5 tbsp oil ● 4 small onions, thinly sliced

1 green chilli, chopped ● 5 ml/1 tsp ground coriander (cilantro)

5 ml/1 tsp ground roasted cumin ● 5 ml/1 tsp garam masala

2.5 ml/½ tsp ground red chilli ● 2.5 ml/½ tsp ground turmeric ● salt

Scrape the bitter gourd, cut into 5 mm/¼ in rounds and scoop out and discard the seeds. Bring the water to the boil with the salt, add the bitter gourd and boil for 1 minute. Drain and repeat 3 times then leave to cool and squeeze out any excess water.

Heat the oil and fry the onion and bitter gourd over a medium heat for 25 minutes until golden brown and crispy. Stir in all the ground spices and cook over a low heat for 5 minutes. Serve hot or cold with paratha or puris, a lentil dish, rice and raita.

South Indian-style Cabbage   Serves 4

1 white cabbage, finely shredded ● 60 ml/4 tbsp mustard oil

5 ml/1 tsp mustard seeds ● 2 onions, chopped

30 ml/2 tbsp chopped fresh coriander (cilantro)

100 g/4 oz desiccated (shredded) coconut ● 150 ml/¼ pt/⅔ cup coconut milk

Blanch the cabbage in boiling water for 3 minutes then drain thoroughly. Heat the oil and fry the mustard seeds until they start crackling. Add the onions and fry until golden. Add half the coriander, the coconut and the

cabbage and stir-fry, gradually adding enough coconut milk to keep the mixture moist. Heat through thoroughly, sprinkle with the remaining coriander and serve at once.

Cabbage and Potato
Serves 4

50 g/2 oz/¼ cup butter ● 1 onion, chopped ● 2 cloves garlic, chopped

5 ml/1 tsp cumin seeds ● 5 ml/1 tsp ground turmeric

450 g/1 lb cabbage, shredded ● 450 g/1 lb potatoes, quartered

2 tomatoes, skinned and chopped ● 1 green chilli, chopped

salt ● 5 ml/1 tsp mango powder ● 5 ml/1 tsp garam masala

30 ml/2 tbsp chopped fresh coriander (cilantro)

Heat the butter and fry the onion, garlic and cumin seeds until golden. Stir in the turmeric, cabbage and potatoes, tomatoes and green chilli. Season with salt and fry for 2 minutes, stirring. Cover and simmer gently for 10-15 minutes. Stir in the mango powder and garam masala, cover and cook for a further 5 minutes. Serve sprinkled with coriander.

Cabbage Poriyal
Serves 4

10 ml/2 tsp oil ● 5 ml/1 tsp mustard seeds ● 5 ml/1 tsp cumin seeds

5 ml/1 tsp split black beans ● 5 ml/1 tsp yellow split peas

1 dried red chilli, halved ● 2.5 ml/½ tsp asafoetida

2-3 curry leaves ● 450 g/1 lb cabbage, chopped ● 2 green chillies, slit

salt ● 30 ml/2 tbsp water ● 30 ml/2 tbsp grated (shredded) coconut

Heat the oil and fry the mustard and cumin seeds, split beans, split peas, chilli, asafoetida and curry leaves until the seeds start crackling. Add the cabbage, chillies, salt and water, cover and simmer over a low heat for about 15 minutes until the vegetables are tender. Stir in the coconut before serving.

Cabbage and Peas
Serves 4-6

60 ml/5 tbsp oil or ghee ● 5 ml/1 tsp mustard seeds

5 ml/1 tsp cumin seeds ● 2 garlic cloves, crushed

1 cm/½ in ginger root, finely chopped ● 1 small onion, finely chopped

5 ml/1 tsp garam masala ● 5 ml/1 tsp ground coriander (cilantro)

2.5 ml/½ tsp ground red chilli ● 2.5 ml/½ tsp ground turmeric

salt ● 225 g/8 oz canned tomatoes, chopped

500 g/18 oz cabbage, shredded ● 150 g/5 oz peas ● 15 ml/1 tbsp lemon juice

Garnish: 1.5 ml/¼ tsp garam masala

15 ml/1 tbsp chopped fresh coriander (cilantro) ● 1 small green chilli, chopped

Heat the oil or ghee and fry the mustard seeds until they start crackling. Add the cumin seeds and fry until browned. Add the garlic, ginger and onion and fry until golden brown. Stir in the garam masala, coriander, chilli, turmeric and salt. Stir in the tomatoes and cabbage, cover and simmer over a medium heat for 10 minutes. Add the peas and simmer for 5 minutes. Mix in the lemon juice. Sprinkle over the garnish and serve hot with dal, rice, raita and chapatis.

Cabbage Parcels   Makes 8

45 ml/3 tbsp oil ● 5 ml/1 tsp mustard seeds ● 2.5 cm/1 in ginger root, chopped

2 green chillies, chopped ● 450 g/1 lb potatoes, cubed

10 ml/2 tsp Sambar Powder (page 15) ● 2-3 curry leaves ● salt

juice of ½ lime ● 8 large cabbage leaves ● 300 ml/½ pt/1¼ cups water

Heat the oil and fry the mustard seeds until they start crackling. Add the ginger and chillies and fry for 1 minute. Add the potatoes, sambar powder, curry leaves and salt, stir well, cover and simmer for 10 minutes, stirring occasionally, until the potatoes are soft. Stir in the lime juice and remove from the heat. Divide the mixture between the cabbage leaves, fold them into parcels and secure with cocktail sticks (toothpicks). Wrap in foil and steam for 10 minutes until soft. Serve at once.

Stuffed Cabbage Leaves   Serves 6

12 cabbage leaves ● 60 ml/5 tbsp oil ● 5 ml/1 tsp mustard seeds

5 ml/1 tsp cumin seeds ● 675 g/1½ lb potatoes, boiled in their skins then chopped

10 ml/2 tsp ground coriander (cilantro) ● 5 ml/1 tsp garam masala

5 ml/1 tsp ground roasted cumin ● 2.5 ml/½ tsp ground red chilli

2.5 ml/¼ tsp ground turmeric ● 1.5 ml/¼ tsp ground mace

1.5 ml/¼ tsp grated nutmeg ● salt ● 100 g/4 oz/⅔ cup raisins

30 ml/2 tbsp lemon juice ● 15 ml/1 tbsp sugar

30 ml/2 tbsp chopped fresh coriander (cilantro) ● 1 small green chilli, chopped

oil for frying

Place the cabbage leaves in a pan and just cover with water. Boil for 2 minutes then drain and leave to dry.

Heat the oil and fry the mustard seeds until they start crackling. Add the cumin seeds and fry for a few seconds until lightly browned. Add the potatoes and fry for 10 minutes until lightly browned. Stir in the spices and cook for 3 minutes. Stir in the raisins, lemon juice and sugar and cook for 2 minutes. Turn off the heat and stir in the coriander and chilli. Place spoonfuls of the filling mixture on the cabbage leaves. Roll them into 5 cm/2 in parcels and secure with cooks' string. Heat the oil in a deep pan and fry the parcels over a medium heat until light golden brown.

Stir-fried Cabbage
Serves 4

60 ml/4 tbsp oil ● 5 ml/1 tsp mustard seeds ● 5-6 curry leaves, torn

2 green chillies, sliced ● 1 large cabbage, thinly sliced

75 g/3 oz grated (shredded) coconut ● juice of 1 lime

Heat the oil and fry the mustard seeds over a medium heat until they start crackling. Add the curry leaves and chillies and fry for a few seconds. Add the cabbage and cook for 5-7 minutes, tossing continuously. Stir in the coconut and cook for 1 minute. Stir in the lime juice before serving.

Carrots and Peas
Serves 4

60 ml/4 tbsp oil ● 5 ml/1 tsp mustard seeds ● 5 ml/1 tsp cumin seeds

2 large cloves garlic, crushed ● 1 cm/½ in ginger root, minced

1 small onion, chopped ● 5 ml/1 tsp ground coriander (cilantro)

2.5 ml/½ tsp garam masala ● 2.5 ml/½ tsp ground red chilli

2.5 ml/½ tsp ground turmeric ● salt ● 225 g/8 oz canned tomatoes, chopped

450 g/1 lb tender carrots, cut into 2.5 cm/1 in pieces ● 250 g/9 oz peas

Garnish: 2.5 ml/½ tsp garam masala

15 ml/1 tbsp chopped fresh coriander (cilantro) ● 1 small green chilli, chopped

Heat the oil in a heavy-based pan and fry the mustard seeds over a medium heat until they start crackling. Add the cumin seeds and fry until lightly browned. Stir in the garlic, ginger and onion and fry over a medium heat until golden brown. Stir in the coriander, garam masala, chilli, turmeric and salt. Stir in the tomatoes and carrots. Reduce the heat to medium-low, cover and cook for 10 minutes until tender, stirring occasionally. Increase the heat and dry off any remaining water. Stir in the peas and cook for a further few minutes until the peas are tender and the oil appears on the surface of the mixture. Sprinkle over the garnish ingredients and serve hot with dal, rice, puris, raita and a fish dish.

Cauliflower Curry
Serves 4

60 ml/4 tbsp ghee ● pinch of asafoetida ● 450 g/1 lb cauliflower florets

300 ml/½ pt/1¼ cups natural (plain) yoghurt ● 1 onion, chopped

2 cloves garlic, chopped ● 4 cloves ● 1 cardamom pod

4 black peppercorns ● 2 bay leaves ● 5 ml/1 tsp coriander (cilantro) seeds

2.5 cm/1 in cinnamon stick ● 5 ml/1 tsp chilli powder

300 ml/½ pt/1¼ cups hot water ● salt

15 ml/1 tbsp chopped fresh coriander (cilantro)

Heat 15 ml/1 tbsp of ghee and fry the asafoetida for a few seconds. Add the cauliflower and fry for 5 minutes then remove from the pan and stir into the yoghurt. Heat the remaining ghee and fry the onion and garlic until golden. Stir in the whole spices and fry for 2 minutes. Add the chilli powder and stir for a few seconds. Add the cauliflower and yoghurt and fry for 5 minutes. Add the water and salt, cover and simmer for 15 minutes. Serve sprinkled with the coriander.

Fried Cauliflower   Serves 4

1 large cauliflower • oil for deep-frying • 30 ml/2 tbsp oil or ghee

5 ml/1 tsp mustard seeds • 5 ml/1 tsp onion seeds • 5 ml/1 tsp cumin seeds

5 ml/1 tsp ground coriander (cilantro) • 5 ml/1 tsp garam masala

5 ml/1 tsp ground roasted cumin • 2.5 ml/½ tsp ground ginger

2.5 ml/½ tsp ground red chilli • 2.5 ml/½ tsp ground turmeric • salt

15 ml/1 tbsp lemon juice • 15 ml/1 tbsp sugar

Garnish: 1.5 ml/¼ tsp garam masala

15 ml/1 tbsp chopped fresh coriander (cilantro) • 1 small green chilli, chopped

Cut the cauliflower into 2.5 cm/1 in florets. Peel the stems thinly and slice 5 mm/¼ in thick. Heat the oil and deep-fry the cauliflower until golden brown. Drain and set aside. Heat the oil in a heavy-based pan and fry the mustard and onion seeds over a medium heat until they start crackling. Add the cumin seeds and fry until lightly browned. Add the coriander, garam masala, cumin, ginger, chilli, turmeric and salt. Stir in the cauliflower. Reduce the heat to low and cook for 10 minutes. Stir in the lemon juice and sugar and cook for a further 2 minutes. Sprinkle over the garnish ingredients and serve hot with puris, dal, raita and biryani.

Cauliflower in Coriander, Mint and Yoghurt   Serves 4-6

4 large garlic cloves • 4 cm/1½ in ginger root • 1 onion, coarsely chopped

salt • 1 medium cauliflower, cut into florets

250 g/9 oz potatoes, cut into 2.5 cm/1 in pieces

450 ml/¾ pt/2 cups natural (plain) yoghurt

100 g/4 oz chopped fresh coriander (cilantro) • 25 g/1 oz fresh mint leaves

90 ml/6 tbsp oil • 90 ml/6 tbsp ghee • 5 ml/1 tsp mustard seeds

5 ml/1 tsp cumin seeds • 5 ml/1 tsp garam masala

5 ml/1 tsp ground coriander (cilantro) • 2.5 ml/½ tsp ground red chilli

2.5 ml/½ tsp ground roasted cumin • 2.5 ml/½ tsp ground turmeric

45 ml/3 tbsp lemon juice

Blend the garlic, ginger, onion and a large pinch of salt to a smooth paste in a blender or food processor. Rub on to the cauliflower and potato pieces and leave to marinate for 30 minutes.

Blend the yoghurt, coriander and mint to a smooth paste and set aside. Heat the oil and fry the marinated vegetables for about 20 minutes until golden. Remove with a slotted spoon and set aside. Heat the ghee and fry the mustard seeds until they start crackling. Add the cumin seeds and fry for a few seconds until lightly browned. Stir in the garam masala, coriander, chilli, cumin, turmeric and a little salt. Stir in the yoghurt paste and bring to the boil. Add the vegetables and cook for 15 minutes until thick. Stir in the lemon juice and serve hot with rice, dal and a meat or chicken dish.

Spiced Cauliflower
Serves 6-8

| 1 cauliflower • 60 ml/4 tbsp ghee • 2 large onions, chopped |
| 1 cm/½ in ginger root, chopped • 4 cloves garlic, chopped • 3 dried red chillies |
| 1 cinnamon stick • 1 bay leaf • 2 green chillies, chopped |
| 4 cloves • 2.5 ml/½ tsp cumin seeds • 3 cardamom pods |
| salt • 300 ml/½ pt/⅔ cups natural (plain) yoghurt • 250 ml/8 fl oz/1 cup water |

Heat half the ghee and fry the cauliflower until lightly browned. Transfer to a casserole and cover with the onion, ginger, garlic and spices. Pour over the yoghurt and water and add the remaining ghee. Cover and cook in a preheated oven at 180°C/350°F/gas mark 4 for about 45 minutes until tender.

Grated Cauliflower
Serves 4-6

| 75 ml/5 tbsp oil or ghee • 5 ml/1 tsp mustard seeds |
| 5 ml/1 tsp onion seeds • 3 large garlic cloves, crushed |
| 2.5 cm/1 in ginger root, finely chopped • 1 onion, finely chopped |
| 1 medium cauliflower, finely grated • 10 ml/2 tsp ground coriander (cilantro) |
| 5 ml/1 tsp ground roasted cumin • 2.5 ml/½ tsp ground red chilli |
| 2.5 ml/½ tsp ground turmeric • 2.5 ml/½ tsp garam masala |
| 1.5 ml/¼ tsp ground mace • 1.5 ml/¼ tsp grated nutmeg • salt |
| **Garnish:** 1.5 ml/½ tsp garam masala |
| 15 ml/1 tbsp chopped fresh coriander (cilantro) • 1 small green chilli, chopped |

Heat the oil or ghee and fry the mustard seeds until they start crackling. Add the onion seeds and fry for a few seconds until browned. Add the garlic, ginger and onion and fry until lightly browned. Add the cauliflower and cook for 5 minutes. Stir in the remaining ingredients. Reduce the heat, cover and cook for 20 minutes until tender, stirring occasionally. Sprinkle with the garnish and serve hot with chapatis, raita and a kofta dish.

Whole Cauliflower
Serves 4-6

1 medium cauliflower, trimmed and stalk removed • oil for deep-frying

60 ml/4 tbsp ghee or oil • 5 ml/1 tsp mustard seeds

1 onion, finely chopped • 4 cloves • 4 black peppercorns

3 bay leaves • 2.5 cm/1 in cinnamon stick • 1 black cardamom pod

3 large garlic cloves • 4 cm/1½ in ginger root, chopped • 1 onion, chopped

45 ml/3 tbsp water • 10 ml/2 tsp ground coriander (cilantro)

5 ml/1 tsp ground roasted cumin • 5 ml/1 tsp ground turmeric

2.5 ml/½ tsp ground red chilli • 2.5 ml/¼ tsp ground mace

1.5 ml/¼ tsp grated nutmeg • salt • 400 g/14 oz canned tomatoes, chopped

50 ml/2 fl oz/3½ tbsp water • 350 g/12 oz potatoes, peeled and cut into chips

225 g/8 oz peas

Garnish: 30 ml/2 tbsp chopped fresh coriander (cilantro)

5 ml/1 tsp garam masala • 1 small green chilli, chopped

Heat the oil in a deep pan and fry the whole cauliflower over a medium heat until golden brown on all sides. Drain and set aside.

Heat the ghee or oil and fry the mustard seeds over a medium heat until they start crackling. Add the onion, cloves, peppercorns, bay leaves, cinnamon and cardamom and fry over a medium heat until golden brown. Blend the garlic, ginger, onion and water to a smooth paste in a blender or food processor. Stir the paste into the pan and cook for a few minutes until golden brown. Stir in the coriander, cumin, turmeric, chilli, mace, nutmeg and salt. Stir in the tomatoes and cook until all the liquid has been absorbed and the ghee appears on the surface of the mixture. Add the water and cook until the water has been absorbed. Place the cauliflower in the pan and baste it thoroughly with the sauce. Cover and cook on a low heat, turning the cauliflower over gently every 5 minutes and cooking and basting with the sauce until the cauliflower is cooked.

While the cauliflower is cooking, heat the deep-frying oil and fry the chips until golden brown. Cook the peas in boiling water for a few minutes until tender. Place the cauliflower in a large serving dish and surround with the chips and peas. Sprinkle over the garnish ingredients and serve hot with puris, dal and pulao.

Benares-style Cauliflower and Potatoes
Serves 6

250 ml/8 fl oz/1 cup water • 1 onion, chopped • 6 cloves garlic, chopped

1 cm/½ in ginger root, chopped • 15 ml/1 tbsp coriander (cilantro) seeds

45 ml/3 tbsp oil • 5 ml/1 tsp cumin seeds • 5 ml/1 tsp caraway seeds

15 ml/1 tbsp garam masala • 5 ml/1 tsp ground turmeric

1 cauliflower, cut into florets • 2 large potatoes, cubed • salt

Blend 45 ml/3 tbsp of water, the onion, garlic, ginger and coriander to a paste in a blender or food processor. Heat the oil and fry the cumin and caraway seeds for 1 minute. Add the purée and fry for 6 minutes until the oil appears on the surface, stirring continuously. Mix in the garam masala and turmeric and stir for 30 seconds. Add the cauliflower, potatoes, salt and remaining water, bring to the boil, cover and simmer for 8-10 minutes until the vegetables are tender, stirring occasionally.

Cauliflower and Peas
Serves 4-6

90 ml/6 tbsp oil or ghee ● 5 ml/1 tsp mustard seeds

2.5 ml/½ tsp cumin seeds ● 2.5 cm/1 in ginger root, minced

1 medium cauliflower, cut into florets ● 10 ml/2 tsp ground coriander (cilantro)

5 ml/1 tsp garam masala ● 5 ml/1 tsp ground roasted cumin

2.5 ml/½ tsp ground red chilli ● 2.5 ml/½ tsp ground turmeric ● salt

150 ml/¼ pt/⅔ cup water ● 250 g/9 oz peas

Garnish: 1.5 ml/¼ tsp garam masala

15 ml/1 tbsp chopped fresh coriander (cilantro) ● 1 small green chilli, chopped

1 lemon, thinly sliced

Heat the oil in a heavy-based pan and fry the mustard seeds over a medium heat until they start crackling. Add the cumin seeds and fry until browned. Add the ginger and cauliflower and fry for 10 minutes until lightly browned. Stir in the coriander, garam masala, cumin, chilli, turmeric, salt and water, bring to the boil, then cover and simmer gently for about 40 minutes or until the cauliflower is tender, stirring occasionally. Stir in the peas and simmer for 5 minutes until tender. Sprinkle over the garnish ingredients and serve hot with dal, rice, raita and a meat curry.

Celery Doroo
Serves 6

12 celery sticks ● 15 ml/1 tbsp ghee ● 1 onion, sliced

2.5 ml/½ tsp garam masala ● 5 ml/1 tsp jaggery ● pinch of salt

2.5 ml/½ tsp ground turmeric ● 600 ml/1 pt/2½ cups coconut milk

300 ml/½ pt/1¼ cups tamarind juice

Masala: 2.5 ml/½ tsp cumin seeds ● 8 dried red chillies

6 cloves garlic ● 1 cm/½ in ginger root

15 ml/1 tbsp grated (shredded) coconut

Grind the masala ingredients. Cut the celery into 10 cm/4 in pieces and tie into bundles of 4. Boil until tender. Heat the ghee and fry the onion until golden. Add the masala paste and fry for 2 minutes. Add the remaining ingredients. Bring to the boil then simmer gently for 15 minutes. Add the celery and simmer for 10 minutes.

Delhi-style Colocasia
Serves 4

90 ml/6 tbsp oil ● 300 g/11 oz colocasia, cut into 2.5 cm/1 in pieces

150 g/5 oz Paneer (page 20), cut into 1.5 cm/½ in squares ● oil for deep-frying

large pinch of asafoetida ● 5 ml/1 tsp cumin seeds

3 cloves garlic, crushed ● 3 bay leaves ● 1.5 cm/½ in ginger root, chopped

1 onion, chopped ● 2.5 ml/½ tsp ajwain ● 5 ml/1 tsp garam masala

5 ml/1 tsp ground coriander (cilantro) ● 5 ml/1 tsp ground roasted cumin

2.5 ml/½ tsp ground red chilli ● 2.5 ml/½ tsp ground turmeric

1.5 ml/¼ tsp ground mace ● 1.5 ml/¼ tsp grated nutmeg ● salt

225 g/8 oz canned tomatoes, chopped ● 150 ml/¼ pt/⅔ cup natural (plain) yoghurt

Garnish: 1.5 ml/¼ tsp garam masala

15 ml/1 tbsp chopped fresh coriander (cilantro) ● 1 green chilli, chopped

Heat 15 ml/1 tbsp of oil and fry the colocasia until golden brown then set aside. Deep-fry the paneer until light golden brown then set aside.

Heat the remaining ghee in a heavy-based pan and fry the asafoetida until it starts sizzling. Add the cumin seeds and fry until browned. Add the garlic, bay leaves, ginger, onion and ajwain and fry until golden. Stir in the ground spices, fried colocasia and tomatoes and cook until all the liquid has been absorbed and the oil appears on the surface. Stir in the yoghurt and paneer and cook until the liquid has been absorbed and the paneer is soft and spongy and the colocasia is tender, adding a little more water while cooking if necessary. Sprinkle over the garnish ingredients and serve hot with puris, dal, raita, rice and a meat dish.

Punjabi-style Fried Colocasia
Serves 4

300 g/11 oz colocasia ● 1.2 l/2 pts/5 cups water ● 60 ml/4 tbsp oil

large pinch of asafoetida ● 5 ml/1 tsp cumin seeds

5 ml/1 tsp garam masala ● 5 ml/1 tsp ground coriandr

5 ml/1 tsp ground ginger ● 5 ml/1 tsp ground roasted cumin

5 ml/1 tsp ajwain ● 2.5 ml/½ tsp ground red chilli

1.5 ml/¼ tsp ground turmeric ● salt

Garnish: 1.5 ml/½ tsp garam masala ● 1 lemon, sliced

Boil the colocasia in the water for 40 minutes until tender then drain, peel and cut into 1.5 cm/½ in rounds. Heat the oil and fry the asafoetida until it starts sizzling. Add the cumin seeds and fry until browned. Add the colo-casia and fry for 10 minutes until golden brown. Stir in the spices and cook over a low heat for 5 minutes. Sprinkle with the garnish ingredients and serve hot with paratha or chapatis, rice, dal and a meat dish.

Lemon Colocasia
Serves 4

300 g/11 oz colocasia ● 1.2 1/2 pts/5 cups water

45 ml/3 tbsp lemon juice ● 5 ml/1 tsp garam masala

5 ml/1 tsp ground roasted cumin ● 2.5 ml/½ tsp ground red chilli ● salt

Simmer the colocasia and water for 40 minutes or until tender then drain and cut into 1.5 cm/½ in thick rounds. Mix with the remaining ingredients and leave to cool. Serve cold with a meal.

Colocasia with Tomato and Onion
Serves 4

75 ml/5 tbsp oil ● 300 g/11 oz colocasia, cut into 2.5 cm/1 in pieces

large pinch of asafoetida ● 3 cloves garlic, crushed

2.5 cm/1 in ginger root, chopped ● 1 onion, chopped

5 ml/1 tsp ground coriander (cilantro) ● 5 ml/1 tsp ground roasted cumin

2.5 ml/½ tsp garam masala ● 2.5 ml/½ tsp ground red chilli

2.5 ml/½ tsp tymol seeds ● 1.5 ml/¼ tsp ground turmeric ● salt

225 g/8 oz canned tomatoes

Garnish: 1.5 ml/½ tsp garam masala

15 ml/1 tbsp chopped fresh coriander (cilantro) ● 1 small green chilli, chopped

Heat half the oil and fry the colocasia until golden brown.

Meanwhile, heat the remaining oil and fry the asafoetida until it starts sizzling. Add the garlic, ginger and onion and fry gently until golden brown. Stir in the spices, salt, tomatoes and colocasia. Cover and simmer gently until all the liquid has been absorbed and the colocasia is tender, adding a little extra water during cooking if necessary. Sprinkle over the garnish ingredients and serve hot with chapatis, dal and a meat dish.

Courgette Bhaji
Serves 4-6

60 ml/4 tbsp oil or ghee ● 5 ml/1 tsp cumin seeds

2 large cloves garlic, crushed ● 1 cm/½ in ginger root, finely chopped

1 small onion, finely chopped ● 5 ml/1 tsp ground coriander (cilantro)

2.5 ml/½ tsp garam masala ● 2.5 ml/½ tsp ground turmeric

1.5 ml/¼ tsp ground red chilli ● salt

450 g/1 lb courgettes (zucchini), cut into 1 cm/½ in pieces

225 g/8 oz canned tomatoes

Garnish: 1.5 ml/¼ tsp garam masala

15 ml/1 tbsp chopped fresh coriander (cilantro) ● 1 small green chilli, chopped

Heat the oil or ghee in a heavy-based pan and fry the cumin seeds until lightly browned. Add the garlic, ginger and onion and fry until lightly browned. Add the coriander, garam masala, turmeric, chilli, salt, courgettes and tomatoes, bring to the boil, cover and cook over a low heat for about 20 minutes until tender, stirring occasionally. Increase the heat and dry off any remaining liquid. Sprinkle with the garnish ingredients and serve hot with lentil, chapatis and raita.

Courgette Foogath
Serves 4

30 ml/2 tbsp ghee ● 225 g/8 oz courgettes (zucchini), sliced

juice of 1 lemon ● ½ green (bell) pepper, sliced

2 tomatoes, skinned and chopped ● 5 ml/1 tsp chilli powder ● salt

Heat the ghee then add all the ingredients and stir gently over a medium heat until sizzling. Serve at once.

Fenugreek Leaves and Potato
Serves 4-6

75 ml/5 tbsp oil ● 5 ml/1 tsp cumin seeds ● 1 onion, finely chopped

1.5 cm/½ in ginger root, finely chopped

500 g/18 oz potatoes, cut into 1.5 cm/½ in pieces

10 ml/2 tsp ground coriander (cilantro) ● 2.5 ml/½ tsp garam masala

2.5 ml/½ tsp ground red chilli ● 2.5 ml/½ tsp ground turmeric ● salt

100 g/4 oz fenugreek leaves, coarsely chopped

Garnish: 2.5 ml/½ tsp garam masala ● 1 small green chilli, chopped

Heat the oil and fry the cumin seeds over a medium heat until golden. Add the onion and ginger and fry until lightly browned. Add the potato pieces and fry for 15 minutes. Stir in the ground spices and fenugreek leaves, cover and cook over a low heat for 10 minutes until the potatoes are tender. Sprinkle over the garnish ingredients and serve hot with chapatis or onion paratha, dal, raita and a kofta dish.

Loki Kofta

450 g/1 lb loki or marrow (squash), peeled and grated

150 ml/¼ pt/⅔ cup water ● 50 g/2 oz/½ cup gram flour

15 ml/1 tbsp chopped fresh coriander (cilantro) ● 2.5 ml/½ tsp garam masala

2.5 ml/½ tsp ground red chilli ● salt ● 12 prunes, stoned

oil for frying

Sauce: 90 ml/6 tbsp oil or ghee ● 1 small onion, finely chopped

4 cloves ● 4 peppercorns ● 2 bay leaves

1 black cardamom pod ● 1.5 cm/½ in cinnamon stick ● 3 large cloves garlic

2.5 cm/1 in ginger root ● 1 medium onion, coarsely chopped

45 ml/3 tbsp water ● 10 ml/2 tsp poppy seeds, ground

5 ml/1 tsp ground coriander (cilantro) ● 5 ml/1 tsp ground roasted cumin

5 ml/1 tsp ground turmeric ● 2.5 ml/½ tsp ground red chilli

1.5 ml/¼ tsp ground mace ● 1.5 ml/¼ tsp grated nutmeg ● salt

225 g/8 oz tomatoes ● 150 ml/¼ pt/⅔ cup natural (plain) yoghurt

200 ml/7 fl oz/scant 1 cup water

Garnish: 2.5 ml/½ tsp garam masala

15 ml/1 tbsp chopped fresh coriander (cilantro) ● 1 small green chilli, chopped

Place the loki and water in a pan and simmer over a medium-low heat for 20 minutes until tender. Increase the heat and dry off any remaining water. Lightly roast the gram flour in a dry frying pan (skillet). Place the loki in a bowl and mix in the flour, coriander, garam masala, chilli and salt to form a dough, adding a little water if necessary. Divide the mixture into 12 equal portions and roll them into balls. Flatten them and place a prune in the centre, bringing the edges over to form rectangles. Heat the oil and deep-fry the koftas until golden brown.

Heat the oil or ghee in a heavy-based pan and fry the onion and whole spices until golden. Blend the garlic, ginger, onion and water to a smooth paste then add it to the pan and fry until golden. Add the poppy seeds and fry for 2 minutes. Stir in the ground spices then the tomatoes and cook until all the liquid has been absorbed and the ghee appears on the surface. Stir in the yoghurt and simmer until all the liquid has evaporated. Add the water, bring to the boil, then simmer gently for 2 minutes. Pour the sauce over the koftas and sprinkle with the garnish ingredients. Serve hot with meat pulao, raita, puris, stuffed aubergine and dal.

Stuffed Loki

Serves 4-6

500 g/18 oz loki or marrow (squash) ● 120 ml/4 fl oz/½ cup oil or ghee

5 ml/1 tsp mustard seeds

Marinade: 225 g/8 oz canned tomatoes

150 ml/¼ pt/⅔ cup natural (plain) yoghurt

3 large cloves garlic, crushed ● 1 cm/½ in ginger root, chopped

1 onion, coarsely chopped ● 5 ml/1 tsp garam masala

5 ml/1 tsp ground roasted cumin ● 2.5 ml/½ tsp ground red chilli

2.5 ml/½ tsp ground turmeric ● salt

Filling: 30 ml/2 tbsp ghee ● 50 g/2 oz/½ cup desiccated (shredded) coconut

150 g/5 oz Khoya (page 19) ● 100 g/4 oz/⅔ cup raisins

50 g/2 oz/½ cup cashew nuts, halved ● 50 g/2 oz/½ cup blanched almonds, halved

15 ml/1 tbsp sugar ● 2.5 ml/½ tsp ground cardamom

Prick the loki all over with a fork and slit it lengthways. Blend all the marinade ingredients to a smooth paste in a blender or food processor. Rub over the loki and leave to marinate for 4 hours.

For the filling, heat the ghee in a heavy-based pan and gently fry the coconut over a medium heat until lightly browned. Mix in the remaining filling ingredients and cook for a further 3 minutes. Lift the marrow from the marinade. Heat the oil or ghee in a heavy-based pan and fry the mustard seeds until they start crack-ling. Add the loki and fry for 2 minutes. Pour in the remaining marinade carefully then cover with a lid as the mixture tends to spit. Cook for 25 minutes or until all the liquid has been absorbed and the loki is tender, stirring occasionally. Remove the lid and cook until the oil or ghee appears on the surface of the mixture. Lift the loki from the sauce and place it on a serving dish. Open the loki and arrange the halves flat on the dish. Spoon the filling on top and pour the sauce around. Serve hot with puris, pulao, raita and dal.

Loki Bhaji

Serves 4

60 ml/4 tbsp oil or ghee ● 5 ml/1 tsp mustard seeds

1 small onion, finely chopped ● 1.5 cm/¼ in ginger root, finely chopped

5 ml/1 tsp ground coriander (cilantro) ● 2.5 ml/½ tsp garam masala

2.5 ml/½ tsp ground roasted cumin ● 2.5 ml/½ tsp ground red chilli

2.5 ml/½ tsp ground turmeric ● salt

500 g/18 oz loki or marrow (squash), cut into 2.5 cm/1 in pieces

225 g/8 oz canned tomatoes ● 150 ml/¼ pt/⅔ cup natural (plain) yoghurt

Garnish: 15 ml/1 tbsp chopped fresh coriander (cilantro)

1.5 ml/¼ tsp garam masala ● 1 small green chilli, chopped

Heat the oil in a heavy-based pan and fry the mustard seeds over a medium heat until they start crackling. Add the onion and ginger and fry until golden brown. Stir in the ground spices, salt, loki, tomatoes and yoghurt. Bring to the boil then cover and simmer gently for 30 minutes until the loki is tender, stirring occasionally. Increase the heat and fry off any remaining liquid. Sprinkle over the garnish ingredients and serve hot with chapatis, dal, rice and a meat or chicken dish.

Stuffed Marrow
Serves 4-6

500 g/18 oz marrow (squash), peeled • 120 ml/4 fl oz/½ cup oil or ghee

5 ml/1 tsp mustard seeds

Marinade: 225 g/8 oz canned tomatoes

150 ml/¼ pt/⅔ cup natural (plain) yoghurt • 3 large cloves garlic, crushed

1 cm/½ in ginger root, chopped • 1 onion, coarsely chopped

5 ml/1 tsp garam masala • 5 ml/1 tsp ground roasted cumin

2.5 ml/½ tsp ground red chilli • 2.5 ml/½ tsp ground turmeric • salt

Filling: 30 ml/2 tbsp ghee

50 g/2 oz/½ cup desiccated (shredded) coconut • 150 g/5 oz Khoya (page 19)

100 g/4 oz/⅔ cup raisins • 50 g/2 oz/½ cup cashew nuts, halved

50 g/2 oz/½ cup blanched almonds, halved • 15 ml/1 tbsp sugar

2.5 ml/½ tsp ground cardamom

Prick the marrow all over with a fork. Slit lengthways and scoop out all the seeds. Blend all the marinade ingredients to a smooth paste in a blender or food processor. Rub over the marrow and leave to marinate for 4 hours.

For the filling, heat the ghee in a heavy-based pan and gently fry the coconut over a medium heat until lightly browned. Mix in the remaining filling ingredients and cook for a further 3 minutes. Lift the marrow from the marinade. Heat the oil or ghee in a heavy-based pan and fry the mustard seeds until they start crac-kling. Add the marrow and fry for 2 minutes. Pour in the remaining marinade carefully then cover with a lid as the mixture tends to spit. Cook for 25 minutes or until all the liquid has been absorbed and the marrow is tender, stirring occasionally. Remove the lid and cook until the oil or ghee appears on the surface of the mixture. Lift the marrow from the sauce and place it on a serving dish. Open the marrow and arrange the halves flat on the dish. Spoon the filling on top and pour the sauce around. Serve hot with puris, pulao, raita and dal.

Mango Curry
Serves 6

10 ml/2 tsp ghee ● 10 ml/2 tsp mustard seeds ● 5 dried red chillies

100 g/4 oz grated (shredded) coconut ● 10 ml/2 tsp ground turmeric

4 large ripe mangoes, cubed ● 600 ml/1 pt/2½ cups water

50 g/2 oz/⅓ cup raisins ● 3 cloves ● 25 g/1 oz/2 tbsp sugar

pinch of salt ● 1 sprig fresh curry leaves

Heat the ghee and fry the mustard seeds and chillies until the seeds start crackling. Add the coconut and turmeric and fry until browned. Add the remaining ingredients and simmer for 10-15 minutes until the mangoes are tender.

Marrow Bhaji
Serves 4-6

75 ml/5 tbsp oil or ghee ● 5 ml/1 tsp mustard seeds

5 ml/1 tsp onion seeds ● 1 small onion, finely chopped

1 cm/½ in ginger root ● 5 ml/1 tsp ground coriander (cilantro)

5 ml/1 tsp ground roasted cumin ● 2.5 ml/½ tsp ground red chilli

2.5 ml/½ tsp ground turmeric ● 2.5 ml/½ tsp garam masala ● salt

900 g/2 lb marrow (squash), peeled and cut into 1 cm/½ in cubes

100 ml/3½ fl oz/6½ tbsp water

Garnish: 2.5 ml/½ tsp garam masala

15 ml/1 tbsp chopped fresh coriander (cilantro) ● 1 small green chilli, chopped

Heat the oil or ghee in a heavy-based pan and fry the mustard seeds over a medium heat until they start crackling. Stir in the onion seeds and fry for a few seconds until lightly browned. Stir in the onion and ginger and fry until lightly browned. Add the coriander, cumin, chilli, turmeric, garam masala and salt. Stir in the marrow and water and bring to the boil. Reduce the heat, cover and cook for 30 minutes until the marrow is tender, stirring occasionally. Increase the heat and dry off any remaining water. Sprinkle with the garnish ingredients and serve hot with dal and rice.

Marrow Kebab
Makes 14

900 g/2 lb marrow (squash), peeled and grated ● 100 ml/3½ fl oz/6½ tbsp water

50 g/2 oz/½ cup gram flour ● 45 ml/3 tbsp chopped fresh coriander (cilantro)

1 small green chilli, chopped ● 5 ml/1 tsp garam masala

5 ml/1 tsp ground roasted cumin ● 1.5 ml/¼ tsp ground red chilli

1.5 ml/¼ tsp ground mace ● 1.5 ml/¼ tsp grated nutmeg ● salt

14 almonds, blanched ● 14 cashew nuts ● 50 g/2 oz/⅓ cup raisins

oil for frying

Cook the marrow and water for 15 minutes until tender then drain well. Place in a strainer and squeeze out all the water. Lightly sift the gram flour and brown it in a dry frying pan (skillet) on a low heat. Place the marrow in a bowl and stir in the gram flour, coriander, chilli, garam masala, cumin, chilli, mace, nutmeg and salt. Mix thoroughly and divide into 14 equal portions. Put an almond, a cashew nut and a few raisins in the centre of each portion, bring the edges over the cover and make it into a round shape. Repeat until you have made all the kebabs. Meanwhile, heat the oil in a heavy-based pan, then gently slip the kebabs into the pan and fry until golden brown. Serve hot with chutney or pulao.

Quick Marrow Kofta
Serves 4

50 g/2 oz/¼ cup gram flour ● 1 marrow (squash), grated ● 2.5 ml/½ tsp salt

1 onion, chopped ● 3 green chillies, chopped

2.5 ml/½ tsp grated ginger root, chopped

15 ml/1 tbsp chopped fresh coriander (cilantro) ● oil for deep-frying

300 ml/½ pt/1¼ cups stock ● 5 ml/1 tsp garam masala

Mix the gram flour with the marrow, salt, onion, chillies, ginger and coriander and knead to a smooth mixture. Make into small round balls. Heat the oil and deep-fry the koftas until golden. Heat the stock then add the koftas and simmer for 10 minutes. Serve sprinkled with garam masala.

Marrow Kofta with Sauce
Makes 14

900 g/2 lb marrow (squash), peeled and grated ● 100 ml/3½ fl oz/6½ tbsp water

50 g/2 oz/½ cup gram flour ● 2.5 ml/½ tsp garam masala

2.5 ml/½ tsp ground roasted cumin ● 2.5 ml/½ tsp ground red chilli

1.5 ml/¼ tsp ground mace ● 1.5 ml/¼ tsp grated nutmeg ● salt

25 g/1 oz/¼ cup blanched almonds ● 25 g/1 oz/¼ cup cashew nuts

50 g/2 oz/⅓ cup raisins ● oil for frying

Sauce: 75 ml/5 tbsp ghee or oil ● 1 small onion, finely chopped

4 large cloves garlic, crushed ● 2.5 cm/1 in ginger root, coarsely chopped

1 onion, coarsely chopped ● 5 ml/1 tsp garam masala

5 ml/1 tsp ground coriander (cilantro) ● 5 ml/1 tsp ground roasted cumin

2.5 ml/½ tsp ground red chilli ● 2.5 ml/½ tsp ground turmeric ● salt

225 g/8 oz canned tomatoes, chopped ● 150 ml/¼ pt/⅔ cup natural (plain) yoghurt

45 ml/3 tbsp water

Garnish: 1.5 ml/¼ tsp garam masala

15 ml/1 tbsp chopped fresh coriander (cilantro) ● 1 small green chilli, chopped

Cook the marrow in the water for about 15 minutes until tender. Drain, reserving the cooking water. Place the marrow in a strainer and squeeze out all the water with the palm of your hand. Lightly brown the gram flour in a dry frying pan (skillet) on a low heat. Put the marrow in a bowl and stir in the gram flour, garam masala, cumin, chilli, mace, nutmeg and salt. Divide the mixture into 14 equal portions. Flatten each portion and place an almond, a cashew and a few raisins in the middle, bring the edges over to cover and shape into a round. Meanwhile, heat the oil, then slip the koftas into the oil and fry until golden brown. Remove with a slotted spoon and put to one side.

To make the sauce, heat the ghee or oil in a heavy-based pan and fry the small onion over a medium heat until golden brown. Blend the garlic, ginger and medium onion to a smooth paste in a blender or food processor. Add to the pan and fry for a few minutes until golden brown. Stir in the garam masala, coriander, cumin, chilli, turmeric and salt. Stir in the tomatoes and cook until all the water has been absorbed and the ghee appears on the surface. Add the yoghurt and cook until all the liquid has been absorbed. Add the water and cook until all the liquid has been absorbed. Make up the reserved marrow cooking liquid to 250 ml/8 fl oz/1 cup with water, if necessary. Add to the pan, bring to the boil and simmer for 2 minutes. Pour over the kofta. Sprinkle with the garnish ingredients and serve hot with puris, cauliflower and chicken.

Mushroom Curry   Serves 4

60 ml/4 tbsp oil or ghee ● 5 ml/1 tsp cumin seeds ● 2.5 ml/½ tsp sesame seeds
2 large cloves garlic, crushed ● 2.5 cm/1 in ginger root, finely chopped
1 onion, finely chopped ● 250 g/9 oz mushrooms, cut into 2.5 cm/1 in pieces
5 ml/1 tsp garam masala ● 5 ml/1 tsp ground coriander (cilantro)
5 ml/1 tsp ground roasted cumin ● 2.5 ml/½ tsp ground red chilli
2.5 ml/½ tsp ground turmeric ● 1.5 ml/¼ tsp ground mace
1.5 ml/¼ tsp grated nutmeg ● salt ● 250 g/9 oz canned tomatoes
250 g/9 oz peas ● 50 g/2 oz/½ cup blanched almonds, halved
50 g/2 oz/⅓ cup raisins
Garnish: 1.5 ml/¼ tsp garam masala
15 ml/1 tbsp chopped fresh coriander (cilantro) ● 1 small green chilli, chopped

Heat the oil in a and fry the cumin and sesame seeds until lightly browned. Add the garlic, ginger and onion and fry gently until golden brown. Stir in the mushrooms and fry for 2 minutes. Stir in the garam masala, coriander, cumin, chilli, turmeric, mace, nutmeg and salt. Stir in the tomatoes, cover and cook over a medium-low heat for 10 minutes, stirring occasionally. Remove the lid and cook until all the liquid has been absorbed and the oil appears on the surface. Stir in the peas, almonds and raisins and cook for a few minutes until tender. Increase the heat to allow any excess liquid to evaporate. Sprinkle over the garnish and serve hot with puris and meat.

Curried Mushrooms, Potatoes and Peas   Serves 6

45 ml/3 tbsp oil ● 1 onion, sliced ● 4 cloves garlic, crushed

2.5 cm/1 in ginger root, grated ● 45 ml/3 tbsp chopped fresh coriander (cilantro)

15 ml/1 tbsp garam masala ● 5 ml/1 tsp ground turmeric

1.5 ml/¼ tsp chilli powder ● 900 g/2 lb potatoes, quartered ● salt

120 ml/4 fl oz/½ cup water ● 900 g/2 lb mushrooms, halved ● 100 g/4 oz peas

Heat the oil and fry the onion until browned. Stir in the garlic, ginger and coriander and fry for 2 minutes. Add the garam masala, turmeric and chilli powder and fry for 1 minute, stirring. Add the potatoes, salt and water, bring to the boil, cover and simmer for 10 minutes until the potatoes are three-quarters cooked, stirring occasionally. Add the mushrooms and peas, cover and cook for 5-8 minutes. Remove the lid, increase the heat and cook until three-quarters of the liquid has evaporated, stirring occasionally. Serve hot with rice and lamb curry.

Curried Mushrooms with Spinach   Serves 6

450 g/1 lb button mushrooms, halved ● 120 ml/4 fl oz/½ cup white wine vinegar

45 ml/3 tbsp clear honey ● 45 ml/3 tbsp oil

2.5 cm/1 in ginger root, grated ● 450 g/1 lb spinach, chopped

5 ml/1 tsp ground cloves ● 2.5 ml/½ tsp chilli powder

1 clove garlic, crushed ● 2.5 ml/½ tsp paprika

Mix together the mushrooms, wine vinegar and honey and leave to marinate for 1 hour. Drain off the liquid. Heat 30 ml/2 tsp of oil and fry the ginger for 30 seconds. Add the mushrooms and fry for 3-4 minutes, stirring, then remove from the pan. Heat the remaining oil and fry the ginger for 1 minute. Add the spinach, cloves, chilli powder and garlic, cover and simmer for 3-4 minutes. Stir in the mushrooms, sprinkle with paprika and simmer, stirring, until well blended.

Okra with Cumin and Garlic   Serves 6

45 ml/3 tbsp oil ● 1 onion, chopped ● 10 cloves garlic, chopped

2 green chillies, chopped ● 5 ml/1 tsp ground turmeric

15 ml/1 tbsp ground cumin ● 1.5 kg/3 lb okra ● salt

Heat the oil and fry the onion, garlic and chillies until browned. Stir in the turmeric and cumin and fry for 2 minutes until the oil appears on the surface. Stir in the okra and salt, cover and simmer gently for 8-10 minutes until the okra is tender, stirring occasionally.

Okra Pachnadi
Serves 6

900 g/2 lb okra ● 6 green chillies ● 30 ml/2 tbsp ghee

2.5 ml/½ tsp cumin seeds ● 3 cloves garlic ● 75 g/3 oz grated (shredded) coconut

600 ml/1 pt/2½ cups water ● salt

150 ml/¼ pt/⅔ cup natural (plain) yoghurt ● 15 ml/1 tbsp coconut oil

2.5 ml/½ tsp mustard seeds ● 2 onions, chopped

1 sprig fresh curry leaves

Cut the okra and chillies into rounds. Heat the ghee and fry them until golden. Grind the cumin seeds, garlic and coconut and add them to the pan with the water. Bring to the boil, and simmer until the sauce is thick. Add the salt and okra and remove from the heat. Stir in the yoghurt. Meanwhile, heat the coconut oil and fry the mustard seeds, onions and curry leaves until soft. Pour over the curry and leave to cool.

Okra Curry
Serves 4

450 g/1 lb okra ● 120 ml/4 fl oz/½ cup ghee ● 4 onions

6 cloves garlic ● salt ● 1.5 ml/¼ tsp ground turmeric

5 ml/1 tsp garam masala ● 5 ml/1 tsp chilli powder

150 ml/¼ pt/⅔ cup natural (plain) yoghurt ● 900 ml/1½ pts/3¾ cups water

15 ml/1 tbsp chopped fresh coriander (cilantro)

Trim the okra and fry in a little ghee until golden. Grind the onions and garlic to a paste. Heat the remaining ghee and fry the paste for 1 minute. Add the salt, turmeric, garam masala and chilli powder, adding a little water from time to time. Add the yoghurt and stir until the ghee appears on the surface. Add the water and simmer for 30 minutes. Add the okra and simmer for 15 minutes. Sprinkle with coriander before serving.

Stuffed Okra
Serves 4

225 g/8 oz okra, slit ● 60 ml/4 tbsp ghee ● 30 ml/2 tbsp chopped onion

15 ml/1 tbsp coriander (cilantro) seeds, crushed ● 2.5 ml/½ tsp grated ginger root

pinch of ground turmeric ● pinch of chilli powder ● salt

10 ml/2 tsp lemon juice ● 1 tomato, sliced

Carefully remove the pulp from the okra. Heat 15 ml/1 tbsp of ghee and fry the onion until golden. Stir in the coriander, ginger, turmeric, chilli powder and salt with the okra pulp and cook for 5 minutes. Stir in the lemon juice, remove from the heat and stuff the okra shells with the mixture. Heat the remaining ghee and fry the stuffed okra carefully for 10 minutes. Serve garnished with tomato.

Crunchy Okra with Onions
Serves 4

250 ml/8 fl oz/1 cup oil ● 4 onions, sliced ● 2 green chillies, chopped

10 ml/2 tsp mango powder ● 2.5 ml/½ tsp garam masala

salt ● 900 g/2 lb okra, chopped

Heat the oil to smoking point then reduce the heat and leave for 5 minutes. Add the onions and fry until crisp and brown, stirring frequently. Remove and drain. Mix the chillies and spices into the onions, crumble them slightly and set aside. Add the okra to the oil and fry for about 20 minutes until browned and crisp. Drain on kitchen paper then mix with the onions.

Fragrant Spicy Okra
Serves 4

45 ml/3 tbsp oil ● 5 ml/1 tsp mustard seeds

2.5 cm/1 in ginger root, chopped ● 2 green chillies, chopped

6 curry leaves, torn ● 10 ml/2 tsp Sambar Powder (page 15)

450 g/1 lb okra, chopped ● salt ● juice of ½ lime

Heat the oil and fry the mustard seeds until they start crackling. Add the ginger, chillies and curry leaves and fry until lightly browned. Add the sambar powder and fry for a few seconds. Add the okra and simmer over a low heat, stirring, for about 10 minutes until half-cooked. Add the salt, stir, cover and cook for a further 10 minutes until soft. Stir in the lime juice before serving.

North Indian Fried Okra
Serves 4

75 ml/5 tbsp oil ● 3 onions, finely chopped

2.5 cm/½ in ginger root, finely chopped

450 g/1 lb tender okra, cut into 1 cm/½ in round pieces

15 ml/1 tbsp ground coriander (cilantro) ● 5 ml/1 tsp ground roasted cumin

5 ml/1 tsp ground turmeric ● 2.5 ml/½ tsp ground red chilli

2.5 ml/½ tsp garam masala ● salt

Garnish: 2.5 ml/½ tsp garam masala ● 1 small green chilli, chopped

Heat the oil and fry the onion and ginger over a medium heat until lightly browned. Add the okra and fry for 5 minutes. Add the coriander, cumin, turmeric, chilli, garam masala and salt, cover and cook on a low heat for 5-7 minutes until tender, turning continuously. Sprinkle with the garnish ingredients and serve hot with paratha or puris, dal, raita, rice and a meat dish.

Stuffed Okra with Nutmeg
Serves 4-6

30 ml/2 tbsp ground coriander (cilantro) ● 15 ml/2 tbsp ground roasted cumin

15 ml/1 tbsp ground mango powder OR 2.5 ml/½ tsp citric acid

10 ml/2 tsp garam masala ● 5 ml/1 tsp ground red chilli

5 ml/1 tsp ground turmeric ● 5 ml/1 tsp ground ginger

2.5 ml/½ tsp ground mace ● 2.5 ml/½ tsp grated nutmeg

1 small green chilli, finely chopped ● salt

500 g/18 oz small, tender okra, slit lengthways ● 60 ml/4 tbsp oil

Mix together all the spices and the chilli and push the stuffing into the slits in the okra. Heat the oil in a heavy-based pan and add the okra. Cover and cook on a low heat for 10 minutes until tender, turning regularly. Serve hot with puris or paratha, rice, lentil, raita and a chicken dish.

Curried Spring Onions
Serves 4

60 ml/4 tbsp oil ● 5 ml/1 tsp mustard seeds ● 2.5 ml/½ cumin seeds

2 onions, chopped ● 2.5 cm/1 in ginger root, grated

3 cloves garlic, crushed ● 30 ml/2 tbsp chopped fresh coriander (cilantro)

5 ml/1 tsp ground turmeric ● 2 green chillies, chopped

350 g/12 oz spring onions (scallions), chopped

100 g/4 oz/1⅔ cup red lentils, soaked ● 5 ml/1 tsp ground cloves

Heat the oil and fry the mustard and cumin seeds until they start crackling. Add the onions and fry until golden. Add the ginger and garlic and fry for 2 minutes, stirring. Add the coriander, turmeric and chillies and fry for 1 minute. Add the spring onions, cover and cook for 2 minutes. Stir in the drained lentils, cover and cook for 4 minutes. Stir in the cloves, cover very tightly and simmer for 20 minutes until well blended, stirring once.

Spring Onions and Tomatoes
Serves 4

60 ml/4 tbsp oil ● 2 onions, chopped ● 2.5 cm/1 in ginger root, grated

2 cloves garlic, crushed ● 225 g/8 oz tomatoes, skinned and chopped

2.5 ml/½ tsp ground turmeric ● 2 green chillies, chopped

450 g/1 lb spring onions (scallions), finely chopped ● 10 ml/2 tsp garam masala

1.5 ml/¼ tsp ground cumin

Heat the oil and fry the onions for 3 minutes. Add the ginger and garlic and fry for 1 minute. Add the tomatoes and fry for 3 minutes. Stir in the turmeric and chillies then add the spring onions, cover and cook for 1 minute. Stir in the garam masala and cumin, cover and simmer gently for about 25 minutes, stirring once or twice during cooking.

Onion Thiyyal
Serves 4

10 ml/2 tsp coriander (cilantro) seeds ● 8 dried red chillies ● ghee

½ coconut, grated (shredded) ● 3 onions, sliced

2.5 ml/½ tsp ground turmeric ● 15 ml/1 tbsp tamarind concentrate

600 ml/1 pt/2½ cups water ● salt ● 1 sprig fresh curry leaves

5 ml/1 tsp mustard seeds

Dry roast the coriander and chillies then grind to a paste. Fry the coconut and half an onion in a little ghee until browned then grind to a paste with the turmeric. Fry the remaining onions in a little ghee. Put the tamarind, water, salt and coriander paste in a pan and bring to the boil. Stir a little water into the coconut paste then stir it into the pan with the fried onions. Simmer over a low heat until the curry thickens. Heat a little ghee and fry the curry leaves and mustard seeds until the seeds start crackling. Pour over the curry before serving.

Piaz Bhaji
Serves 6

15 ml/1 tbsp ghee ● 1 cm/½ in ginger root, sliced

2 cloves garlic, chopped ● 2 green chillies, chopped

225 g/8 oz onions, sliced ● 225 g/8 oz tomatoes, skinned and chopped

2.5 ml/½ tsp ground turmeric ● 2.5 ml/½ tsp garam masala ● salt

Heat the ghee and fry the ginger, garlic and chillies for 2 minutes. Add the onions and tomatoes. Add the turmeric, garam masala and salt and simmer gently until the onions are golden brown, adding a little water if necessary.

Pea Kofta
Serves 6

450 g/1 lb cooked peas ● 3 potatoes, boiled ● 5 ml/1 tsp poppy seeds

25 g/1 oz/¼ cup gram flour ● pinch of salt

ghee for deep-frying ● 1 onion, finely chopped

2 tomatoes, skinned and chopped ● 1.5 ml/¼ tsp cumin seeds, roasted

2.5 ml/½ tsp ground turmeric ● 10 ml/2 tsp ground coriander (cilantro)

5 dried red chillies ● 5 ml/1 tsp garam masala

Grind the peas, potatoes, poppy seeds, gram flour and salt to a paste, shape into balls and deep-fry in hot ghee. Heat a little ghee in a pan and fry the onion, tomato and spices for 5 minutes. Add the koftas and simmer gently for 2 minutes, stirring.

Pea Dopiaza
Serves 4

100 g/4 oz/½ cup ghee ● 1 onion, thinly sliced ● 2 cloves

2 bay leaves ● 1 cardamom pod ● 6 black peppercorns

2.5 ml/½ tsp cumin seeds ● 2.5 cm/1 in cinnamon stick

225 g/8 oz peas ● 2 green chillies, chopped ● 4 tomatoes, quartered

450 g/1 lb small onions, halved ● 10 ml/2 tsp sliced ginger root

150 ml/¼ pt/⅔ cup natural (plain) yoghurt ● 300 ml/½ pt/1¼ cups warm water

salt ● 15 ml/1 tbsp garam masala

30 ml/2 tbsp chopped fresh coriander (cilantro) ● 1 green (bell) pepper, sliced

Heat the ghee and fry the onion until golden then drain and set aside. Add the whole spices, the peas, chillies, tomatoes, onions and ginger and fry for 5 minutes, stirring. Add the yoghurt, water and salt and simmer for 15 minutes. Transfer to a casserole dish and sprinkle with garam masala, coriander and pepper and the fried onion. Cook in a preheated oven at 200°C/ 400°F/gas mark 6 for 10 minutes before serving.

Spicy Green Peas
Serves 4

45 ml/3 tbsp oil ● pinch of asafoetida ● 2.5 ml/½ tsp onion seeds

2.5 ml/½ tsp cumin seeds ● 1 cm/½ in ginger root, grated

2.5 ml/½ tsp ground turmeric ● 5 dried red chillies ● 450 g/1 lb peas

Heat the oil and fry the asafoetida, onion and cumin seeds for 1 minute. Add the ginger and turmeric and fry for 1 minute. Add the peas and chillies and fry for 1 minute then cover and simmer gently for about 5 minutes until the peas are cooked. Remove the lid and fry for a further 1-2 minutes, stirring.

Potato-stuffed Peppers
Serves 6

6 green (bell) peppers ● 3 potatoes ● 50 g/2 oz peas

1 onion, chopped ● 60 ml/4 tbsp ghee

1.5 ml/¼ tsp chilli powder ● 1.5 ml/¼ tsp mango powder

1.5 ml/¼ tsp garam masala ● 1.5 ml/¼ tsp pomegranate seeds ● salt

Cook the peppers in boiling water for about 15 minutes until tender but still crisp, and lighter in colour. Drain and cool. Boil the potatoes and peas until cooked, then drain and mash. Heat 10 ml/2 tsp of ghee and fry the onion until browned. Stir in the potato mixture and the spices and fry for 4 minutes. Cut the stem and seeds out of the peppers and stuff with the potato mixture. Heat the remaining ghee and fry the peppers carefully until browned on all sides.

Stuffed Green Peppers
Serves 4-6

Filling: 45 ml/3 tbsp oil ● 5 ml/1 tsp mustard seeds

5 ml/1 tsp cumin seeds ● 1 kg/2 lb potato, boiled and diced

30 ml/2 tbsp ground coriander (cilantro) ● 5 ml/1 tsp ground roasted cumin

2.5 ml/½ tsp ground red chilli ● 2.5 ml/½ tsp ground turmeric ● salt

100 g/4 oz/⅔ cup raisins ● 30 ml/2 tbsp lemon juice

10 ml/2 tsp sugar ● 2.5 ml/½ tsp garam masala

15 ml/1 tbsp chopped fresh coriander (cilantro) ● 1 small green chilli, chopped

500 g/18 oz small green (bell) peppers

Sauce: 60 ml/4 tbsp oil ● 2.5 ml/½ tsp mustard seeds

1 small onion, finely chopped ● 1 large onion, cut into large pieces

3 garlic cloves ● 1 cm/½ in ginger root

10 ml/2 tsp ground coriander (cilantro) ● 2.5 ml/½ tsp garam masala

2.5 ml/½ tsp ground red chilli ● 2.5 ml/½ tsp ground turmeric

400 g/14 oz canned tomatoes ● salt ● 30 ml/2 tbsp tamarind pulp (page 19)

Garnish: 2.5 ml/½ tsp garam masala

15 ml/1 tbsp chopped fresh coriander (cilantro) ● 1 small green chilli, chopped

Heat the oil in a heavy-based pan and fry the mustard seeds until they start crackling. Add the cumin seeds and diced potatoes and fry over a medium heat for 2-3 minutes. Stir in the coriander, cumin, chilli, turmeric and salt and fry for a further 2-3 minutes. Add the raisins, lemon juice, sugar, garam masala, coriander and chilli and cook for 1 minute. Remove from the heat.

Slice the top off the peppers and scoop out the seeds. Fill the peppers with the potato stuffing and put back the lids. Stand a trivet in a large pan and fill with water to come half way up the trivet. Place the peppers on the trivet, bring the water to the boil then reduce the heat to low, cover and steam for 20 minutes, turning once while cooking.

Meanwhile, make the sauce. Heat the oil in a large frying pan (skillet) and fry the mustard seeds until they start crackling. Add the chopped onion and fry until golden brown. Blend the onion, garlic and ginger to a smooth paste in a blender or food processor. Stir into the pan and fry until golden brown. Add the coriander, garam masala, chilli, turmeric, tomatoes and salt and cook until the oil appears on the top of the mixture. Stir in the tamarind pulp and cook until all the liquid has been absorbed. Reduce the heat to low and add the cooked stuffed peppers to the pan. Cook for 5 minutes over a low heat, basting the peppers with the sauce. Transfer to a serving dish, sprinkle with the garnish ingredients and serve hot with lentils, rice, onion paratha and a chicken dish.

Green Pepper Poriyal
Serves 4

450 g/1 lb green (bell) peppers, chopped ● 30 ml/2 tbsp natural (plain) yoghurt

15 ml/1 tbsp oil ● 5 ml/1 tsp mustard seeds

5 ml/1 tsp cumin seeds ● 2.5 ml/½ tsp asafoetida

2-3 curry leaves ● 30 ml/2 tbsp water ● salt ● 10 ml/2 tsp curry powder

Mix the peppers with the yoghurt and leave to stand for 15 minutes. Heat the oil and fry the mustard and cumin seeds, asafoetida and curry leaves until the seeds start crackling. Add the peppers and yoghurt, water and salt, cover and simmer for about 15 minutes until tender. Sprinkle with the curry powder and simmer for a few minutes before serving.

Peppers with Currants
Serves 4

450 g/1 lb green (bell) peppers ● 5 ml/1 tsp tamarind concentrate

100 g/4 oz grated (shredded) coconut ● 50 g/2 oz/⅓ cup yellow split peas

10 ml/2 tsp sesame seeds ● 45 ml/3 tbsp ghee

100 g/4 oz/⅔ cup currants ● 225 g/8 oz/2 cups peanuts, ground

5 ml/1 tsp jaggery ● 5 ml/1 tsp salt ● 300 ml/½ pt/1¼ cups water

Cut each pepper into 6-8 pieces. Grind the tamarind, coconut, split peas and sesame seeds to a fine paste with a little water. Heat the ghee and fry the peppers for 2 minutes. Add the remaining ingredients. Stir in the paste, cover and simmer for about 30 minutes until the sauce has thickened.

Green Pepper and Potato
Serves 4

60 ml/4 tbsp oil ● pinch of asafoetida ● 2.5 ml/½ tsp mustard seeds

2.5 ml/½ tsp onion seeds ● 250 g/9 oz potatoes, cut into 2.5 cm/1 in pieces

250 g/9 oz green (bell) pepper, cut into 2.5 cm/1 in pieces

5 ml/1 tsp ground coriander (cilantro) ● 5 ml/1 tsp ground roasted cumin

2.5 ml/½ tsp garam masala ● 2.5 ml/½ tsp ground red chilli

2.5 ml/½ tsp ground turmeric ● salt

Garnish: 2.5 ml/¼ tsp garam masala

15 ml/1 tbsp chopped fresh coriander (cilantro)

Heat the oil in a heavy-based pan and fry the asafoetida, mustard and onion seeds over a medium heat until they start crackling. Add the potato pieces and fry until lightly browned. Add the pepper and cook for 1 minute. Stir in the coriander, cumin, garam masala, chilli, turmeric and salt, reduce the heat to low and cook for about 10 minutes until the vegetables are tender, stirring occasionally. Sprinkle with the garnish ingredients and serve hot with dal, rice, puris or chapatis and a kofta dish.

Plantain Poriyal
Serves 4

3 green plantains ● 150 ml/¼ pt/⅔ cup tamarind juice ● 5 ml/1 tsp ground turmeric

salt ● 10 ml/2 tsp oil ● 5 ml/1 tsp mustard seeds

5 ml/1 tsp cumin seeds ● 5 ml/1 tsp split black beans

5 ml/1 tsp yellow split peas ● 1 dried red chilli, halved

1.5 ml/¼ tsp asafoetida ● 2-3 curry leaves ● 2 green chillies, slit

15 ml/1 tbsp curry powder ● 30 ml/2 tbsp grated (shredded) coconut

Peel and chop the plantains and place in a pan with the tamarind juice, turmeric and salt, cover and cook over a low heat until the vegetable is tender and dry. Heat the oil and fry the mustard and cumin seeds, split beans, split peas, chilli, asafoetida and curry leaves until the seeds start crackling. Add the chillies, cooked plantain, curry powder and coconut and cook for 1 minute, stirring well.

Potato, Sago and Cheese Patties
Serves 4

50 g/2 oz sago ● 30 ml/2 tbsp chopped fresh coriander (cilantro)

3 green chillies ● 2.5 cm/1 in ginger root ● 225 g/8 oz Cheddar cheese, grated

225 g/8 oz mashed potatoes ● 25 g/1 oz/¼ cup cornflour (cornstarch)

50 g/2 oz peanuts, crushed ● 100 g/4 oz breadcrumbs ● oil for deep-frying

Put the sago in a bowl and just cover with cold water. Leave to stand for 30 minutes. Grind the coriander, chillies and ginger then mix with the cheese, potato, cornflour, peanuts and sago. Mix well and chill. Shape into walnut-sized balls, roll in breadcrumbs then deep-fry in hot oil until golden brown.

Potato Song
Serves 4

450 g/1 lb potatoes ● 1 lemon-sized tamarind pulp

250 ml/8 fl oz/1 cup water ● 45 ml/3 tbsp coconut oil

5 ml/1 tsp mustard seeds ● 2-3 curry leaves ● 4 onions, finely chopped

15 ml/1 tbsp chilli powder ● 5 ml/1 tsp jaggery ● salt

10 ml/2 tsp ground coriander (cilantro)

1 bunch fresh coriander (cilantro), finely chopped

Boil the potatoes until tender then peel and cut into cubes. Soak the tamarind in the water and extract the juice. Heat the oil and fry the mustard seeds and curry leaves until the seeds start crackling. Add the onions and fry until golden. Add the potatoes and fry for 2-3 minutes. Add the tamarind juice, chilli powder, jaggery and salt and simmer for 2 minutes. Add the ground coriander and simmer until the vegetables are well blended. Serve garnished with coriander.

Fenugreek Potatoes
Serves 4

45 ml/3 tbsp oil ● 2.5 ml/½ tsp cumin seeds

2.5 ml/½ tsp ground turmeric ● 10 ml/2 tsp ground fenugreek ● salt

2 tomatoes, skinned and chopped ● 6 large potatoes, boiled and cubed

juice of ½ lemon

Heat the oil and fry the cumin seeds for 1 minute. Add the turmeric, fenugreek and salt and fry for a few seconds. Add the tomatoes and fry until the oil appears on the surface. Add the potatoes, cover and simmer for about 10 minutes, stirring occasionally. Stir in the lemon juice before serving.

Lime Potatoes
Serves 4

30 ml/2 tbsp butter ● 2.5 ml/½ tsp black pepper

30 ml/2 tbsp tomato purée (paste)

30 ml/2 tbsp chopped fresh coriander (cilantro) ● 2 green chillies, chopped

salt ● 6 large potatoes, boiled and cubed ● juice of 1 lime

Melt the butter and fry all the ingredients except the potatoes and lime juice until the fat appears on the surface. Stir in the potatoes and fry for 5-7 minutes until crisp. Stir in the lime juice before serving.

Poppy Seed Potatoes
Serves 4

60 ml/4 tbsp oil ● 6 large potatoes, cubed ● 30 ml/2 tbsp poppy seeds

2 green chillies ● 2 dried red chillies

2.5 ml/½ tsp ground turmeric ● 2.5 ml/½ tsp sugar ● salt

Heat the oil to smoking point then lower the heat and wait 5 minutes. Fry the potatoes until lightly browned then remove and drain. Dry roast the poppy seeds until they darken slightly then grind them to a paste with the green chillies and a very little water. To the cooking oil, add the red chillies, turmeric, salt and ground paste and fry until the oil appears on the surface and the excess water has evaporated, stirring continuously. Add the potatoes and a little water, cover and simmer for 15 minutes. Stir in the sugar and salt and heat through before serving.

Potato and Carrot Korma
Serves 4

2 large potatoes, chopped ● 2 carrots, chopped

100 g/4 oz green beans, chopped ● 1 large tomato, skinned and chopped

salt ● 50 g/2 oz grated (shredded) coconut ● 6 green chillies

1 onion, chopped ● 1 cm/½ in ginger root, chopped

2.5 ml/½ tsp ground turmeric ● 15 ml/1 tbsp chopped fresh coriander (cilantro)

15 ml/1 tbsp aniseeds ● 1 cinnamon stick ● 4 cloves

2 cardamom pods ● 15 ml/1 tbsp poppy seeds ● 15 ml/1 tbsp ghee

2-3 bay leaves

Place the potatoes, carrots and beans in a pan, just cover with water, bring to the boil and simmer until tender. Add the tomato and salt and simmer for 1-2 minutes. Meanwhile, grind together the coconut, chillies, onion, ginger, turmeric and coriander to a paste with a little water. Grind the aniseeds, cinnamon, cloves, cardamom and poppy seeds to a powder. Stir the paste into the vegetables then sprinkle on the masala. Heat the ghee and fry the bay leaves until slightly darkened then stir them into the pan and simmer for 5 minutes, stirring.

Mashed Potato Poriyal
Serves 4

450 g/1 lb potatoes ● 10 ml/2 tsp oil ● 5 ml/1 tsp mustard seeds

5 ml/1 tsp cumin seeds ● 5 ml/1 tsp split black beans

5 ml/1 tsp yellow split peas ● 1 dried red chilli, halved

2.5 ml/½ tsp asafoetida ● 2-3 curry leaves ● 2 green chillies, slit

2.5 cm/1 in ginger root, chopped ● 2.5 ml/½ tsp ground turmeric ● salt

30 ml/2 tbsp grated (shredded) coconut ● juice of 1 lemon

1 bunch fresh coriander (cilantro), chopped

Boil the potatoes then peel and mash them. Heat the oil and fry the mustard and cumin seeds, split beans, split peas, chilli, asafoetida and curry leaves until the seeds start crackling. Add the green chillies and ginger and fry for a few seconds. Add the potatoes, turmeric, salt and coconut and cook for 3 minutes, stirring. Stir in the lemon juice and serve garnished with the coriander.

Gujrati-style Potatoes
Serves 4

30 ml/2 tbsp ghee ● 5 ml/1 tsp mustard seeds

450 g/1 lb potatoes, quartered ● 10 ml/2 tsp ground coriander (cilantro)

2.5 ml/½ tsp ground turmeric ● 2.5 ml/½ tsp chilli powder

5 ml/1 tsp tamarind concentrate ● 15 ml/1 tbsp jaggery ● salt

½ coconut, grated (shredded) ● 1 bunch fresh coriander (cilantro), chopped

1 green chilli, sliced

Heat the ghee and fry the mustard seeds until they start crackling. Add the potatoes, coriander, turmeric, chilli powder, tamarind, jaggery and salt and fry for 2-3 minutes, stirring. Add just enough water to cover the potatoes and simmer until the potatoes are tender. Add the coconut, coriander and chilli and simmer until the sauce has thickened.

Spicy Potatoes
Serves 4-6

500 g/18 oz small potatoes ● 120 ml/4 fl oz/½ cup ghee or oil

1 small onion, finely chopped ● 4 cloves ● 4 peppercorns

2 bay leaves ● 1 cardamom pod ● 1 cm/½ in cinnamon stick

1 large onion, cut into chunks ● 2 cloves garlic ● 1 cm/½ in ginger root

10 ml/2 tsp ground coriander (cilantro) ● 2.5 ml/½ tsp ground roasted cumin

2.5 ml/½ tsp ground red chilli ● 2.5 ml/½ tsp ground turmeric ● salt

400 g/14 oz canned tomatoes ● 150 ml/¼ pt/⅔ cup natural (plain) yoghurt

375 ml/13 fl oz/1½ cups water

Garnish: 2.5 ml/½ tsp garam masala

15 ml/1 tbsp chopped fresh coriander (cilantro) ● 1 small green chilli, chopped

Prick the potatoes all over with a fork. Heat half the ghee or oil and fry the potatoes until golden brown on all sides. Drain and set aside.

Heat the remaining ghee or oil in a heavy-based pan and fry the chopped onion, cloves, peppercorns, bay leaves, cardamom and cinnamon over a medium heat until golden brown. Blend the onion, garlic and ginger to a smooth paste. Stir into the pan and fry until golden brown. Stir in the coriander, cumin, chilli, turmeric and salt. Stir in the tomatoes and cook until the ghee appears on top of the mixture. Stir in the yoghurt and cook until all the liquid has been absorbed. Add the water and fried potatoes, bring to the boil then cover and cook gently for about 20 minutes until tender. (If you are not serving the dish with rice, reduce the quantity of water to 200 ml/7 fl oz/scant 1 cup.) Sprinkle over the garnish ingredients and serve hot with rice, dal, raita and a chicken or meat dish.

Curried Potato
Serves 6

450 g/1 lb very small potatoes ● 15 ml/1 tbsp ghee ● 5 ml/1 tsp mustard seeds

1 onion, chopped ● 3 green chillies ● 5 ml/1 tsp ground turmeric

2.5 ml/½ tsp ground cumin ● 1 sprig fresh curry leaves ● salt

150 ml/¼ pt/⅔ cup water

Boil the potatoes in their skins until tender then drain. Heat the ghee and fry the mustard seeds until they start crackling. Add the onion and remaining spices and stir well. Add the potatoes, salt and water and simmer until the potatoes are nicely browned and the sauce has thickened.

Whole Potatoes
Serves 4

450 g/1 lb small potatoes ● 175 g/6 oz/¾ cup ghee ● salt

120 ml/4 fl oz/½ cup water ● 1 onion, chopped

2 cloves ● 2 cardamom pods ● 4 black peppercorns

30 ml/2 tbsp tomato purée (paste) ● 150 ml/¼ pt/⅔ cup natural (plain) yoghurt

2.5 ml/½ tsp chilli powder ● 2.5 ml/½ tsp garam masala

15 ml/1 tbsp chopped fresh coriander (cilantro)

Prick the potatoes with a fork. Heat 100 g/4 oz/½ cup of ghee and fry the potatoes for 2 minutes, stirring. Sprinkle with salt and half the water and fry for 5 minutes. Remove from the pan and drain. Heat the remaining ghee and fry the onion until golden. Add the whole spices, tomato purée, yoghurt and chilli powder with the remaining water and a little salt. Cover and simmer for 5 minutes. Add the potatoes, garam masala and coriander, cover and simmer for 10 minutes until the potatoes are tender.

Potato Kebabs
Serves 6

450 g/1 lb potatoes, quartered ● 5 ml/1 tsp salt

30 ml/2 tbsp desiccated (shredded) coconut ● 4 green chillies

4 cloves garlic ● 2 onions ● 1.5 ml/¼ tsp ground turmeric

1.5 ml/¼ tsp cumin seeds ● 10 ml/2 tsp gram flour

10 ml/2 tsp wine vinegar ● 2 eggs, beaten ● 50 g/2 oz/½ cup breadcrumbs

ghee for deep-frying

Boil the potatoes in salted water until tender. Grind the coconut, chillies, garlic, onions, turmeric, cumin seeds and gram flour to a paste, adding enough wine vinegar to make a thick consistency. Drain and finely chop the potatoes and stir into the paste with the eggs. Shape the mixture into balls and roll in the breadcrumbs. Deep-fry in hot ghee until golden brown.

Coconut Kebabs
Serves 6

450 g/1 lb potatoes, boiled and mashed ● ½ coconut, grated (shredded)

2.5 ml/½ tsp sugar ● 5 ml/1 tsp cumin seeds, roasted and ground

15 ml/1 tbsp chopped onion ● 5 ml/1 tsp grated ginger root

1 green chilli, chopped ● 15 ml/1 tbsp lemon juice

15 ml/1 tbsp chopped fresh coriander (cilantro) ● 5 ml/1 tsp salt

5 ml/1 tsp black pepper ● 50 g/2 oz/½ cup breadcrumbs ● ghee for frying

Divide the potatoes into 12 portions and flatten them into discs. Mix together all the remaining ingredients except the breadcrumbs and oil and divide between the potato discs. Fold the potato around the filling then roll in breadcrumbs. Shallow fry in hot ghee and serve hot with chutney.

Potato Matar
Serves 4-6

250 g/9 oz potatoes, cut into 2.5 cm/1 in pieces ● oil for deep-frying

75 ml/5 tbsp oil or ghee ● 1 small onion, finely chopped

3 large garlic cloves ● 1 medium onion, coarsely chopped

1 cm/½ in ginger root ● 175 ml/6 fl oz/¾ cup water

10 ml/2 tsp ground coriander (cilantro) ● 5 ml/1 tsp ground roasted cumin

2.5 ml/½ tsp garam masala ● 2.5 ml/½ tsp ground red chilli

2.5 ml/½ tsp ground turmeric ● salt ● 225 g/8 oz canned tomatoes

150 ml/¼ pt/⅔ cup natural (plain) yoghurt ● 450 g/1 lb peas

Garnish: 2.5 ml/½ tsp garam masala

15 ml/1 tbsp chopped fresh coriander (cilantro) ● 1 small green chilli, chopped

Deep-fry the potato in the oil over a medium heat until golden brown.

Meanwhile, heat the oil or ghee in a heavy-based pan and gently fry the small onion until golden. Blend the garlic, medium onion, ginger and 30 ml/2 tbsp of water to a smooth paste in a blender or food processor. Add it to the pan and fry for a further few minutes until golden brown. Stir in the coriander, cumin, garam masala, chilli, turmeric and salt. Stir in the tomatoes. Simmer until all the liquid has been absorbed and oil appears on the top of the mixture. Stir in the yoghurt and simmer until the liquid has been absorbed. Stir in the remaining water with the potatoes and peas, cover and simmer for 3 minutes. (If you use fresh peas, add them with an extra 150 ml/¼ pt/⅔ cup of water and simmer until tender before adding the potatoes.) Sprinkle over the garnish ingredients and serve hot with rice, dal or raita and a meat or chicken dish.

Photograph opposite: *South Indian-style Potatoes (page 229) and Curried Mushrooms with Spinach (page 211)*

Potato Masala
Serves 4

450 g/1 lb potatoes • 2 onions, chopped • 3 green chillies, chopped

2.5 cm/1 in ginger root, chopped • 2 tomatoes, skinned and chopped

2.5 ml/½ tsp ground turmeric • salt

1 sprig fresh coriander (cilantro), chopped • 250 ml/8 fl oz/1 cup water

Seasoning: 15 ml/1 tbsp oil • 5 ml/1 tsp mustard seeds

5 ml/1 tsp cumin seeds • 5 ml/1 tsp split black beans

5 ml/1 tsp yellow split peas • 1 dried red chilli, halved

2.5 ml/½ tsp asafoetida • 2-3 curry leaves

Boil the potatoes until tender then peel and mash. Heat the seasoning oil and fry the seasoning ingredients until the mustard seeds start crackling. Add the onion, chillies and ginger and fry for 1 minute. Add the tomatoes and fry for 2 minutes. Add the turmeric, salt and water, bring to the boil, cover and simmer for 5 minutes until the onions are cooked. Add the potatoes and cook for 2 minutes until all the ingredients are well blended. Garnish with coriander and serve hot with rice and a meat dish.

Stuffed Potatoes
Serves 4

1 kg/2 lb medium potatoes • 75 ml/5 tbsp oil • 5 ml/1 tsp mustard seeds

5 ml/1 tsp garam masala • 5 ml/1 tsp ground coriander (cilantro)

5 ml/1 tsp ground roasted cumin • 2.5 ml/½ tsp ground red chilli

2.5 ml/½ tsp ground turmeric • salt

250 g/9 oz mixed vegetables, frozen or boiled • 100 g/4 oz/⅓ cup raisins

30 ml/2 tbsp chopped fresh coriander (cilantro) • 1 small green chilli, chopped

75 ml/5 tbsp oil for frying

Boil the potatoes in their skins, peel them and divide them in half. Chop half. Slice 3 mm/1/8 in off the top of the other half and scoop out as much as possible from the potatoes.

Heat the oil in a heavy-based pan and fry the mustard seeds until they start crackling. Add the chopped potatoes and fry over a medium-low heat for about 10 minutes until light golden brown. Stir in the garam masala, coriander, cumin, chilli, turmeric and salt. Stir in the vegetables and cook for 7 minutes. Stir in the raisins, coriander and chilli. Remove from the heat. Stuff the whole potatoes with the mixture and replace the tops. Heat the oil and fry the stuffed potatoes over a medium heat for about 10 minutes until crispy golden brown on all sides. Serve hot with chutney, puris, dal, raita and a kofta dish.

Photograph opposite: *Chicken Biryani (page 278)*

Potatoes and Tomatoes   Serves 4

30 ml/2 tbsp ghee • 1 onion, chopped • pinch of ground turmeric

2.5 ml/½ tsp chilli powder • pinch of garlic powder

1 tomato, skinned and chopped • salt • 450 g/1 lb potatoes

2.5 ml/½ tsp garam masala

Heat half the ghee and fry the onion until golden. Lower the heat and stir in the turmeric, chilli powder and garlic. Add the tomato and salt and fry for 2 minutes, stirring. Add the potatoes, cover and simmer for 10 minutes, stirring occasionally and adding a little water if necessary, until the potatoes are cooked. Sprinkle with garam masala and the remaining ghee.

Bengali-style Potatoes   Serves 4

45 ml/3 tbsp ghee • 5 ml/1 tsp mustard seeds • 2.5 ml/½ tsp cumin seeds

pinch of ground fenugreek • 450 g/1 lb potatoes, cubed

60 ml/4 tbsp water • 100 g/4 oz peas • 10 ml/2 tbsp black pepper

15 ml/1 tbsp chopped fresh coriander (cilantro)

Heat the ghee and fry the mustard seeds until they start crackling. Add the cumin seeds and fenugreek and fry for 1 minute. Add the potatoes and fry for 4-5 minutes until browned. Add the water, cover and simmer for 5 minutes. Add the peas and pepper and simmer, uncovered, until the vegetables are tender. Serve garnished with coriander.

Potato Curry with Tomatoes   Serves 4

500 g/18 oz potatoes • 60 ml/4 tbsp oil or ghee • 2.5 ml/½ tsp mustard seeds

2.5 ml/½ tsp cumin seeds • 5 ml/1 tsp ground coriander (cilantro)

5 ml/1 tsp ground roasted cumin • 2.5 ml/½ tsp garam masala

2.5 ml/½ tsp ground red chilli • 2.5 ml/½ tsp ground turmeric • salt

400 g/14 oz canned tomatoes • 150 ml/¼ pt/⅔ cup water

20 ml/2 tbsp lemon juice

Garnish: 1.5 ml/¼ tsp garam masala

15 ml/1 tbsp chopped fresh coriander (cilantro) • 1 small green chilli, chopped

Boil the potatoes in their skins then drain, peel and cut into 5 mm/¼ in pieces. Heat the oil in a heavy-based pan and fry the mustard seeds over a medium heat until they start crackling. Add the cumin seeds and fry for a few seconds until lightly browned. Stir in the potato pieces and fry until lightly browned. Stir in the coriander, cumin, garam masala, chilli, turmeric and salt. Stir in the tomatoes and cook until the water has been absorbed. Pour in the water, bring to the boil then reduce the heat to low and simmer for 2 minutes. Add the lemon juice. Sprinkle with the garnish.

New Potatoes in their Jackets
Serves 4-6

60 ml/4 tbsp oil • 5 ml/1 tsp mustard seeds • 5 ml/1 tsp cumin seeds

500 g/18 oz small new potatoes, whole

10 ml/2 tsp ground coriander (cilantro)

5 ml/1 tsp ground roasted cumin • 5 ml/1 tsp garam masala

2.5 ml/½ tsp ground turmeric • 1.5 ml/¼ tsp ground red chilli • salt

10 ml/2 tsp ground mango powder OR 2.5 ml/½ tsp citric acid

Garnish: 15 ml/1 tbsp chopped fresh coriander (cilantro)

1 small green chilli, chopped

Heat the oil in a heavy-based pan and fry the mustard seeds over a medium heat until they start crackling. Add the cumin seeds and fry until lightly browned. Stir in the potatoes and fry over a medium heat for 5 minutes, then reduce the heat to medium-low and fry for a further 3 minutes. Stir in the coriander, cumin, garam masala, turmeric, chilli and salt, cover and cook on a low heat for 5 minutes until tender, stirring occasionally. Add the mango powder or citric acid and mix the ingredients together well. Sprinkle over the garnish ingredients and serve hot with dal, plain rice, raita and a green vegetable or fish dish.

Potato Sukhe
Serves 4-6

60 ml/4 tbsp oil • large pinch of asafoetida

5 ml/1 tsp onion seeds • 1 onion, finely chopped

500 g/18 oz potatoes, cooked in their skins then cut into 2 cm/¾ in pieces

10 ml/2 tsp ground coriander (cilantro) • 5 ml/1 tsp ground roasted cumin

2.5 ml/½ tsp garam masala • 2.5 ml/½ tsp ground ginger

2.5 ml/2 tsp ground red chilli • 2.5 ml/½ tsp ground turmeric • salt

Garnish: 2.5 ml/½ tsp garam masala

15 ml/1 tbsp chopped fresh coriander (cilantro)

Heat the oil and fry the asafoetida until it starts sizzling. Add the onion seeds and fry for 5 seconds. Add the onion and fry until lightly browned. Stir in the potato pieces and fry for 5 minutes. Stir in the coriander, cumin, garam masala, ginger, chilli, turmeric and salt and fry over a low heat for 3 minutes. Sprinkle over the garnish ingredients and serve hot with dal, matar paneer, puris or chapatis and a meat dish.

Potatoes with Mustard
Serves 4

45 ml/3 tbsp ghee • 10 ml/2 tsp mustard seeds

15 ml/1 tbsp split black beans • 2-3 curry leaves • 450 g/1 lb potatoes, cubed

pinch of ground turmeric • 10 ml/2 tsp chilli powder

pinch of asafoetida • 45 ml/3 tbsp water • 5 ml/1 tsp lemon juice

Heat the ghee and fry the mustard seeds, split beans and curry leaves until the seeds start crackling. Add the potatoes and stir-fry for 3 minutes. Add the turmeric, chilli powder and asafoetida and fry for 2 minutes. **Sprinkle with water, cover and simmer for about 10 minutes until the potatoes are tender, stirring gently and adding a little more water if necessary. Toss with the lemon juice and serve hot.**

Potato Bhurta
Serves 4

450 g/1 lb potatoes • 100 g/4 oz/½ cup ghee • 1 onion, finely chopped

2 cloves garlic, chopped • 1 green chilli, chopped

5 ml/1 tsp garam masala • pinch of chilli powder • 5 ml/1 tsp grated ginger root

4 spring onions (scallions), chopped • salt

30 ml/2 tbsp chopped fresh coriander (cilantro) • 1 tomato, sliced

Boil the potatoes until tender then peel and mash. Heat the ghee and fry the onion and garlic until golden. Mix in the potato and all the remaining ingredients except the tomato and **coriander and simmer gently for 10 minutes, stirring. Stir half the coriander into the potatoes then serve garnished with the tomato and the remaining coriander.**

Potato Curry
Serves 4

100 g/4 oz/½ cup ghee • 2 onions, chopped • 5 ml/1 tsp cumin seeds

5 ml/1 tsp ground turmeric • 2.5 ml/½ tsp chilli powder

2 cloves garlic, chopped • 2.5 cm/1 in ginger root, grated

30 ml/2 tbsp tomato purée (paste) • 450 g/1 lb potatoes, quartered

100 g/4 oz peas • 300 ml/½ pt/1¼ cups warm water • salt

5 ml/1 tsp green mango powder • 5 ml/1 tsp garam masala

30 ml/2 tbsp chopped fresh coriander (cilantro)

Heat the ghee and fry the onions and cumin seeds until lightly browned. Add the turmeric, chilli powder, garlic, ginger and tomato purée and fry for 1 minute. Add the potatoes and peas and cook for 10 minutes, stir- **ring. Add the water and salt, bring to the boil and simmer for 15 minutes until the potatoes are tender. Sprinkle with the remaining ingredients before serving.**

South Indian-style Potatoes   Serves 4

450 g/1 lb potatoes, diced ● 10 ml/2 tsp ground turmeric

90 ml/6 tbsp mustard oil ● 15 ml/1 tbsp split black beans, crushed

10 ml/2 tsp mustard seeds ● 4 curry leaves ● 3 dried red chillies, halved

5 ml/1 tsp paprika ● 3 onions, sliced

2 tomatoes, skinned and chopped ● salt

Boil the potatoes with the turmeric for a few minutes until just beginning to soften. Meanwhile, heat the oil and fry the split beans and mustard seeds until the seeds start crackling. Add the curry leaves, chillies and paprika and fry for 2 minutes. Add the onion and fry until golden. Add the tomatoes and fry for 5 minutes. Stir in the potatoes and salt and fry for about 2 minutes.

Tandoori Potatoes   Serves 4

450 g/1 lb small new potatoes, scrubbed

150 ml/¼ pt/⅔ cup natural (plain) yoghurt ● 45 ml/3 tbsp oil

15 ml/1 tbsp lemon juice ● 1 clove garlic, crushed

5 ml/1 tsp grated ginger root ● 2 green chillies, chopped

15 ml/1 tbsp chopped fresh mint ● 15 ml/1 tbsp chopped fresh coriander (cilantro)

5 ml/1 tsp garam masala ● 5 ml/1 tsp ground cumin ● 5 ml/1 tsp ground turmeric

5 ml/1 tsp salt ● 45 ml/3 tbsp ghee ● 5 ml/1 tsp mustard seeds

5 ml/1 tsp cumin seeds ● 45 ml/3 tbsp tomato purée (paste)

15 ml/1 tbsp chopped fresh coriander (cilantro)

Rinse and drain the potatoes then place in a bowl. Mix together the yoghurt, oil, lemon juice, garlic, ginger, chillies, spices and salt, stir into the potatoes, cover and marinate overnight.
Heat the ghee and fry the mustard and cumin seeds until they start crackling. Add the tomato purée, potatoes and marinade, bring to a gentle simmer, cover and simmer for about 15 minutes until the potatoes are tender and the sauce has thickened.

Potatoes with Dill   Serves 6

675 g/1½ lb potatoes ● 45 ml/3 tbsp oil ● 1 cm/½ in ginger root, grated

5 ml/1 tsp ground fennel ● 1 green chilli, chopped

5 ml/1 tsp lemon juice ● 30 ml/2 tbsp water ● 5 ml/1 tsp black pepper

50 g/2 oz fresh dill (dill weed), chopped

Boil the potatoes until tender then drain and cut into 1 cm/½ in cubes. Heat the oil and fry the ginger for 1 minute. Add the potatoes, fennel and chilli and fry for 1 minute. Add the lemon juice and water, cover and simmer for 5 minutes. Stir in the pepper and dill and simmer for 3-5 minutes.

Gujrati-style Potato and French Beans

Serves 4

60 ml/4 tbsp oil ● 5 ml/1 tsp mustard seeds ● 5 ml/1 tsp cumin seeds

2 large garlic cloves, crushed ● 1 cm/½ in ginger root, finely chopped

250 g/9 oz potatoes, cut into 1 cm/½ in pieces

250 g/9 oz French beans, cut into 1 cm/½ in pieces

5 ml/1 tsp ground coriander (cilantro) ● 5 ml/1 tsp ground roasted cumin

5 ml/1 tsp garam masala ● 2.5 ml/½ tsp ground red chilli

2.5 ml/½ tsp ground turmeric ● salt ● 100 ml/3½ fl oz/6½ tbsp water

15 ml/1 tbsp lemon juice ● 10 ml/2 tsp sugar

Heat the oil in a heavy-based pan and fry the mustard seeds over a medium heat until they start crackling. Add the cumin seeds and fry until lightly browned. Stir in the garlic, ginger and potatoes and fry for 5 minutes. Stir in the beans and fry for 2 minutes. Stir in the coriander, cumin, garam masala, chilli, turmeric, salt and water. Bring to the boil, cover and simmer over a low heat for 15 minutes until tender, stirring occasionally. Add the lemon juice and sugar and increase the heat to high to dry off any remaining water. Serve hot with paratha, chapatis, dal, rice, raita and a meat dish.

Pumpkin Kofta

Serves 4-6

450 g/1 lb pumpkin, peeled and grated ● 150 ml/¼ pt/⅔ cup water

50 g/2 oz/½ cup gram flour ● 15 ml/1 tbsp chopped fresh coriander (cilantro)

2.5 ml/½ tsp garam masala ● 2.5 ml/½ tsp ground red chilli ● salt

12 prunes, stoned ● oil for frying

Sauce: 90 ml/6 tbsp oil or ghee ● 1 small onion, finely chopped

4 cloves ● 4 peppercorns ● 2 bay leaves

1 black cardamom pod ● 1.5 cm/½ in cinnamon stick

3 large cloves garlic ● 2.5 cm/1 in ginger root

1 medium onion, coarsely chopped ● 45 ml/3 tbsp water

10 ml/2 tsp poppy seeds, ground ● 5 ml/1 tsp ground coriander (cilantro)

5 ml/1 tsp ground roasted cumin ● 5 ml/1 tsp ground turmeric

2.5 ml/½ tsp ground red chilli ● 1.5 ml/¼ tsp ground mace

1.5 ml/¼ tsp grated nutmeg ● salt ● 225 g/8 oz tomatoes, skinned and chopped

150 ml/¼ pt/⅔ cup natural (plain) yoghurt ● 200 ml/7 fl oz/scant 1 cup water

Garnish: 2.5 ml/½ tsp garam masala

15 ml/1 tbsp chopped fresh coriander (cilantro) ● 1 small green chilli, chopped

Place the pumpkin and water in a pan and simmer over a medium-low heat for 20 minutes until tender. Increase the heat and dry off any remaining water. Lightly roast the gram flour in a dry frying pan (skillet). Place the

pumpkin in a bowl and mix in the flour, coriander, garam masala, chilli and salt to form a dough, adding a little water if necessary. Divide the mixture into 12 balls. Flatten them and place a prune in the centre, bringing the edges over to form rectangles. Heat the oil and deep-fry the koftas until golden brown.

Heat the oil or ghee and fry the onion and whole spices until golden. Blend the garlic, ginger, onion and water to a smooth paste then add it to the pan and fry until golden. Add the poppy seeds and fry for 2 minutes. Stir in the ground spices then the tomatoes and cook until all the liquid has been absorbed. Stir in the yoghurt and simmer until all the liquid has evaporated. Add the water, bring to the boil, then simmer gently for 2 minutes. Pour the sauce over the koftas and sprinkle with the garnish ingredients. Serve hot with meat pulao, aubergine and dal.

Pumpkin Bhaji
Serves 4

60 ml/4 tbsp oil or ghee ● 5 ml/1 tsp mustard seeds

1 small onion, finely chopped ● 1.5 cm/¼ in ginger root, finely chopped

5 ml/1 tsp ground coriander (cilantro) ● 2.5 ml/½ tsp garam masala

2.5 ml/½ tsp ground roasted cumin ● 2.5 ml/½ tsp ground red chilli

2.5 ml/½ tsp ground turmeric ● salt ● 500 g/18 oz pumpkin, cut into 2.5 cm/1 in pieces

225 g/8 oz canned tomatoes ● 150 ml/¼ pt/⅔ cup natural (plain) yoghurt

Garnish: 15 ml/1 tbsp chopped fresh coriander (cilantro)

1.5 ml/¼ tsp garam masala ● 1 small green chilli, chopped

Heat the oil in and fry the mustard seeds until they start crackling. Add the onion and ginger and fry until golden brown. Stir in the ground spices, salt, pumpkin, tomatoes and yoghurt. Bring to the boil the cover and simmer gently for 30 minutes until the pumpkin is tender, stirring occasionally. Increase the heat and fry off any remaining liquid. Sprinkle over the garnish ingredients and serve hot with chapatis, dal, rice and a meat or chicken dish.

Spicy Spinach
Serves 6

1.5 kg/3 lb spinach, chopped ● 3 turnips, cubed ● 450 ml/¾ pt/2 cups water

45 ml/3 tbsp oil ● 15 ml/1 tbsp black mustard seeds ● 1 onion, chopped

5 cloves garlic, chopped ● 2.5 cm/1 in ginger root, chopped

5 ml/1 tsp ground turmeric ● 2.5 ml/½ tsp chilli powder

15 ml/1 tbsp garam masala ● salt

Boil the spinach and turnips in the water for about 12 minutes until tender then drain and mash. Heat the oil and fry the mustard seeds until they start crackling. Stir in the onion, garlic and ginger and cook until browned. Add the turmeric, chilli powder, garam masala and salt and fry for 1 minute, stirring. Stir in the vegetables, cover and simmer for 5 minutes until the liquid evaporates, stirring occasionally. Serve hot with chicken.

Spinach and Mustard Leaves

Serves 4

500 g/18 oz spinach leaves, sliced ● 100 g/4 oz mustard leaves, sliced

300 ml/½ pt/1¼ cups water ● 90 ml/6 tbsp ghee

3 large garlic cloves, crushed ● 2.5 cm/1 in ginger root, finely chopped

1 large onion, finely chopped ● 5 ml/1 tsp garam masala

5 ml/1 tsp ground roasted cumin ● 2.5 ml/½ tsp ground red chilli

2.5 ml/½ tsp ground turmeric ● salt

Garnish: 2.5 ml/½ tsp garam masala ● 1 small green chilli, chopped

Place the spinach and mustard leaves and the water in a pan, bring to the boil, cover and cook for 15 minutes until tender. Leave to cool then blend to a smooth paste.

Heat the ghee in a heavy-based pan and fry the garlic, ginger and onion over a medium heat until golden brown. Stir in the ground spices and salt. Mix in the blended spinach paste, bring to the boil, cover and simmer gently for 10 minutes. Sprinkle over the garnish ingredients and serve hot with maize chapatis, tandoori chicken, raita and cauliflower.

Sweetcorn with Peppers

Serves 4

30 ml/2 tbsp desiccated (shredded) coconut ● 4 green chillies

2.5 cm/1 in ginger root ● 4 cloves garlic ● 30 ml/2 tbsp ghee

10 ml/2 tsp mustard seeds ● 1 red (bell) pepper, diced

1 green (bell) pepper, diced ● 400 g/14 oz sweetcorn ● salt

Purée the coconut, chillies, ginger and garlic to a paste with a little water, if necessary. Heat the ghee and fry the mustard seeds until they start crackling. Add the paste and fry for 3-4 minutes, stirring. Add the peppers and sweetcorn and season to taste with salt. Stir-fry for 3 minutes. Reduce the heat and simmer for 10 minutes until the peppers are just tender.

Stuffed Tomatoes

Serves 4-6

500 g/18 oz medium firm tomatoes ● 100 ml/3½ fl oz/6½ tbsp oil

5 ml/1 tsp mustard seeds ● 500 g/18 oz potatoes, cooked, peeled and diced

5 ml/1 tsp garam masala ● 5 ml/1 tsp ground coriander (cilantro)

5 ml/1 tsp ground roasted cumin ● 2.5 ml/½ tsp ground red chilli

2.5 ml/½ tsp ground turmeric ● salt

250 g/9 oz mixed vegetables, frozen or boiled ● 100 g/4 oz/⅔ cup raisins

30 ml/2 tbsp chopped fresh coriander (cilantro) ● 1 small green chilli, chopped

Slice the top off the tomatoes and carefully scoop out and reserve the pulp. Turn the tomatoes upside down on a plate to drain.

Heat 75 ml/5 tbsp of the oil and fry the mustard seeds over a medium heat until they start crackling. Add the potato pieces and fry over a medium-low heat for about 10 minutes until golden brown. Stir in the garam masala, coriander, cumin, chilli, turmeric and salt. Stir in the vegetables and tomato pulp and cook for 7 minutes. Stir in the raisins. Mix in the coriander leaves and chilli and remove from the heat. Stuff the tomatoes with the mixture and put back the tops. Heat the remaining oil and fry the stuffed tomatoes for 2 minutes. Turn them over gently then fry for a further 1 minute. Arrange the tomatoes attractively on a serving plate and spread any remaining filling around the tomatoes. Serve hot with chutney, pulao, puris, dal, raita and a chicken dish.

Tomato Mahashas

Serves 6

900 g/2 lb tomatoes ● 15 ml/1 tbsp ghee ● 4 cloves
4 cardamom pods ● 1 cinnamon stick ● 2 onions, sliced
5 ml/1 tsp ground turmeric ● 5 ml/1 tsp chilli powder
225 g/8 oz/1 cup basmati rice, soaked ● 225 g/8 oz peas
600 ml/1 pt/2½ cups water ● salt
15 ml/1 tbsp chopped fresh coriander (cilantro) ● ½ coconut, grated (shredded)

Slice the tops off the tomatoes and scoop out the inside pulp. Heat the ghee and fry the cloves, cardamom, cinnamon and onions until soft. Add the turmeric, chilli powder, rice, peas, water and salt. Bring to the boil then simmer until the rice is cooked and the water has evaporated. Stuff the tomatoes with the rice mixture and replace the tops. Brush with a little melted ghee and bake in a preheated oven at 180°C/350°F/gas mark 4 for 15 minutes. Serve garnished with coriander and coconut.

Sweet and Sour Tomatoes

Serves 6

30 ml/2 tbsp mustard oil ● 2.5 cm/1 in ginger root, grated
1 clove garlic, crushed ● 50 g/1 lb tomatoes, skinned and chopped
pinch of chilli powder ● 2.5 ml/½ tsp ground turmeric
20 ml/4 tsp jaggery ● 15 ml/1 tbsp raisins
1.5 ml/¼ tsp fenugreek seeds ● 1.5 ml/¼ tsp mustard seeds
1.5 ml/¼ tsp onion seeds ● 2 dried red chillies ● 1.5 ml/¼ tsp aniseeds

Heat half the oil and fry the ginger and garlic until golden. Add the tomatoes, chilli powder, turmeric, jaggery and raisins and simmer gently for 20 minutes. In a separate pan, heat the remaining oil and fry the fenugreek seeds for 1 minute. Add the remaining spices and fry for 1 minute. Stir into the tomatoes and cook for a further 10-15 minutes.

Turnip Kofta
Makes 14

900 g/2 lb turnip, peeled and grated • 100 ml/3½ fl oz/6½ tbsp water

50 g/2 oz/½ cup gram flour • 2.5 ml/½ tsp garam masala

2.5 ml/½ tsp ground roasted cumin • 2.5 ml/½ tsp ground red chilli

1.5 ml/¼ tsp ground mace • 1.5 ml/¼ tsp grated nutmeg

salt • 25 g/1 oz/¼ cup blanched almonds • 25 g/1 oz/¼ cup cashew nuts

50 g/2 oz/⅓ cup raisins • oil for frying

Sauce: 75 ml/5 tbsp ghee or oil • 1 small onion, finely chopped

4 large cloves garlic, crushed • 2.5 cm/1 in ginger root, coarsely chopped

1 onion, coarsely chopped • 5 ml/1 tsp garam masala

5 ml/1 tsp ground coriander (cilantro) • 5 ml/1 tsp ground roasted cumin

2.5 ml/½ tsp ground red chilli • 2.5 ml/½ tsp ground turmeric • salt

225 g/8 oz canned tomatoes, chopped • 150 ml/¼ pt/⅔ cup natural (plain) yoghurt

45 ml/3 tbsp water

Garnish: 1.5 ml/¼ tsp garam masala

15 ml/1 tbsp chopped fresh coriander (cilantro) • 1 small green chilli, chopped

Cook the turnip in the water for about 15 minutes until tender. Drain, reserving the cooking water. Place the turnip in a strainer and squeeze out all the water with the palm of your hand. Lightly brown the gram flour in a dry frying pan (skillet) on a low heat. Put the turnip in a bowl and stir in the gram flour, garam masala, cumin, chilli, mace, nutmeg and salt. Divide the mixture into 14 equal portions. Flatten each portion and place an almond, a cashew and a few raisins in the middle, bring the edges over to cover and shape into a round. Meanwhile, heat the oil, then slip the koftas into the oil and fry until golden brown. Remove with a slotted spoon and put to one side.

To make the sauce, heat the ghee or oil in a heavy-based pan and fry the small onion over a medium heat until golden brown. Blend the garlic, ginger and medium onion to a smooth paste in a blender or food processor. Add to the pan and fry for a few minutes until golden brown. Stir in the garam masala, coriander, cumin, chilli, turmeric and salt. Stir in the tomatoes and cook until all the water has been absorbed and the ghee appears on the surface. Add the yoghurt and cook until all the liquid has been absorbed. Add the water and cook until all the liquid has been absorbed. Make up the reserved marrow cooking liquid to 250 ml/8 fl oz/1 cup with water, if necessary. Add to the pan, bring to the boil and simmer for 2 minutes. Pour over the kofta. Sprinkle with the garnish ingredients and serve hot with puris, pulao, cauliflower and a chicken dish.

Turnip and Peas
Serves 4

60 ml/4 tbsp oil ● 5 ml/1 tsp mustard seeds ● 5 ml/1 tsp cumin seeds

2 large cloves garlic, crushed ● 1 cm/½ in ginger root, minced

1 small onion, chopped ● 5 ml/1 tsp ground coriander (cilantro)

2.5 ml/½ tsp garam masala ● 2.5 ml/½ tsp ground red chilli

2.5 ml/½ tsp ground turmeric ● salt

225 g/8 oz canned tomatoes, chopped

450 g/1 lb tender turnips, cut into 2.5 cm/1 in pieces ● 250 g/9 oz peas

Garnish: 2.5 ml/½ tsp garam masala

15 ml/1 tbsp chopped fresh coriander (cilantro) ● 1 small green chilli, chopped

Heat the oil in a heavy-based pan and fry the mustard seeds over a medium heat until they start crackling. Add the cumin seeds and fry until lightly browned. Stir in the garlic, ginger and onion and fry over a medium heat until golden brown. Stir in the coriander, garam masala, chilli, turmeric and salt. Stir in the tomatoes and turnips. Reduce the heat to medium-low, cover and cook for 10 minutes until tender, stirring occasionally. Increase the heat and dry off any remaining water. Stir in the peas and cook for a further few minutes until the peas are tender and the oil appears on the surface of the mixture. Sprinkle over the garnish ingredients and serve hot with dal, rice, puris, raita and a fish dish.

Turnip Bhurta
Serves 4

50 g/2 oz/¼ cup ghee ● pinch of cumin seeds ● 1 onion, chopped

2 cloves garlic, chopped ● 1 cm/½ in ginger root, grated

2 tomatoes, skinned and quartered ● 450 g/1 lb turnips, boiled and mashed

salt ● 2 green chillies, chopped

2.5 ml/½ tsp garam masala ● 15 ml/1 tbsp chopped fresh coriander (cilantro)

Heat the ghee and fry the cumin seeds, onion, garlic and ginger for 2 minutes. Add the tomatoes, turnips, salt and chillies and cook for 10 minutes, stirring. Sprinkle with the garam masala and coriander before serving.

Watermelon Fries
Serves 6-8

1 medium watermelon ● oil for deep-frying

salt and pepper

Thickly slice the melon and remove the seeds and red flesh, leaving the outer skin with a layer of white flesh. Cut the skin into small pieces and leave in a warm place to dry completely. Store in an airtight container until required. Before serving, deep-fry for about 2 minutes then drain and sprinkle with salt and pepper.

Yam Chips
Serves 4

10 ml/2 tsp ground turmeric • 900 ml/1½ pts/3¾ cups water

900 g/2 lb yam • oil for deep-frying

10 ml/2 tsp chilli powder • 5 ml/1 tsp asafoetida • salt

Mix the turmeric and water. Peel and thinly slice the yam and soak in the turmeric water for 30 minutes. Drain and leave to dry completely. Heat the oil and fry the yam until golden brown. Sprinkle over the spices and salt and store in an airtight container.

Yam Poriyal
Serves 4

450 g/1 lb yam • 2.5 ml/½ tsp ground turmeric • salt

10 ml/2 tsp oil • 5 ml/1 tsp mustard seeds • 5 ml/1 tsp split black beans

5 ml/1 tsp yellow split peas • 1 dried red chilli, halved

2.5 ml/½ tsp asafoetida • 2-3 curry leaves • 3 green chillies, slit

30 ml/2 tbsp grated (shredded) coconut • 15 ml/1 tbsp curry powder

Peel and finely chop the yam and cook with the turmeric and salt and a very little water until tender. Drain and leave to cool. Heat the oil and fry the mustard seeds, split beans, split peas, chilli, asafoetida and curry leaves until the seeds start crackling. Add the chillies and yam and stir well. Stir in the coconut and curry powder and cook for 3 minutes.

Khadi
Serves 4

Khadi: 25 g/1 oz/¼ cup gram flour • 2.5 ml/½ tsp garam masala

2.5 ml/½ tsp ground ginger • 2.5 ml/½ tsp ground red chilli

2.5 ml/½ tsp ground turmeric • salt

450 ml/¾ pt/2 cups natural (plain) yoghurt

Pakora: 100 g/4 oz/1 cup gram flour • 5 ml/1 tsp garam masala

2.5 ml/½ tsp ground red chilli • 2.5 ml/½ tsp oregano seeds

2 small onions, thinly sliced • salt • 15 ml/1 tbsp oil

100 ml/3½ fl oz/6½ tbsp water • oil for frying

60 ml/4 tbsp oil • large pinch of asafoetida

5 ml/1 tsp cumin seeds • 1 l/1¾ pts/4¼ cups water

Tarka: 90 ml/6 tbsp ghee • 2.5 ml/½ tsp mustard seeds

1 small onion, finely chopped • 5 ml/1 tsp garam masala

45 ml/3 tbsp chopped fresh coriander (cilantro) • 1 small green chilli, chopped

Place the gram flour in a bowl and stir in the spices. Gradually blend in the yoghurt.

To make the pakora, stir together the gram flour, garam masala, chilli, oregano seeds, onions and salt. Gradually pour in the oil and water and blend to a smooth batter. Heat the oil in a deep pan over a medium-high heat. Fry tablespoonfuls of the batter until golden brown on both sides. Drain and set aside. Heat the oil in a heavy-based pan and fry the asafoetida over a medium heat until it starts sizzling. Add the cumin seeds and fry for a few seconds until lightly browned. Pour in the yoghurt and flour mixture and half the water. Bring to the boil,

stirring. Add the fried pakoras and remaining water. Bring to the boil, reduce the heat to medium-low then simmer for a further 25 minutes or until the required consistency has been obtained. Indians like to eat kadhi as runny as a soup with plain rice.

While the kadhi is cooking, prepare the tarka. Heat the ghee in a heavy-based pan and fry the mustard seeds until they start crackling. Add the onion and fry until golden brown. Turn off the heat and stir in the garam masala, coriander and chilli. Pour the tarka on the kadhi before serving hot with plain rice, pickle or chutney and stuffed aubergine.

Punjabi Keema   Serves 4-6

60 ml/4 tbsp ghee ● 2 bay leaves ● 2 large cloves garlic, crushed
1 cm/½ in ginger root, finely chopped ● 1 onion, finely chopped
5 ml/1 tsp garam masala ● 5 ml/1 tsp ground roasted cumin
5 ml/1 tsp ground coriander (cilantro) ● 2.5 ml/½ tsp ground red chilli
2.5 ml/½ tsp ground turmeric ● salt ● 225 g/8 oz canned tomatoes
150 g/5 oz Khoya (page 19), broken into pieces ● 100 g/4 oz/⅔ cup raisins
50 g/2 oz/½ cup cashew nuts, halved ● 1.5 ml/¼ tsp ground cardamom
Garnish: 1.5 ml/¼ tsp garam masala
15 ml/1 tbsp chopped fresh coriander (cilantro) ● 1 small green chilli, chopped

Heat the ghee in a heavy-based pan and fry the bay leaves, garlic, ginger and onion over a medium heat until golden brown. Stir in the garam masala, cumin, coriander, chilli, turmeric and salt. Stir in the tomatoes and fry for about 15 minutes until all

the liquid has been absorbed and the ghee appears on the surface. Mix in the khoya, raisins and nuts, reduce the heat to low and cook for a further 2 minutes. Sprinkle over the garnish ingredients and serve hot with pulao, raita and a kofta dish.

Vegetable Sagu
Serves 4

30 ml/2 tbsp ghee ● 5 ml/1 tsp mustard seeds ● 1 dried red chilli, halved

5 ml/1 tsp split black beans ● 2.5 ml/½ tsp asafoetida ● 2-3 curry leaves

1 onion, finely chopped ● 100 g/4 oz mixed vegetables, chopped

2 carrots, chopped ● 1 potato, chopped ● 100 g/4 oz peas

1.5 ml/½ tsp ground turmeric ● salt ● 4-5 green chillies

1.5 ml/½ tsp black pepper ● 15 ml/1 tbsp ground coriander (cilantro)

5 ml/1 tsp cumin seeds ● 1 cinnamon stick ● 2 cloves

1 bunch fresh coriander (cilantro), chopped ● 30 ml/2 tbsp cashew nuts

Heat the ghee and fry the mustard seeds, chilli, split beans, asafoetida and curry leaves over a medium heat until the seeds start crackling. Add the onion and fry for 2 minutes. Add the vegetables, carrots, potato, peas, turmeric and salt and enough water to cover. **Bring to the boil and simmer until the vegetables are tender. Meanwhile, grind the chillies, pepper, coriander, cumin seeds, cinnamon and cloves to a paste. Add to the pan and simmer for 3 minutes. Serve garnished with the coriander and nuts.**

Vegetables in Almond-cardamom Sauce
Serves 6

2.5 ml/½ tsp saffron strands ● 45 ml/3 tbsp hot milk ● 450 ml/¾ pt/2 cups water

50 g/2 oz/½ cup blanched almonds ● 1 onion, chopped ● 5 cloves garlic, chopped

2.5 cm/1 in ginger root, chopped ● 2 green chillies

1.5 ml/¼ tsp grated nutmeg ● 5 ml/1 tsp ground turmeric

5 ml/1 tsp paprika ● 2.5 ml/½ tsp ground red chilli

15 ml/1 tbsp Mughal-style garam masala (page 13) ● 45 ml/3 tbsp oil

225 g/8 oz Paneer (page 20), cubed ● 10 cardamom pods

1 cinnamon stick ● 2.5 ml/½ tsp cloves ● 2.5 ml/½ tsp peppercorns

4 bay leaves ● 2 tomatoes, skinned and coarsely chopped

2 potatoes, diced ● 2 carrots, diced ● 225 g/8 oz cauliflower florets

225 g/8 oz peas ● 450 g/1 lb mushrooms, halved ● salt

45 ml/3 tbsp soured (dairy sour) cream

250 ml/8 fl oz/2 cup natural (plain) yoghurt

15 ml/1 tbsp chopped fresh coriander (cilantro)

Soak the saffron in hot milk for 15 minutes. Purée together 120 ml/4 fl oz/½ cup of water, the almonds, onion, garlic, ginger, chillies, nutmeg, turmeric, paprika, chilli and garam masala. **Heat the oil and fry the**

paneer for about 5 minutes until golden. Remove and drain. Add the cardamom, cinnamon, cloves, peppercorns and bay leaves to the oil and fry until slightly darkened. Add the purée and fry for 10 minutes until the oil appears on the surface, stirring continuously. Add the tomatoes and cook for 3 minutes until soft. Stir in the vegetables and salt and cook for 5 minutes. Pour over the soured cream and yoghurt, add the remaining water and stir well. Cover and simmer for 12 minutes until the vegetables are tender. Stir in the saffron milk and paneer, cover and cook for 5 minutes. Serve garnished with the coriander.

Malabar Mixed Vegetables   Serves 4

30 ml/2 tbsp desiccated (shredded) coconut ● 30 ml/2 tbsp water

3 green chillies, chopped ● 10 ml/2 tsp cumin seeds

5 ml/1 tsp ground turmeric ● 150 ml/¼ pt/⅔ cup coconut milk

675 g/1½ lb mixed vegetables, sliced ● 1 mango, chopped

30 ml/2 tbsp natural (plain) yoghurt ● 10 curry leaves ● salt

60 ml/4 tbsp coconut oil

Blend the coconut, water, chillies, cumin seeds, turmeric and coconut milk to a paste. Blanch the vegetables in boiling water for 4 minutes then strain, leaving enough blanching water to cover the vegetables. Add the mango, yoghurt, curry leaves and paste and simmer gently until the vegetables are tender. Add the salt and coconut oil and serve.

Bombay-style Bhurta   Serves 6

45 ml/3 tbsp oil ● 1 onion, chopped ● 6 cloves garlic, crushed

2 green chillies, chopped ● 2.5 cm/1 in ginger root, chopped

30 ml/2 tbsp cider vinegar ● 30 ml/2 tbsp ground coriander (cilantro)

1.5 ml/¼ tsp ground red chilli ● 10 ml/2 tsp ground turmeric

3 medium aubergines (eggplant), diced ● 450 g/1 lb mushrooms, finely chopped

1 green (bell) pepper, finely chopped ● 225 g/8 oz marrow (squash), chopped

2 turnips, chopped ● 5 tomatoes, skinned and chopped ● salt

Heat the oil and fry the onion, garlic, chillies and ginger until browned. Add the cider vinegar, coriander, chilli and turmeric and fry for 1 minute, stirring. Stir in the vegetables and salt, cover and simmer for 15 minutes until the vegetables are cooked. Remove the lid, increase the heat and cook until the liquid evaporated, stirring constantly. Serve hot with chicken curry and rice.

Sweet and Sour Vegetables   Serves 4-6

675 g/1½ lb mixed vegetables (cauliflower, carrots, green (bell) pepper, aubergine (eggplant) etc.), cut into 4 cm/1½ in pieces

oil for deep-frying

Batter: 100 g/4 oz/1 cup gram flour ● 15 ml/1 tbsp oil

15 ml/1 tbsp chopped fresh coriander (cilantro) ● 5 ml/1 tsp oregano seeds

2.5 ml/½ tsp garam masala ● 2.5 ml/½ tsp ground red chilli ● salt

150 ml/¼ pt/⅔ cup warm water

Sauce: 75 ml/5 tbsp oil or ghee ● 1 small onion, finely chopped

4 large cloves garlic, crushed ● 2.5 cm/1 in ginger root, coarsely chopped

1 onion, coarsely chopped ● 10 ml/2 tsp ground coriander (cilantro)

5 ml/1 tsp garam masala ● 5 ml/1 tsp ground roasted cumin

2.5 ml/½ tsp ground red chilli ● 2.5 ml/½ tsp ground turmeric

1.5 ml/¼ tsp ground mace ● 1.5 ml/¼ tsp grated nutmeg ● salt

225 g/8 oz canned tomatoes, chopped ● 60 ml/4 tbsp wine vinegar

15 ml/1 tbsp clear honey ● 200 ml/7 fl oz/scant 1 cup water

Garnish: 2.5 ml/½ tsp garam masala

15 ml/1 tbsp chopped fresh coriander (cilantro) ● 1 small green chilli, chopped

Beat together all the batter ingredients until smooth. Dip the vegetables into the batter and deep-fry in batches in hot oil until golden brown. Arrange on a serving dish and set aside.

Heat the oil in a heavy-based pan and fry the small onion until golden brown. Blend the garlic, ginger and onion to a smooth paste in a blender or food processor. Stir into the pan with the spices and tomatoes and cook until all the liquid has been absorbed and the oil appears on the surface. Pour in the wine vinegar and cook until all the liquid is absorbed. Add the honey and cook for a further 2 minutes. Add the water and bring to the boil. Simmer over a low heat for 2 minutes. Pour the hot sauce over the vegetables, sprinkle with the garnish ingredients and serve hot with rice, puris, raita and chutney.

Vegetable Scotch   Makes 12

500 g/18 oz mixed vegetables ● 45 ml/3 tbsp oil ● 1 onion, finely chopped

2.5 cm/1 in ginger root, finely chopped ● 5 ml/1 tsp garam masala

5 ml/1 tsp ground roasted cumin ● 2.5 ml/½ tsp ground red chilli ● salt

30 ml/2 tbsp lemon juice ● 30 ml/2 tbsp chopped fresh coriander (cilantro)

1 small green chilli, chopped ● 150 g/5 oz Paneer (page 20), cut into 12

50 g/2 oz/½ cup rice flour ● 75 ml/5 tbsp warm water ● oil for deep-frying

Boil the vegetables in water until tender then drain.

Heat the oil in a heavy-based pan and fry the onion and ginger until lightly browned. Add the cooked vegetables and fry until lightly browned. Stir in the garam masala, cumin, chilli and salt, mix thoroughly and form into a thick paste. Stir in the lemon juice, coriander and chilli. Divide into 12 equal portions. Take one portion at a time and flatten it. Place a piece of paneer on top, bring the edges of the vegetable paste over to cover it and shape it into a rectangle. Mix together the rice flour and warm water to a runny batter and season with salt to taste. Heat the oil in a deep pan. Dip a vegetable scotch in the batter and add it to the hot oil. Fry 5 or 6 at a time until golden brown. Serve hot with chutney and barfi at tea.

Mixed Vegetable Curry   Serves 4

45 ml/3 tbsp oil • 1 onion, chopped • 5 cloves garlic, chopped

1 cm/½ in ginger root, chopped • 1 green chilli • 1 cinnamon stick

15 ml/1 tbsp curry powder • 2.5 ml/½ tsp ground turmeric

1 potato, cubed • 450 g/1 lb broccoli spears • 2 carrots, sliced

1 small cauliflower, cut into florets • 1 large tomato, skinned and chopped

salt • 250 ml/8 fl oz/1 cup water

Heat the oil and fry the onion, garlic, ginger, chilli and cinnamon until the onion is browned. Stir in the curry powder and turmeric and fry for 1 minute. Add the vegetables and salt and stir well. Add the water, bring to the boil, cover and simmer for 10 minutes until the vegetables are tender, stirring occasionally.

Mixed Vegetables   Serves 6

45 ml/3 tbsp oil • 15 ml/1 tbsp black mustard seeds

4 cloves garlic, crushed • 2.5 cm/1 in ginger root, grated

5 ml/1 tsp ground turmeric • 1.5 ml/¼ tsp chilli powder

3 potatoes, cubed • 225 g/8 oz green beans, sliced • 3 carrots, chopped

100 g/4 oz cauliflower florets

Heat the oil and fry the mustard seeds over a medium heat until they start crackling. Add the garlic, ginger, turmeric and chilli powder and fry for 2 minutes. Add the vegetables and salt, cover and simmer for 10-12 minutes until the vegetables are tender. Serve with beef curry and rice.

Mixed Vegetable Korma
Serves 4-6

75 ml/5 tbsp oil ● 5 ml/1 tsp fenugreek seeds

3 large cloves garlic, crushed ● 2.5 cm/1 in ginger root, finely chopped

1 onion, finely chopped ● 90 ml/6 tbsp desiccated (shredded) coconut, ground

5 ml/1 tsp garam masala ● 5 ml/1 tsp ground coriander (cilantro)

5 ml/1 tsp ground roasted cumin ● 2.5 ml/½ tsp ground red chilli

2.5 ml/½ tsp ground tumeric ● 400 g/14 oz canned tomatoes, chopped

500 g/18 oz cauliflower, cut into florets

6 small carrots, cut into 4 cm/1½ in pieces ● 600 ml/1 pt/2½ cups water

1 medium aubergine (eggplant), cut into 1 cm/½ in pieces

1 medium potato, cut into 1 cm/½ in pieces ● 10 ml/2 tsp tamarind pulp (page 19)

Garnish: 1.5 ml/¼ tsp garam masala

15 ml/1 tbsp chopped fresh coriander (cilantro) ● 1 small green chilli, chopped

Heat the oil in a heavy-based pan and fry the fenugreek seeds until lightly browned. Add the garlic, ginger and onion and fry until golden brown. Stir in the coconut, garam masala, coriander, cumin, chilli and turmeric. Stir in the tomatoes and cook until all the liquid has been absorbed and the oil appears on the surface of the mixture. Add the cauliflower and carrots and **200 ml/7 fl oz/scant 1 cup of water and bring to the boil. Reduce the heat to medium-low and cook for 15 minutes. Add the remaining vegetables and water and the tamarind pulp and cook for a further 30 minutes until the vegetables are tender. Sprinkle over the garnish ingredients and serve hot with puris, yoghurt, rice and dal.**

Mixed Vegetables and Potato
Serves 4-6

oil for frying ● 250 g/9 oz medium potatoes, peeled and quartered

75 ml/5 tbsp oil or ghee ● 5 ml/1 tsp mustard seeds

2 bay leaves ● 1 small onion, finely chopped ● 1 onion, coarsely chopped

2 large cloves garlic ● 1 cm/½ in ginger root

5 ml/1 tsp garam masala ● 5 ml/1 tsp ground coriander (cilantro)

5 ml/1 tsp ground roasted cumin ● 2.5 ml/½ tsp ground red chilli

2.5 ml/½ tsp ground turmeric ● 1.5 ml/¼ tsp ground mace

1.5 ml/¼ tsp grated nutmeg ● salt ● 400 g/14 oz canned tomatoes

50 ml/2 fl oz/3½ tsp water ● 500 g/18 oz frozen mixed vegetables, thawed

Garnish: 2.5 ml/½ tsp garam masala

15 ml/1 tbsp chopped fresh coriander (cilantro) ● 1 small green chilli, chopped

Heat the frying oil and fry the potatoes over a medium heat until golden brown. Drain well.

Meanwhile, heat the oil or ghee and fry the mustard seeds over a medium heat until they start crackling. Add the bay leaves and chopped onion and fry until golden brown. Blend the onion, garlic and ginger to a smooth paste in a blender or food processor. Stir into the pan and fry for a few minutes until golden brown. Stir in the garam masala, coriander, cumin, chilli, turmeric, mace, nutmeg and salt. Stir in the tomatoes and cook until all the liquid has been absorbed and the oil appears on the surface of the mixture. Add the water and cook until the liquid is absorbed. Stir in the vegetables and potatoes. Cover and cook over a medium heat for about 15 minutes until the vegetables are tender. Sprinkle with the garnish ingredients and serve hot with onion paratha or puris, rice, dal, raita and a chicken dish.

Kerala-style Vegetable Curry   Serves 6

225 g/8 oz grated coconut ● 120 ml/4 fl oz/½ cup coconut milk

45 ml/3 tbsp water ● 1 onion, chopped ● 5 cloves garlic, chopped

2.5 cm/1 in ginger root, chopped ● 10 ml/2 tsp ground turmeric

2 green chillies ● 250 ml/8 fl oz/1 cup natural (plain) yoghurt

15 ml/1 tbsp coriander (cilantro) seeds ● 10 ml/2 tsp cumin seeds

45 ml/3 tbsp oil ● 15 ml/1 tbsp black mustard seeds

225 g/8 oz green beans ● 225 g/8 oz yams

225 g/8 oz courgettes (zucchini) ● 3 green bananas ● 1 potato

450 g/1 lb pumpkin ● salt ● 2 sprigs fresh curry leaves

20 ml/2 tbsp chopped fresh coriander (cilantro)

Blend the coconut and coconut milk to a paste, adding a little water if necessary. Blend together the water, onion, garlic, ginger, turmeric, chillies, yoghurt, coriander and cumin. Heat the oil and fry the mustard seeds until they start crackling. Stir in the purée and fry for 5 minutes until brown, stirring. Cut the vegetables into 2.5 cm/1 in pieces, add to the pan with the salt and fry for 5 minutes. Add the coconut paste and curry leaves, cover and simmer for 20 minutes until the vegetables are tender.

Mixed Vegetables with Paneer   Serves 6

450 g/1 lb mushrooms, sliced ● 600 ml/1 pt/2½ cups water

45 ml/3 tbsp oil ● 225 g/8 oz Paneer (page 20)

1 onion, finely chopped ● 5 cloves garlic, finely chopped

2.5 cm/½ in ginger root, finely chopped ● 2 green chillies, chopped

15 ml/1 tbsp ground coriander (cilantro) ● 10 ml/2 tsp cumin seeds

5 ml/1 tsp ground turmeric ● 1.5 ml/¼ tsp black pepper

1.5 ml/¼ tsp paprika ● 15 ml/1 tbsp garam masala

1 tomato, chopped ● 225 g/8 oz cauliflower florets

1 potato, diced ● 225 g/8 oz peas

salt ● 30 ml/2 tbsp chopped fresh coriander (cilantro)

Cook the mushrooms in a little of the water for 5 minutes then drain. Heat the oil and fry the cheese until golden then remove and drain. Add the onion, garlic, ginger and chillies and fry for 5 minutes until browned, stirring. Stir in the spices and fry for 5 minutes, stirring. Add the tomato and fry for 5 minutes until the oil appears on the surface. Mix in the vegetables except the mushrooms, the remaining water and salt, bring to the boil, cover and simmer for 8-12 minutes until the vegetables are tender, stirring occasionally. Gently stir in the mushrooms and paneer. Garnish with coriander and serve hot with rice, lamb curry and mango chutney.

Dals

Dal means lentil, and the various types of lentil and pulses are important sources of protein for vegetarians, although they are equally popular among vegetarian and non-vegetarian societies in India and are cooked in every household. They are eaten with rice, chapatis, paratha, vegetables, meat, fish and chicken.

Cooking methods vary in different parts of India. In northern India, urud dal — split black beans — is cooked with garlic, ginger and asafoetida. In eastern India, gram dal — yellow split peas — is cooked with coconut and tamarind. Among southern Indians, it is popular with a variety of vegetables and with tamarind. In the western part of Indian, moong dal — moong beans — is prepared with lemon.

Clean dals before cooking and pick out any grit.

Chick Peas with Tamarind   Serves 4-6

500 g/18 oz chick peas (garbanzos), soaked overnight

50 g/2 oz/⅓ cup yellow split peas, cleaned ● 2.8 l/5 pts/12 cups water

2.5 ml/½ tsp bicarbonate of soda (baking soda) ● salt

75 ml/5 tbsp oil or ghee ● 5 ml/1 tsp cumin seeds

3 large cloves garlic, crushed ● 2.5 cm/1 in ginger root, chopped

1 large onion, finely chopped ● 10 ml/2 tsp ground coriander (cilantro)

5 ml/1 tsp ground roasted cumin ● 5 ml/1 tsp garam masala

2.5 ml/½ tsp ground turmeric ● 2.5 ml/½ tsp ground red chilli

400 g/14 oz canned tomatoes ● 10 ml/2 tsp tamarind pulp (page 19)

Garnish: 30 ml/2 tbsp chopped fresh coriander (cilantro)

1 small green chilli, chopped ● 2.5 ml/½ tsp garam masala

Place the chick peas, split peas, bicarbonate of soda, salt and water in a large pan. If you do not have a pan large enough, add the water gradually. Bring to the boil, skim off any scum and simmer over a medium heat for 1 hour 20 minutes until the chick peas are tender. Drain.

Meanwhile, heat the oil in a heavy-based pan and fry the cumin seeds until lightly browned. Add the garlic, ginger and onion and fry over a medium heat until golden brown. Stir in the coriander, cumin, garam masala, turmeric and chilli. Stir in the tomatoes and cook until all the water has been absorbed and the oil appears on the top of the mixture. Add the tamarind pulp and cook until all the liquid has been absorbed. Stir in the cooked chick peas and simmer over a medium heat for a further 20 minutes until the mixture thickens. Sprinkle with the garnish ingredients and serve hot with nan, tamarind chutney, potato curry and a chopped onion, cucumber and tomato salad.

Chick Peas in Sauce

Serves 4-6

250 g/9 oz/1½ cups chick peas (garbanzos), soaked overnight

2.5 ml/½ tsp bicarbonate of soda (baking soda)

1.75 l/3 pts/7½ cups water ● salt

90 ml/6 tbsp ghee or oil ● 1 small onion, finely chopped

4 cloves ● 4 peppercorns ● 2 bay leaves

1 cm/½ in cinnamon stick ● 2 black cardamom pod

4 cloves garlic ● 2.5 cm/1 in ginger root, coarsely chopped

1 large onion, coarsely chopped ● 45 ml/3 tbsp water

5 ml/1 tsp ground coriander (cilantro) ● 5 ml/1 tsp ground roasted cumin

2.5 ml/½ tsp garam masala ● 2.5 ml/½ tsp ground red chilli

2.5 ml/½ tsp ground turmeric ● 1.5 ml/¼ tsp ground mace

1.5 ml/¼ tsp grated nutmeg ● salt ● 400 g/14 oz canned tomatoes

225 g/8 oz potatoes, boiled and cut into 1 cm/½ in pieces

Garnish: 1.5 ml/¼ tsp garam masala

15 ml/1 tbsp chopped fresh coriander (cilantro)

1 small green chilli, chopped

Place the chick peas in a large pan with the bicarbonate of soda, water and salt. Bring to the boil, skim off any scum, cover and simmer gently for 1 hour until the chick peas are tender.

Meanwhile, heat the ghee or oil in a heavy-based pan and fry the onion, cloves, peppercorns, bay leaves, cinnamon and cardamom until golden brown. Blend the garlic, ginger, onion and water to a smooth paste in a blender or food processor. Add it to the pan and fry for a few minutes until golden brown. Stir in the coriander, cumin, garam masala, chilli, turmeric, mace, nutmeg and salt to taste. Stir in the tomatoes and simmer until all the liquid has been absorbed and the ghee appears on the surface of the mixture. Drain the chick peas then mix them into the sauce. Simmer until the chick peas are thoroughly tender and have absorbed the flavours of the sauce. Stir in the potato and cook for 5 minutes. Sprinkle over the garnish ingredients and serve hot with plain rice, chapatis, raita and okra.

Spiced Chick Peas
Serves 4

225 g/8 oz/1⅓ cups chick peas (garbanzos) ● 600 ml/1 pt/2½ cups water

2.5 ml/½ tsp bicarbonate of soda (baking soda) ● 1 onion, finely chopped

3 cloves garlic, chopped ● 1 tea bag ● 60 ml/4 tbsp ghee

2.5 cm/1 in ginger root, thinly sliced ● 2 tomatoes, chopped

salt ● 2 green chillies, chopped ● 5 ml/1 tsp garam masala

30 ml/2 tbsp tamarind chutney ● 15 ml/1 tbsp chopped fresh coriander (cilantro)

Soak the chick peas overnight in the water with the bicarbonate of soda.

Add half the onion and garlic and the tea bag to the chick peas and bring to the boil in the soaking water. Simmer for 20 minutes until tender. Remove from the heat and discard the tea bag. Heat the ghee and fry the remaining onion and garlic with the ginger until soft. Add the tomatoes, salt, chillies and garam masala and simmer for 2-3 minutes. Add the chick peas and stir well. Cover and simmer gently for 10 minutes. Sprinkle with chutney and coriander and serve hot with plain rice, a beef dish and papadums.

Peshawar-style Chick Peas
Serves 6

450 g/1 lb/2⅔ cups chick peas (garbanzos), soaked overnight

1.5 l/2½ pts/6 cups water ● salt ● 4 black cardamom pods

2 cinnamon sticks ● 6 cloves ● 45 ml/3 tbsp oil

15 ml/1 tbsp ground cumin ● 2.5 ml/½ tsp black pepper

45 ml/3 tbsp ground coriander (cilantro) ● 10 ml/2 tsp garam masala

30 ml/2 tbsp pomegranate seeds ● 45 ml/3 tbsp mango powder

2.5 cm/1 in ginger root, chopped ● 2 green chillies, chopped

1 lemon, cut into wedges

Drain the chick peas then place in a pan with the water, salt, cardamom pods, cinnamon and cloves, bring to the boil then simmer for 30 minutes until tender. Heat the oil and fry the cumin, pepper, coriander, garam masala and pomegranate seeds for 2 minutes. Stir into the chick peas with the mango powder, ginger and chillies then bring to the boil. Garnish with lemon wedges and serve hot with chapatis or plain rice.

Chick Peas with Ginger
Serves 4

2 onions ● 60 ml/4 tbsp ghee ● 2 cloves garlic, chopped

25 g/1 oz ginger root, finely chopped ● 15 ml/1 tbsp black peppercorns, crushed

10 ml/2 tsp ground turmeric

225 g/8 oz/1⅔ cups chick peas (garbanzos), soaked overnight

1 l/1¾ pts/4½ cups non-salty stock

Chop 1 onion and slice the other. Heat 45 ml/3 tbsp of the ghee and fry the chopped onion until soft and lightly browned. Stir in the ginger, peppercorns, turmeric and chick peas and fry for 3 minutes. Add the stock, bring to the boil, cover and simmer for 1 hour, stirring frequently, until the chick peas are tender and slightly mushy. Meanwhile, heat the remaining ghee and fry the sliced onion until crisp and brown. Serve the chick peas garnished with the onion.

Chick Peas with Tomato   Serves 4

60 ml/4 tbsp ghee ● 4 cloves garlic, crushed

3 onions, chopped ● 2 green chillies, chopped

5 ml/1 tsp ground turmeric ● 5 ml/1 tsp paprika

15 ml/1 tbsp ground cumin ● 15 ml/1 tbsp ground coriander (cilantro)

5 ml/1 tsp garam masala ● 5 tomatoes, skinned and chopped

15 ml/1 tbsp chopped fresh mint ● 15 ml/1 tbsp chopped fresh coriander (cilantro)

2 × 450 g/1 lb cans chick peas (garbanzos), drained

salt and pepper

Heat the ghee and fry the garlic, onions and chillies until lightly browned. Add the turmeric, paprika, cumin coriander and garam masala and fry gently for 5 minutes, stirring. Add the tomatoes, mint and coriander and cook for 10 minutes, stirring. Add the chick peas and simmer for 5-10 minutes until the chick peas are well coated in the sauce. Season with salt and pepper before serving.

Mixed Dals   Serves 4

225 g/8 oz/1⅓ cups mixed dals (red lentils, yellow split peas, split black beans)

600 ml/1 pt/2½ cups water● 5 ml/1 tsp ground turmeric

salt ● 30 ml/2 tsp ghee ● pinch of asafoetida

15 ml/1 tbsp finely chopped onion ● 2.5 ml/½ tsp cumin seeds

5 ml/1 tsp chilli powder ● 15 ml/1 tbsp lemon juice

Boil the dals in the water with the turmeric for 30 minutes. Stir in a little salt and simmer for a further 10 minutes. Heat the ghee and fry the asafoetida, onion, cumin seeds and chilli powder until golden. Add to the dals and cook for a further 5 minutes. Sprinkle with lemon juice and serve hot with any main courses.

Punjabi Beans
Serves 4-6

250 g/9 oz red kidney beans, soaked overnight ● 2.8 l/5 pts/12 cups water

salt ● 90 ml/6 tbsp ghee or oil ● 1 small onion, finely chopped

4 cloves ● 4 peppercorns ● 2 bay leaves

1 cm/½ in cinnamon stick ● 1 black cardamom pod ● 3 large cloves garlic

2.5 cm/1 in ginger root, chopped ● 1 onion, chopped

45 ml/3 tbsp water ● 5 ml/1 tsp ground coriander (cilantro)

5 ml/1 tsp ground roasted cumin ● 2.5 ml/½ tsp garam masala

2.5 ml/½ tsp ground red chilli ● 2.5 ml/½ tsp ground turmeric

salt ● 400 g/14 oz canned tomatoes, chopped

150 ml/¼ pt/⅔ cup natural (plain) yoghurt

Garnish: 1.5 ml/¼ tsp garam masala

15 ml/1 tbsp chopped fresh coriander (cilantro) ● 1 small green chilli, chopped

Drain the beans then place them in a large pan with the water and salt. Boil for 10 minutes then reduce the heat, cover and simmer for 1¼ hours until tender.

Meanwhile, heat the ghee or oil in a heavy-based pan and fry the onion, cloves, peppercorns, bay leaves, cinnamon and cardamom over a medium heat until golden brown. Blend the garlic, ginger, onion and water to a smooth paste in a blender or food processor. Stir it into the pan and fry for a few minutes until golden brown. Stir in the coriander, cumin, garam masala, chilli, turmeric and salt. Stir in the tomatoes and cook until all the liquid has been absorbed and the ghee appears on the surface. Stir in the yoghurt and cook until all the liquid has evaporated. Drain the beans and add them to the pan. Cook for a further 15 minutes. Sprinkle with the garnish ingredients and serve hot with rice, chapatis and chicken.

Beans with Ginger and Chilli
Serves 4

250 g/9 oz/1½ cups red kidney beans, soaked overnight

60 ml/4 tbsp ghee ● 2.5 cm/1 in ginger root, chopped

4 cloves garlic, chopped ● 3 green chillies, chopped

60 ml/4 tbsp tomato purée (paste)

150 ml/¼ pt/⅓ cup single (light) cream ● salt and pepper

Drain the beans then place in a pan, cover with water, bring to the boil and boil rapidly for 10 minutes. Reduce the heat and simmer for about 40 minutes until tender then drain thoroughly. Heat the ghee and fry the ginger and garlic for 2 minutes. Add the chillies, tomato purée and cream and cook for 2 minutes. Add the cooked beans and simmer for about 5 minutes until well blended. Season with salt and pepper before serving.

Black Beans and Spinach
Serves 4

100 g/4 oz/⅔ cup split black beans ● 600 ml/1 pt/2½ cups water

pinch of ground turmeric ● salt

225 g/8 oz spinach, chopped ● 30 ml/2 tbsp ghee

15 ml/1 tbsp finely chopped onion ● 2 cloves garlic, crushed

5 ml/1 tsp cumin seeds ● 2.5 ml/½ tsp chilli powder ● pinch of asafoetida

Boil the split beans, water, turmeric and salt then simmer for 30 minutes, stirring occasionally. Add the spinach and cook for 10 minutes. Heat the ghee and fry the onion and garlic until golden. Add the cumin seeds, chilli powder and asafoetida and fry for 1 minute. Pour over the beans and spinach, cover and cook for 5-10 minutes. Serve hot with nan bread or rice.

Spicy Black Beans
Serves 4

75 g/3 oz/½ cup split black beans ● 75 g/3 oz/½ cup yellow split peas

600 ml/1 pt/2½ cups water ● pinch of ground turmeric ● salt

30 ml/2 tbsp ghee ● pinch of asafoetida

5 ml/1 tsp cumin seeds ● 2.5 ml/½ tsp chilli powder

Boil the split beans and split peas in the water with the turmeric for 30 minutes. Add salt and simmer over a low heat for 10 minutes. Heat the ghee and fry the asafoetida, cumin seeds and chilli powder for 2 minutes. Add to the dal and cook for a further 5 minutes. Serve hot with any main courses.

South Indian-style Bean Savoury
Serves 6-8

120 ml/4 fl oz/½ cup water

175 g/6 oz/1 cup split black beans, soaked overnight

salt ● 1 onion, finely chopped

1 cm/½ in ginger root, finely chopped ● 1 green chilli, finely chopped

30 ml/2 tbsp chopped fresh coriander (cilantro) ● 250 ml/8 fl oz/1 cup oil

Grind the water, drained split beans and salt to a fine paste. Stir in the onion, ginger, chilli and coriander (cilantro), divide into about 20 balls and flatten them slightly. Heat the oil and fry the balls over a medium heat for about 2-3 minutes until golden brown and crisp. Drain on kitchen paper and serve hot with coconut chutney.

Split Black Beans
Serves 4-6

350 g/12 oz/3 cups split black beans ● 2.5 ml/½ tsp ground turmeric

900 ml/1½ pts/3¾ cups water ● salt

Tarka: 60 ml/4 tbsp ghee or oil ● large pinch of asafoetida

3 large garlic cloves, crushed ● 2.5 cm/1 in ginger root, chopped

1 large onion, chopped ● 5 ml/1 tsp ground roasted cumin

2.5 ml/½ tsp ground red chilli ● 1.5 ml/¼ tsp ground turmeric

2.5 ml/½ tsp garam masala

Garnish: 15 ml/1 tbsp chopped fresh coriander (cilantro)

2.5 ml/½ tsp garam masala ● 1 small green chilli, chopped

Place the split beans, turmeric, water and salt in a large pan, bring to the boil and skim off any scum. Reduce the heat, cover and simmer over a low heat for 45 minutes until the dal is tender. If any water is left, dry it off on a high heat but don't stir or the dal will become mushy.

Meanwhile, heat the ghee or oil in a heavy-based pan and fry the asafoetida, garlic, ginger and onion over a medium heat until golden brown. Add the cumin, chilli, turmeric and garam masala and stir in the cooked dal. Sprinkle with the garnish ingredients and serve hot with chapatis, stuffed aubergine, potato curry and raita.

Punjabi Black-eye Beans
Serves 4-6

250 g/9 oz black-eye beans, soaked overnight

2.8 l/5 pts/12 cups water ● salt

90 ml/6 tbsp ghee or oil ● 1 small onion, finely chopped

4 cloves ● 4 peppercorns ● 2 bay leaves

1 cm/½ in cinnamon stick ● 1 black cardamom pod ● 3 large cloves garlic

2.5 cm/1 in ginger root, chopped ● 1 onion, chopped

45 ml/3 tbsp water ● 5 ml/1 tsp ground coriander (cilantro)

5 ml/1 tsp ground roasted cumin ● 2.5 ml/½ tsp garam masala

2.5 ml/½ tsp ground red chilli ● 2.5 ml/½ tsp ground turmeric ● salt

400 g/14 oz canned tomatoes ● 150 ml/¼ pt/⅔ cup natural (plain) yoghurt

Garnish: 1.5 ml/¼ tsp garam masala

15 ml/1 tbsp chopped fresh coriander (cilantro)

1 small green chilli, chopped

Drain the beans then place them in a large pan with the water and salt. If you do not have a large enough pan, add the water gradually. Bring to the boil over a medium heat, reduce the heat to medium-low, cover and simmer for 1 hour 20 minutes until the beans are tender.

Meanwhile, heat the ghee or oil in a heavy-based pan and fry the onion, cloves, peppercorns, bay leaves, cinnamon and cardamom over a medium heat until golden brown. Blend the garlic, ginger, onion and water to a smooth paste in a blender or food processor. Stir it into the pan and fry for a few minutes until golden brown. Stir in the coriander, cumin, garam masala, chilli, turmeric and salt. Stir in the tomatoes and cook until all the liquid has been absorbed and the ghee appears on the surface of the mixture. Stir in the yoghurt and cook until all the liquid has evaporated. Drain the beans and add them to the pan. Cook for a further 15 minutes or until the sauce is the consistency you prefer. Sprinkle with the garnish ingredients and serve hot with plain rice, chapatis, cauliflower, raita and a chicken dish.

Split Peas with Tomatoes and Apples   Serves 4-6

250 g/9 oz/1½ cups yellow split peas ● 2.5 ml/½ tsp ground turmeric
salt ● 1.2 l/2 pts/5 cups water
Tarka: 90 ml/4 tbsp ghee ● 5 ml/1 tsp cumin seeds
1 medium onion, finely chopped ● 5 ml/1 tsp garam masala
2.5 ml/½ tsp ground red chilli ● 2.5 ml/½ tsp ground turmeric
400 g/14 oz canned tomatoes, chopped
250 g/9 oz cooking apples, peeled, cored and chopped into 1 cm/½ in pieces
Garnish: 1.5 ml/¼ tsp garam masala
15 ml/1 tbsp chopped fresh coriander (cilantro)
1 small green chilli, chopped

Place the split peas, turmeric, salt and water in a heavy-based pan and bring to the boil over a medium heat. Skim off any scum. Reduce the heat to medium-low, cover and cook for 25 minutes until tender.

Meanwhile, heat the ghee in a heavy-based pan and fry the cumin seeds until lightly browned. Add the onion and fry until golden brown. Stir in the garam masala, chilli and turmeric. Stir in the tomatoes and apple and cook for about 25 minutes until all the liquid has been absorbed and the oil appears on the surface of the mixture. Mix together the tarka and the cooked dal and simmer for 2 minutes. Sprinkle over the garnish ingredients and serve hot with chapatis, rice, stuffed aubergine or okra and raita.

Lentil Kebabs
Serves 6

450 g/1 lb/2½ cups green lentils, soaked overnight ● 15 ml/1 tbsp ghee

1 onion, sliced ● 50 g/2 oz/½ cup gram flour ● 10 ml/2 tsp garam masala

4 eggs, beaten ● 15 ml/1 tbsp natural (plain) yoghurt

2 green chillies, chopped ● salt ● 50 g/2 oz/½ cup breadcrumbs

ghee for frying

Drain the lentils then grind to a fine paste. Heat the ghee and fry the onion until crisp and brown then drain and grind coarsely. Fry the gram flour and garam masala for 1 minute then stir into the lentils with the eggs, yoghurt, chillies, salt and fried onions. Shape the mixture into flat cutlets, roll in breadcrumbs and fry in hot ghee until evenly browned.

Simple Sprouted Lentils
Serves 4

100 g/4 oz/⅔ cup whole green lentils ● 30 ml/2 tbsp oil

2.5 ml/½ tsp cumin seeds ● 2 onions, chopped

2 green chillies, chopped ● pinch of ground turmeric ● 120 ml/4 fl oz/½ cup water

salt and pepper ● juice of 1 lime ● 2.5 ml/½ tsp sugar

Soak the lentils in water overnight then drain and cover with a damp cloth. Leave in a warm place for 8-10 hours until sprouted.

Heat the oil and fry the cumin seeds for 1 minute. Add the onions and chillies and fry until soft but not browned. Add the turmeric, sprouts, water, salt and pepper, stir well, cover and simmer for 10-15 minutes until the sprouts have softened. Stir in the lime juice and sugar before serving.

Nutty Sprouted Lentils
Serves 4

100 g/4 oz/⅔ cups whole green lentils ● 45 ml/3 tbsp fenugreek seeds

45 ml/3 tbsp oil ● 2.5 ml/½ tsp mustard seeds

2.5 ml/½ tsp split black beans ● 2 dried red chillies

2 onions, finely chopped ● 2.5 cm/1 in ginger root, thinly sliced

2 green chillies, chopped ● 5 ml/1 tsp soy sauce ● salt ● 5 ml/1 tsp sugar

45 ml/3 tbsp water ● juice of ½ lime ● 30 ml/2 tbsp roasted peanuts

Soak the lentils and fenugreek seeds in water overnight then drain and cover with a damp cloth. Leave in the warm for 8-10 hours until sprouted.

Heat the oil and fry the mustard seeds, beans and chillies until the seeds start crackling. Add the onions and ginger and fry until browned. Add the chillies, soy sauce, salt and sugar and fry until the oil appears on the surface. Add the lentils and fenugreek seeds and the water, cover and simmer until the lentils are tender. Stir in the lime juice and peanuts.

Lentil Kootu
Serves 4

25 g/1 oz/3 tbsp whole green lentils ● 50 g/2 oz green beans, finely chopped

1 carrot, chopped ● 1 potato, cubed ● 50 g/2 oz peas

5 ml/1 tsp ground tumeric ● salt ● 2-3 curry leaves

Masala: 5 ml/1 tsp oil ● 5 ml/1 tsp cumin seeds

5 ml/1 tsp peppercorns ● 2 dried red chillies

2.5 ml/½ tsp asafoetida ● 30 ml/2 tbsp desiccated (shredded) coconut

Seasoning:10 ml/2 tsp ghee ● 5 ml/1 tsp mustard seeds

2.5 ml/½ tsp cumin seeds ● 5 ml/1 tsp split black beans

1 dried red chilli, halved

Cook the lentils in water for about 20 minutes until tender. Heat the oil for the masala and fry the cumin seeds, peppercorns, chillies and asafoetida for 2 minutes. Add the coconut and grind to a fine paste with a little water. Boil the vegetables with the turmeric and salt until tender. Add the cooked dal and simmer for 2 minutes. Add the ground paste and simmer until well blended. Heat the ghee for the seasoning and fry all the seasoning ingredients until the mustard seeds start crackling. Stir into the lentils and vegetables. Garnish with the curry leaves and serve hot with plain rice and a beef curry.

Mashed Green Lentils
Serves 4

100 g/4 oz/⅔ cup whole green lentils ● 6 green chillies, slit

2.5 ml/½ tsp ground turmeric ● 5 ml/1 tsp tamarind concentrate

salt ● 1 small bunch fresh coriander (cilantro), finely chopped

Seasoning: 10 ml/2 tsp ghee ● 5 ml/1 tsp mustard seeds

1 dried red chilli, halved ● 2.5 ml/½ tsp asafoetida

2-3 curry leaves

Cook the lentils in enough water to cover for about 20 minutes until tender. Heat the seasoning ghee and fry all the seasoning ingredients for 2 minutes. Add the green chillies, turmeric, tamarind and salt and simmer until the raw smell of the tamarind disappears. Add the cooked lentils and simmer until well blended. Garnish with the coriander and serve hot with rice or chapatis.

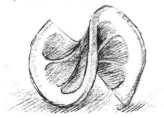

Masoor Dal
Serves 4-6

250 g/9 oz/1½ cups whole green lentils ● 2.5 ml/½ tsp ground turmeric

1.2 1/2 pts/5 cups water ● salt

Tarka: 60 ml/4 tbsp oil or ghee ● 2.5 ml/½ tsp mustard seeds

5 ml/1 tsp cumin seeds ● 1 small onion, finely chopped

2.5 ml/½ tsp ground red chilli ● 225 g/8 oz canned tomatoes

15 ml/1 tbsp lemon juice

Garnish: 15 ml/1 tbsp chopped fresh coriander (cilantro)

2.5 ml/½ tsp garam masala ● 1 small green chilli, chopped

Place the lentils, turmeric, water and salt in a large pan, bring to the boil and skim off any scum. Simmer over a medium heat for 20 minutes.

Meanwhile, heat the oil or ghee in a heavy-based pan and fry the mustard seeds until they start crackling. Add the cumin seeds and onion and fry until golden brown. Stir in the chilli, tomatoes and lemon juice and cook until the water has been absorbed and the ghee appears on the surface. Stir in the cooked dal and simmer for 5 minutes. Sprinkle over the garnish ingredients and serve hot with rice, okra, raita and a meat curry.

Sukha Dal
Serves 6

30 ml/2 tbsp ghee ● 2.5 ml/½ tsp mustard seeds

1.5 ml/¼ tsp asafoetida ● 450 g/1 lb/2⅔ cups whole green lentils, soaked overnight

2 onions, chopped ● 3 green chillies, chopped

100 g/4 oz/1 cup desiccated (shredded) coconut ● 1.5 ml/¼ tsp ground turmeric

salt ● 300 ml/½ pt/1¼ cups hot water ● juice of 1 lemon

2.5 ml/½ tsp chilli powder ● 15 ml/1 tbsp chopped fresh coriander (cilantro)

Heat the ghee and fry the mustard seeds and asafoetida until the mustard seeds start crackling. Add the lentils, onions, chillies, coconut, turmeric and salt. Add the hot water and simmer over a low heat for about 20 minutes until the lentils are tender and the water has been absorbed. Add the lemon juice and sprinkle with chilli powder. Garnish with coriander and serve hot with chapatis or plain rice and a lamb curry.

Lentils, Paneer and Peas
Serves 4-6

100 g/4 oz/⅔ cup moong beans ● 2.5 ml/½ tsp ground turmeric

salt ● 500 ml/17 fl oz/2¼ cups water

Tarka: 30 ml/2 tbsp ghee ● 2.5 ml/½ tsp mustard seeds

2.5 ml/½ tsp cumin seeds ● 2.5 ml/½ tsp onion seeds ● 2.5 ml/½ tsp garam masala

Paneer: 30 ml/2 tbsp ghee ● 1 onion, finely chopped

150 g/5 oz Paneer (page 20), broken into lumps

2.5 ml/½ tsp garam masala ● salt

Peas: 30 ml/2 tbsp ghee ● 2.5 ml/½ tsp cumin seeds ● 250 g/9 oz peas

2.5 ml/½ tsp ground red chilli ● 2.5 ml/½ tsp garam masala ● salt

30 ml/2 tbsp chopped fresh coriander (cilantro) ● 15 ml/1 tbsp lemon juice

Place the beans, turmeric, salt and water in a large saucepan and bring to the boil over a medium heat. Skim off any scum, reduce the heat to low, cover and cook for 20 minutes until the dal is tender. Increase the heat and dry off any remaining water.

To make the tarka, heat the ghee in a heavy-based pan and fry the mustard, cumin and onion seeds until the mustard seeds start crackling. Stir in the garam masala and add to the dal.

To cook the paneer, heat the ghee in a heavy-based pan and fry the onion and paneer over a medium heat until golden brown. Stir in the garam masala and salt and set to one side.

To cook the peas, heat the ghee in a heavy-based pan and fry the cumin seeds over a medium heat until browned. Add the peas and spices and cook for 5 minutes or until tender. Stir in the coriander and lemon juice.

Reheat the beans, paneer and peas. Place a layer of beans on a serving dish and top with the paneer and the peas. Serve hot with sautéed potatoes, raita and puris.

Lentils in Lime
Serves 4

225 g/8 oz/1⅓ cups red lentils, soaked in cold water for 20 minutes

600 ml/1 pt/2½ cups water ● salt ● 30 ml/2 tbsp ghee

pinch of asafoetida ● 5 ml/1 tsp mustard seeds

5 ml/1 tsp chilli powder ● 60 ml/4 tbsp lime juice

Boil the lentils in the water with a little salt for 30 minutes until soft. Heat the ghee and fry the asafoetida and mustard seeds until the seeds start crackling. Pour the mixture over the simmering lentils, cover and simmer over a medium heat for a further 5 minutes. Stir in the chilli powder and lime juice and serve hot as part of a main meal.

Photograph opposite: *Kheema Nan (page 298), Parathas (page 300), Chapatis (page 305) with papadums*

Lentil Curry
Serves 6

350 g/12 oz/2 cups red lentils, soaked in water for 20 minutes

1.5 l/2½ pts/6 cups water ● 5 ml/2 tsp ground turmeric ● 1 cinnamon stick

2.5 ml/½ tsp black peppercorns ● 3 bay leaves ● 6 cardamon pods ● 6 cloves

salt ● 45 ml/3 tbsp vegetable oil 1 onion, thinly sliced

2.5 cm/1 in ginger root, finely chopped ● 4 cloves garlic, thinly sliced

2 green chillies, chopped ● 1 large tomato, skinned and chopped

Boil the lentils with the water, turmeric cinnamon, peppercorns, bay leaves, cardamom, cloves and a little salt for 20 minutes until soft. Heat the oil and fry the onion, ginger, garlic and chillies until browned. Pour over the lentils, add the tomato, cover and simmer for 10 minutes, stirring occasionally. Serve hot with chapatis or pulau rice and a chicken dish.

Lentils, Garlic and Onions
Serves 6

350 g/12 oz/2 cups red lentils, soaked in cold water for 20 minutes

1 l/1pts/4¼ cups water ● 2.5 ml/½ tsp ground turmeric

salt ● 45 ml/3 tbsp oil ● 15 ml/1 tbsp black mustard seeds

10 ml/2 tsp cumin seeds ● 1 onion, finely chopped

6 cloves garlic, finely chopped ● 2.5 ml/½ tsp chilli powder

Boil the lentils in the water with the turmeric and salt for about 20 minutes until tender. Heat the oil and fry the mustard and cumin seeds until the seeds start crackling. Add the onion and garlic and fry until browned. Add the chilli powder and stir for 30 seconds. Pour over the lentils, stir well, cover and simmer for 10 minutes, stirring occasionally. Serve hot with plain rice, papadums and spicy pork.

Lucknow-style Lentils
Serves 6

350 g/12 oz/2 cups red lentils, soaked in cold water for 20 minutes

1.5 l/2½ pts/6 cups water ● salt ● 5 ml/1 tsp ground turmeric

45 ml/3 tbsp oil ● 15 ml/1 tbsp cumin seeds ● 1 onion, chopped

6 cloves garlic, crushed ● 2.5 cm/1 in ginger root, chopped

1.5 ml/¼ tsp chilli powder ● 15 ml/1 tbsp lemon juice

Boil the dal in the water with the salt and turmeric for about 20 minutes until tender. Heat the oil and fry the cumin seeds for 1 minute. Add the onion, garlic and ginger and fry until browned. Add the chilli powder and stir for 30 seconds. Pour over the lentils, mix thoroughly and bring to the boil. Stir in the lemon juice and serve hot with plain rice and lamb.

Photograph opposite: *Cracked Wheat Salad (page 324)*

Courgette and Lentils
Serves 6

450 g/1 lb/2½ cups red lentils, soaked in cold water for 20 minutes

2 1/3½ pts/8½ cups water ● 2.5 ml/½ tsp ground turmeric

1.5 ml/¼ tsp chilli powder ● salt ● 45 ml/3 tbsp oil

1.5 ml/¼ tsp cumin seeds ● 2 onions, finely chopped

4 cloves garlic, finely chopped ● 1 cm/½ in ginger root, chopped

1 large tomato, chopped ● 900 g/2 lb courgettes (zucchini), sliced

15 ml/1 tbsp chopped fresh coriander (cilantro)

Boil the lentils in the water with the turmeric, chilli powder and salt for about 20 minutes until tender. Heat the oil and fry the cumin seeds until golden. Add the onions, garlic and ginger and fry until browned. Add the tomato and fry for 2 minutes. Pour over the lentils, stir well, cover and simmer for 5 minutes. Stir in the courgettes and cook for a further 5 minutes. Garnish with coriander and serve hot as a soup or with chapatis or plain rice.

Madras-style Lentils
Serves 6

350 g/12 oz/2 cups red lentils, soaked in cold water for 20 minutes

1.5 1/2½ pts/6 cups water ● 1.25 ml/½ tsp ground turmeric

salt ● 15 ml/1 tbsp cumin seeds

2.5 ml/½ tsp coriander (cilantro) seeds ● 1.5 ml/¼ tsp fenugreek seeds

1.5 ml/¼ tsp black peppercorns ● 2 dried red chillies

45 ml/2 tbsp oil ● 2 onions, sliced ● 5 cloves garlic, crushed

1 cm/½ in ginger root, chopped ● pinch of asafoetida

3 sprigs fresh curry leaves ● 5 ml/1 tsp tamarind concentrate

1 tomato, skinned and chopped

Boil the lentils in the water with the turmeric and salt for 20 minutes until tender. Dry roast the cumin seeds, coriander and fenugreek seeds, the peppercorns and chillies until lightly coloured then grind to a fine paste. Heat the oil and fry the onions, garlic and ginger until browned. Add the asafoetida and curry leaves and stir for 30 seconds. Stir in the ground spices then pour over the lentils. Add the tamarind and tomato, mix thoroughly and bring to the boil. Simmer for 5 minutes, adding a little more water if necessary. Serve hot with plain rice, papadums and a vegetable dish.

Madras-style Lentils with Vegetables   Serves 6

175 g/6 oz/1 cup red lentils, soaked in cold water for 20 minutes

1.5 l/2½ pts/6 cups water ● 5 ml/1 tsp ground turmeric

salt ● 45 ml/3 tbsp oil ● 15 ml/1 tbsp black mustard seeds

1.5 ml/¼ tsp fenugreek seeds ● 4 dried red chillies ● 1 onion, chopped

1 cm/½ in ginger root, finely chopped ● 4 cloves garlic, crushed

15 ml/1 tbsp ground coriander (cilantro) ● 10 ml/2 tsp ground cumin

1.5 ml/¼ tsp black pepper ● pinch of asafoetida

1 small aubergine (eggplant), cubed ● 225 g/8 oz green beans, coarsely chopped

450 g/1 lb okra ● 2 carrots, sliced ● 1 tomato, chopped

10 ml/2 tsp tamarind concentrate ● 30 ml/1 tbsp chopped fresh coriander (cilantro)

Boil the lentils in the water with the turmeric and salt for 20 minutes until tender. Heat the oil and fry the mustard and fenugreek seeds and the chillies until the mustard seeds start crackling. Add the onion, ginger and garlic and fry until browned. Add the coriander, cumin, pepper and asafoetida and stir for 2 minutes until the oil separates. Pour over the lentils. Add the vegetables and tamarind and stir until well blended. Bring to the boil, cover then simmer gently for 10 minutes until the vegetables are tender, stirring occasionally. Garnish with the coriander and serve hot with plain rice, chutney, papadums and a fish curry.

South Indian-style Lentils with Vegetables   Serves 6

350 g/12 oz/2 cups red lentils ● 1 l/3½ pts/8½ cups water

2.5 ml/½ tsp ground turmeric ● salt ● 15 ml/1 tbsp tamarind concentrate

45 ml/3 tbsp oil ● 15 ml/1 tbsp yellow split peas

15 ml/1 tbsp split black beans ● 4 dried red chillies

1.5 ml/¼ tsp fenugreek seeds ● 1.5 ml/¼ tsp asafoetida

1 large aubergine (eggplant), cubed ● 350 g/12 oz green beans, coarsely chopped

350 g/12 oz courgettes (zucchini) sliced ● 15 ml/1 tbsp black mustard seeds

3 sprigs fresh curry leaves ● 15 ml/1 tbsp chopped fresh coriander (cilantro)

Boil the lentils in the water with the turmeric and salt for 20 minutes until tender. Soak the tamarind in 250 ml/ 8 fl oz/1 cup of water for 10 minutes. Heat 5 ml/1 tsp of the oil and fry the yellow split peas, split black beans, chillies, fenugreek, seeds and asafoetida until golden brown then grind to a powder. Add the vegetables and tamarind water to the lentils and simmer for 5 minutes. Stir in the ground spices and cook for 5 minutes. Heat the remaining oil and fry the mustard seeds until they start crackling. Add the curry leaves and fry for 20 seconds then pour over the lentil mixture, stir thoroughly, add the coriander and bring to the boil. Serve hot with plain rice, papadums and lamb curry.

Marrow and Dal
Serves 4

225 g/8 oz/1⅔ cups yellow split peas, soaked for 20 minutes

900 ml/1½ pts/3¾ cups water ● 225 g/8 oz marrow (squash), cubed

pinch of ground turmeric ● salt ● 5 ml/1 tsp mango powder

30 ml/2 tbsp ghee ● 10 ml/2 tsp cumin seeds ● 2.5 ml/½ tsp cayenne

Boil the split peas in the water for 20 minutes. Add the marrow and turmeric and simmer for 10 minutes. Stir in the salt and mango powder. Heat the ghee and fry the cumin seeds and cayenne for 2 minutes. Pour over the peas and cook for 5 minutes. Serve hot with any main courses.

Aubergine with Yellow Split Peas
Serves 6

450 g/1 lb/2½ cups yellow split peas, soaked in cold water for 20 minutes

1.5 l/2½ pts/6 cups water ● 5 ml/1 tsp ground turmeric ● salt ● 45 ml/3 tbsp oil

5 ml/1 tsp black mustard seeds ● 5 ml/1 tsp cumin seeds ● 1 onion, chopped

4 cloves garlic, crushed ● 1 cm/½ in ginger root, finely chopped

1 green chilli, finely chopped ● 15 ml/1 tbsp ground coriander (cilantro)

1 tomato, skinned and chopped ● 1 aubergine (eggplant), cubed

Boil the split peas in the water with the turmeric and salt for 20 minutes until tender. Heat the oil and fry the mustard and cumin seeds until the mustard seeds start crackling. Add the onion, garlic and ginger and fry until browned. Add the coriander and fry for 2 minutes, stirring constantly. Add the tomato and cook for 4 minutes. Stir into the split peas with the aubergine. Cover and simmer for 10 minutes until the aubergine is tender. Serve hot with plain rice or chapatis, a chicken curry and a spinach dish.

Yellow Split Peas with Vegetables
Serves 6

45 ml/3 tbsp oil ● 2 onions, chopped ● 8 cloves garlic, chopped

2.5 cm/1 in ginger root, chopped ● 4 green chillies, chopped

350 g/12 oz/2 cups yellow split peas, soaked in cold water for 20 minutes

5 ml/1 tsp ground turmeric ● 450 g/1 lb spinach, chopped

3 tomatoes, skinned and chopped ● 450 g/1 lb green beans, chopped

1 aubergine (eggplant), cubed ● 1 potato, cubed

45 ml/3 tbsp chopped fresh dill (dill weed) ● salt ● 1.5 l/2½ pts/6 cups water

Heat the oil and fry the onions, garlic, ginger and chillies until golden. Add the turmeric and fry for 1 minute. Add the split peas, vegetables, dill and salt and stir over a low heat for 5 minutes. Add the water, bring to the boil, cover and simmer for 30-40 minutes until the vegetables and split peas are tender, stirring occasionally. Serve hot with plain rice and a beef curry.

Bengali-style Chola Dal　　　　　　　　Serves 4-6

250 g/9 oz/1½ cups yellow split peas, soaked for 1 hour

2.5 ml/½ tsp ground turmeric ● 1.75 l/3 pts/7½ cups water ● salt

Tarka: 45 ml/3 tbsp oil ● 5 ml/1 tsp cumin seeds

1 small onion, finely chopped ● 1 cm/½ in ginger root, finely chopped

2 bay leaves ● 50 g/2 oz/½ cup desiccated (shredded) coconut

2.5 ml/½ tsp garam masala ● 2.5 ml/½ tsp ground red chilli

1.5 ml/¼ tsp ground turmeric ● 1 small green chilli, finely chopped

5 ml/1 tsp tamarind pulp (page 19) ● 25 g/1 oz/2 tbsp sugar

Garnish: 15 ml/1 tbsp chopped fresh coriander (cilantro)

2.5 ml/½ tsp garam masala

Put the split peas, turmeric, water and salt in a pan and bring to the boil. Skim off any scum, reduce the heat, cover and simmer over a medium heat for about 1 hour until tender.

Meanwhile, heat the oil in a heavy-based pan and fry the cumin seeds until lightly browned. Add the onion, ginger and bay leaves and fry until lightly browned. Stir in the coconut and fry until golden brown. Stir in the garam masala, chilli, turmeric and green chilli and tamarind pulp and bring to the boil. Stir the tarka into the cooked split peas then simmer for a further 10 minutes. Sprinkle over the garnish ingredients and serve hot with plain rice, okra and raita.

Whole Moong Beans　　　　　　　　Serves 4-6

250 g/9 oz/1½ cups whole moong beans, soaked for 1 hour

1.5 l/2½ pts/6 cups water ● large pinch of ground turmeric ● salt

Tarka: 15 ml/3 tbsp oil or ghee ● 5 ml/1 tsp cumin seeds

1 medium onion, finely chopped ● 1 cm/½ in ginger root, finely chopped

2.5 ml/½ tsp ground red chilli ● large pinch of ground turmeric

225 g/8 oz canned tomatoes, chopped

Garnish: 15 ml/1 tbsp chopped fresh coriander (cilantro)

2.5 ml/½ tsp garam masala ● 1 small green chilli, chopped

Place the moong beans, water, turmeric and salt in a pan, bring to the boil and skim off any scum. Reduce the heat, cover and simmer for 50 minutes over a medium heat until tender.

Meanwhile, heat the oil or ghee in a heavy-based pan and fry the cumin seeds until lightly browned. Add the onion and ginger and fry until golden brown. Add the chilli, turmeric and tomatoes and cook for about 40 minutes until all the water has been absorbed and the ghee appears on the surface. Stir in the cooked dal and simmer for a further 10 minutes. Sprinkle with the garnish ingredients and serve hot with rice, chapatis, paneer curry, cauliflower and yoghurt.

Gujrati Sprouted Moong Beans   Serves 6

225 g/8 oz/1⅓ cups whole moong beans, soaked for 24 hours

45 ml/3 tbsp oil ● large pinch of asafoetida

5 ml/1 tsp cumin seeds ● 2 large garlic cloves, crushed

1 cm/½ in ginger root, finely chopped ● 1 small onion, finely chopped

2.5 ml/½ tsp garam masala ● 2.5 ml/½ tsp ground red chilli

2.5 ml/½ tsp ground turmeric ● salt ● 225 g/8 oz canned tomatoes, chopped

500 ml/17 fl oz/2¼ cups water

Garnish: 2.5 ml/½ tsp garam masala

15 ml/1 tbsp chopped fresh coriander (cilantro)

1 small green chilli, chopped ● 1 lemon, chopped

Drain the water from the dal and wrap it in a muslin (cheesecloth) square. Tie it together and leave for 24 hours to sprout. Remove from the cloth.

Heat the oil in a heavy-based pan and fry the asafoetida over a medium heat until it starts sizzling. Add the cumin seeds and fry for a few seconds until lightly browned. Add the garlic, ginger and onion and fry until golden brown. Stir in the garam masala, chilli, turmeric and salt. Stir in the tomatoes, dal and water. Bring to the boil then reduce the heat, cover and simmer for 45 minutes. Increase the heat and dry off any remaining water. Sprinkle over the garnish and serve hot with a kofta dish.

Marrow with Lentils   Serves 4-6

250 g/9 oz/1½ cups red lentils ● 5 ml/1 tsp ground turmeric

1.75 l/3 pts/7½ cups water

250 g/9 oz marrow (squash), peeled and cut into 1 cm/½ in pieces

30 ml/2 tbsp lemon juice ● 75 ml/5 tbsp ghee ● 5 ml/1 tsp cumin seeds

2 large garlic cloves, crushed ● 1 cm/½ in ginger root, finely chopped

1 medium onion, finely chopped ● 45 ml/3 tbsp chopped fresh coriander (cilantro)

5 ml/1 tsp garam masala ● 1.5 ml/½ tsp ground red chilli

1 small green chilli, chopped

Place the lentils in a heavy-based pan with the turmeric, salt and water. Bring to the boil and skim off any scum. Reduce the heat to medium-low, cover and cook for 25 minutes. Add the marrow and cook for a further 25 minutes until tender. Stir in the lemon juice.

Meanwhile, heat the ghee in a heavy-based pan and fry the cumin seeds until lightly browned. Add the garlic, ginger and onion and fry until golden brown. Stir in the coriander, garam masala, chilli and green chilli. Turn off the heat, pour the tarka over the cooked lentils and serve hot with plain rice, chapatis, raita and stuffed aubergine.

Red Lentils
Serves 4-6

250 g/9 oz/1½ cups red lentils, soaked for 1 hour

pinch of ground turmeric ● 2.8 l/5 pts/12 cups water

salt ● 60 ml/4 tbsp ghee or oil ● pinch of asafoetida

2.5 ml/½ tsp fenugreek seeds ● 1.5 ml/½ tsp cumin seeds

1 medium onion, finely chopped ● 2 garlic cloves, crushed

1.5 cm/½ in ginger root, chopped ● 2.5 ml/½ tsp ground red chilli

2.5 l/½ tsp garam masala ● pinch of ground turmeric

225 g/8 oz canned tomatoes, chopped

Garnish: 15 ml/1 tbsp chopped fresh coriander (cilantro)

2.5 ml/½ tsp garam masala ● 1 small green chilli, chopped

Place the lentils, turmeric, water and salt in a pan, bring to the boil and skim off any scum. Simmer over a medium heat for 1½ hours.

Meanwhile, heat the ghee in a heavy-based pan and fry the asafoetida, fenugreek and cumin seeds until brown. Add the garlic, ginger, spices and tomatoes and fry until all the water has been absorbed and the ghee appears on the top. Stir in the cooked dal and simmer for a further 30 minutes. Sprinkle with the garnish ingredients and serve hot with rice, okra, aubergine and matar paneer.

Moong Beans
Serves 4-6

250 g/9 oz/1½ cups moong beans, soaked overnight

2.5 ml/½ tsp ground turmeric ● 1.75 l/3 pts/7½ cups water

salt ● 60 ml/4 tbsp ghee or oil ● 5 ml/1 tsp cumin seeds

1 medium onion, finely chopped ● 2.5 ml/½ tsp ground red chilli

large pinch of ground turmeric ● 2.5 ml/½ tsp garam masala

2.5 ml/½ tsp ground roasted cumin ● 15 ml/1 tbsp lemon juice

Garnish: 15 ml/1 tbsp chopped fresh coriander (cilantro)

2.5 ml/½ tsp garam masala ● 1 small green chilli, chopped

Place the beans, turmeric, water and salt in a pan, bring to the boil and skim off any scum. Reduce the heat to medium-low, cover and simmer for 50 minutes until the beans are tender.

Meanwhile, heat the ghee or oil in a heavy-based pan and fry the cumin seeds until lightly browned. Add the onion and fry until golden brown. Stir in the chilli, turmeric, garam masala and cumin. Stir in the cooked beans and lemon juice and simmer for a further 10 minutes. Sprinkle over the garnish ingredients and serve hot with rice, stuffed aubergine and cauliflower.

Dahi Bara
Makes 16

75 g/3 oz/½ cup split black beans, soaked overnight

25 g/1 oz/3 tbsp whole black beans, soaked overnight

150 ml/¼ pt/⅔ cup water ● 1.5 ml/¼ tsp garam masala

1.5 ml/¼ tsp ground ginger ● 1.5 ml/¼ tsp ground red chilli

pinch of asafoetida ● oil for deep-frying

Dahi: 600 ml/1 pt/2½ cups natural (plain) yoghurt ● salt

30 ml/2 tbsp chopped fresh coriander (cilantro)

5 ml/1 tsp ground roasted cumin ● 1 small green chilli, chopped

Blend the split and whole beans and the water in a blender or food processor to a smooth paste then whisk until spongy. To test whether it is ready, drop 2.5 ml/½ tsp of the mixture into a cup of cold water; if it floats, the mixture is ready. Mix in the spices.

Heat the oil in a deep frying pan (skillet). Dampen your palm and put 15 ml/1 tbsp of the mixture on it, flatten it to 5 mm/1/8 in thick and make a hole in the centre. Gently slip it into the hot oil and fry a few at a time until golden brown. Remove and leave to cool. Drop the baras into boiling water and leave to soak for 20 minutes. Remove and squeeze out excess water.

Whisk the yoghurt until smooth then season to taste with salt. Dip the baras in the yoghurt then arrange in a serving dish then pour over the remaining yoghurt and refrigerate for 2-3 hours. Sprinkle with the garnish ingredients before serving.

Moong Bean Pakori in Yoghurt
Makes 32

50 g/2 oz/⅓ cup split black beans, soaked overnight

50 ml/2 fl oz/3½ tsp water ● 2.5 ml/½ tsp garam masala

1.5 ml/¼ tsp ground red chilli ● small pinch of salt ● oil for deep-frying

Dahi: 450 ml/¾ pt/2 cups natural (plain) yoghurt ● salt

5 ml/1 tsp ground roasted cumin

15 ml/1 tbsp chopped fresh coriander (cilantro)

Blend the beans and water in a blender or food processor to a smooth paste then whisk until spongy. To test whether it is ready, drop 2.5 ml/½ tsp of the mixture into a cup of cold water; if it floats, the mixture is ready. Mix in the spices. Heat the oil then gently slip teaspoonfuls of the batter into the hot oil in a round shape. Fry until golden brown then remove and cool.

Place the pakoris in a pan of boiling water and leave to soak until the water is cold. Remove and drain then squeeze out the remaining water.

Place the yoghurt in a bowl and stir in some salt, half the cumin, half the coriander and all the squeezed pakori. Leave in the refrigerator for 2 hours before serving sprinkled with the remaining cumin and coriander.

Gram Flour Pakori in Yoghurt
Makes 32

100 g/4 oz/1 cup gram flour ● 15 ml/1 tbsp oil

2.5 ml/½ tsp garam masala ● 1.5 ml/¼ tsp ground red chilli

salt ● 75 ml/5 tbsp warm water ● oil for deep-frying

450 ml/¾ pt/2 cups natural (plain) yoghurt ● salt

5 ml/1 tsp ground roasted cumin ● 15 ml/1 tbsp chopped fresh coriander (cilantro)

Place the flour, oil, garam masala, chilli and salt in a bowl and mix thoroughly. Gradually blend in the water to a smooth batter. Heat the oil in a deep frying pan (skillet) on a medium-low heat. Take about 2.5 ml/ ½ tsp of batter and slip it gently in a round shape into the oil. Repeat until all the batter is used up. Fry until golden brown then remove with a slotted spoon and place on a cooling tray.

Meanwhile, bring a large pan of water to the boil. Place all the pakoris into the boiling water, turn off the heat and leave to soak until the water is cold and the pakoris are soft. Remove the pakoris and gently squeeze out the water without spoiling the shape.

Place the yoghurt in a bowl and stir in some salt, half the cumin, half the coriander and all the squeezed pakori. Leave in the refrigerator for 2 hours before serving sprinkled with the remaining cumin and coriander.

Rice Dishes

The world's greatest rice-producing nation, India is famous, in particular, for the long-grain patna and basmati rices which are produced there. In the east and south, they consume the most rice, but lavish biryanis and rice pulao recipes have also originated from the northern parts of India.

Always soak, wash and drain rice before using in the recipes.

Plain Boiled Rice   Serves 4-6

250 g/9 oz/1 cup patna or basmati rice

750 ml/1¼ pts/3 cups water ● 15 ml/1 tbsp ghee

Place the rice, water and ghee in a pan and bring to the boil over a medium heat. Reduce the heat to low, cover the pan and cook for 15 minutes. If any water is left, dry it off on a high heat but don't stir. Turn off the heat and leave for at least 5 minutes before serving. Separate the grains with a fork and serve hot with dal, curries, yoghurt and pickle.

Oven-cooked Rice   Serves 4

225 g/8 oz/1 cup patna or basmati rice

1.2 l/2 pts/5 cups water ● 5 ml/1 tsp oil

Soak the rice for 20 minutes then wash and drain. Bring the water to the boil with the oil. Add the rice and simmer over a medium heat for 5 minutes, stirring occasionally until the rice is three-quarters cooked. Drain and rinse in cold water then leave in a colander for 5 minutes to drain completely. Place in an ovenproof dish, cover and cook in a preheated oven at 200°C/400°F/gas mark 6 for 5-8 minutes. Reduce the oven temperature to 150°C/300°F/gas mark 2 and cook for a further 8 minutes until the rice is cooked and fluffy.

Aromatic Rice   Serves 4

45 ml/3 tbsp ghee ● 3 onions, sliced ● 1 cm/½ in cinnamon stick

3 cardamom pods ● 3 cloves ● 2.5 ml/½ tsp cumin seeds

225 g/8 oz/1 cup long-grain rice, soaked

250 ml/8 fl oz/1 cup water ● salt

Heat the ghee and fry the onions until browned. Add the cinnamon, cardamom pods, cloves and cumin seeds and fry for 1 minute. Add the rice and fry for 2-3 minutes, stirring. Add the water and salt, bring to the boil, cover and simmer gently for about 15 minutes until the rice is cooked.

Aubergine Rice
Serves 6

450 g/1 lb/2 cups long-grain rice ● 60 ml/4 tbsp ghee

1 large onion, chopped ● 4 cloves ● 4 cardamom pods

1 cinnamon stick ● 1.2 l/2 pts/5 cups water ● salt

450 g/1 lb aubergines (eggplant) ● 5 ml/1 tsp mustard seeds

2.5 ml/½ tsp ground turmeric

Masala: 15 ml/1 tbsp ghee ● 15 ml/1 tbsp grated (shredded) coconut

pinch of asafoetida ● 6 peppercorns

5 ml/1 tsp coriander (cilantro) seeds ● 5 ml/1 tsp yellow split peas

5 ml/1 tsp split black beans ● 6 dried red chillies

Garnish: 1 lemon, sliced ● 45 ml/3 tbsp natural (plain) yoghurt

Soak the rice for 20 minutes then drain. Heat half the ghee and fry the onion, cloves, cardamom and cinnamon until lightly browned. Add the rice and fry for 2 minutes. Add the water and salt, cover and simmer for about 10 minutes until tender.

Meanwhile, slice the aubergines lengthways and soak in water. Fry the masala ingredients in the ghee until browned then grind to a coarse powder. Heat half the remaining ghee and fry the mustard seeds until they start crackling. Add the aubergines, sprinkle with salt and turmeric and cook gently until the aubergines are tender. Add the ground spices and stir well. Put the rice back on to the heat and stir in the remaining ghee and the aubergine mixture. Mix well and cook for a few minutes until hot. Serve with yoghurt and slices of lemon.

Black Bean Rice
Serves 4

225 g/8 oz/1 cup long-grain rice ● 600 ml/1 pt/2½ cups water

30 ml/2 tbsp cashew nuts, halved ● 15 ml/1 tbsp ghee ● salt

Masala: 30 ml/2 tbsp split black beans ● 5 ml/1 tsp black peppercorns, crushed

30 ml/2 tbsp sesame seeds ● 30 ml/2 tbsp grated (shredded) copra

Seasoning: 30 ml/2 tbsp ghee ● 5 ml/1 tsp mustard seeds

5 ml/1 tsp split black beans ● 5 ml/1 tsp yellow split peas

1 dried red chilli, halved ● 2.5 ml/½ tsp asafoetida

2 green chillies, finely chopped ● 2-3 curry leaves

Cook the rice in boiling water for about 10 until tender then drain and set aside. Dry roast the masala ingredients until lightly coloured then grind to a fine powder. Heat the ghee and fry the cashew nuts until golden then set aside. Heat the seasoning ghee and fry all the seasoning ingredients except the chillies and curry leaves until the mustard seeds start crackling. Add the green chillies and stir in the rice. Sprinkle with the masala powder and salt. Stir in the curry leaves and garnish with the fried cashew nuts before serving.

Rice with Chick Peas
Serves 6

75 g/6 oz/1 cup chick peas (garbanzos), soaked overnight

2.5 cm/1 in cinnamon stick ● 4 cardamom pods

8 cloves garlic ● 2.5 ml/½ tsp chilli powder

1 green chilli ● 2.5 ml/½ tsp ground turmeric

5 ml/1 tsp mango powder ● 450 g/1 lb/2 cups long-grain rice, soaked

45 ml/3 tbsp oil ● 6 spring onions (scallions), chopped

1 cm/½ in ginger root, grated ● 5 ml/1 tsp cumin seeds

4 bay leaves ● 5 ml/1 tsp black pepper

45 ml/3 tbsp chopped fresh coriander (cilantro)

Place the chick peas, cinnamon, cardamom, garlic, chilli powder, chillies, turmeric and mango powder in a pan and just cover with water. Bring to the boil, cover and simmer for about 2 hours until the peas are tender. Drain, reserving the liquid, and discard the herbs. Make the liquid up to 1 1/1¾ pts/4½ cups with water.

Heat the oil and fry the onions until golden. Add the ginger and fry for 2 minutes. Add the cumin seeds, bay leaves, pepper and chick peas and fry for 3-4 minutes, stirring. Add the rice and fry for 2 minutes, stirring. Add the liquid, bring to the boil then cover and simmer gently for about 30 minutes until the water has been absorbed. Separate the grain with a fork and serve garnished with coriander.

Coconut Rice
Serves 4

225 g/8 oz/1 cup long-grain rice ● 600 ml/1 pt/2½ cups

30 ml/2 tbsp sesame seeds ● 45 ml/3 tbsp ghee

45 ml/3 tbsp cashew nuts, halved ● ½ coconut, grated (shredded)

10 ml/2 tsp oil ● 5 ml/1 tsp mustard seeds ● 5 ml/1 tsp cumin seeds

5 ml/1 tsp split black beans ● 5 ml/1 tsp yellow split peas ● 1 dried red chilli, halved

2.5 ml/½ tsp asafoetida ● 2-3 curry leaves

2 green chillies, finely chopped ● salt

Cook the rice in boiling water for about 10 minutes until tender. Drain and set aside. Dry roast the sesame seeds in a pan then grind. Heat 30 ml/2 tbsp of ghee and fry the cashew nuts until golden. Heat the remaining ghee and fry the coconut until reddish brown. Heat the oil and fry the mustard and cumin seeds, split beans, peas, red chilli, asafoetida and curry leaves until the mustard seeds start crackling. Mix in the green chillies, rice, salt and fried coconut and sprinkle with the ground sesame seeds. Garnish with the nuts and serve hot.

Coloured Rice
Serves 4-6

90 ml/6 tbsp ghee ● 5 ml/1 tsp cumin seeds ● 5 cloves

5 black peppercorns ● 2 bay leaves ● 2.5 cm/1 in cinnamon stick

1 black cardamom pod ● 1 onion, thinly sliced

225 g/8 oz/1 cup patna or basmati rice ● 2 large cloves garlic, crushed

5 ml/1 tsp garam masala ● salt ● 225 g/8 oz peas

500 ml/17 fl oz/2¼ cups water ● 1.5 ml/¼ tsp red food colour

5 ml/1 tsp yellow food colour

Heat the ghee in a heavy-based pan and fry the cumin seeds until lightly browned. Add the cloves, peppercorns, bay leaves, cinnamon, cardamom, onion and garlic and fry until golden brown. Mix in the drained rice and fry for 2 minutes. Stir in the garam masala, salt, peas and water. Bring to the boil, reduce the heat to low, cover and cook for 15 minutes. If any water is left, dry off on a high heat but don't stir; tip the pan to check the water. Turn off the heat. Mix the red colour into one side of the rice with a fork and the yellow colour into the other side. Cover and leave for 5 minutes for serving hot with raita, cauliflower and a chicken dish.

Golden Fried Rice
Serves 6

90 ml/6 tbsp ghee ● 4 onions, finely chopped ● 3 cardamom pods

3 bay leaves ● 10 ml/2 tsp cumin seeds

675 g/1½ lb/3 cups long-grain brown rice, soaked for 20 minutes

1.5 ml/¼ tsp ground turmeric ● 1.5 ml/2½ pts/6 cups boiling water

45 ml/3 tbsp chopped fresh coriander (cilantro)

Heat the ghee until almost smoking then fry the onions until golden brown. Add the cardamom, bay leaves and cumin and fry for 1 minute. Fry the rice and turmeric for about 15 minutes, stirring, until the rice is golden brown. Add the water, cover and simmer for 30 minutes until the rice is tender. Serve sprinkled with coriander.

Rice and Green Beans
Serves 4

100 g/4 oz green beans, halved ● 100 g/4 oz basmati rice

600 ml/1 pt/2½ cups water ● 2.5 ml/½ tsp ground turmeric ● salt

5 ml/1 tsp chilli powder ● 5 ml/1 tsp garam masala ● 15 ml/1 tbsp ghee

pinch of asafoetida ● 5 ml/1 tsp cumin seeds

Soak the beans and rice for 30 minutes. Put the mixture into a pan with the water, turmeric, salt, chilli powder and garam masala and bring to the boil over a medium heat. Reduce the heat to low and simmer for 10 minutes until the beans are tender. Heat the ghee in a separate pan and fry the asafoetida and cumin seeds for 1 minute. Sprinkle over before serving.

Lemon Rice
Serves 4

600 ml/1 pt/2½ cups water ● 225 g/8 oz/1 cup basmati rice

15 ml/1 tbsp lemon juice ● large pinch of salt

30 ml/2 tbsp ghee ● 300 ml/½ pt/1¼ cups coconut milk

2-3 lemon slices ● 15 ml/1 tbsp chopped fresh coriander (cilantro)

Bring the water to the boil, add the rice and simmer for a medium heat for 5-6 minutes. Drain off the water. Stir in the lemon juice and salt and cook for 5 minutes until the rice has soaked up the juice. Meanwhile, heat the ghee in a separate pan. Add the rice, stir carefully once or twice with a fork, pour in the coconut milk, cover and simmer for 5-7 minutes. Drain off any surplus milk. Garnish with lemon slices and coriander before serving.

Lemon and Peanut Rice
Serves 4

25 g/8 oz/1 cup long-grain rice ● 600 ml/1 pt/2½ cups

2 green chillies, finely chopped ● 2.5 cm/1 in ginger root, chopped

45 ml/3 tbsp peanuts ● 2.5 ml/½ tsp ground turmeric

salt ● juice of 2 lemons ● 15 ml/1 tbsp chopped fresh coriander (cilantro)

Seasoning: 10 ml/2 tsp oil ● 5 ml/1 tsp mustard seeds

5 ml/1 tsp cumin seeds ● 5 ml/1 tsp split black beans ● 5 ml/1 tsp yellow split peas

1 dried red chilli, halved ● 2.5 ml/½ tsp asafoetida ● 2-3 curry leaves

Cook the rice in the water for about 10 minutes then drain and set aside. Heat the seasoning oil and fry all the seasoning ingredients until the mustard seeds start crackling. Add the green chillies, ginger and peanuts and fry for 2 minutes. Add the rice, turmeric and salt and mix well. Remove from the heat and stir in the lemon juice. Garnish with coriander and serve hot.

Rice with Lentils and Vegetables
Serves 6

450 g/1 lb/2 cups long-grain rice ● 175 g/6 oz/1 cup red lentils

seeds from 4 cardamom pods ● 4 cloves ● 1 cinnamon stick, crushed

15 ml/1 tbsp cumin seeds ● 1.5 ml/¼ tsp black peppercorns

1.2 l/2 pts/5 cups water ● 5 cloves garlic ● 2.5 cm/1 in ginger root, chopped

2 green chillies ● 45 ml/3 tbsp oil ● 2 onions, thinly sliced

25 g/1 oz/¼ cup blanched almonds ● 25 g/1 oz/⅓ cup raisins

1 potato, diced ● 5 ml/1 tsp ground turmeric ● salt

½ coconut, grated (shredded) ● 450 g/1 lb mushrooms, sliced

30 ml/2 tbsp chopped fresh coriander (cilantro)

Soak the rice and lentils for 20 minutes then drain. Dry roast the cardamom, cloves, cinnamon, cumin and pepper-corns until slightly coloured then purée with 45 ml/3 tbsp of the water, the garlic, ginger and chillies. Heat the oil and fry the onions until brown-ed. Remove from the pan and drain. Add the almonds and raisins and fry until golden brown. Remove from the pan and drain. Add the purée to the pan and stir over a low heat until the oil appears on the surface. Add the rice and lentils, potato, turmeric, salt and coconut and cook for 5 minutes. Add the remaining water and cook for 5 minutes, stirring occasionally. Add the mushrooms and coriander, cover and cook for 6-8 minutes until the liquid has evaporated and the rice and vegetables are cooked. Garnish before serving.

Madras-style Lime Rice
Serves 6

675 g/1½ lb/3 cups long-grain rice, soaked for 20 minutes

1.75 l/3 pts/7½ cups water ● 75 ml/5 tbsp oil ● 5 ml/1 tsp ground turmeric

salt ● 15 ml/1 tbsp black mustard seeds ● 1.5 ml/¼ tsp asafoetida

15 ml/1 tbsp split black beans ● 15 ml/1 tbsp yellow split peas

1 sprig fresh curry leaves ● 4 green chillies, chopped ● juice of 2 limes

Boil the rice in the water with 15 ml/ 1 tbsp of the oil, the turmeric and salt for 10 minutes. Keep warm. Heat the remaining oil and fry the mustard seeds over until they start crackling. Add the asafoetida, split beans and peas and fry until golden brown. Add the curry leaves and chillies and stir for a few seconds. Remove from the heat and pour over the rice. Squeeze over the lime juice and serve hot with Madras-style curries and papadums.

Mango Rice
Serves 4

225 g/8 oz/1 cup long-grain rice ● 600 ml/1 pt/2½ cups water

100 g/4 oz raw mango, grated ● 60 ml/4 tbsp peanuts ● salt ● 2-3 curry leaves

Masala: 5 ml/1 tsp mustard seeds ● 2.5 ml/½ tsp asafoetida

5 dried red chillies ● 2.5 ml/½ tsp ground turmeric

60 ml/4 tbsp grated (shredded) coconut

Seasoning: 45 ml/3 tbsp oil ● 5 ml/1 tsp mustard seeds

15 ml/1 tbsp yellow split peas ● 1 dried red chilli, halved

Cook the rice in boiling water until tender. Drain. Grind the masala ingre-dients to a fine paste with half the mango. Heat the seasoning oil and fry the seasoning ingredients until the seeds start crackling. Add the peanuts and fry until golden. Add the remain-ing mango and simmer for a few minutes. Add the masala and cook until the raw smell disappears. Stir in the rice, salt and curry leaves.

Mustard Seed Rice   Serves 4

225 g/8 oz/1 cup long-grain rice ● 600 ml/1 pt/2½ cups water

45 ml/3 tbsp peanuts ● salt

Masala: 15 ml/1 tbsp mustard seeds ● ½ coconut, grated (shredded)

3 dried red chillies ● 2.5 ml/½ tsp ground turmeric ● 2.5 ml/½ tsp asafoetida

5 ml/1 tsp tamarind concentrate

Seasoning: 15 ml/1 tbsp ghee ● 5 ml/1 tsp mustard seeds

5 ml/1 tsp split black beans ● 10 ml/2 tsp yellow split peas

1 dried red chilli, halved ● 2-3 curry leaves

Cook the rice in boiling water for about 10 minutes until tender then drain and set aside. Grind all the masala ingredients with a little water. Heat the ghee and fry the seasoning ingredients until the mustard seeds start crackling. Add the peanuts and fry for 2 minutes. Add the masala and fry until the raw smell disappears. Add the rice and salt, stir together well and heat through before serving.

Green Pea Rice   Serves 4

225 g/8 oz/1 cup long-grain rice ● 600 ml/1 pt/2½ cups water

225 g/8 oz peas ● 1 small potato, finely chopped

2 small aubergines (eggplant), finely chopped ● 1 green (bell) pepper, finely chopped

5 ml/1 tsp ground turmeric ● 5 ml/1 tsp tamarind concentrate ● salt

Masala: 10 ml/2 tsp oil ● 45 ml/3 tbsp coriander (cilantro) seeds

30 ml/2 tbsp split black beans ● 45 ml/3 tbsp yellow split peas

2.5 ml/½ tsp asafoetida ● 4 dried red chillies

Seasoning: 45 ml/3 tbsp oil ● 10 ml/2 tsp mustard seeds

5 ml/1 tsp split black beans ● 5 ml/1 tsp yellow split peas

2 dried red chillies, halved ● 2-3 curry leaves

Cook the rice in boiling water for about 10 minutes until tender. Drain and set aside to cool. Heat the masala oil and fry all the masala ingredients until lightly coloured. Grind to a fine powder. Heat the seasoning oil and fry the seasoning ingredients until the mustard seeds start crackling. Add the peas, potatoes, aubergines and pepper and simmer over a low heat until the vegetables are tender, adding a little water if necessary. Add the turmeric, tamarind and ground masala with a pinch of salt and fry for a few minutes, stirring. Add the rice and stir until all the ingredients are well blended.

Rice Pongal
Serves 4

225 g/8 oz/1 cup long-grain rice ● 50 g/2 oz/⅓ cup green lentils

900 ml/1½ pts/3¾ cups water ● 2.5 ml/½ tsp ground turmeric

60 ml/4 tbsp ghee ● 30 ml/2 tbsp oil ● 5 ml/1 tsp ground cumin

5 ml/1 tsp ground black peppercorns ● 5 ml/1 tsp asafoetida

2.5 cm/1 in ginger root, grated ● 2-3 curry leaves ● salt

30 ml/2 tbsp grated (shredded) coconut ● 30 ml/2 tbsp cashew nuts, halved

30 ml/2 tbsp ghee

Dry roast the rice and lentils separately until lightly coloured. Wash well, mix together, then cook in the boiling water with the turmeric for about 20 minutes until tender. Drain and set aside. Heat the ghee and oil and fry the cumin, pepper, asafoetida, ginger and curry leaves for 2 minutes. Add the rice and lentils and mix well. Add the salt, coconut and a little water, if necessary. Fry the nuts in the ghee then add to the pan and blend all the ingredients together. Serve hot with coconut chutney.

Saffron Rice
Serves 4

225 g/8 oz/1 cup basmati rice ● 600 ml/1 pt/2½ cups water

225 g/8 oz/1 cup sugar ● 10 ml/2 tsp ghee ● pinch of saffron

6 cloves ● 25 g/1 oz/3 tbsp raisins ● 25 g/1 oz/¼ cup cashew nuts

5 ml/1 tsp ground cardamom

Boil the rice in the water for about 5 minutes until half cooked. Add the sugar and stir well. Lower the heat, add the ghee and continue cooking. Soak the saffron in 15 ml/1 tbsp of hot water for 10 minutes then add to the cooked rice with the cloves, raisins and nuts. Stir well, cover and leave over a low heat for 5-10 minutes. Sprinkle with cardamom before serving.

Southern Yellow Rice
Serves 4

2 onions, sliced ● 45 ml/3 tbsp ghee ● 2-3 curry leaves

225 g/8 oz/1 cup basmati rice ● 600 ml/1 pt/2½ cups coconut milk

2.5 ml/½ tsp peppercorns, crushed ● 4 cloves ● 2 sprigs fresh fennel

2.5 ml/½ tsp ground turmeric ● salt ● 2.5 ml/½ tsp ground cardamom

25 g/1 oz/¼ cup flaked almonds ● 25 g/1 oz/¼ cup cashew nuts, chopped

Heat 30 ml/2 tbsp of ghee and fry most of the onions with the curry leaves until soft. Add the rice and fry for 5 minutes, stirring continuously. Mix all the spices except the cardamom into the coconut milk and add to the rice. Continue to simmer until the rice is tender then stir in the cardamom. Meanwhile, heat the remaining ghee and fry the remaining onion, the almond and cashew nuts and use to garnish the rice before serving.

Spiced Rice
Serves 4

275 g/10 oz/1¼ cups long-grain rice, soaked ● 45 ml/3 tbsp ghee

2.5 cm/1 in cinnamon stick ● 2 bay leaves ● 5 cloves

5 cardamom pods ● 2.5 ml/½ tsp cumin seeds ● salt

Drain the rice and leave to stand. Heat the ghee and fry the whole spices and salt for 2 minutes, stirring. Add the rice and stir until well coated in the seasoned oil. Add just enough water to come 2.5 cm/1 in above the level of the rice, bring to the boil, cover and simmer gently for 20 minutes. Fluff up the rice with a fork before serving.

Hot Spiced Rice
Serves 6

90 ml/6 tbsp oil ● 4 onions, chopped ● 3 cloves garlic, chopped

20 black peppercorns ● 6 cardamom pods ● 4 bay leaves

5 cm/2 in cinnamon stick ● 8 cloves ● 15 ml/1 tbsp grated ginger root

30 ml/2 tbsp garam masala ● 675 g/1½ lb/3 cups long-grain rice, soaked for 20 minutes

15 ml/1 tbsp cumin seeds

Heat the oil and fry half the onions until browned and crisp. Remove from the pan. Add the remaining onions to the pan and fry until golden. Add the peppercorns, cardamom, bay leaves, cinnamon and cloves and fry for 1 minute. Add the ginger and fry for 2 minutes until lightly browned. Add the garam masala and stir well. Drain the rice, reserving the liquid. Make the soaking liquid up to 1.5 l/ 2½ pts/6 cups with water. Add the rice and cumin seeds to the pan and fry for 4-5 minutes, stirring so that the rice is coated in the spiced oil. Add the water, bring to the boil, cover and simmer gently for about 30 minutes until the water has been absorbed. Separate the grains with a fork and serve garnished with the crisp fried onions.

Spicy Sambar Rice
Serves 4-6

225 g/8 oz/1 cup long-grain rice ● 175 g/6 oz/1 cup red lentils

900 ml/1½ pts/3¾ cups water ● 4 onions, sliced

1 green (bell) pepper, diced ● 1 small aubergine (eggplant), diced ● 1 potato, diced

2.5 ml/½ tsp ground turmeric ● 5 ml/1 tsp tamarind concentrate

90 ml/6 tbsp ghee ● 1 small bunch fresh coriander (cilantro), chopped ● salt

Paste: 20 ml/4 tsp oil ● 8 dried red chillies

45 ml/3 tbsp coriander (cilantro) seeds ● 15 ml/1 tbsp yellow split peas

2.5 cm/1 in cinnamon stick ● 5 ml/1 tsp poppy seeds ● 5 cloves

2.5 ml/½ tsp fenugreek seeds ● ½ coconut, grated (shredded)

5 ml/1 tsp asafoetida

Masala: 45 ml/1 tbsp yellow split peas ● 5 ml/1 tsp poppy seeds

15 ml/1 tbsp long-grain rice ● 45 ml/3 tbsp desiccated (shredded) coconut

Seasoning: 30 ml/2 tbsp oil ● 5 ml/1 tsp mustard seeds

5 ml/1 tsp cumin seeds ● 15 ml/1 tbsp split black beans

15 ml/1 tbsp yellow split peas ● 1 dried red chilli, halved ● 2-3 curry leaves

Cook the rice and lentils in the water for about 10 minutes until tender then drain and set aside to keep warm. Heat the oil for the paste and fry all the paste ingredients until lightly coloured then grind together, adding a little water if necessary. Dry roast the masala ingredients until lightly coloured then grind to a powder. Heat the seasoning oil and fry all the seasoning ingredients until the mustard seeds start crackling. Add the onions and fry for 2 minutes. Add the remaining vegetables and fry for 5 minutes until the vegetables are almost cooked. Add the turmeric and tamarind and cook until the vegetables are tender. Add the paste and cook for 2 minutes. Add the rice and lentils, stirring together carefully. Add the ghee and simmer until the mixture blends. Add the masala and remove from the heat. Garnish with coriander and serve hot with papadums.

Rice with Spinach
Serves 4

30 ml/2 tbsp ghee ● 3 dried red chillies, halved ● 2 bay leaves

10 ml/2 tbsp black peppercorns, crushed ● 10 ml/2 tbsp ground coriander (cilantro)

275 g/10 oz/1¼ cups long-grain rice, soaked ● 500 ml/17 fl oz/2¼ cups water

100 g/4 oz spinach, cut into strips

Heat the ghee and fry the chillies, bay leaves, peppercorns and coriander for 1 minute. Stir in the rice and fry for 2-3 minutes, stirring. Add the water, bring to the boil, cover and simmer for 15 minutes. Stir in the spinach and continue to simmer until the rice is tender.

Tomato Rice
Serves 4

30 ml/2 tbsp ghee ● 2 bay leaves ● 2 cardamom pods

1 onion, chopped ● 15 ml/1 tbsp chopped ginger root

3 cloves garlic, crushed ● 10 ml/2 tsp chilli powder

225 g/8 oz/1 cup long-grain rice ● 600 ml/1 pt/2½ cups tomato juice

2 tomatoes, skinned and quartered ● 15 ml/1 tbsp chopped fresh coriander (cilantro)

Heat the ghee and fry the bay leaves and cardamom for 1 minute. Add the onion and fry until soft. Add the ginger, garlic and chilli powder and fry for 1 minute. Add the rice and fry for 2-3 minutes, stirring. Add the tomato juice, bring to the boil, cover and simmer for about 10 minutes until almost cooked. Add the tomatoes and simmer until the rice is tender. Serve garnished with the coriander.

Tomato and Coconut Rice
Serves 4

225 g/8 oz/1 cup long-grain rice ● 600 ml/1 pt/2½ cups

4 tomatoes, skinned and chopped ● 2.5 ml/½ tsp ground turmeric ● salt

2 onions, finely chopped ● 2 green chillies, finely chopped

Masala: 10 ml/2 tsp oil ● 5 dried red chillies

15 ml/1 tbsp yellow split peas ● 5 ml/1 tsp split black beans

1.5 ml/2 tsp fenugreek seeds ● 2.5 ml/½ tsp asafoetida

15 ml/1 tbsp desiccated (shredded) coconut

Seasoning: 30 ml/2 tbsp oil ● 10 ml/2 tsp ghee ● 5 ml/1 tsp mustard seeds

30 ml/1 tbsp peanuts ● 2-3 curry leaves

Cook the rice in boiling water for about 10 minutes until tender. Drain and leave to cool. Purée the chopped tomatoes then strain the juice into a pan with the turmeric and salt and simmer over a low heat until the juice thickens. Heat the masala oil and fry the masala ingredients until slightly darkened. Grind to a fine powder then add to the tomato juice. Set aside. Heat the seasoning oil and ghee and fry all the seasoning ingredients until the mustard seeds start crackling. Add the onions and chillies and fry until golden. Add the rice and tomato juice, mix well and heat through before serving.

Yoghurt Rice
Serves 4

225 g/8 oz/1 cup long-grain rice ● 600 ml/1 pt/2½ cups water

1 mango, skinned and finely chopped ● 1 cucumber, peeled and finely chopped

salt ● 2 green chillies, finely chopped ● 2.5 cm/1 in ginger root, finely chopped

1 bunch fresh coriander (cilantro), chopped

450 ml/¾ pt/2 cups natural (plain) yoghurt ● 120 ml/4 fl oz/½ cup milk

1 carrot, grated

Seasoning: 10 ml/2 tsp oil ● 5 ml/1 tsp mustard seeds

10 ml/2 tsp split black beans ● 10 ml/2 tsp yellow split peas

1 dried red chilli, halved ● 2.5 ml/½ tsp asafoetida ● 2-3 curry leaves

Cook the rice in the water for about 10 minutes until tender then drain and mash. Add the mango, cucumber and salt. Heat the seasoning oil and fry all the seasoning ingredients until the mustard seeds start crackling. Add to the rice with the green chillies, ginger and most of the coriander and mix well. Stir in the yoghurt and milk. Simmer until heated through and well blended then garnish with the remaining coriander and the carrot and serve hot.

Tahri
Serves 4-6

75 ml/5 tbsp ghee ● 5 ml/1 tsp cumin seeds

1 onion, thinly sliced ● 225 g/8 oz/1 cup patna or basmati rice

150 g/5 oz cauliflower, cut into 2.5 cm/1 in florets

150 g/5 oz peas ● 2 medium carrots, cut into 1 cm/½ in slices

1 medium potato, cut into 1 cm/½ in pieces

45 ml/3 tbsp desiccated (shredded) coconut ● 5 ml/1 tsp garam masala

5 ml/1 tsp ground roasted cumin ● 2.5 ml/½ tsp ground red chilli

2.5 ml/½ tsp ground turmeric ● salt ● 500 ml/17 fl oz/2¼ cups water

Garnish: 1 lemon, thinly sliced

Heat the ghee in a heavy-based pan and fry the cumin seeds over a medium heat until browned. Add the onion and fry until golden. Add the rice, vegetables and coconut and fry for 5 minutes. Stir in the garam masala, cumin, chilli, turmeric and salt. Pour in the water, return to the boil. Reduce the heat to low, cover and cook for 15 minutes or until tender. Remove the lid and tip the pan to see if there is any water left, but do not stir. Dry off any remaining water on a high heat. Garnish with lemon slices and serve hot with stuffed aubergine, pickle or chutney and raita.

Chicken Muglai Biryani
Serves 4

500 g/18 oz chicken, skinned and cubed

150 ml/¼ pt/⅔ cup natural (plain) yoghurt ● 3 large cloves garlic

2.5 cm/1 in ginger root ● 150 ml/¼ pt/⅔ cup oil

5 small onions, thinly sliced ● 2 bay leaves ● 5 ml/1 tsp cumin seeds

5 ml/1 tsp garam masala ● 5 ml/1 tsp ground coriander (cilantro)

2.5 ml/½ tsp ground red chilli ● 2.5 ml/½ tsp ground turmeric ● salt

225 g/8 oz canned tomatoes ● 100 ml/3½ fl oz/6½ tbsp water

30 ml/2 tbsp chopped fresh coriander (cilantro)

Rice: 45 ml/3 tbsp ghee ● 5 ml/1 tsp cumin seeds ● 3 bay leaves

150 g/5 oz/cup basmati or patna rice ● 5 ml/1 tsp garam masala

1.5 ml/¼ tsp grated nutmeg ● 1.5 ml/¼ tsp ground mace ● salt

100 g/4 oz/⅔ cup raisins ● 50 g/2 oz/½ cup blanched almonds, halved

50 g/2 oz/½ cup cashew nuts, halved ● 300 ml/11 fl oz water

1.5 ml/¼ tsp saffron ● 45 ml/3 tbsp warm milk

Blend the yoghurt, garlic and ginger to a smooth paste in a blender or food processor. Add the chicken pieces and leave to marinate for 2 hours.

Heat 90 ml/6 tbsp of oil and fry the onions until golden brown. Remove them from the pan. Add the remaining oil and fry the bay leaves and cumin seeds for 1 minute. Add the chicken pieces and fry for 5 minutes. Gradually add the marinade and cook until all the liquid has been absorbed. Stir in the ground spices and salt then the tomatoes and cook until all the liquid has been absorbed and the oil appears on the surface. Add the water, bring to the boil then cover and simmer gently for 15 minutes until tender, stirring occasionally. Stir in the coriander.

Meanwhile, make the rice. Heat the ghee and fry the cumin seeds and bay leaves for 1 minute. Add the rice and fry for 2 minutes. Stir in the ground spices and salt then the raisins and nuts. Add the water and mix thoroughly. Bring to the boil, cover and simmer gently for 10 minutes. Remove from the heat and stand for 5 minutes. Dissolve the saffron in the milk.

Arrange layers of chicken, onion and rice in a heavy-based pan until all the ingredients are used up. Sprinkle over the saffron milk, cover and cook for a further 2-3 minutes over a low heat. Remove from the heat and leave to stand for 5 minutes. Invert on to a serving dish and serve hot with puris, raita, dal and a vegetable kofta curry.

Chicken Biryani   Serves 4

1 chicken, skinned ● 600 ml/1 pt/2½ cups natural (plain) yoghurt

45 ml/3 tbsp ghee ● 3 onions, sliced ● 225 g/8 oz/1 cup long-grain rice, soaked

salt ● 5 ml/1 tsp saffron strands ● 15 ml/1 tbsp hot milk

25 g/1 oz/¼ cup flaked almonds ● 50 g/2 oz/⅓ cup raisins

4 hard-boiled (hard-cooked) eggs, sliced

Marinade: 2 onions, chopped ● 5 cloves garlic, chopped

10 cm/4 in ginger root, chopped ● 1 sprig fresh coriander (cilantro)

1 sprig fresh mint ● 4 cardamom pods ● 2 blades mace

3 cloves ● 10 ml/2 tsp poppy seeds

2.5 cm/1 in cinnamon stick ● 3 green chillies

Clean the chicken and reserve the liver and kidneys. Cut the chicken into 4-6 pieces and slice the liver and kidneys. Grind together the marinade ingredients then mix with the yoghurt, pour over the chicken and leave to marinate for 2 hours.

Heat the ghee and fry the onions until golden. Add to the chicken marinade and mix thoroughly. Place in a pan and cook over a gentle heat for about 45 minutes until tender. Meanwhile, boil the rice in salted water for about 8 minutes until almost cooked.

Layer the rice and chicken in a casserole and dot with ghee. Dissolve the saffron in the milk and sprinkle over the top. Cover tightly with foil and the lid and place the casserole in a large pan half-filled with hot water. Bring to the boil and simmer for 30 minutes. Fry the almonds and raisins in a little ghee and use to garnish the biryani with slices of hard-boiled egg.

Royal Biryani
Serves 4

45 ml/3 tbsp ghee ● 1 onion, chopped

2 tomatoes, chopped ● 2 bay leaves ● 6 black peppercorns

5 cloves ● 5 cardamom pods ● 2.5 cm/1 in cinnamon stick

225 g/8 oz mixed vegetables, diced ● salt ● 225 g/8 oz/1 cup long-grain rice, soaked

600 ml/1 pt/2½ cups vegetable stock

50 g/2 oz Paneer (page 20), cubed and lightly fried

100 g/4 oz/1 cup nuts and fruit, chopped

Heat the ghee and fry the onion until golden. Remove and reserve half the onion. Add the tomato to the pan, stir in the spices and cook for about 5 minutes until the ghee appears on the surface. Add the vegetables and salt, cover and simmer for 5 minutes. Stir in the rice and stock, bring to the boil then simmer gently for 5 minutes. Add the paneer and nuts and mix well. Cover and simmer for a further 5 minutes until all the moisture has gone. Serve hot, sprinkled with fried onion.

Fish Biryani
Serves 4

450 g/1 lb fish ● 3 tomatoes, skinned and chopped

5 ml/1 tsp ground turmeric ● 5 ml/1 tsp cumin seeds

4 green chillies ● 4 cloves garlic ● 1 onion

45 ml/3 tbsp ghee ● 450 g/1 lb/2 cups basmati rice, soaked

750 ml/1¼ pts/3 cups coconut milk ● salt

4 potatoes, boiled and cubed ● 4 hard-boiled (hard-cooked) eggs, sliced

Wash the fish and boil in a little salted water. Bone it and set aside. Grind the turmeric, cumin, chillies, garlic and half an onion. Slice the remaining onion and fry in the ghee until lightly browned. Stir in the rice and fry for 2 minutes. Add the coconut milk and enough water to bring the liquid 2.5 cm/1 in above the level of the rice. Simmer for about 8 minutes until the rice is almost cooked. Add the ground paste, fish and salt, mix gently and reduce the heat. Cover and simmer until the rice is dry. Serve garnished with potato and hard-boiled egg.

Lamb Mughlai Biryani Serves 4-6

4 large cloves garlic ● 2.5 cm/1 in ginger root

150 ml/¼ pt/⅔ cup natural (plain) yoghurt

60 ml/4 tbsp chopped fresh coriander (cilantro)

500 g/18 oz lamb, cut into 2.5 cm/1 in pieces

60 ml/4 tbsp ghee or oil ● 1 onion, finely chopped

10 ml/2 tsp ground coriander (cilantro) ● 5 ml/1 tsp garam masala

5 ml/1 tsp ground roasted cumin ● 2.5 ml/½ tsp ground red chilli

2.5 ml/½ tsp ground turmeric ● salt ● 225 g/8 oz canned tomatoes

100 ml/3½ fl oz/6½ tbsp water

Rice: 75 ml/5 tbsp ghee ● 5 ml/1 tsp cumin seeds

2 onions, thinly sliced ● 6 cloves ● 6 black peppercorns

1 black cardamom pod ● 1.5 cm/½ in cinnamon stick

225 g/8 oz patna or basmati rice ● 5 ml/1 tsp garam masala

5 ml/1 tsp ground roasted cumin ● salt

400 ml/14 fl oz/1¾ cups water ● 100 g/4 oz/⅔ cup raisins

50 g/2 oz/½ cup blanched almonds, halved ● 50 g/2 oz/½ cup cashew nuts, halved

1.5 ml/¼ tsp saffron ● 45 ml/3 tbsp lukewarm milk

Blend the garlic, ginger, yoghurt and coriander to a smooth paste. Rub the paste into the lamb and leave to marinate for 2 hours.

Heat the ghee in a heavy-based pan and fry the onion until golden brown. Add the meat, cover and cook for 15 minutes, stirring occasionally. Remove the lid and dry off the liquid then fry the meat until golden brown. Stir in the ground spices and salt then the tomatoes and water. Bring to the boil and simmer gently for 15 minutes until tender. Increase the heat and cook until all the liquid has been absorbed and the ghee appears on the surface.

To prepare the rice, heat the ghee in a heavy-based pan and fry the cumin seeds until lightly browned. Add the onion and whole spices and fry until golden brown. Add the rice and fry for 2 minutes. Stir in the ground spices then the water. Bring to the boil, cover and simmer gently for 7 minutes. Gently mix in the raisins and nuts.

Arrange thin layers of meat and rice in a heavy-based pan. Dissolve the saffron in the milk and sprinkle over the top. Cover and cook over a low heat for a further 5 minutes. Invert on to a serving dish and serve hot with raita and a vegetable dish.

Vegetable Biryani
Serves 4-6

60 ml/4 tbsp oil or ghee ● 2.5 ml/½ tsp cumin seeds

2 large cloves garlic, crushed ● 1 cm/½ in ginger root, finely chopped

1 onion, finely chopped ● 60 ml/4 tbsp desiccated (shredded) coconut

5 ml/1 tsp garam masala ● 5 ml/1 tsp ground coriander (cilantro)

5 ml/1 tsp ground roasted cumin ● 2.5 ml/½ tsp ground red chilli

2.5 ml/½ tsp ground turmeric ● salt ● 400 g/14 oz canned tomatoes

250 g/9 oz frozen sweetcorn, thawed

150 g/5 oz Paneer (page 20), cut into 1 cm/½ in pieces

30 ml/2 tbsp chopped fresh coriander (cilantro) ● 30 ml/2 tbsp lemon juice

15 ml/1 tbsp chopped fresh mint

Rice: 90 ml/6 tbsp ghee ● 5 ml/1 tsp cumin seeds

1 onion, thinly sliced ● 4 cloves ● 4 black peppercorns

2.5 cm/1 in cinnamon stick ● 2 bay leaves ● 1 black cardamom pod

225 g/8 oz/1 cup patna or basmati rice, washed and drained

5 ml/1 tsp garam masala ● 5 ml/1 tsp ground roasted cumin

salt ● 100 g/4 oz/1 cup raisins

50 g/2 oz/½ cup blanched almonds, halved ● 50 g/2 oz/½ cup cashew nuts, halved

500 ml/17 fl oz/2¼ cups water

To finish: 2.5 ml/½ tsp ground saffron ● 45 ml/3 tbsp warm milk

Heat the oil or ghee in a heavy-based pan and fry the cumin seeds until lightly browned. Add the garlic, ginger and onion and fry until golden brown. Stir in the coconut and fry for 2 minutes. Stir in the garam masala, coriander, cumin, chilli, turmeric and salt. Stir in the tomatoes, sweetcorn and paneer. Cook for about 20 minutes until all the liquid has been absorbed. Stir in the coriander, lemon juice and mint. Remove from the heat and set aside.

Meanwhile, cook the rice. Heat the ghee in a heavy-based pan and fry the cumin seeds until lightly browned. Add the onion, cloves, peppercorns, cinnamon, bay leaves and cardamom and fry until golden brown. Mix in the rice and fry for 2 minutes. Stir in the garam masala, cumin and salt. Stir in the raisins, nuts and water and bring to the boil. Reduce the heat to low, cover and cook for 10 minutes. Dissolve the saffron in the warm milk.

To assemble the dish, layer the vegetables and rice in a heavy-based pan and pour over the saffron milk. Cover and cook over a low heat for 5 minutes. Before serving, place a serving dish on the saucepan and carefully turn them over. Tap a little with a spoon on the pan and gently lift it off, leaving the biryani in the serving dish. Serve hot with raita, salad, and potatoes and peas.

Apple Pulao

3 apples, peeled, cored and cut into 8

1.5 l/3 pts/7½ cups water ● 350 g/12 oz/1 cup sugar

2.5 ml/½ tsp ground saffron ● 45 ml/3 tbsp ghee ● 2 bay leaves

2 cinnamon sticks ● 8 cloves ● 5 ml/1 tsp cardamom seeds

225 g/8 oz basmati rice, soaked ● 50 g/2 oz/½ cup flaked almonds

50 g/2 oz/⅓ cup raisins

Put the apples and 450 ml/¾ pt/2 cups of water in a pan, bring to the boil and simmer for 4 minutes then drain. Put the sugar and a further 450 ml/¾ pt/2 cups of water in a separate pan, add the apple pieces, bring to the boil and add the saffron. Simmer for 30 minutes until about one-third of the syrup remains. Heat the ghee and fry the bay leaves, cinnamon, cloves and cardamom for 1-2 minutes. Add the rice, almonds and raisins and fry for 3 minutes. Add the remaining water, bring to the boil then simmer for 15 minutes until the rice is almost cooked. Remove from the heat, make a well in the centre and spoon in the apple pieces with a little syrup. Cover with rice and pour the remaining syrup on top. Cook on a low heat for about 15 minutes until the rice is cooked.

Aubergine and Mushroom Pulao
Serves 4

30 ml/2 tbsp ghee ● 1 onion, chopped

5 ml/1 tsp cumin seeds ● pinch of asafoetida

600 ml/1 pt/2½ cups stock ● 225 g/8 oz/1 cup basmati rice, soaked

50 g/2 oz aubergine (eggplant), chopped and par-boiled

50 g/2 oz mushrooms, chopped ● salt ● 2.5 ml/½ tsp cayenne

5 ml/1 tsp garam masala ● 1 lemon, sliced

Heat the ghee and fry the onion until golden. Stir in the cumin and asafoetida. Add the stock and bring to the boil. Add the rice and vegetables and season with salt and cayenne. Cover and simmer for 15 minutes until the rice is tender. Remove the lid, sprinkle with garam masala and cook for 5 minutes. Serve garnished with the lemon slices.

Basmati Pulao
Serves 6

450 g/1 lb/2 cups basmati rice, soaked for 20 minutes

seeds from 6 cardamom pods ● 1.5 ml/¼ tsp cloves

3 bay leaves ● 1 cinnamon stick

2.5 ml/½ tsp black peppercorns ● 1 onion, thinly sliced

3 cloves garlic, sliced ● 15 ml/1 tbsp oil

1.2 l/2 pts/5 cups water ● salt

Preheat the oven to 200°C/400°F/gas mark 6. Place all the ingredients in a large pan and bring to the boil. Cover and simmer gently for 7-10 minutes until the rice is three-quarters cooked. Drain and transfer to a casserole dish.

Cover with foil and the lid. Reduce the oven temperature to 150°C/300°F/gas mark 2 and cook for 5-8 minutes. Turn off the heat and leave the casserole for a further 5 minutes before serving hot.

Carnataka Pulao
Serves 6

900 g/2 lb boneless lamb, cubed • 450 ml/¾ pts/2 cups natural (plain) yoghurt

salt • 45 ml/3 tbsp water • 5 ml/1 tsp ground turmeric

5 ml/1 tsp paprika • seeds from 8 cardamom pods • 1 cinnamon stick

6 cloves • 15 ml/1 tbsp ground coriander (cilantro)

15 ml/1 tbsp ground cumin • 1.5 ml/¼ tsp grated nutmeg

1.5 ml/¼ tsp ground mace • 1.5 ml/¼ tsp ground red chilli

8 cloves garlic, chopped • 5 cm/2 in ginger root, chopped

3 green chillies • 30 ml/2 tbsp chopped fresh coriander (cilantro)

120 ml/4 fl oz/½ cup oil • 8 onions, sliced

Rice: 5 ml/1 tsp saffron strands • 45 ml/3 tbsp hot milk

900 g/2 lb/2 cups long-grain rice, soaked • 2.8 l/5 pts/12 cups water

15 ml/1 tbsp oil • 6 cloves • 5 ml/1 tsp ground cardamom

1 cinnamon stick • 2.5 ml/½ tsp black peppercorns

salt • 30 ml/2 tbsp raisins • 3 potatoes, peeled and cubed

Mix the meat with the yoghurt and salt and leave to marinate. Purée the remaining meat ingredients except the oil and onions. Heat the oil and fry the onions until browned and crisp then remove from the pan, leave to cool then crush. Mix half the crushed onions with 30 ml/2 tbsp of oil from the pan and the marinated meat and set aside for 3 hours.

Reheat the oil in the pan and add the meat and marinade. Bring to the boil, cover and simmer gently for 1 hour, stirring occasionally, until the meat is tender and the sauce thick. Remove from the heat.

Meanwhile, dissolve the saffron in the hot milk. Bring the rice to the boil with the water, oil, cloves, cardamom, cinnamon, peppercorns and salt and simmer for 4 minutes. Drain. Spread the meat in a greased casserole dish, top with the raisins and potatoes and sprinkle with the saffron milk. Sprinkle over half the remaining onions then add the rice and the remaining onions. Seal with foil then the lid and cook in a preheated oven at 150°C/300°F/gas mark 2 for 45 minutes until the meat is tender. Turn off the heat and leave in the oven for a further 5 minutes. Serve hot with tomato chutney and papadums.

Benares-style Pulao
Serves 6

450 g/1 lb/2 cups basmati rice ● 2.8 l/5 pts/12 cups water

45 ml/3 tbsp oil ● salt ● 1 onion, chopped

5 cloves garlic, crushed ● 1 cm/½ in ginger root, grated

1 cinnamon stick ● seeds from 5 cardamom pods

8 cloves ● 2.5 ml/½ tsp black peppercorns ● 2 bay leaves

1 small cauliflower, cut into florets ● 225 g/8 oz peas

2.5 ml/½ tsp ground turmeric ● 1.5 ml/¼ tsp ground red chilli

Boil the rice and water in a large pan with 15 ml/1 tbsp of oil and a pinch of salt over a medium heat for 5 minutes, stirring occasionally, until the rice is three-quarters cooked. Drain and set aside. Preheat the oven to 200°C/400°F/gas mark 6. Heat the remaining oil and fry the onion, garlic and ginger over a medium heat until browned. Add the cinnamon, cardamom, cloves, peppercorns and bay leaves and fry for 2 minutes, stirring. Stir in the cauliflower, peas, turmeric, chillies and a little more salt. Cover and simmer for 5 minutes. Spread the cooked rice in a large casserole dish and stir in the cauliflower mixture. Cover tightly with foil and the lid. Reduce the oven temperature to 150°C/300°C/gas mark 2 and bake in the oven for 5-7 minutes. Turn off the heat and leave in the oven for 5 minutes. Serve hot with mango chutney, curry and papadums.

Pulao with Carrots and Beans
Serves 6

675 g/1½ lb/3 cups long-grain rice, soaked for 20 minutes

45 ml/3 tbsp oil ● 5 ml/1 tsp cumin seeds

2 bay leaves ● 1 cinnamon stick ● 4 black cardamom pods

2.5 ml/½ tsp black peppercorns ● 1.5 ml/¼ tsp cloves

3 large carrots, cut into strips ● 450 g/1 lb green beans, cut into strips

225 g/8 oz peas ● 5 ml/1 tsp ground turmeric

1.5 ml/¼ tsp ground red chilli ● salt ● 900 ml/1½ pts/3¾ cups water

Preheat the oven to 200°C/400°F/gas mark 6. Wash and drain the rice. Heat the oil in a flameproof casserole and fry the cumin, seed, bay leaves, cinnamon, cardamom, peppercorns and cloves over a medium heat for 10 seconds. Add the carrots, beans, peas, turmeric, ground chillies and salt and fry for 3 minutes. Add the rice and stir together well. Add the water and bring to the boil. Reduce the oven temperature to 150°C/300°F/gas mark 2. Cover the casserole tightly and cook in the oven for about 10 minutes until the rice and vegetables are tender. Serve hot with coriander chutney, raita and papadums.

Cauliflower Pulao

Serves 4

50 g/2 oz/¼ cup ghee ● 1 onion, chopped ● pinch of asafoetida

2.5 ml/½ tsp cumin seeds ● 4 bay leaves ● 2.5 cm/1 in cinnamon stick

8 cloves ● 4 cardamom pods ● 225 g/8 oz/1 cup basmati rice, soaked

100 g/4 oz cauliflower florets, par-boiled ● 600 ml/1 pt/2½ cups water ● salt

5 ml/1 tsp ground turmeric ● 2.5 ml/½ tsp black pepper ● 1 tomato, sliced

Heat the ghee and fry the onion and asafoetida until golden. Stir in the cumin seeds, bay leaves, cinnamon, cloves and cardamom then add the rice and cauliflower and stir well. Pour in the water with the remaining ingredients except the tomato, bring to the boil then simmer gently for about 10 minutes until the rice is soft and the water has evaporated. Serve garnished with the tomato.

Egg Pulao

Serves 4-6

75 ml/5 tbsp ghee ● 1 onion, thinly sliced ● 4 cloves

4 black peppercorns ● 2 bay leaves ● 1.2 cm/½ in cinnamon stick

1 black cardamom pod ● 5 ml/1 tsp garam masala ● 5 ml/1 tsp ground roasted cumin

salt ● 225 g/8 oz/1 cup basmati or patna rice

150 g/5 oz/⅔ cup raisins ● 50 g/2 oz/½ cup blanched almonds, halved

50 g/2 oz/½ cup cashew nuts, halved ● 500 ml/17 fl oz/2¼ cups water

Eggs: 4 large tomatoes ● 15 ml/1 tbsp ghee

5 ml/1 tsp cumin seeds ● 6 hard-boiled (hard-cooked) eggs, coarsely chopped

2.5 ml/½ tsp garam masala ● 2.5 ml/½ tsp ground red chilli

2.5 ml/½ tsp ground turmeric ● salt

60 ml/4 tbsp chopped fresh coriander (cilantro)

30 ml/2 tbsp chopped fresh mint ● 15 ml/1 tbsp lemon juice

oil for frying

Garnish: 12 radishes, cut into flowers

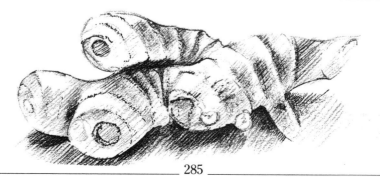

Heat the ghee in a heavy-based pan and fry the onion and whole spices until golden brown. Add the rice and fry for 2 minutes. Stir in the ground spices then the raisins, nuts and water. Bring to the boil, cover and simmer gently for 10 minutes until the rice is tender and the water has been absorbed.

Meanwhile, cut a slice off the top of the tomatoes and scoop out the pulp. Heat the ghee and fry the cumin seeds until browned. Add the egg, ground spices and salt then mix in the tomato pulp and remaining ingredients except the whole tomatoes. Cook gen-

tly for 3 minutes, stirring occasionally. Spoon half the egg mixture into the tomatoes. Heat the frying oil and gently fry the stuffed tomatoes for 2 minutes.

Mix the remaining egg mixture into the cooked rice. Before serving, place a serving dish on the saucepan and carefully turn them over. Tap a little with a spoon on the pan and gently lift it off, leaving the pulao in the serving dish. Arrange the tomatoes and radish flowers attractively over the top and serve hot with raita, mushrooms, dal and a kofta dish.

Fish Pulao
Serves 6

100 g/4 oz/½ cup ghee ● 450 g/1 lb fish fillets, cut into chunks

150 ml/¼ pt/⅔ cup water ● salt ● 4 onions, sliced

675 g/1½ lb/3 cups long-grain rice, soaked

600 ml/1 pt/2½ cups coconut milk ● juice of ½ lemon

Masala: 10 ml/2 tsp coriander (cilantro) seeds, roasted

4 dried red chillies ● 5 ml/1 tsp cumin seeds

2.5 ml/½ tsp ground turmeric ● 4 cloves

1 bunch fresh coriander (cilantro) ● 1 cm/½ in ginger root, grated

100 g/4 oz/½ cup desiccated (shredded) coconut

Grind together all the masala ingredients. Heat 45 ml/3 tbsp of ghee and fry the masala until it bubbles and turns slightly red. Add the fish, salt and water, cover and simmer until the fish is tender. Remove the fish from the pan and keep it warm. Reserve the sauce. Heat the remaining ghee and fry the onions until soft. Add the rice

and a little salt and mix well. Pour in the fish sauce, coconut milk, lemon juice and simmer until the rice is almost cooked and the water is absorbed, adding a little more water during cooking if necessary. Arrange the fish pieces on top of the rice, cover and continue to simmer over a low heat until the rice is tender.

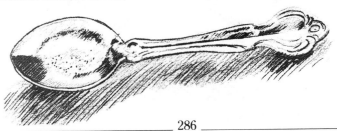

Fruit and Nut Pulao
Serves 4

45 ml/3 tbsp ghee ● 1 onion, chopped ● 5 ml/1 tsp ground cumin

seeds from 4 cardamom pods, crushed ● 2 bay leaves

2.5 cm/1 in cinnamon stick ● 5 ml/1 tsp ground turmeric

225 g/8 oz/1 cup long-grain rice, soaked and drained

salt and pepper ● 50 g/2 oz dried apricots, sliced ● 50 g/2 oz dried peach, sliced

50 g/2 oz/½ cup pistachios, chopped ● 50 g/2 oz/½ cup cashew nuts, chopped

Heat the ghee and fry the onion until soft and lightly browned. Add the cumin, cardamom, bay leaves, cinnamon and turmeric and fry for 2 minutes, stirring. Stir in the rice and fry for 2 minutes, stirring until well coated in seasoned oil. Season with salt and pepper and pour in enough water to come 2.5 cm/1 in above the level of the rice. Sprinkle with the fruit and nuts, cover and simmer gently for 20 minutes. Fluff up the rice with a fork before serving.

Hyderabad-style Chicken Pulao
Serves 6

900 g/2 lb chicken breasts and legs ● 45 ml/3 tbsp oil

1 onion, chopped ● 5 cloves garlic, chopped

2.5 cm/1 in ginger root, chopped ● 8 cardamom pods ● 12 cloves

4 bay leaves ● 2.5 ml/½ tsp black peppercorns ● 1 cinnamon stick

1.5 ml/¼ tsp grated nutmeg ● 15 ml/1 tbsp ground coriander (cilantro)

1.5 ml/¼ tsp ground red chilli ● 45 ml/3 tbsp soured (dairy sour) cream

150 ml/8 fl oz/½ cup natural (plain) yoghurt ● salt

Rice: 450 g/1 lb/1 cup long-grain rice, soaked ● 45 ml/3 tbsp oil

1 onion, chopped ● 25 g/1 oz/¼ cup blanched almonds ● 50 g/2 oz/⅓ cup raisins

Remove the skin from the chicken. Heat the oil and fry the onion, garlic and ginger over a medium heat until browned. Add the cardamom, cloves, bay leaves, peppercorns and cinnamon and fry for 3 minutes. Add the nutmeg, coriander and chilli and cook for 2 minutes. Lightly whisk the soured cream and yoghurt, pour over the spices and cook for 2-3 minutes, stirring. Mix in the chicken pieces and salt. Cover and simmer gently for 20-25 minutes until the chicken is tender, stirring occasionally.

Cook the rice in boiling water for about 10 minutes then drain. Heat the oil and fry the onion over a medium heat until browned and crisp then remove and drain. Add the almonds and raisins to the pan and fry until the almonds are golden. Remove and drain. Place the chicken in a casserole dish and spread the rice over the top. Garnish with the onions, almonds and raisins, cover tightly with foil and the lid and bake in a preheated oven at 150°C/300°F/gas mark 3 for 15 minutes. Turn off the heat and leave the casserole in the oven for a further 10 minutes. Serve hot with vegetables, mint chutney and papadums.

Hyderabad-style Lamb Pulao   Serves 6

900 g/2 lb boneless lamb, cubed ● 250 ml/8 fl oz/1 cup natural (plain) yoghurt

5 ml/1 tsp ground turmeric ● 1.5 ml/¼ tsp ground red chilli ● salt

1.2 l/2 pts/5 cups water ● 100 g/4 oz grated (shredded) coconut

1 onion, chopped ● 5 cloves garlic, chopped ● 1 cm/½ in ginger root, chopped

2 green chillies, chopped ● 15 ml/1 tbsp garam masala

1.5 ml/¼ tsp grated nutmeg ● 15 ml/1 tbsp coriander (cilantro) seeds

10 ml/2 tsp cumin seeds ● 45 ml/3 tbsp oil ● 5 cardamom pods

2 cinnamon sticks ● 2.5 ml/½ tsp black peppercorns

1.5 ml/¼ tsp cloves ● 2 bay leaves ● 2 potatoes, peeled and cubed

900 g/2 lb/4 cups long-grain rice, soaked ● 225 g/8 oz peas

30 ml/2 tbsp chopped fresh mint ● 30 ml/2 tbsp chopped fresh coriander (cilantro)

Place the lamb in a bowl with the yoghurt, turmeric, chillies and salt. Purée 120 ml/4 fl oz/½ cup of water, the coconut, onion, garlic, ginger, chillies, garam masala, nutmeg, coriander and cumin seeds, adding a little more water if necessary. Heat the oil and fry the cardamom, cinnamon, peppercorns, cloves and bay leaves until slightly darkened. Mix in the purée and simmer for 8-10 minutes, stirring, until the oil appears on the surface. Add the meat and yoghurt, cover and simmer for 30 minutes, stirring occasionally. Add the potatoes and remove from the heat.

Preheat the oven to 200°C/400°F/ gas mark 6. Boil the rice in 2.8 l/5 pts/ 12 cups of water for 5 minutes then drain. Stir in the peas. Transfer the meat to a casserole dish and sprinkle with mint and coriander. Spread over the rice, cover with foil and the lid and bake in the oven for 15 minutes. Reduce the oven temperature to 150°C/300°F/gas mark 2 and cook for a further 20 minutes. Turn off the heat and leave the casserole in the oven for a further 5 minutes. Serve hot with papadums, spinach, dal and mango chutney.

Kashmir-style Chicken Pulao   Serves 6

1.5 kg/3 lb chicken, cut into portions ● 2.8 l/5 pts/12 cups water

25 g/1 oz/¼ cup pistachios ● 10 ml/2 tsp fennel seeds ● 30 ml/2 tbsp cumin seeds

5 ml/1 tsp paprika ● 15 ml/1 tbsp garam masala

45 ml/3 tbsp natural (plain) yoghurt ● 5 ml/1 tsp saffron strands

45 ml/3 tbsp hot milk ● 75 ml/5 tbsp oil ● 2 onions, chopped

25 g/1 oz/¼ cup blanched almonds ● 50 g/2 oz/⅓ cup raisins

3 cardamom pods ● 2 cinnamon sticks ● 2.5 ml/½ tsp cloves

2 bay leaves ● 2.5 ml/½ tsp black peppercorns

1.5 ml/¼ tsp grated nutmeg ● 5 cloves garlic, chopped ● salt

30 ml/2 tbsp chopped fresh mint ● 675 g/1½ lb/3 cups long-grain rice, soaked

Boil the chicken wings, neck and giblets in 250 ml/8 fl oz/1 cup of the water to make 250 ml/8 fl oz/1 cup of stock. Grind the pistachios, fennel and cumin seeds, paprika and garam masala then whisk them into the yoghurt. Soak the saffron in the hot milk for 15 minutes.

Heat 60 ml/4 tbsp of the oil and fry 1 onion until browned then remove and drain. Fry the almonds and raisins until golden. Add the cardamom, cinnamon, cloves, bay leaves, peppercorns, nutmeg and garlic for 1-2 minutes. Mix in the ground spices and cook for 1-2 minutes, stirring. Add the chicken, salt and strained stock, cover and simmer for 15 minutes, stirring occasionally until the chicken is half-cooked and the gravy is thick. Stir in the mint. Boil the rice in the remaining water and oil for 8 minutes until almost cooked then drain. Transfer the chicken to a casserole and cover with the rice. Garnish with the almonds, onions and raisins and pour over the saffron milk. Cover tightly with foil and the lid and bake in a preheated oven at 200°C/400°F/gas mark 6 for 15 minutes. Reduce the oven temperature to 150°C/300°F/gas mark 2 and cook for a further 15 minutes. Serve with spinach, papadums and onion relish.

Meatball Pulao   Serves 6

2 slices bread ● 150 ml/¼ pt/⅔ cup milk

2 onions ● 450 g/1 lb minced (ground) lamb

juice of ½ lemon ● 2 eggs ● 100 g/4 oz/1 cup breadcrumbs

ghee for deep-frying ● 5 ml/1 tsp cumin seeds ● 2 black cardamom pods

450 g/1 lb/2 cups long-grain rice, soaked ● 1.2 1/2 pts/5 cups water

Seasoning: 2 green chillies ● 5 ml/1 tsp coriander (cilantro) seeds

4 cloves garlic ● 2.5 ml/½ tsp ginger root ● 5 ml/1 tsp garam masala

Tomato sauce: 15 ml/1 tbsp ghee ● 3 cloves ● 1 cinnamon stick

4 cloves garlic ● 450 g/1 lb tomatoes, skinned ● 10 ml/2 tsp chilli powder

25 g/1 oz/½ cup plain (all-purpose) flour ● 300 m/1½ pt/10 cups coconut milk

Grind together the seasoning ingredients. Soak the bread in the milk for 15 minutes then squeeze out the excess. Mince 1 onion then mix it with the bread, meat, ground spices, lemon juice and 1 egg. Shape the mixture into small balls, dip in beaten egg, roll in breadcrumbs and deep-fry in hot oil until golden brown.

Heat 15 ml/1 tbsp ghee, slice the remaining onion and fry it until soft. Add the cumin seeds, cardamom and rice and stir together well. Add the rice and water, bring to the boil, cover and simmer until the rice is almost cooked. Transfer to a casserole dish, gently place the meatballs into the rice, cover and cook in a preheated oven at 180°C/350°F/gas mark 4 for about 15 minutes until almost dry.

To make the sauce, heat the ghee and fry the cloves, cinnamon and garlic for 2 minutes. Add the tomatoes and cook until soft. Add the chilli powder and mix well, squashing the tomatoes with the back of a spoon. Bring to the boil, add the flour and coconut milk and simmer until thick and creamy. Serve the pulao with the sauce poured over.

Mussel Pulao
Serves 6

450 g/1 lb mussels, scrubbed and bearded

45 ml/3 tbsp ghee • 10 black peppercorns

2 cinnamon sticks • 75 g/3 oz grated (shredded) coconut

5 ml/1 tsp coriander (cilantro) seeds • 2 onions, chopped

5 cloves garlic, chopped • 450 g/1 lb/2 cups long-grain rice, soaked

900 ml/1½ pts/3¾ cups water • 600 ml/1 pt/2½ cups coconut milk

salt • 4 dried red chillies, ground

Place the mussels in a large pan and cover with water. Bring to the boil then simmer for about 5 minutes until the shells have opened. Remove the mussels from the shells, discarding any that have not opened. Heat 5 ml/1 tsp of ghee and fry the peppercorns and cinnamon for 2 minutes then grind them together. Heat 15 ml/1 tbsp ghee and fry the coconut until lightly browned then grind. Heat 15 ml/1 tbsp of ghee, fry the coriander seeds then grind. Heat the remaining ghee and fry the onions and garlic until soft. Add the fried spices and rice. Add the water, coconut milk and salt, bring to the boil, cover and simmer for about 10 minutes until almost cooked. Toss the mussels with the chillies then add to the rice with the coconut and mix well. Transfer to a casserole dish, cover tightly and cook in a preheated oven at 180°C/350°F/gas mark 4 for 15 minutes until the rice is dry. Serve with tomato chutney.

Mango Pulao
Serves 4

30 ml/3 tbsp ghee • 4 bay leaves

2.5 ml/½ tsp cardamom seeds • 225 g/8 oz/1 cup basmati rice, soaked

150 ml/¼ pt/⅔ cup water • 2 mangoes, peeled and stoned

sugar • 50 g/2 oz chopped nuts and fruit

2-3 drops of rose water

Heat the ghee and fry the bay leaves and cardamom for 2 minutes. Add the rice and cook over a medium heat for 5 minutes. Add the water and bring to the boil. Simmer gently for 10 minutes until the water has been absorbed. Add the mango, sugar, nuts and fruit and blend together carefully. Cover and simmer gently for 10 minutes until the rice is tender. Sprinkle with rose water before serving.

Mushroom Pulao
Serves 4

45 ml/3 tbsp ghee ● 10 cardamom pods ● 5 cloves

1 cinnamon stick ● 225 g/8 oz button mushrooms, sliced

450 g/1 lb long-grain rice, soaked and drained ● salt and pepper

Heat the ghee and fry the cardamom, cloves, cinnamon and mushrooms for 2 minutes, stirring. Add the rice and stir for 3 minutes until well coated in the seasoned ghee. Pour in enough water to come 2.5 cm/1 in above the level of the rice, bring to the boil, cover and simmer gently for about 20 minutes until tender. Fluff the rice grains with a fork and season with salt and pepper before serving.

Onion Pulao
Serves 4

15 ml/1 tbsp ghee ● 5 ml/1 tsp cumin seeds

15 ml/1 tbsp chopped onion ● 1 dried red chilli, chopped

2 cloves ● 1 cinnamon stick ● 225 g/8 oz/1 cup basmati rice, soaked

600 ml/1 pt/2½ cups water ● salt ● 225 g/8 oz baby onions, par-boiled

Heat the ghee and fry the cumin seeds, onion and chilli for 2 minutes. Add the cloves, cinnamon and rice and fry for a further 3 minutes, stirring. Add the water and salt, bring to the boil and simmer for 10 minutes. Add the onions, cover and simmer for a further 10 minutes until the rice is cooked.

Pink Pulao Rice
Serves 4

225 g/8 oz/1 cup basmati rice, soaked ● 1 large beetroot (red beets)

60 ml/4 tbsp ghee ● 5 ml/1 tsp mustard seeds

5 ml/1 tsp black pepper ● 2.5 ml/½ tsp cumin seeds

15 ml/1 tbsp yellow split peas ● 15 ml/1 tbsp split black beans

6 green chillies ● 2 aubergines (eggplant), cubed

2 onions, chopped ● 1 sprig fresh curry leaves ● salt

2.5 ml/½ tsp ground turmeric ● ½ coconut, grated (shredded)

50 g/2 oz/½ cup cashew nuts ● juice of 1 lemon

Cook the rice in boiling water for about 15 minutes until tender then drain. Boil the beetroot until tender then remove the skin. Heat 15 ml/1 tbsp of ghee and fry the mustard seeds, pepper, cumin seeds, split peas, split beans and chillies until browned. Add the aubergines, onions and curry leaves and cook until soft. Add the beetroot and cook for 2 minutes. Add the salt, turmeric and coconut and fry for a few seconds. Stir in the cooked rice. Fry the nuts in the remaining ghee and add to the rice. Sprinkle with lemon juice, cover and simmer over a low heat for 5-10 minutes before serving.

Prawn Pulao

Serves 4-6

45 ml/3 tbsp ghee ● 5 ml/1 tsp cumin seeds ● 4 cloves

4 black peppercorns ● 2 bay leaves ● 1 cardamom pod

1.5 cm/1 in cinnamon stick ● 2.5 ml/½ tsp garam masala ● salt

500 ml/17 fl oz/2¼ cups water

Prawns (shrimp): 60 ml/4 tbsp oil ● 1 onion, thinly sliced

3 large cloves garlic, crushed ● 5 ml/1 tsp ground coriander (cilantro)

5 ml/1 tsp ground roasted cumin ● 2.5 ml/½ tsp ground red chilli

2.5 ml/½ tsp ground turmeric ● 225 g/8 oz canned tomatoes

150 ml/¼ pt/⅔ cup natural (plain) yoghurt

50 g/2 oz/½ cup desiccated (shredded) coconut ● salt

250 g/9 oz large peeled prawns (shrimp)

Garnish: 15 ml/1 tbsp chopped fresh coriander (cilantro)

5 ml/1 tsp garam masala ● 1 small green chilli, chopped ● 45 ml/3 tbsp milk

Heat the ghee in a heavy-based pan and fry the cumin seeds until lightly browned. Add the whole spices and rice and stir for 2 minutes until the mixture no longer sticks to the pan. Add the garam masala, salt and water, bring to the boil then reduce the heat to minimum, cover and simmer for 15 minutes.

Meanwhile, prepare the prawns. Heat the oil and fry the onion and garlic until golden brown. Add the ground spices, tomatoes, yoghurt, coconut and salt to taste and stir over a low heat for 2 minutes. Add the prawns and cook over a medium heat until all the liquid has been absorbed and the oil appears on the surface. Don't stir the mixture too often or the prawns will become mushy. Remove from the heat and sprinkle with garnish ingredients.

Arrange the cooked rice and prawns in layers in a large heavy-based pan. Pour in the milk and heat gently for 3 minutes until the liquid has been absorbed. Before serving, place a serving dish on the saucepan and carefully turn them over. Tap a little with a spoon on the pan and gently lift it off, leaving the pulao in the serving dish. Serve hot with raita, bitter gourd, aubergine, moong beans and chapatis.

Prawn and Coconut Pulao

Serves 6

900 g/2 lb large peeled prawns (shrimp) ● 5 ml/1 tsp ground turmeric

1.5 ml/¼ tsp ground red chilli ● 45 ml/3 tbsp oil

1 onion, chopped ● 6 cardamom pods ● 2 cinnamon sticks

1.5 ml/¼ tsp cloves ● 2.5 ml/½ tsp black peppercorns ● 2 bay leaves

salt ● 450 g/1 lb/2 cups long-grain rice, soaked

120 ml/4 fl oz/½ cup coconut cream ● 450 ml/¾ pt/2 cups water ● 225 g/8 oz peas

Preheat the oven to 200°C/400°F/gas mark 6. Mix the prawns with the turmeric and chillies. Heat the oil and fry the onion until browned. Remove from the pan and drain. Add the cardamom, cinnamon, cloves, peppercorns and bay leaves to the pan and fry until slightly darkened. Stir in the prawns and salt. Add the rice, coconut cream and water, cover and simmer for 8-10 minutes, stirring occasionally. Remove from the heat and stir in the peas. Cover tightly. Reduce the oven temperature to 150°C/300°F/gas mark 2 and bake in the oven for 7-10 minutes until the liquid is absorbed. Garnish with the fried onions and serve with vegetable curry, coconut chutney and papadums.

Prawn and Tamarind Pulao   Serves 6

30 ml/2 tbsp ghee • 1 onion, sliced • 3 cloves garlic, sliced

25 g/1 oz grated (shredded) coconut • 6 cloves • 6 black peppercorns

2 sticks cinnamon • 450 g/1 lb/2 cups long-grain rice, soaked

1.2 1/2 pts/5 cups water • pinch of salt

450 g/1 lb peeled prawns (shrimp) • 15 ml/1 tbsp tamarind concentrated

5 ml/1 tsp chilli powder • 5 ml/1 tsp ground turmeric

Heat half the ghee and fry the onion, garlic and coconut until lightly browned. Add the cloves, peppercorns and cinnamon and fry for 2 minutes. Add the rice and fry until well coated in the oil and spices. Add the water and salt, bring to the boil then simmer over a medium heat until the rice is three-quarters cooked. Heat the remaining ghee in a separate pan and fry the prawns, tamarind, chilli powder and turmeric for 3 minutes. Add this to the rice. Transfer to a casserole dish, cover and cook in a preheated oven at 150°C/300°F/gas mark 2 for 15-20 minutes until the rice is dry.

Sweet Pulao   Serves 4

15 ml/1 tsp ghee • 6 cardamom pods • 4 cloves

225 g/8 oz/1 cup basmati rice, soaked • 150 ml/¼ pt/⅔ cups water

25 g/1 oz/2 tbsp sugar • 50 g/2 oz/½ cup chopped fruit and nuts

1.5 ml/¼ tsp saffron strands, crushed

Heat the ghee and fry the cardamom and cloves for 30 seconds. Stir in the rice and cook for 5 minutes. Add the water, bring to the boil then simmer for 10 minutes until the water has been absorbed. Stir in the sugar and nuts, cover and simmer gently for 10 minutes until the rice is tender and the grains are separated. Serve sprinkled with saffron.

Sindhi Pulao
Serves 6

100 g/4 oz/½ cup ghee ● 225 g/8 oz onions, chopped

675 g/1½ lb boneless lamb, cubed ● 150 ml/¼ pt/⅔ cups natural (plain) yoghurt

15 ml/1 tbsp coriander (cilantro) seeds ● 6 cardamom pods

30 ml/2 tbsp cumin seeds ● salt ● 15 ml/1 tbsp chilli powder

450 g/1 lb/2 cups long-grain rice, soaked ● 3 bay leaves

15 ml/1 tbsp peppercorns ● 50 g/2 oz/½ cup pistachios

50 g/2 oz/½ cup blanched almonds

Heat 60 ml/4 tbsp of ghee and fry the onions until browned. Remove and reserve half the onions. Add the meat to the pan and fry until golden brown. Add the yoghurt and simmer for 5 minutes. Grind together the coriander, cardamom and cumin seeds. Add to the meat with salt and chilli powder. Cover and simmer until the meat is tender and the gravy thick.

Heat 45 ml/3 tbsp of ghee in a separate pan and fry the bay leaves, peppercorns, drained rice and salt for 3 minutes. Add the reserved onion. Remove the pan from the heat and spoon three-quarters of the rice on to a dish. In the pan, put layers of rice, cooked meat, chopped onion and nuts. Pour over enough water to come 2.5 cm/1 in above the level of the rice and simmer until the rice is cooked and the water has been absorbed.

Tricolour Pulao
Serves 4

100 g/4 oz/½ cup ghee ● 2 onions, chopped ● 4 cloves

8 black peppercorns ● 2 bay leaves ● 2 cardamom pods

2.5 cm/1 in cinnamon stick ● 2.5 ml/½ tsp black cumin seeds

5 ml/1 tsp garam masala ● 2.5 ml/½ tsp chilli powder

5 ml/1 tsp grated ginger root ● 2 cloves garlic, crushed

60 ml/4 tbsp natural (plain) yoghurt ● 225 g/8 oz/1 cup basmati rice, soaked

75 g/3 oz peas ● 600 ml/1 pt/2½ cups water ● salt

50 g/2 oz Paneer cubes (page 20), fried ● pinch of saffron strands

few drops of food colour ● 30 ml/2 tbsp chopped nuts ● 2 tomatoes, sliced

Heat half the ghee and fry half the onions with the whole spices for 1 minute. Stir in the garam masala, chilli powder, ginger, garlic and yoghurt. Add the rice and peas and stir well. Pour in the water, add the salt, bring to the boil then simmer over a low heat for 10-15 minutes until the rice is tender. Remove from the heat and stir in the paneer. Divide the rice into 3 portions. Sprinkle one with the saffron and different food colours over the other 2. Return the pan to a low heat, cover and cook for 5 minutes. Heat the remaining ghee and fry the remaining onion until golden. Remove the onion from the pan and reserve. Fry the nuts in the same ghee and reserve. Spoon the rice into a serving dish, sprinkle with onion and nuts and serve garnished with the tomatoes.

Vegetable Pulao
Serves 6

450 g/1 lb/2 cups long-grain rice, soaked for 15 minutes

2 1/3½ pts/8½ cups water ● 120 ml/4 fl oz/½ cup oil

salt ● 225 g/8 oz peas ● 5 cloves garlic

2.5 cm/1 in ginger root, chopped ● seeds from 5 cardamom pods

2 green chillies ● 5 cloves ● 1 cinnamon stick, broken

5 ml/1 tsp ground turmeric ● 15 ml/1 tbsp poppy seeds

4 onions, sliced ● 30 ml/2 tbsp chopped fresh mint

5 ml/1 tsp saffron strands ● 45 ml/3 tbsp hot milk

25 g/1 oz/½ cup blanched almonds ● 25 g/1 oz/⅓ cup raisins

2 carrots, diced ● 2 potatoes, diced ● 1 small cauliflower, cut into florets

1 tomato, chopped ● 1 green (bell) pepper, cut into rings

30 ml/2 tbsp chopped fresh coriander (cilantro)

Boil the rice in the water with 15 ml/1 tbsp of oil and salt over a medium heat for 5 minutes until the rice is three-quarters cooked. Drain and mix in the peas. Purée together the garlic, ginger, cardamom, chillies, cloves, cinnamon, turmeric, poppy seeds, onions and mint. Soak the saffron strands in the hot milk for 15 minutes. Heat the remaining oil and fry the almonds, and raisins until lightly browned. Remove from the pan and drain. Add the purée to the pan and fry for 5 minutes, stirring occasionally. Stir in all the vegetables except the peas, 120 ml/4 fl oz/½ cup of water and salt and mix thoroughly. Cover and simmer gently for 5 minutes until the vegetables are half-cooked.

Preheat the oven to 200°C/400°F/gas mark 6. Turn the vegetables into a lightly greased casserole dish and garnish with the coriander. Spread the peas and rice in an even layer over the top and garnish with the almonds and raisins. Cover with foil and the lid. Reduce the oven temperature to 150°C/300°F/gas mark 2 and cook for 7-10 minutes. Serve hot.

Vegetable Pulao with Nuts

Serves 4-6

90 ml/6 tbsp ghee ● 5 ml/1 tsp cumin seeds ● 1 onion, thinly sliced

5 cloves ● 5 black peppercorns ● 2 bay leaves

2.5 cm/1 in cinnamon stick ● 1 black cardamom pod

225 g/8 oz/1 cup patna or basmati rice ● 5 ml/1 tsp garam masala

1.5 ml/¼ tsp ground mace ● 1.5 ml/¼ tsp grated nutmeg ● salt

250 g/9 oz peas ● 150 g/5 oz carrots, grated in long strips

75 g/3 oz/½ cup raisins ● 50 g/2 oz/½ cup cashew nuts, halved

600 ml/1 pt/2½ cups water

Garnish: 250 g/9 oz potatoes, cut into chips ● oil for deep-frying

Heat the ghee in a heavy-based pan and fry the cumin seeds until lightly browned. Add the onion, cloves, peppercorns, bay leaves, cinnamon and cardamom and fry until golden brown. Stir in the drained rice and fry for 2 minutes. Stir in the garam masala, mace, nutmeg and salt. Stir in the peas, carrots, raisins, nuts and water and bring to the boil. Reduce the heat to low, cover and cook for 15 minutes. Tip the pan to see if any water is left but do not stir; dry off any excess water on a high heat.

Meanwhile, heat the oil and fry the chips until crispy and golden. Drain. Turn off the heat under the pulao and stand for 5 minutes before garnishing with the chips and serving hot with aubergine and kofta.

Kedgeree

Serves 6

60 ml/4 tbsp ghee ● 2 cinnamon sticks ● 4 cardamom pods

5 ml/1 tsp ground turmeric ● 2 onions, sliced

450 g/1 lb/2 cups long-grain rice, soaked

4 cloves garlic, chopped ● 1 cm/½ in ginger root, chopped

2.5 ml/½ tsp garam masala ● 2.5 ml/½ tsp chilli powder

25 g/1 oz/¼ cup flaked almonds ● 450 g/1 lb white fish fillets, cubed

1 tomato, skinned and chopped ● juice of 1 lemon

25 g/1 oz/3 tbsp raisins ● salt ● 2 hard-boiled (hard-cooked) eggs, sliced

Heat 30 ml/2 tbsp of ghee and fry the cinnamon, cardamom, turmeric and 1 onion for 1 minute. Add the rice and fry until golden brown. Add water to come 2.5 cm/1 in above the level of the rice, bring to the boil then simmer gently for about 8 minutes.

Meanwhile, heat the remaining ghee and fry the remaining onion with the garlic, ginger, garam masala, chilli powder and almonds. Add the fish and tomato and sprinkle over the lemon juice. Simmer until the fish is tender. Add the fish to the rice and stir in the raisins and salt. Leave over a low heat until the rice is completely cooked. Serve garnished with hard-boiled egg.

Breads and Papadums

Wheat breads play an important part in a northern Indian meal menu. There are three basic types: dry breads such as chapati, roti and nan; shallow-fried breads such as paratha; and deep-fried bread such as puri. All of these breads can be served plain or stuffed. South India's famous breads are dosa and idli and they are made with lentils and rice.

Papadums are available ready-made and are easy to bake, fry or microwave ready to go with your Indian meal. Although not easy, however, it is possible to make them even if you cannot dry them out in the hot sun.

Nan   Makes 8

30 ml/2 tbsp fresh yeast or 5 g/¼ oz/1 sachet dried yeast

120 ml/4 fl oz/½ cup warm milk ● 30 ml/2 tbsp sugar

120 ml/4 fl oz/½ cup natural (plain) yoghurt ● 1 large egg, lightly beaten

45 ml/3 tbsp oil plus extra for brushing ● salt

450 g/1 lb/4 cups plain (all-purpose) flour plus extra for brushing

45 ml/3 tbsp warm water (optional) ● 15 ml/1 tbsp black onion seeds

Dissolve the yeast in 45 ml/3 tbsp of the warm milk. Stir in 5 ml/1 tsp of sugar and leave to rest in a warm place for 10 minutes until frothy. Lightly beat the yoghurt and add the remaining sugar and milk, the egg, 45 ml/3 tbsp of oil and salt to taste. Stir in the yeast mixture and flour and mix to a dough. Knead for 10-15 minutes until smooth, using the extra water if necessary and dusting with flour to prevent sticking. Cover the dough with a damp cloth and set aside for 4 hours until doubled in size.

Punch down the dough and knead it for 2 minutes until smooth. Divide it into 8 equal balls and roll out to 20 cm/8 in circles. Brush with a little oil and sprinkle with onion seeds. Place 2 breads on greased baking sheets and bake in a preheated oven at 240°C/475°C/gas mark 9 for 3 minutes until the bread has puffed and turned golden brown. Repeat with the remaining breads.

Kheema Nan
Makes 12

1 quantity nan dough (page 297) ● 30 ml/2 tbsp oil

1 small onion, finely chopped ● 250 g/9 oz minced lamb

5 ml/1 tsp ground coriander (cilantro) ● 5 ml/1 tsp ground roasted cumin

2.5 ml/½ tsp garam masala ● 2.5 ml/½ tsp ground red chilli

salt ● 100 ml/3½ fl oz/6½ tbsp water

30 ml/2 tbsp chopped fresh coriander (cilantro)

1 small green chilli, chopped ● 2.5 ml/½ tsp garam masala

Prepare the dough as for ordinary nan (page 297).

Heat the oil and fry the onion until golden brown. Stir in the meat, ground spices, salt and water, bring to the boil, cover and simmer gently for 15 minutes until the meat is tender. Remove the lid and dry off any remaining liquid over a high heat. Leave to cool. Mix in the coriander, chilli and garam masala.

Punch down the dough and knead it for 2 minutes until smooth. Divide it into 12 equal balls and roll out to 20 cm/8 in circles. Divide the filling mixture into 12 portions and place one on each round of dough. Seal the edges together over the filling. Place 2 breads on greased baking sheets and bake in a preheated oven at 240°C/ 475°C/gas 9 for 3 minutes until the bread has puffed and turned golden brown. Repeat with the remaining breads.

Khameera Nan
Makes 8

450 g/1 lb/4 cups plain (all-purpose) flour ● pinch of salt

5 ml/1 tsp aniseeds ● 45 ml/3 tbsp butter or margarine

1 egg, beaten ● 150 ml/¼ pt/⅔ cup warm milk

2.5 ml/½ tsp dried yeast ● ghee for deep-frying

Mix together the flour, salt and aniseeds. Rub in the butter or margarine until the mixture is crumbly then gradually add the egg and milk. Add the yeast and knead thoroughly. Cover with a damp cloth and leave in a warm place until doubled in size.

Divide the dough into 8 equal portions and roll out to 2 cm/¾ in thick. Cover and leave to rise again until doubled in size. Deep-fry in hot ghee until brown on both sides. Drain on kitchen paper and cover with silver foil before serving.

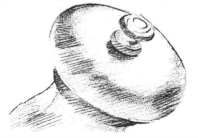

Dosa
Makes 12

150 g/5 oz/⅔ cup long-grain rice, soaked overnight

300 ml/½ pt/1 cup water ● 50 g/2 oz/⅓ cup split black beans, soaked overnight

salt ● 150 ml/¼ pt/⅔ cup water

Filling: 75 ml/5 tbsp oil ● 5 ml/1 tsp mustard seeds

5 ml/1 tsp cumin seeds ● 900 g/2 lb cooked potatoes, diced

5 ml/1 tsp garam masala ● 5 ml/1 tsp roasted cumin ● 2.5 ml/½ tsp ground ginger

2.5 ml/½ tsp ground red chilli ● 2.5 ml/½ tsp ground turmeric ● salt

400 g/14 oz canned tomatoes ● 200 ml/7 fl oz/scant 1 cup water

60 ml/4 tbsp lemon juice ● 60 ml/4 tbsp chopped fresh coriander (cilantro)

1 small green chilli, chopped ● oil for frying

Drain the rice then blend it with half the water in a blender or food processor until smooth. Drain the dal and blend it with the remaining water until smooth. Mix together the rice and dal and whisk for 5 minutes. Cover and leave in a warm place to rise for 24 hours.

Heat the oil and fry the mustard seeds over a medium heat until they start crackling. Add the cumin seeds and fry for a few seconds. Add the potato pieces and fry for 10 minutes until light brown. Stir in the ground spices and salt. Stir in the tomatoes and cook until all the liquid has been absorbed. Stir in the water, bring to the boil then simmer gently for 3 minutes. Stir in the lemon juice, coriander and pepper.

Place a flat frying pan (skillet) over a medium-low heat. Whisk the rice mixture for 2 minutes then add a pinch of salt and the water to make a smooth, runny batter. Smear the pan with oil then pour in about 45 ml/3 tbsp of batter and spread it over the pan. Cook for 2 minutes until the edges begin to lift then pour in 10 ml/2 tsp of oil around the edges. Turn over the dosa and spoon in another 10 ml/2 tsp of oil. Cook until golden brown. Cook the remaining dosa in the same way.

Spread the filling over half of each dosa, fold into a semi-circle and serve hot with chutney.

Idli
Makes 12

150 g/5 oz/⅔ cup long-grain rice, soaked overnight

75 g/3 oz/½ cup split black beans, soaked overnight

250 ml/8 fl oz/1 cup water ● large pinch of salt

Mix together the drained rice, dal and water in a blender or food processor and blend to a smooth, thick paste. Place in a bowl and whisk for 5 minutes. Cover and keep in a warm place for 24 hours.

Bring a large pan of water to the boil and grease 12 idli containers. Pour 30 ml/2 tbsp of mixture into each container and place them in the pan. Cover and steam for 30 minutes until tender. Serve hot with vegetable korma.

Roghni Nan
Serves 4-6

10 ml/2 tsp dried yeast ● 10 ml/2 tsp sugar ● 30 ml/2 tbsp lukewarm water

500 g/18 oz/4½ cups plain (all-purpose) flour ● 75 g/3 oz/⅓ cup margarine or ghee

1.5 ml/¼ tsp bicarbonate of soda (baking soda) ● large pinch of salt

120 ml/4 fl oz/½ cup lukewarm milk ● 30 ml/2 tbsp natural (plain) yoghurt

15 ml/1 tbsp milk ● 15 ml/1 tbsp sesame seeds ● 15 ml/1 tbsp onion seeds

Mix the yeast, sugar and water in a small bowl, cover and leave in a warm place for 30 minutes until frothy.

Place the flour in a bowl and rub in the margarine or ghee and the bicarbonate of soda. Mix in the salt, milk, yoghurt and yeast mixture and knead for 5-10 minutes until springy and satiny. Cover and leave in a warm place for 3-4 hours or until doubled in size.

Roll half the dough into a 15 cm/9 in strip then divide it into 6 equal portions. Repeat with the other half. Flatten each portion with the palm into an oval shape about 5 mm/¼ in thick and arrange 4 or 5 nan on a greased baking sheet. Brush the tops with milk and sprinkle with sesame and onion seeds. Repeat with the remaining nan. Bake in a preheated oven at 240°C/475°F/gas mark 9 for 7-9 minutes until golden brown, repositioning the sheets during cooking if necessary.

Paratha
Makes 12

225 g/8 oz/2 cups wholewheat flour plus extra for dusting

100 g/4 oz/1 cup plain (all-purpose) flour ● 5 ml/1 tsp cardamom seeds ● salt

250 ml/8 fl oz/1 cup warm water, milk or buttermilk ● 120 ml/4 fl oz/½ cup oil

Mix the flours, cardamom seeds and salt. Work in the water, milk or buttermilk and 15 ml/1 tbsp of oil to make a dough. Knead for 10 minutes. Cover with a damp cloth and leave to rest for 20 minutes.

Divide the dough into 12 equal balls and roll out to 15 cm/6 in rounds. Heat a frying pan (skillet) over a medium heat. Brush each paratha with a little oil, fold in half then brush with oil and fold again to make a triangle. Dust with flour and flatten with a rolling pin to a 15 cm/6 in triangle. Pour a little oil into the pan and fry a paratha for about 1 minute until it starts to puff up. Turn over, brush with oil and cook for a further 1 minute. Remove from the pan and keep warm while you fry the remaining paratha.

Garlic Paratha

Makes 8

225 g/8 oz/2 cups wholewheat flour plus extra for dusting

5 cloves garlic, crushed ● 5 ml/1 tsp cardamom seeds

salt ● 120 ml/4 fl oz/½ cup oil ● 250 ml/8 fl oz/1 cup warm water or milk

Mix the flours, garlic, cardamom and salt. Add 15 ml/1 tbsp of oil and the water or milk to make a dough. Knead for 10 minutes until smooth. Cover with a damp cloth and leave to rest for 20 minutes.

Divide the dough into 8 equal portions and roll out to a 18 cm/7 in circle. Heat a frying pan (skillet) over a medium heat and brush with a little oil. Gently place the bread in the pan and fry for 2-3 minutes until golden brown and crisp. Turn over and brush with a little more oil and fry for a further 2-3 minutes. Remove and keep warm while you fry all the paratha.

Fenugreek Paratha

Makes 12

175 g/6 oz fresh fenugreek leaves, finely shredded ● salt

large pinch of chilli powder ● 5 ml/1 tsp mango powder

350 g/12 oz/3 cups wholewheat flour ● 250 ml/8 fl oz/1 cup water ● ghee

Sprinkle the fenugreek leaves with salt, chilli and mango powders and set aside. Mix the flour with just enough water to make a pliant dough then divide it into 12 small balls. Flatten each one and spread with fenugreek. Wrap it up carefully and then flatten again. Roll out each paratha into a thin round. Heat the ghee in a frying pan (skillet) and fry the paratha until golden brown and crisp on both sides.

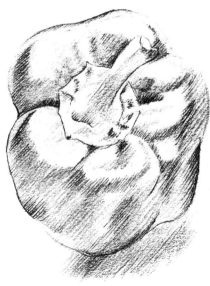

Mooli Paratha
Makes 9

275 g/10 oz/2½ cups brown chapati flour ● 15 ml/1 tbsp oil ● salt

150 ml/¼ pt/⅔ cup lukewarm water

450 g/1 lb large white radish, scraped and grated

30 ml/2 tbsp chopped fresh coriander (cilantro)

5 ml/1 tsp garam masala ● 2.5 ml/½ tsp ground red chilli

1 green chilli, chopped ● oil for frying

Place **250 g/9 oz/1¼ cups of flour in a bowl** with the oil and a large pinch of salt. Blend in the water and knead for 5 minutes until springy and satiny. Cover and leave for 30 minutes.

Mix together the remaining ingredients except the oil and season with salt. Heat a flat frying pan (skillet) over a medium heat. Divide the dough into 18 equal portions. Roll them in the palm of your hands, dust with the remaining flour and roll into 5 cm/ 2 in rounds. Squeeze any excess water from the filling. Place a round on a floured board, spoon some filling into the centre, place a second round on top and seal the edges. Sprinkle with flour and roll out thinly. Immediately place in the hot frying pan (skillet) and cook both sides until lightly browned. Pour in 10 ml/2 tsp of oil and fry the first side until golden brown. Add a little more oil and fry the second side. Repeat with the remaining paratha.

Onion Paratha
Makes 12

550 g/1¼ lb/5 cups chapati flour ● 1 medium onion, finely chopped

1 small green chilli, finely chopped

30 ml/2 tbsp chopped fresh coriander (cilantro)

15 ml/1 tbsp oil ● 5 ml/1 tsp garam masala

5 ml/1 tsp oregano seeds ● 2.5 ml/½ tsp ground red chilli

salt ● 250 ml/8 fl oz/1 cup lukewarm water

oil for frying ● butter or ghee

Place **500 g/18 oz/4½ cups of flour in a large bowl** and add the onion, chilli, coriander, oil and spices. Gradually blend in the water to make a soft dough. Knead for 5 minutes until the dough is springy and satiny. Cover and leave for 30 minutes.

Heat a frying pan (skillet) over a medium heat. Divide the dough into 12 equal portions and roll them into balls, dust with flour and flatten into circles. Smear half of the circles with butter or ghee and fold in half. Smear the half again and fold again into a triangle. Sprinkle with flour and roll out to 2.5 mm/⅛ in thick, keeping the triangular shape. Place the paratha on the hot frying pan (skillet) and cook both sides dry like a chapati. Then pour 10 ml/2 tsp of oil over it and fry the first side until lightly browned. Make 6 or 7 slits on the paratha and pour on some more oil. Fry the other side until light golden. Serve hot with pickle, butter and natural (plain) yoghurt.

Paratha Stuffed with Cauliflower

Makes 6

450 g/1 lb cauliflower, finely chopped ● 2 onions, finely chopped

2 green chillies, finely chopped ● 15 ml/1 tbsp pomegranate seeds, crushed

1 cm/½ in ginger root, grated ● 15 ml/1 tbsp chopped fresh coriander (cilantro)

2.5 ml/½ tsp garam masala ● 450 g/1 lb/4 cups wholewheat flour

30 ml/2 tbsp ghee ● pinch of salt ● 300 ml/½ pt/1¼ cups water

Soak the cauliflower in salted water for 30 minutes. Strain and squeeze out any liquid. Mix the cauliflower with the onions, chillies, pomegranate seeds, ginger, coriander and garam masala. Mix the flour, ghee, salt and enough water to make a stiff dough. Knead well, cover with a damp cloth and leave to stand for 10 minutes.

Divide the dough into 6 equal portions and roll out each one into a thick round. Spread with a little ghee. Spoon the filling into the centre of each one and fold over. Roll into balls, then roll out as thinly as possible. Brush with a little ghee and fry on both sides until lightly browned. Serve hot.

Paratha Stuffed with Potato

Makes 8

4 medium potatoes, boiled, peeled and mashed

30 ml/2 tbsp chopped fresh coriander (cilantro)

2.5 ml/½ tsp basic garam masala ● 1.5 ml/¼ tsp ground red chilli

juice of ½ lemon ● salt

225 g/8 oz/2 cups wholewheat flour plus extra for dusting

salt ● 175 ml/6 fl oz/¾ cup warm water or milk ● 45 ml/3 tbsp oil

Mix together the potatoes, coriander, garam masala, chilli, lemon juice and salt and divide into 8 equal portions.

Mix together the flour and salt then work in the water to make a firm dough. Knead for 10 minutes until smooth. Cover with a damp cloth and leave to stand for 20 minutes.

Divide the dough into 8 equal balls and make holes in the centre. Fill with stuffing then cover the filling evenly

with dough. Gently flatten each ball and roll out to 15 cm/6 in circles. Heat a frying pan (skillet) over a medium heat and brush with a little oil. Gently place 1 bread on the hot pan and cook for 1 minute until golden brown. Turn over, brush with a little more oil and cook for a further 1 minute until browned and crisp. Keep warm while you fry the remaining paratha.

Spiced Potato Paratha
Makes 11

250 g/9 oz/2¼ cups chapati flour plus extra for dusting

15 ml/1 tbsp oil ● large pinch of salt ● 150 ml/¼ pt/⅔ cup warm water

450 g/1 lb potatoes, boiled, peeled and mashed

30 ml/2 tbsp chopped fresh coriander (cilantro)

15 ml/1 tbsp lemon juice ● 5 ml/1 tsp dried pomegranate seeds

2.5 ml/½ tsp garam masala ● 2.5 ml/½ tsp ground red chilli

2.5 ml/½ tsp ajwain ● 1 cm/½ in ginger root, finely chopped

1 small onion, finely chopped ● 1 small green chilli, finely chopped

salt ● oil for frying

Place the flour in a bowl and rub in the oil. Mix in the salt and add enough water to make a soft dough. Knead for 5 minutes until the dough is soft and smooth. Cover with a damp cloth and leave to rest for 30 minutes.

Mix together all the remaining ingredients and divide into 11 equal portions. Divide the dough into 11 equal balls, dust with flour and flatten into a small round. Place portions of the filling on the dough and bring the edges together. Flatten, dust with flour and roll out thinly. Heat a frying pan (skillet) and dry-fry the paratha on both sides. Brush the first side with oil, turn over and fry until light golden brown. Make 6 small slits on the paratha, brush with oil, turn again and fry until light golden. Serve hot.

Paratha Stuffed with Spinach
Makes 12

450 g/1 lb spinach, chopped ● 2 green chillies, finely chopped

225 g/8 oz/2 cups wholewheat flour plus extra for dusting

250 ml/8 fl oz/1 cup warm milk or water ● 175 ml/6 fl oz/¾ cup oil ● salt

Cook the spinach in a little water until soft then drain and mash with a fork. Mix in the chillies.

Mix together the flour, milk or water, 15 ml/1 tbsp of oil and the salt to a firm dough. Knead for 8 minutes until smooth then divide into 12 equal balls and roll out to 12 cm/5 in circles. Spread the spinach paste over the bread, fold in half, then in half again to make a triangle. Brush lightly with oil and gently roll out to a 15 cm/6 in triangle, dusting with flour to prevent sticking. Heat a frying pan (skillet) over a medium heat and brush with a little oil. Gently place a paratha in the pan and fry for 2 minutes. Turn over and brush with oil then fry for another 1 minute until golden brown and crisp on both sides. Keep warm while you fry the remaining paratha.

Paratha Stuffed with Mozzarella and Chicken   Makes 8

225 g/8 oz/2 cups wholewheat flour plus extra for dusting

salt ● 250 ml/8 fl oz/1 cup warm water or milk

120 ml/4 fl oz/½ cup oil ● 1 large chicken breast, boned and cut into pieces

250 ml/8 fl oz/1 cup water ● 45 ml/3 tbsp oil

1 small onion, finely chopped ● 3 cloves garlic, grated

5 mm/¼ in ginger root, finely chopped ● 1 green chilli, finely chopped

2.5 ml/½ tsp ground coriander (cilantro) ● 1.5 ml/¼ tsp ground cumin

50 g/2 oz Mozzarella cheese, grated

Mix the flour, salt, water and 15 ml/ 1 tbsp oil to make a dough. Knead for 10 minutes until smooth. Cover with a damp cloth and leave to rest for 20 minutes.

Cook the chicken in the water with a pinch of salt for about 15 minutes until cooked. Finely chop the chicken and set aside.

Heat the oil and fry the onion, garlic, ginger and chilli over a medium heat until the onion is browned. Stir in the coriander and cumin and fry for 1 minute. Add the chicken and fry for 2-3 minutes, stirring and mixing thoroughly. Remove from the heat and set aside.

Knead the dough for 1 minute, divide it into 8 balls and roll out to 15 cm/6 in circles. Spread the chicken mixture over the circles and sprinkle with Mozzarella. Fold the breads in half, brush with oil and fold in half again to make a triangle. Dust with flour and gently roll out to make an 18 cm/7 in triangle. Heat a frying pan (skillet) over a medium heat and brush with a little oil. When the oil is hot, gently place 1 bread in the pan and fry for 2-3 minutes. Turn and brush with a little oil. Fry for 2-3 minutes until golden brown and crisp on both sides. Remove from the pan and keep warm while you fry the remaining paratha.

Chapatis   Makes 12

350 g/12 oz/3 cups wholewheat flour plus more for dusting ● salt

250 ml/8 fl oz/1 cup warm milk, water or buttermilk ● 15 ml/1 tbsp oil

Mix together the flour, salt and milk, water or buttermilk to form a dough. Place the dough on a floured surface and knead in the oil. Knead for 10 minutes until smooth then cover with a damp cloth and leave to stand at room temperature for 15-20 minutes.

Divide the dough into 12 balls. Coat each one with flour and flatten to form a round. Roll out to about 15 cm/6 in

in diameter. Heat an iron griddle or frying pan (skillet) over a high heat then reduce the heat to medium. Place 1 chapati in the hot pan and fry for about 30 seconds until the top begins to puff. Turn over the chapati and fry for a further 30-40 seconds until the surface starts to puff. Remove from the pan and fry the remaining chapatis in the same way. Serve immediately.

Maize Chapatis

Makes 10

150 g/5 oz/1¼ cups maize flour ● 150 l/¼ pt/⅔ cups lukewarm water ● ghee

Place the flour in a bowl and blend in the water to a smooth dough. Cover and leave for 30 minutes.

Divide the dough into 10 equal portions, roll each one into a ball and flatten with your fingers to about 5 cm/ 2 in diameter. Heat a flat frying pan (skillet) over a medium heat and smear with ghee. Place the chapati in the pan and fry until light golden brown on both sides. Smear with ghee before serving.

Roti

Makes 8

450 g/1 lb/4 cups wholewheat flour ● 300 ml/½ pt/1¼ cups water ● ghee

Save a little flour for dredging. Gradually mix the water into the remaining flour until you have a stiff dough. Knead well until smooth, cover with a damp cloth and leave to stand for 20 minutes.

Knead the dough again then divide it into 8 portions and roll them into thick rounds. Take 1 at a time, spread a little ghee on the surface, roll it into a ball then roll it out again, keeping the remaining dough covered while working. Take 1 round, brush both sides with ghee then fry lightly on a frying pan (skillet) then transfer to a hot grill to finish cooking. Serve straight from the grill, brushed with a little more ghee.

Egg Roti

Makes 8

450 g/1 lb/4 cups wholewheat flour ● 300 ml/½ pt/1¼ cups water

ghee ● 16 eggs ● salt and pepper ● chilli powder (optional)

Save a little flour for dredging. Gradually mix the water into the remaining flour until you have a stiff dough. Knead well until smooth, cover with a damp cloth and leave to stand for 20 minutes.

Knead the dough again then divide it into 8 portions and roll them into thick rounds. Take 1 at a time, spread a little ghee on the surface, roll it into a ball then roll it out again, keeping the remaining dough covered while working.

Take 1 round, brush both sides with ghee then fry lightly in a frying pan (skillet) on both sides. Break 2 eggs on to one side and let them spread out over the roti. Sprinkle with salt, pepper and chilli powder, if using. Add a little more ghee to the edges of the roti then turn it over when the eggs have set slightly. Fry until golden brown on both sides.

Gram Flour Roti
Makes 8

450 g/1 lb/4 cups gram flour ● 1 small onion, finely chopped

2 green chillies, thinly sliced ● 2.5 ml/½ tsp pomegranate seeds

15 ml/1 tbsp ghee ● 450 ml/¾ pt/2 cups warm water ● ghee for frying

Mix the flour, onion, chillies, pomegranate seeds and ghee then gradually work in enough water to make a stiff dough. Knead well until smooth, then divide into 8 portions and roll them into thick rounds. Brush both sides with ghee then fry until lightly browned on both sides.

Onion Roti
Makes 8

450 g/1 lb/4 cups wholewheat flour ● 3 onions, finely chopped

6 green chillies, finely chopped ● 15 ml/1 tbsp chopped fresh coriander (cilantro)

1 sprig fresh curry leaves, finely chopped

pinch of bicarbonate of soda (baking soda)

salt ● 600 ml/1 pt/2½ cups water ● ghee

Mix the flour, onions, chillis, coriander, curry leaves, bicarbonate of soda and salt to taste. Gradually blend in enough water to make a batter just thick enough to pour. Lightly grease a frying pan (skillet) and add just enough batter to cover it thinly, spreading the batter with the back of a spoon, if necessary. Pour a little ghee around the edge to prevent sticking and fry until lightly browned on the underside. Flip over and brown the other side. Cook the remaining roti in the same way.

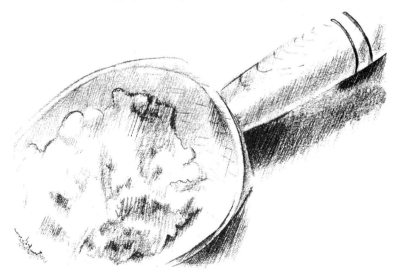

Roti Stuffed with Potato · Makes 8

15 ml/1 tbsp ghee ● 2 onions, finely chopped

450 g/1 lb potatoes, boiled, peeled and chopped

4 green chillies, finely chopped

30 ml/2 tbsp chopped fresh coriander (cilantro)

1 cm/½ in ginger root, grated

5 ml/1 tsp coriander (cilantro) seeds, roasted and ground

2.5 ml/½ tsp black pepper ● 5 ml/1 tsp pomegranate seeds

900 g/2 lb/8 cups wholewheat flour ● pinch of salt ● 750 ml/1¼ pts/3 cups water

Heat the ghee and fry the onions until soft. Stir in the potatoes, chillies, coriander, ginger, coriander seeds, pepper and pomegranate seeds. Remove from the heat and mash coarsely with a fork.

Mix the flour and salt and gradually work in enough water to make a stiff dough. Knead well until smooth, then divide into 8 portions and roll each one into a thick round. Spoon the filling on to the centre of each round, fold them over and roll into a ball. Roll out again as thinly as possible. Heat a frying pan (skillet) and fry the roti until browned on both sides.

Roti Stuffed with Carrots · Makes 8

225 g/8 oz/2 cups wholewheat flour plus more for dusting ● salt

250 ml/8 fl oz/1 cup warm water or milk ● 175 ml/6 fl oz/¾ cup oil

2.5 ml/½ tsp black mustard seeds ● 1 small onion, finely chopped

2 cloves garlic, crushed ● 5 mm/¼ in ginger root, finely chopped

1 green chilli, finely chopped ● 2 large carrots, finely grated

Mix the flour, salt and water or milk with 15 ml/1 tbsp of the oil to make a firm dough. Knead for 10 minutes until smooth. Cover with a damp cloth and leave to stand for 20 minutes.

Heat 45 ml/3 tbsp of oil in a frying pan (skillet) and fry the mustard seeds over a medium heat until they start crackling. Add the onion, garlic, ginger and chilli and fry until the onion is soft and browned. Add the carrots and season with salt. Fry for 5 minutes until the liquid has evaporated.

Knead the dough again, divide it into 8 equal portions and roll out each one into a 13 cm/5 in circle. Spread spoonfuls of the carrot mixture over the bread, fold the dough in half and brush with oil. Fold the dough again to make a triangle and dust with flour. Roll out with a rolling pin to make an 18 cm/7 in triangle, dusting with flour to prevent sticking.

Heat a frying pan (skillet) over a medium heat and brush with oil. Fry the roti one at a time for about 2 minutes until brown and crisp. Turn the roti over, brush with oil and fry for 1 minute until crisp. Keep warm while you fry the remaining roti.

Roti Stuffed with Meat and Mint   Makes 8

30 ml/2 tbsp oil ● 1 small onion, finely chopped

2 cloves garlic, finely chopped ● 5 mm/¼ in ginger root, finely chopped

2.5 ml/½ tsp garam masala

225 g/8 oz/½ lb lean minced (ground) beef, lamb or turkey ● salt

15 ml/1 tbsp chopped fresh mint

100 g/4 oz/1 cup plain (all-purpose) flour plus more for dusting

100 g/4 oz/1 cup wholewheat flour ● 250 ml/8 fl oz/1 cup warm water or milk

120 ml/4 fl oz/½ cup oil ● salt

Heat the oil and fry the onion, garlic and ginger over a medium heat until lightly browned. Add the garam masala and fry for 40 seconds. Add the meat, salt and mint and fry for 4-5 minutes until the meat is evenly browned. Reduce the heat, cover and cook for 5-7 minutes until the meat is cooked. Remove from the heat.

Mix together the flours, water, 15 ml/1 tbsp of oil and a pinch of salt to make a firm dough. Knead for 10 minutes then cover with a damp cloth and leave to rest for 20 minutes.

Knead the dough again, divide it into 8 equal portions and roll out each one into a 13 cm/5 in circle. Spread spoonfuls of the filling mixture over the bread, fold the dough in half and brush with oil. Fold the dough again to make a triangle and dust with flour. Roll out with a rolling pin to make an 18 cm/7 in triangle, dusting with flour to prevent sticking.

Heat a frying pan (skillet) over a medium heat and brush with oil. Fry the roti one at a time for about 3 minutes until brown and crisp. Turn the roti over, brush with oil and fry for 2 minutes until crisp. Keep warm while you fry the remaining roti.

Puri   Makes 8

225 g/8 oz/2 cups plain (all-purpose) flour ● pinch of salt

175 ml/6 fl oz/¾ cup water ● ghee for deep-frying

Reserve a little flour for dredging. Mix the rest with the salt and gradually add enough water to make a stiff dough. Divide the dough into 8 equal balls and roll them into thin circles.

Heat the ghee in a pan and deep-fry the puris 2 at a time. Drain on kitchen paper and serve hot or store in an air-tight container.

Wholewheat Puri   Makes 12

225 g/8 oz/2 cups wholewheat flour plus extra for dredging

100 g/4 oz/1 cup plain (all-purpose) flour ● salt

750 ml/1¼ pts/3 cups oil ● 250 ml/8 fl oz/1 cup warm water, milk or buttermilk

Mix the flours, salt, 30 ml/2 tbsp of the oil and water, milk or buttermilk to make a firm dough. Knead for 10 minutes until smooth. Cover with a damp cloth and leave to rest for 20 minutes.

Divide the dough into 12 equal balls and coat them with flour. Roll out to 15 cm/6 in circles.

Heat the remaining oil in a wok over a high heat. When the oil is hot, gently drop in 1 puri. The puris will sink to the bottom. Hold a spatula over the bread for a few seconds to help it cook then gently press the bread for a few seconds to help it puff up. Once it starts to puff, cook for about 15 seconds then turn it over and cook for a further 10-15 seconds. Drain on kitchen paper while you cook the remaining puris.

Leavened Puri
Makes 12

350 g/12 oz/3 cups plain (all-purpose) flour ● pinch of salt

30 ml/2 tbsp ghee plus extra for deep-frying

2.5 ml/½ tsp bicarbonate of soda (baking soda)

90 ml/6 tbsp natural (plain) yoghurt ● warm water

Rub together the flour, salt and ghee. Stir in the baking powder and yoghurt and just enough water to make a pliable dough. Knead until the dough is springy and does not stick to the fingers. Cover with a damp cloth and leave overnight in a warm place to rise.

Knead the dough again, divide into 12 equal portions and form into thick rounds. Heat the ghee and deep-fry the puris 2 at a time until golden. Drain on kitchen paper then serve hot.

Savoury Puri
Makes 8

225 g/8 oz/2 cups plain (all-purpose) flour ● pinch of salt

5 ml/1 tsp cumin seeds ● 5 ml/1 tsp black pepper ● 1 clove garlic

15 ml/1 tbsp chopped fresh coriander (cilantro)

5 green chillies ● 15 ml/1 tbsp ghee plus extra for deep-frying

150 ml/¼ pt/⅔ cup warm water

Mix the flour, salt, cumin seeds and pepper. Grind the garlic, coriander and chillies together and stir into the flour with the ghee. Mix in just enough water to make a firm dough. Divide the dough into 8 equal portions and roll out to thin circles. Heat the ghee and deep-fry the puris until golden brown.

Til Puri
Makes 16

450 g/1 lb/4 cups plain (all-purpose) flour ● 30 ml/2 tbsp sesame seeds

10 ml/2 tsp salt ● 10 ml/2 tsp sugar ● 10 ml/2 tsp celery seeds

10 ml/2 tsp caraway seeds ● 10 ml/2 tsp black pepper ● 10 ml/2 tbsp onion seeds

300 ml/½ pt/1¼ cups water ● ghee for deep-frying

Mix together all the dry ingredients. Add just enough warm water to make a firm dough, divide into 16 equal portions and roll out to thin circles. Heat the ghee and deep-fry the puris until golden brown on both sides.

Banana Puri
Makes 12

225 g/8 oz/2 cups plain (all-purpose) flour

100 g/4 oz/1 cups gram flour ● 5 ml/1 tbsp chilli powder

1.5 ml/¼ tsp ground turmeric ● 5 ml/1 tsp cumin seeds

pinch of salt ● 15 ml/1 tbsp ghee plus extra for deep-frying

3 ripe bananas ● 5 ml/1 tsp sugar

Mix the flours, chilli powder, turmeric, cumin and salt then knead in the ghee. Mash the bananas with the sugar, work into the flour mixture and knead until soft. Divide into 12 equal balls and roll then out into thin circles. Heat the ghee and deep-fry the puris until crisp and golden brown on both sides.

Puri Stuffed with Green Beans
Makes 8

50 g/2 oz skinless dried green beans ● 10 ml/2 tsp oil

5 ml/1 tsp cumin seeds ● pinch of garam masala● 2.5 ml/½ tsp salt

pinch of chilli powder ● 225 g/8 oz/2 cups plain (all-purpose) flour

5 ml/1 tsp ghee plus extra for deep-frying ● 150 ml/¼ pt/⅔ cup warm water

Soak the beans overnight. Drain off the water and grind the b̆eans. Heat the oil and fry the cumin seeds and garam masala for 2 minutes. Add the bean paste and stir in the salt and chilli powder. Cook for 5 minutes over a medium heat, stirring constantly, until the moisture has evaporated. Remove from the heat.

Mix the flour with the ghee and add enough water to make a pliable dough. Divide the dough into 8 equal balls and flatten them slightly. Place a portion of the filling on each one, roll into a ball then flatten again to 7.5 cm/3 in rounds. Heat the ghee and deep-fry two puris at a time until golden. Drain on kitchen paper and serve hot.

Potato Katchori
Makes 20

Dough: 250 g/9 oz/1¼ cups chapati flour ● 25 g/1 oz/2 tbsp margarine

30 ml/2 tbsp natural (plain) yoghurt ● 5 ml/1 tsp ajwain

large pinch of salt ● 100 ml/3½ fl oz/6½ tbsp warm water

Filling: 450 g/1 lb potatoes

30 ml/2 tbsp chopped fresh coriander (cilantro)

1 green chilli, finely chopped ● 5 ml/1 tsp ground roasted cumin

2.5 ml/½ tsp garam masala ● 1.5 ml/¼ tsp ground red chilli

salt ● oil for deep-frying

Put the flour into a bowl and mix in the margarine. Add the yoghurt, 2.5 ml/½ tsp of the ajwain, salt and water and mix to a soft dough. Knead for 5 minutes until springy and satiny. Cover with a damp cloth and leave to rest for 30 minutes.

Boil the potatoes in their skins then peel and mash them. Mix in the remaining ingredients except the oil and divide into 20 equal portions. Heat the oil over a medium heat.

Divide the dough into 20 equal balls then flatten them slightly. Lightly oil the work surface and roll the balls into 5 cm/2 in circles. Place a portion of filling on each one and shape the dough around it. Flatten again then roll out thinly. Heat the oil and gently slide a katchori into the oil, pressing it down with a slotted spoon until it swells slightly. Fry both sides until lightly browned.

Khasta Katchori
Makes 20

1 quantity Potato Katchori dough (this page)

100 g/4 oz/⅔ cup split black beans, soaked overnight

50 ml/2 fl oz/2½ tbsp water ● 15 ml/1 tbsp oil

large pinch of asafoetida ● 5 ml/1 tsp garam masala

5 ml/1 tsp ground roasted cumin ● 2.5 ml/½ tsp ground ginger

2.5 ml/½ tsp ground red chilli ● salt ● oil for deep-frying

Prepare the dough as for the potato katchori recipe (above) and divide into 20 equal portions. Drain the split beans then blend coarsely with the water. Heat the oil and fry the asafoetida for a few seconds. Add the split beans and fry for 6 minutes until lightly browned. Stir in the ground spices and cook over a low heat for 3 minutes. Cool then divide into 20 portions.

Roll a portion of dough into a ball on the palm of your hands. Flatten it,

place a few drops of oil on a board and roll it into a small circle. Place a portion of filling on the dough and seal the edges. Flatten it and roll it to a 5 cm/2 in circle. Repeat with the remaining katchori.

Heat the oil and carefully slip a katchori into the oil. Gently press it down with a slotted spoon and it should swell up like a balloon. Fry 3-4 katchori together until golden brown on both sides, turning twice.

Bhutoora
Makes 22

5 ml/1 tsp dried yeast ● 5 ml/1 tsp sugar ● 30 ml/2 tbsp warm water

25 g/1 oz/2 tbsp margarine ● 500 g/18 oz/4½ cups plain (all-purpose) flour

120 ml/4 fl oz/½ cup natural (plain) yoghurt ● salt

100 ml/3½ fl oz/6½ tbsp warm water ● oil for frying

Mix the yeast, sugar and water and leave in a warm place for 15 minutes until frothy. Rub the margarine into the flour. Stir in the yoghurt, salt, yeast mixture and water and knead for 10 minutes until the dough is springy and smooth. Cover with a damp cloth and leave to rise in a warm place for 3-4 hours until doubled in size.

Divide the dough into 22 equal balls. Either rub a little oil on to the palms of your hands and flatten the ball, turning it quickly from one palm to the other until it is about 1 mm thick, or roll out.

Heat the oil and slide the bhutoora gently into the oil, pressing down with a slotted spoon. It will rise like a balloon. Fry until both sides are lightly browned. Drain on kitchen paper and keep warm while you fry the remaining bhutoora.

Pudha
Makes 6

100 g/4 oz/1 cup gram flour ● 1 small onion, finely chopped

30 ml/2 tbsp chopped fresh coriander (cilantro)

5 ml/1 tsp garam masala ● 2.5 ml/½ tsp ground red chilli ● salt

200 ml/7 fl oz/scant 1 cup lukewarm water ● oil for frying

Place the flour, onion, coriander, spices and salt in a bowl then gradually blend in the flour to a smooth batter. Heat a frying pan (skillet) over a medium heat then smear the pan with 15 ml/1 tbsp oil. Spoon 45 ml/3 tbsp of batter into the pan and spread to 1 mm thick. Cook for 2-3 minutes until crispy golden brown then turn over the pudha and pour 10 ml/2 tsp of oil around the edges. Fry the second side until golden brown. Serve hot with chutney, tea or lassi.

Sago Papadums
Makes 25

900 ml/1½ pts/3¾ cups water ● 100 g/4 oz/1 cup sago ● 2.5 ml/½ tsp salt

Boil the water in a pan, stir in the sago and salt, lower the heat and simmer for 15 minutes, stirring constantly, until the mixture thickens. Drop tablespoonfuls of the mixture on to a greased plastic sheet and spread it into circles. Leave in a warm place to dry completely then store in an airtight container. Deep-fry as Potato Papadum (page 314).

Potato Papadums

Makes 14

250 g/9 oz potatoes ● 2.5 ml/½ tsp garam masala

1.5 ml/¼ tsp ground red chilli ● 1.5 ml/¼ tsp black pepper

salt ● 1 large plastic bag ● 1 small plastic bag ● oil for smearing and deep-frying

Cook the potatoes in their skins until tender then peel and mash them thoroughly. Stir in the spices and divide into 14 equal portions. Smear both the bags with oil and place the large bag on the work surface. Roll 1 portion of potato into a ball, place on the plastic, cover with the other bag and roll it into a 10 cm/4 in circle. Remove the small bag, smear it again with oil and continue to roll out all the papadums. Leave exposed to the air for 1 day to dry out.

Place the papadums on greased baking trays and place in the oven about 30 cm/12 in above the pilot light. Leave for 3 days to dry out, turning them over every day. When dried, store in an airtight container.

Just before serving, heat the oil in a deep frying pan (skillet) over a medium-low heat. Gently slip a papadum into the hot oil and fry for a few seconds until lightly browned on both sides. Serve hot or at room temperature. Do not fry in advance otherwise the papadums will go soft.

Spiced Lentil Papadums

Makes 8

25 g/1 oz split black beans, ground ● 15 black peppercorns, coarsely ground

1.5 ml/¼ tsp ground red chilli ● salt ● 100 ml/3½ fl oz/6½ tbsp water

Place all the ingredients in a pan and cook over a medium heat for 3 minutes until the water has been absorbed, stirring continuously. Leave to cool

slightly then shape into 8 equal portions. Roll, dry and fry as Potato Papadums (above), or grill (broil) for a few seconds. Serve immediately.

Rice Papadums

Makes 10

25 g/1 oz/2 tbsp long-grain rice, ground ● large pinch of salt

100 ml/3½ fl oz/6½ tbsp water ● 1 large plastic bag ● 1 small plastic bag

oil for smearing and deep-frying

Combine all the ingredients in a pan over a medium heat and cook for 1 minute until all the water has been

absorbed. Leave to cool slightly then shape into 10 equal portions. Roll, dry and fry as Potato Papadums (above).

Spiced Rice Papadums
Makes 20

225 g/8 oz/2 cups rice flour ● 600 ml/1 pt/2½ cups water

2.5 ml/½ tsp salt ● pinch of ground cumin

2.5 ml/½ tsp bicarbonate of soda (baking soda)

Put all the ingredients into a bowl and whisk thoroughly to a smooth batter. Transfer to a pan and bring to the boil over a medium heat. Lower the heat and continue cooking. Remove 15 ml/ 1 tbsp of the mixture and spread it over a greased metal plate then place the plate on top of the pan as a lid. The mixture will soon firm up into a disc. Remove the disc and place it on a greased plastic sheet to dry out. Continue to make the papadums in the same way. Store in an airtight container. Deep-fry as Potato Papadums (page 314).

Tapioca Papadums
Makes 22

50 g/2 oz tapioca ● large pinch of salt

500 ml/17 fl oz/2¼ cups water

red, yellow, green or blue food colour (optional)

oil for frying

Place the tapioca, salt, water and a few drops of food colour, if using, into a pan over a medium heat and stir continuously until all the water has been absorbed and the mixture leaves the edges of the pan. Remove from the heat.

Drop spoonfuls of the tapioca on to a greased baking sheet; they will spread thinly into 7.5 cm/3 in circles. If they do not, the tapioca is overcooked. Add an extra 100 ml/3½ fl oz/ 6½ tbsp of water and boil it again. Leave the papadums on the tray to dry for 1 day. Turn them over and leave to dry again.

Just before serving, heat the oil in a deep frying pan (skillet) over a medium heat. Gently slip a papadum into the hot oil and it will treble in size. Fry it for a few seconds until lightly browned on both sides. Serve hot or at room temperature.

Salads and Salad Dressings

Fresh and crisp and made with different varieties of vegetables, salads can be served with any course. Most vegetables for Indian salads are chopped raw and seasoning lightly, but some may be boiled or sautéed. Cucumber, tomato, carrot and green chillies are particular favourites, and sprouted whole green lentils make a nutritious, crunchy addition.

To sprout green lentils, wash and soak them in water for at least 6 hours, then drain, cover with a damp cloth and keep in a dry, warm place for a further 6-10 hours.

The basic salad dressing on page 324 can be adapted to suit individual taste. Store it in an airtight jar or bottle in the refrigerator.

Bean Salad   Serves 4-6

150 ml/¼ pt/⅔ cup wine vinegar ● 2.5 ml/½ tsp sugar

2.5 ml/½ tsp salt ● 2 onions, sliced into rings

100 g/4 oz/⅔ cup chick peas (garbanzos), soaked overnight

100 g/4 oz red kidney beans, soaked overnight

225 g/8 oz/½ lb French beans, chopped ● 1 green (bell) pepper, finely chopped

30 ml/2 tbsp Basic Salad Dressing (page 324) ● 2-3 lettuce leaves

Place the wine vinegar in a bowl and stir in the sugar and salt. Add the onion rings and leave to soak for 6-8 hours, by which time they should have turned a delicate pink.

Drain the chick peas and kidney beans, place in separate pans and cover with cold water. Bring to the boil and boil rapidly for 10 minutes then cover and simmer for about 1 hour until tender. Cook the French beans in boiling water for about 10 minutes until tender. Drain and refresh under cold water.

Drain all the ingredients and mix with the pepper. Pour over enough dressing to coat the beans and toss together well and chill for 2 hours. Just before serving, line a bowl with the lettuce and fill with the salad. Sprinkle with a little more dressing before serving.

Beansprout Salad
Serves 4

45 ml/3 tbsp walnut halves ● 6 radishes, sliced

15 ml/1 tbsp raisins ● ½ cucumber, sliced ● 100 g/4 oz beansprouts

juice of 2 lemons ● 15 ml/1 tbsp chopped fresh mint ● salt

Mix all the ingredients together and toss lightly.

Broccoli Salad with Mushrooms
Serves 6

1.2 1/2 pts/5 cups water ● 675 g/1½ lb broccoli florets

60 ml/4 tbsp oil ● 2.5 cm/1 in ginger root, thinly sliced

100 g/4 oz mushrooms ● pinch of chilli powder

10 ml/2 tsp mustard seeds, crushed

6 cloves garlic, crushed ● 30 ml/2 tbsp lemon juice

100 g/4 oz cherry tomatoes ● 30 ml/2 tbsp clear honey

Bring the water to the boil, add the broccoli and boil for 1 minute. Drain well. Heat the oil and fry the ginger and mushrooms for 3 minutes. Add the broccoli, chilli powder and mustard seeds and fry for 1 minute, stirring. Remove from the pan and leave to cool. Mix together the garlic, lemon juice, tomatoes and honey. Stir in the broccoli mixture and chill for 30 minutes before serving.

Nutty Chicken Salad
Serves 6

1 medium chicken ● 1 bay leaf ● 4 large boiled potatoes, cubed

juice of ½ lime ● 1 green (bell) pepper, cut into strips

1 green chilli, chopped ● 45 ml/3 tbsp finely shredded cabbage

300 ml/½ pt/1¼ cups mayonnaise ● salt and pepper

175 g/6 oz/1½ cups walnut halves ● 5-6 lettuce leaves

Place the chicken in a heavy-based pan and fill with water to come half way up the leg. Add the bay leaf, bring to the boil, cover and simmer for about 1½ hours until the chicken is tender. Drain and leave to cool. Remove the meat and shred or cube it. Put the potatoes into a bowl and toss in the lime juice. Stir in the chicken and all the remaining ingredients except the walnuts and lettuce. Just before serving, arrange the leaves on a serving place, stir the walnuts into the salad and pile on top of the lettuce.

Crunchy Cabbage Salad   Serves 4

1 medium cabbage, finely shredded • 60-90 ml/4-6 tbsp grated (shredded) coconut

juice of 1 lime • 30 ml/2 tbsp oil • 1 dried red chilli • 5 ml/1 tsp mustard seeds

Mix together the coconut and cabbage, stir in the lime juice and chill. Heat the oil and fry the chilli until dark in colour. Discard the chilli then add the mustard seeds to the oil, cover and fry for a few seconds until they start crackling. Add the oil to the cabbage and toss together well. Chill before serving.

Carrot and Grape Salad   Serves 6

3 large carrots, cut into strips • 225 g/8 oz seedless grapes

30 ml/2 tbsp oil • 5 ml/1 tsp mustard seeds, crushed • 15 ml/1 tbsp clear honey

15 ml/1 tbsp wine vinegar • 15 ml/1 tbsp lemon juice

5 ml/1 tsp paprika • pepper

Toss the carrots and grapes with the remaining ingredients and refrigerate for 30 minutes before serving.

Chick Pea and Spinach Salad   Serves 6

250 g/9 oz/1½ cups chick peas (garbanzos), soaked overnight in 900 ml/1½ pts/ 3 cups water

3 cloves garlic ᴐ pinch of ground turmeric • 2.5 ml/½ tsp chilli powder

5 ml/1 tsp ground ginger • pinch of black pepper

100 g/4 oz spinach, chopped • 30 ml/2 tbsp oil

10 ml/2 tsp mustard seeds, crushed • 75 ml/5 tbsp lemon juice

5 ml/1 tbsp clear honey • 5 ml/1 tsp garlic powder

Drain the chick peas, reserving the soaking water, and place them in a large pan. Make up the soaking water to 1.2 l/2 pts/5 cups then add it to the chick peas with the garlic, turmeric, half the chilli powder, half the ginger and the pepper. Bring to the boil then cover and simmer gently for about 2 hours until the chick peas are tender but not mushy. If necessary, remove the lid for the last few minutes of cooking to allow excess water to evaporate. Toss the spinach with the oil. Add the remaining chilli powder and ginger, the mustard seeds, lemon juice, honey and garlic powder, toss lightly and leave to marinate for at least 30 minutes. Fold together the chick peas and spinach, cover and chill thoroughly before serving.

Chick Pea and Green Tomato Salad
Serves 6

175 g/6 oz/1 cup chick peas (garbanzos), soaked overnight in 450 ml/¾ pt/ 2 cups water

2.5 ml/½ tsp ground cumin • pinch of asafoetida

2.5 ml/½ tsp garlic powder • 2.5 ml/½ tsp chilli powder

5 ml/1 tsp grated ginger root • 8-10 small green tomatoes, coarsely chopped

75 ml/5 tbsp wine vinegar • 45 ml/3 tbsp clear honey

Put the chick peas and soaking water, 175 ml/6 fl oz/¾ cup water, the cumin, asafoetida, garlic, chilli powder and ginger in a large pan and bring to the boil. Cover and simmer for about 2 hours until the chick peas are tender. Mix together the tomatoes, wine vinegar and honey and leave to marinate for 30 minutes. Drain the chick peas and spoon into a serving bowl. Drain the tomatoes and stir into the chick peas. Leave to cool and serve at room temperature or chill before serving.

Cauliflower Salad with Mushrooms
Serves 6

1.2 1/2 pts/5 cups water • 675 g/1½ lb cauliflower florets

60 ml/4 tbsp oil • 2.5 cm/1 in ginger root, thinly sliced

100 g/4 oz mushrooms • pinch of chilli powder

10 ml/2 tsp mustard seeds, crushed • 6 cloves garlic, crushed

30 ml/2 tbsp lemon juice • 100 g/4 oz cherry tomatoes

30 ml/2 tbsp clear honey

Bring the water to the boil, add the cauliflower and boil for ½ minute. Drain well. Heat the oil and fry the ginger and mushrooms for 3 minutes. Add the cauliflower, chilli powder and mustard seeds and fry for 1 minute, stirring. Remove from the pan and leave to cool. Mix together the garlic, lemon juice, tomatoes and honey. Stir in the cauliflower mixture and chill for 30 minutes before serving.

Cucumber in Soy Dressing
Serves 4

20 ml/4 tsp sesame seeds • 1 cucumber, cut into chunks

45 ml/3 tbsp soy sauce • 20 ml/4 tsp wine vinegar • pinch of cayenne

2.5 ml/½ tsp cayenne • 2.5 ml/½ tsp sugar • 1 clove garlic, crushed

15 ml/1 tbsp sesame oil

Dry roast the sesame seeds until lightly browned. Place the cucumber in a bowl. Mix together the remaining ingredients, pour over the cucumber and leave to stand for 30 minutes to 1 hour. Serve sprinkled with sesame seeds.

Cucumber Salad
Serves 4

30 ml/2 tbsp green lentils • 1 cucumber, peeled and finely chopped

30-45 ml/3-4 tbsp grated (shredded) coconut • 1 green chilli, finely chopped

1 small bunch fresh coriander (cilantro), chopped • 15 ml/1 tbsp lemon juice

salt • 10 ml/2 tsp oil • 5 ml/1 tsp mustard seeds

5 ml/1 tsp cumin seeds • 5 ml/1 tsp split black beans

5 ml/1 tsp yellow split peas • 2.5 ml/½ tsp asafoetida

1 dried red chilli, halved • 2-3 curry leaves

Soak the green lentils in water for 1 hour. Mix together the cucumber, coconut, green chilli, coriander, lemon juice and salt. Drain the lentils and stir them in.

Heat the oil and fry all the remaining ingredients until the mustard seeds start crackling. Add to the salad and mix well. Serve chilled or at room temperature.

Fruit Salad

1 melon • 1 large boiled potato, narrow at the top • 2 cloves

4 black peppercorns • 2 strips marrow (squash) skin • 4 peaches

1 mango, diced • 4 plums, thickly sliced • 250 g/9 oz seedless grapes

Cut the melon in half and then cut the second half so that you have one piece larger than the other in a boat shape then scoop out the seeds. Place the 'boat' in the centre of a large serving platter. Cut off the bottom of the potato so that it will stand up then make it into a person by using the cloves for eyes, a shape from a piece of plum for a mouth, peppercorn but-tons and a scarf from a piece of plum. Put the girl in the middle of the boat. Make the strips of marrow skin into the shape of oars and fix them to the boat with cocktail sticks (toothpicks). Quarter and stone the peaches then arrange all the fruit attractively around the boat. Serve as a dessert or aperitif.

Sprouted Green Lentil Salad
Serves 4

275 g/10 oz/1¾ cups whole green lentils • 2 small onions, chopped

salt and pepper • 15-30 ml/1-2 tbsp Basic Salad Dressing (page 324)

Wash and soak the lentils in water for at least 6 hours, then drain, cover with a damp cloth and keep in a dry, warm place for a further 6-10 hours. The len-tils should sprout.

Mix the sprouted lentils with the onion, season with salt and pepper and toss with the salad dressing.

Photograph opposite: *Onion and Spinach Pakoras (page 336) and Peanut Raita (page 361)*

Mixed Salad
Serves 6

2 onion, finely chopped ● 2 boiled potatoes, cubed ● 2 tomatoes, chopped

2 hard-boiled (hard-cooked) eggs, chopped ● 1 cucumber, peeled and cubed

100 g/4 oz/1 cup sprouted green lentils (page 320) ● 100 g/4 oz/½ cup cottage cheese

juice of 1 lime ● salt and pepper ● 30 ml/2 tbsp oil

100 g/4 oz/1 cup roasted peanuts, ground ● 30 ml/2 tbsp sugar

juice and grated rind of 1 lime ● 250 ml/8 fl oz/1 cup water

Mix together the onion, potatoes, tomatoes, eggs, cucumber, lentils and cottage cheese. Sprinkle with the lime juice, season with salt and pepper and toss well. Chill. Heat the oil and stir in the peanuts, sugar and lime rind and juice. Cook for a few minutes, stirring, until the mixture thickens slightly. Adjust the seasoning to taste. Pour over the salad and toss before serving.

Mixed Salad with Moong Beans
Serves 6

100 g/4 oz/¾ cup moong beans, soaked for 12 hours

3 onions, thinly sliced ● 90 ml/6 tbsp lemon juice

15 ml/1 tbsp chopped fresh coriander (cilantro) ● 2.5 ml/½ tsp black pepper

1 green (bell) pepper, cut into rings ● 3 tomatoes, sliced

4 green chillies, halved and seeded ● 10 radishes, trimmed

Rinse the soaked beans thoroughly then place in a bowl and cover with a damp cloth. Leave to stand for 12 hours. Sprinkle the cloth with water and leave to stand for a further 24 hours until the beans have sprouted and swollen. Mix the beans with the lemon juice, coriander and pepper. Arrange the onions on a serving dish and sprinkle with half the beans. Arrange the pepper and tomato slices alternately over the top and sprinkle with the remaining beans. Serve garnished with the chillies and radishes.

Onion and Cumin Salad
Serves 6

5 ml/1 tsp ground cumin ● 3 onions, thinly sliced ● 45 ml/3 tbsp lemon juice

100g/4 oz watercress leaves ● 6 green chillies, halved and seeded

Dry roast the cumin for 1 minute then mix with the onions, lemon juice and watercress. Stir in the chillies. Arrange the salad on a large plate and serve with chicken.

Photograph opposite: *Hot Indian Chutney (page 366) and Mango Chutney (page 376)*

Onion and Chilli Salad
Serves 6

6 large onions, sliced into rings ● 6 green chillies, halved

45 ml/3 tbsp chopped fresh mint ● 45 ml/3 tbsp lemon juice

Arrange the onions and chillies on a plate. Mix together the mint and lemon juice and spoon over the onions.

Onion, Tomato and Cucumber Salad
Serves 4

1 onion, cut into rings ● ½ cucumber, thinly sliced

2 firm tomatoes, thinly sliced ● pinch of salt

juice of ½ lemon ● 1 small green chilli, chopped (optional)

Arrange the onion, cucumber and tomato on a serving plate and sprinkle with salt and lemon juice. Serve sprinkled with chilli, if liked.

Pea and Potato Salad
Serves 4

2 boiled potatoes, cubed ● 100 g/4 oz/1 cup cooked peas

1 cucumber, peeled and cubed ● 1 apple, chopped

2-3 spring onions (scallions), sliced ● 2 hard-boiled (hard-cooked) eggs, chopped

salt and pepper ● 60 ml/4 tbsp tomato purée (paste)

60 ml/4 tbsp mayonnaise ● 30 ml/2 tbsp cream

Mix together all the salad ingredients and season with salt and pepper. Blend together the tomato purée, mayonnaise and cream and stir into the salad. Chill before serving.

Vegetable Salad
Serves 4

1 carrot, finely chopped ● 1 cucumber, peeled and finely chopped

1 tomato, finely chopped ● 1 green chilli, finely chopped

1 small bunch fresh coriander (cilantro), finely chopped ● 10 ml/2 tsp oil

5 ml/1 tsp mustard seeds ● 5 ml/1 tsp cumin seeds

5 ml/1 tsp split black beans ● 1 dried red chilli, halved

2.5 ml/½ tsp asafoetida ● 2-3 curry leaves

30 ml/2 tbsp lemon juice ● salt

Mix together the vegetables and coriander.

Heat the oil and fry the mustard and cumin seeds, split beans, chilli, asafoetida and curry leaves until the mustard seeds start crackling. Stir them into the salad with the lemon juice and salt. Serve cold or at room temperature.

Watercress and Apple Salad   Serves 4-6

1 hard dessert apple ● 15 ml/1 tbsp lemon juice

salt and pepper ● pinch of ground cumin ● pinch of cayenne pepper

1.5 ml/¼ tsp sugar ● 30 ml/2 tbsp oil ● 2 bunches watercress

20 ml/4 tsp red wine vinegar ● 20 ml/4 tsp soy sauce

Peel, quarter and core the apple then slice. Sprinkle with lemon juice, salt, pepper, cumin, cayenne, sugar and 5 ml/1 tsp of the oil. Arrange the slices on serving plates. Toss the watercress with the wine vinegar, soy sauce and remaining oil and season with pepper. Arrange with the apple slices and serve.

Watermelon Salad   Serves 6

1 watermelon ● 1 bunch radishes ● 2 cucumbers

1 banana ● 15 ml/1 tbsp lemon juice ● 8 firm tomatoes

250 g/9 oz seedless grapes ● 4 green chillis

Cut 2 small triangles for eyes and a small half-moon shape for a smiling mouth in the watermelon and place it in the centre of a large serving platter. Use a cocktail stick (toothpick) to stick 1 radish on to the face as a nose. Cut the others into flower shapes. Cut 2 quarters of a cucumber and use a cocktail sticks (toothpicks) to fix them to the melon as arms. Thinly slice the remainder. Slice the banana and toss in the lemon juice. Cut the tomatoes into flowers. Arrange the cucumber slices around the platter then arrange the radish and tomato flowers, banana, grapes and chillis attractively around the plate.

Cracked Wheat Salad
Serves 6

175 g/6 oz/1½ cups cracked wheat ● 15 ml/1 tbsp wine vinegar

15 ml/1 tbsp lemon juice ● 10 ml/2 tsp clear honey

1 cucumber, thinly sliced ● 12 cherry tomatoes

225 g/8 oz spinach, cut into strips ● 225 g/8 oz lettuce, cut into strips

45 ml/3 tbsp groundnut (peanut) oil ● 2.5 ml/½ tsp black pepper

10 ml/2 tsp grated ginger root ● 15 ml/1 tbsp sesame seeds ● 5 ml/1 tsp paprika

Cover the wheat with water and leave to soak for 1 hour. Mix together the wine vinegar, lemon juice and honey, add the cucumber and tomatoes and leave to marinate for 15 minutes. Remove the cucumber and tomatoes and set aside. Toss the spinach and lettuce with 15 ml/1 tbsp of oil then add to the wine vinegar marinade and toss with pepper. Drain the wheat in a colander lined with muslin (cheesecloth) and squeeze out excess water.

Heat the remaining oil and fry the ginger for 30 seconds. Add the wheat, sesame seeds and paprika and fry for 2-3 minutes, stirring. Leave to cool for a few minutes. Arrange the greens on a serving plate and spoon the wheat into a mound on the top. Arrange the cucumber and tomatoes attractively around the edge and garnish with a little paprika. Serve at room temperature or chilled.

Basic Salad Dressing
Makes about 250 ml/8 fl oz/1 cup

120 ml/4 fl oz/½ cup oil ● 30 ml/2 tbsp white wine vinegar

30 ml/2 tbsp lime juice ● 5 ml/1 tsp sugar ● 5 ml/1 tsp mustard powder

2.5 ml/½ tsp salt ● 1 clove garlic, crushed ● 2.5 ml/½ tsp black pepper

Whisk together all the ingredients until well blended. Store in an airtight jar in the refrigerator. Just before serving, shake the dressing ingre-

dients together and spoon 1-2 tablespoons over the salad before tossing well.

Snacks

Snacks play an important part in an Indian household, especially in the late afternoon and in the summer when days are long and late suppers are usual. Afternoon tea, or 'tiffin', includes a variety of nibbles and the Indian housewife can always produce sev and nimkis from her larder. In India, friends and relations may visit you at any hour of the day, and the host always offers them something to eat and drink.

Sev Puri   Serves 4

12 Puris (page 309) ● 2 boiled potatoes, chopped

1 onion, finely chopped ● ½ cup Sev (page 353)

45 ml/3 tbsp chutney ● 1 green mango, chopped

15 ml/1 tbsp chopped fresh coriander (cilantro)

Arrange the puris on a plate and top with the potatoes and onion then the sev. Add chutney to taste and garnish with the mango and coriander.

Batato Puri   Serves 4

12 Puris (page 309) ● 3 boiled potatoes, chopped

60 ml/4 tbsp natural (plain) yoghurt ● salt

5 ml/1 tsp chilli powder ● 15 ml/1 tbsp chutney

15 ml/1 tbsp chopped fresh coriander (cilantro) ● 5 ml/1 tsp ground cumin

Arrange the puris on a plate and make a hole in the centre of each. Stuff the potatoes into the puris and sprinkle with salt and chilli powder then a little chutney. Garnish with coriander and cumin and serve at once.

Dosas
Makes 15-20

350 g/12 oz/3 cups par-boiled rice, soaked overnight

175 g/6 oz/1 cup split black beans, soaked overnight

10 ml/2 tsp fenugreek seeds, soaked overnight ● salt ● oil for frying

Mix together the soaked rice, split beans and fenugreek seeds and salt to make a smooth batter. Leave to stand for at least 12 hours until the mixture ferments and increases in volume.

Heat a heavy-based pan and sprinkle on a few drops of water. If it sizzles, it is ready for use. Smear a little oil on the pan and heat to smoking point. Pour a ladleful of batter over the pan and spread quickly to about 15 cm/6 in. Pour a teaspoonful of oil around the edges, increase the heat and cook for 2 minutes until golden brown. Turn over and fry for 2 minutes until browned. Serve hot with coconut chutney.

Fenugreek Dosas
Makes 15-20

350 g/12 oz/3 cups par-boiled rice, soaked overnight

175 g/6 oz/1 cup split black beans, soaked overnight

10 ml/2 tsp fenugreek seeds, soaked overnight

salt ● 1 onion, finely chopped ● 1 tomato, skinned and chopped

15 ml/1 tbsp chopped fresh coriander (cilantro) ● oil for frying

Mix together the soaked rice, split beans and fenugreek seeds and salt to make a smooth batter. Leave to stand for at least 12 hours until the mixture ferments and increases in volume.

Mix together the onion, tomato and coriander. Heat a heavy-based pan and sprinkle on a few drops of water. If it sizzles, it is ready for use. Smear a little oil on the pan and heat to smok-ing point. Pour a ladleful of batter over the pan and spread quickly to about 15 cm/6 in. Pour a teaspoonful of oil around the edges and sprinkle over the onion mixture. Increase the heat and cook for 2 minutes until golden brown. Turn over and fry for 2 minutes until browned. Serve hot with chutney.

Spicy Dosas
Makes 15-20

100 g/4 oz/½ cup long-grain rice ● 50 g/2 oz/⅓ cup red lentils

600 ml/1 pt/2½ cups water ● ½ coconut, grated (shredded)

5 dried red chillies ● 2.5 ml/½ tsp asafoetida ● salt ● oil for frying

Soak the rice and lentils in the water for 2 hours. Grind to a fine batter with the coconut, chillies, asafoetida and salt, adding a little water if necessary.

Heat a heavy-based pan and smear with oil. Pour a ladleful of batter into the pan and spread to a 15 cm/6 in circle. Pour a spoonful of oil around the edges and cook for about 2 minutes until each side is golden. Serve hot with chutney.

Vegetable Dosas
Makes 15-20

350 g/12 oz/3 cups par-boiled rice, soaked overnight

175 g/6 oz/1 cup split black beans, soaked overnight

10 ml/2 tsp fenugreek seeds, soaked overnight

salt ● 15 ml/1 tbsp ghee ● 5 ml/1 tsp mustard seeds

2.5 ml/½ tsp ground turmeric ● 1 onion, chopped

225 g/8 oz potatoes, boiled and diced ● 6 curry leaves, chopped

2.5 ml/½ tsp salt ● 2.5 ml/½ tsp chilli powder ● oil for frying

Mix together the soaked rice, split beans and fenugreek seeds and salt to make a smooth batter. Leave to stand for at least 12 hours until the mixture ferments and increases in volume.

Heat the ghee and fry the mustard seeds until they start crackling. Add the turmeric, onion, potatoes, curry leaves, salt and chilli powder, cover and simmer for 5 minutes.

Heat a heavy-based pan and sprinkle on a few drops of water. If it sizzles, it is ready for use. Smear a little oil on the pan and heat to smoking point. Pour a ladleful of batter over the pan and spread quickly to about 15 cm/6 in. Pour a teaspoonful of oil around the edges, increase the heat and cook for 2 minutes until golden brown. Turn over and put 30 ml/2 tbsp of the spice mixture down the centre of the dosa, fold in half and fry for 2 minutes until browned. Serve hot with chutney.

Coconut Dosas
Makes 15-20

900 g/2 lb/4 cups long-grain rice, soaked overnight

225 g/8 oz grated (shredded) coconut ● 4 green chillies, chopped

1 cm/½ in ginger root, grated ● 4 onions, sliced

30 ml/2 tbsp oil ● 15 ml/1 tbsp chopped fresh coriander (cilantro)

5 ml/1 tsp chopped fresh curry leaves ● salt ● 30 ml/2 tbsp ghee

Drain and wash the rice then grind it to a paste with the coconut, chillies and ginger. Fry the onions in a little oil until soft then add to the rice with the coriander and curry leaves. Season with salt. Heat a little oil at a time and cook tablespoonfuls of the batter to make pancakes. Cook until lightly browned on the underside then flip over, add a little ghee to the pan and fry until browned.

Semolina Dosas
Makes 15-20

100 g/4 oz/1 cup plain (all-purpose) flour ● 100 g/4 oz/1 cup semolina

100 g/4 oz/1 cup rice flour ● 10 ml/2 tsp cumin seeds

3 green chillies, chopped ● 250 ml/8 fl oz/1 cup natural (plain) yoghurt

salt ● 30 ml/2 tbsp chopped fresh coriander (cilantro)

2-3 curry leaves, chopped ● 120 ml/4 fl oz/½ cup water ● oil for frying

Mix the flours, cumin seeds, chillies, yoghurt, salt, coriander and curry leaves. Stir in just enough water to make a stiff dough, cover and leave to stand for 2 hours.

Add more water to the dough and mix to a thin, pouring consistency.

Heat a heavy-based pan and smear with oil. Pour a ladleful of batter into the pan and spread to a 15 cm/6 in circle. Pour a spoonful of oil around the edges and cook for about 2 minutes until each side is golden. Serve hot with coconut chutney.

Wholewheat Dosas
Makes 15-20

225 g/8 oz/2 cups wholewheat flour ● 100 g/4 oz/1 cup rice flour

salt ● 120 ml/4 fl oz/½ cup buttermilk ● water

2 green chillies, finely chopped ● 45 ml/3 tbsp chopped fresh coriander (cilantro)

10 ml/2 tsp oil ● 2.5 ml/½ tsp mustard seeds ● 2.5 ml/½ tsp cumin seeds

pinch of asafoetida ● 2-3 curry leaves, chopped ● oil for frying

Mix the flours, salt and buttermilk then add just enough water to make a batter of pouring consistency. Add the chillies and coriander. Heat the oil and fry the remaining ingredients until the mustard seeds start crackling. Pour into the dosa batter.

Heat a heavy-based pan and smear with oil. Pour a ladleful of batter into the pan and spread to a 15 cm/6 in circle. Pour a spoonful of oil around the edges and cook for about 2 minutes until each side is golden. Serve hot with coconut chutney.

Jaggery Dosas
Makes 15-20

100 g/4 oz jaggery ● 250 ml/8 fl oz/1 cup water

225 g/8 oz/2 cups wholewheat flour ● 100 g/4 oz/1 cup rice flour ● oil for frying

Heat the jaggery and water in a heavy-based pan until blended. Strain and leave to cool. Add the jaggery syrup to the flours to make a batter of pouring consistency, adding a little water if necessary.

Heat a heavy-based pan and smear with oil. Pour a ladleful of batter into the pan and spread to a 15 cm/6 in circle. Pour a spoonful of oil around the edges and cook for about 2 minutes until each side is golden. Serve hot with coconut chutney.

Potato Dosas
Makes 15-20

100 g/4 oz/1 cup rice flour ● 2 large potatoes, boiled and mashed

120 ml/4 fl oz/½ cup natural (plain) yoghurt ● 2 green chillies, chopped

45 ml/3 tbsp chopped fresh coriander (cilantro) ● salt ● oil for frying

Mix together all the ingredients except the oil and add just enough water to make a batter of pouring consistency.
Heat a heavy-based pan and smear with oil. Pour a ladleful of batter into the pan and spread to a 15 cm/6 in circle. Pour a spoonful of oil around the edges and cook for about 2 minutes until each side is golden. Serve hot with chutney.

Red Lentil Dosas
Makes 15-20

50 g/2 oz/⅓ cup split black beans ● 50 g/2 oz/⅓ cup red lentils

50 g/2 oz/⅓ cup yellow split peas ● 100 g/4 oz/½ cup long-grain rice

450 ml/½ pt/2 cups water ● 60 ml/4 tbsp grated (shredded) coconut

1 onion, finely chopped ● 2.5 ml/½ tsp asafoetida

30 ml/2 tbsp chopped fresh coriander (cilantro)

salt ● oil for frying

Soak the split beans, lentils, peas and rice in the water for 2 hours. Grind coarsely. Stir in the coconut, oinion, asafoetida, coriander and salt and mix to a smooth batter.
Heat a heavy-based pan and smear with oil. Pour a ladleful of batter into the pan and spread to a 15 cm/6 in circle. Pour a spoonful of oil around the edges and cook for about 2 minutes until each side is golden. Serve hot with chutney.

Green Lentil Dosas
Makes 15-20

225 g/8 oz/1⅓ cups green lentils ● 50 g/2 oz/¼ cup long-grain rice

4 green chillies, chopped ● 1 onion, chopped

30 ml/2 tbsp grated (shredded) coconut ● 1 potato, boiled and mashed

30 ml/2 tbsp chopped fresh coriander (cilantro)

2.5 ml/½ tsp asafoetida ● salt ● oil for frying

Soak the lentils and rice for 2 hours. Grind coarsely with the chillies then mix in the coconut, potato, coriander, asafoetida and salt and mix to a thick batter.
Heat a heavy-based pan and smear with oil. Pour a ladleful of batter into the pan and spread to a 15 cm/6 in circle. Pour a spoonful of oil around the edges and cook for about 2 minutes until each side is golden. Serve hot with chutney.

Vadas

100 g/4 oz/⅔ cup split black beans ● 450 ml/¾ pt/2 cups water

4 green chillies, chopped ● 5 ml/1 tsp asafoetida ● salt

30 ml/2 tbsp chopped fresh coriander (cilantro) ● oil for deep-frying

Soak the split beans in the water for 2 hours. Add the chillies, asafoetida and salt and grind to a smooth dough, adding a very little water. Mix in the coriander. Take a ladleful of dough on the palm of your left hand and flatten it with your right hand. Make a hole in the centre, slip the dough into hot oil and fry until browned and crisp. Drain on kitchen paper and serve hot with chutney.

Cabbage Vadas
Makes 15-20

100 g/4 oz/⅔ cup split black beans ● 450 ml/¾ pt/2 cups water

4 green chillies, chopped ● 5 ml/1 tsp asafoetida ● salt

50 g/2 oz cabbage, finely chopped ● 30 ml/2 tbsp peas

30 ml/2 tbsp chopped fresh coriander (cilantro) ● oil for frying

Soak the split beans in the water for 2 hours. Add the chillies, asafoetida and salt and grind to a smooth dough, adding a very little water. Mix in the cabbage, peas and coriander. Take a ladleful of dough on the palm of your left hand and flatten it with your right hand. Make a hole in the centre, slip the dough into hot oil and fry until browned and crisp. Drain on kitchen paper and serve hot with chutney.

Yoghurt Vadas
Makes 15-20

175 g/6 oz/1 cup split black beans ● 450 ml/¾ pt/2 cups water

8 green chillies ● salt ● 45 ml/3 tbsp grated (shredded) coconut

5 ml/1 tsp cumin seeds ● 1 l/1¾ pts/4¼ cups natural (plain) yoghurt

10 ml/2 tsp oil ● 5 ml/1 tsp mustard seeds ● 5 ml/1 tsp cumin seeds

1 dried red chilli, halved ● 5 ml/1 tsp split black beans

2.5 ml/½ tsp asafoetida ● 2-3 curry leaves, chopped

Soak the split beans in the water for 2 hours. Grind to a fine paste with 4 chillis and salt. Grind the coconut, remaining chillies and cumin seeds to a paste then stir it into the yoghurt. Heat the oil and fry the remaining ingredients until the seeds start crackling. Stir into the yoghurt. Take a ladleful of bean dough on the palm of your left hand and flatten it with your right hand. Make a hole in the centre, slip the dough into hot oil and fry until browned and crisp. Drain on kitchen paper and pour over the yoghurt mixture before serving.

Masala Vadas
Makes 15-20

75 g/3 oz/½ cup red lentils ● 75 g/3 oz/½ cup split black beans

75 g/3 oz/½ cup yellow split peas ● 600 ml/1 pt/2½ cups water

5 dried red chillies ● 4 green chillies, chopped ● 2.5 ml/½ tsp asafoetida

1 onion, finely chopped ● 2.5 cm/1 in ginger root, grated

30 ml/2 tbsp chopped fresh coriander (cilantro) ● salt ● oil for frying

Soak the lentils, split beans and split peas in the water for 2 hours then grind to a coarse batter with the red chillies. Add the green chillies, asafoetida, onion, ginger and coriander. Take a ladleful of dough on the palm of your left hand and flatten it with your right hand. Make a hole in the centre, slip the dough into hot oil and fry until browned and crisp. Drain on kitchen paper and serve hot with chutney.

Mysore Vadas
Makes 15-20

50 g/2 oz/½ cup rice flour ● 50 g/2 oz/½ cup semolina

50 g/2 oz/½ cup plain (all-purpose) flour ● 45 ml/3 tbsp melted ghee

4 green chillies, chopped ● 1 onions, chopped

30 ml/2 tbsp chopped fresh coriander (cilantro) ● 2.5 ml/½ tsp asafoetida

salt ● water ● oil for frying

Mix together all the ingredients except the oil, adding enough water to make a stiff dough. Take a ladleful of dough on the palm of your left hand and flatten it with your right hand. Make a hole in the centre, slip the dough into hot oil and fry until browned and crisp. Drain on kitchen paper and serve hot with mint chutney.

Potato Vadas
Makes 15-20

4 potatoes, boiled and mashed ● 50 g/2 oz/½ cup gram flour

25 g/1 oz/¼ cup rice flour ● 6 green chillies, finely chopped

1 cm/½ in ginger root, finely chopped ● 2.5 ml/½ tsp asafoetida

2-3 curry leaves, chopped ● 30 ml/2 tbsp chopped fresh coriander (cilantro)

10 ml/2 tsp oil ● 5 ml/1 tsp mustard seeds ● oil for frying

Mix together the potatoes, flours, chillies, ginger, asafoetida, curry leaves and coriander. Heat the oil and fry the mustard seeds until they start crackling. Pour into the potato mixture and mix well to a stiff dough. Take a ladleful of dough on the palm of your left hand and flatten it with your right hand. Make a hole in the centre, slip the dough into hot oil and fry until browned and crisp. Drain on kitchen paper and serve hot with mint chutney.

Sago Vadas
Makes 15

50 g/2 oz/½ cup sago ● 120 ml/4 fl oz/½ cup buttermilk

50 g/2 oz/½ cup gram flour ● 5 ml/1 tsp chilli powder

2.5 ml/½ tsp asafoetida ● 2 green chillies, chopped

30 ml/2 tbsp chopped fresh coriander (cilantro)

5 ml/1 tsp ghee ● salt ● oil for frying

Soak the sago in the buttermilk for 1 hour. Stir in the flour, chilli powder, asafoetida, chillies, coriander and ghee to make a stiff dough. Take a ladleful of dough on the palm of your left hand and flatten it with your right hand. Make a hole in the centre, slip the dough into hot oil and fry until browned and crisp. Drain on kitchen paper and serve hot with mint chutney.

Semolina Vadas
Makes 15-20

100 g/4 oz grated (shredded) coconut ● 4 green chillies, finely chopped

1 cm/½ in ginger root, grated ● 2.5 ml/½ tsp sugar

5 ml/1 tsp cumin seeds ● 200 g/7 oz semolina

15 ml/1 tbsp natural (plain) yoghurt ● 120 ml/4 fl oz/½ cup water

oil for frying

Mix together all the ingredients, adding just enough water to make a batter of thick dropping consistency. Heat a heavy-based pan and smear with a little oil. Pour a ladleful of batter into the pan and spread as thinly as possible. Make a hole in the centre and pour in a teaspoon of oil. Cook until golden brown on the underside then turn over and fry until golden and crisp. Drain on kitchen paper and serve hot with chutney.

Rice Idlis
Makes 15-20

225 g/8 oz/2 cups par-boiled rice ● 175 g/6 oz/1 cup split black beans ● salt

Soak the rice and split beans separately for 5-6 hours. Grind separately to coarse batters then mix them together, add salt and leave to ferment for at least 8 hours.

Without stirring the batter, pour it into greased idli moulds or egg poaching cups and steam over boiling water for about 20 minutes until soft and fluffy. Serve hot with coconut chutney.

Semolina Idlis
Makes 15-20

45 ml/3 tbsp ghee ● 100 g/4 oz/1 cup semolina

2.5 cm/1 in ginger root, grated ● 2 green chillies, finely chopped

30 ml/2 tbsp chopped fresh coriander (cilantro)

120 ml/4 fl oz/½ cup natural (plain) yoghurt ● salt

30 ml/2 tbsp cashew nuts, chopped ● 5 ml/1 tsp mustard seeds

5 ml/1 tsp cumin seeds ● 2-3 curry leaves, chopped

Heat 30 ml/1 tbsp of ghee and fry the semolina until golden. Stir in the ginger, chillies, coriander, yoghurt and salt and add just enough water to mix to a batter of thick, pouring consistency. Heat 15 ml/1 tbsp of ghee and fry the nuts until golden. Add the batter. Heat the remaining ghee and fry the mustard and cumin seeds and curry leaves until the seeds start crackling. Add to the batter.

Without stirring the batter, pour it into greased idli moulds or egg poaching cups and steam over boiling water for about 20 minutes until soft and fluffy. Serve hot with coconut chutney.

Kancheepuram Idlis
Makes 15-20

175 g/6 oz/1½ cups par-boiled rice ● 175 g/6 oz/1 cup split black beans

2.5 ml/½ tsp asafoetida ● 5 ml/1 tsp black pepper ● 5 ml/1 tsp ground ginger

5 ml/1 tsp cumin seeds ● salt ● 45 ml/3 tbsp gingelly oil

45 ml/3 tbsp ghee ● 2-3 curry leaves, chopped ● oil for frying

Soak the rice and split beans in water for 2 hours. Grind to a coarse batter and add the asafoetida, pepper, ginger, cumin seeds and salt and leave to ferment for 24 hours.

Heat the oil and ghee and fry the curry leaves for a few seconds. Stir into the batter. Pour into a heavy-based pan, cover and cook over a gentle heat for about 20 minutes until set. Cut into triangles and serve with coconut chutney.

Cheese Bondas
Serves 4

300 ml/½ pt/1¼ cups milk ● 100 g/4 oz/1 cup plain (all-purpose) flour

75 g/3 oz/⅓ cup butter ● 100 g/4 oz Mozzarella cheese, grated

3 eggs, beaten ● 5 ml/1 tsp chilli powder ● salt ● ghee for deep-frying

Warm the milk then gradually beat in the flour. Add the butter and stir until thickened. Remove from the heat and stir in the cheese. Add the eggs, chilli powder and salt. Leave to cool. Divide the mixture into 6-8 balls. Heat the oil and fry the balls until golden brown. Drain on kitchen paper and serve hot with tomato sauce.

Potato Bondas
Serves 6

450 g/1 lb potatoes ● 45 ml/3 tbsp oil ● 2.5 ml/½ tsp mustard seeds

15 ml/1 tbsp split black beans ● 50 g/2 oz/½ cup cashew nuts, chopped

1.5 ml/¼ tsp ground turmeric ● 2 onions, chopped ● 6 green chillies, chopped

2.5 cm/1 in ginger root, grated ● 1 sprig fresh curry leaves

salt ● juice of ½ lemon ● 225 g/8 oz/2 cups gram flour

5 ml/1 tsp chilli powder ● 2.5 ml/½ tsp salt ● 150 ml/¼ pt/⅔ cup water

oil for deep-frying

Boil the potatoes then drain and dice. Heat the oil and fry the mustard seeds until they start crackling. Add the split beans and nuts and fry until golden. Add the turmeric, onions, chillies, ginger and curry leaves and cook until soft. Add the potatoes and salt and fry for 2 minutes, stirring. Add the lemon juice and stir well. Shape the mixture into small balls. Mix the flour, chilli powder and salt then add enough water to make a thick batter. Heat the oil. Dip the potato balls in the batter then fry a few at a time in the hot oil until golden. Drain on kitchen paper and serve with chutney.

Mysore Bondas
Serves 4

100 g/4 oz/⅔ cup split black beans ● 450 ml/¾ pt/2 cups water

5 ml/1 tsp black peppercorns ● 50 g/2 oz grated (shredded) coconut

2.5 ml/½ tsp asafoetida ● salt ● 3 curry leaves ● oil for deep-frying

Soak the split beans in the water for 2 hours. Grind to a smooth batter with the remaining ingredients then shape into small balls. Heat the oil and fry the balls until golden. Drain on kitchen paper and serve hot with coconut chutney.

Vegetable Bondas
Serves 4

100 g/4 oz/⅔ cup yellow split peas ● 450 ml/¾ pt/2 cups water

4 dried red chillies ● 5 ml/1 tsp asafoetida ● salt

50 g/2 oz cauliflower florets ● 50 g/2 oz peas

1 onion, chopped ● 2-3 curry leaves, chopped ● oil for deep-frying

Soak the peas in the water for 2 hours. Grind them to a thick batter with the chillies, asafoetida and salt. Mix the vegetables and curry leaves into the batter. Heat the oil. Drop spoonfuls of the batter into the oil and fry until golden. Drain on kitchen paper and serve hot with chutney.

Potato Pakoras
Serves 4

225 g/8 oz/2 cups gram flour ● pinch of bicarbonate of soda (baking soda)

300 ml/½ pt/1¼ cups water ● salt ● 4 green chillies, chopped

10 ml/2 tsp pomegranate seeds, crushed

15 ml/1 tbsp fenugreek leaves, chopped (optional)

oil for deep-frying ● 450 g/1 lb potatoes, boiled and chopped

Mix the flour, bicarbonate of soda and water to a batter. Add the salt, chillies, pomegranate seeds and fenugreek, if using. Whisk thoroughly then leave to stand for 10 minutes. Heat the oil to smoking point. Dip the potato pieces in the batter then slide into the hot oil a few at a time and fry until golden. Drain on kitchen paper and serve hot with chutney.

Cheese Pakoras
Serves 4

175 g/6 oz/1½ cups gram flour ● 150 ml/¼ pt/⅔ cup water ● salt

5 ml/1 tsp chilli powder ● 15 ml/1 tbsp chopped fresh coriander (cilantro)

225 g/8 oz Paneer (page 20), cubed ● oil for deep-frying

Mix the flour and water to a batter. Stir in the salt, chilli powder and coriander, whisk thoroughly then leave to stand for 10 minutes. Dip the paneer in the batter and fry a few at a time in hot oil until golden. Drain on kitchen paper and serve hot or cold with chutney.

Corn Pakoras
Makes 12

150 g/5 oz sweetcorn kernels ● 400 ml/14 fl oz/1¾ cups water

2 sliced bread ● 150 g/5 oz mashed potatoes ● 50 g/2 oz/⅓ cup raisins

45 ml/3 tbsp chopped fresh coriander (cilantro) ● 15 ml/1 tbsp lemon juice

5 ml/1 tsp garam masala ● 5 ml/1 tsp ground cumin

5 ml/1 tsp ground red chilli ● 1 small green chilli, chopped

salt to taste ● oil for frying

Place the corn and water in a pan, bring to the boil and cook for about 3 minutes until tender. Drain well. Dip the bread slices in water for 30 seconds then squeeze out all the water with the palms of your hands. Place the bread in a bowl with the cooked corn and the remaining ingredients. Mix thoroughly then divide into 12 equal portions.

Put a few drops of oil on the palm of your hand. Take one portion of the corn mixture and roll it into a smooth round shape. Continue with the remaining pakoras while you heat the oil over a medium heat. Gently slip 6 pakoras into the hot oil and fry until golden brown on all sides, turning a few times while cooking. Serve hot with chutney and barfi at tea.

Onion Pakoras
Serves 4

pinch of bicarbonate of soda (baking soda) • 10 ml/2 tsp ghee

100 g/4 oz/1 cup gram flour • 50 g/2 oz/½ cup rice flour

30 ml/2 tbsp ghee • 3 onions, finely chopped • 1 potato, finely chopped

2.5 cm/1 in ginger root, finely chopped • 3 green chillies, chopped

5 ml/1 tsp chilli powder • 1 bunch fresh coriander (cilantro), chopped

salt • oil for deep-frying

Mix the soda with the ghee until frothy then add all the remaining ingredients and mix to a stiff batter, adding a little water. Heat the oil and drop spoonfuls of the batter into the oil and fry until golden. Drain on kitchen paper and serve hot with tomato ketchup or chutney.

Onion and Spinach Pakoras
Serves 4-6

Batter: 250 g/9 oz/1¼ cups gram flour, sifted • 15 ml/1 tbsp oil

30 ml/2 tbsp chopped fresh coriander (cilantro)

15 ml/1 tbsp dried pomegranate seeds • 5 ml/1 tsp garam masala

5 ml/1 tsp ground red chilli • 5 ml/1 tsp ground roasted cumin

5 ml/1 tsp oregano seeds • 1 small green chilli, chopped

salt to taste • lukewarm water

Vegetables: 1 medium onion, thinly sliced

50 g/2 oz spinach, chopped • oil for deep-frying

Place the flour in a bowl and rub in the oil. Mix in the spices then gradually blend in the water to make a thick batter. Stir the onion and spinach into the batter. Heat the oil over a medium heat. Place tablespoonfuls of the mixture into the hot oil, 7 or 8 at a time and fry until golden brown on all sides, pressing and turning them over until cooked. Serve hot at tea with chutney and barfi.

Vegetable Pakoras
Serves 4-6

Batter: 250 g/9 oz/1¼ cups gram flour, sifted • 15 ml/1 tbsp oil

30 ml/2 tbsp chopped fresh coriander (cilantro)

15 ml/1 tbsp dried pomegranate seeds • 5 ml/1 tsp garam masala

5 ml/1 tsp ground red chilli • 5 ml/1 tsp ground roasted cumin

5 ml/1 tsp oregano seeds • 1 small green chilli, chopped

salt to taste • lukewarm water

Vegetables: 1 aubergine (eggplant), cut into strips • 1 carrot, cut into strips

2 courgettes (zucchini), cut into strips • oil for deep-frying

Place the flour in a bowl and rub in the oil. Mix in the spices then gradually blend in the water to make a thick batter. Dip the vegetables into the batter. Heat the oil over a medium heat. Place the battered vegetable strips into the hot oil, a few at time and fry until golden brown on all sides, pressing and turning them over until cooked. Serve hot at tea with chutney and barfi.

Paneer Pakoras

Makes 16

3 large cloves garlic ● 2.5 cm/1 in ginger root

1 green chilli ● 15 ml/1 tbsp chopped fresh coriander (cilantro)

5 ml/1 tsp garam masala ● 5 ml/1 tsp oregano seeds ● salt

2 quantities Paneer (page 20), cut into 16 pieces

Batter: 50 g/2 oz/½ cup gram flour, sifted

30 ml/2 tbsp chopped fresh coriander (cilantro) ● 7.5 ml/1½ tbsp oil

2.5 ml/½ tsp garam masala ● 1.5 ml/¼ tsp ground red chilli

75 ml/5 tbsp lukewarm water ● oil for deep-frying

Blend the garlic, ginger, chilli, coriander, garam masala, oregano seeds and salt to a smooth paste in a blender or food processor. Rub the mixture over the paneer and leave for 30 minutes to marinate. Place the flour in a bowl and rub in the oil. Add the remaining batter ingredients then work in the water to make a smooth, runny batter. Heat the oil in a deep frying pan (skillet) over a medium heat. Dip the marinated pakora in the batter then place it in the hot oil. Fry about 8 pakoras together, turning them over until golden brown. Serve hot with chutney as a starter or tea dish.

Prawn Pakoras

Serves 4-6

50 g/2 oz/½ cup gram flour ● 30 ml/2 tbsp water ● 2 onions, sliced

5 green chillies, chopped ● 5 ml/1 tsp pomegranate seeds

pinch of bicarbonate of soda (baking soda)

salt ● 450 g/1 lb peeled prawns (shrimp)

ghee or oil for deep-frying

Place the flour in a bowl and add just enough water to make a batter. Stir in the remaining ingredients. Heat the ghee or oil and drop teaspoonfuls of the batter into the oil and fry until golden brown. Drain on kitchen paper and serve hot with tomato sauce or chutney.

Cashew Nut Pakoras
Serves 4-6

450 g/1 lb/4 cups cashew nuts ● 450 g/1 lb/4 cups gram flour

5 ml/1 tsp ground turmeric ● 5 ml/1 tsp chilli powder

2.5 ml/½ tsp salt ● 150 ml/¼ pt cup oil

1 sprig fresh curry leaves, chopped ● ghee or oil for deep-frying

Chop the nuts. Mix the flour, turmeric, chilli powder and salt. Heat the oil, add the flour and mix well. Add the chopped nuts and curry leaves and mix well. Leave to cool slightly then make into small balls. Heat the ghee or oil and fry the balls until golden. Drain and serve hot or cold.

Sweet and Sour Pakoras
Serves 4

225 g/8 oz/2 cup gram flour ● 300 ml/½ pt/1¼ cups water

2.5 ml/½ tsp salt ● 1 green chilli, chopped

pinch of bicarbonate of soda (baking soda)

ghee or oil for deep-frying ● 150 ml/¼ pt/⅔ cup natural (plain) yoghurt

5 ml/1 tsp garam masala ● 5 ml/1 tsp tamarind concentrate

Place the flour in a bowl and gradually mix in enough water to make a medium-thick batter. Stir in the salt, chilli and bicarbonate of soda. Heat the ghee or oil and drop spoonfuls of the batter into the oil and fry until golden. Remove and drain on kitchen paper than soak in warm water for 10 minutes. Squeeze out the pakoras then mix into the yoghurt with the garam masala and tamarind.

Khandwi
Serves 4

300 ml/½ pt/1¼ cups natural (plain) yoghurt ● 600 ml/1 pt/2½ cups water

275 g/10 oz/2½ cups gram flour ● 5 green chillies, ground

2.5 cm/1 in ginger root, ground ● 2.5 ml/½ tsp salt

2.5 ml/½ tsp ground turmeric ● 15 ml/1 tsp sesame oil

5 ml/1 tsp mustard seeds

10 ml/2 tsp chopped fresh coriander (cilantro)

10 ml/2 tsp desiccated (shredded) coconut

Beat the yoghurt then beat in the water until milky. Mix in the gram flour and stir until all the lumps disappear. Add the chillies and ginger, salt and turmeric. Pour into a pan, bring to the boil then simmer for 15 minutes. Remove from the heat and pour into a large baking tray so that it forms a thin layer. Leave to cool then cut into strips and roll up. Arrange the rolls in a serving dish. Heat the sesame oil and fry the mustard seeds until they start crackling. Pour over the rolls and serve garnished with the coriander and coconut.

Curry Puffs
Serves 6

15 ml/1 tbsp ghee • 2 onions, chopped

225 g/8 oz minced (ground) meat • 10 ml/2 tsp garam masala

2.5 ml/½ tsp salt • 5 ml/1 tsp cornflour (cornstarch)

225 g/8 oz/2 cups self-raising flour • pinch of salt

75 g/3 oz/⅓ cup cooking fat or ghee • 45 ml/3 tbsp cold water

oil for deep-frying

Heat the ghee and fry half the onions until browned. Add the meat and fry for 2 minutes. Add the remaining onion, garam masala and salt, cover and fry gently until the meat is tender and the water has evaporated. Mix the cornflour to a smooth paste with a little water then stir it into the meat. Bring to the boil, lower the heat and simmer for 3 minutes. Mix the flour and salt then rub in the fat and mix to a pastry with just enough water. Roll out thinly and cut into 10 cm/4 in rounds. Put the meat mixture on one half and fold the pastry over, sealing the edges with water. Heat the oil and fry the puffs until browned on both sides. Drain on kitchen paper and serve hot.

Sagolet
Serves 6

100 g/4 oz sago • 2.5 ml/½ tsp salt

600 ml/1 pt/2½ cups warm water • 1 large potato, boiled and mashed

1 small onion, chopped • 2 green chillies, chopped

25 g/1 oz desiccated (shredded) coconut, toasted • 2-3 dried mint leaves

15 ml/1 tbsp lemon juice • 2.5 ml/½ tsp black pepper

oil for deep-frying

Soak the sago and salt in the water for 30 minutes then drain. Mix together all the ingredients then shape the mixture into small balls and deep-fry until golden brown. Serve with tomato sauce.

Coriander Potatoes
Serves 4

1 bunch fresh coriander (cilantro) leaves, coarsely chopped

1 onion, coarsely chopped • 1 small green chilli

juice of 1 large lemon • 2.5 ml/½ tsp ground red chilli

2.5 ml/½ tsp garam masala • salt

250 g/9 oz small new potatoes or potatoes cut into 1 cm/½ in pieces, boiled

Blend all the ingredients except the potatoes to a fine paste in a blender or food processor. Mix in the potato pieces and chill for 1-2 hours before serving cold with a meal, or as a snack.

Gujrati-style Dhokla
Serves 4-6

50 g/2 oz/⅓ cup yellow split peas, soaked overnight

25 g/1 oz/2 tbsp long-grain rice, soaked overnight

60 ml/4 tbsp natural (plain) yoghurt • 5 ml/1 tsp ground roasted cumin

2.5 ml/½ tsp Eno • 2.5 ml/½ tsp garam masala

2.5 ml/½ tsp ground red chilli • 2.5 ml/½ tsp ground turmeric

2.5 ml/½ tsp ground ginger • salt

Tarka: 30 ml/2 tbsp oil • 5 ml/1 tsp mustard seeds

30 ml/2 tbsp chopped fresh coriander (cilantro)

30 ml/2 tbsp desiccated (shredded) coconut • 1 small green chilli, chopped

Blend together the split peas, rice and yoghurt to a smooth paste in a blender or food processor. Cover and keep in a warm place overnight.

Place a trivet in a large saucepan, fill with water to come just below the trivet and bring to the boil. Mix the ground spices into the yoghurt batter and pour the batter into a greased heatproof dish so that it is about 2 cm/¾ in deep. When the water starts boiling, place the dish on the trivet, cover and cook for about 15 minutes until the dokhla has doubled in size and is soft and spongy. Cut into 2.5 cm/1 in cubes.

Heat the oil and fry the mustard seeds until they start crackling. Add the coriander, coconut, chilli and dokhla pieces and cook for a further 1 minute. Serve hot or cold at tea or a meal with chutney.

Gujrati-style Dokri
Serves 4-6

100 g/4 oz/1 cup gram flour • 90 ml/6 tbsp natural (plain) yoghurt

2.5 ml/½ tsp garam masala • 2.5 ml/½ tsp ground ginger

2.5 ml/½ tsp ground red chilli • 2.5 ml/½ tsp ground turmeric

1 small green chilli, chopped (optional) • salt • 2.5 ml/½ tsp Eno

Tarka: 30 ml/2 tbsp oil • pinch of asafoetida

2.5 ml/½ tsp mustard seeds • 2.5 ml/½ tsp cumin seeds • 2.5 ml/½ tsp sesame seeds

5 ml/1 tsp sugar • 2.5 ml/½ tsp citric acid

Blend the flour and yoghurt to make a smooth batter. Mix in the garam masala, ginger, chilli, turmeric, green chilli, salt and Eno. Cover overnight.

Place a trivet in a large saucepan, fill with water to come just below the trivet and bring to the boil. Pour the batter into a greased heatproof dish. When the water starts boiling, place the dish on the trivet, cover and cook for 15 minutes until the dokri has doubled in size and is spongy. Remove from the heat and cut it into 2.5 cm/1 in pieces.

Meanwhile, heat the oil in a heavy-based pan and fry the asafoetida and mustard seeds until they start crackling. Add the cumin and sesame seeds and fry for a few seconds. Mix in the dokri. Remove from the heat and mix in the sugar and citric acid. Serve hot or cold at tea with chutney.

Potato Samosas   Makes 16

200 g/7 oz/1¾ cups plain (all-purpose) flour

5 ml/1 tsp lemon juice ● salt ● 75 ml/3 tbsp lukewarm water

Filling: 45 ml/3 tbsp oil ● 5 ml/1 tsp cumin seeds

500 g/18 oz potatoes, boiled in their skins then chopped

5 ml/1 tsp garam masala ● 5 ml/1 tsp ground roasted cumin

2.5 ml/½ tsp ground ginger ● 2.5 ml/½ tsp ground red chilli

2.5 ml/½ tsp ground turmeric

salt ● 225 g/8 oz peas ● 30 ml/2 tbsp lemon juice

15 ml/1 tbsp sugar ● 60 ml/4 tbsp chopped fresh coriander (cilantro)

1 small green chilli, chopped

Batter: 15 ml/1 tbsp plain (all-purpose) flour

15-30 ml/1-2 tbsp water ● oil for frying

Sift **150 g/5 oz/1¼ cups of flour** into a bowl and mix in the lemon juice and salt. Work in the water to form a dough then knead for 5 minutes until the dough is springy and satiny. Cover and set aside for 30 minutes.

To make the filling, heat the oil in a heavy-based pan and fry the cumin seeds until lightly browned. Add the potato pieces and fry for 10 minutes until light golden brown. Stir in the garam masala, cumin, ginger, chilli, turmeric and salt. Stir in the peas and simmer for about 3 minutes until tender. Stir in the lemon juice and sugar and cook for 2 minutes. Remove from the heat and stir in the coriander and chilli. Leave to cool then divide into 16 equal portions.

Make a runny batter with the flour and a little water and set aside.

Divide the dough into 8 equal portions and roll each one into a ball. Dust with flour then roll into circles. Place a circle on a floured board, smear the top with oil, sprinkle with flour and top with another circle. Repeat this until you have 4 circles one on top of each other. Sprinkle with flour then roll out thinly. Heat a flat frying pan (skillet) over a medium heat. Reduce the heat to low and place the rolled circles in it. Fry for 10-20 seconds until dry, turn over and remove the first layer. Immediately turn over again and remove the second layer and continue until both sides of all the layers are cooked. Place on a cooling tray and cover with a tea cloth. Cook the remaining dough.

Cut the rounds in half and overlap the flat sides to form a cone shape. Brush the edges with the batter and seal them firmly. Fill the cones with the potato mixture, brush the edges with batter and seal firmly. Heat the oil in a deep pan over a medium heat. Gently slip 5 or 6 samosas into the hot oil, reduce the heat to medium-low and fry gently until crispy light golden brown on all sides.

Vegetable Samosas
Serves 8

2 green chillies ● 2 cloves garlic ● 2.5 cm/1 in ginger root

2.5 ml/½ tsp ground turmeric ● 1.5 ml/¼ tsp ground coriander (cilantro)

2.5 ml/½ tsp ground cumin ● 15 ml/1 tbsp oil ● 1 onion, sliced

100 g/4 oz peas ● 100 g/4 oz carrots, chopped

100 g/4 oz potato, chopped ● 2.5 ml/½ tsp salt ● 15 ml/1 tbsp water

2 sprigs fresh coriander (cilantro), chopped ● juice of 1 lime

100 g/4 oz/1 cup wholewheat flour ● 225 g/8 oz/2 cups plain (all-purpose) flour

pinch of salt ● 60 ml/4 tbsp water ● oil for deep-frying

Grind the spices to a paste. Heat the oil and fry the onion until browned. Add the peas, carrots and potatoes and fry for 2 minutes. Add the ground spices, salt and water, cover and simmer until the vegetables are tender and the water is absorbed. Add the coriander and lime juice.

Mix the flours and salt and add enough water to make a soft dough. Divide the dough into small balls then roll them out into 8 cm/3 in circles. Cut in half and shape into cones, sealing the edges together with a little water. Spoon the vegetable mixture into the cones and seal the edges carefully. Deep-fry in the hot oil until browned.

Moghlai Samosas
Serves 6

450 g/1 lb minced (ground) meat ● 2 large onions, chopped

5 cloves garlic, chopped ● 4 green chillies, chopped

1 bunch fresh coriander (cilantro), chopped ● 15 ml/1 tbsp ghee

5 ml/1 tsp ground turmeric ● 2.5 ml/½ tsp salt

juice of ½ lemon ● 275 g/10 oz/2½ cups plain (all-purpose) flour

pinch of salt ● 60 ml/4 tbsp water ● oil or ghee for deep-frying

Cook the meat, onions, garlic, chillies, coriander, ghee, turmeric and salt in a large pan until the meat is dry and tender. Add the lemon juice and leave to cool.

Mix the flour and salt then add enough water to make a stiff dough. Divide into walnut-sized balls then roll out 2 of the balls together into a circle. Brush one circle with melted ghee and press the other on top the roll out the circles until very thin. Dry fry in a heavy-based pan until dry but not browned. While still hot, pull the 2 pieces of pastry apart then cut into 3 cm/1¼ in strips.

Fold the short edge of the pastry strips over twice to form a pocket, fill this with mince then fold the strip over and over in a triangle shape, sealing the edges with a little water.

Deep-fry in the hot oil until crisp and brown. Serve hot with chutney.

Keema Samosas
Makes 16

200 g/7 oz/1¾ cups plain (all-purpose) flour • 5 ml/1 tsp lemon juice

salt • 75 ml/3 tbsp lukewarm water

Filling: 45 ml/3 tbsp oil • 2 large cloves garlic, crushed

1.5 cm/½ in ginger root, finely chopped • 1 small onion, finely chopped

5 ml/1 tsp garam masala • 5 ml/1 tsp ground roasted cumin

2.5 ml/½ tsp ground turmeric • salt • 450 g/1 lb lean lamb, diced • 450 g/1 lb peas

100 ml/3½ fl oz/6½ tbsp water • 30 ml/2 tbsp lemon juice

10 ml/2 tsp sugar • 30 ml/2 tbsp chopped fresh coriander (cilantro)

1 small green chilli, chopped

Batter: 15 ml/1 tbsp plain (all-purpose) flour

15-30 ml/1-2 tbsp water • oil for frying

Sift 150 g/5 oz/1¼ cups of flour into a bowl and mix in the lemon juice and salt. Work in the water to form a dough then knead for 5 minutes until the dough is springy and satiny. Cover and set aside for 30 minutes.

To make the filling, heat the oil in a heavy-based pan and fry the garlic, ginger and onion until lightly browned. Stir in the ground spices, salt, meat and water, bring to the boil then cover and simmer over a medium heat for 20 minutes until the meat is tender. Add the peas, sugar and lemon juice and cook for a few minutes until the peas are tender. Stir in the coriander and chilli and set aside to cool.

Make a runny batter with the flour and a little water and set aside.

Divide the dough into 8 equal portions and roll each one into a ball. Dust with flour then roll into circles. Place a circle on a floured board, smear the top with oil, sprinkle with flour and top with another circle.

Repeat this until you have 4 circles one on top of each other. Sprinkle with flour then roll out thinly. Heat a flat frying pan (skillet) over a medium heat. Reduce the heat to low and place the rolled circles in it. Fry for 10-20 seconds until dry, turn over and remove the first layer. Immediately turn over again and remove the second layer and continue until both sides of all the layers are cooked. Place on a cooling tray and cover with a teacloth. Cook the remaining dough.

Cut the rounds in half and overlap the flat sides to form a cone shape. Brush the edges with the batter and seal them firmly. Fill the cones with the filling mixture, brush the edges with batter and seal firmly. Heat the oil in a deep pan over a medium heat. Gently slip 5 or 6 samosas into the hot oil, reduce the heat to medium-low and fry gently until crispy light golden brown on all sides. Serve hot with chutney at tea.

Peanut Uppuma
Serves 6

15 ml/1 tbsp oil or ghee ● 2.5 ml/½ tsp mustard seeds

4 green chillies, chopped ● 1 onion, sliced

5 ml/1 tsp ground turmeric ● pinch of asafoetida

25 g/1 oz desiccated (shredded) coconut ● 350 g/12 oz/3 cups peanuts, chopped

salt ● 15 ml/1 tbsp chopped fresh coriander (cilantro)

Heat the oil and fry the mustard seeds until they start crackling. Add the chillies, onion, turmeric and asafoetida and fry until browned. Add the coconut and peanuts, cover and cook for 5 minutes. Remove the lid and cook, stirring, until the mixture is soft and cooked through. Serve sprinkled with coriander.

Vegetable Rava Uppuma
Serves 4

100 g/4 oz semolina ● 45 ml/3 tbsp ghee ● 5 ml/1 tsp mustard seeds

5 ml/1 tsp cumin seeds ● 5 ml/1 tsp split black beans

5 ml/1 tsp yellow split peas ● 2.5 ml/½ tsp asafoetida

1 dried red chilli, halved ● 2-3 curry leaves ● 2 onions, chopped

1 cm/½ in ginger root, chopped ● 2 green chillies, chopped

1 potato, chopped ● 1 green (bell) pepper, chopped

1 carrot, chopped ● 2.5 ml/1 tsp ground turmeric ● salt

750 ml/1¼ pts/3 cups water ● juice of 1 lemon

15 ml/1 tbsp chopped fresh coriander (cilantro)

Dry roast the semolina until lightly browned then set aside. Heat the ghee and fry the mustard and cumin seeds, split beans, split peas, asafoetida, chilli and curry leaves until the mustard seeds start crackling. Add the onions, ginger and chillies and fry for 2 minutes. Add the vegetables, tur-meric and salt and fry for 1 minute. Add the water, bring to the boil, cover and simmer gently until the vege-tables are tender. Gradually add the semolina, stirring carefully. Simmer until the water has been absorbed. Add the lemon juice and stir in the coriander before serving.

Masala Uppuma Serves 6

2 cinnamon sticks • 5 ml/1 tsp coriander (cilantro) seeds

pinch of cumin seeds • 4 dried red chillies

15 ml/1 tbsp ground turmeric • juice of 4 lemons

225 g/8 oz semolina • 60 ml/4 tbsp ghee • 10 ml/2 tsp mustard seeds

60 ml/4 tbsp yellow split peas • 60 ml/4 tbsp split black beans

50 g/2 oz/½ cup cashew nuts • 2 onions, chopped

45 ml/3 tbsp chopped fresh coriander (cilantro)

450 ml/¾ pt/2 cups boiling water • 100 g/4 oz grated (shredded) coconut • salt

Dry roast the cinnamon, coriander and cumin seeds, chillies and turmeric until lightly coloured then grind them and stir into the lemon juice. Dry roast the semolina until lightly coloured then set aside. Heat the ghee and fry the mustard seeds over a medium heat until they start crackling. Add the split peas, split beans and nuts and fry for a few seconds. Add the onions and fry for 5 minutes. Add the coriander and cook for 5 minutes. Add the water, spice mixture, coconut and salt, bring to the boil then simmer for 10 minutes. Gradually add the semolina, stirring continuously, until the mixture forms a thick paste. Cover and simmer gently for 5 minutes, stirring occasionally.

Sundal Serves 4

175 g/6 oz/1 cup chick peas (garbanzos), soaked overnight

10 ml/2 tbsp oil • 5 ml/1 tsp mustard seeds

5 ml/1 tsp split black beans • 1 dried red chilli, halved

2.5 ml/½ tsp asafoetida • 30 ml/2 tbsp grated (shredded) coconut

½ mango, chopped • 1 green chilli, chopped • juice of 1 lemon • salt

Cook the chick peas in boiling water for about 1 hour until tender then drain. Heat the oil and fry the mustard seeds, split beans, chilli and asafoetida until the seeds start crackling. Add the remaining ingredients and simmer for 2 minutes, stirring. Serve hot or cold.

Mysore Kodumbalai Serves 4

450 g/1 lb/4 cups rice flour • 100 g/4 oz/1 cup maize flour

50 g/2 oz/½ cup semolina • 5 ml/1 tsp cumin seeds • salt

100 g/4 oz grated (shredded) coconut • 6 green chillies

45 ml/3 tbsp chopped fresh coriander (cilantro) • 1 onion, sliced

pinch of asafoetida • 15 ml/1 tbsp jaggery • 90 ml/6 tbsp ghee

Mix the flours, semolina, cumin seeds and salt. Grind the coconut with the chillies, coriander, onions, asafoetida and jaggery to a chutney consistency. Melt half the ghee and pour it into the flour. Add the ground ingredients then gradually stir in enough water to make a stiff dough. Knead well. Take lumps of dough and roll into long noodles then shape them into spirals on a greased plate. Heat the remaining ghee and fry the spirals until golden brown.

Potato Patties
Makes 12

Potato mixture: 450 g/1 lb mashed potatoes

15 ml/1 tbsp chopped fresh coriander (cilantro)

5 ml/1 tsp pomegranate seeds ● 2.5 ml/½ tsp garam masala

2.5 ml/½ tsp ground red chilli ● 2.5 ml/½ tsp ground roasted cumin

1 small green chilli, chopped (optional) ● salt

Pea filling: 30 ml/2 tbsp oil ● 2.5 ml/½ tsp mustard seeds

2.5 ml/½ tsp cumin seeds ● 5 ml/1 tsp ground roasted cumin

1.5 ml/¼ tsp ground red chilli ● 1.5 ml/¼ tsp ground turmeric

salt ● 250 g/9 oz peas ● 30 ml/2 tbsp lemon juice

15 ml/1 tbsp chopped fresh coriander (cilantro)

5 ml/1 tbsp garam masala ● oil for frying

Place the potato mixture ingredients in a bowl and blend thoroughly. Divide into 12 equal portions. To make the filling, heat the oil in a heavy-based pan and fry the mustard seeds until they start crackling. Add the cumin seeds and fry for a few seconds until lightly browned. Stir in the cumin, chilli, turmeric and salt. Stir in the peas and cook for about 5 minutes until the peas are cooked. Add the lemon juice, coriander and garam masala, remove from the heat and divide the mixture into 12 equal portions. Take one portion of potato and roll it into a ball. Flatten the ball and place a portion of the pea mixture in the centre. Bring the edges over and smoothly cover the filling. Roll into a ball again and flatten until it is a 1 cm/½ in thick circle. Repeat with the remaining mixture.

Heat a flat frying pan (skillet) over a medium heat and smear with 30 ml/2 tbsp of oil. Place 5-6 patties on it and fry until golden brown. Turn them over carefully, pour 30 ml/2 tbsp of oil around the patties and fry the other side until golden brown. Serve hot with chutney for tea.

Mathi
Makes 24

100 g/4 oz/1 cup plain (all-purpose) flour ● pinch of salt

25 g/1 oz/2 tbsp margarine ● 2.5 ml/½ tsp tymol seeds

1.5 ml/¼ tsp black peppercorns, crushed ● 75 ml/5 tbsp lukewarm water

oil for deep-frying

Place the flour and salt in a bowl and rub in the margarine. Add the tymol seeds, peppercorns and water and knead to a dough. Knead for 5 minutes until satiny and spongy. Cover and leave for 30 minutes.

Heat the oil in a deep pan. While the oil is heating, divide the dough into 24 equal portions, roll them into balls then press into thin circles about 5 cm/2 in in diameter. Make 6 to 8 small slits in the circle with a pointed knife. Fry a few mathis at a time in the hot oil until light brown on all sides. Remove with a slotted spoon and place on a cooling tray. Repeat until you have fried all the mathis. Serve hot or cold with pickle or chutney at tea. They will store in an airtight container for up to 2 weeks.

Gujrati-style Batata Wada
Makes 12

450 g/1 lb mashed potatoes ● 30 ml/2 tbsp chopped fresh coriander (cilantro)

30 ml/2 tbsp lemon juice ● 15 ml/1 tbsp dried pomegranate seed

2.5 ml/½ tsp garam masala ● 2.5 ml/½ tsp ground red chilli

2.5 ml/½ tsp ground roasted cumin ● 2.5 cm/1 in ginger root, finely chopped

1 small green chilli, finely chopped ● salt

Batter: 50 g/2 oz/½ cup gram flour ● 5 ml/1 tsp oil

1.5 ml/¼ tsp garam masala ● 1.5 ml/¼ tsp ground red chilli

salt ● 75 ml/5 tbsp lukewarm water ● oil for deep-frying

Place the mashed potatoes in a bowl and mix in the coriander, lemon juice, pomegranate seed, garam masala, chilli, cumin, ginger, green chilli and salt. Divide the mixture into 12 equal portions and shape into balls. Place the gram flour in a bowl and mix in the oil, garam masala, chilli and salt. Gradually work in the water to make a smooth, runny batter. Heat the oil in a deep frying pan (skillet) over a medium heat. Dip the potato balls in the batter until completely covered. Fry a few at a time in the hot oil until golden brown on all sides, turning occasionally. Serve hot with chutney and barfi at tea.

Gol Guppa with Coriander Sauce

Makes 24

Dough: 50 g/2 oz/½ cup brown chapati flour ● 25 g/1 oz/3 tbsp semolina

2.5 ml/½ tsp lemon juice ● pinch of salt ● lukewarm water ● oil for deep-frying

Filling: 75 g/3 oz cooked chick peas (garbanzos)

75 g/3 oz cooked potatoes

15 ml/1 tbsp chopped fresh coriander (cilantro) ● salt

Sauce: 15 ml/1 tbsp chopped fresh coriander (cilantro)

15 ml/1 tbsp chopped fresh mint ● 300 ml/½ pt/1¼ cups water

10 ml/2 tsp sugar ● 2.5 ml/½ tsp garam masala

2.5 ml/½ tsp ground red chilli ● 2.5 ml/½ tsp ground roasted cumin

15 ml/1 tbsp tamarind concentrate ● 15 ml/1 tbsp lemon juice ● salt

Mix together all the dough ingredients and knead to a smooth dough. Knead for 3-5 minutes until the dough is springy and satiny. Cover and leave for 30 minutes.

Place the filling ingredients in a bowl and mix thoroughly. Roll the dough into a ball with the palm of your hands then flatten it. Place a few drops of oil on the work surface then roll into a thin circle. Cut out several 6 cm/2½ in circles and arrange them on a damp tea towel. Cover with a second damp tea towel and leave to stand for 5 minutes. Heat the oil in a deep frying pan (skillet) over a medium-high heat. Press one circle into the hot oil and as soon as it comes up like a balloon, add another one. Fry 4-5 together until golden brown and crispy, turning frequently. Remove from the heat and leave to cool on a cooling tray.

Blend the coriander, mint and 60 ml/4 tbsp of water to a smooth paste in a blender or food processor. Pour the remaining water into a jug and add the remaining sauce ingredients. Mix thoroughly then dilute to taste and chill in the refrigerator for 2-3 hours before using.

Make a hole in the centre of each gol guppa and fill it with the filling mixture. Dip it in the sauce and eat it at once so that it is not soggy.

Gol Guppa with Chutney

Makes 24

Dough: 50 g/2 oz/½ cup brown chapati flour ● 25 g/1 oz/3 tbsp semolina

2.5 ml/½ tsp lemon juice ● pinch of salt ● lukewarm water

Filling: 75 g/3 oz cooked chick peas (garbanzos)

75 g/3 oz cooked potatoes ● 15 ml/1 tbsp chopped fresh coriander (cilantro)

salt ● oil for deep-frying ● 150 ml/¼ pt/⅔ cup natural (plain) yoghurt

30 ml/2 tbsp cold milk ● tamarind chutney (page 381)

Garnish: 2.5 ml/½ tsp garam masala ● 2.5 ml/½ tsp ground red chilli

2.5 ml/½ tsp ground roasted cumin ● salt

Mix together all the dough ingredients, adding the water gradually until you have a smooth dough. Knead for 3-5 minutes until the dough is springy and satiny. Cover and leave for 30 minutes.

Place the filling ingredients in a bowl and mix thoroughly. Roll the dough into a ball with the palm of your hands then flatten it. Place a few drops of oil on the work surface then roll into a thin circle. Cut out several 6 cm/2½ in circles and arrange them on a damp tea towel. Cover with a second damp tea towel and leave to stand for 5 minutes. Heat the oil in a deep frying pan (skillet) over a medium-high heat. Press one circle into the hot oil and as soon as it comes up like a balloon, add another one. Fry 4-5 together until golden brown and crispy, turning frequently. Remove from the heat and leave to cool on a cooling tray.

Blend the coriander, mint and 60 ml/4 tbsp of water to a smooth paste in a blender or food processor. Pour the remaining water into a jug and add the remaining sauce ingredients. Mix thoroughly then dilute to taste and chill in the refrigerator for 2-3 hours before using.

Make a hole in the centre of each gol guppa and fill it with the filling mixture. Dip it in the yoghurt or pour the yoghurt in it with a spoon then spoon in some tamarind chutney. Sprinkle over the garnish ingredients and eat it at once so that it is not soggy.

Namkeen Phool   Makes 11

100 g/4 oz/1 cup plain (all-purpose) flour ● pinch of salt

25 g/1 oz/2 tbsp margarine ● 2.5 ml/½ tsp tymol seeds

75 ml/5 tbsp lukewarm water ● 30 ml/2 tbsp milk ● oil for deep-frying

Place the flour and salt in a bowl and rub in the margarine. Mix in the tymol seeds and water to make a dough. Knead for 5 minutes until satiny and spongy. Cover and leave for 30 minutes.

Heat the oil in a deep pan. While the oil is heating, divide the dough into 11 portions. Roll out 1 portion thinly into a circle and cut out 3 circles increasing in size. Place the largest on the work surface, brush with milk and top with the centre circle. Brush that with milk and top with the smallest circle. Make a dent in the centre and slit the circle into 8 equal portions without cutting through to the centre. Repeat with the rest of the dough. Deep-fry a few flowers at a time until golden brown, turning a few times during cooking. Leave to cool and serve cold at tea with a sweet.

Dalmod   Serves 4

Sev: 150 g/5 oz/1¼ cups gram flour ● 10 ml/2 tsp oil

2.5 ml/½ tsp garam masala ● 2.5 ml/½ tsp ground red chilli

2.5 ml/½ tsp tymol seeds ● salt

100 ml/3½ fl oz/6½ tbsp lukewarm water ● oil for deep-frying

Chevda: 100 g/4 oz flaked rice ● oil for frying

Chick peas (garbanzos) or lentils:

100 g/4 oz/⅔ cup chick peas (garbanzos), soaked overnight ● oil for deep-frying

Cashew nuts: 100 g/4 oz/1 cup cashew nuts ● oil for deep-frying

Peanuts: 150 g/5 oz fresh shelled peanuts ● oil for deep-frying

Tarka: 15 ml/1 tbsp oil ● 5 ml/1 tsp mustard seeds

5 ml/1 tsp garam masala ● 5 ml/1 tsp ground roasted cumin

2.5 ml/½ tsp ground red chilli ● salt ● 150 g/5 oz/1 cup raisins

15 ml/1 tbsp sugar ● 5 ml/1 tsp citric acid

To make the sev, place the flour in a bowl, rub in the oil then mix in the spices and salt. Gradually work in the water to a smooth batter. Heat the oil. Using a sev machine or an icing bag, slowly drop a long strip of the batter into the hot oil and fry until light golden brown. Remove with a slotted spoon, leave to cool then break into 2.5 cm/1 in pieces.

To make the chevda, heat the oil and place handfuls of the flaked rice into the hot oil. Immediately turn them over and take them out.

To cook the chick peas, heat the oil over a high heat and fry the chick peas until crispy and golden brown. Chick peas tend to pop so cover the pan while frying.

To cook the cashew nuts, heat the oil over a medium-low heat and fry the nuts until golden brown.

To cook the peanuts, heat the oil over a medium heat and fry the nuts until crispy and golden brown.

To make the tarka, heat the oil and fry the mustard seeds until they start crackling. Stir in the ground spices, salt and raisins. Remove from the heat and leave to cool slightly, then mix in the sugar and citric acid. Add all the cooked ingredients and mix thoroughly. Cool and store in an airtight container for up to 2 weeks. Serve at tea or as a nibble with drinks.

Papri   Makes 24

225 g/8 oz/2 cups plain (all-purpose) flour

5 ml/1 tsp lemon juice ● 5 ml/1 tsp ajwain

120 ml/4 fl oz/½ cup lukewarm water ● large pinch of salt

oil for frying ● 15 ml/1 tbsp natural (plain) yoghurt, whisked

5 ml/1 tsp tamarind chutney ● garam masala ● ground red chilli

ground roasted cumin

Place 200 g/7 oz/1¾ cups of flour in a bowl and mix in the remaining ingredients to form a soft dough. Knead for 5 minutes until springy and satiny. Cover and leave for 30 minutes.

Divide the dough into 24 equal portions. Roll them into balls, flatten them then roll then into circles on an oiled board. Smear the top with oil, sprinkle with flour and fold in half.

Smear the top again with oil and sprinkle with flour and fold again. Then roll out thinly to a triangle shape of about 5 mm/¼ in thick.

Heat the oil and fry a few papri at a time until golden brown and crispy, turning frequently while cooking. Spoon over the yoghurt and chutney, sprinkle with garam masala, chilli and cumin and serve hot.

Onion Bhaji
Makes 12

75 g/3 oz/¾ cup gram flour ● 150 ml/¼ pt/⅔ cup natural (plain) yoghurt

15 ml/1 tbsp lemon juice ● 5 ml/1 tsp garam masala

5 ml/1 tsp ground roasted cumin ● 2.5 ml/½ tsp ground red chilli

2.5 ml/½ tsp ground turmeric ● 2.5 ml/½ tsp ajwain ● salt

30 ml/2 tbsp chopped fresh coriander (cilantro)

1 small green chilli, chopped ● 4 onions, sliced ● oil for deep-frying

Place the gram flour in a bowl then mix in the yoghurt to make a smooth, runny batter. Mix in the ground spices and salt, cover and leave in a warm place for 4-5 hours.

Mix the coriander, lemon juice, chilli and onion into the batter. Heat the oil and whisk the batter a little more. Gently slip spoonfuls of the batter into the oil to form a round shape. Fry a few bhajis at a time until golden brown, making sure they are cooked through. Serve hot with chutney before a meal or at tea.

Mushroom Bhaji
Makes 12

75 g/3 oz/¾ cup gram flour ● 150 ml/¼ pt/⅔ cup natural (plain) yoghurt

15 ml/1 tbsp lemon juice ● 5 ml/1 tsp garam masala

5 ml/1 tsp ground roasted cumin ● 2.5 ml/½ tsp ground red chilli

2.5 ml/½ tsp ground turmeric ● 2.5 ml/½ tsp ajwain ● salt

30 ml/2 tbsp chopped fresh coriander (cilantro)

1 small green chilli, chopped ● 100 g/4 oz mushrooms, sliced

oil for deep-frying

Place the gram flour in a bowl then mix in the yoghurt to make a smooth, runny batter. Mix in the ground spices and salt, cover and leave in a warm place for 4-5 hours.

Mix the coriander, lemon juice, chilli and mushrooms into the batter. Heat the oil and whisk the batter a little more. Gently slip spoonfuls of the batter into the oil to form a round shape. Fry a few bhajis at a time until golden brown, making sure they are cooked through. Serve hot with chutney before a meal or at tea.

Cauliflower Bhaji

Makes 12

75 g/3 oz/¾ cup gram flour ● 150 ml/¼ pt/⅔ cup natural (plain) yoghurt

15 ml/1 tbsp lemon juice ● 5 ml/1 tsp garam masala

5 ml/1 tsp ground roasted cumin ● 2.5 ml/½ tsp ground red chilli

2.5 ml/½ tsp ground turmeric ● 2.5 ml/½ tsp ajwain ● salt

30 ml/2 tbsp chopped fresh coriander (cilantro)

15 ml/1 tbsp lemon juice ● 1 small green chilli, chopped

100 g/4 oz cauliflower, cut into small florets ● oil for deep-frying

Place the gram flour in a bowl then mix in the yoghurt to make a smooth, runny batter. Mix in the ground spices and salt, cover and leave in a warm place for 4-5 hours.

Mix the coriander, lemon juice, chilli and cauliflower into the batter.

Heat the oil and whisk the batter a little more. Gently slip spoonfuls of the batter into the oil to form a round shape. Fry a few bhajis at a time until golden brown, making sure they are cooked through. Serve hot with chutney before a meal or at tea.

Aubergine Bhaji

Makes 12

75 g/3 oz/¾ cup gram flour ● 150 ml/¼ pt/⅔ cup natural (plain) yoghurt

15 ml/1 tbsp lemon juice ● 5 ml/1 tsp garam masala

5 ml/1 tsp ground roasted cumin ● 2.5 ml/½ tsp ground red chilli

2.5 ml/½ tsp ground turmeric ● 2.5 ml/½ tsp ajwain ● salt

30 ml/2 tbsp chopped fresh coriander (cilantro)

15 ml/1 tbsp lemon juice ● 1 small green chilli, chopped

100 g/4 oz aubergine (eggplant), chopped ● oil for deep-frying

Place the gram flour in a bowl then mix in the yoghurt to make a smooth, runny batter. Mix in the ground spices and salt, cover and leave in a warm place for 4-5 hours.

Mix the coriander, lemon juice, chilli and aubergine into the batter.

Heat the oil and whisk the batter a little more. Gently slip spoonfuls of the batter into the oil to form a round shape. Fry a few bhajis at a time until golden brown, making sure they are cooked through. Serve hot with chutney before a meal or at tea.

Photograph opposite: *Gulab Jamun (page 412) and Jalebis (page 413)*

Mharashtrian-style Poha
Serves 4-6

60 ml/4 tbsp oil ● large pinch of asafoetida

2.5 ml/½ tsp mustard seeds ● 1.5 cm/¼ in ginger root, finely chopped

1 onion, finely chopped ● 1 medium potato, chopped

100 g/4 oz rice flakes ● 2.5 ml/½ tsp garam masala

2.5 ml/½ tsp ground red chilli ● 2.5 ml/½ tsp ground turmeric

salt ● 60 ml/4 tbsp desiccated (shredded) coconut

100 g/4 oz peas ● 30 ml/2 tbsp lemon juice

30 ml/2 tbsp chopped fresh coriander (cilantro) ● 1 green chilli, chopped

Heat the oil and fry the asafoetida and mustard seeds until they start crackling. Add the ginger, onion and potato and fry until golden brown. Stir in the rice flakes, ground spices, salt and coconut and cook for 5 minutes. Stir in the peas and cook for about 5 minutes until tender. Add the lemon juice, coriander and chilli and serve hot with a meal or at tea with chutney.

Sagarpare
Serves 4-6

150 g/5 oz/1¼ cups plain (all-purpose) flour ● large pinch of salt

40 g/1½ oz margarine ● 2.5 ml/½ tsp ajwain

100 ml/3½ fl oz/6½ tbsp lukewarm water ● oil for deep-frying

Place the flour and salt in bowl and rub in the margarine. Add the ajwain and water and mix to a dough. Knead for 5 minutes until satiny and spongy. Cover and leave for 30 minutes.

Heat the oil in a deep pan. Roll the dough into a ball then roll out to 5 mm/¼ in thick. Cut through the circle in parallel lines about 1.5 cm/½ in apart then cut at right angles in the same way to form diamond shapes. Fry in the hot oil until golden brown. Serve hot or cold at tea with barfi, rasgulla or any sweet.

Sev
Serves 4-6

225 g/8 oz/2 cups gram flour ● 300 ml/½ pt/1¼ cups water

pinch of bicarbonate of soda (baking soda) ● salt ● oil for deep-frying

Mix together the flour, water and bicarbonate of soda with a pinch of salt and knead to a stiff, smooth dough. Roll out thinly and cut into long strips or use a pasta machine.

Heat the oil and drop the strips into the hot oil. Fry until brown and crisp them drain and leave to cool. Store in an airtight container.

Photograph opposite: *Pistachio Kulfi (page 423) and Fruit Kulfi (page 422)*

Stuffed Bread Rolls
Makes 18

450 g/1 lb mashed potatoes ● 225 g/8 oz peas, rinsed in hot water

1 onion, finely chopped ● 1 green chilli, chopped

100 g/4 oz/⅔ cup raisins ● 30 ml/2 tbsp lemon juice

30 ml/2 tbsp chopped fresh coriander (cilantro) ● 5 ml/1 tsp garam masala

2.5 ml/½ tsp ground red chilli ● salt ● 9 slices bread, halved

oil for deep-frying

Mix together all the ingredients except the bread and oil and divide into 18 equal portions. Roll them into oblong shapes and set aside.

Fill a pan with warm water. Put half a slice of bread in it and soak for about 30 seconds. Remove and press gently between your palms to squeeze out the water. Repeat with the remaining bread. Place a portion of filling on the bread and gently roll the bread around the mixture.

Heat the oil and fry a few stuffed bread rolls at a time until golden brown. Serve hot at tea with chutney and barfi or as a starter.

Nimkis
Serves 4-6

225 g/8 oz/2 cups wholewheat flour ● salt ● 30 ml/2 tbsp ghee

ghee or oil for deep-frying

Sift together the flour and salt and rub in the ghee. Add sufficient water to make a soft dough, roll into small balls then roll these out to thick circles. Sprinkle a little flour on each circle then fold into quarters, dampen the edges and press together. Heat the oil or ghee and fry until browned.

Bread Chops

6 slices bread ● 2 large potatoes, boiled and mashed

5 ml/1 tsp chopped fresh coriander (cilantro)

1 green chilli, chopped ● 1 onion, chopped

2.5 ml/½ tsp salt ● ghee for frying

Soak the bread in water for a few minutes then squeeze out the water. Mash the bread with the potatoes, coriander, chilli, onion and salt. Divide into 8 portions and shape into short, fat discs with greased hands. Heat 15 ml/1 tbsp of ghee at a time and fry the discs in batches until lightly browned on both sides. Serve hot with chutney.

Flour Nuggets
Serves 4

30 ml/2 tbsp ghee ● 100 g/4 oz/1 cup plain (all-purpose) flour

salt and pepper ● 1.5 ml/¼ tsp cardamom seeds

ghee for deep-frying

Rub the ghee into the flour, salt, pepper and cardamom. Add a little water to make a stiff dough and roll it out to a large, thin round. Cut into strips them chop these into uneven pieces. Heat the ghee and deep-fry the nuggets to golden brown. Drain on kitchen paper and serve hot or cold.

Gram Flour Rings
Serves 4-6

450 g/1 lb/4 cups gram flour ● salt ● 2.5 ml/½ tsp chilli powder

5 ml/1 tsp cardamom seeds ● 100 g/4 oz/½ cup ghee ● ghee for deep-frying

Mix the flour, salt, chilli powder and cardamom seeds. Rub in the ghee and add enough water to make a stiff dough. Divide in half and roll out into thin round discs. Roll the discs then chop the roll into small rings. Heat the ghee and deep-fry the rings until golden. Drain on kitchen paper and serve hot with chutney.

Potato Pouches
Serves 4-6

6 medium potatoes ● 15 ml/1 tbsp ghee ● 5 ml/1 tsp chopped onion

pinch of cumin seeds ● 25 g/1 oz Paneer (page 20) ● 4 tomatoes

salt and pepper ● 15 ml/1 tbsp chopped fresh coriander (cilantro)

Boil the potatoes in water until just tender then drain. Cut in half and scoop out most of the flesh. Heat the ghee and fry the onion and cumin seeds for 1 minute. Add the potato flesh, paneer, 1 of the tomatoes, chopped, salt and pepper. Arrange the potato skins on a baking tray and fill with the cooked mixture. Slice the remaining tomatoes and arrange on top of the potatoes. Sprinkle with coriander and grill (broil) for 10 minutes.

Savoury Discs
Serves 4-6

150 g/5 oz/⅔ cup ghee ● 450 g/1 lb/2 cups plain (all-purpose) flour

10 ml/2 tsp cumin seeds ● salt ● 150 ml/¼ pt/⅔ cup water

5 ml/1 tsp black pepper ● ghee for deep-frying

Rub the ghee into the flour, cumin and salt then add enough water to make a stiff dough. Divide into 24 portions, sprinkle with pepper and roll out to a flat round disc. Heat the ghee to smoking point then deep-fry until golden. Drain on kitchen paper and serve hot or cold.

Chaklis
Serves 6

100 g/4 oz/½ cup gram flour ● 350 g/12 oz/3 cups rice flour

15 ml/1 tbsp chilli powder ● 2.5 ml/½ tsp asafoetida

2.5 ml/½ tsp salt ● 25 g/1 oz/2 tbsp butter

150 ml/¼ pt/⅔ cup water ● 15 ml/1 tbsp sesame seeds ● oil for deep-frying

Mix the flours, chilli powder, asafoetida, salt, butter and sesame seeds. Stir in enough water to make a soft dough. Heat the oil to smoking point. Place the dough in an icing bag and press small spirals of dough into the hot oil. Fry until crisp and brown, then drain on kitchen paper and serve hot with chutney.

Fried Corn
Serves 6-8

225 g/8 oz sweetcorn ● 300 ml/½ pt/1¼ cups milk

45 ml/3 tbsp ghee ● salt and pepper

Bring the corn and milk to the boil and simmer until the corn is dry and the milk has evaporated. Heat the ghee and add the cooked corn. Fry gently until the aroma arises, sprinkle with salt and pepper and serve hot.

Potato Chat
Serves 6

900 g/2 lb small potatoes ● 4 green chillies, chopped

5 ml/1 tsp mango powder ● 5 ml/1 tsp garam masala

5 ml/1 tsp roasted ground cumin ● 2.5 ml/½ tsp salt

150 ml/¼ pt/⅔ cup lemon juice ● 15 ml/1 tbsp chopped fresh coriander (cilantro)

Boil the potatoes in their skins then peel and slice into rounds. Place in a serving bowl and mix in all the other ingredients.

Spinach Chat
Serves 6

100 g/4 oz/1 cup gram flour ● 150 ml/¼ pt/⅔ cup water ● salt

2.5 ml/½ tsp chilli powder ● ghee for deep-frying ● 225 g/8 oz spinach

Add enough water to the flour to make a thin batter then stir in the salt and chilli powder. Heat the ghee. Dip the spinach leaves in the batter then slide into the hot ghee and fry until golden. Drain on kitchen paper and serve with chutney.

Potato Bundle
Serves 4

100 g/4 oz/1 cup gram flour ● 150 ml/¼ pt/⅔ cup water

450 g/1 lb potatoes, boiled ● 2.5 ml/½ tsp salt ● 1 onion, chopped

1 green chilli, chopped ● 2.5 ml/½ tsp chilli powder

2.5 ml/½ tsp grated ginger root ● 2.5 ml/½ tsp garam masala

10 ml/2 tsp chopped fresh coriander (cilantro) ● oil for deep-frying

Mix the gram flour with the water to make a thick batter and leave to stand. Mash the remaining ingredients together and divide into small round balls. Heat the oil. Dip the balls in batter then deep-fry until golden. Drain on kitchen paper and serve hot or cold with chutney.

Green Potatoes
Serves 4-6

450 g/1 lb potatoes

90 ml/4 tbsp chopped fresh coriander (cilantro)

10 ml/2 tsp salt ● 4 green chillies ● 90 ml/6 tbsp lemon juice

Boil the potatoes then peel and dice. Grind the remaining ingredients to a paste and mix well with the potato. Leave to stand for 5 minutes before serving.

Raitas

Raitas are yoghurt-based side dishes. They make a cool and refreshing accompaniment to spiced foods, reducing the effect of hot spices and producing a cooling effect on the body. Also, the proteins in yoghurt can be easily digested and absorbed by the human body. Yoghurt is extensively used in Indian cuisine, so it is worth making your own; you will find a recipe on page 20. Butter is often extracted from the yoghurt when it is made in Indian kitchens and buttermilk is formed, which is used as a cold drink after a meal.

Banana and Nut Raita
Serves 4

600 ml/1 pt/2½ cups natural (plain) yoghurt ● 30 ml/2 tbsp ghee, melted

2.5 ml/½ tsp mustard seeds ● 15 ml/1 tbsp minced peanuts

½ green chilli, minced ● 2.5 ml/½ tsp cumin seeds ● 3 firm bananas, thickly sliced

15 ml/1 tbsp chopped fresh coriander (cilantro) ● 30 ml/2 tbsp oil

30 ml/2 tbsp flaked almonds ● 2.5 ml/½ tsp garam masala

Beat the yoghurt lightly and place in a serving bowl. Heat the ghee and fry the mustard seeds until they start crackling. Add the peanuts and fry for 1 minute, stirring. Add the chillies and cumin seeds then stir in the bananas. Remove from the heat and stir into the yoghurt with the coriander. Heat the oil and fry the almonds until golden brown. Drain off excess oil then stir the almonds into the yoghurt. Dry roast the garam masala for a few seconds until darkened then sprinkle over the raita before serving.

Coconut Raita
Serves 4

45 ml/3 tbsp grated (shredded) coconut ● 4 green chillies

1 cm/½ in ginger root, chopped ● 1 bunch fresh coriander (cilantro), chopped

250 ml/8 fl oz/1 cup natural (plain) yoghurt ● salt ● 10 ml/2 tsp oil

5 ml/1 tsp mustard seeds ● 5 ml/1 tsp yellow split peas

2.5 ml/½ tsp split black beans ● 1.5 ml/¼ tsp cumin seeds

1 dried red chilli, halved ● 1.5 ml/¼ tsp asafoetida ● 2 curry leaves

Grind the coconut, chillies, ginger and a few coriander leaves to a paste. Add to the yoghurt with salt and taste and mix well. Heat the oil and fry the remaining ingredients until the mustard seeds start crackling and the split peas are golden. Add the raita and serve garnished with the remaining coriander.

Spicy Cucumber Raita
Serves 4-6

1 cucumber ● 600 ml/1 pt/2½ cups natural (plain) yoghurt ● pepper

2 green chillies, chopped ● 45 ml/3 tbsp chopped fresh coriander (cilantro)

5 ml/1 tsp cumin seeds ● 2.5 ml/½ tsp garam masala

Peel the cucumber and grate it coarsely. Squeeze out the excess moisture. Beat the yoghurt then stir in the cucumber and pepper and spoon into a serving bowl. Sprinkle with the chillies and coriander. Dry roast the cumin seeds for a few seconds until golden then grind and sprinkle over the yoghurt. Dry roast the garam masala for a few seconds until darkened then sprinkle over the raita and serve.

Cucumber and Onion Raita
Serves 2

1 cucumber, peeled and cubed ● 1 small onion, cut into rings

salt ● 5 ml/1 tsp dried soya ● pepper

15 ml/1 tsp lime juice ● 5 ml/1 tsp honey

150 ml/¼ pt/⅔ cup natural (plain) yoghurt

Sprinkle the cucumber and onion with salt and leave to drain for 15 minutes. Place in a bowl. Beat together the remaining ingredients, fold into the cucumber and onion and chill for 15 minutes before serving.

Fruit Raita
Serves 4

10 ml/2 tsp gelatine ● 30 ml/2 tbsp water ● 75 ml/5 tbsp caster (superfine) sugar

600 ml/1 pt/2½ cups natural (plain) yoghurt ● 2 small apples, peeled and cubed

30 ml/2 tbsp chopped walnuts ● 2.5 ml/½ tsp ground cinnamon

Dissolve the gelatine in the water. Mix the sugar into the yoghurt then whisk in the gelatine and leave until the yoghurt begins to thicken. Stir in the apples and walnuts and leave to set in the refrigerator. Serve sprinkled with cinnamon.

Sprouted Lentil Raita
Serves 4

100 g/4 oz/1 cup sprouted green lentils (page 253)

450 ml/¾ pt/2 cups natural (plain) yoghurt ● salt and pepper

2 green chillies, chopped ● 5 ml/1 tsp ground cumin ● juice of 1 lime

Mix together all the ingredients and chill before serving.

Mango Raita

3 ripe mangoes ● 600 ml/1 pt/2½ cups natural (plain) yoghurt

salt ● sugar ● 45 ml/3 tbsp grated (shredded) coconut

4 green chillies ● 15 ml/1 tbsp ghee

2.5 ml/½ tsp mustard seeds ● 1 small onion, chopped

Peel and cube the mangoes. Beat the yoghurt until smooth then season to taste with salt and sugar. Grind the coconut and chillies to a paste then stir into the yoghurt with the mango cubes. Heat the ghee and fry the mus-tard seeds until they start crackling. Add the onion and fry until lightly browned. Add the yoghurt mixture and remove from the heat. Serve with rice dishes.

Mint and Aubergine Raita

1 aubergine (eggplant), cut into 2.5 cm/1 in pieces

450 ml/¾ pt/2 cups natural (plain) yoghurt

pinch of ground red chilli ● 2.5 ml/½ tsp ground roasted cumin

salt ● 15 ml/1 tbsp chopped fresh mint

1 small onion, thinly sliced ● 1 spring onion, thinly sliced

Steam the aubergine for 10 minutes then mash it with a fork and set aside to cool. Mix together the remaining ingredients, stir in the mashed aubergine and chill before serving.

Okra Raita

10 ml/2 tsp oil ● 5 ml/1 tsp mustard seeds ● 5 ml/1 tsp cumin seeds

5 ml/1 tsp split black beans ● 5 ml/1 tsp yellow split peas

1 dried red chilli, halved ● 1.5 ml/¼ tsp asafoetida

2 curry leaves ● 225 g/8 oz/½ lb okra, chopped ● salt

300 ml/½ pt/1¼ cups natural (plain) yoghurt

Heat the oil and fry the mustard and cumin seeds, split beans, split peas, chilli, asafoetida and curry leaves until the mustard seeds start crack-ling. Add the okra and simmer over a low heat until the okra is tender. Season to taste with salt and simmer for 2 minutes. Add the yoghurt and blend together well. Serve cold or at room temperature.

Peanut Raita
Serves 4

30 ml/2 tbsp roasted peanuts ● 300 ml/½ pt/1¼ cups natural (plain) yoghurt

salt ● 2.5 ml/½ tsp black pepper

5 ml/1 tsp cumin seeds, roasted and ground ● 1 green chilli, finely chopped

15 ml/1 tbsp chopped fresh coriander (cilantro)

Chop the peanuts into small pieces. Beat the yoghurt until smooth then stir in the peanuts, salt, pepper and cumin seeds and blend together well. Sprinkle with the chilli and coriander and chill before serving.

Potato Raita
Serves 4

300 ml/½ pt/1¼ cups natural (plain) yoghurt ● salt and pepper

4 boiled potatoes, peeled and grated ● 1 green chilli, chopped

2.5 ml/½ tsp chilli powder ● 5 ml/1 tsp cumin seeds, roasted and ground

15 ml/1 tbsp chopped fresh mint

Whisk the yoghurt until smooth. Stir in the salt, pepper, potatoes and chilli powder. Sprinkle with the cumin and mint and chill before serving.

Minted Potato Raita
Serves 4

15 ml/1 tbsp ground coriander (cilantro) ● 30 ml/2 tbsp chopped fresh mint

2.5 ml/½ tsp pomegranate seeds ● 1 green chilli, seeded ● juice of 1 lime

450 ml/¾ pt/2 cups natural (plain) yoghurt ● 3 boiled potatoes, cubed ● salt

Grind the coriander, mint, pomegranate seeds, chilli and lime juice to a paste. Mix into the yoghurt with the potatoes and season to taste with salt. Chill well before serving.

Spicy Potato Raita
Serves 4

3 boiled potatoes, cubed ● 450 ml/¾ pt/2 cups natural (plain) yoghurt

salt and pepper ● 2 green chillies, chopped ● 15 ml/1 tbsp oil

5 ml/1 tsp mustard seeds ● 1 tomato, skinned and chopped ● 2 curry leaves

Mix the potatoes with the yoghurt, salt, pepper and chillies. Heat the oil and fry the mustard seeds until they start crackling, then add the tomato and curry leaves and fry until the fat appears on the surface and the tomatoes are cooked. Stir in the yoghurt.

Potato and Onion Raita
Serves 4-6

600 ml/1 pt/2½ cups natural (plain) yoghurt

50 g/2 oz potato, boiled in its skin and cut into 5 mm/¼ in pieces

1 small onion, finely chopped ● ½ small green chilli, chopped

salt ● 2.5 ml/½ tsp ground roasted cumin ● 1.5 ml/¼ tsp ground red chilli

1.5 ml/¼ tsp garam masala ● 15 ml/1 tbsp chopped fresh coriander (cilantro)

Whisk the yoghurt with a fork until smooth. Stir in the potato, onion, chilli and salt. Store in the refri-gerator until required. Sprinkle with the remaining ingredients before serving.

Potato, Cucumber and Coriander Raita
Serves 4

1 cucumber, peeled and grated ● salt ● 1 boiled potato, cubed

450 ml/¾ pt/2 cups natural (plain) yoghurt

30 ml/2 tbsp chopped fresh coriander (cilantro)

1 spring onion, thinly sliced ● 1.5 ml/¼ tsp ground red chilli

2.5 ml/½ tsp ground roasted cumin ● pinch of black pepper ● pinch of garam masala

Sprinkle the cucumber with salt and leave to drain for 15 minutes. Squeeze off any excess liquid and place in a bowl. Stir in the potato, yoghurt, cori-ander, spring onion, chilli, cumin, pepper and salt to taste. Sprinkle on the garam masala and chill before serving.

Radish Raita
Serves 4

10 white radishes, grated ● salt

450 ml/¾ pt/2 cups natural (plain) yoghurt ● pepper

2 green chillies, finely chopped ● 5 ml/1 tsp ground cumin ● lemon juice (optional)

Sprinkle the radish with salt and leave to drain for 30 minutes. Squeeze out any excess water then stir into the yoghurt with salt, pepper, chillies, cumin. Add lemon juice if wished. Chill before serving.

Spinach Raita
Serves 4

225 g/8 oz/½ lb fresh spinach, trimmed and finely chopped

450 ml/¾ pt/2 cups natural (plain) yoghurt ● 1 small onion, thinly sliced

5 ml/1 tsp ground roasted cumin ● 1.5 ml/¼ tsp ground red chilli

pinch of black pepper ● salt

Steam the spinach in a pan without water for about 5 minutes until soft. Strain. Mix together the remaining ingredients, stir in the spinach then chill until ready to serve. Serve with chicken curry and rice.

Tomato Raita
Serves 6

15 ml/1 tbsp oil ● pinch of asafoetida

5 ml/1 tsp yellow split peas, crushed ● 1 cm/½ in ginger root, grated

1 bunch spring onions (scallions), chopped

225 g/8 oz tomatoes, skinned and chopped

600 ml/1 pt/2½ cups natural (plain) yoghurt ● 2.5 ml/½ tsp garam masala

30 ml/2 tbsp chopped fresh coriander (cilantro) ● 2 green chillies, chopped

Heat the oil and fry the asafoetida and peas for 2 minutes. Add the ginger and fry for 2-3 minutes. Add the spring onions and fry for 1 minute. Stir in the tomatoes then remove from the heat. Beat the yoghurt then stir it into the tomato mixture and transfer to a serving bowl. Dry roast the garam masala for a few seconds until darkened then stir into the raita. Sprinkle with the coriander and chillies and chill before serving.

Tomato and Onion Raita
Serves 4

2 tomatoes, skinned and chopped ● ½ cucumber, peeled and grated

4 radishes, thinly sliced ● 4 spring onions (scallions), thinly sliced

450 ml/¾ pt/2 cups natural (plain) yoghurt

pinch of ground red chilli ● salt ● 2.5 ml/½ tsp paprika

Mix together all the ingredients except the paprika. Sprinkle with the paprika and chill until ready to serve.

Tomato, Cucumber and Onion Raita
Serves 4-6

500 g/17 fl oz/2¼ cups natural (plain) yoghurt

150 g/5 oz tomatoes, cut into 1 cm/½ in pieces

1 small onion, finely chopped ● ½ cucumber, cut into 1 cm/½ in pieces

salt ● 2.5 ml/½ tsp ground roasted cumin

15 ml/1 tbsp chopped fresh coriander (cilantro) ● 1 small green chilli, chopped

Whisk the yoghurt until smooth. Stir in the tomatoes, onion, cucumber, salt and cumin. Chill in the refrigerator. Sprinkle with the remaining ingredients before serving.

Marrow Raita
Serves 4

225 g/8 oz/½ lb marrow (squash), peeled and grated

300 ml/½ pt/1¼ cups water ● 450 ml/¾ pt/2 cups natural (plain) yoghurt

salt ● 5 ml/1 tsp ground roasted cumin

30 ml/2 tbsp chopped fresh coriander (cilantro) ● 1 small green chilli, chopped

Place the marrow and water in a pan over a medium heat and cook for 10 minutes until tender. Strain through a colander, squeezing out any excess water with your hands. Place the yoghurt in a bowl and whisk with a fork until smooth. Add the marrow, salt and half the remaining ingredients. Chill in the refrigerator for 2-3 hours before serving sprinkled with the remaining garnish.

Raita Mould
Serves 6-8

30 ml/2 tbsp gelatine ● 120 ml/4 fl oz/½ cup water

1.75 l/3 pts/7½ cups natural (plain) yoghurt ● 1 small cucumber, peeled and chopped

5 ml/2 tsp salt ● 1 small apple, peeled and chopped

1 small green (bell) pepper, chopped ● 2 green chillies, seeded and chopped

5 ml/1 tsp celery salt ● salt ● pinch of mustard powder

5 ml/1 tsp sugar ● ½ small cabbage, finely shredded

Dissolve the gelatine in the water then stir it into the yoghurt and leave until the yoghurt starts to thicken. Mix in all the remaining ingredients except the cabbage, spoon into a mould and leave to set in the refrigerator. Turn out on to a serving plate and serve surrounded with the shredded cabbage.

Vegetable Raita
Serves 4

1 cucumber, peeled and finely chopped ● 1 tomato, skinned and finely chopped

1 onion, finely chopped ● 1 green chilli, finely chopped

1 small bunch fresh coriander (cilantro), chopped

450 ml/¾ pt/2 cups natural (plain) yoghurt ● salt ● 10 ml/2 tsp oil

5 ml/1 tsp mustard seeds ● 5 ml/1 tsp cumin seeds

5 ml/1 tsp split black beans ● 5 ml/1 tsp yellow split peas

2.5 ml/¼ tsp asafoetida ● 1 dried red chilli, halved ● 2 curry leaves

Mix together the cucumber, tomato, onion, chilli, half the coriander, the yoghurt and salt. Heat the oil and fry the remaining ingredients until the mustard seeds start crackling. Add to the yoghurt and garnish with the remaining coriander. Serve cold or at room temperature.

Bundi Raita

Serves 4-6

50 g/2 oz/½ cup gram flour ● 5 ml/1 tsp oil

1.5 ml/¼ tsp garam masala ● 1.5 ml/¼ tsp ground red chilli ● salt

45 ml/3 tbsp warm water ● oil for frying

600 ml/1 pt/2½ cups natural (plain) yoghurt ● 5 ml/1 tsp roasted cumin seeds

15 ml/1 tbsp chopped fresh coriander (cilantro)

Place the flour in a bowl and rub in the oil. Mix in the spices and salt then gradually work in enough water to make a smooth batter, adding a little more if necessary. Heat the oil in a frying pan (skillet). Place half the batter on a slotted spoon and keep it about 20 cm/8 in above the pan and tap or stir the spoon so that lots of small droplets fall into the hot oil. Reduce the heat to medium-low and turn the droplets constantly with a slotted spoon until golden brown. Repeat with the remaining batter. Drain and transfer the bundi to boiling water then leave to cool.

Take handfuls of bundis out of the water, drain and gently press with the palm of your hands to squeeze out the remaining water. Whisk the yoghurt until smooth then stir in the bundis and chill. Serve sprinkled with cumin seeds and coriander.

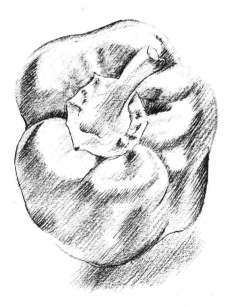

Chutneys, Pickles and Relishes

No Indian meal is complete without a pickle and chutney. They add an extra taste to a meal and help to increase the appetite. There are no special guidelines as to which chutney goes with which dish, they are all interchangeable according to one's own preference. They are served with both snacks and main meals. There are two types of chutney: cooked and uncooked. The former keep very well in airtight jars like any other preserve, whereas uncooked chutneys should be eaten within a day or two of making them.

Apple Chutney
Makes 900 g/2 lb

4 large cloves garlic ● 5 cm/2 in ginger root

250 ml/8 fl oz/1 cup wine vinegar ● 800 g/1¾ lb/3½ cups sugar

seeds from 6 black cardamom pods ● 2.5 ml/½ tsp black peppercorns

2.5 ml/½ tsp cloves ● 500 g/18 oz firm apples, peeled and grated in long strips

10 ml/2 tsp ground red chilli ● 10 ml/2 tsp salt

Blend the garlic, ginger and 45 ml/ 3 tbsp of wine vinegar to a smooth paste in a blender or food processor. Heat the remaining wine vinegar in a heavy-based pan over a medium heat. Add the sugar and boil until the sugar has dissolved. Skim off any scum. Coarsely grind the cardamom seeds, peppercorns and cloves then add them to the pan with the remaining ingredients and bring to the boil. Reduce the heat to medium-low and cook, uncovered, until the mango is tender and the chutney is thick. Leave to cool uncovered then pot in clean screw-top jars.

Hot Indian Chutney
Makes 1 kg/2 lb

350 g/12 oz cooking apples, peeled, cored and sliced

225 g/8 oz onions, finely chopped ● 350 g/12 oz brown sugar

750 ml/1¼ pts/3 cups malt vinegar ● 225 g/8 oz raisins

2 cloves garlic, crushed ● 10 ml/2 tsp salt ● 15 ml/1 tbsp ground ginger

15 ml/1 tbsp mustard seeds ● 15 ml/1 tbsp paprika

10 ml/2 tsp coriander (cilantro) seeds, crushed

Place all the ingredients in a large pan and stir over a gentle heat until the sugar has dissolved. Bring to the boil then simmer gently for about 2 hours until the chutney is thick. Spoon into warmed jars, cover and store for 2-3 months before serving.

Aubergine Kasaundi
Makes 900 g/2 lb

100 g/4 oz jaggery ● 150 ml/¼ pt/⅔ cup wine vinegar

5 ml/1 tsp cardamom seeds ● 1 cm/½ in cinnamon stick ● 5 cloves

8 peppercorns ● 10 cloves garlic ● 5 cm/2 in ginger root

10-15 dried red chillies ● 15 ml/1 tbsp oil ● 5 ml/1 tsp ground turmeric

675 g/1½ lb aubergines (eggplants), sliced

30 ml/2 tbsp mustard seeds, ground ● 30 ml/2 tbsp salt

Crush the jaggery and soak in the wine vinegar. Grind the cardamom seeds, cinnamon, cloves and peppercorns. Grind the garlic, ginger and chillies to a paste with a little wine vinegar. Heat the oil and fry the paste and turmeric for 1 minute. Add the aubergine and cook until soft. Add the jaggery and wine vinegar, mustard seeds and salt, stir well then simmer over a low heat until the mixture thickens. Sprinkle with the ground spices. Leave to cool. Store in airtight jars.

Aubergine Pickle
Makes 1.75 kg/4 lb

1.75 l/3 pts/7½ cups wine vinegar ● 10 g/¼ oz dried red chillies

15 ml/1 tbsp ground turmeric ● 25 g/1 oz ginger root, sliced

12 cloves garlic, sliced ● 300 ml/½ pt/1¼ cups gingelly oil

5 ml/1 tsp fenugreek seeds ● 5 ml/1 tsp cumin seeds

5 ml/1 tsp mustard seeds ● 2 sprigs fresh curry leaves

1.5 kg/3 lb small aubergines (eggplants), quartered

8 green chillies ● 5 ml/1 tsp sugar ● salt

Grind the red chillies, turmeric, half the ginger and half the garlic with 150 ml/¼ pt/⅔ cups of wine vinegar. Heat the oil and fry the fenugreek, cumin and mustard seeds, curry leaves and remaining garlic and ginger until browned. Add the ground paste and fry until dry. Add the aubergines and green chillies and pour in enough wine vinegar to cover the vegetables. Add the sugar and salt and simmer until the aubergines are tender and the oil floats to the top. Leave to cool. Store in airtight jars.

Banana Chutney
Makes about 1 kg/2 lb

500 g/18 oz bananas, peeled and sliced ● 50 g/2 oz/⅓ cup raisins

50 g/2 oz/⅓ cup stoned dates, chopped

225 g/8 oz cooking apples, peeled, cored and chopped

2.5 ml/½ tsp salt ● 75 g/3 oz/⅓ cup demerara sugar ● 10 ml/2 tsp ground ginger

pinch of cayenne ● 150 ml/¼ pt/⅔ cup distilled vinegar

Place all the ingredients in a large pan and stir over a low heat until the sugar has dissolved. Bring to the boil then simmer gently, stirring occasionally, for about 45 minutes until the chutney is thick and pulpy. Spoon into warmed jars, cover and store for 2-3 months before serving.

Carrot Chutney
Makes 450 g/1 lb

450 g/1 lb carrots, grated ● 1 onion, grated

45 ml/3 tbsp chopped fresh mint ● 2.5 cm/1 in ginger root, finely chopped

7.5 ml/1½ tsp salt ● 60 ml/4 tbsp lemon juice

Mix together all the ingredients, adding just enough lemon juice to moisten. Cover and chill until required. The chutney will keep for up to 2 days in the refrigerator.

Cauliflower Pickle
Makes 900 g/2 lb

900 g/2 lb cauliflower, cut into florets ● salt

15 ml/1 tbsp mustard seeds ● 50 g/2 oz mango powder

15 ml/1 tbsp chilli powder ● 10 ml/2 tsp ground turmeric

5 ml/1 tsp aniseeds ● 90 ml/6 tbsp mustard oil

Cook the cauliflower in boiling salted water until just tender. Drain and leave to cool. Grind together the spices and mustard oil to a paste. Toss the cooked cauliflower in the paste and leave to marinate for 1 day in a warm place. Store in airtight jars.

Green Chilli Pickle
Makes about 450 ml/¾ pt

225 g/8 oz green chillies, halved and seeded

300 ml/½ pt/1¼ cups oil ● 15 ml/1 tbsp paprika ● 5 ml/1 tsp ground turmeric

15 ml/1 tbsp fennel seeds ● 15 ml/1 tbsp mustard seeds ● 30 ml/2 tbsp salt

Place the chillies in a dry jar. Warm the oil slightly then stir in the remaining ingredients and leave to cool for 10 minutes. Pour over the chillies and mix well. Cover with muslin (cheesecloth) and leave to stand for 2-3 days in a warm place, stirring occasionally. Remove the muslin and put on the lid. Leave in a cool place for 2 weeks before serving.

Chilli Chutney
Makes 150 g/5 oz

1 bunch fresh coriander (cilantro) • 1 bunch fresh mint

6-7 green chillies • 5 ml/1 tsp chilli powder

2.5 ml/½ tsp cumin seeds, roasted • pinch of asafoetida

10 ml/2 tsp mango powder • salt • juice of 1 lemon

Grind together all the ingredients except the lemon juice, seasoning to taste with salt. Mix in the lemon juice. Serve with any main courses.

Coriander Chutney
Makes 450 g/1 lb

1 bunch fresh coriander (cilantro), coarsely chopped

1 medium onion, coarsely chopped • 1 small green chilli

juice of 1 large lemon • 2.5 ml/½ tsp ground red chilli

2.5 ml/½ tsp garam masala • salt

Blend all the ingredients to a smooth paste in a blender or food processor then store in an airtight jar for up to 2 weeks.

Coriander and Coconut Chutney
Makes 200 g/7 oz

100 g/4 oz fresh mint, chopped • 100 g/4 oz fresh coriander (cilantro), chopped

½ small coconut, grated (shredded) • 10 cloves garlic, chopped

1-2 green chillies, chopped • juice of 1 lemon • salt

Grind all the ingredients together, seasoning to taste with salt. Chill before serving.

Coriander and Mint Chutney
Serves 4

15 g/1 oz fresh coriander (cilantro) • 15 g/½ oz fresh mint leaves

60 ml/4 tbsp lemon juice • 5 ml/1 tsp pomegranate seeds

2.5 ml/½ tsp garam masala • 2.5 ml/½ tsp ground red chilli

1 small green chilli • 1 large clove garlic • 1 onion, coarsely chopped

30 ml/2 tbsp water • salt

Blend all the ingredients to a smooth paste in a blender or food processor. Refrigerate for 1 hour before serving.

Coconut Chutney

Makes 450 g/1 lb

150 ml/¼ pt/⅔ cup natural (plain) yoghurt

75 g/3 oz/¾ cup desiccated (shredded) coconut

60 ml/4 tbsp lemon juice ● 25 g/1 oz fresh coriander (cilantro) leaves

15 g/½ oz fresh mint leaves

15 ml/1 tbsp yellow split peas, soaked in warm water for 4 hours

5 ml/1 tsp ground roasted cumin ● 2.5 ml/½ tsp ground red chilli

1.5 cm/½ in ginger root, coarsely chopped ● 1 small green chilli

salt ● 15 ml/1 tbsp oil ● pinch of asafoetida ● 2.5 ml/½ tsp mustard seeds

5 ml/1 tsp split black beans, soaked in warm water for 4 hours

Blend all the ingredients except the oil, asafoetida, mustard seeds and split beans in a blender or food processor to a smooth paste. Place in a bowl. Heat the oil and fry the asafoetida and mustard seeds until the mustard seeds start crackling. Add the split beans and fry until light brown. Mix into the ground chutney and pour into an airtight jar.

Coconut and Garlic Chutney

Makes 200 g/7 oz

2 coconuts, grated (shredded) ● 2 bulbs garlic, chopped

30 ml/2 tbsp chopped fresh coriander (cilantro)

2 green chillies, seeded and chopped ● salt

Brown the grated coconut in a heavy-based frying pan (skillet). Grind all the ingredients together and store in an airtight jar.

South Indian Coconut Chutney

Makes 450 g/1 lb

225 g/8 oz grated (shredded) coconut

450 ml/¾ pt/2 cups natural (plain) yoghurt ● 45 ml/3 tbsp water

45 ml/3 tbsp oil ● 5 ml/1 tsp black mustard seeds

2.5 ml/½ tsp asafoetida ● 6 dried red chillies ● salt

Place the coconut, yoghurt and water in a blender or food processor and blend to a fine mixture. Heat the oil and fry the mustard seeds and asafoetida until the seeds start crackling. Add the chillies and cook for 30 seconds until they darken in colour. Stir in the coconut purée and season to taste with salt. Bring to the boil and simmer for 2-3 minutes, stirring continuously. Leave to cool. Serve with vegetable dishes.

Hot Coriander Relish

Makes 100 g/4 oz

1 bunch fresh coriander (cilantro) ● 1 onion, chopped

2 tomatoes, chopped ● 5 mm/¼ in ginger root, chopped

4 green chillies ● 15 ml/1 tbsp lemon juice

45 ml/3 tbsp water ● salt

Purée all the ingredients to a fine mixture. Serve as a dip for snacks and appetizers.

Cucumber, Onion and Tomato Relish

Makes 100 g/4 oz

½ cucumber, peeled and chopped ● 1 onion, chopped

3 green chillies, thinly sliced ● 1 tomato, skinned and chopped

juice of 1 lemon ● 2.5 ml/½ tsp ground cumin

45 ml/3 tbsp chopped fresh coriander (cilantro)

45 ml/3 tbsp chopped (bell) pepper

Mix together all the ingredients and leave to stand for 30 minutes. Serve with tandoori-style dishes.

Date and Orange Chutney

Makes about 1.5 kg/3½ lb

225 g/1 lb oranges ● 350 g/12 oz dates, stoned

225 g/8 oz onions, chopped ● 100 g/4 oz/⅔ cup raisins

350 g/12 oz granulated sugar ● 15 ml/1 tsp salt

pinch of cayenne ● 750 ml/1¼ pts/3 cups malt vinegar

Finely grate the orange rind, remove and discard the pith and pips and slice the oranges. Put the orange rind and flesh in a large pan with all the remaining ingredients. Stir over a gentle heat until the sugar has dissolved then bring to the boil and simmer gently, stirring occasionally, for about 45 minutes until thick. Spoon into warmed jars, seal and store for 2-3 months before eating.

Pickled Fish

Serves 6-8

450 g/1 lb plaice fillets, chopped ● 30 ml/2 tbsp ground turmeric

salt ● 1.2 l/2 pts/5 cups white wine vinegar

600 ml/1 pt/2½ cups mustard oil ● 60 ml/4 tbsp chilli powder

9 cloves garlic, crushed ● 2.5 cm/1 in ginger root

Sprinkle the plaice with turmeric, salt and a little of the wine vinegar and leave to marinate for 1 hour. Heat the oil and fry the fish then drain well. Grind the chilli powder, garlic and ginger to a paste with a little wine vinegar. Heat the oil and fry the paste for 2 minutes. Add the fish and remaining wine vinegar and simmer for 10 minutes until thickened. Cool and store in an airtight jar.

Spicy Pickled Fish

Makes 1.5 kg/3 lb

900 g/2 lb white fish fillets, diced ● 5 ml/1 tsp salt

1.2 l/2 pts/5 cups gingelly oil ● 50 g/2 oz/1 cup dried red chillies

50 g/2 oz coriander (cilantro) seeds ● 12 peppercorns

5 ml/1 tsp cumin seeds ● 2 bulbs garlic ● 10 cm/4 in ginger root

7.5 ml/1½ tsp ground turmeric ● 900 ml/1½ pts/3¾ cups wine vinegar

Sprinkle the fish with salt. Heat 300 ml/½ pt/1¼ cups of oil and fry the fish until crisp and dry. Set aside. Heat 15 ml/1 tbsp of oil and fry the chillies, coriander, peppercorns and cumin seeds until browned. Grind together the garlic, ginger, turmeric and a little wine vinegar to a fine paste.

Heat the remaining oil and fry the paste and ground spices until dry. Add the wine vinegar and mix well. Simmer until the mixture thickens. Leave to cool. Stir in the fish pieces then store in airtight jars.

Fish Roe Pickle

Makes 675 g/1½ lb

450 g/1 lb fresh fish roe ● 60 ml/4 tbsp chilli powder

30 ml/2 tbsp ground turmeric ● 30 ml/2 tbsp salt

300 ml/½ pt/1¼ cups groundnut (peanut) oil ● 450 ml/¾ pt/2 cups wine vinegar

45 ml/3 tbsp mustard seeds, ground

Clean the fish roes and sprinkle with 15 ml/1 tbsp of chilli powder, 10 ml/ 2 tsp of turmeric and the salt. Mix well then leave to stand for 30 minutes.

Heat the oil and fry the roes well on both sides. Leave to cool then cut into 2.5 cm/1 in pieces and pack in layers in a pickling jar. Mix the remaining spices with the wine vinegar then pour over the roes. Seal tightly and shake the jar well. Leave to stand for 1 week before using.

Hot Garlic Pickle
Makes 1.75 kg/4 lb

1.75 kg/2 lb garlic ● 225 g/8 oz salt

10 ml/2 tsp ground turmeric ● 5 ml/1 tsp mustard seeds

5 ml/1 tsp fenugreek seeds ● 5 ml/1 tsp aniseeds

5 ml/1 tsp nigella seeds ● 5 ml/1 tsp cumin seeds

225 g/8 oz mango powder ● 100 g/4 oz chilli powder ● mustard oil

Soak the garlic in water for 15 minutes then rub off the skins. Dry thoroughly then pound lightly to mash but not pulp. Mix the garlic with the salt and turmeric and leave to marinate in a warm place for 1 day.

Roast all the seeds lightly in a heavy-based pan then grind coarsely. Add to the garlic with the mango and chilli powders then spoon the mixture into a large jar. Add just enough oil to cover all the ingredients. Cover with muslin and leave for 6 days in a warm place. Transfer to smaller airtight jars for storing.

Ginger Chutney
Makes 675 g/1½ lb

225 g/8 oz jaggery ● 900 ml/1½ pts/3¾ cups wine vinegar

100 g/4 oz/2 cups dried red chillies ● 5 ml/1 tsp fenugreek seeds

10 cm/4 in ginger root ● 3 cloves garlic

350 g/12 oz/2 cups raisins ● 30 ml/2 tbsp salt

Boil the jaggery in 600 ml/1 pt/ 2½ cups of wine vinegar to make a syrup. Dry roast the chillies and fenugreek then grind them to a powder. Then grind in the ginger, garlic and raisins. Mix together the syrup, the remaining wine vinegar, the spices and salt and place in a large earthenware jar. Leave to marinate in a warm place for 2 weeks.

Ginger and Green Chilli Pickle
Makes 450 g/1 lb

100 g/4 oz ginger root ● 50 g/2 oz green chillis

175 ml/6 fl oz/¾ cup lemon juice ● 10 ml/2 tsp salt

5 ml/1 tsp garam masala ● 5 ml/1 tsp ground red chilli

Cut the peeled ginger into strips 1.5 cm/½ in long and 5 mm/⅛ in thick. Place in a jar with the remaining ingredients, making sure there is enough lemon juice to cover the ginger and chilli. Put the lid on the jar and shake it twice daily for about a month until the pickle is ready. The pickle will mature quicker if the jar is left in the sun, but open the lid slightly to avoid condensation.

Gooseberry Pickle
Makes 150 g/5 oz

2.5 ml/½ tsp asafoetida ● 5 ml/1 tsp fenugreek seeds

120 ml/4 fl oz/½ cup gingelly oil ● 2.5 ml/½ tsp ground turmeric

20 ml/4 tsp chilli powder ● 10 ml/2 tsp mustard seeds

100 g/4 oz gooseberries, chopped ● 30 ml/2 tbsp salt

Dry roast the asafoetida and fenugreek seeds until lightly coloured. Heat the oil and fry the mustard seeds, turmeric and chilli powder until the seeds start crackling. Add the gooseberries, salt and roasted spices and simmer for a few minutes, stirring, until well blended. Leave to cool.

South Indian-style Green Chutney
Makes 150 ml/¼ pt/⅔ cup

50 g/2 oz chopped fresh coriander (cilantro)

100 g/4 oz/1 cup grated (shredded) coconut ● 4 green chillies

1 onion, chopped ● 5 mm/¼ in ginger root, chopped ● 3 cloves garlic

1.5 ml/¼ tsp tamarind concentrate ● 120 ml/4 fl oz/½ cup water ● salt

Place all the ingredients in a blender or food processor and blend to a fine paste. Serve in a small bowl as a dip with snacks or appetizers.

Guava Relish
Makes 100 g/4 oz

2.5 cm/1 in ginger root, sliced ● 30 ml/2 tbsp chopped fresh coriander (cilantro)

4 green chillies, halved ● 5 ml/1 tsp salt ● 4 guavas ● 60 ml/4 tbsp lemon juice

Grind all the ingredients to a paste, adding the lemon juice a little at a time to reach the desired consistency.

Lamb Pickle
Makes 1.5 kg/3 lb

900 g/2 lb lamb, cubed ● 225 g/8 oz onions ● 1 bulb garlic

225 g/8 oz ginger root ● 450 ml/¾ pt/2 cups mustard oil

450 ml/¾ pt/2 cups wine vinegar ● 15 ml/1 tbsp chilli powder

15 ml/1 tbsp mango powder ● 5 ml/1 tsp cumin seeds

6 cardamom pods ● 6 cloves ● 2.5 ml/½ tsp grated nutmeg

2.5 ml/½ tsp ground mace ● 30 ml/2 tbsp salt

Place the meat in a heavy-based pan and cook over a low heat until the liquid from the meat dries up. Grind the onions, garlic and ginger to a paste. Heat the oil and fry the paste until browned. Add the mix and fry for 2 minutes. Add half the wine vinegar and all the remaining spices and simmer for 10 minutes, stirring continuously. Remove from the heat, stir in the remaining wine vinegar and leave to cool. Store in airtight jars.

Lemon Pickle
Makes 450 g/1 lb

900 g/2 lb soft-skinned lemons ● 75 g/3 oz/⅔ cup salt

10 ml/2 tsp ground ginger ● 10 ml/2 tsp ground red chilli

10 ml/2 tsp ground roasted cumin ● 10 ml/2 tsp tymol seeds

5 ml/1 tsp black pepper ● pinch of asafoetida

Cut half the lemons into eighths and squeeze the juice from the remainder. Place the lemon pieces in a jar then add the remaining ingredients, making sure all the lemon pieces are covered with juice. Put the lid on the jar and shake it well to mix the spices but do not stir. Shake the jar twice daily for about a month until the pickle is ready. The pickle will mature quicker if the jar is left in the sun, but open the lid slightly to avoid condensation.

Spicy Lemon Pickle
Makes 150 g/5 oz

150 ml/¼ pt/⅔ cups water ● 100 g/4 oz jaggery

10 ml/2 tsp salt ● 1.5 ml/½ tsp coriander (cilantro) seeds

2.5 ml/½ tsp garam masala ● 5 ml/1 tsp fennel seeds

2.5 ml/½ tsp nigella seeds ● 15 lemons, quartered

Put all the ingredients except the lemons into a pan and cook over a medium heat for 10 minutes. Place the lemon quarters into a glass jar and spoon in the cooked mixture. Shake the jar thoroughly and leave in a warm place for about 1 week until the lemon skin is tender, shaking at least once a day and before each use.

Lemon and Date Chutney
Makes 900 g/2 lb

24 large lemons ● 100 g/4 oz salt ● 675 g/1½ lb jaggery

12 cloves garlic ● 45 ml/3 tbsp cumin seeds

350 g/12 oz/2 cups dates, shredded ● 600 ml/1 pt/2½ cups wine vinegar

Quarter the lemons, sprinkle with salt and place in a large pickling jar. Cover tightly and leave to stand for 3 days.

Spread the pieces in a large, flat tray and leave to dry in a warm place for 5 days.

Mince the lemons. Grind together the jaggery, garlic and cumin seeds. Mix together all the ingredients to form a thick syrup with a consistency like custard, using a little more or less wine vinegar if necessary. Pour into airtight jars and store for 2 weeks before use.

Lentil Chutney
Makes 100 g/4 oz

30 ml/2 tbsp ghee ● 50 g/2 oz/⅓ cup red lentils ● 3 dried red chillies

2.5 ml/½ tsp asafoetida ● 60 ml/4 tbsp grated (shredded) coconut ● salt

Heat the oil and fry the lentils, chillies and asafoetida for 5 minutes. Add the coconut and salt to taste. Grind everything to a fine paste.

Lime Pickle
Makes 900 g/2 lb

900 g/2 lb limes, quartered ● 100 g/4 oz salt ● 900 ml/1½ pt/3¾ cups water

900 g/2 lb/4 cups sugar ● 30 ml/2 tbsp black pepper

Rub the limes with salt and leave to stand for 30 minutes. Put the limes into a pan with the remaining ingredients and stir over a low heat until the sugar has dissolved. The whole mixture will be quite watery. Boil rapidly until setting point is reached. A spoonful of the pickle dropped on to a cool saucer will wrinkle when pressed. Store in airtight jars.

Mango Chutney
Makes 900 g/2 lb

4 large cloves garlic ● 5 cm/2 in ginger root

250 ml/8 fl oz/1 cup wine vinegar ● 800 g/1¾ lb/3½ cups sugar

seeds from 6 black cardamom pods ● 2.5 ml/½ tsp black peppercorns

2.5 ml/½ tsp cloves ● 500 g/18 oz firm mango, peeled and grated in long strips

10 ml/2 tsp ground red chilli ● 10 ml/2 tsp salt

Blend the garlic, ginger and 45 ml/ 3 tbsp of wine vinegar to a smooth paste in a blender or food processor. Heat the remaining wine vinegar in a heavy-based pan over a medium heat. Add the sugar and boil until the sugar has dissolved. Skim off any scum. Coarsely grind the cardamom seeds, peppercorns and cloves then add them to the pan with the remaining ingredients and bring to the boil. Reduce the heat and cook, uncovered, until the mango is tender and the chutney is thick. Store in screw-top jars.

Mango and Redcurrant Chutney
Makes 1.75 kg/4 lb

900 g/2 lb green mangoes ● 450 g/1 lb redcurrants

225 g/8 oz ginger root ● 1.75 kg/4 lb sugar

450 ml/¾ pt/2 cups vinegar ● 45 ml/2 tbsp chilli powder ● 15 ml/1 tbsp salt

Peel and slice the mangoes. Grind half the redcurrants and ginger together. Thinly slice the remaining ginger. Put all the ingredients except the mangoes in a pan and simmer, stirring, for 15 minutes. Add the mangoes and simmer until the mixture has a jam-like consistency and the mangoes are tender. Leave to cool. Store in airtight jars.

Sweet Mango Chutney
Makes 900 g/2 lb

6 green mangoes • 250 ml/8 fl oz/1 cup cider vinegar

225 g/8 oz/1 cup light brown sugar • 10 cloves garlic, sliced

2.5 cm/1 in ginger root, thinly sliced • 5 ml/1 tsp ground red chilli • salt

Peel and slice the mangoes. Place all the ingredients in a pan and bring to the boil. Reduce the heat and simmer gently for 30-40 minutes, stirring occasionally, until thick. Leave to cool. Store in airtight jars.

Sindhi Mango Chutney
Makes 1.75 g/4 lb

1.1 kg/2½ lb green mangoes • 675 g/1½ lb/3 cups sugar

450 ml/¾ pt/2 cups vinegar • 5 ml/1 tsp nigella seeds

1 bulb garlic • 15 ml/1 tbsp chilli powder

15 ml/1 tbsp salt • 10 ml/2 tsp black peppercorns

Peel and slice the mangoes. Place the sugar and vinegar in a pan and stir over a low heat until the sugar has dissolved. Add all the remaining ingredients and simmer over a low heat for about 2 hours until the mangoes are soft and the chutney has turned reddish-brown and thick. Leave to cool. Store in airtight jars in a cool, dry place.

Mango Ambel
Makes 450 g/1 lb

4 green mangoes • 15 ml/1 tbsp mustard oil

2 dried red chillies, seeded and crushed • 5 ml/1 tsp mustard seeds

15 g/1 oz/2 tbsp sugar • 1.5 ml/¼ tsp salt

900 ml/1½ pts/3¾ cups water

Peel the mangoes and cut the flesh into thin strips. Heat the oil and fry the chillies for a few seconds. Add the mustard seeds and fry until they start crackling. Add the mango and fry for 5 minutes. Add the sugar and salt and cook, stirring, until brown. Add the water and bring to the boil then simmer for a few minutes. Check and adjust the taste. Leave to cool then chill well before serving.

Mint Chutney
Makes 150 ml/⅓ pt/⅔ cup

60 ml/4 tbsp chopped fresh mint • 60 ml/4 tbsp chopped fresh coriander (cilantro)

2-3 green chillies, seeded and chopped • juice of 1 lime

5 ml/1 tsp pomegranate seeds • 5 ml/1 tsp sugar • salt

Grind all the ingredients together, seasoning to taste with salt. Chill before serving.

Sweet Mint Chutney   Makes 150 ml/¼ pt/⅔ cup

100 g/4 oz/1 cup fresh mint leaves ● 1 onion, chopped

5 mm/¼ in ginger root, chopped ● 2 tomatoes, skinned and chopped

4 green chillies, chopped ● 30 ml/2 tbsp light brown sugar

15 ml/1 tbsp lemon juice ● salt

Combine all the ingredients in a blender or food processor and blend to a fine paste. Serve in a small bowl as an **accompaniment to lamb dishes, snacks or any meal.**

Onion Relish   Serves 4

1 onion, cut into thin rings ● juice of 1 lemon

2.5 ml/½ tsp paprika ● salt and pepper

Toss all the ingredients together well, cover and leave to marinade for 1 **hour. Chill for 1 hour before serving.**

Onion Chutney   Makes 150 ml/¼ pt/⅔ cup

30 ml/2 tbsp oil ● 2 dried red chillies ● 3 green chillies

10 ml/2 tsp black mustard seeds ● 20 ml/4 tsp split black beans

2.5 ml/½ tsp asafoetida ● 3 onions, finely chopped

1 small bunch fresh coriander (cilantro) ● 5 ml/1 tsp tamarind concentrate ● salt

Heat 15 ml/1 tbsp of oil and fry the chillies, mustard seeds, split beans and asafoetida until the seeds start crackling. Heat the remaining oil and **fry the onions until golden. Grind all the ingredients to a fine paste. Serve with any main courses.**

Peach Chutney   Makes about 1 kg/2 lb

2.5 cm/1 in ginger root, bruised ● 6 peaches, skinned, stoned and sliced

100 g/4 oz/⅔ cup sultanas (golden raisins) ● 3 onions, finely chopped

15 ml/1 tbsp salt ● 350 g/12 oz/1½ cups granulated sugar

300 ml/½ pt/1¼ cups malt vinegar ● 15 ml/1 tbsp mustard seeds

finely grated rind and juice of 1 lemon

Tie the ginger in a piece of muslin (cheesecloth) and tie to the pan handle with a piece of string. Put all the ingredients into the pan and stir over a gentle heat until the sugar has dis- **solved. Bring to the boil then simmer gently, stirring occasionally, for about 1 hours until thick. Discard the ginger, spoon into warm jars, seal and store for 2-3 months before eating.**

Peach and Apple Murabha
Serves 4

150 g/5 oz peaches, peeled, quartered and stoned

150 g/5 oz Granny Smith apples, peeled, cored and quartered

150 g/5 oz/⅔ cup sugar ● 100 ml/3½ fl oz/6½ tbsp water

2.5 ml/½ tsp ground cardamom ● 5 ml/1 tsp citric acid

Prick the peaches and apples all over with a fork. Bring the sugar and water to the boil and stir until the sugar is dissolved. Add the fruit, bring to the boil then simmer gently for 10 minu- **tes. Stir in the cardamom and citric acid and remove from the heat. Leave to cool then pour into an airtight jar.**

Green Pepper Chutney
Makes 900 g/2 lb

225 g/8 oz tamarind ● 675 ml/1½ pts/3¾ cups vinegar

100 g/4 oz ginger root, grated ● 1 bulb garlic, chopped

15 ml/1 tbsp mustard seeds ● 12 dried red chillies

3 green chillies ● 300 ml/½ pt/1¼ cups oil ● salt

450 g/1 lb green (bell) peppers, chopped ● 225 g/8 oz/1 cup sugar

Soak the tamarind in half the vinegar for 30 minutes. Strain through a sieve and extract the pulp; discard the seeds. Grind the ginger, garlic, mustard seeds and chillies in the remaining vinegar. Heat the oil and fry the ground spices and salt for 10 minutes. **Add the peppers, sugar and tamarind pulp. Cook over a low heat until the liquid has evaporated and the oil floats to the top, stirring occasionally. Leave to cool. Store in airtight jars for at least a week before serving with any main courses.**

Pepper and Coconut Pickle
Makes 225 g/8 oz

30 ml/2 tbsp oil ● 1 sprig fresh curry leaves, chopped

½ coconut, grated ● 2 dried red chillies ● 5 ml/1 tsp mustard seeds, ground

pinch of fenugreek seeds, ground ● 4 green (bell) peppers, cut into strips

15 ml/1 tbsp vinegar ● 5 ml/1 tsp sugar ● salt

Heat the oil and fry the curry leaves, coconut, chillies, mustard and fenugreek seeds until browned. Add the peppers, vinegar, sugar and salt and **simmer over a low heat until the peppers are tender. Serve as a fresh pickle.**

Prawn Pickle
Makes 900 g/2 lb

4 onions ● 10 dried red chillies

900 g/2 lb peeled prawns (shrimp) ● 2 bulbs garlic

2.5 ml/½ tsp black peppercorns ● 300 ml/½ pt/1¼ cups water

5 ml/1 tsp salt ● 450 ml/¾ pt/2 cups gingelly oil

450 ml/¾ pt/2 cups vinegar ● 75 g/3 oz ginger root

2.5 ml/½ tsp mustard seeds ● 15 ml/1 tsp ground turmeric

2.5 ml/½ tsp cumin seeds ● 8 green chillies

1 sprig fresh curry leaves ● 15 ml/1 tbsp sugar

Grind the onions, red chillies, pepper and 4 clove of garlic to a smooth paste. Put into a pan with the prawns, water and salt. Bring to the boil then simmer until the water has evaporated. Remove from the heat. Heat half the oil and fry the prawns until well browned. Grind the prawns with 30 ml/2 tbsp of vinegar, half the ginger, 12 cloves of garlic, the mustard seeds, turmeric and cumin seeds. Slice the remaining ginger, garlic and green chillies. Add the remaining oil to the oil in which the prawns were fried and fry the sliced ingredients. Add the curry leaves and ground paste and fry, stirring continuously, for 2 minutes. Add the vinegar, season with salt and bring to the boil. Add the prawns and sugar and simmer, stirring occasionally, until the oil floats to the top. Leave to cool. Store in airtight jars.

Sweet Chutney
Makes 225 g/8 oz

100 g/4 oz tamarind ● 300 ml/½ pt/1¼ cups water

100 g/4 oz jaggery ● 5 ml/1 tsp chilli powder

5 ml/1 tsp coriander (cilantro) seeds ● 5 ml/1 teaspoon aniseeds

5 ml/1 tsp cumin seeds, roasted ● salt

15 ml/1 tbsp chopped fresh coriander (cilantro)

Soak the tamarind in hot water then strain and extract the pulp. Grind the jaggery with all the remaining ingredients except the coriander, adding a little water to make the consistency you prefer. Serve garnished with coriander.

Tomato and Onion Chutney
Makes about 2.3 kg/5 lb

15 ml/1 tbsp mustard seeds ● 900 g/2 lb tomatoes, skinned and chopped

450 g/1 lb onions, chopped ● 2 cloves garlic, chopped

900 g/2 lb cooking apples, peeled, cored and sliced

225 g/8 oz/1⅓ cups raisins ● 350 g/12 oz/1½ cups granulated sugar

30 ml/2 tbsp curry powder ● 5 ml/1 tsp cayenne ● 20 ml/4 tsp salt

900 ml/1½ pts/3¾ cups vinegar

Tie the mustard seeds in a piece of muslin and tie on the handle of a preserving pan. Place all the ingredients in the pan and heat gently until the sugar has dissolved, stirring. Bring to the boil then simmer gently for about 3 hours until very thick. Discard the mustard seeds and spoon the chutney into airtight jars. Store for 2-3 months before eating.

Tomato, Onion and Coriander Relish   Serves 4-6

225 g/8 oz tomatoes, chopped • 1 onion, finely chopped

1 green chilli, seeded and chopped • 30 ml/2 tbsp chopped fresh coriander (cilantro)

15 ml/1 tbsp lemon juice • salt and pepper

Toss all the ingredients well together, cover and chill for 1 hour before serving. Can be stored in the refrigerator for 2 days.

Tricolour Chutney   Makes 150 ml/¼ pt/⅔ cup

4 red radishes, sliced • 4 spring onions (scallions), chopped

2 green chillies, chopped • 5 cm/2 in ginger root, grated

salt • 2.5 ml/½ tsp black pepper • juice of 1 lemon

30 ml/2 tbsp chopped fresh coriander (cilantro)

Mix together all the ingredients except the coriander and stir to blend thoroughly. Chill before serving garnished with the coriander.

Tamarind Chutney   Makes 675 g/1½ lb

100 g/4 oz dry tamarind • 300 ml/½ pt/1¼ cups water

225 g/8 oz/1 cup sugar • 5 ml/1 tsp garam masala

5 ml/1 tsp ground roasted cumin • 2.5 ml/½ tsp ground red chilli

salt • 75 g/3 oz/½ cup raisins • 5 dried dates, thinly sliced

Soak the tamarind overnight in the water or boil it for 15 minutes over a medium-low heat. Sieve the pulp and discard the seeds and sticks; the waste should not exceed 15 ml/1 tbsp. Place the pulp, sugar and spices in a pan over a high heat, bring to the boil then simmer gently for 10 minutes. Add the raisins and dates and cook for a further 2-3 minutes. Leave to cool then spoon into airtight jars.

Tamarind Sauce

Makes 50 g/2 oz

25 g/1 oz tamarind pulp ● 150 ml/¼ pt/⅔ cups warm water

5 ml/1 tsp salt ● 5 ml/1 tsp chilli powder

Soak the tamarind in the water for 15 minutes. Rub it in the water and blend the two together. Rub through a sieve and discard the husk. Stir in the salt and chilli powder. Chill before serving.

Fruity Tamarind Chutney

Makes 675 g/1½ lb

100 g/4 oz dry tamarind ● 300 ml/½ pt/1¼ cups water

225 g/8 oz/1 cup sugar ● 5 ml/1 tsp garam masala

5 ml/1 tsp ground roasted cumin ● 2.5 ml/½ tsp ground red chilli

salt ● 100 g/4 oz apples, peeled and chopped

150 g/5 oz peach, peeled and chopped ● 2 bananas, sliced

Soak the tamarind overnight in the water or boil it for 15 minutes over a medium-low heat. Sieve the pulp and discard the seeds and sticks; the waste should not exceed 15 ml/1 tbsp. Place the pulp, sugar and spices in a pan over a high heat, bring to the boil then simmer gently for 10 minutes. Add the apple and peach and cook for a further 2-3 minutes. Add the banana and cook for 1 minute. Leave to cool then spoon into airtight jars.

Tomato Chutney

Makes 900 g/2 lb

75 g/3 oz ginger root, coarsely chopped ● 50 g/2 oz cloves garlic, chopped

300 ml/½ pt/1¼ cups vinegar ● 800 g/1 lb canned tomatoes

300 g/11 oz/1¼ cups sugar ● 5 ml/1 tsp garam masala

5 ml/1 tsp ground red chilli ● 5 ml/1 tsp salt ● 1.5 ml/¼ tsp ground mace

1.5 ml/¼ tsp grated nutmeg ● 100 g/4 oz/⅔ cup raisins

Blend the ginger and garlic to a smooth paste with a little of the vinegar in a blender or food processor. Place in a pan with all the remaining ingredients except the raisins, bring to the boil then cook, uncovered, for 40 minutes, stirring occasionally. Add the raisins and cook over a low heat for 10 minutes until thick. Leave to cool then spoon into airtight jars.

Tangy Tomato Chutney Makes 900 g/2 lb

900 g/2 lb tomatoes, skinned and chopped ● 225 g/8 oz/1 cup sugar

4 cm/2 in ginger root, ground ● 10 cloves garlic, ground

10 ml/2 tsp onion seeds ● 120 ml/4 fl oz/½ cup white wine vinegar

5 ml/1 tsp chilli powder ● salt

Simmer the tomatoes in a pan over a low heat until the juices start to run. Add the sugar and stir briskly to dissolve it completely. Add the remaining ingredients, seasoning to taste with salt. Stir well and simmer over a low heat until thickened, stirring occasionally.

Hot Tomato Chutney Makes 900 g/2 lb

60 ml/4 tbsp mustard oil ● 3-4 dried red chillies, seeded and chopped

5 ml/1 tsp mustard seeds ● 1 bulb garlic, chopped

900 g/2 lb tomatoes, skinned and chopped ● 100 g/4 oz/½ cup sugar

45 ml/3 tbsp vinegar

Heat the mustard oil and fry the chillies for 1 minute. Add the mustard seeds and fry until they start crackling. Add the garlic and stir well then add the tomatoes and fry until the juices start to run. Add the sugar and vinegar. Stir well then simmer over a low heat until thick. Store in the refrigerator.

Sweet Tomato Chutney Makes 900 g/2 lb

6 cloves garlic, chopped ● 2.5 cm/1 in ginger root, chopped

2 onions, chopped ● 900 g/2 lb tomatoes, skinned and chopped

300 ml/½ pt/1¼ cups vinegar ● 175 g/6 oz/¾ cup sugar

15 ml/1 tbsp raisins ● 5 ml/1 tsp ground cardamom

5 ml/1 tsp salt ● 5 ml/1 tsp chilli powder ● 2 bay leaves

Cook the garlic, ginger and onions over a low heat until soft. Add the tomatoes and simmer until the juices start to run. Add the remaining ingredients and stir over a low heat until the chutney thickens. Leave to cool. Remove the bay leaves and store in an airtight jar.

Pickled Turnips and Dates   Makes 1.5 g/3 lb

15 ml/1 tbsp fennel seeds • 15 ml/1 tbsp coriander (cilantro) seeds

2.5 ml/½ tsp fenugreek seeds • 450 g/1 lb sugar

600 ml/1 pt/2½ cups water • 900 g/2 lb turnips, diced

225 g/8 oz/1 cups dried dates, chopped • 15 ml/1 tbsp salt

5 ml/1 tsp cayenne • 5 ml/1 tsp mustard seeds • pinch of ground turmeric

Dry roast the fennel, coriander and fenugreek seeds in a heavy-based pan until lightly coloured then grind together. Put the sugar and water in a pan and bring to the boil, stirring. Add the turnips and dates and simmer gently for about 15 minutes until the water has evaporated. Stir in the remaining ingredients and blend thoroughly. Leave to cool. Store in airtight jars.

Vegetable Pickle   Makes 2 kg/5 lb

900 g/2 lb turnips, sliced • 450 g/1 lb cauliflower, cut into florets

450 g/1 lb carrots, sliced • 225 g/8 oz peas • 2 bulbs garlic

50 g/2 oz ginger root • 50 g/2 oz onions, chopped

300 ml/½ pt/1¼ cups mustard oil • 15 ml/1 tbsp chilli powder

10 ml/2 tsp garam masala • 5 ml/1 tsp mustard seeds, ground

2.5 ml/½ tsp ground turmeric • salt • 250 ml/8 fl oz/1 cup vinegar

450 g/1 lb jaggery

Cook all the vegetables in boiling water for 5 minutes to soften. Drain and pat dry. Grind the garlic, ginger and onions to a paste. Heat the oil and fry the paste for 1 minute. Add the remaining spices and salt and fry until the oil rises to the surface. Leave to cool. Mix in all the vegetables then pour into a large glass jar and leave in a warm place for 2-3 days, shaking well every day.

Heat the vinegar and jaggery and simmer until it forms a syrup. Leave to cool. Mix with the vegetables and leave to marinate for a further 2 days. Transfer to smaller airtight jars to store.

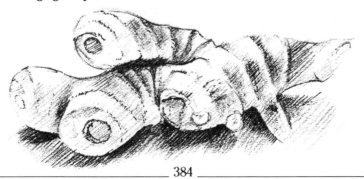

Mixed Vegetable Pickle
Makes 1.75 kg/4 lb

2.25 1/4 pts/10 cups water ● 450 g/1 lb cauliflower florets

450 g/1 lb fresh peas, shelled ● 450 g/1 lb small carrots, diced

450 g/1 lb turnips, sliced ● 15 g/½ oz cloves garlic

15 g/½ oz ginger root ● 1 onion, coarsely chopped ● 45 ml/3 tbsp water

150 ml/¼ pt/⅔ cup mustard oil ● 5 ml/1 tsp black cardamom

5 ml/1 tsp mustard seeds ● 5 ml/1 tsp black peppercorns

100 g/4 oz/½ cup salt ● 15 ml/1 tbsp garam masala

15 ml/1 tbsp ground red chilli ● 5 ml/1 tsp ground turmeric

225 g/8 oz/1 cup sugar ● 120 ml/4 fl oz/½ cup vinegar

Bring the water to the boil and add the vegetables. Return to the boil then remove from the heat, drain and spread the vegetables on a clean cloth. Leave overnight to dry then place in a bowl.

Blend the garlic, ginger, onion and water to a smooth paste in a blender or food processor. Heat the oil, add the paste and fry until golden brown. Grind the cardamom, mustard seeds and peppercorns to a powder. Remove the pan from the heat and stir in all the ground spices then add the vegetables and shake the saucepan to mix but do not stir. Place in a jar and leave in the sun for 2 days with the lid slightly unscrewed to avoid condensation.

Place the sugar and vinegar in a pan and bring to the boil then simmer until the sugar has dissolved. Leave to cool then add to the vegetables and shake the jar twice daily for 2 days.

Vegetable Sauce
Makes 450 g/1 lb

30 ml/2 tbsp sambar powder (pages 15/16) ● 600 ml/1 pt/2½ cups water

salt ● 5 ml/1 tsp tamarind juice ● 225 g/8 oz mixed vegetables, chopped

15 ml/1 tbsp chopped fresh coriander (cilantro)

Put the sambar powder and water into a pan and bring to the boil. Stir in the salt and tamarind juice and simmer for 5-7 minutes. Add the vegetables and continue to simmer for about 10 minutes until they are tender and the gravy is of the required consistency. Garnish with coriander and serve hot.

Desserts and Sweets

Indian desserts are very rich, and many of them are milk-based. A small portion is a delicious way to finish a meal. Use a non-stick saucepan if possible because some of them stick to the pan very easily.

Sweets play an important role in India. No function or festival is celebrated without sweets. Sweets are always distributed among relatives, friends and neighbours whenever a child is born, a marriage takes place, on birthdays or other celebrations. It is a lovely way to encourage celebration and bring people closer together.

Pineapple Salad   Serves 6

175 ml/6 fl oz/¾ cup pineapple juice ● 15 ml/1 tbsp arrowroot

60 ml/4 tbsp clear honey ● few drops of kewra or rose water

1 pineapple, sliced ● 2 apples, cored and sliced ● 2 bananas, sliced

30 ml/2 tbsp raisins ● 30 ml/2 tbsp pine nuts, chopped

15 ml/1 tbsp lemon juice ● 50 g/2 oz strawberries

120 ml/4 fl oz/½ cup soured (dairy sour) cream

Bring the pineapple juice to a boil. Mix the arrowroot and honey and stir into the juice. Simmer for 15 minutes. Add the kewra or rose water and simmer for 3 minutes then pour into a large bowl. Add the prepared fruit to the juice then gently stir in the raisins, pine nuts and lemon juice. Cover and refrigerate for about 2 hours, stirring occasionally. Stir in the strawberries and serve with a dollop of soured cream.

Fruit Chat   Serves 4-6

100 g/4 oz apples ● 100 g/4 oz pears ● 100 g/4 oz guavas

100 g/4 oz seedless grapes ● 3 bananas ● 30 ml/2 tbsp lemon juice

15 ml/1 tbsp sugar ● 5 ml/1 tsp garam masala

2.5 ml/½ tsp ground red chilli ● salt

Cut the apple, pear and guavas into 2.5 cm/1 in pieces, separate the grapes and slice the bananas. Place in a bowl with the remaining ingredients, toss together gently and serve cold. You can substitute other fruits of your choice, such as pineapple, orange, papaya, apricot, peach and melon.

Yoghurt with Fresh Fruits
Serves 4

450 ml/¾ pt/2 cups natural (plain) yoghurt ● 45 ml/3 tbsp sugar

2 bananas, thickly sliced ● 100 g/4 oz seedless grapes

2 peaches, peeled and cubed

Whisk the yoghurt until smooth and place in a serving dish. Stir in the sugar then the fruits and chill before serving.

Bhapa Dohi
Serves 6-8

300 ml/½ pt/1¼ cups natural (plain) yoghurt

400 g/14 oz condensed milk ● 50 g/2 oz/⅔ cup raisins

25 g/1 oz/¼ cup blanched almonds, chopped ● 25 g/1 oz/¼ cup cashew nuts, chopped

15 ml/1 tbsp pistachios, chopped ● 2.5 ml/½ tsp ground cardamom

Whisk the yoghurt until smooth then mix in the remaining ingredients and pour into a heatproof bowl and cover with a lid. Stand the bowl on a trivet in a pan half-filled with water. Bring the water to the boil then reduce the heat to low, cover and cook for 50 minutes. Serve cold.

Kalakand
Makes 20

100 g/4 oz/1 cup full-cream milk powder

75 ml/5 tbsp double (heavy) cream, whipped

10 ml/2 tsp ghee, melted ● 2.5 ml/½ tsp ground cardamom

2.5 ml/½ tsp kewra or rose water ● 75 g/3 oz/⅓ cup sugar

50 ml/2 fl oz/3½ tbsp water ● 15 ml/1 tbsp blanched almonds, finely chopped

15 ml/1 tbsp pistachios, finely chopped

Mix together the milk powder, cream, 5 ml/1 tsp of ghee, the cardamom and kewra or rose water. Bring the sugar, water and remaining ghee to the boil and simmer until it is ready to set. A drop in cold water will set and stay at the bottom. Add the syrup and half the nuts to the milk mixture and stir until smooth and cool. Shape the mixture into a ball and flatten on a greased plate to about 1.5 cm/½ in thick. Decorate with the remaining chopped nuts and leave to set for 2-3 hours. Cut into squares or triangles and serve cold as a dessert or snack.

Chenamurgi

Makes 225 g/8 oz

150 g/5 oz Paneer (page 20) ● 75 g/3 oz/⅓ cup sugar

45 ml/3 tbsp water ● 2.5 ml/½ tsp kewra or rose water

1.5 ml/½ tsp ground cardamom

Cut the paneer into 2.5 cm × 5 mm/ 1 × ¼ in pieces. Dissolve the sugar in the water over a medium heat. Add the paneer pieces and stir gently until the syrup is ready to set. A drop in cold water will set and stay at the bottom. Remove from the heat, stir in the essence and cardamom and continue to stir until the pieces are cool and coated with sugar. Serve cold at tea with samosas, tamarind chutney and barfi.

Kale Jamun

Makes 20

100 g/4 oz/1 cup full-cream milk powder ● 75 g/3 oz Paneer (page 20), mashed

30 ml/2 tbsp ghee, melted ● 30 ml/2 tbsp plain (all-purpose) flour

15 ml/1 tbsp semolina ● large pinch of bicarbonate of soda (baking soda)

100 ml/3½ fl oz/6½ tbsp lukewarm milk ● 25 g/1 oz/1½ tbsp sultanas (golden raisins)

6 blanched almonds, finely chopped ● 6 pistachios, finely chopped

5 ml/1 tsp yellow food colour ● 2.5 ml/½ tsp ground cardamom

1.5 ml/¼ tsp saffron ● ghee and oil for deep-frying

225 g/8 oz/1 cup sugar ● 200 ml/7 fl oz/scant 1 cup water

5 ml/1 tsp kewra or rose water

Mix together the milk powder, paneer, ghee, flour, semolina and bicarbonate of soda. Stir in the milk to form a soft dough, cover and leave for 30 minutes. Mix together the sultanas, almonds, pistachios, food colour, cardamom and saffron. Shape the dough into 20 equal portions and roll into balls. Place a little of the filling on each one and roll again. Heat the oil and fry the jamun over a medium-low heat until dark golden brown, turning frequently. Remove with a slotted spoon and leave to cool.

Meanwhile, bring the sugar and water to the boil over a medium heat. As soon as the sugar has dissolved, turn off the heat and add the jamun. Return to the boil then simmer gently for 5 minutes. Remove from the heat, add the kewra or rose water and shake the pan to coat the jamun in the syrup. Serve hot or cold as a dessert or at tea.

Kheer
Serves 4

1.75 l/3 pts/7½ cups milk ● 25 g/1 oz/2 tbsp patna or basmati rice

60 ml/4 tbsp sugar ● 25 g/1 oz/1½ tbsp sultanas

25 g/1 oz/3 tbsp blanched almonds, finely chopped ● 12 pistachios, chopped

2.5 ml/½ tsp ground cardamom ● 1.5 ml/¼ tsp ground saffron

5 ml/1 tsp rose or kewra water

Bring the milk to the boil then reduce the heat to medium-low, add the rice and simmer for 1 hour, stirring occasionally. Mix in half the nuts, the cardamom and saffron and simmer gently for 45 minutes or until the rice is at the desired consistency. Remove from the heat and mix in the rose or kewra water. Serve hot sprinkled with the remaining nuts.

Kheer 2
Serves 6

50 g/2 oz/⅓ cup basmati rice ● 450 ml/¾ pt/2 cups water

2.25 l/4 pts/10 cups milk ● 5 cardamom pods ● 225 g/8 oz/1 cup sugar

25 g/1 oz/3 tbsp flaked almonds ● 2.5 ml/½ tsp ground cardamom

1.5 ml/¼ tsp grated nutmeg ● 15 ml/1 tbsp rose water

Cook the rice in boiling water over a medium heat for 5-6 minutes until one-quarter cooked. Drain. Bring the milk and cardamom pods to the boil, add the rice and simmer for 30-40 minutes until the rice is soft and the milk very thick, stirring occasionally at first then continuously as the mixture thickens. Add the sugar, almonds, cardamom and nutmeg and simmer for a further 5 minutes, stirring continuously. Remove from the heat, discard the cardamom pods and sprinkle with rose water. Serve warm or chilled.

Quick Kheer
Serves 4

300 ml/½ pt/1¼ cups milk ● 425 g/15 oz canned rice pudding

25 g/1 oz/1½ tbsp blanched almonds, finely chopped

25 g/1 oz/1½ tbsp pistachios, finely chopped

25 g/1 oz/1½ tbsp sultanas ● 15 ml/1 tbsp sugar

2.5 ml/½ tsp ground cardamom ● 5 ml/1 tsp rose or kewra water

Boil the milk, add the rice pudding, half the nuts, the sultanas, sugar and cardamom. Return to the boil then simmer gently for 7 minutes. Stir in the rose or kewra water and serve sprinkled with the remaining nuts.

Carrot Kheer
Serves 8

2.5 ml/½ tsp saffron threads ● 1 1/1¾ pts/4¼ cups milk

225 g/8 oz/1 cup sugar ● 1.5 ml/¼ tsp ground cardamom

25 g/1 oz/3 tbsp flaked almonds ● 25 g/1 oz/2 tbsp margarine

1.5 kg/3 lb carrots, grated

Soak the saffron in 60 ml/4 tbsp of hot milk. Boil the remaining milk, sugar, cardamom, almonds and margarine over a medium heat for 5-6 minutes, stirring occasionally. Add the carrots and mix thoroughly. Simmer for a further 20 minutes until the mixture thickens and the carrots are glazed and sticky. Pour the saffron milk over the mixture and stir for 2 minutes. Serve warm or cold.

Almond Kheer
Serves 6-8

350 g/12 oz/2 cups blanched almonds ● 2.25 1/4 pts/10 cups milk

225 g/8 oz/1 cup sugar ● 5 ml/1 tsp ground cardamom

pinch of ground saffron

Soak the almonds in hot water for 3 hours then drain and slice. Heat the milk in a large pan, add the sugar and boil until thickened slightly. Add the almonds, cardamom and saffron and serve hot.

Horseradish Kheer
Serves 8

2 large white horseradishes, grated ● 15 ml/1 tbsp ghee

1.5 1/2½ pts/5½ cups milk ● 450 g/1 lb/2 cups sugar

50 g/2 oz/⅓ cup raisins ● 5 ml/1 tsp ground cardamom

Cook the radishes in boiling water until tender, drain. Heat the ghee and fry the radishes until lightly browned. Heat the milk in a separate pan, add the radishes and simmer over a low heat until the milk begins to thicken. Add the sugar and raisins and cook, stirring continuously, until it reaches the desired consistency. Remove from the heat, stir in the cardamom, cover and leave to cool. Serve hot or chilled.

Lotus Seed Kheer
Serves 8

100 g/4 oz lotus seeds ● 1.2 1/2 pts/5 cups milk

100 g/4 oz/½ cup sugar ● 5 ml/1 tsp ground cardamom

Remove the hard covering from the seeds then chop them coarsely. Bring the milk to the boil and add the seeds. Simmer until the seeds are soft and thoroughly mixed with the milk. Add the sugar and bring to the boil. Sprinkle with cardamom before serving.

Cauliflower Kheer
Serves 6

450 g/1 lb cauliflower florets, grated ● 600 ml/1 pt/2½ cups milk

5 ml/1 tsp ground cardamom ● 225 g/8 oz/1 cup sugar

50 g/2 oz/½ cup flaked almonds ● 50 g/2 oz/⅓ cup raisins

50 g/2 oz/½ cup desiccated (shredded) coconut ● 50 g/2 oz/½ cup pistachios, chopped

Bring the cauliflower, milk and cardamom to the boil and simmer until the milk thickens. Add the sugar, almonds, raisins and coconut and simmer for 10 minutes. Pour into a bowl and serve sprinkled with the pistachios.

Vermicelli Kheer
Serves 6

30 ml/2 tbsp ghee ● 75 g/3 oz vermicelli

450 ml/¾ pt/2 cups milk ● 75 g/3 oz/⅓ cup sugar

25 g/1 oz/3 tbsp sultanas (golden raisins) ● 5 ml/1 tsp ground cardamom

Heat the ghee and fry the vermicelli until golden brown. Pour in the milk and bring to the boil. Simmer for 5-10 minutes. Add the sugar and sultanas and simmer, stirring occasionally, until the desired consistency is obtained. Sprinkle with cardamom before serving.

Channa Dal Kheer
Serves 4

225 g/8 oz/1⅓ cups yellow split peas, soaked for 10 minutes

1 coconut ● 450 g/1 lb jaggery

15 ml/1 tbsp ghee ● 5 ml/1 tsp ground cardamom

Cook the split peas in boiling water for about 20 minutes until tender. Meanwhile, take a small piece of coconut and chop it. Grind the remaining coconut and pour over 300 ml/½ pt/1¼ cups of hot water then squeeze to extract the thick milk. Repeat twice more. When the peas are almost tender, add the thin coconut milks and the jaggery and simmer for 20 minutes until well cooked. Leave to cool for 5 minutes. Stir in the thick coconut milk. Fry the coconut bits in the ghee until browned then stir into the kheer with the cardamom. Serve cold.

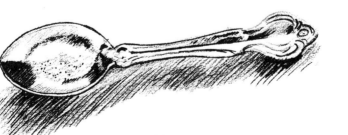

Rasgulla
Makes 14

1.2 1/2 pts/5 cups milk ● 30 ml/2 tbsp lemon juice

350 g/12 oz/1½ cups sugar ● 2.25 1/4 pts/10 cups water

10 ml/2 tsp semolina ● 5 ml/1 tsp kewra or rose water

Boil the milk then add the lemon juice and remove from the heat. Leave for 2 minutes to separate. Strain through a muslin cloth and reserve the whey for cooking lentils or vegetables. Rinse the curd or paneer with cold water then press under a heavy object to squeeze out all the water for 30 minutes.

Bring the sugar and water to the boil then leave to simmer. Mix the semolina into the paneer with the palm of your hand until it is soft and springy. Divide into 14 equal balls. Add the paneer balls to the boiling syrup and cook for 1 hour until the syrup is reduced by three-quarters. Leave to cool then chill for 3-4 hours and stir in the kewra or rose water just before serving. Serve cold as a dessert or at tea with samosa and pakora.

Rasmalai
Makes 14

1.2 1/2 pts/5 cups milk ● 30 ml/2 tbsp lemon juice

350 g/12 oz/1½ cups sugar ● 2.25 1/4 pts/10 cups water

10 ml/2 tsp semolina ● 10 ml/2 tsp kewra or rose water

1.5 ml/¼ tsp ground cardamom ● 300 ml/½ pt/2½ cups double (heavy) cream, whipped

25 g/1 oz/¼ cup pistachios, finely chopped

Boil the milk then add the lemon juice and remove from the heat. Leave for 2 minutes to separate. Strain through a muslin (cheesecloth) and reserve the whey for cooking lentils or vegetables. Rinse the curd or paneer with cold water then press under a heavy object to squeeze out all the water for 30 minutes.

Bring the sugar and water to the boil then leave to simmer. Mix the semolina into the paneer with the palm of your hand until it is soft and springy. Divide into 14 equal balls.

Add the paneer balls to the boiling syrup and cook for 1 hour until the syrup is reduced by three-quarters. Leave to cool then chill for 3-4 hours and stir in 5 ml/1 tsp of the kewra or rose water just before serving. Mix the remaining kewra or rose water and the cardamom into the cream. Dip each rasgulla into the cream mixture and place them on a serving dish. Pour over the remaining cream and sprinkle with the pistachios. Serve cold as a dessert or at tea.

Mallpuha
Makes 6

25 g/1 oz/¼ cup full-cream milk powder ● 25 g/1 oz/¼ cup plain (all-purpose) flour

120 ml/4 fl oz/½ cup lukewarm water ● 6 blanched almonds, finely chopped

6 pistachios, finely chopped ● 2.5 ml/½ tsp ground cardamom

25 g/1 oz/2 tbsp sugar ● 50 ml/2 fl oz/3½ tbsp water

ghee and oil for frying

Mix together the milk powder and flour. Gradually mix in the water to form a smooth batter. Mix in the nuts and cardamom. Bring the sugar and water to the boil then simmer until the sugar has dissolved. Remove from the heat. Heat 10 ml/2 tsp of oil and ghee in a frying pan (skillet). Spread 15 ml/ 1 tbsp of batter thinly in the pan and cook for 1 minute. Turn it over, pour a further 10 ml/2 tsp of oil around it and cook until golden brown. Dip in the syrup and place on a serving plate. Cook the remaining mallpuha in the same way and serve hot or cold as a dessert.

Seviya
Serves 4-6

30 ml/2 tbsp ghee ● 50 g/2 oz vermicelli

1.2 1/2 pts/5 cups milk ● 50 g/2 oz/¼ cup sugar

1.5 ml/¼ tsp ground cardamom ● 25 g/1 oz/1½ tbsp sultanas

25 g/1 oz/¼ cup blanched almonds, finely chopped

25 g/1 oz/¼ cup pistachios, finely chopped

Heat the ghee in a large heavy-based pan and fry the vermicelli over a medium heat until golden brown. Pour in the milk and sugar and simmer for 45 minutes over a medium-low heat until the mixture is a little runnier than canned rice pudding. Stir in the cardamom, sultanas and half the nuts. Transfer to a serving dish, sprinkle with the remaining nuts and serve hot as a dessert.

Aloo Jamun
Makes 20

225 g/8 oz mashed potatoes ● 50 g/2 oz/½ cup full-cream milk powder

50 g/2 oz/⅓ cup semolina ● 2.5 ml/½ tsp ground cardamom

45 ml/3 tbsp milk ● ghee and oil for frying

225 g/8 oz/1 cup sugar ● 200 ml/7 fl oz/scant 1 cup water

5 ml/1 tsp rose water

Mix together the potatoes, milk powder, semolina, cardamom and milk to a soft dough. Cover and leave for 30 minutes. Divide the dough into 20 portions and roll into sausage shapes. Heat equal quantities of oil and ghee and fry the jamun over a medium heat until golden brown, turning frequently. Do not fry them too quickly or they will not be cooked through. Remove with a slotted spoon and cool.

Meanwhile, bring the sugar and the water over a medium heat, stirring until the sugar dissolves. Remove from the heat and add the jamun to the syrup. Return to the boil, reduce the heat and simmer for 5 minutes. Remove from the heat and stir in the rose water, shaking the pan to coat the jamun in syrup. Serve hot or cold.

Halwa
Serves 6

150 g/6 oz/¾ cup ghee ● 150 g/5 oz/1¼ cups gram flour

150 ml/¼ pt/⅔ cup water ● 150 g/6 oz/¾ cup sugar

25 g/1 oz/3 tbsp pistachios, sliced ● 25 g/1 oz/3 tbsp flaked almonds

5 ml/1 tsp ground cardamom

Heat the ghee and fry the gram flour over a low heat for 5 minutes, stirring continuously. Add the water and continue to stir until it has been absorbed. Add the sugar and half of each of the nuts and blend thoroughly. Simmer until the mixture is thick then stir in the remaining nuts. Sprinkle with cardamom and serve hot.

Beetroot Halwa
Serves 8-10

4 beetroots (red beets), peeled and diced ● 225 g/8 oz/1 cup sugar

60 ml/4 tbsp ghee ● 50 g/2 oz/⅓ cup raisins

50 g/2 oz/½ cup cashew nuts, chopped ● 5 ml/1 tsp ground cardamom

Cook the beetroots in boiling water until tender. Drain then mash until smooth. Put the beetroot and sugar in a pan and simmer over a low heat until the mixture thickens. Gradually add the ghee, stirring all the time until the halwa is almost solid. Add the raisins, nuts and cardamom and spoon into a serving dish to cool.

Carrot Halwa
Serves 8

900 g/2 lb carrots, grated ● 600 ml/1 pt/2½ cups milk

200 g/7 oz/scant 1 cup sugar ● 60 ml/4 tbsp ghee

50 g/2 oz/½ cup blanched almonds, halved ● 50 g/2 oz/⅓ cup sultanas

25 g/1 oz/¼ cup pistachios, halved ● 150 g/5 oz Khoya (page 19)

5 ml/1 tsp ground cardamom

Place the carrots and milk in a heavy-based pan and bring to the boil over a high heat. Reduce the heat to medium and simmer until all the milk has been absorbed, stirring occasionally. Add the sugar and continue to simmer until the liquid has been absorbed. Pour in the ghee and cook gently for 10 minutes. Stir in the nuts, khoya and cardamom and simmer for 5 minutes. Serve hot.

Carrot and Honey Halwa
Serves 8-10

2.4 1/6 pts/15 cups milk ● 450 g/1 lb/2 cups light brown sugar

100 g/4 oz/½ cup margarine ● 50 g/2 oz/½ cup flaked almonds

50 g/2 oz/½ cup pistachios, chopped ● 1.5 kg/3 lb carrots, grated

100 g/4 oz clear honey ● 10 ml/2 tsp ground cardamom

Boil two-thirds of the milk with the sugar for 20 minutes until reduced to one-quarter of the original quantity, stirring continuously. Lower the heat and simmer for about 1 hour, stirring continuously, until the thick becomes a thick, creamy fudge. Transfer to a greased bowl and leave to cool.

Heat the margarine and fry the almonds and pistachios until lightly browned. Add the carrots, cover and cook for 10-12 minutes until tender. Add the milk fudge and remaining milk and simmer for 20-30 minutes, stirring occasionally, until the milk has been absorbed and the halwa is moist. Add the honey and cardamom and stir until the sugar has dissolved and the carrots are glazed and sticky. Cook for 2-3 minutes, stirring continuously. The halwa should be thick. Pour into a lightly greased platter and leave to cool then cut into 5 cm/2 in squares. Serve hot or cold.

Cashew Nut Halwa
Serves 6-8

350 g/12 oz/3 cups cashew nuts, soaked in cold water

1 coconut, grated ● 675 g/1½ lb/3 cups sugar

120 ml/4 fl oz/½ cup water ● 15 ml/1 tbsp ghee

few drops of vanilla essence (extract)

Drain the nuts then grind to a paste with the coconut. Boil the sugar and water for about 5 minutes until it forms a thick syrup. Add the paste, ghee and vanilla essence and mix over a low heat until the mixture is semi-solid. Spread into a greased baking tray and cut into shapes.

Coloured Halwa
Makes 12

50 g/2 oz/½ cup cornflour (cornstarch) ● 750 ml/1¼ pts/3 cups water

100 g/4 oz/½ cup sugar ● 2.5 ml/½ tsp green, pink or yellow food colour

90 ml/4 tbsp ghee ● 50 g/2 oz/½ cup blanched almonds, halved

25 g/1 oz/¼ cup cashew nuts, halved ● 25 g/1 oz/¼ cup pistachios, halved

2.5 ml/½ tsp ground cardamom

Dissolve the cornflour in the water then mix with the sugar and food colour and stir over a medium heat until the mixture thickens and becomes transparent. Add 30 ml/2 tbsp of ghee and stir for 2 minutes. Stir in the remaining ghee, the nuts and cardamom and stir for a further 5 minutes until the mixture comes away from the base of the pan. Remove from the heat and spread the mixture about 2.5 cm/1 in thick on a greased plate. Leave to set for 3-4 hours then cut into 2.5 cm/1 in squares.

Dal Halwa
Serves 8-10

900 g/2 lb/5 cups green lentils, soaked overnight ● 675 g/1½ lb sugar

250 ml/8 fl oz/1 cup water ● 450 g/1 lb Khoya (page 19), broken into chunks

675 g/1½ lb/3 cups ghee ● 100 g/4 oz/1 cup flaked almonds

100 g/4 oz/1 cup melon seeds ● 15 ml/1 tbsp ground cardamom

silver leaves to decorate

Wash the soaked lentils well then grind to a paste. Boil the sugar with the water to make a thin syrup. Place the khoya in a heavy-based pan and toast for 5 minutes. Heat the ghee in a deep pan and fry the lentil paste. Simmer until the ghee appears on the surface, stirring constantly. Add the khoya, almonds, melon seeds and cardamom and fry for 5 minutes. Add the syrup and cook, stirring, until the syrup dried up. Turn out into a flat dish and decorate with silver leaves. Serve hot.

Egg Halwa
Serves 6-8

12 eggs ● 450 g/1 lb/2 cups sugar ● 5 ml/1 tsp ground saffron

100 g/4 oz/½ cup ghee or butter ● 10 ml/2 tsp ground cardamom

50 g/2 oz/⅓ cup raisins ● few drops of vanilla essence (extract)

100 g/4 oz/1 cup flaked almonds ● 100 g/4 oz/1 cup pistachios

Whisk the eggs for about 10 minutes until frothy. Add the sugar and saffron and whisk for a further 5 minutes. Heat the ghee or butter and fry the cardamom for 1 minutes then remove from the heat. Add the eggs and raisins and cook, stirring gently, until the ghee begins to rise to the top. Stir in the vanilla essence then pour into a greased baking tin and spread evenly. Sprinkle with nuts then allow to cool. Cut into squares to serve.

Mango Halwa
Serves 8-10

1.75 l/3 pts/7½ cups mango juice ● 900 g/2 lb/4 cups sugar

2.25 l/4 pts/10 cups milk ● 450 g/1 lb ghee

100 g/4 oz/1 cup flaked almonds ● 50 g/2 oz/½ cup pistachios, chopped

50 g/2 oz/⅓ cup raisins

Heat the mango juice, sugar and milk in a large pan and simmer until it reaches a paste-like consistency. Gradually add the ghee, stirring well to prevent the mixture sticking to the pan. Pour the mixture into a greased baking tray, flatten out evenly then sprinkle with the nuts and raisins. Leave to cool then cut into diamond-shaped pieces.

Marrow Halwa
Serves 6-8

1 large marrow (squash) ● 600 ml/1 pt/2½ cups milk

100 g/4 oz/½ cup ghee ● 450 g/1 lb/2 cups sugar

225 g/8 oz Khoya (page 19) ● 2.5 ml/½ tsp ground saffron

600 ml/1 pt/2½ cups double (heavy) cream, whipped

50 g/2 oz/½ cup blanched almonds or pistachios, chopped

Peel the marrow, halve it and remove the seeds. Grate into a large pan, add the milk then boil until the milk is absorbed and the marrow is tender, adding a little water if necessary. Heat the ghee and fry the cooked marrow with the sugar, khoya and saffron over a low heat until the mixture forms a thick mass. Pour into a flat dish and spread evenly. Pour over the cream and sprinkle with nuts and cut into squares to serve.

Nut Halwa
Serves 8-10

1.5 kg/3 lb/6 cups peanuts ● 450 g/1 lb/2 cups sugar

2.5 ml/½ tsp ground cardamom ● pinch of ground saffron

50 g/2 oz/⅓ cup raisins ● 900 g/2 lb/4 cups ghee

150 g/5 oz/1¼ cups cashew nuts, chopped

Soak the nuts in water for 1 hour. Drain, peel and grind to a thick liquid. Bring the paste to the boil and simmer until reduced to half the quantity. Add the remaining ingredients except the cashew nuts and simmer, stirring constantly, until the mixture thickens. Turn out on to a greased dish and garnish with the cashew nuts. Serve hot or cold, cut into cubes.

Potato Halwa
Serves 8-10

450 g/1 lb potatoes, peeled and grated ● 450 g/1 lb shelled peas

175 g/6 oz/¾ cup sugar ● 250 ml/8 fl oz/1 cup water

100 g/4 oz/½ cup ghee ● 225 g/8 oz/2 cups chopped mixed nuts

50 g/2 oz/⅓ cup raisins ● 5 ml/1 tsp ground cardamom

few silver leaves for garnish

Place the potatoes in a pan, just cover with water, bring to the boil and simmer for a few minutes. Drain off the water. Boil the peas in water until tender then drain and mash coarsely. Put the sugar in a pan, add the water and boil for about 5 minutes to a thick syrup. Heat a little ghee and fry the nuts until lightly browned.

Heat the remaining ghee and fry the potatoes and peas for 5 minutes. Add the syrup and cook, stirring, for 15 minutes. Stir in the nuts, raisins and cardamom and serve warm, garnished with silver leaves.

Creamy Pumpkin Halwa
Serves 8-10

1 large ripe pumpkin ● 300 ml/½ pt/1¼ cups milk

100 g/4 oz/½ cup ghee ● 225 g/8 oz Khoya (page 19)

450 g/1 lb/2 cups sugar ● pinch of ground saffron

few drops of rose water ● 100 g/4 oz/1 cup blanched almonds, chopped

100 g/4 oz/1 cup pistachios, chopped ● 100 g/4 oz/1 cup pumpkin seeds, chopped

600 ml/1 pt/2½ cups double (heavy) cream

Remove the seeds and pith and grate the pumpkin flesh. Put into a pan with the milk and simmer gently until the milk is absorbed. Heat the ghee in a large pan and fry the mixture until it turns reddish in colour. Add the sugar and khoya and fry gently until the sugar has dissolved and the mixture

is thick. Pour into a large dish and spread evenly. Sprinkle with saffron, rose water, nuts and seeds. Whisk the cream and make an even pattern of dollops over the top. Leave to cool then cut into squares so you have a dollop of cream on each piece.

Pumpkin Halwa
Serves 8

900 g/2 lb pumpkin, grated ● 600 ml/1 pt/2½ cups milk

200 g/7 oz/scant 1 cup sugar ● 60 ml/4 tbsp ghee

50 g/2 oz/½ cup blanched almonds, halved ● 50 g/2 oz/⅓ cup sultanas

25 g/1 oz/¼ cup pistachios, halved ● 150 g/5 oz Khoya (page 19)

5 ml/1 tsp ground cardamom

Place the pumpkin and milk in a heavy-based pan and bring to the boil over a high heat. Reduce the heat to medium and simmer until all the milk has been absorbed, stirring occasionally. Add the sugar and continue to simmer until the liquid has been absorbed. Pour in the ghee and cook gently for 10 minutes. Stir in the nuts, khoya and cardamom and simmer for 5 minutes. Serve hot.

Semolina Halwa   Serves 6-8

100 g/4 oz/⅔ cup semolina ● 100 ml/3½ fl oz/6½ tbsp ghee

25 g/1 oz/¼ cup gram flour ● 500 ml/17 fl oz/2¼ cups water

100 g/4 oz/½ cup sugar ● 50 g/2 oz/⅓ cup sultanas

25 g/1 oz/¼ cup blanched almonds, halved ● 25 g/1 oz/¼ cup cashew nuts, halved

25 g/1 oz/¼ cup pistachios, halved ● 5 ml/1 tsp ground cardamom

Cook the semolina in a pan over a low heat for 1 minute. Stir in the ghee and flour, increase the heat to medium-low and stir continuously until golden brown. Add the water and sugar and stir until the water has been absorbed and the ghee appears on the surface of the mixture. Mix in the nuts and cardamom and cook for a further 3 minutes. Serve hot as a dessert or at breakfast with pakora.

Sohan Halwa   Serves 8-10

900 g/2 lb/4 cups sugar ● 1.2 1/2 pts/5 cups water

150 ml/¼ pt/⅔ cup milk ● 225 g/8 oz/2 cups cornflour (cornstarch)

few drops of red or yellow food colour ● 100 g/4 oz/½ cup ghee

225 g/8 oz/2 cups blanched almonds ● 100 g/4 oz/1 cup pistachios

50 g/2 oz cardamom seeds, crushed

Dissolve the sugar in half the water and boil for 5 minutes. Add the milk and boil for a further 5 minutes. Remove from the heat and strain through muslin (cheesecloth). Dissolve the cornflour in the remaining water and add to the syrup. Cook over a medium heat until it begins to form lumps then add the food colour, stirring continuously and adding a little ghee every time the mixture starts sticking to the bottom of the pan until all the ghee has been added and the mixture leaves the sides of the pan. Reserve a few almonds and pistachios for decoration and add the remainder to the mixture with the cardamom. Flatten into a greased dish, sprinkle with the reserved nuts and leave to cool. Cut into shapes and store in an airtight container.

Almond Payasam
Serves 6

100 g/4 oz/1 cup blanched almonds ● 2 l/3½ pts/8½ cups milk

100 g/4 oz/½ cup sugar ● seeds from 4 cardamom pods, crushed

5 ml/1 tsp ground saffron ● 5 ml/1 tsp grated nutmeg

Soak the almonds in hot water for 2 hours. Grind to a fine paste. Boil the milk until it reduced by a quarter. Add the remaining ingredients and simmer for 5 minutes, stirring. Pour into a greased dish and chill.

Carrot and Cashew Payasam
Serves 4

50 g/2 oz/½ cup cashew nuts ● 225 ml/8 fl oz/1 cup warm milk

1.5 l/2½ pts/6 cups milk ● 30 ml/2 tbsp ghee

225 g/8 oz carrots, grated ● 100 g/4 oz/½ cup sugar

seeds from 6 cardamom pods, crushed

Soak the cashew nuts in the warm milk for 30 minutes. Boil the remaining milk in a heavy-based pan until reduced to half the quantity. Meanwhile, heat the ghee and fry the carrots for 5 minutes. Grind to a paste with the soaked nuts. Add the paste to the milk with the sugar and cardamom and simmer until blended. Turn into a dish and leave to cool.

Milk Payasam
Serves 4

2.8 l/5 pts/12 cups milk ● 25 g/1 oz/2 tbsp long-grain rice

100 g/4 oz/½ cup sugar ● 5 ml/1 tsp ground cardamom

5 ml/1 tsp ground saffron

Boil the milk with the rice in a heavy-based pan until the milk reduces to half quantity, stirring continuously. Add the sugar, cardamom and saffron and stir well. Serve hot or chilled.

Vermicelli Payasam
Serves 4

2 l/3½ cups/8½ cups milk ● 50 g/2 oz/¼ cup ghee

30 ml/2 tbsp cashew nuts, halved ● 15 ml/1 tbsp raisins

100 g/4 oz vermicelli ● 100 g/4 oz/½ cup sugar

seeds from 4 cardamom pods, crushed ● 2.5 ml/½ tsp ground saffron

Boil the milk in a heavy-based pan until reduced to three-quarters of the quantity. Meanwhile, heat the ghee and fry the nuts and raisins for a few minutes. Remove from the pan. In the same ghee, fry the vermicelli until it turns reddish. Add to the milk and simmer until the vermicelli is tender. Add the sugar, cardamom and saffron and turn into a serving dish. Garnish with the nuts and raisins and serve hot or chilled.

Sweet Pongal
Serves 4

50 g/2 oz/⅓ cup red lentils ● 100 g/4 oz/½ cup long-grain rice

250 ml/8 fl oz/1 cup milk ● 600 ml/1 pt/2½ cups water

350 g/12 oz/1½ cups ground jaggery ● 60 ml/4 tbsp ghee

25 g/1 oz/¼ cup cashew nuts ● 25 g/1 oz/3 tbsp raisins

5 ml/1 tsp ground cardamom ● 5 ml/1 tsp ground cloves

2.5 ml/½ tsp grated nutmeg ● pinch of ground saffron

Dry roast the lentils in a heavy-based pan for 2 minutes. Add the rice, milk and water, bring to the boil then simmer for about 25 minutes until tender. Dissolve the jaggery in 150 ml/¼ pt/ ⅔ cup of water and simmer over a low heat until the jaggery melts. Strain. Heat the syrup until it becomes sticky then add the cooked rice and lentils. Heat the ghee and fry the nuts and raisins. Add to the rice mixture with the cardamom, cloves, nutmeg and saffron and stir until the ingredients are well blended. Serve hot.

Basundi
Serves 4

2.8 l/5 pts/12 cups milk ● 100 g/4 oz/½ cup sugar

5 ml/1 tsp ground cardamom ● 2.5 ml/½ tsp ground saffron

30 ml/2 tbsp chopped pistachios

Boil the milk in a heavy-based pan until it is reduced to one-third of the quantity. Add the sugar and simmer for 5 minutes. Add the cardamom and saffron and pour into a bowl. Garnish with the pistachios and serve chilled.

Seviyan
Serves 6

100 g/4 oz/1 cup fine vermicelli ● 2.5 ml/½ tsp saffron strands

500 ml/17 fl oz/2¼ cups milk ● 50 g/2 oz/¼ cup margarine

150 g/6 oz/¾ cup sugar ● 25 g/1 oz/¼ cup flaked almonds

25 g/1 oz/3 tbsp raisins ● 2.5 ml/½ tsp ground cardamom

Break the vermicelli into 2.5 cm/1 in pieces. Soak the saffron in 60 ml/4 tbsp of hot milk for 15 minutes. Heat the margarine and fry the vermicelli for about 5 minutes until golden brown. Add the milk and bring to the boil, stirring. Add the saffron milk. Cover and simmer gently for about 8 minutes until the vermicelli is tender, stirring occasionally. Add the sugar, almonds, raisins and cardamom and stir thoroughly for 1 minute. Serve warm or chilled.

Milk Delight

Makes 20

675 ml/1¼ pts/3 cups milk ● 450 g/1 lb/2 cups sugar

100 g/4 oz/½ cup ghee ● 25 g/1 oz/3 tbsp semolina

Mix all the ingredients in a heavy-based pan and simmer over a low heat until thick. Rub a little extra ghee over a serving plate. Pour the mixture on to the plate and cut into squares. Leave to cool before serving.

Carrot Murabha

Serves 6-8

450 g/1 lb carrots, sliced ● 450 g/1 lb/2 cups sugar ● 4 cloves

2 cinnamon sticks ● 2 cardamom pods ● 300 ml/½ pt/1¼ cups water

Cook the carrots in boiling water until tender. Drain, reserving the water. Add the sugar, cloves, cinnamon and cardamom to the water and boil to a thick syrup. Remove and discard the whole spices. Add the carrots and boil again until the syrup is thick again. Leave to stand overnight. Boil again if the syrup thins down too much. Serve cold.

Laddus

Makes 15-20

675 g/1½ lb/3 cups sugar ● 300 ml/½ pt/1¼ cups water

few strands of saffron ● 5 ml/1 tsp ground cardamom

275 g/10 oz/2½ cups gram flour ● oil for deep-frying

30 ml/2 tbsp ghee ● 10 cashew nuts, chopped

15 ml/1 tbsp raisins ● 30 ml/2 tbsp sugar diamonds

Boil the sugar and water until it forms a thick syrup. Stir in the saffron and cardamom and set aside. Add enough water to the flour to make a thick batter of dropping consistency. Heat the frying oil. Drop a ladleful of batter through a draining spoon with pea-sized holes into the oil and fry until crisp. Add to the sugar syrup and continue to fry the remaining batter.

Melt the ghee and fry the nuts and raisins. Add to the syrup with the sugar diamonds and mix well. Leave to cool then shape into small balls.

Semolina Laddus

Makes 15

150 g/6 oz/1 cup semolina ● 100 g/4 oz/½ cup ghee

275 g/10 oz/2½ cups sugar ● 5 ml/1 tsp ground cardamom

30 ml/2 tbsp cashew nuts, chopped ● 30 ml/2 tsp raisins

Toast the semolina in 30 ml/2 tbsp of the ghee in a heavy-based pan until light golden. Stir in the sugar and cardamom. Heat the remaining ghee and fry the cashew nuts and raisins for 2 minutes. Add to the semolina mixture and stir over a low heat until very thick. Shape into balls.

Semolina Pudding
Serves 4

60 ml/4 tbsp ghee ● 100 g/4 oz/⅔ cup semolina

300 ml/½ pt/1¼ cups boiling water ● 275 g/10 oz/1¼ cups sugar

5 ml/1 tsp ground cardamom ● few saffron strands

15 ml/1 tbsp raisins ● 25 g/1 oz/¼ cup cashew nuts, halved

Heat 45 ml/3 tbsp of the ghee and fry the semolina until golden. Add the hot water and simmer for 2 minutes. Add the sugar, cardamom and saffron and simmer until all the ingredients are well blended. Heat the remaining ghee and fry the raisins and nuts for 2 minutes. Stir into the pudding and serve hot.

Kalkass
Serves 4-6

1 coconut ● 150 g/5 oz/1¼ cups plain (all-purpose) flour

100 g/4 oz/½ cup ghee ● 450 g/1 lb/2 cups sugar

300 ml/½ pt/1¼ cups water ● 5 ml/1 tsp ground cardamom

Grate the coconut and grind the flesh. Reserve the milk. Mix the coconut milk with the flour and knead to a soft dough, with a little extra water if necessary. Roll marble-sized pieces of dough into balls then flatten with a fork. Heat the ghee and fry the rolls until golden brown. Meanwhile, boil the sugar and water until it forms a syrup. Place the fried balls in a bowl and pour over the hot syrup. Shake the bowl so that the syrup covers the rolls. Sprinkle with cardamom and leave to cool.

Malabar Banana Dessert
Serves 6

6 cooking bananas ● 30 ml/2 tbsp butter

2 eggs ● 150 ml/¼ pt/⅔ cup milk ● 50 g/2 oz/¼ cup sugar

15 ml/1 tbsp ground almonds ● 225 g/8 oz/2 cups grated (shredded) coconut

15 ml/1 tbsp raisins ● few drops of vanilla essence (extract) ● 12 cloves

Steam the bananas in their skins until soft. Peel them and arrange them in a flat dish. Cut in half lengthways and remove the seeds. Mash to a smooth dough with a little butter then shape into 12 balls. Beat the eggs with the milk, sugar and almonds. Stir in the coconut and raisins to blend well and add the vanilla essence. Melt a little butter and scramble the egg mixture until frothy. Flatten the banana balls, pile a teaspoon of the egg mixture in the centre then shape the banana around the filling. Stick a clove in the top of each ball and chill them overnight. Serve cold with cream or dip in batter and fry in hot ghee and serve hot.

Pudalamboo
Serves 6-8

225 g/8 oz/1⅓ cups split black beans ● 50 g/2 oz/½ cup cashew nuts, ground

5 ml/1 tsp ground cardamom ● 600 ml/1 pt/2½ cups coconut milk

450 g/1 lb/2 cups sugar ● oil for deep-frying

Soak the split beans in water for 1 hour then drain well and grind to a paste with a little water. Stir in the cashew nuts and cardamom. Mix together the coconut milk and sugar. Shape the bean paste into small balls. Heat the oil and fry the balls until golden brown. Place in the coconut milk and leave to soak for 1 hour before serving.

Suseum
Serves 4-6

225 g/8 oz sweet potatoes ● 5 ml/1 tsp ground cardamom

100 g/4 oz/½ cup sugar ● 25 g/1 oz/¼ cup desiccated (shredded) coconut

salt ● 60 g/2½ oz/½ cup rice flour ● pinch of ground turmeric

30 ml/2 tbsp water ● oil for deep-frying

Boil the potatoes until tender then peel and mash. Mix in the cardamom, sugar, coconut and a pinch of salt and make the paste into small balls. Mix the flour, turmeric and a pinch of salt then add enough water to make a thick batter. Dip the balls in the batter and fry in the hot oil until golden. Drain and serve hot.

Sweet Potato Bondas
Serves 6-8

450 g/1 lb sweet potatoes ● 100 g/4 oz/½ cup sugar

120 ml/4 fl oz/½ cup water ● 5 ml/1 tsp ground cardamom

225 g/8 oz/2 cups gram flour ● salt ● oil or ghee for frying

Boil the potatoes until tender then peel and mash. Boil the sugar and water to a syrup. Add the potato and cardamom and mix well. Divide the mixture into small balls. Add just enough water to the flour to make a thin batter and season with salt. Dip the potato balls in the batter and fry in hot oil until golden. Place in the syrup and serve warm.

Kerwai
Serves 6-8

450 g/1 lb/2 cups ghee ● 75 g/3 oz/¾ cup blanched almonds, chopped

45 ml/3 tbsp peanuts ● 45 ml/3 tbsp raisins

5 ml/1 tsp ground cardamom ● 2.5 ml/½ tsp grated nutmeg

2.5 ml/½ tsp vanilla essence (extract) ● 12 frying bananas

75 g/3 oz/⅓ cup sugar

Heat a little ghee and fry the almonds, peanuts and raisins for 3 minutes then stir in the cardamom, nutmeg and vanilla essence. Heat a little more ghee and fry the peeled bananas until lightly browned. Add the sugar and keep stirring until the mixture forms a lump. Remove from the heat and mix well. Shape the mixture into small balls then flatten and fill with the fruit filling and press the banana mixture round to enclose the filling. Heat the remaining ghee and fry the balls until golden brown on all sides. Serve hot.

Labanga Latika
Serves 6

225 g/8 oz/1 cup sugar ● 600 ml/1 pts/2½ cups water

225 g/8 oz/2 cups plain (all-purpose) flour ● 24 cloves

100 g/4 oz/½ cup ghee

Filling: 600 ml/1 pt/2½ cups milk ● 50 g/2 oz/¼ cup sugar

25 g/1 oz/3 tbsp raisins ● 5 ml/1 tsp ground cardamom

Boil the sugar and water to a thick syrup. Add just enough water to the flour to make a stiff dough. Roll the dough into 10-12 small balls and press them flat.

To make the filling, boil the milk and sugar until it forms lumps. Add the raisins and cardamom and mix well.

Place spoonfuls of the filling on the balls then shape them over to cover the filling and make small rectangles. Stick a clove on either side to keep them closed. Heat the ghee and fry over a low heat until crisp and golden. Drain and arrange on a serving plate. Pour over the syrup and serve cold.

Parsi Rava
Serves 8-10

175 g/6 oz/1½ cups blanched almonds ● 100 g/4 oz/1 cup pistachios

100 g/4 oz/⅔ cup raisins ● 100 g/4 oz/½ cup ghee

2.25 1/4 pts/10 cups milk ● 225 g/8 oz/1 cup sugar

225 g/8 oz/1⅓ cups semolina ● 2.5 ml/½ tsp grated nutmeg

2.5 ml/½ tsp ground cardamom ● 45 ml/3 tbsp rose water

Soak the almonds, pistachios and raisins in hot water until soft then drain and slice. Heat 15 ml/1 tbsp of ghee and fry the nuts and raisins for 2 minutes. Boil 1.2 1/2 pts/5 cups of milk until reduced by half. Boil the remaining milk with the sugar. Heat the remaining ghee in a large pan and fry the semolina over a low heat for 3 minutes, stirring continuously. Add the thickened milk then the sweetened milk, stirring all the time. Add the nutmeg, cardamom and rose water then stir in half the nuts and raisins. Continue to cook until thick. Turn out on to a flat dish and garnish with the reserved nuts and raisins. Cut into squares and serve warm.

Rabarhi
Serves 8

1.2 1/2 pts/5 cups milk ● 50 g/2 oz/¼ cup sugar

5 ml/1 tsp kewra or rose water ● 5 ml/1 tsp ground cardamom

15 ml/1 tbsp chopped almonds ● 15 ml/1 tbsp chopped pistachios

Bring the milk to the boil then simmer slowly for at least 2 hours, stirring frequently and letting the cream thicken at the edges of the pan. Add the sugar and stir until the milk is less than a quarter of the original amount. Scrape the cream back into the milk. Stir in the kewra or rose water and pour into a glass dish. Garnish with cardamom, almonds and pistachios and serve hot or chilled.

Bhapa Dahi
Serves 8

1.5 1/2½ pts/6 cups natural (plain) yoghurt

400 g/14 oz sweetened condensed milk

Beat the yoghurt then blend in the milk. Pour the mixture into a heat-proof bowl and stand in a pan filled with hot water to come half way up the sides of the bowl. Boil gently for 1 hour, topping up with boiling water as necessary. Leave to cool then chill before serving.

Sweet Yellow Rice
Serves 4-6

150 g/5 oz/⅔ cup patna or basmati rice ● 200 ml/7 fl oz/scant 1 cup water

150 g/5 oz/⅔ cup sugar ● 150 ml/¼ pt/⅔ cup water

50 g/2 oz/⅓ cup raisins ● 25 g/1 oz/¼ cup blanched almonds, chopped

25 g/1 oz/¼ cup cashew nuts, chopped

25 g/1 oz/¼ cup desiccated (shredded) coconut

15 ml/1 tbsp ghee ● 5 ml/1 tsp ground cardamom

5 ml/1 tsp yellow food colour ● 1.5 ml/¼ tsp saffron

Garnish: 50 g/2 oz Khoya (page 19)

Place the rice and water in a pan, bring to the boil then reduce the heat to low and cook for 7 minutes until all the water has been absorbed and the rice is not quite cooked.

Place the sugar, water, raisins, nuts, coconut, ghee, cardamom, food colour and saffron in a pan, bring to the boil then stir in the rice. Reduce the heat to low, cover and cook for 7 minutes until the rice is cooked and the water has been absorbed. Gently mix in half the khoya then sprinkle with the remaining khoya and serve hot.

Shagarpare
Serves 6-8

50 g/2 oz/¼ cup margarine ● 150 g/5 oz/1¼ cups plain (all-purpose) flour

100 ml/3½ fl oz/6½ tbsp lukewarm water ● oil for deep-frying

225 g/8 oz/1 cup sugar ● 2.5 ml/½ tsp ground cardamom

100 ml/3½ fl oz/6½ tbsp water

Rub the margarine into the flour then mix in the water and knead for 5 minutes until satiny and spongy. Cover and leave for 30 minutes.

Heat the oil. Roll the dough into a ball then roll out to a circle about 5 mm/¼ in thick. Cut both ways across the circle to make 1.5 cm/½ in diamond shapes. Fry over a medium heat until golden brown. Remove with a slotted spoon.

Meanwhile, boil the sugar, cardamom and water and stir until the sugar has dissolved. Remove from the heat. Add the shagarpare to the syrup and boil until the syrup is ready to set. A drop in cold water will set and stay at the bottom. Remove from the heat and turn the shagarpare in the syrup until coated. Serve cold as a dessert, snack or at tea with gulab jamun, pakora, samosas and chutney.

Sheeıni
Serves 6-8

25 g/1 oz/2 tbsp margarine ● 100 g/4 oz/1 cup gram flour

100 ml/3½ fl oz/6½ tbsp lukewarm water ● oil for deep-frying

225 g/8 oz/1 cup sugar ● 2.5 ml/½ tsp ground cardamom

100 ml/3½ fl oz/6½ tbsp water

Rub the margarine into the flour then mix in the water to a smooth batter. Heat the oil. Place half the batter in a vermicelli machine and let the batter fall in long strips into the oil. Fry over a medium-low heat until golden brown then remove and drain.

Meanwhile, boil the sugar, cardamom and water and stir until the

sugar has dissolved. Remove from the heat. Add the shagarpare to the syrup and boil until the syrup is ready to set. A drop in cold water will set and stay at the bottom. Remove from the heat and turn the shagarpare in the syrup until coated. Serve cold as a dessert, snack or at tea with gulab jamun, pakora, samosas and chutney.

Barfi Churmura
Makes 22

100 g/4 oz/1 cup brown chapati flour ● 50 g/2 oz/½ cup semolina

25 g/1 oz/¼ cup gram flour, sifted ● 75 g/3 oz/⅓ cup margarine or ghee

50 ml/2 fl oz/3½ tbsp warm water ● ghee and oil for frying

60 ml/4 tbsp sugar ● 50 ml/2 fl oz/3½ tbsp water

50 g/2 oz/½ cup blanched almonds, halved ● 15 ml/1 tbsp pistachios, halved

2.5 ml/½ tsp ground cardamom

Place the chapati flour, semolina and gram flour in a bowl. Rub in the margarine or ghee and mix well. Pour in the water and knead until the dough is springy and satiny. Cover and set aside for 30 minutes.

Heat equal quantities of ghee and oil in a heavy-based pan. While the fat is heating, divide the dough into 12 equal portions and roll them into balls. Flatten to about 5 mm/¼ in thick and fry for about 10 minutes until crispy and golden brown. Remove with a slotted spoon and place on a cooling rack to cool. Coarsely grind them in a coffee grinder.

Place the sugar and water in a pan over a medium heat and boil until it forms a syrup. When a drop in cold water sets and stays at the bottom, it is ready. Remove from the heat and stir in the ground mixture, nuts and cardamom. Spread on a greased square plate about 2.5 cm/1 in thick and leave in a cold place for 3-4 hours to set. Cut into squares or triangles.

Almond Barfi
Makes 12

50 g/2 oz/¼ cup sugar ● 50 ml/2 fl oz/3½ tbsp water

100 g/4 oz/1 cup ground almonds ● 1.5 ml/¼ tsp ground cardamom

Boil the sugar and water together for 2-3 minutes until a drop in a cup of cold water sets and stays at the bottom. Turn off the heat. Stir in the almonds and cardamom and mix thoroughly until smooth and cool. Form into a ball, place on a greased plate and flatten into a square about 5 mm/⅛ in thick. Cut into squares or triangles.

Three-coloured Barfi
Makes 20

First layer: 25 g/1 oz/¼ cup pistachios, coarsely ground

15 ml/1 tbsp ghee, melted ● 50 g/2 oz/½ cup full-cream milk powder

45 ml/3 tbsp double (heavy) cream, whipped ● 25 g/1 oz/2 tbsp sugar

30 ml/2 tbsp water ● 2.5 ml/½ tsp green food colour

2.5 ml/½ tsp kewra or rose water

Second layer: 25 g/1 oz/¼ cup coarsely ground almonds

15 ml/1 tbsp ghee, melted ● 50 g/2 oz/½ cup full-cream milk powder

45 ml/3 tbsp double (heavy) cream, whipped ● 25 g/1 oz/2 tbsp sugar

30 ml/2 tbsp water

Third layer: 25 g/1 oz/¼ cup desiccated (shredded) coconut

15 ml/1 tbsp ghee, melted ● 15 ml/1 tbsp full-cream milk powder

45 ml/3 tbsp double (heavy) cream, whipped ● 2.5 ml/½ tsp ground cardamom

25 g/1 oz/2 tbsp sugar ● 30 ml/2 tbsp water ● 2.5 ml/½ tsp yellow food colour

1.5 ml/¼ tsp ground saffron ● silver decorations

Place the pistachios and 5 ml/1 tsp of ghee over a medium-low heat and fry for 3 minutes until light brown. Mix the milk powder and cream with 5 ml/1 tsp of ghee then add the fried pistachios. Boil the sugar, water, food colour and remaining ghee in the same pan until the syrup is ready to set. A drop in cold water will set and stay at the bottom. Stir in the milk mixture and the kewra or rose water and continue to stir until smooth and cool. Spread on a greased plate and shape into a square about 1.5 cm/½ in thick.

Place the almonds and 5 ml/1 tsp of ghee over a medium-low heat and fry for 3 minutes until light brown. Mix the milk powder, cream and 5 ml/1 tsp of ghee then add the fried almonds. Boil the sugar, water and remaining ghee in the same pan until the syrup is ready to set. A drop in cold water will set and stay at the bottom. Stir in the milk mixture and continue to stir until smooth and cool. Spread over the first layer.

Place the coconut and 5 ml/1 tsp of ghee over a medium-low heat and fry for 3 minutes until light brown. Mix the milk powder, cream and 5 ml/1 tsp of ghee then add the fried coconut. Boil the sugar, water, remaining ghee and saffron in the same pan until the syrup is ready to set. A drop in cold water will set and stay at the bottom. Stir in the milk mixture and continue to stir until smooth and cool. Spread over the second layer, decorate with silver decorations and leave to set for 3-4 hours. Cut into squares or triangles and serve cold as a dessert or at tea.

Cashew Nut Barfi
Makes 20

100 g/4 oz/½ cup sugar ● 50 ml/2 fl oz/3½ tbsp water

225 g/8 oz/2 cups cashew nuts, finely ground ● 5 ml/1 tsp rose or kewra water

silver decorations

Bring the water and sugar to the boil then simmer until it forms a syrup. A drop in cold water will set and stay at the bottom. Stir in the nuts, remove from the heat and stir until smooth and cool. Stir in the rose or kewra water. Shape into a round and spread on a greased plate about 1 cm/½ in thick. Leave to set for 3-4 hours then cut into 2.5 cm/1 in squares and garnish with silver decorations. Serve as a dessert or snack.

Coconut Barfi
Makes 15

225 g/8 oz/1 cup sugar ● 250 ml/8 fl oz/1 cup water

100 g/4 oz/1 cup grated (shredded) coconut ● 5 ml/1 tsp ground cardamom

30 ml/2 tbsp cashew nuts, chopped

Boil the sugar and water to a thick syrup. Remove the scum then stir in the coconut and cardamom and mix well. Stir over a low heat until the mixture is a thick, pouring consistency. Stir in the cashew nuts and pour the mixture evenly into a greased baking tray. Leave to cool for a few minutes then cut into diamond shapes. Store in an airtight container.

Coconut and Chocolate Barfi
Makes 24

100 g/4 oz/1 cup full-cream milk powder

75 ml/5 tbsp double (heavy) cream, whipped

20 ml/1½ tbsp ghee ● 1.5 ml/¼ tsp ground cardamom

75 g/3 oz/¾ cup desiccated (shredded) coconut ● 75 g/3 oz/⅓ cup sugar

2.5 ml/½ tsp yellow food colouring ● 50 ml/2 fl oz/3½ tbsp water

100 g/4 oz milk chocolate

Mix together the milk powder, whipped cream, 5 ml/1 tsp of ghee and the cardamom. Fry the coconut and 15 ml/1 tbsp of ghee over a low heat until lightly browned. Stir in the milk mixture. Put the sugar, remaining ghee, food colour and water in a separate pan, bring to the boil then boil for 2-3 minutes until it is ready to set. A drop in cold water will set and stay at the bottom. Pour the syrup into the milk, remove from the heat and stir until smooth and cold. Shape the mixture into a ball and flatten it on a greased plate to about 1 cm/½ in thick. Melt the chocolate and pour it over the barfi then leave to set for 3-4 hours. Cut into squares or diamonds and serve cold after a meal or at tea.

Gram Flour Barfi
Makes 15

450 g/1 lb/2 cups ghee ● 100 g/4 oz/1 cup gram flour ● 450 g/1 lb/2 cups sugar

Melt half the ghee then stir in the gram flour until well blended. Place the sugar into a heavy-based pan and just cover with water. Boil to a thick syrup then strain to remove the scum. Melt the remaining ghee. Stir the flour mixture into the syrup and stir over a low heat, gradually adding the melted ghee. Stir over a low heat until the ghee appears on the surface and the mixture froths up. Pour quickly on to a greased baking sheet and leave to cool slightly. Cut into pieces. Leave to cool completely then store in an airtight container.

Marrow Barfi
Serves 6

450 g/1 lb marrow (squash), peeled and grated ● 450 g/1 lb/2 cups sugar

150 ml/¼ pt/⅔ cup milk ● 675 g/1½ lb Khoya (page 19)

5 ml/1 tsp ghee ● 15 ml/1 tbsp pistachios, chopped ● 15 ml/1 tbsp flaked almonds

Put the marrow in a pan with the sugar and milk and simmer for 10-15 minutes until thick. Remove from the heat and mix in the khoya. Sprinkle the nuts over a baking tray and spread the marrow mixture evenly over the nuts. Leave to cool. Cut into shapes to serve.

Peanut Barfi
Makes 15

175 g/6 oz/¾ cup sugar ● 100 g/4 oz/1 cup peanuts, coarsely chopped

45 ml/3 tbsp ghee

Melt the sugar in a heavy-based pan then simmer until thick. Stir in the peanuts then spread over a lightly greased baking sheet and flatten with a greased rolling pin. Cut into squares while still hot then leave to cool.

Gujiya
Makes 16

25 g/1 oz/2 tbsp margarine ● 100 g/4 oz/1 cup plain (all-purpose) flour

50 ml/2 fl oz/3½ tbsp water

Filling: 10 ml/2 tsp ghee ● 50 g/2 oz/⅓ cup sultanas

25 g/1 oz/¼ cup blanched almonds, finely chopped

15 ml/1 tbsp pistachios, finely chopped

75 g/3 oz Khoya made with full-cream milk powder (page 19)

75 g/3 oz/⅓ cup sugar ● 2.5 ml/½ tsp ground cardamom

1.5 ml/¼ tsp saffron strands, soaked in 15 ml/1 tbsp warm milk

ghee and oil for deep-frying

Rub the margarine into the flour. Mix in the water and knead for 5 minutes to form a soft, springy dough. Cover and leave for 30 minutes. Heat the ghee and fry the sultanas and nuts for 2 minutes. Add the khoya, sugar, cardamom and saffron and cook for a further 3 minutes, stirring continuously. Leave to cool. Heat equal quantities of ghee and oil over a medium-low heat. Divide the dough and filling into 16 equal portions, shape the dough into balls then flatten to about 10 cm/4 in in diameter. Place a portion of filling on each dough circle, fold them in half and seal together into semi-circles. Slip a few gujiya into the hot fat from the side of the pan and fry until golden brown, turning several times. Serve hot or cold after a meal or at tea.

Simple Gulab Jamun   Serves 6

1.2 1/2 pts/5 cups milk ● 100 g/4 oz/1 cup plain (all-purpose) flour

pinch of salt ● 2.5 ml/½ tsp baking powder

450 g/1 lb/2 cups sugar ● 300 ml/½ pt/1¼ cups water

few drops of vanilla essence (extract) ● ghee for deep-frying

Boil the milk until it thickens to the consistency of a thick batter, stirring continuously. Mix in the flour, salt and baking powder and knead to a soft dough, adding a little more flour if the dough is sticky. Shape into small balls. Boil the sugar and water to a thin syrup and add the vanilla essence. Heat the ghee and fry the balls until golden brown. Drain on kitchen paper then place in the syrup to soak. Serve warm or cold.

Gulab Jamun   Makes 20

100 g/4 oz/1 cup full-cream milk powder ● 30 ml/2 tbsp ghee, melted

30 ml/2 tbsp plain (all-purpose) flour ● 15 ml/1 tbsp semolina

large pinch of bicarbonate of soda (baking soda)

100 ml/3½ fl oz/6½ tbsp lukewarm milk

15 ml/1 tbsp sultanas ● 6 blanched almonds, finely chopped

5 pistachios, finely chopped ● 2.5 ml/½ tsp ground cardamom

ghee and oil for deep-frying ● 250 g/9 oz/1 cup sugar

200 ml/7 fl oz/scant 1 cup water

Mix together the milk powder, ghee, flour, semolina and bicarbonate of soda. Pour in the milk and knead to a soft dough. Cover and leave for 30 minutes. Divide into 20 equal portions and roll into balls. Mix together the sultanas, almonds, pistachios and cardamom. Place a little filling on each piece of dough then roll them round again. Heat equal quantities of oil and ghee and fry the gulab over a medium-low heat, turning frequently. Do not fry them too fast or they will not be cooked on the inside. Remove with a slotted spoon and leave to cool.

Meanwhile, bring the sugar and water to the boil over a medium heat and stir until the sugar has dissolved. Remove from the heat. Add the fried gulab to the syrup, return to the boil then simmer gently for 5 minutes. Serve hot or cold after a meal or at tea with samosas or pakora.

Yeast Jalebi
Serves 4-6

5 ml/1 tsp dried yeast ● 250 ml/8 fl oz/1 cup lukewarm water

100 g/4 oz/1 cup plain (all-purpose) flour ● 5 ml/1 tsp lemon juice

150 g/5 oz/⅔ cup sugar ● 5 ml/1 tsp yellow food colouring

ghee and oil for deep-frying

Mix the yeast with 15 ml/1 tbsp of water and leave in a warm place for 20 minutes until frothy. Mix the flour, lemon juice and the yeast mixture then gradually work in 150 ml/¼ pt/⅔ cup of water to make a smooth batter. Cover and leave to rise for 1 hour until doubled in size. Place the sugar and remaining water and bring to the boil. Stir in the food colouring and leave to simmer gently.

Heat equal quantities of oil and ghee over a medium heat. Mix the batter then pour it into a piping bag or syringe with a plain nozzle. Hold the syringe 15 cm/6 in above the fat and gently but quickly form spirals in the hot fat. Fry a few jalebies together until golden brown then transfer to the syrup and leave to soak for 30 seconds on each side. Remove from the syrup and place on a serving plate. Serve hot at breakfast, after a meal or as a snack.

Jalebis
Serves 6-8

450 g/1 lb/4 cups plain (all-purpose) flour ● 5 ml/1 tsp baking powder

1.25 kg/3 lb/6 cups sugar ● 300 ml/½ pt/1¼ cups water

450 g/1 lb/2 cups ghee ● 5 ml/1 tsp ground saffron

Sift the flour and baking powder then add enough warm water to make a thick dough. Boil the sugar with the water to form a thick syrup. Heat the ghee to boiling point. Place the dough in an icing bag and squeeze out in small spirals into the hot ghee. Fry until golden brown. Remove from the fat and place in the syrup to soak for 5-10 minutes.

Banana Jalebis
Serves 6-8

3.5 kg/4 lb cooking bananas ● 30 ml/2 tbsp ghee

900 g/2 lb/4 cups sugar ● 250 ml/8 fl oz/1 cup water

juice of 2 lemons ● pinch of saffron, soaked in water

oil or ghee for deep-frying

Halve the bananas lengthways without removing the skin then boil in a little water until tender. Leave to cool then remove the skins. Chop the bananas to a thick paste, adding a little water if necessary. Knead well with a little ghee. Boil the sugar and water to form a syrup then add the lemon juice and strain. Stir in the saffron. Heat the ghee. Place the dough in a piping bag and pipe into the hot ghee in small spirals. Fry until golden then remove from the ghee and place in the syrup to soak for 5-10 minutes.

Iced Custard-apple
Serves 8

75 g/3 oz/⅓ cup sugar ● 1.75 l/3 pts/7½ cups milk

5 ml/1 tsp cornflour (cornstarch) ● 100 g/4 oz cooked apple, chopped

Boil the sugar and milk until it has reduced to three-quarters of the quantity. Blend the cornflour with a little milk then blend it into the sugar-milk and stir over a low heat until the mixture thickens. Remove from the heat and stir in the apple. Leave to cool then chill and whisk before serving.

Shahi Tukri
Serves 8

12 slices white bread ● 60 ml/4 tbsp ghee

600 ml/1 pt/2¼ cups milk ● 5 ml/1 tsp cardamom seeds

225 g/8 oz/1 cup sugar ● 2.5 ml/½ tsp ground saffron

225 g/8 oz Khoya (page 19) ● 10 ml/2 tsp vanilla essence (extract)

25 g/1 oz/¼ cup blanched almonds, chopped ● 15 ml/1 tbsp chopped pistachios

4 glacé cherries, chopped

Cut the crusts off the bread and cut the slices into squares. Fry on the ghee until golden. Remove from the pan. Boil the milk with the cardamom seeds, sugar and saffron until the sugar has dissolved. Add the fried bread to the milk and leave to soak for a few minutes. Remove the bread with a slotted spoon. Mix the khoya in to the milk and heat gently for 5 minutes. Add the bread slices and continue to cook, stirring, until the mixture thickens, turning the slices over a few times. Add the vanilla essence then remove from the heat and leave to cool a little. Spread carefully into a greased baking dish and sprinkle with the nuts and cherries. Leave to cool then cut into squares to serve.

Puran Poli
Serves 8

450 g/1 lb/2⅔ cups yellow split peas ● 450 g/1 lb/2 cups sugar

seeds from 12 cardamom pods, ground ● 4 cloves

450 g/1 lb/4 cups plain (all-purpose) flour ● ghee

Boil the split peas in water until tender and the water has been absorbed. Add the sugar and simmer until the sugar has dissolved. Add the cardamom and cloves and simmer until it forms a thick syrup. Meanwhile, sift the flour and mix in about 10 ml/2 tsp of ghee. Add just enough water to mix to a thick dough then knead well and divide into 5 cm/2 in balls. Grind the pea mixture to a thick paste and roll into the same number of balls as you have dough balls. The pea balls should be twice the size of the dough balls. Flatten the dough balls and carefully stuff with the pea balls, sealing carefully. Melt a little ghee in a pan and fry the balls until golden brown.

Parsi Custard
Serves 8

2.8 l/5 pts/12 cups milk ● 225 g/8 oz Khoya (page 19)

225 g/8 oz/1 cup sugar ● 100 g/4 oz/1 cup ground almonds

6 eggs, beaten ● 12 egg yolks, beaten

5 ml/1 tsp ground cardamom ● 5 ml/1 tsp grated nutmeg

10 ml/2 tsp vanilla essence (extract) ● 100 g/4 oz pumpkin seeds, blanched

Boil the milk and sugar until the milk is reduced to half the quantity. Add the khoya and ground almonds then stir in the eggs and egg yolks, cardamom, nutmeg and vanilla essence. Pour into a greased baking dish and garnish with the pumpkin seeds. Bake in a preheated oven at 180°C/350°F/gas mark 4 for 30 minutes until the pudding is set and the seeds have browned. Leave to cool then chill before serving.

Cardamom Balushahi
Makes 12

200 g/7 oz/1¾ cups plain (all-purpose) flour

large pinch of bicarbonate of soda (baking soda)

50 g/2 oz/¼ cup margarine or ghee ● 100 ml/3½ fl oz/6½ tbsp lukewarm water

ghee and oil for deep-frying ● 150 g/5 oz/⅔ cup sugar

100 ml/3½ fl oz/6½ tbsp water ● 1.5 ml/¼ tsp ground cardamom

Mix the flour and bicarbonate of soda in a bowl then rub in the margarine or ghee. Add the water and knead to a soft, springy dough. Divide the dough in 12 equal portions, roll them into balls and flatten to 1.5 cm/½ in thick, pressing in the centre with your finger. Heat equal quantities of ghee and oil in a frying pan (skillet) over a medium heat. Slip the balushahi into the fat then turn off the heat and leave until the fat stops simmering. Turn them over and heat again on a medium heat. As soon as the fat starts boiling, turn off the heat. Repeat until the balushahi are risen and golden brown. Remove with a slotted spoon and drain.

Place the sugar, water and cardamom in a pan and bring to the boil. As soon as the sugar has dissolved, add the balushahi and simmer until the syrup is ready to set. A drop in a cup of cold water will set and stay at the bottom. Turn off the heat and keep turning and coating the balushahi until they are cold and well coated with syrup.

Balushahi

Serves 6

75 g/3 oz/¾ cups ghee ● 675 g/1½ lb/3 cups plain (all-purpose) flour

900 g/2 lb/4 cups sugar ● 300 ml/½ pt/1¼ cups ● ghee for deep-frying

Rub the ghee into the flour then add enough water to make a soft dough. Divide into small balls, flatten slightly and make dents in the centre. Boil the sugar and water to make a thick syrup. Heat the ghee and add the balushahi. Remove the pan from the heat until the ghee stops simmering. Return to the heat and bring back to the boil. Repeat this process until the balushahi are well risen and layers appear. Use a slotted spoon to transfer the balushahi into a bowl and pour over the hot syrup. Shake well to cover well then leave to cool.

Falooda

Serves 4

50 g/2 oz/½ cup cornflour (cornstarch) ● 300 ml/½ pt/1¼ cups water

25 g/1 oz/2 tbsp sugar ● 5 ml/1 tsp kewra essence (extract) or rose water

1.5 ml/¼ tsp red, yellow or green food colouring (optional)

crushed ice or ice-cream

Place a colander over a bowl of ice cold water. Mix the cornflour and 250 ml/8 fl oz/1 cup of water in a pan and bring to the boil, stirring constantly, until the mixture is thick and transparent. Remove from the heat and place in a pasta machine to make long ribbons, placing them in the colander. Alternatively, roll out and cut into ribbons. Leave for 3-4 hours then drain.

Meanwhile dissolve the sugar in the remaining water over a medium heat. Leave to cool then add the essence or rose water and the food colouring.

To serve, half fill glasses with crushed ice or ice cream then fill with the falooda. Pour over the cold syrup and eat with a spoon.

Bundi Ke Ladoo

Makes 12

150 g/5 oz/1¼ cups gram flour ● 30 ml/2 tbsp melted ghee

175 ml/6 fl oz/¾ cup lukewarm water ● 275 g/10 oz/1¼ cups sugar

250 ml/8 fl oz/1 cup water ● 5 ml/1 tsp yellow food colour

2.5 ml/½ tsp ground cardamom ● 1.5 ml/½ tsp ground saffron

ghee and oil for deep-frying ● 12 pistachios, finely chopped

Place the flour in a bowl, work in the ghee then mix in the water to make a smooth, runny batter. Place the sugar, water, food colour, cardamom and saffron in a pan and bring to the boil over a medium heat. As soon as the sugar has dissolved, reduce the heat to low and leave it to simmer. Heat equal quantities of ghee and oil over a medium heat. Take a slotted spoon, place about 30 ml/2 tbsp of batter on it and hold the spoon about 15 cm/6 in above the pan. Stir the batter with your fingers so that droplets fall into the fat. Turn them until golden brown, then remove them with a slotted spoon and transfer to the hot syrup. Repeat until all the batter is used. Increase the heat and cook the syrup until it has been absorbed and the droplets are soft. Leave to cool. Divide into 12 equal portions and shape into rounds with the palm of your hands, using damp hands if necessary. Place a little pistachio on each ladoo. Serve cold.

Basin Ke Ladoo
Makes 10

30 ml/2 tbsp semolina ● 100 g/4 oz/1 cup gram flour, sifted

100 g/4 oz/½ cup ghee ● 50 g/2 oz/½ cup blanched almonds, coarsely chopped

50 g/2 oz/⅓ cup sultanas ● 2.5 ml/½ tsp ground cardamom

50 g/2 oz/¼ cup sugar

Place the semolina in a deep frying pan (skillet) over a medium-low heat and stir for 3 minutes. Add the gram flour and ghee and fry for 12 minutes until light golden, stirring continuously. Remove from the heat, stir in the nuts, sultanas and cardamom and leave to stand for 5 minutes. Stir in the sugar and leave to cool. Divide the mixture into 10 equal portions and leave to stand for 6-8 hours. Roll the ladoos into a ball on the palm of your hand. Store in an airtight container for up to 1 month.

Malpuras
Serves 6

350 g/12 oz/3 cups plain (all-purpose) flour ● 350 g/12 oz/2 cups semolina

350 g/12 oz/1½ cups sugar ● 2.5 ml/½ tsp ground cardamom

1.2 1/2 pts/5 cups natural (plain) yoghurt ● pinch of ground saffron

30 ml/2 tbsp ghee

Blend all the ingredients except the ghee to make a thickish batter. Cover and leave to stand overnight.

Mix the batter again and add a further 75 g/3 oz/½ cup of semolina and mix well. Heat the ghee and drop tablespoonfuls of the batter into it. When the edges begin to brown, turn them over and cook the other side. Drain well and leave to cool. The edges should be crisp and the centres soft.

Mysore Pak
Serves 8

450 g/1 lb/2 cups sugar ● 300 ml/½ pt/1¼ cups water

450 g/1 lb/2 cups gram flour ● 675 g/1½ lb/3 cups ghee ● pinch of ground cardamom

Boil the sugar and water to a thick syrup. Add 90 ml/6 tbsp of ghee then the gram flour and remaining ghee and stir over a medium heat until the ghee appears on the surface, stirring continuously. Pour on to a greased flat dish and sprinkle with cardamom. Leave to cool then cut into 2.5 cm/1 in squares.

Ras Malai
Serves 6

30 ml/2 tbsp ghee ● 225 g/8 oz Khoya (page 19)

225 g/8 oz Paneer (page 20) ● 225 g/8 oz/1 cup sugar

1.5 l/2½ pts/6 cups milk ● pinch of ground saffron

100 g/4 oz/1 cup chopped mixed nuts ● pinch of ground cardamom ● rose water

Heat the fry and fry the khoya for 10 minutes over a low heat. Add the paneer and sugar and blend thoroughly then cook for a further 10 minutes. Remove from the heat and divide into 12. Bring the milk to the boil, lower the heat and simmer until reduced by half. Remove from the heat and sprinkle with the saffron, nuts and cardamom. Add the khoya pieces, cover and leave to stand for 5 minutes. Sprinkle with rose water before serving.

Cream Cheese Patties
Serves 4

Cream sauce: 1.2 l/2 pts/5 cups milk ● 450 g/1 lb/2 cups sugar

Patties: 1.2 l/2 pts/5 cups milk ● 30 ml/2 tbsp lemon juice

10 ml/2 tsp plain (all-purpose) flour ● pinch of baking powder

Syrup: 1.2 l/2 pts/5 cups milk ● ½ cinnamon stick

10 ml/2 tsp ground cardamom ● 450 g/1 lb/2 cups sugar

Garnish: 15 ml/1 tbsp flaked almonds ● 15 ml/1 tbsp chopped pistachios

Boil the milk and sugar for the sauce over a medium heat for 15 minutes, stirring continuously. Simmer gently for 40 minutes until reduced to about 250 ml/8 fl oz/1 cup, stirring constantly. Leave to cool.

Boil the milk for the patties over a medium heat for 5 minutes. Add the lemon juice and stir for 15 seconds until the milk curdles. Drain in muslin (cheesecloth) for about 1 hour. Knead for 5-6 minutes until the cheese has a dough-like consistency. Add the flour and baking powder and knead to a smooth dough. Divide into 16 portions, roll into balls and flatten.

For the syrup, boil the milk, cinnamon and cardamom for 10 minutes. Stir in the sugar and simmer for 5 minutes. Add the patties to the milk syrup and simmer for 20 minutes until the patties puff up and float to the surface. Remove from the heat and leave to cool. Discard the cinnamon stick and chill until ready to serve.

Remove the patties from the milk and arrange on a serving dish. Pour over the syrup and garnish with almonds and pistachios. Chill for 2-3 hours before serving.

Sweet Pancakes
Serves 6

225 g/8 oz/2 cups rice flour ● 225 g/8 oz/1 cup sugar

5 ml/1 tsp ground cardamom ● 30 ml/2 tbsp ghee

45 ml/3 tbsp milk ● 50 g/2 oz/½ cup sesame seeds ● ghee for deep-frying

Put the rice flour, sugar and cardamom into a bowl and rub in 30 ml/2 tbsp of ghee. Add just enough milk to make a stiff dough and knead well. Cover with a damp cloth and leave to stand for 20 minutes. Knead again then divide into small balls. Sprinkle the sesame seeds on the work surface and roll the balls into thin discs over the seeds. Heat the ghee and fry the pancakes until golden. Drain on kitchen paper and serve hot or cold.

Jaggery Pancakes
Serves 6

225 g/8 oz/1 cup plain (all-purpose) flour ● 2.5 ml/½ tsp salt

2.5 ml/½ tsp ground turmeric ● 250 ml/8 fl oz/1 cup gingelly oil

5 ml/1 tsp ground cardamom

Filling: 175 g/6 oz/1 cup yellow split peas ● 50 g/2 oz/⅓ cup red lentils

1 coconut, grated ● 1.5 kg/3 lb ground jaggery

Mix the flour, salt, turmeric and 45 ml/3 tbsp of oil with just enough water to make a firm dough. Pour the remaining oil over the dough and set aside.

Cook the split peas and lentils in boiling water for about 30 minutes until tender but not overcooked. Roast the grated coconut in a dry pan for a few minutes until lightly browned. Add the jaggery and simmer over a low heat until melted. Add the lentils and peas and simmer, stirring, until the mixture blends and thickens. Set aside to cool. Grind the filling to a paste.

Mix the oil into the dough, divide into small balls and flatten. Place spoonfuls of the filling on the dough and fold over to enclose the filling. Flatten again. Heat a heavy-based pan and fry the balls in a very little oil. Serve hot or cold with ghee.

Sesame Snaps
Serves 4-6

100 g/4 oz/1 cup sesame seeds ● 100 g/4 oz/½ cup sugar ● 5 ml/1 tsp ghee

Toast the sesame seeds in a dry pan until lightly browned. Put the sugar in a pan and cook over a low heat until melted. Add the sesame seeds and blend thoroughly. Spread in a greased baking tray as thinly as possible. Cut into shapes and leave to cool.

Sesame Toffee
Serves 4

450 g/1 lb/4 cups sesame seeds ● 150 g/6 oz/¾ cups sugar

120 ml/4 fl oz/½ cup water ● 225 g/8 oz/2 cups desiccated (shredded) coconut

Toast the sesame seeds in a pan until lightly browned. Boil the sugar and water to a syrup. Add the coconut and simmer over a low heat until the syrup is thick and sticky. Stir in the sesame seeds and remove from the heat. Shape into small balls and store in an airtight container.

Almond Fudge
Serves 8

225 g/8 oz/2 cups blanched almonds ● 1.2 l/2 1/2 pts/5 cups milk

225 g/8 oz/1 cup sugar ● 2.5 ml/½ tsp ground cardamom

15 ml/1 tbsp margarine or oil

Purée the almonds with 250 ml/8 fl oz/ 1 cup of the milk. Heat the remaining milk with the sugar and cardamom over a medium heat for 8-10 minutes until thick, stirring continuously. Add the almond paste and margarine or oil and cook for 15-20 minutes until thick and smooth. Spread evenly in a greased baking dish and leave to cool. Cut into squares to serve.

Carrot Fudge
Serves 8

900 g/2 lb carrots, minced ● 1.5 l/2½ pts/6 cups milk

few saffron strands ● 675 g/1½ lb/3 cups sugar ● 175 g/6 oz/1 cup raisins

5 ml/1 tsp ground cardamom ● 50 g/2 oz/½ cup blanched almonds, chopped

Boil the carrots with 300 ml/½ pt/1¼ cups of milk until tender. Leave to cool. Dissolve the saffron in a little milk and add to the carrots with the remaining milk. Simmer until the milk has been absorbed then add the sugar and stir over a low heat until the mixture thickens. Remove from the heat and stir in the raisins, cardamom and almonds. Spread into a flat dish and leave to cool. Cut into squares to serve.

Cashew Fudge
Serves 8

225 g/8 oz/2 cups cashew nuts ● 1.2 l/2 1/2 pts/5 cups milk

225 g/8 oz/1 cup light brown sugar ● 2.5 ml/½ tsp ground cardamom

15 ml/1 tbsp margarine

Soak the nuts in boiling water for 1 hour then drain. Purée with 250 ml/ 8 fl oz/1 cup of the milk. Heat the remaining milk with the sugar, cardamom and margarine over a medium heat for about 15 minutes, stirring continuously, until the sugar has dissolved and the mixture is thick. Add the cashew paste and mix thoroughly. Cook over a low heat for 4-5 minutes, stirring, until the mixture is thick and sticky. Spread evenly in a greased baking tray and leave to cool. Cut into squares to cool.

Coconut Fudge
Serves 8

250 ml/8 fl oz/1 cup milk ● 30 ml/2 tbsp margarine

450 g/1 lb/2 cups sugar ● 1 coconut, grated (shredded) ● 5 ml/1 tsp ground cardamom

Bring the milk and margarine to the boil over a medium heat. Stir in the sugar, coconut and cardamom and cook, stirring continuously for 8 minutes until the coconut is thick and glazed. Spread evenly in a flat baking tray and leave to cool. Cut into squares to serve.

Ice Cream

Indian ice cream, kulfi, is creamy and delicious — and easy to make. Kulfi moulds have a distinctive cone-like shape, but if you don't have these, any moulds will do. Chuskies are the Indian equivalent of ice lollies.

Kulfi   Serves 4

450 ml/¾ pt/2 cups evaporated milk ● 50 g/2 oz/½ cup blanched almonds

75 g/3 oz/⅓ cup sugar ● 5 ml/1 tsp almond essence (extract)

Blend together 30 ml/2 tbsp of the evaporated milk with the almonds in a mixing bowl. Mix in the remaining evaporated milk and the sugar. Add the almond essence and pour the mixture into an ice cream mould. Freeze for about 3 hours until firm.

Kulfi 2   Serves 4-6

2.25 1/4 pts/10 cups milk ● 60 ml/4 tbsp sugar

50 g/2 oz/½ cup flaked almonds ● 15 ml/1 tbsp sliced pistachios

5 ml/1 tsp ground cardamom ● 10 ml/2 tsp rose water

Rinse a heavy-based pan with cold water. Pour in the milk and sugar, bring to the boil, then simmer gently to reduce the milk to 300 ml/½ pt/1¼ cups, stirring occasionally. Stir in the nuts and cardamom and leave to cool. Stir in the rose water. Pour into conical kulfi containers or small plastic cups, cover and freeze, stirring every 20-30 minutes to prevent the nuts settling to the bottom. Cut into rounds to serve.

Quick Kulfi   Serves 4

300 ml/½ pt/1¼ cups imitation cream (vegetable oil non-dairy cream)

400 ml/14 fl oz/1¾ cups evaporated milk ● 45 ml/3 tbsp sugar

50 g/2 oz/½ cup flaked almonds ● 15 ml/1 tbsp sliced pistachios

10 ml/2 tsp rose water ● 5 ml/1 tsp ground cardamom

Whisk the cream, evaporated milk and sugar until thick. Add the remaining ingredients and mix thoroughly. Pour into conical kulfi containers or small plastic cups, cover and freeze, stirring every 20-30 minutes to prevent the nuts settling to the bottom. Cut into rounds to serve.

Kulfi with Cardamom
Serves 6-8

1.5 l/2½ pts/6 cups milk ● 25 g/1 oz/2 tbsp sugar

100 g/4 oz/1 cup flaked almonds ● seeds from 16 cardamom pods, ground

2-3 drops of almond essence (extract)

Bring the milk to the boil and simmer until it is reduced by at least half, stirring all the time to prevent burning. Stir any skin that forms back into the milk. Stir in the sugar until dissolved. Remove from the heat and add the almonds and cardamom. Stir in the almond essence. Leave to cool then pour into moulds and freeze for about 3 hours until firm.

Kulfi with Nuts
Serves 4

600 ml/1 pt/2½ cups full-cream milk ● pinch of saffron threads

10 ml/2 tsp rose water ● 2.5 ml/½ tsp ground cardamom

15 ml/1 tbsp flaked almonds, crushed ● 15 ml/1 tbsp chopped nuts

100 g/4 oz/½ cup sugar ● 250 ml/8 fl oz/1 cup single (light) cream

Bring the milk to the boil and simmer until it is reduced by at least half, stirring all the time to prevent burning. Meanwhile, steep the saffron in the rose water. Remove the milk from the heat and add the remaining ingredients, one at a time, finally stirring in the cream. Whisk thoroughly and leave to cool. Pour into moulds and freeze until firm.

Fruit Kulfi
Serves 4

1 mango ● 4 large peaches ● 4 raspberries

300 ml/½ pt/1¼ cups condensed milk ● 90 ml/6 tbsp double (heavy) cream

sugar to taste ● 2.5 ml/½ tsp kewra or rose water

Bring a saucepan of water to the boil. Remove from the heat and drop in the mango and peaches. When the water cools, remove the fruit, stone and skin them. Purée with the raspberries then blend in the condensed milk, cream and sugar to taste. Whisk until smooth. Pour into moulds and freeze until firm. Sprinkle with kewra or rose water before serving.

Pistachio Kulfi
Serves 4

225 g/8 oz/2 cups pistachios ● 300 ml/½ pt/1¼ cups milk

250 ml/8 fl oz/1 cup single (light) cream ● 25 g/1 oz/2 tbsp sugar

pinch of salt ● 2.5 ml/½ tsp kewra water

Grind the pistachios finely with a little milk. Stir into the remaining milk in a pan and bring to the boil. Add the cream and simmer over a medium heat for 10 minutes. Stir in the sugar and salt and cook for a further 5 minutes. Remove from the heat and leave to cool. Pour into moulds and freeze until firm. Sprinkle with kewra water before serving.

Mango Ice Cream
Makes 2 l/3½ pts

60 ml/4 tbsp custard powder ● 100 g/4 oz/½ cup sugar

1.2 l/2 pts/5 cups gold top milk ● 300 ml/½ pt/1¼ cups double (heavy) cream

2 large ripe mangoes, peeled and diced ● 5 ml/1 tsp vanilla essence (extract)

Mix the custard powder and sugar with a little milk. Bring the remaining milk to the boil, stir in the custard powder mixture and return to the boil. Reduce the heat to low and simmer for 2 minutes. Remove from the heat, cover and leave to cool. Whip the cream until stiff. Stir the cream, mangoes and vanilla essence into the milk, pour into a box and freeze until firm. When firm, remove and whisk until smooth and spongy. Return to the freezer for 1 hour before serving.

Lychee Chuski
Serves 6

225 g/8 oz/½ lb lychee flesh ● 600 ml/1 pt/2½ cups water

50 g/2 oz/¼ cup sugar ● 5 ml/1 tsp rose water

Blend the lychees and water in a blender or food processor for 1 minute. Stir in the sugar and kewra water and blend again. Pour into lolly moulds and freeze on sticks.

Mango Chuski
Serves 6

300 ml/½ pt/1¼ cups mango pulp ● 300 ml/½ pt/1¼ cups water

25 g/1 oz/2 tbsp sugar ● pinch of ground cumin

2.5 ml/½ tsp finely chopped fresh mint ● pinch of salt ● 6 saffron threads

Put all the ingredients into a large bowl and mix thoroughly. Pour into lolly moulds and freeze on sticks.

Melon and Ginger Sorbet
Serves 6

225 g/8 oz/1 cup caster sugar • 1.2 l/2 pts/5 cups water

75 g/3 oz ginger root, thinly sliced • 30 ml/2 tbsp lemon juice

2 medium melons • 2 egg whites

Heat the sugar and water in a large pan over a gentle heat until dissolved. Bring to the boil and boil for 5 minutes. Remove from the heat ad add the ginger and lemon juice. Leave to cool then strain. Purée the melon flesh until smooth then mix into the syrup and pour into a freezer container. Freeze for about 2 hours until slushy, stirring occasionally. Whisk the egg whites until stiff then fold them into the fruit and freeze until firm, stirring occasionally. Place in the refrigerator for about 30 minutes before serving.

Lime and Lemon Sorbet
Serves 4-6

225 g/8 oz/1 cup caster sugar • 750 ml/1¼ pt/3 cups water

grated rind and juice of 4 limes • grated rind and juice of 2 lemons • 1 egg white

Heat the sugar and water over a gentle heat, stirring until the sugar dissolves. Bring to the boil and boil for 5 minutes. Stir in the lime and lemon rind and juice and leave to cool. Pour into a freezer container and freeze for 2-3 hours until slushy, stirring occasionally. Whisk the egg white until stiff then fold it into the mixture and return to the freezer until firm, stirring occasionally. Transfer to the refrigerator for 30 minutes before serving.

Drinks

Most parts of India have long and very hot summers and intense heat waves, therefore soft, cold drinks play an enormous part in the people's lives. Mostly, people like to make and preserve different types of 'sharbat', 'dhandai' and 'lassi' at home. The reason for this is that one can make them cheaper than buying them in the shops, and they can be made according to individual taste. For special occasions, alcohol is sometimes added to the soft drinks.

Tea is also synonymous with India. India and Sri Lanka are the largest producers of fine teas in the world. Black Assam tea is grown in the foothills of the Himalayas and is strong, pungent and full-bodied. Darjeeling, cultivated under snow-capped mountains, is known for its exquisite flavour and distinctive aroma. The teas of Nilgiris — the Blue Hills in southern India — have a bright, brisk quality with distinctive flavours.

In the cooler parts of India, the people often add spices to their teas, not just for flavouring but also to induce heat in the body. Spiced teas are particularly welcome after a satisfying Indian meal.

Almond Squash   Serves 4

50 g/2 oz/½ cup blanched almonds, soaked overnight

250 ml/8 fl oz/1 cup water ● 150 g/5 oz/⅔ cup sugar ● cold milk ● ice cubes

Drain the almonds and blend with half the water to a smooth paste in a blender or food processor. Place the paste in a pan with the remaining water and the sugar and bring to the boil. Reduce the heat to low and simmer for 2 minutes. Cool then chill to ice cold. To serve, dilute with milk to taste and serve with ice cubes.

Cherry Squash   Serves 4

450 g/1 lb cherries ● 450 ml/¾ pt/2 cups water ● 225 g/8 oz/1 cup sugar

7.5 ml/1½ tsp citric acid ● 5 ml/1 tsp cherry essence (extract)

Put the cherries and water in a large pan and bring to the boil. Reduce the heat and simmer gently for about 15 minutes until tender. Cool then rub through a sieve and collect the juice in a clean pan. Add the sugar and citric acid, bring to the boil, skim off any scum and simmer for 5 minutes over a medium-low heat. Leave to cool then stir in the cherry essence. Dilute with cold water to taste.

Ginger Cordial
Makes about 4.5 l/8 pts

25 g/1 oz ginger root, bruised ● 225 g/8 oz/1 cup granulated sugar

5 ml/1 tsp tartaric acid ● ½ lemon, sliced ● 2.3 l/4 pts/10 cups boiling water

Put the ginger, sugar, tartaric acid and lemon in a bowl and cover with boiling water. Stir well until the sugar has dissolved then cover and leave to stand for 3-4 days. Strain through muslin (cheesecloth) into bottles and seal. Leave for 2 days before drinking. Store in the refrigerator for up to 10 days.

Lemon Squash
Serves 8

120 ml/4 fl oz/½ cup lemon juice ● 150 g/5 oz/⅔ cup sugar

120 ml/4 fl oz/½ cup water ● 5 ml/1 tsp citric acid

Place all the ingredients in a pan over a medium heat and bring to the boil. Reduce the heat to medium-low, skim off any scum and simmer for 3 minutes. Leave to cool. To serve, dilute to taste with cold water and serve with ice. Store in an airtight bottle.

Lemon Barley Water
Makes about 450 ml/¾ pt/2 cups

50 g/2 oz pearl barley ● 50 g/2 oz/¼ cup sugar ● juice of 2 lemons

Put the barley into a pan, just cover with cold water and bring to the boil. Strain off the water and rinse the barley under cold, running water. Return the barley to the pan with 600 ml/1 pt/2½ cups of water, bring to the boil, cover and simmer for 1 hour. Strain the liquid into a jug, add the sugar and leave to cool. Stir in the lemon juice and store in the refrigerator.

Lime Thirst Quencher
Serves 6

450 g/1 lb/2 cups sugar ● 250 ml/8 fl oz/1 cup water

250 ml/8 fl oz/1 cup lime juice

Put the sugar and water into a pan over a low heat and stir until the sugar dissolves. Bring to the boil, skim off any scum then strain through muslin (cheesecloth) or a fine sieve. Stir in the lime juice, cool and store in an airtight bottle. To serve, dilute with water and serve with crushed ice.

Orange Squash
Serves 8

375 ml/13 fl oz/1½ cups fresh orange juice, strained

225 g/8 oz/1 cup sugar ● 250 ml/8 fl oz/1 cup water

Place all the ingredients in a pan over a medium heat and bring to the boil. Skim off any scum, reduce the heat simmer for 10 minutes. Cool. To serve, dilute with cold water and serve with ice. Store in an airtight bottle.

Strawberry Squash
Serves 8

450 g/1 lb strawberries ● 150 ml/8 fl oz/1 cup water

225 g/8 oz/1 cup sugar ● 7.5 ml/1½ tsp citric acid

Put the strawberries and water in a pan and bring to the boil. Reduce the heat to medium-low and simmer for 5 minutes until tender. Leave to cool. Mash the mixture then strain through muslin (cheesecloth) or a fine sieve into a clean pan. Stir in the sugar and citric acid and bring to the boil. Skim off any scum then simmer gently for 5 minutes. Leave to cool. To serve, dilute to taste with cold water. Store in an airtight bottle.

Rose-flavoured Nimbu Pani
Serves 4

juice of 3 lemons ● 30 ml/2 tbsp sugar ● 15 ml/1 tbsp rose water

600 ml/1 pt/2½ cups water ● crushed ice

Stir the lemon juice and sugar together until dissolved, then stir in the rosewater and water. Pour into 4 glasses and serve with crushed ice.

Mango Shake
Serves 6-8

2 mangoes, peeled and coarsely chopped ● 90 ml/6 tbsp sugar

5 ml/1 tsp vanilla essence (extract) ● ice cubes

Blend all the ingredients in a blender or food processor until everything is mixed thoroughly and foam appears on the top.

Mango Juice
Serves 4

1 large mango ● 30 ml/2 tbsp lime juice ● 15 ml/1 tbsp caster sugar

pinch of salt ● crushed ice ● ½ lime, sliced

Squeeze the mango to soften it then spear it on a fork and hold it over a flame (or place it under the grill) until the skin is scorched. Leave to cool slightly then peel it. Scrape the pulp into a blender with the lime juice, sugar and salt and blend well. Pour into chilled glasses and dilute with cold water. Add ice and lime slices to decorate.

Mango Panna
Serves 6-8

450 g/1 lb green mangoes ● 250 ml/8 fl oz/1 cup water

5 ml/1 tsp ground roasted cumin ● pinch of garam masala ● pinch of salt

pinch of black pepper ● 50 g/2 oz/¼ cup sugar

Cut the tops off the mangoes and let the oily substance ooze out. Wash well. Put the mangoes and water into pan, bring to the boil, cover and simmer for about 40 minutes until the skin and seeds have separated from the pulp (or you can do this in a pressure cooker). Discard the skin and seeds and purée the pulp in a blender or food processor. Stir in the spices, salt, pepper and sugar. Cool then chill. To serve, put 3-4 tablespoons of the concentrate into a glass and top up with ice and water.

Orange and Pineapple Whisk
Serves 4

1 banana ● 90 ml/6 tbsp orange juice ● 90 ml/6 tbsp pineapple juice

45 ml/3 tbsp clear honey ● 25 g/1 oz/¼ cup sugar

salt and pepper ● 300 ml/½ pt/1¼ cups water

2 drops of almond essence ● crushed ice ● orange slices

Mash the banana in a deep bowl. Stir in the fruit juices and whisk thoroughly. Stir in the honey, sugar, a pinch of salt and pepper, the water and almond essence (extract) and whisk again. Serve in tall glasses, topped with crushed ice and garnished with orange slices.

Payasam
Serves 4

6 ripe mangoes ● 450 ml/¾ pt/2 cups coconut milk

100 g/4 oz/½ cup sugar ● 2.5 ml/½ tsp ground cardamom

pinch of ground saffron ● 5 ml/1 tsp ghee ● 2-3 cashew nuts ● ice cubes

Peel the mangoes, squeeze out and retain the pulp. Add a little hot water to the mango stones and wash them clean of all pulp, then add this to the pulp with the coconut milk, sugar, cardamom and saffron. Heat the ghee in a separate pan and fry the cashew nuts for a few minutes. Add them to the milk mixture and serve cold with ice cubes.

Badam Sherbet
Serves 8

150 g/5 oz/1¼ cups blanched almonds ● 900 g/2 lb/4 cups sugar

300 ml/½ pt/1¼ cups water ● 10 cardamom pods

few drops of kewra or rose water ● few drops of almond essence (extract)

Soak the almonds overnight in cold water. Drain the almonds then grind them to a fine paste with a little water. Place in a large pan with the sugar and water, bring to the boil then simmer gently, stirring continuously. Grind the cardamom pods with 15 ml/1 tbsp of water. Strain through muslin (cheesecloth) into the almond syrup, stir well and skim any scum off the top. Simmer until the syrup thickens then remove from the heat and strain through muslin (cheesecloth) or a fine sieve. Leave to cool. Stir in the kewra or rosewater and the almond essence. To serve, dilute with iced water and serve with crushed ice.

Party Punch
Serves 12

6 oranges or citrus fruit ● 4 limes ● 25 g/1 oz/2 tbsp sugar

1 pear ● 2 apples ● 2 small bananas

100 g/4 oz/¼ lb grapes ● 30 ml/2 tbsp ginger juice

soda water ● fizzy orange drink ● 2-3 mint leaves

Extract the juice from the oranges and 3 of the limes. Thinly slice the remaining lime. Add the sugar to the juice. Peel and chop the remaining fruit and add to the juice with the ginger juice. Chill for at least 4 hours. To serve, put 2-3 tablespoons of the fruit mixture into a glass and top with equal quantities of soda water and orange drink. Garnish with mint leaves and lime slices.

Honey Milk
Serves 4

1.2 1/2 pts/5 cups milk ● 60 ml/4 tbsp clear honey ● 2.5 ml/½ tsp grated nutmeg

Bring the milk to the boil then remove from the heat and stir in the honey. Leave to cool then chill. Serve sprinkled with nutmeg.

Dhandai
Serves 6

1.2 1/2 pts/5½ cups milk ● 50 g/2 oz/¼ cup sugar

25 g/1 oz/¼ cup blanched almonds ● 15 ml/1 tbsp pistachios

5 ml/1 tsp kewra or rose water ● 2.5 ml/½ tsp yellow food colour (optional)

1.5 ml/¼ tsp ground cardamom ● 1.5 ml/¼ tsp ground saffron

large pinch of ground mace ● large pinch of grated nutmeg ● ice cubes

Pour the milk into a large jug and stir in the sugar until dissolved. Stir in all the remaining ingredients until well blended. Serve chilled with a meal or instead of tea in the summer.

Almond and Pistachio Milk
Serves 6

1.75 l/3 pts/7½ cups milk ● 2.5 ml/½ tsp saffron strands

90 ml/6 tbsp clear honey ● 25 g/1 oz/¼ cup flaked almonds

25 g/1 oz/¼ cup blanched pistachios, chopped ● 2.5 ml/½ tsp ground cardamom

1.5 ml/¼ tsp ground cloves ● 30 ml/2 tbsp rose water ● 6 ice cubes

Place all the ingredients except the ice cubes in a pan, bring to the boil then simmer over a medium heat for 25 minutes. Remove from the heat and leave to cool. Blend with the ice cubes for 2 minutes until whipped and creamy. Serve in wine glasses.

Almond Milk
Serves 4

225 g/8 oz/2 cups blanched almonds ● 600 ml/1 pt/2½ cups milk

50 g/2 oz/¼ cup sugar ● pinch of ground cardamom

4 drops of kewra or rose water ● 30 ml/2 tbsp crushed flaked almonds

Grind the almonds to a paste with a little of the milk. Add the remaining milk and bring to the boil. Stir in the sugar, cardamom and kewra or rose water and simmer for 10 minutes. Serve hot, sprinkled with crushed almond flakes.

Saffron and Almond Milk
Serves 6

5 ml/1 tsp saffron strands ● 60 ml/4 tbsp hot milk

50 g/2 oz/½ cup flaked almonds ● 1.75 l/3 pts/7½ cups milk

2.5 ml/½ tsp ground cardamom ● 75 g/3 oz/⅓ cup soft light brown sugar

6 ice cubes

Soak the saffron strands in the hot milk for 15 minutes. Blend the saffron milk with the almonds, milk, cardamom and sugar for 1-2 minutes until whipped and creamy. Add the ice cubes and blend for 20 seconds. Serve in wine glasses.

Exotic Milk Shake
Serves 6-12

900 g/2 lb mixed fruit (peaches, apricots, plums, oranges, pineapple etc.)

600 ml/1 pt/2½ cups milk ● 45 ml/3 tbsp sugar

5 ml/1 tsp kewra or almond essence (extract) ● ice cubes, crushed

150 ml/¼ pt/⅔ cup double (heavy) cream, whipped ● 6-12 cherries

Extract the juice from the fruit using a liquidiser or juice extractor, as appropriate. Blend together the milk, sugar and essence. Just before serving, stir in the fruit juice. Fill glasses three-quarters full of milk shake, top with the cream and garnish with a cherry.

Guava Milk Shake
Serves 4

2 ripe or canned guavas ● 25 g/1 oz/2 tbsp sugar

600 ml/1 pt/2½ cups milk ● 5 ml/1 tsp rose water

crushed ice ● 2 sprigs fresh mint

Crush the guavas, stir in the sugar and whisk together for 2 minutes. Add the milk and whisk for a further 3 minutes. Rub through a sieve then chill in the refrigerator. Before serving, sprinkle with rose water, stir in some crushed ice and garnish with mint sprigs.

Spicy Fountain
Serves 4

15 ml/1 tbsp fennel seeds ● 30 ml/2 tbsp rose petals ● 30 ml/2 tbsp poppy seeds

50 g/2 oz melon seeds ● 5 cardamom pods ● 8 black peppercorns

12 blanched almonds ● 300 ml/½ pt/1¼ cups milk

50 g/2 oz/¼ cup sugar ● 600 ml/1 pt/2½ cups water ● crushed ice

Grind the spices and almonds to a paste with a little water. Strain through muslin (cheesecloth) then stir in the milk, sugar and water and stir until the sugar has dissolved. Serve with crushed ice.

Strained Milk
Serves 6

900 ml/1½ pts/3¾ cups milk ● juice of 1 lemon

sugar ● pinch of saffron strands

Bring the milk to the boil then remove from the heat and add the lemon juice. The mixture will curdle. Strain through muslin (cheesecloth) into a clean pan and stir in the lemon juice, sugar to taste and the saffron. Simmer over a medium heat for 5 minutes. Serve hot.

Cold Coffee Cooler
Serves 4

750 ml/1¼ pts/3 cups milk ● 30 ml/2 tbsp coffee powder

sugar ● 4 drops of vanilla essence ● 8 ice cubes, crushed

Heat a few tablespoons of the milk and pour over the coffee and sugar. Stir to dissolve, then leave to infuse for a few minutes. Blend all the ingredients except the ice in a blender or food processor until whipped and creamy. Serve immediately with crushed ice.

Creamed Coffee
Serves 4

60 ml/4 tbsp coffee powder ● 600 ml/1 pt/2½ cups water

pinch of ground cardamom ● 25 g/1 oz/2 tbsp sugar

60 ml/4 tbsp double (heavy) cream, whisked

Blend the coffee to a paste with a little water in a pan, then pour in the remaining water and bring to the boil. Simmer over a medium heat for 20 minutes. Stir in the cardamom and sugar. Serve piping hot, topped with cream.

Chocolate Coffee
Serves 4

30 ml/2 tbsp coffee powder ● 10 ml/2 tsp cocoa ● 30 ml/2 tbsp sugar

300 ml/½ pt/1¼ cups water ● 300 ml/½ pt/1¼ cups milk

15 ml/1 tbsp drinking chocolate

Blend the coffee, cocoa and sugar to a paste with a little water in a pan. Bring the remaining water to the boil in a separate pan with the milk, stir in the paste and simmer gently for 5 minutes, stirring occasionally. Serve hot, sprinkled with a little chocolate powder.

Buttermilk Refresher
Serves 4

600 ml/1 pt/2½ cups buttermilk

10 ml/2 tsp cumin seeds, roasted and coarsely ground

salt ● 15 ml/1 tbsp chopped fresh mint ● 8 ice cubes, crushed

Mix together all the ingredients and whisk well. Chill before serving in tall glasses garnished with a few shreds of mint.

Watermelon Surprise
Serves 4

1 watermelon, chopped ● 30 ml/3 tbsp vanilla ice cream

60 ml/4 tbsp milk ● sugar ● 4 fresh mint leaves, lightly crushed

8 ice cubes, crushed

Blend all the ingredients together in a blender or food processor until smooth and frothy. Dilute with extra milk, if necessary. Serve immediately.

Mango-yoghurt Drink
Serves 6

3 ripe mangoes ● 750 ml/1¼ pts/3 cups natural (plain) yoghurt

45 ml/3 tbsp light soft brown sugar ● 6 ice cubes

Peel the mangoes and remove the seeds. Blend with the yoghurt and sugar in a blender or food processor until whipped and creamy. Add the ice cubes and blend for 30 seconds. Serve in wine glasses. You can replace the mangoes with 1 medium papaya if you prefer.

Coconut Nectar
Serves 6

600 ml/1 pt/2½ cups milk ● 300 ml/½ pt/1¼ cups natural (plain) yoghurt

30 ml/2 tbsp sugar ● 30 ml/2 tbsp honey

50 g/2 oz/½ cup desiccated (shredded) coconut

50 g/2 oz/⅓ cup sultanas (golden raisins) ● few drops of rose water

Whisk together the milk and yoghurt in a deep bowl. Stir in the sugar until it dissolves then stir in the honey, coconut and sultanas. Mix together thoroughly then serve sprinkled with rose water.

Sandalwood Drink
Serves 6

1.75 l/3 pts/7½ cups water ● 5 cloves ● 5 cardamom pods

2.5 ml/½ tsp saffron strands ● 4 drops of sandalwood essence (extract)

225 g/8 oz/1 cup light soft brown sugar ● juice of 1 lemon

250 ml/8 fl oz/1 cup natural (plain) yoghurt

1.2 l/2 pts/5 cups tonic or soda water

Put the water, cloves, cardamom pods, saffron and sandalwood essence in a pan, bring to the boil then simmer over a medium heat for 5 minutes. Stir in the sugar until dissolved, then boil until the syrup thickens. Remove from the heat, stir in the lemon juice and leave to cool.

Purée the syrup and yoghurt in a blender or food processor for 1 minute until it becomes frothy. Pour into a bowl, mix with the tonic or soda water and serve cold with ice cubes.

Lassi   Serves 6

450 ml/¾ pt/2 cups natural (plain) yoghurt ● 60 ml/4 tbsp sugar

100 ml/3½ fl oz/6½ tbsp cold water ● 12 ice cubes

Blend the yoghurt and sugar in a blender or food processor until smooth. Add the water and ice cubes to taste and blend for a further 2 minutes until the mixture is frothy. Pour into tall glasses and serve immediately.

Rose Lassi   Serves 6

1.2 1/2 pts/5 cups natural (plain) yoghurt ● 30 ml/2 tbsp rose water

75 g/3 oz light soft brown sugar ● 6 ice cubes

Blend the yoghurt, rosewater and sugar in a blender or food processor until smooth. Add the ice cubes and blend for 1 minute until the mixture is frothy. Pour into tall glasses and serve immediately.

Iced Lemon or Lime Tea   Serves 4

600 ml/1 pt/2½ cups water ● 15 ml/1 tbsp tea leaves

sugar ● crushed ice ● 20 ml/4 tsp lemon or lime juice ● lemon or lime slices

Put the water into a pan and bring to the boil. Put the tea leaves into a tea pot and pour over the boiling water, cover and leave to stand for 2 minutes. Stir in the sugar to taste and leave to cool. Stir in the lemon or lime juice. Put plenty of ice into 4 serving glasses, pour in the cool tea and serve garnished with lemon or lime slices.

Iced Lime Tea   Serves 4

4 glasses of water ● 15 ml/1 tbsp tea leaves ● sugar ● juice of 2 limes ● ice cubes

Put the water into a pan and bring to the boil. Stir in the tea, remove from the heat, cover and leave to infuse for 3 minutes. Strain into a jug and stir in the sugar to taste. Leave to cool then chill. Before serving, squeeze the juice of half a lime into 4 glasses, add a few ice cubes and pour in the tea. Stir together before serving.

Iced Aniseed Tea   Serves 4

30 ml/2 tbsp aniseeds ● 450 ml/¾ pt/2 cups strong black tea

milk or cream ● sugar ● crushed ice

Put the aniseeds and 250 ml/8 fl oz/1 cup of water into a pan and bring to the boil. Simmer until tender. Strain the liquid and stir in the tea. Leave to cool. Add milk or cream and sugar to taste and pour into 4 glasses half-filled with crushed ice.

Satsuma Tea
Serves 4

600 ml/1 pt/2½ cups water ● rind of 1 satsuma ● sugar

30 ml/2 tbsp single (light) cream

Bring the water to the boil in a pan, add the rind and simmer for 1 minute. Remove from the heat, stir in the **sugar to taste, strain and serve hot, topped with cream.**

Cardamom Tea
Serves 6

1.5 1/2½ pts/6 cups water ● 12 cardamom pods

30 ml/2 tbsp Darjeeling or Assam tea ● 250 ml/8 fl oz/1 cup milk

50 g/2 oz/¼ cup light soft brown sugar

Put the water and cardamom in a pan, bring to the boil then simmer for 5 minutes. Remove from the heat, cover and leave to infuse for 5 minutes. Add **the tea, return to the boil and boil for 2 minutes. Stir in the milk and sugar, remove from the heat, strain and serve immediately.**

Cinnamon Tea
Serves 6

3 cloves ● 1 cm/½ in cinnamon stick ● 1.2 1/2 pts/5 cups water

15 ml/3 tbsp Darjeeling tea ● 50 g/2 oz/¼ cup sugar

60 ml/4 tbsp orange juice ● juice of 1 lemon ● cinnamon sticks

Bring the cloves, cinnamon and water to the boil. Put the tea into a large bowl, pour over the spiced water and leave to infuse for 5 minutes. Stir in **the sugar until dissolved then add the fruit juices. Reheat gently before serving, but do not allow to boil. Strain and serve with cinnamon sticks.**

Princely Tea
Serves 4

300 ml/½ pt/1¼ cups water ● 30 ml/2 tbsp tea leaves

300 ml/½ pt/1¼ cups milk ● 3 cardamom pods

15 ml/1 tbsp soft light brown sugar ● pinch of saffron threads

Put the water into a pan and bring to the boil. Add the tea, cover and simmer for 2 minutes. Bring the milk and cardamom to the boil in a separate **pan then stir in the sugar. Strain the tea into the milk, cover and simmer gently for 5 minutes. Serve hot, sprinkled with saffron threads.**

Spicy Himalayan Tea   Serves 6

15 ml/1 tbsp fennel seeds ● 6 cardamom pods ● 12 cloves

1 cinnamon stick ● 5 mm/¼ in ginger root, chopped

2.5 ml/½ tsp black peppercorns ● 2 bay leaves

90 ml/6 tbsp soft light brown sugar ● 1.5 l/2½ pts/6 cups water

30 ml/2 tbsp Darjeeling tea ● 250 ml/8 fl oz/1 cup milk

Place all the ingredients except the tea and milk in a pan and bring to the boil. Cover and simmer for 20 minutes. Remove from the heat, stir in the tea and leave to infuse for 10 minutes. Add the milk, return to the boil then strain and serve immediately.

Spiced Tea   Serves 6

1.5 l/2½ pts/6 cups water ● 250 ml/8 fl oz/1 cup milk

1 cinnamon stick ● 6 cardamom pods ● 6 cloves

5 mm/¼ in ginger root, chopped ● 50 g/2 oz/¼ cup light soft brown sugar

30 ml/2 tbsp Darjeeling or Assam tea

Put the water and milk into a pan and bring to the boil. Stir in the spices and sugar and boil for 5 minutes. Remove from the heat, cover and pan and leave to infuse for 10 minutes. Add the tea and bring back to the boil. Cover and simmer gently for 5 minutes. Strain and serve immediately.

Index